Educating for Diversity

212-529-2103
212-529-2103

Educating for Diversity

An Anthology of Multicultural Voices

Edited by
CARL A. GRANT

University of Wisconsin-Madison

SPONSORED BY
ASSOCIATION OF TEACHER EDUCATORS

Allyn and Bacon
Boston • London • Toronto • Sydney • Tokyo • Singapore

Editor-in-Chief, Education: *Nancy Forsyth*
Series Editor: *Virginia Lanigan*
Editorial Assistant: *Nihad Farooq*
Cover Admninistrator: *Suzanne Harbison*
Composition Buyer: *Linda Cox*
Manufacturing Buyer: *Megan Cochran*
Marketing Representative: *Ellen Mann*
Production Coordinator: *Eleanor Sabini*
Editorial-Production Service: *TKM Productions*

Copyright © 1995 by Allyn & Bacon
A Simon & Schuster Company
Needham Heights, MA 02194

This book is printed on recycled, acid-free paper.

Library of Congress Cataloging-in-Publication Data

Educating for diversity : an anthology of multicultural voices /
    Association of Teacher Educators ; edited by Carl A. Grant.
        p.   cm.
    Includes bibliographical references and index.
    ISBN 0-205-16573-7
    1. Multicultural education--United States.   2. Pluralism (Social
sciences)--Study and teaching--United States.   I. Grant, Carl A.
II. Association of Teacher Educators.
LC1099.3.E38   1994
370.19'6'610973--dc20
                                                            94-34094
                                                            CIP

Printed in the United States of America
10 9 8 7 6 5 4 3 2 1   99 98 97 96 95 94

Contents

Part II: American Diversity: Ethnic Vignettes   33

Foreword

Our nation's classrooms are beginning to reflect the growing diversity of a student population whose ethnicity, culture, background, and needs vary more than at any other time in our history. This richness provides an opportunity to learn from each other, to expand our horizons, and to move forward, hand in hand, to guarantee a better life for all people. It also provides a challenge to many of our nation's teachers and teacher-education institutions alike to acquire both an understanding and an appreciation of the backgrounds, needs, and contributions of many groups who contribute to our schools' "rainbow."

At the 1992 Annual Meeting in Orlando, Florida, the Association of Teacher Educators (ATE) passed a resolution that reaffirmed ATE's commitment to diversity in education. *Educating for Diversity: An Anthology of Multicultural Voices* is a significant contribution toward providing *all* teachers with a better understanding of *all* students. Carl A. Grant should be praised for his efforts in bringing together a well-known, talented, and experienced group of educators to share their knowledge and experiences with us.

The ATE takes great pride in presenting *Educating for Diversity: An Anthology of Multicultural Voices.* I invite you to share this book with your colleagues *and* students, so that we can truly praise the diversity that enriches our society.

D. John McIntyre
President, Association of Teacher Educators

D. John McIntyre is a professor in the department of curriculum and instruction and director of the Teaching Skills Laboratory at Southern Illinois University at Carbondale. He has a B.A. from Otterbein College, a M.A. from Ohio State University, and an Ed.D. from Syracuse University. McIntyre taught junior high school English in Gahanna, Ohio. He has conducted extensive research in teacher education, especially in the area of field experience, and has authored approximately 50 journal articles and book chapters. He has been a recipient of ATE's Award for Outstanding Research in Teacher Education, named an Outstanding Leader in Teacher Education, and appears in *Who's Who in American Education.* McIntyre was 1991–1992 president of the Association of Teacher Educators.

Preface

Multicultural education was just emerging as a theme in school practice and curricula in 1977 when William Smith, then National Director of the Peace Corps, asked the late Harry N. Rivlin, who was retiring as Dean of the Fordham University School of Education, to form a Teacher Corps component on cultural pluralism. During the ensuing 18 years, interest in multicultural education literally exploded as the nation's consciousness of its diversity was awakened. In those years, immigration to the United States did indeed expand—but what is especially noteworthy was the shift in geographic origins from Europe to Central and South America, the Caribbean, and important parts of Asia: Peoples of color replaced White Europeans as the larger part of the immigrant population.

Of enormous importance, too, was increasing expression on the part of African and Hispanic Americans of their concern for recognition as integral and contributing parts of the American culture. The impact and popularity of the television series "Roots" confirmed both the self-expression of the African-American community and recognition of it by the broader society. A result of this demand for legitimization of a long-suppressed culture found parallel expression in Native-American peoples and in the emergence into mainstream political, social, and cultural participation of Asian-American groups as well.

Thus, *cultural pluralism,* a term introduced by Horace Kallen and publicized by Randolph Bourne just before World War I, while gaining slow acceptance for well over half a century (witness the popularity of Paul Robeson's singing of John Latouche and Earl Robinson's *Ballad for Americans*), finally burst like a star rocket. It also brought attention to women's issues, the disabled, and the rights of other long-neglected cultural groups in the national community, such as gays and lesbians.

Yet the reality of America's diversity is not yet matched in many quarters by either perceptions of its existence or the recognition of the value of real and potential contributions of the varied components of the population. New York City's Mayor David Dinkins speaks hopefully of the "gorgeous mosaic," and Rev. Jesse Jackson of his Rainbow Coalition, but interethnic and interracial disturbances continue to vitiate the scene, and to turn at times the American Dream into a nightmare for various minority groups. The task of making the mosaic "gorgeous," of building respect in the mainstream for *all* minorities, remains unfinished. Simple-minded prejudice, economic competition, and ignorance of the ways of others combine to maintain explosive situations that all Americans must try to resolve.

It is in this context that education has a crucial dual role to play: to build an atmosphere of positive human relations on the one hand and to remove negative stereotypes and prejudices on the other. These are the themes of multicultural education: to help us all perceive more accurate pictures of persons in cultures different from our own; to understand that "different" means neither better nor worse but simply "not the same"; to prize the differences among cultures, because those differences enrich the American scene; and—in the realizing of all these processes—to build attitudes of genuine brotherhood that transcend mere toleration.

The task is not made easier in the light of some issues that have arisen. In some instances, excessive zeal to build a positive self-concept has resulted in the growth of a chauvinistic ethnocentrism, which is the *opposite* of multiculturalism. Without a positive self-concept, the person who does not value himself or herself is not likely to value those who differ from him or her. Yet, a self-concept based on chauvinistic attitudes of superiority over all others—or hostility to other cultures, whatever their perceived faults—is not likely to produce a positive attitude toward other elements in the "gorgeous mosaic."

Still another issue—one raised by Arthur M. Schesinger, Jr. (*The Disuniting of America*) and other responsible students of the current scene of American culture—is the concern over possible diminution of the basic political and social values that are our inheritance from western Europe through our English forebears. Will a new emphasis on other cultures undermine such institutions as our political democracy and our judicial system or our belief in the scientific method and our literary cultural heritage? Adherence to these values may appear like a form of ethnocentrism, but a distinction *must* be made between the maintenance of core values as a positive factor and exclusion of other cultures as a negative. Whereas substituting one set of values for another is only another expression of ethnocentrism, adding to our rich mix still other cultural perspectives is a prime example of cultural pluralism.

Educating for Diversity: An Anthology of Multicultural Voices comes at a strategic time. Many school systems are studying their curricula with a view toward correcting previous programs that have been in reality monocultural—that have ignored the contributions, or even the very existence, of substantial minorities within our society. In stressing the monocultural, schools in all parts of the country have presented a distorted view of America as the inheritor of a culture that came solely from western Europe, with a strongly White Anglo-Saxon Protestant thrust. The need for a more inclusionary ethos has been evident for a long time, but curricula and textbooks have consistently proved slow to update. To help dispel the pall of ignorance that covers too many of the neighbors of children in the schools, this book provides school administrators, teachers, and mature readers in secondary schools with a base of information about a variety of cultures in America, extending from Native Americans to recent immigrant groups. It contains a considerable number of vignettes describing these cultures, and it also goes deeply into matters of curriculum and instruction.

The eloquence of Earl Robinson's words in *Ballad for Americans* seems appropriate:

Are you an American?

I'm just an Irish, Negro, Jewish Italian,
French and English, Spanish, Russian,
Chinese, Polish, Scotch, Hungarian,
Litvak, Swedish, Finnish, Canadian,
Greek and Turk, and Czech and double Czech American!

And that ain't all. He was baptized
Baptist, Methodist, Congregationalist,
Lutheran, Atheist, Roman Catholic,
Orthodox Jewish, Presbyterian, Seventh
Day Adventist, Mormon Quaker, Christian Scientist.

You sure are something.
Our country's strong, our country's young
And her greatest songs are still unsung.
From her plains and mountains we have sprung
To keep the faith with those who went before....

Ballad for Americans was written in 1938. Written today, it would be even *more* inclusive!

Milton J. Gold
March 1994

Milton J. Gold served as associate director of the multicultural component of the New York State Teacher Corps Network. He is Dean Emeritus of Programs in Education at Hunter College of the City University of New York, former director of curriculum for the Washington State Education Department, and has taught in the public schools of New York City. He is currently a research associate of the Center for Advanced Study in Education of the City University.

Acknowledgments

This project has taken the great efforts of a few terrific people. First and foremost, I wish to extend great thanks to Nadine Goff, who greatly assisted me with editing and content suggestions, and who worked on each chapter with the care she gives her own writing and research. Gloria Chernay, executive director of the Association of Teacher Educators, deserves a huge bouquet for her efforts in coordinating this project between Allyn and Bacon and ATE. Virginia Lanigan is also most deserving of appreciation for her efforts in working out the details of this project. I also wish to acknowledge the following reviewers for their valuable insights and comments: Kenneth Cushner, Kent State University; Mike Davis, St. Cloud State University; Samuel Kellams, University of Virginia; Cameron McCarthy, University of Illinois at Urbana-Champaign; Theresa McCormick, Iowa State University; Barbara Merino, University of California, Davis; Trevor Phillips, Bowling Green State University; Tony R. Sanchez, Purdue University; and Arlette Ingram Willis, University of Illinois at Urbana-Champaign. Margaret Tierney must also be thanked for researching and updating some of the material. Finally, a big thanks to Amy Hutler for typing and copying portions of the manuscript.

Introduction

Those who say, "The more things change, the more they are the same" are optimists. They do not seem to be talking about our willingness to accept and understand one another and our differences. Thanks to the knowledge revolution of the 1980s and 1990s, it has been easier to recognize and to analyze our interdependency, as well as to identify social values that differ from our traditional ones. But we seem to be reacting to these differences with fear, loathing, or despair. Bob Dylan's song correctly stated "The times they are a-changing," but I regret to add that the directions of the changes do not appear positive. Our attitudes about our differences may even be *worse* than they were in the early 1970s.

My pessimism stems from attempts to develop teachers who are sensitive to the many cultures that characterize our country. From 1971 to 1972, and again from 1973 to 1979, I served as the National Director of the federally funded Teacher Corps Program, authorized under Title V of the Higher Education Act of 1965. Teacher Corps was established in 1966 as part of efforts to improve the educational opportunities of poor children in both urban and rural areas. Teachers were to be prepared with specific training and a special commitment to improving the school experiences of these children.

Teacher Corps came into immediate contact with America's minorities, so many of whom lived in poverty. As a consequence of prejudice, racism, discrimination, and other factors, we were failing as a nation to realize fully the potential wealth that lies in diversity. Because of the close connection between poverty and minority group membership, Teacher Corps realized early in its history an obligation to help build respect for diversity in our nation's schools. This respect for diversity is fundamental, for without it all those who are "different" (culturally, racially, religiously, ethnically, or physically) are all too often excluded from full participation in our society.

The Teacher Corps Program was disestablished by Congress with the passage of the Consolidation Act of 1981; its funds were included in Chapter II of the Elementary/Secondary Act. Many colleges of education and schools across the country have attempted, however, to continue to implement the concepts and practices that grew out of those 15 years of Teacher Corps program activities.

During the summer of 1974 and the following winter, a number of meetings were held in my office (and subsequently across the country) planning the design of a Corps Members Training Institute (CMTI). The CMTI brought together all of the new interns enrolled in the federally funded projects across the country and U.S. territories in an initial eight-week training program at a single Institution of Higher Education (IHE). The rationale was to make the best minds, newest materials, and most talented instructors available to all of these interns and team leaders, prior to their matriculation in the local IHE and in the school district where they would remain for the next two years. The focuses of the content areas for the CMTI were (1) teaching and learning theory, (2) exceptionality, (3) organizational behavior theory, and (4) multicultural education and/or education that is multicultural.

The meeting in my office addressed only one content area: multiculturalism. Assembled at that historic meeting were the people who made possible the publication of early multicultural materials, including *In Praise of Diversity:* Floyd Waterman, Paul Collins, Jim Steffenson, Milt Gold, Carl Grant, and Harry Rivlin. That original group conceived the framework for the initial design of the multicultural strand for the CMTI of 1975 and 1976. In fact, CMTI served as the developmental testing ground. To say that we owe them a debt of gratitude for filling a major void of relevant materials in useful form is an understatement. Further, the wisdom of Bob Stevenson and the Association of Teacher Educators (ATE) to publish the final product of those years of work has justified itself. The fact that the original document received highly complimentary book reviews in academic circles speaks for itself.

In the preface of *In Praise of Diversity,* I wrote:

> *"I hear America singing, its varied carols I hear." Walt Whitman heard the diverse strains of America's cultural symphony and celebrated the wonderful richness that springs from difference. How long will it take the rest of the nation to recognize and accept the pluralism that marks our culture, to tolerate difference, and to prize the value and potential of diversity!*
>
> *A challenge confronts us all to throw off the monoculturalism that has oppressed us all, majority and minority alike, and to find instead a new respect, for the many heritages which feed America's culture. First to tolerate, then to respect, and ultimately to prize and use the differences that to so great a degree and for so long have been swept under the rug and ignored!*
>
> *For, to the extent to which minority cultures have been ignored, they have been implicitly demeaned.*

As I prepared the manuscript and reflected on the kinds of changes that occurred in the 15 or so years since those days, I did not have the same sense of confidence that I did back then. Not only has it seemed that more things have changed, but—regrettably—that more things have worsened. This makes the need for this book all the more important— indeed, more urgent! Since 1987 alone, the number of complaints of racial harassment on high school and college campuses has multiplied tenfold. Too, the number of new and different minority immigrants has increased substantially: In a certain California school district, 54 different languages are being spoken! More and more attitudes in America's society have become conflicting, and the negative aspects are being demonstrated in explosive, explicit behavior (witness, for example, the 1992 Los Angeles riots).

There is a much greater need for understanding and tolerance of difference today than was the case in the mid to late 1970s. The universe of people with differences has expanded tremendously, but the degree of tolerance of differences has by proportion all too quickly lessened. The goal of *Educating for Diversity: An Anthology of Multicultural Voices* is to help develop a respect for, and an appreciation of, diversity—in order to stamp out the fears, prejudice, and discrimination that stem from inadequate understanding of the *positive values* of difference, of diversity, and of pluralism. Milton Gold, Carl Grant, and Harry Rivlin must be praised for establishing the groundwork to meet that goal. It is incumbent upon the editor of this volume to lift this work to its next higher level.

William L. Smith

William L. Smith was a teacher, guidance counselor, and school administrator before becoming a civil servant in the U.S. Office of Education in 1969. He is a senior executive who has served under five presidents. He has been the associate commissioner for educational personnel development, the national director of the Teachers Corps Program, and the last U.S. Commissioner of Education. He is the author of 38 articles and chapters in major publications and books. He has received many honors, including five honorary degrees, three distinguished leadership awards, and two presidential rank awards. Smith enjoys both a national and international reputation as a scholar, leader, and program developer in his field. He is also a highly respected federal official.

This Book: Its Purposes and Contents

When Milton Gold, Harry Rivlin, and I came together to develop multicultural materials for Teacher Corps and to edit *In Praise of Diversity* in 1977, it was at a time when the United States was developing a new recognition of its ethnic roots. Alex Haley's monumental book *Roots* was published in 1976, and the television series based on that book first aired in January 1977. No longer was the search for family history the province of White Americans attempting to qualify for membership in patriotic societies like the Daughters of the American Revolution (DAR), which had once denied Marion Anderson the opportunity to perform at Constitution Hall simply because she was Black. Haley's book inspired Americans of all races and ethnic heritages to reclaim their family history.

In 1995, the United States is in a similar position. The 1990 census confirmed that our country is "browning." The Hispanic population is increasing rapidly and the Asian-American and Pacific-Islander populations are also growing. Additionally, there is a significant growth in the number of Americans whose roots are in the Middle East and Central America. Estimates of the growth of the student population of color includes an increase from 24 percent in 1976 to 30 to 40 percent by the year 2000. In addition, Romero, Mercado, and Vazques-Faria have reported that over 30 million students speak a native language other than English, or come from homes where English is not spoken. Furthermore, as I argued in an article in the *Phi Delta Kappan* (September 1990), the diversity equation can no longer be centered around "Black and White." The contact thesis proposed by Allport as a way of eliminating or reducing prejudice must now take into account interactive contact across and among numerous ethnic and cultural groups.

As teachers were in 1977, teacher educators and classroom teachers in 1995 are in need of authentic, insightful, and illuminating materials to inform them about cultural diversity and the issues of race, class, and gender in order that they might have a better understanding of their students and thereby be more effective and affective in their teaching. Central and key to *Educating for Diversity: An Anthology of Multicultural*

Voices, as it was in *In Praise of Diversity* in 1977, are the ethnic vignettes. These vignettes are written by members of various ethnic groups (or, in some cases, in collaboration with an author from another group) in order to (1) provide a historical and cultural snapshot of an ethnic group member "coming to be" an American; (2) develop an understanding of the cultural contributions of each ethnic group to the broader American culture; (3) provide a picture of the diversity and richness that characterizes America and makes it the unique country that it is; (4) present the ethnic, cultural, gender, linguistic, and socioeconomic issues and problems that these ethnic groups have experienced and continue to encounter; and (5) serve as a "curriculum" that educators can study to learn and examine the similarities and differences among the Americans discussed in the vignettes.

Beside the ethnic vignettes, *Educating for Diversity: An Anthology of Multicultural Voices* provides a discussion of the "diversity" that goes beyond race and ethnicity. We are seeing more and more students from mixed race families, and, if human nature remains as it always has been, this student population will continue to increase. It is time that teachers understand and accept their biracial students for the richness and specialness they bring to the classroom. Also, more students in our classroom than we may know come from gay and lesbian homes. These students must be prized just as other students are prized. Often, however, they feel isolated and alone. Praising diversity means total acceptance of students from the homes of gay and lesbian families, and the affirmation of their rights as Americans.

With the recent passage of the Americans with Disabilities Act (1990), the United States has taken a huge step toward extending civil rights to everyone. Many students with disabilities can now look to a brighter future in employment and increased access to public facilities and telecommunications. To make certain that the future is bright, it is important that teachers understand the needs of culturally and linguistically diverse students with disabilities.

Awareness and understanding of diversity is essential, acceptance and appreciation of diversity is important, but advocacy and affirmation of diversity is a must. *Educating for Diversity: An Anthology of Multicultural Voices* includes chapters on curriculum, instruction, policy, and home-school relationships. These chapters were especially written to assist educators who represent different role groups (e.g., teachers, administrators, policy makers, professors) to advocate and affirm diversity in their daily work.

Finally, an important purpose of this book is to recognize and celebrate the efforts and deeds of countless individuals, many whom we will never know, who, sometime at a cost to their own life or welfare, stood tall and faced up to those who sought to destroy or deny the beauty, value, and richness in every regard that come with human and ethnic diversity.

Ethnic Vignettes

The 17 vignettes in this book provide readers with the opportunity to become aware of and appreciate the ethnic diversity of their fellow citizens and to hear a firsthand account of what it is like to be or become an American.

The instruction to the authors of the vignettes was: "Imagine there is a group of teachers seated before you. What would you want them to know about your ethnic background and cultural history that would be useful as they teach students about your cultural background?" Each vignette has its own style and personality; each author heard and interpreted these instructions in her or his own way. Such independence can be frightening to an editor of a volume of this size, and perhaps it initially unnerved me. However, this independence exemplifies "diversity," and brings an authenticity to the essays.

If there is a central feature of the vignettes, it is that most of the authors insisted that they provide a "history" of their ethnic group. Many argued that the available history of their ethnic group that is in text material is inaccurate and unfair—filled with sins of "omission and commission." They stood fast and protested (rightly so) when I took my editorial pen to them. Enjoy the vignettes as you read them, but remember they are only "vignettes." Look upon them as single chapters of a good, good book. Finally, it needs to be mentioned that there were some vignettes that I requested but that were not included in *Educating for Diversity: An Anthology of Multicultural Voices* because the authors were overcommitted and could not make the deadline. We hope to include them in a future volume.

Carl A. Grant

Carl A. Grant is a Hoef-Bascom professor in the Department of Curriculum and Instruction and the Department of Afro-American Studies at the University of Wisconsin-Madison. He has written or edited 15 books or monographs in multicultural education and/or teacher education. These include *Research and Multicultural Education, Making Choices for Multicultural Education* (with Christine E. Sleeter), *After the School Bell Rings* (with Christine E. Sleeter), *Bringing Teaching to Life*, and *Community Participation in Education*. He has also written more than 100 articles, chapters in books, and reviews. Several of his writings and programs that he directed have received awards. He is a former classroom teacher and administrator. Grant was a Fulbright Scholar in England in 1982–1983, researching and studying multicultural education. In 1990, the Association of Teacher Educators selected him as one of the 70 leaders in teacher education. In 1993, Grant became president of the National Association for Multicultural Education (NAME).

Part I

Diversity Redux

Praising Diversity in School

Social and Individual Implications

CARL A. GRANT

Politicians, ecologists, demographers, and educators are among the host of people using the word *diversity* with increasing frequency. Throughout the history of the United States, all these groups have as a matter of course responded to diversity, although, unfortunately, often in negative ways. For instance, although people claim to value individuality, our schools have often been forces for conformity. The purpose of this chapter is to discuss both social/political diversity and individual/human diversity and make clear what these types of diversity imply for education and educational policy in the United States today.

In order to do this, it is first necessary to make clear what exactly is meant by *diversity*—not only by definition but also by connotation. Then, it will be useful to examine how diversity has been viewed throughout the history of our nation. After this, we shall be ready to look at some of the people who are using the term today, and what they mean when they use it, whether in a straightforward or a convoluted sense. Finally, we can zero in on an appropriate definition and the implications of diversity for today's schools. During this process, we shall examine both social/political diversity and human/individual diversity, with particular emphasis on how our public schools should and do respond to the issues that continue to arise as both the population of the United States and the students in its public schools become increasingly diverse.

"We are all interested in the origins of words, and their rise and fall....We are all in some sense political, and so is language" (McCrum, Cran, & MacNeil, 1986, p. 14). Throughout the history of this nation, some words have become political footballs (or, if you prefer, hot potatoes). They are appropriated by various factions and tossed about with wild abandon in the hope of making some sort of political point. *Multicultural* and *diversity* are among the words being used with increased frequency, although there is often disagreement about just what they mean. Consider the following excerpt from an article on census data in the *Chicago Sun-Times* that manages to use both words in the same sentence:

> *The greater diversity also follows two decades of immigration that has brought a striking new multiculturalism to many coastal and Sun Belt cities but left many smaller communities in the Midwest relatively untouched.*

Although this appears to be a simple statement of fact, to some people it is good news, while others see it as not-so-good news.

The *American Heritage Dictionary* defines *diversity* as "variety or multiformity." *Roget's Thesaurus* uses "assort," "vary," and "difference" as synonyms for *diversity*. Neither, however, assigns a value—either positive or negative—to the word.

There are some words that, for whatever reason (sound, definition, spelling), have a special meaning for certain individuals. *Diversity* is among the words that have a special meaning to me because I believe that it describes something positive and valuable. Diversity, in the context of this chapter, as well as in the whole collection of chapters herein, is a positive concept. I value diversity; I believe it is something positive. Diversity means that you and I don't have to try to be the same as everyone else. We can be different—and acting and looking different is even more than merely okay, it's a good thing.

Diversity, as defined here, demands the awareness, acceptance, and affirmation of cultural and ethnic differences. In addition, it promotes both the appreciation of human differences and the belief that, in order for students to think critically—especially about life circumstances and opportunities that directly and indirectly impact their lives and the lives of their family members, community, and country—they must affirm both *social* diversity (cultural pluralism) and *human* diversity.

Diversity and Cultural Pluralism

Diversity has been incorporated, in theory, in the principles of cultural pluralism. Gordon (1961) argued that cultural pluralism was a *fact* in U.S. society *before* it became a theory. As newly arriving immigrants sought out and settled with their own national kind, they formed national and ethnic colonies. Gordon (1978) described cultural pluralism as the belief that there is strength in variety, and that the United States as a whole benefits from the contributions of different groups of people. He further observed: "Cultural pluralism involves giving and taking and, more importantly, the sharing of and mutual respect for ideas, customs and values" (p. 64). In a similar manner, Rose (1964) observed, "America can be seen as a mosaic of ethnic groups, a 'nation of nations,' each retaining its unique qualities while contributing to the over-all pattern" (p. 56).

Diversity, although symbolized as respected and natural within our society, and in some ways accepted as normal (e.g., religious differences), nevertheless both as a concept and in practice is not actually affirmed. "Mainstreaming," "fitting in," and the reluctance (or outright refusal) to accept people who differ by color, language, ethnicity, sexual preference, and/or socioeconomic status shape the prevailing attitudes and behavior of our society. Praise and respect for diversity must become the spirit that motivates people of color, White ethnic groups, and other marginalized groups of people to believe in the American creed—essential dignity for every individual, equality for all humankind, and the guarantee of the inalienable rights of freedom, justice, and equal opportunity for every American. These beliefs must be genuine because they are the very cornerstone of democracy in this country.

Diversity versus Conformity: A Long Chapter in U.S. History

From the days when a wide variety of Native-American tribes lived freely on this continent, the geographic areas that came together to form this nation teemed with diversity. The arrival of people from different European countries and the establishment of colonies on the North American continent merely expanded an already existing diversity of peoples in the lands that would eventually become the United States.

Colonial life during the seventeenth and eighteenth centuries exhibited variety in people, customs, and industry. For years, some historians and social scientists have argued that it was because of its diversity that the United States was strengthened as a nation. John Dewey, Jane Addams, Horace Kallen, and Louis Adamic were among those who argued this point of view, while many others were advocating the concept and policy of "Americanization" or "Anglo conformity." Indeed, Anglo conformity and Americanization, especially of new immigrants to this country, has been espoused since early in this nation's history by such leaders as George Washington, John Adams, and Benjamin Franklin. George Washington wrote to John Adams a pertinent letter that included the following statement: "My opinion, with respect to immigration, is that except of useful mechanics and some particular descriptions of men or professions, there is no need of encouragement, while the policy or advantage of its taking place in a body (I mean the settling of them in a body) may be much questioned; for, by so doing, they retain the language, habits and principles (good or bad) which they bring with them" (Rose, 1964, p. 149).

In an article on cultural pluralism, Seymour Itzkoff (1966) wrote that "Benjamin Franklin himself was suspicious of any other tongue but English and wanted the schools to wean the Pennsylvania Dutch from their foreign accents." On the other hand, Dewey and many others recognized the value of ethnic diversity to this country. Dewey in particular saw the important role that education needed to play in teaching respect for diversity, and for that reason I quote him extensively here:

> *I want to mention only two elements in the nationalism which our education should cultivate. The first is that the American nation is itself complex and compound. Strictly speaking it is interracial and international in its make-up. It is composed of a multitude of peoples speaking different tongues, inheriting diverse traditions, cherishing varying ideals of life. This fact is basic to our nationalism as distinct from that of other peoples. Our national motto, "One from Many," cuts deep and extends far. It denotes a fact which doubtless adds to the difficulty of getting a genuine unity. But it also immensely enriches the*

possibilities of the result to be attained. No matter how loudly any one proclaims his Americanism, if he assumes that any one racial strain, any one component culture, no matter how early settled it was in our territory, or how effective it has proved in its own land, is to furnish a pattern to which all other strains and cultures are to conform, he is a traitor to an American nationalism. (1916a, p. 205)

When Dewey wrote that statement in 1916 in "Nationalizing Education," the climate in the United States was one of heightened Americanism. In many cases, there was outright hostility toward immigrant groups. Novelist E. L. Doctorow, describing immigrants during this period, wrote in *Ragtime* (1974):

They went into the streets and were somehow absorbed in the tenements. They were despised by New Yorkers. They were filthy and illiterate.... They lived too many to a room. There was no sanitation. The streets reeked of shit. Children died of mild colds or slight rashes. Children died on beds made from two kitchen chairs pushed together. They died on floors. Many people believed that filth and starvation and disease were what the immigrant got for his moral degeneracy. (pp. 13, 15)

The role of schools at this time was to teach immigrants Anglo conformity. Many native-born, nonindigenous Americans believed that the growing number of immigrants arriving on U.S. shores threatened national unity. This perceived threat to national unity caused the government to take legislative action to halt or greatly restrict immigration. Among the results of this legislation were the following:

- In 1902, the Chinese Exclusion Act was made permanent.
- In 1917, the U.S. Congress enacted a law requiring adult immigrants to pass a literacy test; this same law also created the Asiatic Barred Zone, which prohibited immigration from most of Asia and the Pacific Islands.
- In 1921, the U.S. government enacted an emergency law that limited immigration from southern and eastern Europe.
- In 1922, the U.S. Supreme Court ruled that the naturalization of immigrants applied to White people only.

Asian immigrants were the victims of special laws to keep them out of the United States. However, when they *were* permitted to enter (often because they were needed as laborers), they were usually viewed as strangers. This view is still prevalent today in many segments of society.

Ronald Takaki (1989) explained that point in *Strangers from a Different Shore:*

Asian newcomers encountered a prevailing vision of America as essentially a place where European immigrants would establish a homogeneous white society and where nonwhites would have to remain "stranger."...But the Asian immigrants chose not to let the course of their lives be determined completely by the "necessity" of race and class in America....Throughout their history in this country, Asians have been struggling in different ways to help America accept its diversity. (pp. 472–473)

Takaki (1989) further added:

[Today, Asian Americans] have greater freedom than did the earlier immigrants to embrace their own "diversity"—their own cultures as well as their own distinctive physical characteristics, such as their complexion and the shape of their eyes....But in many painful ways, they still find themselves unjustly viewed and treated as "strangers from a different shore." (p. 474)

"Diversity" in the United States of the 1990s

Before concluding this discussion on the meaning of diversity, it is important that some observations be made about how and why the term is being used more and more, as both word and concept, in political and social contexts. For some people, *diversity* is a much less threatening, safer (kinder and gentler) term than "antiracist education," or "multicultural education." By "kinder and gentler," I mean that the word does not directly suggest that one's political or social attitudes are in need of significant change. In fact, it suggests, as stated earlier, variety and multiformity. This sometimes seems to imply that *just a little* change or adjustment—developing tolerance—is *all* that's needed in the traditional institutional structures to make room for "different folk." For other people, the increasing use of *diversity* as both a word and a concept in education means that the melting-pot theory is being abandoned, and that the social and political implications associated with it— "melting away" both cultural differences and the striving for Anglo conformity—are being abandoned because they were the source of much human degradation.

The use of *diversity* in educational discussion and writing therefore demands an accompanying clarity of meaning and purpose. For example, in a recently published book by Sonia Nieto (1992), titled *Affirming Diversity*, the author acknowledged diversity but chose to focus on only certain aspects of it: "Nevertheless, although I refer in the text to many kinds of differences, I am particularly concerned with race, ethnicity, and language" (p. xxviii).

Cushner, McClelland, and Safford (1992) defined *diversity* in a somewhat different manner:

Our definition of diversity, at least for classroom and school purposes, encompasses not only those individuals whose ethnic heritage originates in another country, but also those among us who may have special educational and other needs (the hearing impaired, the visually impaired), those who may share significantly different lifestyles (rural and urban children, children who live in extreme poverty, drug dependents), those whose identity is critically influenced by their gender, and those who are significantly influenced by variations in class and religion. By this definition, everyone in a pluralistic society such as the

> *United States is multicultural to some degree and each person may have a distinct subjective culture, including unique value systems, norms of behavior, modes of interaction, socialization practices, linguistic patterns, and so forth. (p. 24)*

Debate about the meaning of *diversity* is to be expected, and this is as it should be, for debate stimulates excellence in research and scholarship. It is important, however, that readers make certain that they understand precisely *how* the term is being used when they study *any* author's work.

Social/Political Diversity and the Role of the School

> *As in an orchestra, every type of instrument has its special timbre and tonality, found in its substances and form; as every type has its appropriate theme and melody in the whole symphony, so in society each ethnic group is the natural instrument, its spirit and culture are its theme and melody, and the harmony and dissonances and discords of them all make the symphony of civilization, with this difference. (Kallen, 1915)*

The meanings, including the positive values previously described, given to *diversity*—difference, variety, or multiformity—should convey to a student that (within school policy and procedures) he or she can be wholly and confidently himself or herself. It is not necessary to follow the "in" crowd, to adhere to peer pressure, or to follow the mainstream view of social and political school life, without a close critical inquiry and analysis. A student can move to the beat of a *different* drum, one that resonates a rhythm that inspires because it communicates respect, understanding, and acceptance for his or her home and community. To allow for these things in schools, diversity must mean that students are (1) presented with a *range* of academic and social choices, (2) encouraged to examine and evaluate *alternatives*, (3) encouraged to seek *different* points of views, and (4) taught that there is *strength and unity* in diversity.

What, then, is the role of the school in respecting and prizing racial, ethnic, and linguistic diversity? Given disturbingly recurring events in our society (e.g., the racial unrest in our cities and on our campuses, the growing number of haves and have-nots, and the increasing percentage of the population consisting of people of color), it is extremely important for educators to understand the role of the schools, as well as the significance of this role as they develop an action plan.

It is obvious to me that the public K–12 education system must become a more active player in promoting social equality and cultural pluralism, and in preparing students to work toward these goals. Since racism, classism, and sexism are embedded within the social fabric of society, the schools' curriculum and instruction must prepare students to bring about positive social change to correct these inequities. The curriculum must include current social issues and examine prejudice, discrimination, and differential treatment of groups of people in all institutions of U.S. life, as well as consider the bases for inequities in individuals' daily lives. The curriculum must also provide knowledge about the history, ideas, and beliefs of the diverse groups that have contributed to the growth and development of the United States. The various and conflicting viewpoints that are a part of our culturally pluralistic society must be examined in the schools, because if they are not, the resultant misunderstanding, frustration, and anger may lead to continuing and worsening turmoil on our streets. Similarly, critical thinking must be taught, but its teaching must include much more than mere cogitation on what will provide the correct answer on an academic examination. It must encompass consideration of issues that affect students' present and future lives—for example, Why is our nation moving toward a two-class society, and how will this affect my life circumstances and opportunities? If my mother is Black and my father is White, am I Black or White or neither?

Some will argue that, yes, the school has a role to educate and to help students understand and appreciate diversity, but that it should not be required to take on the *major* share of this enormous responsibility. They will argue that public schools need to concentrate on teaching reading, math, science, history, art, and music. In addition, they will argue that public schools are having to take on so many *other* social responsibilities. Their arguments are not without merit, for when our nation is in crisis, it is the schools that all too often are called on to assume major societal responsibility for the cure (and, I might add, to accept major blame for the societal failure).

In 1916, John Dewey wrote the following in an article entitled "The School and Social Preparedness":

> *Yet it is back to the schools, to the teachers, the text-books, the courses of study, the school-room methods of teaching and discipline, that education comes and with education the larger part of the conscious direction of our social affairs. The public school is the willing packhorse of our social system; it is the true hero of the refrain: Let George do it. Whenever any earnest group of people want something which is threatened preserved or something which is stable altered, they unite to demand that something or other be taught in the public school. (1916b, p. 191)*

Dewey's observations are correct. Society always turns to the schools to be our "packhorse" in time of crisis. However, I would add that the need for the schools to respond to society's crises is even more important today than it was decades ago, because of the increasing weakness of *other* social institutions, such as the home and organized religion. Thus, it is important that both educators *and* students accept the responsibility to be active participants in society's efforts to accept and advocate the positive values of social equality and equity.

Human/Individual Diversity

Labels and Individual Diversity

Theoretically, in U.S. schools each and every student is a prized human being. In practice, however, human diversity is not given the acceptance and affirmation it deserves there in spite of the use of many school slogans and terms to the contrary. For example, it is common to hear teachers espousing such words as *color blindness* and *equality*, and making such statements as *I treat everyone the same*, and *I love all my students*. The currency of such words and statements is often either counterfeit or lacking in full value when applied to students of color. When a teacher is *genuinely* "color blind" toward students, he or she does not recognize and prize any one of them for his or her personal and individual racial and/or ethnic characteristics. Also, if "everyone is treated the same," a student's learning and understanding about his or her own multiple-group membership (e.g., race, ethnicity, gender) isn't enhanced, and, as a result, his or her concept of self could be devalued, or at least not enriched.

The individual diversity and humanness that each and every student brings to school must be accepted and affirmed. Those who tend to see (or want to see) every group, and every member of that group, as the same, miss or deny the beauty of human diversity and variety. Lewontin (1982), in his book *Human Diversity*, denounced this absurdity when he stated, "Despite the similarities that appear when we observe human beings from a philosophical distance, our everyday experience reveals that there is an extraordinary amount of variation among us, too. We differ in height, weight, hair texture, skin color, features and expression, posture, gait, and costume. We have not the slightest difficulty in picking out the faces of a friend from a large crowd of faces even at a glance" (p. 1).

Other words and terms are often used by educators to identify and label individual students with the belief that it will help those students. However, some of these labels have created more educational problems than they have contributed to educational solutions. *Culturally disadvantaged* and *culturally deprived*, two terms used in the 1960s and 1970s, encouraged teachers to believe that students of color and students who came from low-income families didn't have a culture, and so were unable to achieve the level of academic success of White students. These terms encouraged teachers to view most students of an ethnic group of color in a stereotypical or generalized manner, thereby not respecting and giving credit to each student's individual worth and ability. Frank Riessman, author of *The Culturally Deprived Child* (1962), recognized the damage done by the title of his book when he criticized the title in the opening line of the first chapter of his next book, *The Inner-City Child* (1976): "Since 1962, when I wrote *The Culturally Deprived Child*—the book with the very bad and misleading title...."

Although the appellation sounds more positive, an increasing number of Asian-American scholars have been speaking out regarding the practice of viewing (stereotyping) all Asian-American students as "model students"—passive, quiet, and intelligent. Bob Suzuki (1989) argued, "As positive as the model minority image may seem, Asian Americans have suffered significant negative fallout from this stereotype. It is, in fact, a liability, as Asian scholars have been saying for years."

Recent studies show that many Asian Americans, especially recent immigrants, are far from realizing the American Dream. Southeast Asians, such as the Hmong and Mien refugees, are probably having the most difficult time making ends meet, often living on welfare and showing signs of strain. Although many Korean immigrants have become economically successful by becoming self-employed entrepreneurs, they have also been found to suffer from overwork, depression, and other psychological disorders (Suzuki, 1989, pp. 13, 19).

Presently, there is another term that has a negative impact on the human diversity that many students of color bring to school because it stereotypes them on the basis of an educational and social profile. That term is *at risk*. This term was first used in the report by the National Commission on Excellence in Education, *A Nation at Risk*, when it addressed the educational problems of the United States. The report used the term as follows: "Our Nation is at risk.... We report to the American people that while we can take justifiable pride in what our schools and colleges have historically accomplished and contributed to the United States and the well-being of its people, the educational foundations of our society are presently being eroded by a raising tide of mediocrity that threatens our very future as a Nation and a people" (p. 5).

At risk, as it is used presently by many educators, no longer refers to a nation, but rather to students who are most often of color and poor, and whose first language isn't English. Thus, certain characteristics of student diversity (e.g., color, language, ethnicity, and socioeconomic class) label an individual as a potential educational winner or loser. Furthermore, the term often sticks to a student and clouds teachers' perceptions of that person as he or she moves through the grades. Finally, *whether or not* the student needs a great deal of assistance, the "at risk" label (which students find out about) can bring forth a self-fulfilling prophecy.

Body Size, Standards of Beauty, and Diversity

There is another area of human diversity that needs to be better understood and respected in schools, because how teachers deal with it can influence a student's feelings about himself or herself. This is the area of body size (height and weight) and physical beauty. Television, Hollywood, and Madison Avenue are powerful forces in deciding on the standards of beauty for society. These institutions declare and perpetuate the image of what kind of body characteristics are attractive and therefore most accepted. Similarly, athletic sports define the body size necessary to participate in the organized games that lead to becoming a school sports hero. Schools reflect and perpetuate these ideas mainly through their hidden curriculum (e.g., members of the cheering squad or golf team) of the model person and the model sport. Because of such propagandized criteria, many students feel put down, their human/individual diversity and variance from "the standard" making them less worthy and acceptable as human beings.

Teachers as well as parents tell students that beauty is only skin deep and that it is the inner person that really counts. However, students are reminded most everywhere they look that this simply is not the case. During a visit to a school on the West Coast where the student composition was 45 percent Hispanic, 35 percent White, 12 percent African American, and 8 percent Asian American, I observed a microcosmic English class that had demographics very similar to that of the whole school. Displayed around the room were student projects that included magazine pictures. The majority of the photos showed tall, slender, White males and females; only a few were of tall, slender, African-American males and females. Representations of the other ethnic groups were conspicuously absent, as were evidences of a variety of different body sizes and shapes.

Schools must make conscientious efforts to ensure that they celebrate different models of human diversity. For example, schools' cheerleaders and drum-majorette squads need to reflect the true populations of the schools more closely, whenever that is practicable. Wall posters and pictures need to focus more on a healthy person than on a so-called beautiful person. Schools also need to sponsor more of a variety of athletic teams for both boys and girls in order to enable more students to participate. These teams should promote physical conditioning and playing for *fun*, and provide an opportunity for larger numbers of children to demonstrate their skills before peers, parents, relatives, and teachers.

As recently as 1960, many western European ideas about beauty were reinforced via standardized tests. For example, the version of the Terman's Stanford-Binet Intelligence Test of that time discriminated against members of the lower class, southern Europeans, and African Americans through the inclusion of derogatory content. That version asked children to determine "Which is Prettier?" and counterposed portraits of non-White people against those of White Anglo-Saxon individuals. According to the test, the correct choice was the Anglo-Saxon representative in both examples.

Double Consciousness and Diversity

Prizing human diversity requires understanding the "double consciousness" that many students of color experience as they enter schools with a large population of White students and teaching staff. DuBois, in *The Souls of Black Folk*, addressed this double-consciousness feeling experienced by people of color. He wrote:

> The Negro is a sort of seventh son, born with a veil, and gifted with second-sight in this American world, a world which yields him no true self consciousness, but only lets him see himself through the revelation of the other world. It is a peculiar sensation, this double-consciousness, this sense of always looking at one's self through the eyes of others, of measuring one's soul by the tape of a world that looks on in amused contempt and pity. One ever feels his twoness—an American, a Negro; two souls, two thoughts, two unreconciled strivings; two warring ideals in one dark body, whose dogged strength alone keeps it from being torn asunder. (pp. 16–17)

Recently, my daughter was required to read *Native Son* for an English class in which she was the only student of color. It was the class's first assignment. From time to time, during her reading of the book, we discussed the different characters and the social and political setting of the story. The second book she had to read for that class was *The Autobiography of Malcolm X*. We discussed this book, too, but there was a difference in the nature of the discussion: This time she was much more "turned on." Reading *Malcolm X* encouraged her to visit the library to read newspaper accounts describing his life and death. She was also eager for me to read her report on the book.

Shortly after she had completed the reading of *Malcolm X*, I had to go to her school to drop off something she had left at home. At the school, a chance meeting with her English teacher took place. She complimented my daughter's report on *Malcolm X*, but wondered why the report on *Native Son* was never turned in. She said that she knew my daughter had read the book because of her active class participation, which especially included trying to explain the Black point of view of the story. I listened, somewhat puzzled by this rush of information. I thanked the teacher and said, "I will ask her about the *Native Son* report." Of more concern to me, however, was her comment about trying to explain the Black point of view.

To make a long story short, my daughter and I discussed why the *Native Son* report hadn't been completed. Listening to her reason, I concluded that her continuous effort of having to try to explain a Black point of view regarding *Native Son* to an all-White class (many of whom she was trying to develop friendships with, since she had recently transferred to the school) and teacher wore her down and made her want to forget the novel. Also, since *Native Son* was the first novel in the course, and the students were attacking the Black protagonist, she was immediately put on the defensive.

Later, when I saw the English teacher, I discussed with her what I reasoned had happened and suggested, that the next time there were only one or two African-American students in the class, she should consider starting with *Malcolm X*, because that story provides many African-American students with a sense of personal power and respect. In her English class, my daughter experienced DuBois's words: "One ever feels his twoness— an American, a Negro; two souls, two thoughts, two unreconciled strivings; two warring ideals in one dark body..." (1961, p. 17).

Gender, Language, and Diversity

Before I conclude this discussion of human diversity, it is important that I give specific attention to gender and language. School life can affect how a student values and under-stands his or her own gender, and thereby both influences career paths and develops an understanding of power relationships. Whereas it is important in valuing human diversity that the recognition of gender be considered of paramount significance, it is equally important that a student's gender not prevent him or her from equality in all of life's opportunities. Lewontin (1982) noted:

> *Gender differences are not the direct consequence of chromosomal and hor-monal differences but arise from the socialization and self-images of people, identified from birth by their external appearance, as male or female. That is, gender differences are based upon, but are not caused by, sex differences. Parents identify a baby as female, socialize it as a female, and make it aware, at an early age, of its own female identify. In this way, individual people and society interact to determine each person's gender identity. (p. 139)*

Schools must be alert to the way in which society socializes students because of their gender, and offer policies and practices that encourage socialization and development based on a student's ability and career goals, not on gender.

In many high schools, science and mathematics courses are taught by male teachers, and language and writing courses are taught by female teachers. It is important that these staffing patterns be changed to show greater diversity. However, until this change occurs, it is important that teachers make students—both male and female—aware of opportuni-ties in all professions and occupations, including those that at one time mainly hired people based on their gender. Similarly, it is important for teachers to point out to students incidents of gender discrimination that occur in employment situations, in order that they may become aware of this discrimination and participate in efforts to eliminate it.

Students also need to know that in the U.S. Department of Labor there is a "glass ceiling" office, and that this office is dedicated to the elimination of gender bias at the highest levels of employment in corporate America. Additionally, students need to know that although there have been slight increases in female median income, the gap between the median incomes of males and females continues to widen.

Females of color are often put into a double bind. Their human diversity is often put down because of two of their multiple-group characteristics—race and gender. Females of color must be prized for both their race and gender. They need to have the opportunity to learn about and read about people such as themselves throughout the school curriculum, and to participate in school events (e.g., plays, assemblies) that celebrate and discuss collectively both of these characteristics. The importance of such an experience has been illuminated for adults by such authors as Alice Walker (*The Color Purple*), Ntozake Shange (*For Colored Girls...*), Gloria Naylor (*The Women of Brewster Place*), Terry McMillan (*Waiting to Exhale*), Louise Erdrich (*Tracks*), and Sandra Cisneros (*House on Mango Street*). These authors have received wide acclaim, especially from women of color, because they speak directly to the issue of being both female and of color. In articulate voices that are clear and forceful, these authors celebrate and discuss publicly their gender and ethnicity in a way that, for decades, has only been heard within female-of-color friendship groups. The opportunity to participate in the aforementioned school events, and the encouragement to do so, along with high expectations by teachers during participation, all are important.

Females of color must in fact be encouraged to become actively involved in a variety of school affairs and events, and to take leadership roles therein. Most of what they see, with a few exceptions (e.g., Oprah Winfrey, Connie Chung, Whitney Houston), tells them that the "world" is White and male or White and female. The choice of events such as school plays must not put females of color at a disadvantage when trying out for a leading role. Teachers must not claim a "gender color blindness." Females of color are very much aware of their gender and their race, and to attempt to relegate it to obscurity, or to marginalize it, doesn't prize diversity.

The beauty of females of color must be celebrated no less in quality, quantity, and kind than that of White females. Many of the classic paintings that feature White females, especially in our older school buildings, need to share the wall space with contemporary paintings of women of color. *All* decorations need to be examined for sexism. An overall count of the number of paintings of women of color and White women, and the way these women are portrayed (e.g., active versus passive, decision makers versus followers), needs to be taken in order to make certain that equality exists and diversity is celebrated.

Language

According to the U.S. Bureau of the Census (1984), there are more than 35 million linguistic-minority persons in the United States. Of this number, 10.5 million are under the age of 17, and 19.5 million are not fluent in English. A student's language is an important factor in defining his or her individual diversity. Language can serve to indicate a student's culture and station in life, and can influence his or her academic achievement and self-concept development. Trueba (1991) stated that research studies of English literacy acquisition since the early 1970s have shown a significant correspondence between cultural congruency and effective learning, and that language and effective teacher-student communication are essential to the fostering of cognitive growth in children (p. 154). Trueba also pointed out the need for teachers to understand the language diversity that each student brings: "Without knowing the children's language, the teacher cannot bridge the instructional gap and adapt instructional design for culturally different children" (p. 154).

In spite of these research results on English literacy, many teachers and school administrators seem to believe only that the way for nonnative students to achieve academically is by knowing English. Similarly, many believe that since other immigrants had to learn English, no exception should be made for recent immigrants. These educators tend to forget that in order for the United States to maintain its global respect and leadership, it must have citizens who are fluent in the languages of the different countries we work with if we are to live harmoniously in the "global village."

Presently, many students whose first language isn't English are without teachers who can teach them academics in their native language or who can help them to continue to increase their knowledge of their own language while they are learning English. The absence of bilingual teachers curtails the academic potential of non-English-speaking students, and severely limits the development of an important aspect of their cultural diversity—their native language.

Conclusion

As our nation continues to change, new challenges and demands to understand, appreciate, and affirm diversity will arise. Unless there are major improvements in other societal institutions, schools will be required to play a major role in preparing students to deal with this change. Teachers must do what must be done—and what must be done is to educate all of our students to praise diversity.

References

Cushner, K., McClelland, A., & Safford, P. (1992). *Human diversity in education*. New York: McGraw-Hill.

Dewey, J. (1916a). Nationalizing education. In J. A. Boydston (Ed.), *John Dewey: The middle works 1899–1924*. Carbondale and Edwardsville: Southern Illinois University Press.

Dewey, J. (1916b). The School and social preparedness. In J. A. Boydston (Ed.), *John Dewey: The middle works 1899–1924*. Carbondale and Edwardsville: Southern Illinois University Press.

Doctorow, E. L. (1974). *Ragtime*. New York: Vintage Books.

DuBois, W. E. B. (1961). *The souls of black folk*. Greenwich, CT: Fawcett Publications

Gordon, M. M. (1978). *Human nature, class, and ethnicity*. New York: Oxford University Press.

Itzkoff, S. W. (1966). Curriculum pluralism in urban education, *School and Society, 94,* 385.

Kallen, H. M. (1915). Democracy versus the melting pot. *The Nation, 100*, 190–194.

Lewis, N. (Ed.). (1961). *The new Roget's thesaurus.* New York: Berkley.

Lewontin, R. (1982). *Human diversity.* New York: Scientific American Books.

McCrum, R., Cran, W., & MacNeil, R. (1986). *The story of English.* New York: Penguin.

National Commission on Excellence in Education. (1983). *A Nation at risk:The imperative of education reform.* Washington, DC: U.S. Government Printing Office.

Nieto, S. (1992). *Affirming diversity.* New York: Longman.

Riessman, F. (1962). *The culturally deprived child.* New York: Harper & Row.

Riessman, F. (1976). *The inner-city child.* New York: Harper & Row.

Rose, P. I. (1964). *They and we: Racial and ethnic relations in the United States.* New York: Random House.

Suzuki, B. H. (1989, November/December). Asian Americans as the model minority. *Change.*

Takaki, R. (1989). *Strangers from a different shore.* Boston: Little, Brown.

Trueba, H. T. (1991). Learning needs of minority children: Contributions of ethnography to educational research. In L. Malave & G. Duquette (Eds.), *Language, culture and cognition.* Philadelphia: Adeaode.

U.S. Bureau of the Census (1984). *1980 census: Current population report.* Washington, DC: U.S. Government Printing Office.

About the Author

Carl A. Grant is a Hoef-Bascom professor in the Department of Curriculum and Instruction and the Department of Afro-American Studies at the University of Wisconsin-Madison. He has written or edited 15 books or monographs in multicultural education and/or teacher education. These include *Research and Multicultural Education, Making Choices for Multicultural Education* (with Christine E. Sleeter), *After the School Bell Rings* (with Christine E. Sleeter), *Bringing Teaching to Life*, and *Community Participation in Education.* He has also written more than 100 articles, chapters in books, and reviews. Several of his writings and programs that he directed have received awards. He is a former classroom teacher and administrator. Grant was a Fulbright Scholar in England in 1982–1983, researching and studying multicultural education. In 1990, the Association of Teacher Educators selected him as one of the 70 leaders in teacher education. In 1993, Grant became president of the National Association for Multicultural Education (NAME).

Chapter 2

Population Dynamics and Ethnic Attitudes

The Context of American Education in the Twenty-First Century

MICHAEL C. THORNTON

Introduction

Since the early 1970s, we have witnessed a momentous demographic transformation in the landscape of U.S. society: Most immigration to the United States has come from non-European regions. Although many factors are contributing to the rapid rise in the number of people of color in this country (including, for example, higher birth rates and larger families), immigration has been the most publicized. Taken together, these trends foretell that by early in the twenty-first century, people of African, Asian, Hispanic, and Native-American heritages will be the majority of the work force in places like California and New York, and also the majority of the populations of several states. By the year 2010, at least one in three Americans will be from a racial minority group, although at that time such a term may, in many instances, be inappropriate. Thus, it is clear that over the next several decades, groups of color inevitably will assume an ever-increasing influence on our society.

This increasing influx of Americans of varying worldviews, colors, and cultures is ushering in what might be called a new millennium in American life. However, the beginning phases of this new era have created mixed reactions, exacerbating the existing crisis in interracial relations. There are clear signs that liberalism is stagnating, with some suggesting that we have reached an impasse between support for the principles of racial equality and a willingness to implement policy to bring it about. All the easy integration has been done (Schuman, Steeh, & Bobo, 1988). This lack of support for implementation reflects in part the shrinking centrality of race in political discourse and its perceived relative insignificance for life in the United States. However, this trend toward intransigence in racial issues is of course nothing new, nor is the ebb and flow between practice and ideals. "The pervasive gap between our aims and what we actually do," stated President Truman's Committee on Civil Rights in 1947, "is a kind of moral dry rot which eats away at the emotional and rational bases of democratic beliefs" (U.S. President's Committee on Civil Rights, 1947, p. 139).

The "browning of America" brings with it many challenges, most of which involve conflict. In the process of preparing for such a new world, if history is any judge, our educational institutions will be called on to lead the way. This chapter will explore how the new demographics appear to have affected intergroup relations and attitudes. These factors in turn will be examined for what they imply for the nature of education and educational institutions as they attempt to accomplish the task of making this a society where true diversity is at least tolerated, but hopefully more valued and perhaps even seen as indispensable to a healthy world.

Changing Demographics

As we have seen, the changing scenery of the U.S. social life in recent decades is due in no small way to the influx of a multitude of people from throughout the world. As Lieberson and Waters (1988, pp. 780–781) suggested, immigration patterns are reflections of several factors, including government policies facilitating immigration to the United States from certain regional sources while simultaneously obstructing it from elsewhere; differences within groups in rates of natural increase; and the age and sexual composition of immigrant groups, both of which affect the contraction or growth of a group's relative position in society. The ethnic composition of U.S. society has also been influenced by the acquisition of overseas territories (e.g., Puerto Rico) and overseas economic and military involvement in places such as Asia and South and Central America.

Immigration Patterns

Since about 1950, perhaps the most fundamental influence on the ethnic composition of U.S. society has been the passage of the Immigration and Naturalization Act of 1965 (which actually went into effect in 1968). This legislation brought about a major shift in the sources of U.S. immigration. As Table 1 indicates, in the 20 years prior to this legislation, almost 90 percent of immigration originated from European or North American sites. Non-White immigration was negligible. Following the implementation of the new law, European immigration dropped to almost a third of its prior rates, while Asian immigration almost tripled. These trends increased through the 1980s, although since 1989 immigration from North America has become an increasingly larger part of overall immigration. When Asian and Mexican rates were examined in separate analyses, the proportion of overall immigration from these areas increased from 23 percent for the period 1951 to 1970 to 53 percent for the period 1971 to 1980, and to approximately 65

TABLE 1   Immigration to the United States by Region of Origin, 1951 to 1991 (in thousands)

Region	1951 to 1970	1971 to 1980	1981 to 1990	1991	1951 to 1991
Europe	2,400	800	416	135	3,751
Asia	580	1,588	2,759	358	5,285
America	2,700	1,983	3,550	1,211	9,444
Other	120	122	613	123	978
Total Immigration	5,800	4,493	7,338	1,827	19,458

Source: Data are from U.S. Department of Justice, Immigration and Naturalization Service. Annual reports, 1945 to 1977; Statistical Yearbook of the Immigration and Naturalization Service, 1978 to 1990; INS Fact Book, 1993.

percent of total immigration during the 1980s. When immigration from all sources of non-European heritage are combined, one in two immigrants during the years immediately following the passage of legislation was non-White, while during the recent era two out of three are what we now call "people of color" (Latinos/Hispanics, Asians, and Africans).

Current population estimates indicate that there are 28 million Black Americans, 1.5 million Native Americans, 7 million Asian Americans, and 20 million Hispanic Americans (Harrison, Wilson, Pine, Chan, & Buriel, 1990). These figures represent a doubling of the Asian-American population since 1980 (most Asians here now were born overseas) and a more than 50 percent increase in Hispanic Americans (who are primarily of Mexican heritage), who now make up almost 10 percent of all Americans.

Geographical Distribution

Although the numbers are impressive, they say nothing about how these populations are distributed, a pattern which contributes to the complexity of interracial relations in late twentieth-century American life. In part because they tend to migrate to established communities, partially encouraged to do so by the family reunification focus of past law, these groups are concentrated in particular areas—unlike most of the largest White ethnic groups, that are fairly well distributed throughout the country. The largest Asian-American groups live primarily on the Pacific coast, with pockets in the Midwest and New York. Mexican-American and Native-American populations are primarily in the Southwest, Puerto Ricans in the Northeast, and Cubans in the Mid-Atlantic and South Atlantic states. Blacks remain concentrated in the South. All these groups also tend to be urban residents.

Lieberson and Waters (1988, p. 788) noted that the index of dissimilarity (which ranges from 0 to 100, with 0 signifying that a group's geographical distribution is identical to that of the rest of the population, and with 100 revealing a population totally segregated from other groups in society) indicates that groups vary tremendously in how residentially integrated they are into society. The range is from a low of 4 (Irish) to a high of 61 (Mexicans). The most segregated groups, with index values of over 50, are Filipinos, Japanese, Portuguese, Puerto Ricans, and Mexicans. Other ethnic minorities fall within a wide range: Native Americans (17), Hispanics (30), Cubans (49), and Blacks (23).

Along with distinctive regional distributions, we also find varying urban dispersion patterns. In San Jose, minorities will be Mexican and Asian; in Miami, they will be primarily Cuban and Black; and Los Angeles will have Mexicans and Blacks. Other cities will have one primary minority group, such as Denver and Houston with Mexicans, and Chicago, Atlanta, and New York with primarily Blacks (Lieberson & Waters, 1988, pp. 798–799).

The new immigration pattern since 1965 has exacerbated interracial relations by widening the number and variety of participants on the playing field, most of whom are obviously different from the general population. By the nature of these dispersion patterns, few areas of the country will have the same configuration of groups interacting. In many cases, the focus of attention is no longer on how Whites and some other group get along, but how two (or three) ethnic minority populations interact. In many cases, Whites may even be an insignificant factor in the formula. Thus, how we deal with the issue of interracial conflict has become ever more complicated, as well as group- and geographically specific.

Part of the resulting friction is attributed to genuine culture conflict and misunderstandings due to language barriers. However, a number of other, perhaps more significant, dynamics also explain recent race relations. As noted earlier, the influx of these new groups has occurred over a very short period of time, from 1965 to 1985, and within a narrow range of communities. Such developments probably will always lead to resentment, fear, and hostility, revealing underlying prejudices and racism born of preexisting stereotypes.

Additionally, in this situation, other things occurred simultaneously to exacerbate relations. As growing numbers of racial minorities arrived on these shores, we also witnessed a decline in U.S. economic dominance, with many so-called countries of color (e.g., Japan, Korea, and Saudi Arabia) now achieving preeminence and a concomitant decline in job security and increased job competition both at home and internationally. Many business and political leaders have chosen to interpret these events in causative terms: "Our" decline is due to "their" predominance, and thus "they" are responsible for the present predicament.

Research on racial attitudes suggests that fear and feeling threatened are dispositions associated with higher rates of racial intolerance (Giles & Evans, 1984). Consequently, we have seen increasing rates of violence against Asians and "Arabs" (who often are Iranian and therefore not Arab). This underlying apprehension of losing economic control to "foreigners" also can be seen in the nature of new legislation directed at ensuring that this remains a predominantly "White" nation. Recent events have heightened pressure in Congress to return to traditional immigrant patterns, going so far as to create a new ethnic-diversity preference for immigration from such nations as Ireland and Poland.

A casual examination of media sources might suggest that racial intolerance is somehow more virulent and pervasive among groups of color. Witness the recent coverage of orthodox Jews fighting Blacks in Crown Heights, Blacks boycotting Korean grocery stores in New York and Los Angeles, and Hispanics rioting against a local government run by Blacks in Washington, DC. Spotlighting these cases serves to exaggerate the level and extent of interracial conflict, especially between racial minorities. Evidence is not available to explore how prevalent conflict among minorities may be. Nevertheless, most hate-related events involve Whites venting their anger at Blacks, Jews, and homosexuals. Recent events suggest that the recipients of such treatment now also include significant numbers of Asians, and possibly Hispanics (U.S. Commission on Civil Rights, 1986).

While seemingly a new problem, this sort of tension over the changing nature of the population composition has shaped the history of U.S. ethnic relations for more than 100 years. To a large degree this is part of the ebb and flow of American life. What makes it different is that it is no longer a "Negro" or "Chinese" problem, but is far more comprehensive.

✓*White Racial Attitudes*

How the general population feels about various racial groups is a complicated issue. Despite recent developments, racial attitudes among the general population over time have changed for the better, particularly in the level of support given to principles of racial equality. Nevertheless, there are many signs indicating that the general population continues to have ambiguous feelings about interracial interactions. Levels of support for implementation, for example, run far behind support of the principles. In fact, unlike questions of principle, those about implementation (feelings about what steps the government might take to combat segregation or discrimination or to reduce racial inequalities in income or statue) have not shown a consistently positive trend over time (Schuman et al., 1988).

Social-distance research also suggests that attitudes have changed, though in a complex way. Feelings of social distance involve an unwillingness of in-group members to accept or approve a given degree of intimacy in interaction with any member of an out-group (Williams, 1964). Social-distance scales reveal a relative consistency of group rankings from year to year. Although generally making progress since the 1940s, racial minorities remain somewhere between the middle and the bottom of the social hierarchy. Recent scales reveal that (after considering other White ethnic groups) Whites are most accepting of American Indians, then (in order) African Americans, Mexican Americans, and Japanese Americans, followed by other Asian-American groups (i.e., Chinese and Filipinos) (Owen, Eisner, & McFaul, 1981).

Recent Gallup polls reveal a broad pattern of prejudice against diverse ethnic minorities. Substantial numbers of Whites continue to be inhospitable to various groups. More than 1 in 10 Americans would not welcome Koreans, Hispanics, Indians, Pakistanis, or Vietnamese as neighbors. Particular segments of the general community are least accepting of all. Southern Whites are less tolerant than other Whites in their acceptance of Black, Hispanic, and Asian populations (Gallup, 1988, 1990). Almost twice as many southern versus northern Whites would not welcome a member of these groups into their neighborhood. Those over age 50 are least likely to accept any group except Koreans and

Hispanics, who are least desired as neighbors by those 18 to 29 years of age. Those from the Northeast are most accepting of all these groups. Based on this poll, Whites are most accepting of Blacks, then Koreans, Hispanics, Indians, and Paskistanis, and, finally, Vietnamese (Gallup, 1990, pp. 67–74).

A recent study that examined White views toward Asian, Hispanic, and Black Americans tells us a little more about the underlying dynamics of White attitudes toward racial minorities (Bobo & Kluegel, 1991). Whites viewed Asian Americans much less negatively (e.g., they are seen as economically successful, self-supportive, and hard working) than they did Hispanics and Blacks, although they felt equally distant toward Hispanics and Asian Americans, a trend supported by other research (Dyer et al., 1989; Owen et al., 1981). Although Whites viewed Asian Americans less favorably than themselves, Asian Americans were seen to be far ahead of Blacks and Hispanics. Nevertheless, all three groups were seen as less intelligent, more violence prone, lazier, and more likely to live off welfare than Whites. Indeed, the *majority* of Blacks and Hispanics were seen to possess the negative qualities just mentioned.

Of course, not all Whites hold similar viewpoints. Evidence from research also points to qualities associated with positive attitudes toward racial minority groups. Age is an important influence, with younger people adopting more racially egalitarian positions than older people (Condran, 1979; Schuman et al., 1988; Bobo & Kluegel, 1991). However, much of the change observed since 1945 has occurred within—not between—cohorts (e.g., Firebaugh & Davis, 1988; Schuman & Bobo, 1988). Regional differences are well established; non-Southerners are more liberal (Middleton, 1976; Reed & Black 1985; Tuch, 1987). Rural versus urban disparities in tolerance have been a matter of resurgent interest (Stouffer, 1955; Tuch, 1987; Wilson, 1985).

The impact of social class variables and of ethnicity on intergroup attitudes have been addressed qualitatively (Wellman, 1977) and through survey data (Giles & Evans, 1984), and it has been found that the working class generally expresses greater prejudice. Cummings (1980) found this trend particularly among White ethnics in direct labor market competition with Blacks. Greeley's (1985) analysis of National Opinion Research Center data showed modest variation in anti-Black attitudes by ethnicity, but concluded that there was no credible evidence of a unique White ethnic anti-Black backlash. Education remains the single-most important influence on racial tolerance (Bobo & Licari, 1989).

Racial Attitudes among Blacks

While our understanding of White views of Blacks has a long tradition in academic circles, there have been few systematic efforts at examining White attitudes toward non-Black groups, and Black and other racial minority views of other groups. This lack of information is particularly problematic given differing determinants of Black attitudes when compared to those that influence White views (Tuch, 1988; Thornton & Taylor, 1988a, 1988b). The need for this type of information is only heightened by growing contact and conflict between new and established minority groups. The media and many social commentators seem to assume that Black and Hispanic, Black and Arab, and Black and Asian perceptions and interactions are, at best, conflictual. At worst—for the last relationship—they involve the broadest, deepest, and most sustained animosity of any group (Zinsmeister, 1987, 1988; Salholz, 1988; Chavira, Monroe, & Woodbury, 1991). Few commentators talk of potential efforts at coalition building or positive interactions (Jabara & Saleh, 1983; Henry, 1980; Dreyfuss, 1979) unless they are historical accounts (Shankman, 1982).

Aside from a few historical and anecdotal pieces (e.g., Grinde & Taylor, 1984; Forbes, 1984; Shankman, 1982), most work on minority perceptions have focused on Black attitudes, and usually toward Whites. These attitudes have been evaluated directly through measures of alienation, or indirectly with questions about interracial contact, such as marriage and integration (Schuman et al., 1988). Generally, Blacks are more accepting of interracial contact than are Whites. Studies using direct measures find that higher education and higher incomes characterize Blacks who hold liberal racial attitudes (Williams, 1964; Noel & Pinkney, 1964). Males are also described as more tolerant than females (Williams, 1964). However, we must note that these findings come from studies conducted during the 1960s!

Age has an ambiguous effect on racial attitudes. Early evidence associated youth with greater tolerance (Cothran, 1951, Noel, 1964; Noel & Pinkney, 1964; Williams, 1964). Later works described both older and younger Blacks as most likely anti-Semitic (Selznick & Steinberg, 1969), or older Blacks as closer to Whites and Jews (Paige, 1970; Tsukashima, 1978; Tsukashima & Montero, 1976). Region of residence also has an important influence on attitudes, with non-Southerners as more liberal (Williams, 1964; Noel, 1964; Noel & Pinkney, 1964; Stouffer, 1955). At least one study has identified urban residents as less anti-White (Paige, 1970).

Other works highlight less direct measures of attitudes among Blacks. Measures of interracial marriage and school integration (Tuch, 1988; Wilson, 1986), alienation (Schuman & Hatchett, 1974; Campbell & Schuman, 1968) or militancy (Marx, 1967) depict the highly educated, males, non-Southerners, middle income, and urban dwellers as more positive toward Whites than their counterparts. With one exception (Wilson, 1986), this research indicates that older Blacks feel closer to Whites than do their younger compatriots.

The historical and anecdotal evidence on Black views of other racial minorities indicates a range of perceptions. Blacks hold favorable attitudes toward Japanese Americans (Maykovich, 1971) but generally hold negative perceptions of Asian Americans as a group (Lee, 1987; Shankman, 1982; Thornton & Taylor, 1988a, 1988b). By contrast, Black servicemen hold more positive attitudes, especially in comparison to White attitudes, toward Vietnamese (Fiman, Borus, & Stanton, 1975; Borus, 1973). Research on Black and Hispanic interactions stress the political arena and indicate both antagonistic and cooperative relationships (McClain & Karnig, 1990; Willie, 1986; Barbaro, 1977). One recent poll indicates that Blacks are more accepting of Hispanics than is the reverse (Gallup, 1988, pp. 47–51). Another Gallup poll (1990) found Blacks were least likely to accept a Vietnamese as a neighbor, followed by Koreans and Hispanics, and were most accepting of Indians and Pakistanis.

Whichever sociodemographic characteristics are associated with Black racial attitudes toward other ethnic minorities is unclear. Fiman and associates (1975) indicated that older soldiers were more liberal in their views toward Vietnamese than were their younger counterparts. Thornton and Taylor (1988b) found that education, income, age, sex, and urbanicity are determinants of attitudes toward Asian Americans. Certain subgroups were most likely to hold positive attitudes toward this group. Among them were older, male, and rural respondents, and those with lower incomes and educations. Nevertheless, which determinants are significant is dependent on the target group analyzed. For example, income was a significant factor in attitudes toward Africans, but it was *not* toward Asian Americans. Urban residence had opposing effects (Thornton & Taylor, 1988ab).

In analysis using the National Study of Black Americans data set, Thornton (1991) discovered that Black adult feelings of closeness to other minorities (i.e., Africans, West Indians, Hispanics, American Indians, and Asian Americans) is hierarchical in nature. These adults feel closest to other Blacks (i.e., Africans and West Indians), who are followed by American Indians, Hispanic Americans, and then Asian Americans. Of those on the lower end of the rankings, approximately one in three black adults felt close to Hispanic Americans and one in four to Asian Americans. These results also identified characteristics associated with feeling close—results that stand in sharp contrast to those predictive of racial tolerance among Whites. Males were always more tolerant than females. Age was related positively to feeling close to all groups but Hispanics. Increased education and income were affiliated with views toward only three groups. The more educated felt closer to American Indians and Asian Americans; higher income brought with it more distance from African Americans, Northeasterners were more accepting than southerners of all groups except African Americans, while those living in the West felt closer than southerners to non-Black groups (i.e., Asian, Hispanic, and Native American).

The Role of Educational Institutions

It is clear that we still know little about how various racial minority groups perceive one another. This blind spot in our knowledge is particularly problematic, given recent developments in the racial composition of our school systems—particularly those in the larger urban centers. In 1988, for example, Chicago was 60 percent Black and 24 percent Hispanic, Miami was 33 percent Black and 44 percent Hispanic, Los Angeles was 18 percent Black and 57 percent Hispanic, and Dallas was 48 percent Black and 31 percent Hispanic (Salholz, 1988, p. 29). Of course, these figures do not do justice to the complexity of the issue because they do not include Asians and other recent immigrants from Europe and Africa.

Despite this demographic trend, little attention has been given to exploring the mutual perceptions of minorities within the school context. Some recent studies may shed some light on the underlying dynamics, however. For example, different racial groups have contrasting perspectives on diversity. Bowler, Rauch, and Schwarzer (1986) found among a number of high school students (Black, Asian, Filipino, Indochinese, Hispanic, and White) in the San Francisco area that Black and White students were much less racially tense (less uneasy in the presence of others) than were Asian and Indochinese children. Increased tension among the latter may be related to their length of residence in this country. Those who felt most tense were from Asia—fairly recent arrivals with little interracial contact. Blacks, on the other hand, were the most seasoned in cross-group contact. A distant second and third in this category were Hispanics and Filipinos, respectively. The Asian groups and Whites were at the other extreme, having little interracial contact.

Recent studies also reinforce what has (to many informed observers, at least) been a common conviction all along—that there may be some relationship between a willingness to have contact and having an open mind. It seems that Blacks and Hispanics are the most open to these endeavors, while Whites and Asians are least accepting of cross-group interactions. These patterns suggest that groups have strengths and weaknesses that they bring to interracial situations. The underlying causes for these patterns await further examination, but at least one reason may be related to both the length of stay in America and some cultural artifacts. Many Asian groups have very different norms concerning intergroup interactions. These patterns would be most pronounced among recent immigrants, but would be enhanced given the adjustment needs as well. Presumably, with time, those norms inhibiting interaction would be gradually replaced by greater acceptance.

Other work speaks in part to this possibility. Lambert and Taylor (1988) examined attitudes about multiculturalism of parents with children in large public schools in the Detroit area. The participants in the study chosen from four major ethnic groups living in Hamtramck, Michigan (Polish Americans, Arab Americans, Albanian Americans, and Black Americans) and from five major ethnic groups living in Pontiac (Black Americans, working-class and middle-class White Americans, Arab Americans, Puerto Rican Americans, and Mexican Americans). All groups but the middle-class Whites were respondents from lower working-class backgrounds. The authors found little support among these groups for assimilation as a viable strategy for newcomers to these shores. The participants for this study were very supportive of the practice of multiculturalism and the retaining of one's cultural heritage. Only White working-class parents were hostile to these ideas. Retaining one's cultural heritage was an idea that found strong support even among those of Polish ancestry, many of whom were third generation. With few exceptions, these parents wanted their families to be bicultural.

How multiculturalism was to be supported differed by the group in question. Some groups saw schools playing important roles in encouraging multiculturalism, and bilingualism in particular. Arabs and Albanians were especially favorable to the idea of their language being used in public school systems, and Puerto Rican parents wanted schools to take a strong role in promoting bilingualism. In contrast, Mexican-American parents felt that bilingualism should be supported via community-based language classes, whereas White and Black parents felt that languages other than English should be kept at home, the latter feeling nonetheless that their own children should develop full bidialectal skills involving both Black English and standard American English.

Further, Lambert and Taylor (1988) found differing mutual perceptions among the groups examined. Both Albanians and Arabs felt negative attitudes toward other groups, but particularly toward Blacks. Puerto Rican and Mexican parents held relatively favorable intergroup attitudes, much like White middle class and Black respondents who felt favorable toward all groups. Black parents held attitudes generally comparable to those of the socially dominant group in both communities (the Polish in Hamtramck and the middle class in Pontiac). Moreover, Black parents were aware of now other groups viewed them. Of those they perceived to be favorable toward them, they expressed mutual respect and appreciation. Nevertheless, they did not reciprocate hostile sentiments, even against those groups they perceived as disliking them (i.e., members of the White working class, Arabs, and Albanians). The only group hostile to all others were White working class in Pontiac.

Here, too, the evidence suggests that many of these attitudes reflected cultural influences from the mother country. For example, Arab and Albanian parents were more fatalistic and likely to stress the importance of remaining close to the nuclear family than was the case for Polish parents. Perhaps boundaries being so close-knit enhances the drawing of clear boundaries between family and others who are different.

Aside from the streets, the only place these diverse groups will probably meet is within the walls of our educational institutions. However, these institutions are ill prepared to deal with changing demographics and the new configurations of racial groups involved. These new realities force us to look at the idea of an education that is multicultural (cf., Grant, Boyle, & Sleeter, 1980) in a very different light from that cast on past efforts. Demographic changes make it more difficult to find administrators and teachers of color among a shrinking pool of applicants. In part, this trend is explained by the constricting numbers of college-bound racial minorities (especially Blacks and Hispanics), due both to cuts in college grants and the more general economic malaise in communities of color (see, e.g., Irvine, 1988). Additionally, in many of our urban centers the number of White students available to participate in efforts to enhance diversity are also in short supply—in part because they are leaving urban centers where most racial minorities still reside but also because their parents are having fewer children. Effective efforts for diversity in many urban schools now mean a refocusing on not only teaching White students about growing numbers of racial minority groups but also on enlightening these minority groups about one another—an effort in some sense hampered by the presence of primarily White faculty and administrators. Particularly problematic has been the growing presence of economically disadvantaged minority students in school systems that face increasing financial difficulties. We need a better understanding of how we both do and can deal with this new situation.

Although not providing any answers to the financial dilemmas faced by many school systems, perhaps social-science research may be helpful in giving us a clearer idea of things that might help in this context. In reviewing the literature on intergroup attitudes, Brewer and Kramer (1985) suggested that certain observations emerging out of this research are applicable to interracial relations in schools. This research indicates that group membership influences attributions we make about our own and others' behavior, intentions, and values, suggesting that the "subjective culture" (Triandis, 1972) one brings to contact situations may be as important as the structure of the situation—much like the idea of "open-mindedness" discussed in Bowler and colleagues (1986).

Information gained when interacting with others may be either rejected or assimilated to conform to prior expectations, unless alternative knowledge structures have been provided in advance of contact (Brewer & Kramer, 1985). Thus, prior assumptions (i.e., stereotypes) about the group one interacts with may be used to explain away good and/or bad behavior that is (or is not) consistent with the stereotype in operation; these assumptions become self-fulfilling prophecies. For example, if I believe that people in your group are all violence prone, any nonviolent behavior on your part will be explained as your "waiting for the right moment"; violent behavior is attributed to "what can you expect of those people." Resegregation that occurs within many schools may have at its foundation cultural and racial baggage (i.e., prejudices and stereotypes) that students bring with them to school (Gerard & Miller, 1975; Miller, Rogers, & Hennigan, 1983). Intercultural training methods such as the "cultural assimilator" (see Landis & Brislin, 1983) may provide a model for interventions along these lines.

Another key factor identified as potentially important in reducing in-group biases is the presence or cross-cutting category distinctions. With a number of organizing categories available (e.g., race, ethnicity, nationality, social class, sex), competing bases for in-group and out-group classifications reduce the importance of any one category membership as a source of social identity and intergroup comparisons. Thus, the diversity available in school systems today presents us with a golden opportunity to mix classes by race, culture, social class, and sex. Yet, rarely are desegregation efforts sensitive to the need for salient cross-cutting categories schemes that realign individuals along these different dimensions. Even cooperative learning programs are usually designed with the intent of subsuming existing social groupings under a common overarching category, rather than creating alternative category alignments. Without being aware of the importance of these many diverse and cross-cutting categories, the traditional method may allow realignment to reinforce old patterns. Thus, the greater the diversity of students and staff by color, class, and sex, the more affective the intergroup relations.

Some other possibilities arise out of the preceding discussion. Any type of program aiming to increase positive interactions must be tailored to the specific groups in contact, which differ by city, state, and region. A national program will work unevenly. Responding to situational needs means that efforts must be better informed about unique histories and qualities of the ethnic groups involved. For many groups, that consists of information about effects of immigration on attitudes. For example, several of the studies discussed previously suggest that some of the most recent immigrant groups are most uneasy about interracial interactions, particularly with certain other groups. Part of the hostility may have more to do with having to interact with many new groups in a manner not previously required of them (Lambert & Taylor, 1988; Bowler et al., 1986). Alternatively, some of my own work suggests that some groups may have more of a natural rapport with specific other groups. For example, Blacks generally feel much closer to American Indians than they do to Asian Americans, whom they feel less close to than Hispanics. These feeling toward Native Americans are in part due to a long history of biological (and often political) joinings between the two groups; in fact, at one point in history, many Blacks claimed an Indian rather than an African heritage (Thornton, 1991).

One other key factor seldom mentioned is the importance of leadership. Leaders set the tone for any institution. Effective leadership would provide clear-cut rewards and sanctions for those who make honest efforts in moving the organization toward the desired goals. It still seems the rule that we more penalize than reward those who seek to enhance diversity. We often do so by requiring that they confine such efforts to after-hours or on top of other responsibilities. It also occurs too often that the conveyor of the message of valuing diversity only has to convey, but not necessarily instill, those values within themselves. Good leadership can also ensure that the messenger practices what she or he preaches.

Conclusion

As a society, we have seldom rewarded efforts to develop such sophisticated approaches to multiculturalism. Because these efforts are seldom rewarded, we have little experience in this area, and so programs that have been developed have not adequately conveyed the diversity and complexity of American life. In large measure, this failure is related to a lack of understanding of the dynamics of life for so-called racial minorities—especially when it comes to understanding qualities of life unique to each. While this is all too involved to explore further here, suffice it to say that the limitations of many such programs and perspectives are related to the focus on two groups, usually Blacks and Whites, *or* Whites and Asian Americans, *or* Hispanic Americans and Whites. Given the predictable demographic changes in our society over the next decades, such dichotomous comparisons are inadequate in bringing us to a more multidimensional understanding of the complex interracial relationships involved in our social landscape. There must be a move to a more comprehensive perspective of both individual racial groups and various combinations of racial groups.

In the final analysis, people of color have been the objects of this understanding, but not its subjects. This tendency has meant that when racial minorities are discussed, most probably the concern is their relationship with Whites; how people of color feel about one another has rarely been the subject of discussion. The problem with this tactic has been that it simplifies race relations; they are obviously much more complex than "White and other." Despite recent media coverage, there have been among groups of color many positive and constructive coalitions and attitudes crossing racial boundaries. Some evidence indicates that many Blacks feel a special rapport with other groups of color predicated on a belief about a shared experience as racial minorities. The biological and political intersection of Blacks and Native Americans has led to synergetic coalitions. From Black support provided Asian Americans in their early efforts to enter America, to fits of coalition building between Hispanics and Blacks in the Southwest, people of color have interacted with one another in ways unique to each of their respective histories (Shankman, 1982; Thornton & Taylor, 1988a, 1988b).

Thus, while the context and quality of intergroup relations may appear to be group specific, certain patterns transcend racial boundaries. These patterns reveal striking similarities in the behavior of all contending groups, with respect to orientation to power differentials, social conflict, and altering of social structures. There is a deepening sense of disillusionment, rage, alienation, and distrust in the United States that transcends both class and ethnic boundaries.

Universities can also provide an important avenue to understanding these intersections in intergroup relations. Ethnic studies programs, in particular, provide important gateways for assessing this new tomorrow. In real life, people of color have had mixed interactions, but at least they interact. Academics in ethnic studies seem bounded by their own experiences, not making those connections with other minorities; we've "ghettoized" ourselves. In part, this reflects our recent development as academic disciplines. Nevertheless, given the new realities of contact among and between many of us in everyday life, developing and exploring our differences and connections with others of color is imperative. Reestablishing coalitions and alliances across racial and ethnic boundaries is the most effective way to ensure the survival of democratic principles and ideals, the resolution of crises in intergroup relations, and improvement in the state of all groups. Without this synergism, we will make more difficult the war that we each fight. To wage this campaign, we need to begin by reassessing strategies and approaches for changing the conditions of these groups. Although the conditions experienced by groups may be similar, strategies alleviating the conditions each faces may not be equally appropriate.

As part of this reassessment, we must also begin to break down walls between our respective communities of color and continue to rid ourselves of those artificial barriers that are in large measure based on our ignorance of one another. We need to do so to be able to deal with the real discord between us, and move on to strengthen the bonds that bind us to one another.

Our institutions of learning play a key role in this effort. Given a legal requirement that all our citizens must attend school, these institutions are in a unique position to educate all Americans in such a way as to subvert those forces that keep us apart—a goal that is no longer a nicety but instead a necessity as we prepare to enter the new multicultural century. Schools must take the lead in bringing diverse peoples together in mutual explorations, must convey the message that we all have important things to learn from one another, and must help us confront our fears by helping to eradicate many of the stereotypes we all hold. If an important goal for schools is to help prepare good citizens, then the task of helping people to overcome their fears of people who appear different is a vital role in this preparation. Although this is no easy task, and these institutions cannot alone cope with the enormity of this problem, our educational systems can—and must—serve as a beacon to guide us into a future that can be wonderfully alive with growth as well as with growing pains. If schools can get people to see greater diversity as a strength, we can begin to see that each of us is deserving of respect, and commence working together for a better world—but we need each other to do so. In helping America to see variety as the spice of life, schools would bring us closer to making this planet Earth a place we would be proud to pass on to those who follow.

References

Barbaro, Fred. 1977. "Ethnic Resentment." Pp. 77–94 in *Black/Brown/White Relations,* edited by Charles Willie. News Brunswick, New Jersey: Transaction Press.

Bobo, Lawrence, and Frederick Licari. 1989. "Education and Political Tolerance: Testing the Effects of Cognitive Sophistication and Target Group Affect." *Public Opinion Quarterly* 53: 285–308.

Bobo, Lawrence, and James Kluegel. 1991. "Modern American Prejudice: Stereotypes, Social Distance, and Perceptions of Discrimination Toward Blacks, Hispanics and Asians." Paper presented at the Annual Meetings of the American Sociological Association, Cincinnati, Ohio.

Borus, Jonathan. 1973. "Reentry: Adjustment Issues Facing the Vietnam Returnee." *Archives of General Psychiatry* 28: 501–506.

Bowler, Rosemarie, Stephen Rauch, and Ralf Schwarzer. 1986. "Self-Esteem and Interracial Attitudes in Black High School Students." *Urban Education* 21: 3–19.

Brewer, Marilyn, and Roderick Kramer. 1985. "The Psychology of Intergroup Attitudes and Behavior." *Annual Review of Psychology* 36: 219–243.

Campbell, Angus, and Howard Schuman. 1968. *Racial Attitudes in Fifteen American Cities.* Ann Arbor, Michigan: SRC.

Chavira, Richardo, Sylvester Monroe, and Richard Woodbury. 1991. "Browns vs Blacks." *Time* July 29: 14–16.

Condran, John. 1979. "Changes in White Attitudes Toward Blacks, 1963–1977." *Public opinion Quarterly* 43: 463–476.

Cothran, Tilman. 1951. "Negro Conceptions of White People." *American Journal of Sociology* 56:458–467.

Cummings, Scott. 1980. "White Ethnics, Racial Prejudice and Labor Market Segmentation." *American Journal of Sociology* 85: 938–958.

Dreyfuss, Joel. 1979. "Blacks and Hispanics: Coalition or Confrontation?" *Black Enterprise* July: 21–23.

Dyer, James, Arnold, Vedlitz, and Stephen Worchel. 1989. "Social Distance Among Racial and Ethnic Groups in Texas: Some Demographic Correlates." *Social Science Quarterly* 70:, 607–616.

Fiman, Byron, Jonathan Borus, and M. Stanton. 1975. "Black-White and American-Vietnamese Relations Among Soldiers in Vietnam." *Journal of Social Issues* 31: 39–48.

Firebaugh, Glenn, and Kenneth Davis. 1988. "Trends in Antiblack Prejudice, 1972–1984: Region and Cohort Effects." *American Journal of Sociology* 94: 251–272.

Forbes, Jack. 1984. "Mulattos and People of Color in Anglo-North America: Implications for Black-Indian Relations." *Journal of Ethnic Studies* 12: 17–61.

Gallup, George. 1990. *The Gallup Poll: Public Opinion, 1989.* Wilmington, Delaware: Scholarly Resources, Inc.

Gallup, George. 1988. *The Gallup Poll: Public Opinion, 1987.* Wilmington, Delaware: Scholarly Resources, Inc.

Gerard, H., and N. Miller. 1975. *School Desegregation.* New York: Plenum.

Giles, Michael, and A. Evans. 1984. "External Threat, Perceived Threat and Group Identity." *Social Science Quarterly* 65: 50–66.

Grant, Carl, Marilynne Boyle, and Christine Sleeter. 1980. *The Public School and the Challenge of Ethnic Pluralism.* New York: Pilgrim Press.

Greeley, Andrew. 1985. "School Desegregation and Ethnicity." Pp. 133–155 in *School Desegregation: Past, Present and Future,* edited by Walter Stephan and Joe Feagin. New York: Plenum.

Grinde, D., and Q. Taylor. 1984. "Red Vs. Black: Conflict and Accommodation in the Post Civil War Indian Territory, 1865–1907." *American Indian Quarterly* 8: 211–229.

Harrison, Algea, Melvin Wilson, Charles Pine, Samuel Chan, and Raymond Buriel. 1990. "Family Ecologies of Ethnic Minority Children." *Child Development* 61: 347–362.

Hellwig, D. 1979. Black Reactions to Chinese Immigration and the Anti-Chinese Movement: 1850-1910. *Amerasia Journal* 6: 25–44.

Henry, Charles. 1980. "Black-Chicano Coalitions: Possibilities and Problems." *Western Journal of Black Studies* 4: 222–233.

Irvine, Jacqueline. 1988. "An Analysis of the Problem of Disappearing Black Educators." *Elementary School Journal* 88: 503–513.

Jabara, Abdeen, and Noel Saleh. 1983. "Blacks and Iraqis Collide in Detroit." *Freedomways:* 179–185.

Konecni., V. 1979. "The Role of Aversive Events in the Development of Intergroup conflict." In *The Social Psychology of Intergroup Relations,* edited by W. Austin and S. Worchel. Monterey, CA: Brooks/Cole.

Lambert, Wallace, and Donald Taylor. 1988. "Assimilation versus Multiculturalism: The Views of Urban Americans." *Sociological Forum* 3: 72–88.

Landis, D., and R. Brislin. Eds. 1983. *Handbook of Intercultural Training.* Vols 1–3. Elmsford, NY: Pergamon.

Lee, L. 1987. "International Migration and Refugee Problems: Conflict Between Black Americans and Southeast Asian Refugees. *Journal of Intergroup Relations* 14: 38–50.

Lieberson, Stanley, and Mary Waters. 1988. "The Location of Ethnic and Racial Groups in The United States." *Sociological Forum* 2: 780–810.

McClain, Paula, and Albert Karnig. 1990. "Black and Hispanic Socioeconomic and Political Competition." *American Political Science Review* 84: 535–545.

Marx, Gary. 1967. *Protest and Prejudice: A Study of Belief in the Black Community.* New York: Harper.

Maykovich, Minako. 1971. "Reciprocity in Racial Stereotypes: White, Black and Yellow." *American Journal of Sociology* 77: 876–897.

Middleton, Russell. 1976. "Regional Differences in Prejudice." *American Sociological Review* 25: 94–117.

Miller, N., M. Rogers, and K. Hennigan. 1983. "Increasing Interracial Acceptance: Using Cooperative Games in Desegregated Elementary Schools." *Applied Social Psychology Annual* 4:199–216

Noel, Donald. 1964. "Group Identification among Negroes: An Empirical Analysis." *Journal of Social Issues* 20: 71–84.

Noel, Donald, and Alphonso Pinkney. 1964. Correlates of Prejudice: Some Racial Differences and Similarities." *American Journal of Sociology* 69: 609–622.

Owen, Carolyn, Howard Eisner, and Thomas McFaul. 1981. "A Half-Century of Social Distance Research: National Replication of the Bogardus Studies." *Sociology and Social Research* 66:80–99.

Paige, Jeffrey. 1970. "Changing Patterns of Anti-White Attitudes among Blacks." *Journal of Social Issues* 26: 69–86.

Reed, John, and Merle Black. 1985. "How Southerners Gave Up Jim Crow." *New Perspectives.* Fall: 15–19.

Salholz, Eloise. 1988. "A Conflict of the Have-Nots." *Newsweek* December 12: 28–29.

Schuman, Howard, and Lawrence Bobo. 1988. "Survey-based Experiments on White Racial Attitudes Toward Residential Integration." *American Journal of Sociology* 94: 273–299.

Schuman, Howard, and Shirley Hatchett. 1974. *Black Racial Attitudes.* Ann Arbor, Michigan: ISR.

Schuman, Howard, Charlotte Steeh, and Lawrence Bobo. 1988. *Racial Attitudes in America.* Cambridge: Harvard University Press.

Selznick, Gertrude, and Stephen Steinberg. 1969. *The Tenacity of Prejudice: Anti-Semitism in Contemporary America.* New York: Harper and Row.

Shankman, Arnold. 1982. *Ambivalent Friends: Afro-American Views of the Immigrant.* Westport, CT: Greenwood Press.

Stouffer, Samuel. 1955. *Communism, Conformity and Civil Liberties.* New York: Doubleday.

Thornton, Michael. 1991. "Social Correlates of Intergroup Attitudes." Unpublished paper, Department of Afro-American Studies, University of Wisconsin.

Thornton, M., and R. Taylor. 1988a. "Intergroup Perceptions: Black American Feelings of Closeness to Black Africans." *Ethnic and Racial Studies* 11: 139–150.

Thornton, M., and R. Taylor. 1988b. "Intergroup Attitudes: Black American Perceptions of Asian Americans." *Ethnic and Racial Studies,* 11: 474–488.

Triandis, H. 1972. *The Analysis of Subjective Culture.* New York: Wiley.

Tsukashima, Ronald. 1978. *The Social and Psychological Correlates of Black Anti-Semitism.* San Fransico: R and E Research Associates.

Taukashima, Ronald, and Darrel Montero. 1976. "The Contact Hypothesis: Social and Economic Contact and Generational Changes in the Study of Black Anti-Semitism." *Social Forces* 55: 149–165.

Tuch, Steven. 1988. "Race Differences in the Antecedents of Social Distance Attitudes." *Sociology and Social Research* 72: 181–184.

Tuch, Steven. 1987. "Urbanism, Region and Tolerance Revisited: The Case of Racial Prejudice." *American Sociological Review* 52: 504–510.

U.S. Commission on Civil Rights. 1986. *Recent Activities Against Citizens and Residents of Asian Descent.* Publication number 88. Washington, DC: U.S. Government Printing Office.

U.S. President's Committee on Civil Rights. 1947. *To Secure These Rights.* New York: Simon and Schuster.

Wellman, David. 1977. *Portraits of White Racism.* New York: Oxford University Press.

Williams, Robin. 1964. *Stranger Next Door.* Englewood Cliffs, New Jersey: Prentice-Hall.

Willie, Charles. 1986. *Race, Ethnicity and Socioeconomic Status.* New York: General Hall.

Wilson, Thomas. 1986. "The Asymmetry of Racial Distance between Blacks and Whites." *Sociology and Social Research* 70: 161–163.

Wilson, Thomas. 1985. "Urbanism and Tolerance: A Test of Some Hypotheses Drawn from Wirth and Stouffer." *American Sociological Review* 50: 117–123.

Zinsmeister, Karl. 1988. Asians and Blacks: Bittersweet Success. *Current* 300: 9–16.

Zinsmeister, Karl. 1987. "Asians: Prejudice from Top and Bottom." *Public Opinion* (July/August): 8–10, 59.

About the Author

Michael C. Thornton is a sociologist in the Department of Afro-American Studies, University of Wisconsin-Madison. His primary research areas focus around racial group identification and intergroup perceptions. Current projects involve exploring subdimensions of identity among Black adults and examining the influence of religious affiliations, feelings of racial group autonomy, and interacial contact on Black adult attitudes toward a number of ethnic minority groups, including Asian and Native Americans and Africans.

Part *II*

American Diversity: Ethnic Vignettes

African-American Culture and Contributions in American Life

GENEVA GAY

During the 1970s Broadway play, *Don't Bother Me, I Can't Cope,* the cast sang a song titled "They Keep A-Coming." Several years later, Stevie Wonder composed "Black Man." These musicians brought to the popular-culture forum messages that enlightened scholars, both Black and White, have long shared through professional journals, books, research, and teaching. They spoke of the ongoing creative and societal efforts of African Americans in the United States under adverse circumstances. Despite a wealth of sociological, anthropological, literary, historical, and experiential data to corroborate these contributions, however, some people still refuse to acknowledge them. They simply will not concede that African Americans, in fact, do own a rich and distinctly cultural heritage—one representing a synergy of their African origins and African Americans' unique experiences in the United States—that has spawned many significant advances in American life.

African Americans have survived being kidnapped from their native homeland, the atrocities of human bondage, and the persistent conditions of discrimination and oppression to make an indelible imprint on the fabric of the cultures of not only the United States but also many other nations. Indeed, whether in art, music, politics, science, technology, literature, or economics; whether in colonial or contemporary times; whether in bondage or in freedom; whether in times of peace or war; whether individually or collectively, the presence of African Americans has been a persistent force in the shaping of "the good old USA"—and in myriad places and times.

The magnitude, breadth, and significance of these influences first became visibly evident in the mid-1700s. After a century and a half of the seeming obscurity and anonymity that had surrounded them since their first forced arrival in 1619, Africans in North America emerged during the American Revolution era to become major players in shaping the culture and character of the United States. Fueled by the oral ethics of their struggle for freedom and dignity, and endowed with a variety of creative gifts, they "forced an entrance onto the stage of American history as movers and shapers...as soldier and sailor, founder of the Black church; as scientist, writer, poet, artist, captain, physician, frontiersman, and rebel" (Kaplan & Kaplan, 1989, pp. 4–5). This tradition of active, diversified, and creative participation in American life has continued ever since.

In addition to their contributions to mainstream society, African Americans have developed a distinct culture, complete with its own system of institutions, behavior, values, beliefs, customs, traditions, and communication styles. Over time, there has emerged among them a heightened sense of group consciousness, identity, and common destiny, plus a recognition of the strength of collective values and actions (Jaynes & Williams, 1989). These are expressed in poetry, songs, folklore, stories, cartoons, plays, speeches, autobiographies, novels, art, newspapers, and magazines (Berry & Blassingame, 1982).

Yet, African Americans are *not* a monolithic group, and their culture is *not* static. Variations in how individuals express their common-core cultural traits *do* exist among African Americans because of such factors as time, location, economics, education, and personal circumstances. Both the group's cultural traits and specific expressions of them are continually evolving and being revitalized by the persistence of many of the forces that stimulated their original inception. Thus, African Americans created effective ways to affirm and vitalize their dual identity—as people of African heritage who are systematically denied equal access to opportunities, and as Americans who also believe in the promises and the ideals of democracy.

In sociological terms, these two sets of creative forces are called acculturation and enculturation. *Acculturation* deals with the ways in which Africans adapted to and accommodated mainstream societal values and demands, whereas *enculturation* involves the perpetuation and transmission of African traditions across generations. These processes and the results they have generated need to be understood if one is to acquire both accurate knowledge of and a better appreciation of the African-American presence in the United States—and in the other Americas.

This chapter has three major purposes: (1) to provide a conceptual framework for understanding the nature and character of African-American culture and contributions within the context of the United States; (2) to summarize some of the key patterns of their contributions that demonstrate the persistence and pervasiveness of the African-American presence in and influence on American life; and (3) to explain the centrality of the ancestral African past in shaping African-American culture and other responses to American conditions in both historical and contemporary times. (The last two purposes, which corroborate and illustrate the first, are so voluminous that they far exceed the limits of this chapter. Information can be obtained by consulting the publications mentioned in this chapter and the references listed at the end.)

It is imperative to know a people's past in order to better understand its present conditions and future potential. Therefore, a combined historical and socioanthropological orientation is used to discuss the development of African-American culture and to explain its impact on the United States. Specific issues examined are the heritages that Africans brought with them, their adjustments to conditions in the Americas, their cultural creations, the contributions they may have made to U.S. society, and the implications of all of these for teaching and learning in schools.

The African Legacy

The first Africans brought to the United States were far from being simple, naive, childlike, or uncivilized peoples—as they have often been portrayed. In addition, they most certainly were not slaves at the point of capture. Even those who had experienced enslavement in Africa had not even come close to encountering the levels of dehumanization that they would ultimately suffer in the United States. These captured Africans were not "young" in the ways of civilization. They had experienced a rich history of social, cultural, economic, and political developments that began long before many of the civilizations of western Europe. As Lerone Bennett (1975) suggested, slavery was not imposed on undifferentiated raw material; it was imposed on a people with a rich cultural heritage, an honorable tradition, and a clearly defined point of view. Faulkner (1977, p. xi) added that "the first blacks did not come to these shores empty-handed.... They brought an inner strength that could not be broken; they revealed a depth of spirituality that has seldom been matched for its simplicity of expression, its richness of speech, its vibrant imagery."

The African heritage and cultural memory are central to understanding the shaping of an African-American culture in the United States, and the impact that generations of African descendants have had on the American experience (Berry & Blassingame, 1982). Some key sources of information about these legacies and creations are Lerone Bennett's *Before the Mayflower* (1987), *From Slavery to Freedom* by John Hope Franklin and Alfred Moss (1988), *There Is a River* by Vincent Harding (1981), and *The Negro Almanac*, by Harry Ploski and James Williams (1983).

By 1441, when the Portuguese left West Africa with the first shipload of human cargo, Africa already had seen the rise and fall of many great kingdoms and cultures. Archeological evidence from the Olduvai Gorge, the Nile Valley, and the Sahara confirms the following:

> *The African ancestors of American blacks were among the major benefactors of the human race. [They] were on the scene and acting when the human drama opened....For some 600,000 years Africa and Africans led the world. [They] were among the first people to use tools, paint pictures, plant seeds, and worship gods.*
>
> *In the beginning, then, and for a long time afterwards black people marched in the front ranks of the emerging human processing. They founded empires and states. They extended the boundaries of the possible. They made some of the critical discoveries and contributions that led to the modern world. (Bennett, 1987, p. 5)*

The earliest centers of civilization included Kush (modern northern Sudan), Egypt, Nubia, and Axum (modern Ethiopa) in East Africa; the Zimbabwe, Bantu, and Kongo Kingdoms in South and Southeast Africa; smaller independent kingdoms in the coastal rain-forest area, such as old Yoruba, Ife, Benin, Nok, Dahomey, and Asanti; and the great kingdoms of Ghana, Mali, and Songhay in West Africa. The latter kingdoms were located in those areas of the continent that subsequently became the "slaving region" of European traders, and the sources of most of the ancestors of African Americans. These empires had reached their peaks and were sliding into decline by the time Europeans began arriving in the New World. Songhay, the last of the great West African kingdoms, ended in 1591, 16 years before settlement began in the first English colony at Jamestown, Virginia. The African kingdoms of antiquity accomplished some remarkable achievements in commerce, construction, agriculture, science, politics, arts and crafts, and education. The summary of those presented here are based on the research and writings of Herskovits (1958), Franklin and Moss (1988), Bennett (1975, 1987), Brooks (1971), Harding (1981), Drake (1987), and Asante and Asante (1985).

Some of the most distinguished rulers of ancient Egypt were, according to St. Clair Drake (1987), "indubitably Negro." Among these were Djoser, who is credited with being highly skilled in medicine; Cheops, who built the Great Pyramid of Gizeh (Giza); Chefren, for whom the head of the Sphinx was modeled; Akhenaten (Amenhotep) and his queen (Nefertiti, renowned for her great beauty); and the boy pharoah, Tutankhamen, who is known affectionately in modern times as King Tut, a result of the popularity that surrounded the excavation of his tomb and the world-traveled exhibitions of its contents.

Africans were among the world's first artists, iron makers, weavers, and users of plants for medicine. They also developed well-planned cities with great halls, palaces, and temples at Meroe, Kilwa, Jenne, Walata, Kumbi, Gao, and Timbuktu. These cities became cosmopolitan centers of domestic and international exchange in culture, education, politics, business, and trade, where people from West and North Africa, Europe, and Asia mingled freely. Timbuktu was so renowned for these affairs that Bennett (1987, p. 19) described it as "Paris, Chicago, and New York blended into an African setting."

Franklin and Moss (1988) provided a cogent summary of the way of life that existed among Africans when the Europeans began arriving on the continent to claim their human cargo. It was a life of complexities, culture, and accomplishment:

> *The basic problem of existence had been solved; political, economic, and social institutions were, on the whole, stable [and] well-defined concepts of law and order prevailed. The divisions of labor and the practice of specialization in occupations display[ed] a remarkable versatility and variety of talents and tastes…. The deep loyalty and attachment of the individual to the family approached reference…everywhere [there were] pronounced proclivities to artistic expression…that reflect[ed] the finer things of life…. The song and dance played important parts in their social life [and their] oral literature…served as educational devices, sources of amusement, and guides for the administration of government and the conduct of religious ceremonies. (pp. 24–25)*

The first Africans brought to the Americas were far from homogeneous. They came from different tribal groups and cultural backgrounds, spoke different languages and dialects, and reflected different aspects of the African worldview. Among them were Bambaras, Malinkas, Fons, Dinkas, Ewes, Bakongos, Ibos, and Yorubas. They were royalty, warriers, statesmen, and priests, but most were average citizens, farmers, artisans, musicians, weavers, miners, traders, and herders. Some were Muslims, but most were ancestor and nature worshippers. Some, enslaved or imprisoned by *their* kinspeople as casualties of tribal wars, had been sold to traders, but most were, as one might expect, victims of European piracy and kidnapping.

Some of the original Africans transported to the Americas came from the northern, eastern, and central regions of the content, but most came from the West Coast. This area comprises the modern-day nations of Ghana, Dahomey, Nigeria, Togo, Sierra Leone, Liberia, Senegal, Angola, and Zaire (Berry & Blassingame, 1982). They had already known complex social and political systems, and experienced the demands of accommodating different cultural values, beliefs, and practices, as a result of diversified peoples they encountered through war, travel, and/or trade. The first transported Africans came to the New World not as slaves but (by way of Europe) as indentured servants and/or as crew members of Spanish and Portuguese expeditions. They arrived in Latin America more than 100 years before reaching North America. It was not until the 1640s that slavery became a legal institution in the English colonies. The first Africans had arrived some 20 years earlier, in 1619, as indentured servants.

Despite much cultural and ethnic diversity among the original Africans, some commonalities and shared experiences also existed among them. The centripetal and organizing forces of their aboriginal life-styles were a clan-based political system, the extended family, and an agricultural economy. Within this structural framework, cooperation and mutual aid were prized; the wisdom, experience, and authority of elders were revered; cultural values and traditions were transmitted through song, folklore, story telling, and dance; priests and griots (oral historians) were the keepers and conveyers of tribal histories; religion, music, arts, and crafts permeated and reflected everyday life activities; and an approach to life and living existed in which all people and things were intertwined to make for group solidarity, cultural cohesion, unity, and continuity (Asante & Asante, 1985; Bennett, 1975, 1987; Drake, 1987; Franklin & Moss, 1988). Their shared experience of capture, the Middle Passage, and bondage as human chattel added to fostering feelings of kinship, common destiny, and camaraderie among the diversified lot of Africans brought to the New World.

These cultural commonalities and shared experiences allowed the Africans to draw upon them in developing survival strategies for coping with their circumstances in the New World. They also enabled them to set aside their tribal differences and cooperate in creating new customs, traditions, and values that reflected their more basic *communal* values. The new creations made them neither totally African nor fully American, but a combination of both. They led to the birth of the African American—a bicultural people who, according to W. E. B. DuBois (1969), have a double consciousness and a dual identity, must always be aware of their two souls (thoughts and sources), and must constantly strive to reconcile the two sets of forces into a single being.

Response to American Conditions

Africans reacted to New World conditions in both similar and different ways. They did not simply accept their fate or quietly acquiesce and conform to being held in bondage. Invariably, they resisted continuously, creatively, and aggressively through conspiracies, rebellions, escapes, and sabotage. The specific forms and substance of these reactions were a function of many interactive factors. Among them were particular African backgrounds, the time of arrival, the geographic location in the New World, the organization and operation of the plantations on which they lived, the numerical ratio of Blacks to Whites, and the degree and kinds of interactions that Blacks had with each other and with Whites.

Undoubtedly, the first generations of Africans in North America felt more compelled than did subsequent generations to try to re-create their original customs and traditions. After all, they had experienced Africa more personally and intimately, their memories and points of reference were more deeply entrenched in their origins, and they were brought more directly to the English colonies. They knew no other languages, religions, or values. They were, indeed, *transplanted* Africans. The only things that separated them from their origins were the atrocities of ethnic separation and the personal humiliations they suffered during the Middle Passage.

Subsequent generations had the benefit of their predecessors' experiences in the Americas to add to their African memories as they fashioned ways to survive in the New World. Additionally, many of them had experienced stopovers in the Caribbean to be trained or "seasoned" for the kind of work they would have to perform in the United States. Thus, by the time they arrived, they were already six or seven steps removed from their origins. They had been captured or sold, forcefully separated from their ethnic kinspeople and marched across the continent fastened together in coffles, humiliated and depersonalized in the cargo bays of slave ships, transported across the Atlantic, processed through seasoning camps in the Caribbean, moved to the United States, sold again on the U.S. auction blocks, and dispersed to various plantations.

Although slavery in Latin America as an institution was no less morally reprehensible than slavery in the United States, some conditions were different there, which created a climate somewhat more conducive to both the survival of African traditions (enculturation) and the adoption of European customs and culture (acculturation). These included the concentration of large numbers of Africans in the same area; the influx of Africans directly from the continent, which revitalized cultural memories and legacies; the tendency to keep families together; the less pervasive idea of the inferiority of Africans; and the more liberal practices of manumission and interracial marriages among Africans, Europeans, and Indians.

Africans in the United States did not assimilate into mainstream social structures to the same extent as did their Latin American kinfolk, nor did they retain their African legacies to the same degree of completeness or authenticity. There were fewer opportunities for large numbers of Blacks to interact with each other or to be reaffirmed by Africans arriving directly from the African continent. Thus, replenishing the indigenous cultural memories by newcomers was less potent in the United States than in the Caribbean and in Latin America.

In another sense, however, the acculturative forces *were* equally active. Contrary to what some early historians claimed, the culturally uprooted and geographically displaced Africans did *not* become merely inadequate imitations of their European captors, nor were they passive bystanders in the construction of an identity as Africans in America. Instead, they were creators of themselves. The same energy and imagination that prompted them to create a tradition of struggle to resist bondage and the denigration of their human dignity also led them to develop a cultural system to satisfy their emotional, social, political, economic, and esthetic needs. They meshed African, European, and American customs, values, and traditions together to create another distinctive cultural system.

Often, too, these displaced innocents couched African substance and nuances in European forms, and masked messages of affinity, escape, sabotage, and survival in rituals of song, dance, and worship (Pasteur & Toldson, 1982). For example, rituals of Christianity provided a protective exterior beneath which "vital aspects of Africanity, which some considered eccentric in movement, sound, and symbolism, could be practiced more openly" (Stuckey, 1987, p. 35) and without threat of reprisal from masters. These decisions and techniques stemmed as much from the need for self-protection and the desire to make sense and order out of the various forces impinging upon them, as from the impulses of cultural creation.

Out of this synthesis emerged the African American, who was—and is—"in part European, in part African, in part X" (Bennett, 1975, p. 145). Bennett cautioned us never to forget that African Americans were present and active in their own creation—that they are the products of tenacious traditions that worked in and through them as they forged a new identity. The synthesis they fashioned was based on a practical philosophical perception of struggle, and was an effective tool of survival. This blend of old and new cultural influences continued, in modified forms, exemplifying many of the African traditions of group solidarity, pragmatism, spirituality, versatility, and estheticism.

A New Culture Emerges

Alternative institutions and life-styles in the United States had to be developed because African ancestral ways could not be transplanted and sustained in their original forms in the New World. Another factor contributing to the creation of a new culture was the fact that mainstream European institutions were inaccessible to the Africans. Since their sociopsychological needs for identity, community, personal integrity, and survival could not be suspended until Whites opened their cultural systems to them, the Africans had no other choice but to fashion their own. It was in response to these primordial needs and their living conditions that Africans in the Americas came together by whatever expeditious means, initially to endure the harshness of slavery, and eventually to develop an order and structure to life that would sustain their humanity. They created and institutionalized codes of behavior and strategies for maintaining community cohesion; for dealing with oppression, discrimination, and exploitation; for articulating and transmitting values, beliefs, customs, and traditions; and for surviving in a larger society that at worst considered them chattels, and at best treated them as second-class citizens.

A driving force underlying these creative processes was *Pan-Africanism*, a powerful feeling of kinship that transcended ancestral ethnic affiliations. The efforts of Africans from diverse tribal backgrounds to transform themselves into a single people and to pool their energies to effective challenge slavery meant appropriating the best from the many different ethnic origins (Stuckey, 1987). The results were the first steps toward cultural survival, regeneration, and creation. They laid the foundations for the emergence of an African-American culture in the United States.

A clear sense of peoplehood among African descendants in the United States began to surface full-bloom between 1787 and 1837, a period that Lerone Bennett (1975, p. 121) calls the "Black Pioneer Period." It was grounded in shared memories of the motherland, common destinies, self-affirmation as people of African ancestry, and an insatiable desire to be free (Stuckey, 1987). Negative experiences—enslavement, the continuous presence of racism and poverty, and displacement due to migration—joined these influential forces in stimulating the creation of an alternatiave cultural system. Out of the efforts of the Black pioneer institution makers

> *came a people, an orientation, and a culture...characterized by an "ethos of mutuality".... More concretely, the culture was based on mutual aid, stressing communal values and the responsibility of each to all and of all to each. Although most blacks were desperately poor, the community ideal required sharing, and, to a great extent, this ideal was lived. In many cases, blacks handled their own welfare cases and provided structures for the care of the sick and the lame and the unfortunate. (Bennett, 1975, p. 136)*

Both physical survival and cultural regeneration demanded cooperative strategies, creative imagination, and astonishing tenacity.

It was during this formative period that the pioneer shapers of African-American culture began to crystallize their efforts to create a cultural system in visible and tangible forms. Whereas previous actions to subvert slavery and preserve their cultural identity had been largely covert, they now became more overt, direct, confrontational, and formalized. The leaders recognized and responded to the primal law that in order to be and become, people must have institutions, rituals, structures to regulate relationships, and some means to communicate. The Black founding leaders responded to these needs by creating churches, lodges, fraternal orders, schools, insurance companies, newspapers, folk customs, rituals and ceremonies, songs, a language, and various forms of escape from bondage.

The institutions they founded sprang from the psychological, social, political, economic, and physical contexts of their being of African ancestry and treated as outsiders who were hardly human. These institutions, like their art forms, answered psychological and physical needs. Among the noteworthy first formal institutions were the Free African Society (Philadelphia), out of which emerged the First African Church of St. Thomas (Philadelphia) and the Bethel AME Society (Philadelphia), the African Masonic Lodge No. 459 (Boston), and the Prince Hall School (Boston). All were in operation before 1800. The first Black newspapers and magazines to enjoy widespread readership came a little later. Still, by 1838, three notable publications were gaining influence: *Freedom's Journal, Mirror of Liberty* (a magazine), and *National Reformer* (Bennett, 1975, 1987; Harding, 1981).

By the time the pioneer framers of African-American culture were finished laying its foundations, not only had more publications appeared but early colleges had also been established. Some of the most prestigious and popular newspaper were *New Orleans Tribune, Chicago Defender, Pittsburgh Courier, Baltimore Afro-American, New York Amsterdam News, Cleveland Call & Post*, and *Atlanta Daily World*. Among the earliest colleges were Cheyney, Avery, and Lincoln University in Pennsylvania; Wilberforce in Ohio; Atlanta University in Georgia; Fisk in Tennessee; Morehouse in Georgia; Hampton in Virginia; Howard in Washington, DC; Talladege in Alabama; and Morgan State in Maryland. Most of these newspapers and colleges are still operational.

The pioneers also began to identify recurrent themes, issues of concern, and strategies of response; thus, they commenced to further shape their unique orientations, values, perceptions, and perspectives into a distinctly African-American philosophy. Key elements in these were the right of self-determination, respect for human dignity, the inherent merit of struggle, equal rights, communal effort, cultural preservation, and creative survival. These gifted leaders were inspired to action by both the memories of their African heritage and the promise of democratic principles that was reverberating throughout the world. Their American heritage led them to *believe* and *demand* that these principles should apply to Blacks as well as to Whites.

Those individuals who emerged from the masses during the Black Pioneer Period to distinguish themselves as leaders in masterminding African-American culture and freedom were a diversified lot. They included both Blacks and Whites, the enslaved and the free. The Black pioneers were men and women of different temperaments and persuasions, but generally they shared a common set of experiences, heritages, and visions. They were common folk whose only claim to fame in the unfolding drama of the creation of an African-American culture in the United States (and elsewhere) was that they endured. It was precisely their daily living conditions *while* enduring that the leaders were committed to changing. They were African, West Indian, and mulatto, but most were "full-blooded African Americans." In philosophy and strategy, they could be termed separatists, nationalists, Pan-Africanists, integrationists, and pluralists—but all of them were basically humanists who demanded recognition of their inalienable human rights.

The masses and leaders pooled their talents, experiences, and energies to shape the contours of their emerging culture. Initially, they constructed a life-style out of adaptations to African origins and cultural borrowing from European ethnic groups. It was further refined upon later contact and interactions with other groups such as American Indians and immigrants from Mexico and South America. The resulting synergy of forms, substance, and institutions is the legacy that the African pioneers who shaped African-American culture entrusted to their descendants to practice, perpetuate, and embellish. The process of regeneration goes on.

Cultural Perseverance

During the intervening years since the Black Pioneer Period, African-American culture has experienced both stability and continuity in the midst of change. Stability and continuity are natural and expected imperatives if a culture is to maintain its vitality as well as its functionality while undergoing altering circumstances. They are even more so for cultures that operate in very close proximity and interaction with others.

Change and continuity are apparent in most (if not all) basic cultural institutions. For example, remnants of the early Black mutual-aid societies and insurance companies remain, but now they are more social. That is, their financial functions have been assumed largely by employment and related fringe benefits of our technological society—the social-welfare system, workers' compensation, social security, and health-care programs. Service functions are now being performed by public schools, civil rights organizations, political lobbyists, and daycare centers. In general, the African-American family continues to struggle under the weight of extraordinary economic and psychological burdens. The church, however, remains as an anchor point within African-American communities, and it is their most authentic cultural institution. Colleges created by African Americans continue the tradition to educate the greatest number of those Blacks who gain access to higher education, even though many schools and students alike continue to have serious financial problems. African-American newspapers and magazines are not as prominent or vital as they once were as vehicles of cultural expression; other media—records, radio, literature, television, art—have emerged to supplement or replace them. And so it goes.

The spoken word (Nommo), in its various literal and symbolic forms, has always been a fundamental element of African-American culture. It is the quintessential conduit of cultural expression and the ultimate symbol and source of cultural essence. The cultural uses to which it is applied embody both the artifice and esthetics of the ethos and infrastructures of creative survivalism that African Americans developed over time. This is understandable, considering that their African-based culture is primarily aural as well as oral, and that (during slavery) words were often the only tools that Blacks had at their disposal for self-defense against the wrath of the oppressive mainstream society. Therefore, it is not surprising that those media that are most conducive to oral expression are the arenas in which the African-American presence is most prominently displayed. These include songs, dance, art, drama, folklore, story telling, poetry, and sermons.

The credibility, durability, and viability of African-American culture, as a functional alternative in U.S. society, have been questioned incessantly by some nonmembers since the culture's inception. These skeptics variously contend that it is merely an inadequate imitation of the dominant Eurocentric culture; that it is more of a culture of poverty and a response to oppression than anything else; and that African Americans are *purely* Americans since any remnants of their African heritage were destroyed by slavery and their permanent separation from Africa. Skeptics also maintain that once our nation's problems are solved, this so-called culture will cease to be. These arguments fail to understand the fundamental essence and inherent vitality of African-American culture.

There is no reason to believe that the survival of African-American culture is in danger. This is true for several reasons. First, it has a long history of cohesion and stability, so its foundations are solid. The same ingenuity and creativity that guided its initial formation are still active among its members. Second, it serves some of the most basic human needs such as identity, community, personal worth, and emotional affirmation for millions of people. They will not readily allow anything to jeopardize this fundamental means of their continuity. Third, there are mechanisms in place within the African-American cultural community that ensure its survival and vitality today as much as did in the past. These are the myriad ways in which the people replenish and revitalize their sense of cultural peoplehood and transmit cultural values. One of these is the compelling need and the related practices of periodically "going home" and "returning to their roots" to be rejuvenated—visits to relatives in areas where Black culture began—and family reunions. Also, African-American scholars, artists, literary writers, politicians, social activists, church leaders, and educators are increasingly turning their professional energies to promoting cultural consciousness. In great numbers, they are actively vindicating, articulating, celebrating, and disseminating their cultural perspectives.

A fourth—and if unfortunate—source of renewal for African-American culture is the continued discriminatory practices that deny them unrestricted access to mainstream societal institutions and opportunities. Just as their ancestors had to create a cultural system to fill such voids and assure affirmation of their human identity, contemporary African Americans must do likewise. At some level of consciousness, mainstream society must know that it *needs* African-American (and other ethnic group) cultures in order to continue to enrich itself and extend its own social, political, economic, esthetic, and moral potential. Unquestionably, the mark of the African American is deep in the fabric of everything American (Bennett, 1975).

Samples of the African-American Presence in American Culture

The creation of a cultural system composed of a synthesis of forms and content and imbued with an African esthetic is an extraordinary contribution in and of itself. The gifts of Blacks to American life and culture go far beyond that, however. African Americans have been a central force in building the United States since their arrival on its shores. Their group influence has been fundamental, pervasive, continuous, and ingenious. They have labored in the fields and factories, fought on foreign and domestic battlegrounds, and enriched the nation with their inventions and art, language and literature, religion and recreation. Specific *individual* contributions have been varied, and here is not the place for such an inventory. However, a few are offered to illustrate their patterns, range, and diversity. Other examples are readily available from histories, anthologies, and encyclopedias such as Ploski and Williams's (1983) *The Negro Almanac*, Bennett's (1987) *Before the Mayflower*, Franklin and Moss's (1988) *From Slavery to Freedom*, Raymond Corbin's (1986) *1999 Facts About Blacks*, and other references found at the end of this chapter.

The African-American presence was first felt during the Spanish and Portuguese explorations to and through the New World. They were among the crew members of such early European voyagers as Columbus, Balboa, Pizarro, and Cortés. They sailed with the Spanish conquistadors who landed in Mexico, Peru, and Chile. They joined the pioneers who prepared the way for Europeans to settle the western frontier of what eventually became the United States. Thus, they helped blaze trails from the West Indies to the Atlantic shores, through the Midwest, and across the Sierra, Rocky, and Cascade Mountains to the California coast. Cowboy lore and escapades all bear the indelible imprint of more than 5,000 Blacks.

Throughout much of our history, African Americans have been a strong force in the ranks of the unskilled and semiskilled workers who bedrocked the rapid rise of the United States from a small, agrarian country to one of the most highly technologically developed and politically powerful nations in the world. For too long a time, they held the primary responsibility for cultivating cotton and tobacco in the South, proper compensation denied. Then, finally free to seek other means of employment, and with the mechanism of farm and related work leading to the demise of cotton as king, many African Americans migrated to midwestern and northern cities, where they joined other laborers in assembly lines, stockyards, steel mills, coal mines, and railroad companies in building industrial America. They also serviced the homes, restaurants, and kitchens of America's middle class through such occupations as porters, domestics, nursemaids, and cooks. They mothered, fed, comforted, and otherwise cared for upper-class White American family members while simultaneously having to teach, socialize, and protect their own children and themselves. All these tasks were most often performed without adequate economic resources, psychological security, and/or government support.

African Americans have always actively pursued the American democratic principles of freedom, equality, and justice, and have participated in campaigns of all kinds toward these ends—military, political, social, and educational. They have served in all of the country's wars. At least 5,000 Blacks fought in the colonial army in the Revolutionary War; over 186,000 joined the Union forces in the Civil War; more than 400,000 served in World War I; and nearly 900,000 saw action in World War II.

African Americans constituted over 9 percent of the total armed forces in the Vietnam War. Also, of the 260,000 military personnel deployed by mid-December 1990 to conduct Operation Desert Shield, 29.8 percent of the Army, 21.3 percent of the Navy, 16.9 percent of the Marine Corps, and 13.9 percent of the Air Force were African Americans (Berry & Blassingame, 1982; Franklin & Moss, 1988; U.S. General Accounting Office, 1991). Such individuals as Dorie Miller, Daniel "Chappie" James, Mary Elizabeth Bowser, Samuel L. Gravely, Jr., Benjamin O. Davis, Hazel Johnsohn, and General Colin Powell are reminders of the thousands of African Americans who have served valiently in America's defense.

Through elective office, appointments, pressure politics, and social activism, African Americans have exerted influence to improve their own and others' conditions at home. The national roster of *Black Elected Officials* (1991) has reported that the number, range, and prominence of public offices held by African Americans all have increased steadily since 1970. By January 1991, there were approximately 7,370 African Americans elected to hold office in Congress, state legislatures, county and city governments, law enforcement, and public school systems and college governance boards. This included 24 congressional representatives from 13 states; 1 governor; 415 state legislators serving 44 states; and 215 mayors, two-thirds of whom lead southern cities and 35 of whom operate in cities with a population of 50,000 or more.

Officeholders by appointment—such as federal judges, commissioners, and presidential cabinet members—add considerably to these numbers. They call to mind such luminaries as Justice Thurgood Marshall, A. Leon Higginbotham, Jr., and Louis W. Sullivan. With the election of L. Douglas Wilder as governor of Virginia, African Americans have been elected to every type of public office except president and vice president of the United States. Familiar names among the list of Black mayors include David Dinkins (New York), Thomas Bradley (Los Angeles), Coleman Young (Detroit), Maynard Jackson (Atlanta), Norman Rice (Seattle), Sharon Pratt Kelly (Washington, DC), W. Wilson Goode (Philadelphia), Willie W. Herenton (Memphis), and Carrie Perry (Hartford).

These political accomplishments surely are significant and worthy of recognition. However, they represent only a beginning. The overall percentage of African-American elected officials is still greatly disproportionate to the Black population, and most are elected in communities that have high concentrations of African Americans.

The social-activist groups and movements organized under the tutelage of African Americans have been widely diversified in structure, philosophy, and activities. They range from complete assimilation, to separatism and return-to-Africa initiatives, to cultural consciousness and ethnic revivalism, to repudiating *any* affiliation with Blackness, to vindicating the cultural vitality of the African and slavery experiences, to promoting pan-humanism and social reconstruction within the context of democratic principles! Yet, all of them were motivated by a common theme and vision: to achieve greater equity, respect, recognition, dignity, and rights for African Americans.

The social-activist legacies represented include slave revolts, abolitionist organizations, underground railroads, school desegregation, freedom marches, voter registration campaigns, boycotts, sit-ins, federal court class-action cases, legislative lobbying, and a potent body of protest ethics, literature, philosophy, music, and values. These movements are symbolically represented by individuals such as Gabriel Prosser, Richard Allen, Frederick Douglass, Harriet Tubman, Marcus Garvey, Martin Luther King, Jr., Sojourner Truth, Jesse Jackson, Rosa Parks, and Ida B. Wells. The movements are represented by such organizations as the National Association for the Advancement of Colored People (NAACP), Unified Negro Improvement Association (UNIA), the Urban League, Southern Christian Leadership Conference (SCLC), Congress of Racial Equality (CORE), Student Nonviolent Coordinating Committee (SNCC), and the Rainbow Coalition. Movements are also represented by events such as the 1960 North Carolina A&T State University students' sit-in at a Woolworth lunch counter, the 1963 march on Washington, the 1955 Montgomery bus boycott, and the 1954 *Brown* v. *Board of Education* Supreme Court decision.

African-American contributions to popular culture as transmitted through music, dance, media, athletics, language, and fashion are classic. Black performing arts have been on the cutting edge of mainstream popular-culture creativity throughout most of the country's history. They convey the unique ethnic esthetics of African Americans, as well as enrich the forms of mainstream pop artists. The shared heritages of Africa, slavery, field work, subservience, defiance, shame, pride, joy, celebration, sacrifice, protest, and perseverance are evinced in the works of popular artists as symbolic declarations of cultural survival (Shaw, 1990).

Of all the African-American gifts, these are probably the most familiar to the general public; therefore, a detailed description of them is not included. Suffice it to say that Thomas A. Dorsey, Sugar Ray Leonard, Magic Johnson, Aretha Franklin, the Temptations, Florence Joyner, Duke Ellington, Arsenio Hall, and CeCe and BeBe Winan have many notable companions. The music of contemporary pop, rhythm and blues, hip-hop, and rapper artists is a multimillion-dollar business. Its influence is extended by the fact that many other musicians are "crossing over," imitating African-American performing styles (and, of course, African Americans are doing likewise). Thus, Michael Jackson, Fresh Prince, Anita Baker, M. C. Hammer, and Whitney Houston appeal to Black and White listeners alike. The increasing numbers and successes of these "cross-over" performers are testimony to the fact that modifications in both cultural systems are destined to take place as African Americans and Anglo Americans (and others) interact. This is as much true today as it was in the past. So it is that the processes of Black cultural creation, renewal, and perpetuation in the United States are both reciprocal and dialectic. As African Americans are influencing and thus helping to shape U.S. culture, so too are they being influence by the broader American context.

A new generation of African-American filmmakers has emerged recently to bring their ethnic group's cultural esthetics and experiences to bear on the film, television, and home videotape industries. Their products are sources of pride, insight, criticism, and controversy; and they make movies into a medium for transmitting social messages and ethnic images, as well as a source of culturally diverse entertainment. This development has generated such names as Spike Lee, Robert Townsend, Debbie Allen, and John Singleton. They are embellishing, refining, and refocusing what predecessors such as Spencer Williams, Gordon Park, Sidney Poitier, Harry Belafonte, Charles Gordone, Lorraine Hansberry, and Amir Baraka started. They visualize on screen what their compatriot artists try to capture in paintings, sculpture, and photography and what writers characterize in folktales, poems, novels, biographies, autobiographies, and scholarly treatises. All give voice to the complex dynamics, different perspectives, and multiplicity of the African-American experience—or, as Wormley and Fenderson (1969) might say, "the many shades of Black."

The artistic and literary achievements of African Americans are not limited to the popular-culture media, however. They have left their imprint on "high culture" as well, in the form of stellar performances by stage actors, operatic songsters, classic and modern dancers, and award-winning poets and writers. In fashioning this presence, they have simultaneously given voice to ethnic issues and transcended the boundaries of their ethnicity to address the technical qualities of their respective art forms, solely by way of art for art's sake. Their specific contributions are magnified by their being at once African Americans, artists, and Americans. They represent a rich legacy of fiction, poetry, autobiographies, folklore, religious songs, operas, plays, and stage performances on and off Broadway. This tradition evokes the names of individuals such as Paul Robeson, Leontyne Price, Alvin Ailey, Marian Anderson, Katherine Durham, James Earl Jones, Langston Hughes, James Weldon Johnson, Zora Neale Hurston, Gwendolyn Brooks, James Baldwin, Alice Walker, Maya Angelou, and Alex Haley.

The gifts of African Americans in science and technology are greatly underestimated because slaves were not given patents for their inventions and were not allowed to assign them to their masters. Since many of their most basic inventions predate 1834, when the first patent was granted to a Black (Henry Blair) in the United States, the list of contributions will remain forever incomplete. Yet, those that have been documented and properly assigned demonstrate, as in other areas of creative endeavor, a consistent presence and a wide diversity in the range of specific accomplishments. They cover the spectrum from inventions to improve everyday life, to the most advanced technological and scientific improvements. The inventory includes saddles, lawn mowers, ironing boards, mops, folding chairs, lawn sprinklers, elevators, automatic gearshifts, street sweepers, air-conditioning units, mechanical refrigeration, seed planters, automatic railcar couplers, the railway telegraph, gas inhalators, traffic lights, the ultraviolet spectrograph cameras, engine lubricators, curing salts, open-heart surgery, syphilis diagnosis, cortisone for treating arthritis, blood plasma, and synthesized hysostigmine for treating glaucoma.

Although the roll call of individuals is headed by the dean of African-American inventors, George Washington Carver, he is by no means alone. Among his reputable companions are Frederick McKinley Jones, Jan Matzeliger, Norbert Rillieux, Andrew Beard, Granville Woods, Elijah McCoy, William Hinton, George Carruthers, Daniel Hale Williams, Charles Drew, and Percy Julian.

Neither the areas of contributions nor the list of names of the individuals discussed here are exhaustive. They are, as promised, merely samples and symbolic representations of how the African-American presence is woven deeply and pervasively throughout the fabric of U.S. society. They enrich the lives of everyone in the United States, illuminate the diversity of African-American accomplishments, indicate the power of their creativity even under adverse circumstances, and attest to the centrality of their role in the unfolding American story. As they have given freely of their talents and ingenuity, African Americans deserve to be treated in kind. Their culture and contributions should be known, acknowledged, respected, and celebrated by all other Americans.

Educational Implications

The information discussed in this chapter has several implications for teaching about the culture and contributions of African Americans. Since the themes, specific facts, and lists of renowned individuals is incomplete, they need to be supplemented by in-depth study. What are some of the directions that should be pursued?

First, the major premise—the place of African Americans in the history, culture, and development of the United States—should be examined more thoroughly. The focus here has been on African Americans without a corollary examination of the total American experience. A better understanding and appreciation of both can be achieved by studying them in relationship to each other. In fact, America's story—in all its splendor, potential, and strife—is incomplete without consideration of the African Americans' presence in its making. For example, how the contributions of Charles Drew improved the overall practice of medicine, how George Corruthers's inventions enhanced advancement in space exploration, how the African influence helped determine the contours of American jazz music traditions—all need to be understood and appreciated.

The incomplete information presented here provides a framework for organizing facts and areas of emphasis in studying African-American presence in the United States. Each area of influence, and the individuals who made significant contributions to it, that are mentioned need to be studied in greater depth. The list also should be extended to include other areas—such as religion, education, sports, philosophy, labor, and law—as well as numerous unnamed individuals. The study of all of these requires multi- and interdisciplinary analyses from both historical and contemporary perspectives. Concepts, principles, content, and techniques from the social, behavioral, and natural sciences; from history; from the expressive and performing arts; and from the literary and communications arts should, of course, be applied to the study of the African-American experience.

Curricula designed for students should be a combination of cognitive, affective, and action activities integrated into the subjects they are studying, and they should include a variety of data sources such as scholarly research, oral histories, personal experiences, and ethnic literature. In the classroom, African-American voices have been too long silenced or distorted about their own experiences. Therefore, the information sources selected to teach their culture and contributions should be highly varied and should allow African Americans to tell *their own* multiple stories in their own diverse voices, and according to their own unique cultural styles and esthetics.

A third set of themes throughout this chapter that bears closer scrutiny has to do with the character of African-American culture. These are African retentions, and the cohesion, stability, continuity, and changes in the lives of African Americans that has developed across time and place. Students should examine how events and circumstances have impinged on the overall lives of African Americans. Critical incidents, major events, and significant documents also should be a central part of the study of African Americans.

Among them should be specific things such as slavery, constitutional amendments, judicial decisions extending citizenship rights, domestic and foreign wars, economic depressions, physical diaspora and psychological displacement, diseases and epidemics, the Harlem Renaissance and the cultural revivals of the 1950s, 1960s, and 1980s, the civil rights movement, and busing and school desegregation.

African American culture and contributions have not developed in isolation and are not mutually exclusive in that they are the dominion of African Americans. Rather, they and their gifts are but one of the many strands that make up the fabric of the American (and human) cultural mosaic. As such, they are available for everyone to know and to enjoy—and they enrich all our lives. What they have done for America and themselves, and what American has done to them, illuminates the past, informs the present, and directs the future (Quarles, 1988). This is true in both society and the schools. Therefore, the study of African-American culture and contributions should be an integral part of the education of *all* students in *all* grades, subjects, and settings. It makes no difference whether students are from African, Asian, Hispanic, Anglo, or Native-American ancestry. All need to know the African-American experience, and can benefit from understanding how their respective lives, legacies, and futures are interwoven with it.

Another teaching implication closely related to making the African-American experience accessible to all students is demonstrating how it is both alike and different from those of other ethnic groups in the United States. Comparative analyses of various ethnic histories, heritages, cultures, and contributions should be present and actively engaged in shaping the American story. Although each experienced and responded to them differently, certain commonly recurring themes have persisted across their separate experiences. Among these are cultural modifications, diaspora, oppression and racism, exploitation, ethnic identity, ingenuity and creativity, and biculturalism. Studying these issues in schools helps students to appreciate both similarities and differences among ethnic groups and to develop a deeper understanding of the American experience. Both are imperative for creating better-quality lives and a more desirable national society in an ever more ethnically, culturally, racially, and socially pluralistic and interdependent world.

Conclusion

African Americans are a bicultural people; they are at once African descendants and Americans made in the United States of America. The culture they have created since they were captured in Africa and transported to the New World, and the contributions they have made to American society and humankind, have resulted from a combination of enculturative and acculturative forces—the drive to perpetuate their unique identity while simultaneously demanding their full rights as citizens of the United States. Contrary to the mistaken notions held by some that one dimension of this dual identity is contradictory to—or cancels out—the other, this has not been the case. In fact, one complements the other; a dialectic relationship exists between the two. They enrich each other.

Who African Americans are, what they have accomplished thus far, and what they will achieve in the future all are a direct result of their experiences in the United States. Similarly, what the United States is *and might be* are affected by the influence of African Americans. Neither of these stories can be fully told, with accuracy and integrity, without telling the other and showing how both stories are interrelated. Therefore, all students should learn to know and appreciate the culture and contributions of African Americans. This chapter was designed to assist in that process by providing an overview of some of the major African-American historical highlights, the African-based foundations of the Black culture, and a framework for understanding African Americans' perpetual and pervasive presence in shaping the mainstream culture of the United States. Hopefully, this will be a useful reference point for students and teachers as they chart directions for more in-depth explorations of African-American history, heritage, culture, and contributions.

References

Asante, Molefi K, & Asante, Kariamu W. (Eds.). (1985). *African culture: The rhythms of unity*. Westport, CT: Greenwood Press.

Bennett, Lerone, Jr. (1975). *The shaping of Black America*. Chicago: Johnson Publishing.

Bennett, Lerone, Jr. (1987). *Before the Mayflower: A history of Black America* (6th ed.). Chicago: Johnson Publishing.

Berry, Mary Frances, & Blassingame, John W. (1982). *Long memory: The Black experience in America*. New York: Oxford University Press.

Black elected officials: A national roster. (1991). 20th Anniversary Edition. Washington, DC: Joint Center of Political and Economic Studies Press.

Brooks, Lester. (1971). *Great civilizations of ancient Africa*. New York: Four Winds Press.

Corbin, Raymond M. (1986). *1999 facts about Blacks: A sourcebook of African-American accomplishments*. Hampton, VA: Beckham House.

Drake, St. Clair. (1987). *Black folk here and there: An essay in history and anthology* (Vol. 1). Los Angeles: University of California, Center for Afro-American Studies.

DuBois, W. E. B. (1969). *The souls of Black folk*. New York: New American Library.

Faulkner, William J. (1977). *The days when the animals talked: Black American folktales and how they came to be*. Chicago: Follett.

Franklin, John Hope, and Moss, Alfred A., Jr. (1988). *From slavery to freedom: A history of Negro Americans* (6th ed.). New York: Alfred A. Knopf.

Harding, Vincent. (1981). *There is a river: The Black struggle in America*. New York: Vintage Books.

Herskovits, Melville J. (1958). *The myth of the Negro past*. Boston: Beacon Press.

Jaynes, Gerald D., & Williams, Robin M., Jr. (Eds.). (1989). *A common destiny: Blacks and American society*. Washington, DC: National Academy Press.

Kaplan, Sidney, & Kaplan, Emma N. (1989). *The black presence in the era of the American Revolution* (rev. ed.). Amherst: The University of Massachusetts Press.

Pasteur, Alfred B., & Toldson, Ivory L. (1982). *Roots of soul: The psychology of Black expressiveness*. Garden City, NY: Anchor Press.

Ploski, Harry A., & Williams, James (Eds.). (1983). *The Negro almanac: A reference work on the African American* (4th ed.). New York: John Wiley & Sons.

Quarles, Benjamin. (1988). *Black mosaic: Essays in Afro-American history and historiography*. Amherst: The University of Massachusetts Press.

Shaw, Harry B. (Ed.). (1990). *Perspectives of Black popular culture*. Bowling Green, OH: Bowling Green State University Press.

Stuckey, Sterling. (1987). *Slave culture: Nationalist theory and the foundations of Black America*. New York: Oxford University Press.

U.S. General Accounting Office. (1991, February). *Military personnel: Composition of the active duty forces by race and gender*. Washington, DC: U.S. General Accounting Office.

Wormley, Stanton L., & Fenderson, Lewis H. (Eds.). (1969). *Many shades of Black*. New York: William Morrow.

About the Author

Geneva Gay is professor of education at the University of Washington's Department of Curriculum–Instruction. She received her B.A. in Comprehensive Social Studies, and her M.A. in History from the University of Akron, in Ohio, and her Ph.D. in Curriculum and Instruction (Secondary Education), from the University of Texas in Austin. Gay has held a number of professional positions in education, including high school social studies teacher in Ohio's public schools and professor of education and curriculum and instruction at the University of Texas at Austin and Purdue University. She holds memberships in many professional associations, such as the American Education Research Association, Association for the Study of Afro-American Life and History, Professors of Curriculum, National Alliance of Black School Educators, and Association for Supervision and Curriculum Development. She has written over 75 published articles and books, including "Racism in America: Imperatives for Teaching Ethnic Studies," in James A. Banks's *Teaching Ethnic Studies: Concepts and Strategies*. She is a professional consultant to school districts, state departments of education, colleges and universities, and professional organizations nationwide, on the meaning and need for multicultural education, curriculum design and implementation, and other related areas of education.

Chapter 4

Diversity and Our Dilemma

Reflections of an African-American Couple

KIMBERLY CASH TATE   *WILLIAM F. TATE*

On any given day, the newspapers are likely to carry a story that says African American students are demonstrating on the campus of one or more predominantly white colleges and universities. The students invariably protest the conditions at their particular institutions, and there is a striking similarity to their complaints. They often contend that they have experienced racist incidents, that there are too few African American faculty and staff, and that the curriculum diminishes or ignores the contributions of their ancestors. (Harvey, 1993, p. 96)

Most recently, we [both African Americans] joined the teacher education faculty at a predominantly white campus in the Midwest.... How well would we survive in this new environment? What professional wellness issues, implications, and insights would be extrapolated from this experience? (Tillman & Wheeler, 1993, p. 76)

As African-American students cry out for diversity, what is the price that African-American professors must pay in answering their plea? If more of these professors join the faculty ranks at predominantly White campuses, thereby creating a more diverse environment, will they and their families actually be sacrificing the experiences and cultural realities to which they have become accustomed?

In this chapter, we explore, from two perspectives, how such a move by an African-American professor to a predominantly White campus affected our family. Further, we detail our attempts to survive as well as cope with issues of professional wellness in an environment that lacks diversity.

Kim's Story

As the plane descends on the darkness of the nation's capital, I cannot contain my enthusiasm. I lean over my husband to catch a glimpse of the radiant lights blazing through the cloud of the window. My mind races with plans of places to go: Tower Records to purchase a compact disc that I have not been able to find, a shopping excursion to Tysons Corner and Tysons II, a trip to the Corcoran Gallery to view a popular exhibit, not to mention the family members that I did not see on the last visit. Suddenly, I sink in my seat, saddened that my stay is limited to two days and angry that I have been relegated to the legions of "visitors" to the city.

For almost three years, we have been calling Madison, Wisconsin, our home. It offered career opportunities that, at the time, seemed especially attractive to two students simultaneously completing their graduate programs. We knew that, as African Americans, we would not consider Madison the most ideal place to live. Still, its coldness was a rude awakening, precipitating in me a sudden grief over what I had all my life experienced as ordinary: diversity and variety. Not until I moved away did I become aware of the idyllic circumstances in which I was raised. Prince George's County, Maryland, boasts one of the largest Black populations of any suburban jurisdiction in the country. Admittedly, the privilege of attending schools with high enrollments of African Americans, most of whom continued on to college, never seemed particularly special. It was, after all, my home. Now, I credit Madison with forever casting away the familiarity of diversity. Instead, I live in perpetual awareness that very few people look as I do.

As we deplane the aircraft at Washington National Airport, I become reacquainted with that which in the past had been taken for granted, one of which is the mere fact that we had a choice of three major airport hubs within which to land. With wide eyes, I observe fellow African Americans representing various airlines, working in airport gift shops and restaurants, offering to help with our luggage, and inquiring whether we are in need of taxi service. We proceed, with the other "visitors," to the rent-a-car location.

Before I even fasten my seat belt, I engage in the more important function of setting the radio stations of my choice. Why is it, I wonder, that the metropolitan area of Washington, DC, has the market to bear at least five radio stations targeted to African Americans while Madison pretends that it cannot accommodate one?

Rather than dwell on the deprivations, I delight in my current state and allow myself to drift with the melodies. My husband often is amazed at the revival of my spirit as it is quenched with the sounds of music. For him, the adage "out of sight, out of mind" has been translated to "out of earshot, out of mind," so that he is not as troubled by the fact that we do not have a radio station to our liking in Madison. For me, music has always been a passion, my calm in emotional storms, my passport to sentimental journeys, my partner in celebration. In Madison, I am most reminded of my absent crutch when I am driving and instinctively push the buttons on the radio dial. Always met with displeasing sounds, I am forced to resort to listening to the same cassette tapes. My craving is so great that at times, while driving on the east side of Madison, I tune in to a Milwaukee radio station, content to feign enjoyment through the static of a distant signal. During these moments, I face a haunting image of myself looking from behind bars and out into a cultural landscape of people enjoying simple pleasures that are not so simple to find in Madison. In DC, in our rent-a-car, I escape momentarily.

We are always unable to visit with as many friends and family as we would like on one trip. Thus, we attempt to dine with a different friend or to stop at the house of a different relative on each visit. Invariably, a well-intentioned friend will ask, "So when are you moving back?" or "So why did you buy a house in Madison? You're not staying there, are you?" Donning my veil of positivism, I usually retort something like, "Well, it's not so bad. We couldn't have asked for a better start to our careers and we're also close to Bill's family in Chicago." I often decline to add that it is only when we visit Chicago that I feel close to home again; or that I was elated when I happened to find a competent hairstylist familiar with "Black hair"; or that the Fox station in Madison was one of the first to cancel its syndication of the "The Arsenio Hall Show"; or that we have to drive 90 miles one way to attend concerts in Milwaukee compared to the 15-minute drive we had once enjoyed. Were I ever to allow my veil to fall, I am afraid that the tears of frustration would fall along with it. This trip home is no different.

We gather with friends at a seafood restaurant at the Baltimore harbor, always delighting in the opportunity to partake of the fresh seafood offered by the coast. The conversation, of course, turns to life in Madison, and it's only natural. Cities such as Atlanta, Houston, Detroit, Chicago, and Philadelphia strike familiar chords among our circles. The high populations of African Americans in those and a handful of other cities permit basic information about those cities to become common knowledge. At the least, an African American will know someone who has been to that city and he or she will have a fair picture of that city's mood. On the other hand, numerous cities in this country harbor scant numbers of African Americans, rendering those places foreign to many. I daresay that Madison is close to that model. It certainly is not a city that our friends or families would have visited or lived in at one time or even know others before us to have lived. We have weathered, it seems, a new frontier and are looked to as purveyors of knowledge about this foreign land.

"So what is it like?" they ask sincerely. We give our pat answer of Madison being a "college town" surrounded by beautiful lakes. They proceed curiously with, "But what is it really like? You know, for African Americans." The looks my husband and I exchange reveal what our friends suspect. Our friends then attempt to raise our spirits by reminding us that had we stayed in Washington, we may not be in the same position careerwise. We all agree that if our careers are the priority, we made the right move; but we also know that our friends would probably not switch positions with us even if it meant a career boost.

The purpose of this trip is my being sworn in to the District of Columbia Bar. Having passed the Wisconsin bar exam two years ago, my deadline for waiving in had almost expired. Fortunately, my firm thought it advantageous to have me become a member of the DC Bar, and I had my own sentimental reasons for filling out the paperwork. I made time for a lunch visit with my adopted mentor, Denise Randall.[1] In 1991, Denise became the first African American to start from the bottom and work her way up to partner at one of the largest law firms in the country. We met during my first year of law school at George Washington University, from which she had graduated a few years before. As is her nature, she was "giving back" by agreeing to talk to the Black Law Student's Association about the climate of her firm and her experiences as a litigator. She was about seven months pregnant, dressed in a brilliant red dress, causing her to stand out from the conservative scenarios painted for us as law students. I cannot remember the exact message of her exchange, but I will always remember her open, inviting demeanor. She offered her business card, I later called her to go to lunch, and we have since kept in touch.

I had not seen Denise in over two years. During our last lunch together, early in 1991, we had debated the dilemma that was consuming that period of my life. Bill was nearing graduation from the doctoral program at the University of Maryland and his offer of choice had come from the number-one school in his field, the University of Wisconsin. "You'd be a fool not to take it," he was told. While he was open to the prospect of investigating this proposition, I was battling the idea of moving from an area I loved to a city that offered neither warm winters nor cultural enrichment. I was, in short, distraught. I had sought solace from a number of individuals, hoping to be enlightened by wisdom that had not yet occurred to me. Mostly, though, I heard tales of woe as close friends lamented the passing of our weekend get-togethers and our daily, extended toll-free calls. "I can't believe Bill can't find a job with all the universities and colleges in this area," they would proclaim. I found myself justifying his position, regurgitating the words that he would use when I posed the same questions.

Tired of partisan input from family and friends, my lunch with Denise had been a welcome respite. She did not see the move as traumatic as I. Although she could not deny the disadvantage of Madison's lack of diversity, she saw an opportunity for me to be a "big fish in a little pond." Denise offered a slight glimmer of anticipation in an otherwise dim prospect. Soon after that lunch, I received an offer that I, too, would have been a fool to pass up, making the move to Madison equally beneficial for both of our careers.

Two and a half years later, Denise and I now meet again for lunch, this time at a restaurant on the corner of 18th and M Streets. "How's Madison?" she asks casually, unaware of the mixture of emotions she has just stirred. I am honest about my dissatisfaction and about my lingering desire to return to Washington. "As a matter of fact, I am looking for a litigator with your level of experience," she offers. Great. Now I am moved to imagining myself working for a prestigious law firm, under the tutelage of an accomplished partner who is African American and a woman, in the nation's capital. I quickly shirk the dream as too remote.

Denise and I share war stories about litigation in particular and law firm culture in general. I find it paradoxical that although she practices in the District of Columbia, she, too, is very much in the minority at her firm. The difference for her is that when she leaves her office to go to lunch, or to do any number of activities, she will be reaffirmed with the presence of many African Americans. Conversely my minority status is constant and it is a reality that strikes when I least expect it.

Such a circumstance hit a couple of months ago. I belong to an African-American lawyer's organization in Madison. A subcommittee of that group met in the cafeteria of my building at work. Seven of us gathered at a table and I noticed a male coworker in the distance. Not two minutes after I had returned to my office, this coworker thought it his prerogative to inquire into the purpose of my meeting. I had only 10 minutes to eat lunch and prepare for an appointment with a client, so I told him that I did not have time for his inquisition at the moment. He returned twice more that day, his demeanor inappropriately overwrought. At his third appearance, I remarked half-jokingly that he had not been in my office that often in the past year. Undaunted, he launched immediately into a litany of questions about my meeting: What were we doing? Who were those people? What kind of group is this? Although he sensed my obvious incredulity at his interrogation, he sunk deeper into insensitivity by offering that he feels nervous when a group of people of the same race gather together. "What about the umpteen times you and two or three other White men meet in one of your offices?" I asked. He responded, "We're talking about business." The fact that they are, of course, not always talking about business was irrelevant; his implication that we could not have been talking about "business" as well was insulting. The sad truth to this episode, I told him, was that had we been in some other city, such as Chicago, he would not have been so shocked and taken aback at the sight of seven African Americans sitting together in a cafeteria.

I leave an inspired lunch with Denise and head to the District of Columbia Court of Appeals for the swearing-in ceremony. I note with pride the number of African-American attorneys in attendance, as well as the number of African-American judges who serve the District. It takes only a couple of minutes to stand, raise my right hand, and recite the oath, but the length of the ceremony belies its importance. In addition to being an alumnus of a university in the city, I now am connected officially to its legal community. Although I remind myself that I may never practice law in DC, somewhere inside I know that I am laying the foundation for what I hope will materialize in the future.

For early December in Washington, my wool coat is a few degrees out of place. I savor the balminess, though, longing to bottle it and take it with me. On this our last night in town, we pay a visit to my father, stepmother, and three younger brothers. The mood is festive as we engage in discussions ranging from current family matters to the disappointing performance of the Redskins this season. I wander over to my brothers, ages 10, 13, and 15 and congratulate them on their achievements in school. When I delve into their reasons for enjoying school, they cite favorite teachers, favorite subjects, friends, and an all-time favorite—recess. Not one mentions the richness of attending top-notch schools in Prince George's County, in which great percentages of students and faculty are African American. They take this existence for granted, as I did, and I allow them their naivete.

If my experience is any indication, I know that my brothers' familiarity with diversity will serve them well. As an African-American child who often saw African-American professional workers, I inevitably developed an inner sense of pride. It instilled in me the confidence to excel at predominantly White universities, both as an undergraduate and as a law student. And now, although I am the only African American in a law firm of approximately 150 lawyers, I have never doubted my self-worth or felt insecure about my minority status. I credit the foundation laid for me and I know that my brothers, whether they realize it or not, have the advantage of that same foundation.

As we ride to National Airport for the return trip, my mood can best be described as a balloon deflating slowly. Just as the balloon loses the air that gives it life, I slowly lose all attachment to an African-American existence—my life line. I never shed tears or complain loudly. It is more a silent ache that causes damage in areas unseen. I believe though, that if spirits were tangible, I would know the extent of the destruction.

Bill's Story: The Return Trip

Our plane lands at Chicago O'Hare Airport and we prepare for a two-hour layover. I purchase coffee and local newspapers, and we attempt to relax in the waiting area of our departing gate. As I browse through the metro section of the paper, I read familiar stories of the city's failure to educate its African-American students. The schools receive low marks in academic achievement and attendance. As an educator, these stories disturb me. However, they also validate my own fortune in being able to attend a Chicago elementary school that works. I wonder why other schools can't do the same.

I have come to understand that values and political ideology greatly impact and influence the school experience of children. My elementary education was built on the philosophical tenet of centricity. My school's doctrine and practice were to prepare students to view and understand the world from the perspective of an African person in America. That is, my family, cultural, and community experiences served as building blocks to knowledge about society. One example from my school experience illustrates the school administration's commitment to the centric perspective.[2]

It was a routine Thursday afternoon in my fifth-grade class. The class spent this time preparing for Friday's spelling and vocabulary tests. One word on the spelling test list was *raccoon*. My teacher, a White male, shared with our class that his father referred to raccoons as *coons*. By coincidence, my father, a graduate student at the time, had recently discussed with me Bogle's analysis of the portrayal of African Americans in films. I was intrigued by our discussion and read the book. In his analysis, Bogle described the coon as one of three variants—toms, bucks, and coons—constructed to portray the African American as an amusement object or buffoon. My teacher's remark triggered a frantic mental search for the following statement by Bogle (1989): "The pickaninny was the first of the coon types to make its screen debut. It gave the Negro [sic] child actor his place in the black pantheon. Generally, he was a harmless, little screwball creation whose eyes popped, whose hair stood on end with the least little excitement, and whose antics were pleasant and diverting." (p. 7).

At this moment, I was uncomfortable. I momentarily lost focus. I can't remember what was said next by my teacher. I had to know whether my teacher understood the dual meaning of the word *coon*. Did he think of my classmates and me as coons? Why didn't he mention the "other" meaning of coon? Throughout the school year, he had emphasized that some words had several meanings. So I raised my hand and waved as if I were saying goodbye. It seemed as if hours passed before he noticed me. I informed him and the class that coon had another meaning. I went on to describe Bogle's book and the other definition of coon. My teacher turned a shade of red. He looked as dazed as I felt. It did not take more than a few seconds to recognize that my teacher was quite upset. He asked me to step outside of the classroom. Once outside the room, he suggested that I apologize to the class for my remarks. I told him no, that my statement was based on my father's college experience, as his were based on his father's experience. In my eyes, my father's graduate school experience was equally as relevant as his father's notion of coon. We were not communicating. I lost this battle. He sent me to the office.

I sat in the office next to the school secretary for several minutes. I figured at the very least a suspension was pending. Finally, the school principal returned to the office. He asked me what I had done to be sent to the office. I explained to him the events that led to my removal from class. He smiled and told me that it was appropriate to point out the dual meaning of the word. In fact, he asked me to retell the story to the school's assistant principal. The assistant principal shook her head. I am not sure she believed the story. However, she suggested that I write a paper on the topic and present it to my class.

Two important events occurred after my discussion with the school's administrators. First, the teacher asked me to prepare and present a report on Bogle's book. Second, the teacher did not return to the faculty the following year. Many years after that incident, I talked with the principal about several of my former teachers—including my fifth-grade teacher. I inquired why he had left the faculty. He smiled and said, "Philosophical differences." I often speculate on the nature of these philosophical differences. Perhaps it was the inability of my teacher to neither recognize nor discuss the dual level of consciousness required of an African American that resulted in a tension between the school's centric philosophy and his "colorblind" approach to pedagogy.

I avoided suspension—a frequent outcome for many outspoken African-American males in today's schools. Instead, I was rewarded for being scholarly and understanding the social construction of the African American. My academic career was launched in fifth grade. How many other African-American students could benefit from a centric education? Before I could launch into deeper thought on this question, an announcement moved me to action. "All passengers on flight 5409 to Madison, please board at gate 3A." My wife and I gathered our bags and boarded the plane. The flight to Madison will be quick. I wonder what developments are taking place in our new hometown. I reach into the plane's magazine section and grab a Madison newspaper left from the previous flight. The lead article is entitled "Dual Education: How Madison schools stack the deck against African-American students." The article is based on a study conducted by a policy "think tank" that is considered more closely associated with conservative ideologies. They found that Madison's schools have developed an efficient system of removing, segregating, and punishing African-American students. This has been my greatest fear. Before I accepted the position at the University of Wisconsin, I wondered about the school environment for my yet to be born children. My own elementary education was a lesson in the importance of school administrators and teachers supporting African-American students. How would Madison schools treat my children? This continues to be a major consideration in the debate about whether to stay in Madison. I vowed to myself and my wife that I would get involved with the school district.

Unfortunately, my interactions with the Madison school administration have been less than cordial. During my first year, the NAACP chapter conducted a survey of African-American teachers in the Madison school district. The survey revealed that an overwhelming majority of respondents believed their White colleagues did not know how to teach African-American students. In response, the acting superintendent of schools stated that children of lower socioeconomic status were difficult to educate. His remarks were in direct contrast to my own elementary school experience. I responded with the following remarks:

> *Using children's socio-economic status as a rationale for poor achievement is not a very wise position for educators who are accountable to all the people of Madison. The economic deprivation argument provided by the acting superintendent is no different from the cultural deprivation theories of the 1960s and 1970s. These theories hold that the reason some students fail is because their home environments or cultures are deficient. Thus school administrators have no reason to provide curriculum, teacher in-service, or other capacity-building*

> *initiatives that may meet the needs of all children. This simply is not acceptable.*
> *Failure to address the needs of all children is taxation without representation.*
> *As a citizen of Madison I will not tolerate an education system that ignores the*
> *needs of lower economic and/or culturally diverse students. Let's move from the*
> *rhetoric of economic deprivation to discussion and reform of a system that is*
> *drowning in apathy. (Tate, 1992a, p. 9A)*

The acting superintendent did not appreciate my remarks. He responded with a letter outlining the district's initiatives to improve the performance of "economically deprived children." He wrote: "I will not take personal issue with some of your statements because that would serve no purpose. As indicated earlier, I hope this clarifies some of the District's efforts. In the future, I would urge you not to make judgments on out of context, incomplete media reporting." He was right. His letter was more telling than the newspaper article reporting his position on educating children of color. In conjunction, a series of letters to the editor appeared to support the acting superintendent's position.

Directly following my response, one Madisonian stated:

> *The recent survey of Madison's black educators is another verse to the same old*
> *song. Preaching the "multiculturism" line, they do more to separate than unite.*
> *American history is about uniting people of different backgrounds, cultures, and*
> *religions, not celebrating difference. While my particular ethnic heritage may*
> *differ from others, my American culture remains the same as every other Ameri-*
> *can. Multiculturalism is really no culture at all. (Sannes, 1992, p. 9A)*

I was flooded with calls of both denial and support. One citizen wrote that I knew nothing about the Madison schools. A teacher commented that many hard-working educators were committed to African-American education. Further, in her opinion, I knew nothing about the schools. Little did she know that I had just conducted a mathematics staff development for the district. Moreover, I was a member of a committee to establish a new school in the district. Fortunately, many of my colleagues supported my letter. They encouraged me to continue my efforts. Others stated it was a waste of time. One suggested I concentrate on my research. Did this colleague understand that the philosophy undergirding my research is social justice? How could I remain silent? My lessons from elementary school form the basis for a critical awareness of myself and my position in society. I realize that my fifth-grade teacher's color-blind pedagogy is consistent with the mindset and actions of many educators of my community. I felt the need to assume the same kind of leadership exhibited by my elementary school principal. Somehow every child should receive an education that builds on their experiences and that looks to prepare them to succeed in a democratic/capitalistic society. That means each child should be prepared to defend his or her rights. I could not remain silent. My education and my belief in a centric education moved me to action. I decided to write the editor of the *Wisconsin State Journal*. He published my remarks.

> *I have been defined by others (letters to the editor) as a critic of the Madison*
> *Metropolitan School District. I would like to clarify and define myself and my*

stance on several issues. First, I am not a critic of the school district. Rather, I am an advocate of children who have been disenfranchised as the result of many factors, including the subtractive nature of the school system. I recognize the hard work and effort by schoolteachers and administrators....However, school systems are made up of many people. Everyone must be fully committed to educating all children. That includes the citizens of Madison. In the letter that followed my comments in the July 24 State Journal, *Norman Sannes stated that "American history is about uniting people from different backgrounds, cultures, religions, not celebrating differences." Why, then, does Sannes advocate the removal of students from mainstream classes? Further, why was there no outcry about this position? Sannes would have you believe disuniting children from the mainstream is the answer. Could it be there is something wrong with the system? I concur with the comments of Josephine M. Zell in another letter. She appealed to every citizen to visit and become involved with the schools. I believe that teachers like Zell, who are committed to activism and advocacy, rather than policies that disunite, have the real solution for schools. (Tate, 1992b, p. 9A)*

I wonder if the acting superintendent understood how he perpetuated and supported a negative perception of African Americans. Philosophically, he was very similar to my fifth-grade teacher. Both were unable to understand and support children different from themselves. Each of these educators tacitly supported educational approaches—color-blind pedagogy and economic deprivation theory—that were detrimental to the education of African-American children.

Will Madison's schools change to incorporate the centric philosophy of my elementary school? Should my wife and I wait around to find out? Where would we go? Do my colleagues and students understand the price we pay to diversify the university community?

The plane has touched down. It moves slowly toward the gate—just like educational and social change. The answer to these and many other questions will have to wait. It's time to go home.

Postscript

At press time, Kimberly Cash Tate has found shelters of solace in Madison. Besides the great fortune of enjoying her job, her spirits are lifted through her church, the Greater Madison African American Lawyers' Organization, and the monthly pot-luck lunches enjoyed with her "sisters."

Endnotes

1. This name was changed to protect the identity of the individual.

2. For additional discussion of this school, see Tate (in press).

References

Bogle, D. (1989). *Toms, coons, mulattoes, mammies, and bucks: An interpretive history of blacks in American films* (originally published in 1973). New York: Continuum.

Harvey, W. B. (1993, February 25). Why African American students are protesting. *Black Issues in Higher Education, 9* (26), 96.

Korris, S. (1994, February 11–17). Dual education: How Madison schools stack the deck against African-American students. *Isthmus, 19* (6), 1, 8–9.

Sannes, N. C. (1992, July 24). Multicultural tune is old. Letter to the editor. *Wisconsin State Journal,* 9A.

Tate, W. F. (in press). From inner city to ivory tower. *Urban Education.*

Tate, W. F. (1992a, July 24). Schools have window of opportunity [letter to the editor]. *Wisconsin State Journal,* 9A.

Tate, W. F. (1992b, August 9). Professor "defines" his school stance [letter to the editor]. *Wisconsin State Journal,* 9A.

Tillman, J., & Wheeler, P. (1993, May 6). Professional wellness for African American faculty at predominately white universities: Inconvertible reality. *Black Issues in Higher Education, 10* (5), 76.

About the Authors

Kimberly Cash Tate is a graduate of The George Washington University National Law Center, where she was a member of the *Journal of International Law and Economics.* Upon completion of her studies, she clerked for the Honorable Barbara B. Crabb of the United States District Court for the Western District of Wisconsin. She is now an associate at Michael, Best, & Friedrich, a large midwestern law firm specializing in commercial litigation. She is a member of the Wisconsin State Bar and the District of Columbia Bar.

William F. Tate is an assistant professor in the department of curriculum and instruction at the University of Wisconsin-Madison. He received his Ph.D. from the University of Maryland in mathematics education. He teaches courses in mathematics and urban education. His research interests include educational equity and the political and cultural dimensions of mathematics and mathematics education. He is a member of several national committees, including the Research Advisory Committee of the National Council of Teachers of Mathematics. He was the recipient of the University of Wisconsin's Anna J. Cooper Postdoctoral Fellowship (1991–1992). Tate also was awarded a Ford Foundation Fellowship to study at the University of Ghana. "Race, Retrenchment, and the Reform of School Mathematics," in *Phi Delta Kappan* (February 1994), reflects his interest on educational equity. His forthcoming chapter in the National Council of Teachers of Mathematics 1994 yearbook entitled "Diversity, Reform, and the Professional Knowledge of Mathematics Teachers: The Need for Multicultural Clarity" reflects his interest in the professional development of teachers.

Chapter **5**

The Central American Experience

LILLIAN RODRÍGUEZ POST   KATHRYN PRICE

The seven separate nations that make up Central America—Belize, Guatemala, Honduras, Nicaragua, El Salvador, Costa Rica, and Panamá—emerged in the mid-1800s after more than 300 years of European colonization of indigenous peoples. The Spanish language dominates, with the exception of Belize (English) and a number of enclaves where indigenous languages are still in use. With this resulting national diversity, it is impossible to definitely characterize a "typical" Central American; however, that nonexistent individual is likely to be young, Catholic, at either end of the economic scale, and a member of an extended family that recognizes certain obligations and benefits.

From the conquistadors to Iran-Contra, the history of the Central American people has been intertwined with the fortunes and misfortunes of one or another influential outside entity. Whether this powerful force has been a sixteenth-century Spaniard in search of riches or individuals to enslave, a nineteenth-century transnational corporation acquiring farm land through railway concessions, or a modern-day collusion of foreign interests and self-serving insiders, the effect has been similar: A few have benefited while many have lost—property, individual rights, even life. A long history of colonization, foreign political intervention, war, and multinational corporate activity has created conditions in many parts of Central America that understandably encourage migration. At various times in recent years, for example, significant numbers of residents from Guatemala, El Salvador, and Nicaragua have sought refuge and/or economic stability elsewhere.

As difficult as it is to abandon family, friends, and property, the physical dangers of war and the loss of individual rights essentially prevent any other choice. In many cases, the decision to migrate may not even be directly prompted by political situations, but rather related to the worsening economic conditions that invariably follow extended periods of upheaval. Individuals and families may also elect to migrate in order to join relatives who left previously and have settled outside their homeland. For a great many, regardless of the totality of precipitating factors, economic survival alone plays a major role in the decision to migrate. Such neighboring countries as Costa Rica and Honduras may well be initial destinations of this kind of migration, because these nations have enjoyed relatively strong economies and fewer periods of the intense political instability that have plagued Guatemala, El Salvador, and Nicaragua.

Ultimately, large-scale migrations and generalizations concerning them are reduced to individual experiences—to personal stories that reflect uniqueness while forming part of an overall trend. Regardless of country or culture of origin, the success that a refugee or immigrant experiences in the country of destination more than likely will largely depend on how well he or she is able to "make sense of" new expectations and cultural demands. Different societies place varying values on the importance of loyalty to the family, government, institutions, and the church. Taking a look at one Central American's story will show, to some extent at least, how transplanted beliefs and practices can take hold and form the substance of the migrating individual's new interrelationships.

Lillian's Story

Lillian Rodríguez is a Nicaraguan woman who left Central America in the late 1970s, shortly after her marriage to a United States Peace Corps worker. She grew up as the second youngest of five children. When she was very young, her father sold his farming land and moved the family to the nearby town of Estelí. There, he worked in the tanning business and also as a shoemaker. Her mother baked bread and tortillas for the children to sell.

In her youth, Lillian had almost no contact with North Americans, except for some Catholic priests who worked as missionaries. At the same time, her recollection is that nearly everything used in Nicaragua—clothes, household products, appliances—was supplied by the United States. She grew up surrounded by English words in advertising and commercials, and in the Hollywood version of the United States that played at the theater in town. Lillian and her contemporaries realized that the images of the United States portrayed in movies and through advertising didn't truly reflect life in the States—but then, such visions formed the *only* view of that life available to them.

The effect of the "familiarity" that Central Americans feel with United States culture, even if based on secondhand images, combines with the physical proximity of North America to exert a definite pull northward. According to Lillian, going to the United States is like going up to the "main house." There is the strong sentiment that it should be the duty of the United States to take care of those in its own backyard rather than becoming involved in far-off places. This attitude is a call for a sense of affinity toward citizens of Latin America, rather than for intervention, and helps explain the continual flow of Hispanics north to the United States.

Like many of her friends, Lillian received training as a teacher in a two-year certification program after finishing high school. She admits now that she was not drawn to the profession for any particular personal reason, but rather went with the "flow" determined by her family and peers. With time, she has come to believe that it was within her destiny to teach, because it allowed her the power to create change. Her experiences as a primary teacher provide a glimpse in the challenges that she and other Hispanic immigrants have faced as they have interacted with the United States school system.

Lillian's teaching assignment took her to Quilalí, a small town in the northern part of her country, close to the border with Honduras. The town was basically one main road with houses on either side. As in many such communities, the school building served as the center of all activity for the town. Virtually every event or issue related in some way to the school, reflecting communitywide interest in the lives and well-being of the children. Correspondingly, just about everyone in the community—immediate family, relatives, and neighbors—was responsible for educating the children. Since the performance of the child reflects on the larger group, when a child achieves, that success is shared and enjoyed by all; and when there are difficulties, everyone feels at least some responsibility for the disappointment. It is rarely possible to carry this level of group "ownership" over to participation in United States schools.

Although *some* semblance of extended-family and community support for schools may exist here and there in the United States, these involved groups generally function outside of majority-culture parameters, and do not wield the influence necessary to affect educational decisions. Apart from the obvious linguistic barriers to their "ownership" aims, Hispanic parents with little formal education may also have difficulty in forming partnership relations with staff, even when mechanisms exist for encouraging family involvement. The United States school that is able to overcome these obstacles and empower the Hispanic family in this supportive role taps a formidable resource indeed.

The trade-off for this all-encompassing support from the family was the allegiance that the individual—in this case, the student—owed to it. This was apparent as Lillian established contact with her students' families, and sought their cooperation when, for instance, a child's absences became problematic.

It was common for parents to keep children out of school because they were needed to help at home, either in the fields or to watch younger children so that the parents could work. Some children were taken out quite regularly during the planting and harvesting times; for many families, this practice was a desperate necessity, basic to maintaining their wherewithal. In such cases, it was often quite difficult for Lillian to argue that, according to the schools, the family didn't come ahead of education.

Most assuredly, when transplanted to the United States, the "needed more at home" attitude contributes immensely to the appearance of a cavalier attitude about attendance. Be that as it may, the family need may still be legitimate, even though less crucial to actual survival. For example, for the Hispanic family, having the child available to translate at a medical appointment or to provide child care so a parent doesn't miss work without question represents a very real need. Correctly gauging the degree of need, and intervening in effective ways, can occur only when teachers are aware of home issues that interfere with overall student achievement.

At the center of community life, the Nicaraguan school traditionally has provided various services to area residents. In farming regions such as Quilalí, the school might possess agricultural equipment for special projects on the part of students. Developing one such project brought Lillian's husband-to-be to the area; he was a Peace Corps worker from a small farming town in Wisconsin. When parents saw the results of his demonstration project at the school, they enlisted his help with their own crops. The success of the resulting collaboration was clearly due to three factors that characterized his approach to the community—factors that also can serve as guidelines to any educator seeking rapport with a culturally or linguistically different parent population. First and foremost, it was obvious that he respected the Nicaraguan way of life, and even enjoyed it. Second, he made every effort to communicate in Spanish. Finally, he clearly relayed his belief in the power of knowledge to bring about positive change, while providing access to that knowledge.

Lillian Rodríguez and Arthur Post were married in 1976 in the midst of a deepening political conflict that pitted pro-government, United States-backed forces against Sandinista rebels. As a U.S. citizen, Post was soon asked to leave the country; the two left for his family farm outside Madison.

Like that of many other immigrants and refugees, Lillian's move to the United States was complicated by the fact that she was leaving her extended family at a difficult and highly dangerous time. By then, the war in Nicaragua had spread to all parts of the country, touching every home. Lillian's family, like many others, was divided by the war; some members supported the existing government, while others backed the opposition. Her younger sister joined the guerrillas, and lost her life for their cause right at the beginning of the conflict, in 1977. She was 19 years old.

For the next few years, Lillian remained very focused on events back home and eventually was able to return various times to Nicaragua in spite of the military activity. At some personal risk, she had traveled back for her sister's funeral, taking her newborn son. Although she was very clearly pulled between staying longer in Nicaragua and returning to the United States, her father convinced her that her "American" son would be in danger should they remain, so she reluctantly left.

Lillian's ongoing concern for her family's well-being led her to return again to Nicaragua, in both the late seventies and the early eighties. At different times she was even able to bring her two brothers and an uncle back to the United States, thinking they might take advantage of new opportunities. Her brothers eventually left, but her uncle married and moved to California.

By the early eighties, the situation in Nicaragua looked more hopeful; the literacy efforts in particular stood out as a major accomplishment of the Sandinista government. In 1985, however, the United States embargo effectively brought the country to a halt. For an economy based on United States trade, the inability to secure needed spare parts, basic goods, and credit meant, in Lillian's words, "death for the Nicaraguan people." Life worsened drastically, and immigrants could only watch helplessly from a distance.

Lillian's experiences in making the transition to a new country are typical in many ways of those lived by most refugees and immigrants in that there is a tremendous preoccupation with loved ones left behind. Concern for their safety and well-being often is coupled with guilt over having migrated, to the point where much mental energy remains focused on the home country. As a result, there is a great deal of ongoing anxiety that often interferes with making such important adjustments as learning the language, adapting to new routines, and becoming aware of different expectations and obligations. For those who experienced trauma, the death of family members, and/or loss of property in their flight, the accompanying mental anguish can be overwhelming, taking precedence over providing for both present and future needs.

The fact that Lillian sought to bring family members to the United States also fits into a major trend. In some U.S. communities where settlement by Central Americans is highest, virtually all new migration is made up of extended family of previous immigrants. The clear advantage that these later arrivals enjoy is that support networks already exist; it was the earlier immigrants who established needed contacts for securing housing, finding employment, locating medical services, and enrolling in school.

The size and productivity of these ethnic communities can be seen throughout the United States, but most especially in California, New York, Texas, and Florida, where (*in toto*) more than half of the new immigrants over the past 10 years have settled. In addition, certain *cities* have emerged as primary destinations for particular groups: Guatemalans are concentrated in Los Angeles, Salvadorans in Washington, DC, and Nicaraguans in Miami. Lillian points out that it was to her advantage to arrive at a time and place in which foreigners were viewed as novelties, rather than as subjects of concern or fear, as has become the case in many large urban areas. Despite results that prove otherwise, the perception today remains that newcomers, and particularly those in low-income areas, represent a drain on the local economy.

In reality, these migrations traditionally have a *positive* effect, as younger workers fill cheap labor slots and as businesses catering to ethnic preferences are created. Significantly, however, many Central American families receive no government assistance whatever, even though they qualify based on income, because they do not enjoy legal-resident status. Thus, they of course are careful to avoid contact with government agencies and services. Naturally, this reluctance to interact can affect all relationships with "outside" entities, including those with schools. There is often a strong desire to remain low-profile in order to avoid detection, prosecution, and possible deportation. Educators seeking greater rapport with those families will have to accept the possibility that issues relating to legal status may interfere with school-involvement efforts. Unless school staff members are willing to assist these families in *obtaining* legal status, they will have to work around the limitations created by this barrier to school participation.

Lillian experienced other advantages that eased her adjustment to the new culture. Because she came as the wife of an established community member, she was not responsible for resolving all of the basic issues relating to daily living (as discussed earlier). She and her children also were not forced to contend with the debilitating poverty that characterizes life for a significant percentage of the United States immigrant and refugee population. Finally, although not unaffected by the struggles faced by her family in Nicaragua, Lillian was not physically or emotionally traumatized before or during her departure from her country. Subsequently, she did not have to cope with potentially incapacitating mental-health needs that might have delayed or even prevented successful adaptation. (Lillian's case was also unusual in that she was able to travel back to her home country with relative ease. For most newcomers, personal economics and war conditions preclude return visits.)

Regardless of the degree to which Lillian's special circumstances eased her adjustment to the United States, her transition was hardly free of difficulties and frustrations. For any non-English speaker, communication is an especially vital issue. The acute sense of powerlessness one suffers without adequate language cannot be underestimated—not daring to answer a phone or initiate a conversation, fearing that crucial messages will be misunderstood, negotiating absolutely every detail with uncertainty. The experience is challenging enough for someone who is basically "together" and benefits from a support system; for those dealing with refugee shock, minus a history of formal education, and struggling financially, acquiring a new language can easily seem impossibly daunting.

In addition to coping with language difficulties, Lillian found life on a midwestern farm to be isolating. Although her husband speaks Spanish, she was essentially cut off from contact with other Hispanics (a situation she had to work hard to remedy). Fortunately, the very physical and hands-on nature of running a farm and household provided Lillian with a useful forum for acquiring a second language; her communication needs were immediate and highly practical, and of the utmost relevance to the tasks of the moment.

Eventually, Lillian and her husband had three children: two boys and a girl. There was never any doubt that theirs would be a bilingual home. The children have always heard both Spanish and English spoken at home, and while they are now most proficient at the latter, they understand Spanish in conversation, even if they respond in English. Developing and maintaining a sense of Latin heritage, however, has proved more problematic. Like many Hispanic parents raising children in areas with few immigrants, Lillian has made a concerted effort to seek out other Spanish speakers and cultural events so that her children might interact and gain exposure. Happily, as the Central American community has grown, that endeavor has become easier; today, a fair number of cultural and political groups now function nearby, in Madison.

One ongoing issue concerns what Lillian describes as "classism" within and among the various Hispanic groups—the unwillingness of some to associate with others. Non-Hispanics need to be sensitive to this diversity within the Spanish-speaking world, both among various nations and within a specific nationality. The differences between rural and urban citizens, educated and illiterate, mestizo and indigenous, and landed and poor are as significant as those between two separate nations. Those seeking the collaboration of the Hispanic community need to recognize and acknowledge the range of backgrounds represented, in order to effectively form partnerships that meet a variety of purposes.

At the time Lillian's oldest child enrolled in the local primary school, he spoke Spanish more fluently than English. He was tested in English, and placed in special education as the result of his test scores. He spent a year in the program, exiting when his fluency in English increased sufficiently to allow him to participate in the regular classroom. He apparently has no recollection of this placement, and has not been adversely affected academically, socially, or emotionally by his initial assessment. Lillian excuses the decision made by the school as understandable, given that personnel had not dealt previously with bilingual children. Noting that her other two children (who entered school more fluent in English) were placed directly in regular classrooms, Lillian explains that her fears regarding labeling never materialized, and that all of her children have been treated fairly by the school system.

Lillian's son's experience does indicate, however, an approach in assessment of non-"mainstream" students that should be viewed with great caution. Nationwide, Hispanic students (as well as African-American and Native-American students) are overrepresented in special education, even when allowance is made for the negative effect of environmental factors related to income levels (such as poor prenatal care and exposure to lead and other toxins). The inability of traditional educational practice to meet these students' needs is a real threat to their academic potential, cultural uniqueness, and self-esteem.

Lillian recognizes that her children have avoided other pitfalls that face Hispanic students as well. They have always been part of the same peer group in their community and have enjoyed genuine acceptance by that group. They have not faced the kind of negative pressure from friends that can pull them away from family values and educational goals. By contrast, large numbers of Central American youth are challenged by outside pressures that undermine both parental wishes and school expectations. In many cases, teenagers from Nicaragua and other countries have been sent on their own to live with relatives and friends, for a variety of reasons: to receive a more comprehensive education, to avoid military service, or perhaps because there is an element of prestige attached to having a child studying in the States. These students are at additional risk of being influenced by forces beyond the control of family and school. Often they have not been adequately prepared to manage the level of responsibility required, and are easily swayed in negative ways.

Even when a Central American student is living with his or her immediate family in the United States, the influence of friends and peers is substantial. In their native country, the family can usually "protect" its members because the family is so extensive, and there is a group level of responsibility for each individual. Although children may logically feel that this "pressure" from relatives is simple interference, the support it provides is nevertheless a powerful force in countering undesired and potentially destructive behaviors.

As is often the case in a new culture, even those parents willing to show the strongest support for educational values may be at a complete loss as to how to effectively promote academic goals and otherwise serve as advocates for their children's needs. They may not feel sufficient confidence in approaching a school, due to their own level of English fluency, hesitancy to reveal their lack of formal schooling, discomfort because of economic status, or belief that they do not possess the skills necessary to help their children succeed academically. Too, educational priorities often are second to more urgent needs, such as those created by the stresses of refugee trauma and living in poverty.

As a result of all such factors, Hispanic parents are especially isolated from the kind of partnerships with schools that result in meaningful involvement and, ultimately, in decision-making power. Without outreach in Spanish, and ongoing efforts to support parents in their role as teachers of their children, schools will *have* to accept their share of responsibility for the failure of Hispanic students to reach their maximum academic potential. The clearest evidence of this lack of collaboration is the dropout rate for Spanish-speaking students, which in many school districts is the highest for any ethnic group.

The school should *never* make the assumption that a parent does not care. To do so ignores the all too obvious fact that *all* parents desire success for their children. Rather, educators need a thorough understanding of the barriers that Hispanic parents face, a sincere appreciation of the cultural strengths that these families can bring to home-school partnerships, and a jointly designed plan for effective collaboration. When these crucial components are finally in place, the Central American parents' inherent faith in the role of U.S. schools will be fully mobilized, and their children will at long last receive the support they need and deserve.

About the Authors
Lillian Rodríguez Post is a former resident of Nicaragua, where she taught primary school. She is a graduate of the Escuela Normal de Esteli and currently farms with her husband in Mount Horeb, Wisconsin.

Kathryn Price is a graduate of the University of Wisconsin. She is a home-school coordinator with the Madison Metropolitan School District. Her work focuses on parent-involvement programs for low-income families.

Chapter 6

The Role of Social History in Research and Practice

One Chicana's Perspective

LILLIAN VEGA CASTANEDA

Introduction

The educational system in the United States has consistently explored the possibility and, in some cases, policies aimed at increasing the opportunities for ethnic and racial minorities to obtain an equal educational opportunity—equal to that of White, middle-class, mainstream students. This series of attempts is grounded in both a historical and contemporary context. Simply put, we are still trying to improve the opportunities for a quality education, and, by extension, a higher quality of life (e.g., in profession and ultimately in earnings) for our nation's disenfranchised, the children of color, those who are visibly distinct—ethnically, racially, linguistically, or culturally. The U.S. public schools serve as the primary agents for articulating, shaping, and predicting the future successes, failures, and possibilities (or lack of) for all students. These predictions are reflected in choices made regarding curricula, approaches to teaching and learning, philosophies, and designs of programs and implementation. For better or for worse, the schools hold many answers toward increasing opportunities for the children of color, ethnic, and linguistic minorities.

As in the seventies and eighties, the nineties mark a continued search for excellence in education. Issues involving low achievement scores on standardized tests, curriculum planning and implementation, and improvement of teacher preparation and performance, through stricter and more focused certification requirements, are at the forefront of the agenda. Yet, minority students continue to fail in the educational system.

As an associate professor at a state university, and coordinator of an education program specifically designed to prepare teachers to deal effectively with ethnically, linguistically, and culturally diverse children, the following is offered as one individual's story, growing up "Chicano" in the United States, searching for a way to define who I wanted to be (and am), along with the many obstacles I faced and the invisible boundaries I crossed. This vignette describes my search and the impact on current work with ethnically, racially, culturally, and linguistically diverse children. My experiences have helped to shape how I think about and study children in and out of school, their families, curriculum planning, and teaching. Perhaps my reflections as a student, teacher, parent, teacher trainer, and researcher will provide an impetus for teachers, administrators, policy makers, and researchers to think about their "thinking" toward children of color, ethnic and linguistic minorities, who do not "fit" the mainstream context.

The first section discusses the notion of sociohistoric context. An example of how sociohistoric context may or may not be acknowledged in an academic context is given. The second section focuses on my educational experiences as a Mexican-American student growing up in the sixties. A description of how I began to identify as a "Chicana" follows. Connections are made regarding the role of social history in framing an approach to research on ethnically, linguistically, and racially distinct students. In the third section, I describe how these occurrences have impacted my research, teaching, approach, and perspective.

Sociohistoric Context

I am the product of a large nuclear family. My father worked to support the family as a self-employed sewer contractor. He was born in Tyrone, New Mexico, in 1920. His parents immigrated to the United States from Piños, Zacatecas. My grandfather entered the United States in 1914. In 1974, as I interviewed him for my senior (college) thesis, he told me that he paid two cents to cross the border at El Paso, Texas. My grandparents raised their children in strict Catholic tradition. My father's first language is Spanish, and he is bilingual and biliterate.

My mother was born in Los Angeles in 1927. Her father and mother were born in New Mexico. I am unable to trace the maternal line into Mexico, but am aware that her father was a railroad worker for Southern Pacific. He died a young man, leaving my mother as a very young child. My mother's birth name is Alvina, yet, upon entering the U.S. school system, her teacher "changed" it to "Evelyn," thus beginning the process of "Americanization." My father entered the U.S. school system as Enrique, to become Henry. In conversations with my parents, I learned that children were often punished for speaking Spanish in school. Children were punished for such an infraction by spankings along with verbal warnings. Thus, it is not surprising that my parents chose not to teach me, or my two brothers and five sisters, to speak Spanish.

Given this information, one may ask why it matters. So what? What difference does it make? To some, this partial description of my family's social history may be viewed merely as a personal anecdotal narrative. Personal narrative, reflection, and connections made to one's experiences are often viewed as inferior to "objective," "analytical," and "abstract" forms of academic discourse. This was clearly the case throughout my doctoral studies. During one doctoral course, the use of narrative form in academic discourse was used by one group of students, while another group engaged in what they believed to be a higher-level abstract form. The seminar was organized such that students read a series of articles based on a theme. Several guiding questions were posed to assist in the readings. During the seminar, a guest presenter (usually one of the authors of an assigned reading) would present his or her work to the class. Next, the students would divide into groups and discuss the readings.

What occurred reflects the distinction between discourse interwoven with personal narrative and related life experiences versus a form of discourse void of personal reflection. One group based its discussion only on the assigned readings. They came to self-identify as being the "academic abstract" group. The other group consisted mainly of minorities and a few White women. This group was viewed as "less academic," relying on experiential thinking. During the course of the seminar, the White female members moved back and forth between the two groups.

Cazden and Hymes (1980) wrote of a similar experience. They pointed out, "They highlighted the possibility that one form of inequality of opportunity in our society has to do with rights to use narrative, with whose narratives are admitted to have a cognitive function" (p. 126). The authors continued:

> *We tend to depreciate narrative as a form of knowledge, and personal narrative particularly, in contrast to other forms of discourse considered scholarly, scientific, technical, or the like. This seems to me part of a general predisposition in our culture to dichotomize forms and functions of language use, and to treat one side of the dichotomy as superior, the other side as something to be disdained, discouraged, diagnosed as evidence or cause of subordinate status. Different dichotomies tend to be conflated, so that standard: non-standard, written: spoken, abstract: concrete, context-independent: context-free, technical/formal narrative tend to be equated. (p. 129)*

By extension, social history (i.e., those experiences rooted in a historical context for a given population or individual) tends to differentiate between various perspectives and accounts. An illustration of this proposition is that social studies texts still teach American history from a largely Eurocentric perspective. Social history and life experiences play a major role in my current thinking regarding the research of children of color, socially, culturally, linguistically distinct from the mainstream of society. In short, my sociohistoric and life experiences have impacted my perspective as an individual, a woman, an educator, a parent, and a Chicana. The following accounts of several childhood experiences inform my present thinking surrounding the education of Chicano children and other children of color. For sure, these experiences impact my perspective on designing research and practice, curriculum, and instruction. Although "pure research" argues that researchers should pursue inquiry devoid of "subjective" contexts, I argue that all researchers are impacted by their specific, sociohistorical experiences and perspectives. Because of the undeniable acceptance of a Eurocentric tradition in higher education, what is termed "objective" and "pure" is based on the majority culture's definition of objectivity.

At the age of 6, I entered the first grade at St. Anthony's Elementary School. The classroom and my utter confusion and inability in deciphering the written word remain vivid in my memory. Several children in the group (termed "the slow group" and assigned the name of the Crackerjacks) would sit quietly as Sister Miriam Mark printed a list of words on the chalkboard. The slate was clean, green, without a mark. I recall the neatness and exactness of her printing. Each child was expected to say the words to Sister as she pointed. I recall the desire to "read" and to "get it right." At the end of the first grade, I was termed a slow learner and recommended for retention. However, retention was not to happen for me. My mother pulled me out of the school at the end of the year and placed me in a public school.

That summer, and during the second grade, I recall the evenings that I sat with my mother on her bed and "read." My mother made flash cards, read to me, and had me read with her. She was a very patient teacher, who herself had been forced to drop out of high school in the tenth grade because of harassment from other students. Had it not been for her patience, caring, love, and understanding, I may have been lost in the school system.

Another incident occurred at the public school where my mother had enrolled me in the second grade. I remember my teacher telling me that I talked "funny." For the next two years, I worked with a speech teacher on articulation. I practiced saying words, sentences, tongue twisters, and rhymes. In retrospect, I wonder if my accent may have been interpreted as different—deficient to that of the mainstream. Yet, I am a native English speaker, and the notion of language "difference" cannot serve as a reasonable rationale for the assignment of the label. This is especially important to note because English is my first language. Thus, language difference could not explain the teacher's actions. If language difference was not at issue, perhaps the way I "used" language and "pronounced" words was.

The final example of confusion in the classroom revolves around an incident I experienced as a fourth-grader. I was back at St. Anthony's in Mrs. Wilson's class. On one particular morning, the whole class was taking a standardized test. We had been told to stay in our seats and to be quiet. That morning, I was feeling very sick. I attempted to complete the test but could not. I remember thinking that I could either raise my hand and ask to be excused or I could sit quietly and throw up at my desk.

I opted for the first choice. I raised my hand. Mrs. Wilson saw me raise my hand and did not call on me. Finally, I got out of my seat to make a quick run for the restroom—only to be met with a firm hand on my backside. I ran and cried all the way to the restroom, sick. Mrs. Wilson sent the "smartest girl in class," Suzanne, to see what I was "up to." When I returned, the teacher asked me in a very gentle tone, "But honey, why didn't you tell me?"

Phillips (1983), a pioneer in exploring how differences in cultural background may block opportunity for positive communication and learning in the classroom, has provided an excellent example of how culturally different students are subject to feelings of confusion in the classroom: "When I went to junior high, it was hard for me to read, cause in grade school I was too scared to read...because...in grade school you were taught, 'Be quiet and listen,' you know? And then they'd want you to answer and if you was quiet, they'd get mad at you anyway. So, you know, you was all mixed up, unless you was teacher's pet or something" (p. 107).

My childhood experiences are not unique. But if these things happened to me, a middle-class, English-only speaker, third-generation Mexican-American, one can only imagine what may happen to working-class, monolingual, immigrant students. It is because of this shared experience that I am drawn to the study of Chicano, Latino, and other minority children in the school and home/community setting. This focus and interest in how minority children interact with one another and the adults in and out of school is grounded in a sociohistoric perspective.

As a Chicano researcher, my sociohistoric experience has led me to reflect on what might have occurred differently in Mrs. Wilson's fourth-grade class had I known how to "get the teacher's attention" in a culturally congruent, acceptable way. Perhaps Sister Miriam Mark was unaware that children and adult learners acquire knowledge and understanding in a variety of ways, in different situations, and that how children learn is largely determined by their sociocultural experiences and informal learning and communication in the home/community context, prior to the onset of formal schooling.

In *Minority Education and Caste* (1978), Ogbu has compared the contradiction between the American ideal of education as the "greatest equalizer" to the daily reality faced by a large number of minority children. While minority children have a "traditionally low" performance level on standardized tests, and many scholars have argued this based on a cultural deprivation model, Ogbu suggested a different view, one based on an American "caste system or system of racial stratification" (p. 3). He asserted that minority children achieve at a lower rate than mainstream children because of their "birth ascribed status as subordinate minorities."

Evolution of a Chicano Consciousness

> *Like calaveras bailando—the humorous, dancing skeletons of Mexican folklore that teach us to celebrate life by laughing at death—the partygoers laughed and danced, recalling for an evening the lost intensity of their tumultuous youth.*
>
> *It was a reunion of sort for the Chicano movement.*
>
> *A decade had passed since the death of the movement. In the interim, most of the young Chicano "revolutionaries" had joined the establishment as lawyers, business executives, college professors or bureaucrats. But they were still bound together by the political rite of passage that had forged their generation's Chicano identity.*
>
> *It raised a question each had wrestled with in different ways. Though the dream of Aztlan had faded, would its legacy be strong enough to sustain a generation's commitment to change? (Hernandez, 1983)*

The sixties witnessed a monumental social movement for change in the United States. The social protest movement of the time came in the form of diverse interests and groups. Mainstream youth, along with their anti-war sentiments and critical evaluation of the "establishment," became the active force in a social and political protest movement, which questioned the fundamental principles on which the nation was founded. The late sixties and early seventies also witnessed the awakening of rights for gays, women, blacks, and Chicanos. Various student groups were formed on college campuses across the nation (e.g., Students for a Democratic Society, Black Student Union, National Organization for Women, and El Movimiento Estudiantil Chicanos de Aztlan).

In 1967, I entered the ninth grade at San Gabriel High School in middle-class Alhambra, California. Although not referred to as *integration*, I was bused into this upper-middle class, White, public school at the age of 14. It was my first experience in sustained activity with upper-middle class mainstream culture. I recall that I made a conscious effort to befriend several Anglo girls, so that I would have a few friends from the "inside." In fact, most of my friends from Ivar Street adopted this strategy.

As a freshmen in high school, I had decided to take courses that would prepare me for entrance to college. My understanding of the term *college prep* was that it was a path for serious students. Was I not a serious student? My counselor, Mrs. Goddard, informed me that I was not college material. Early in the school year, she called me into her office. She told me that I would not be allowed to take college-prep courses because my scores on the high school assessment were too low. That day, she changed my course schedule to reflect typing and home economics.

When I told my parents of the change, my mother contacted Mrs. Goddard. I don't recall the exact chain of events, but I was allowed to take the courses for college-bound students. I remember sitting in Mrs. Goddard's office as she signed my course change cards. She said, "Well, I can't stop you from signing up, but you'll never make it. Trust me."

In spite of the warning, I excelled in high school. I was well liked by my teachers and had my share of friends, Mexican-American and White. I even joined the drill team, Spanish Club, and Future Business Leaders of America. I didn't have any visible problems with which to contend. As a teen, I went to different extracurricular functions with Mexican-American and White friends. Although I would never identify myself as a "sellout," I clearly felt that I was the same as my Anglo peers in terms of upward mobility and opportunity. I felt that friendship could withstand the obstacles presented by racial differences.

Several incidents occurred that served as a catalyst for me to rethink my relationships with my Anglo peers. I had become friends with a member of the drill team who was also enrolled in the same Spanish class. This individual lived in "upper crust" North San Gabriel. She was a warm, soft-spoken, kind individual. I used to help her with her Spanish. Although I had not been raised to consciously speak Spanish, I still had a receptivity to the language, as I heard it on a daily basis in the community setting. On one occasion, she invited me and several others to her home after a game. I remember the large rooms and elegant furniture in her home. More clearly, I recall the look on her mother's face when Joan introduced me. Her mother looked at me and through me, as if a zombie had just walked into her home. She did not welcome me, say hello, or nod. I remember looking at Mrs. Kelm, knowing that I would not get the same welcome that she extended to the others. After that evening, Joan never spoke to me again. She never said "hi" even if she passed me face to face in the hall or class.

As a junior in Mr. McCallister's U.S. History class, I continued to excel. I remember thinking that I wanted always to do my best, because, in the end, it would pay off. Mr. McAllister urged me to think about majoring in history when I entered the university. I took his recommendation to heart. Yet, during my junior year I began to change my outlook and perspective as a Mexican-American student in a predominantly White school. San Gabriel High School was my first real encounter with overt racism, prejudice, and mistreatment, where it was crystal clear that being Mexican American was to be undesirable.

One key incident in my adolescent life served as a catalyst in the formation of a Chicano consciousness and perspective—one that has impacted my current thinking. During the second semester, I did what many adolescents do. I changed my appearance by adopting the dress code of the counterculture. I began to read the newspaper regularly to keep informed of national events. I had also let Mr. McAllister down. He said to me, "What ever happened to that nice, well-groomed young lady I used to know?" Several things had happened, but this one stands out.

I had enrolled in U.S. Government during the summer of 1970. As I entered the classroom, I became acutely aware that, for some reason, I was the only Mexican American in class. I thought to myself, Where are the others? Walking past a group of students, a boy, a popular one and member of the student council, looked at me and said in a very loud voice, "Oh, look, there's a *Mexican* in our class." From that time on, I made a conscious effort (perhaps a paradigm shift) never to apologize for myself, my culture, or the color of my skin. That summer, during that class, each student was assigned to make a formal presentation on a political or social issue relevant to the time. I prepared and delivered a speech on the United Farm Workers Movement and its leader, Cesar Chavez. These combined experiences led to the beginning of my consciousness and transformation as a Chicana learning to succeed as a subordinate minority in a White society (Ogbu, 1974).

Theory, Research, and Practice

The underachievement of Chicano and other minority children across the educational continuum remains a major area of concern. The high dropout rate and low achievement scores on standardized tests (at the elementary, secondary, and postsecondary levels) are current and timeless issues. For example, why do such disproportionate numbers of Chicano students continue the cycle of failure, 25 years after the advent of the Chicano movement and the accompanying demands for equal educational opportunity?

The demands for equal educational opportunity for minority children *were* addressed, as pointed out by Hymes (1981):

> *The civil rights movement stimulated attention to the educational needs of Black children. Lack of adequate knowledge of the actual language situation led to mistaken efforts on the part of many liberal and conservative alike.*
>
> *The bilingual education of Spanish-speaking Americans has followed a similar course. Political mobilization and regard for equity have led to pro-*

grams which had little in the way of precedent and basic research on which to draw.

In general, one sees a recurrent pattern of a surge of attention to a language situation, because of social and political concerns, and then a lapse. (p. vi)

The early "mistaken efforts" took the form of programs that were based on cultural deprivation, cultural disadvantages, and culture of poverty models. It was theorized that minority children came from a culture that lacked experiences necessary for the development of their thinking and language skills. Programs were designed to enrich the minority children's cultural and language experiences. A major intervention strategy was through the use of language development activities in the school setting. This practice was based on the rationale that, if a student received large doses of language enrichment, this would translate into improved academic achievement:

This was a decade when a great deal of research was devoted to the perceptual, cognitive, and linguistic processes of poor black children. Cultural and linguistic deprivation, said to result, in part, from maladaptive mother-child interactional styles, had been cited as factors contributing to these children's poor school performance and low scores on IQ and standardized achievement tests. Based on these studies, legislation and federal monies created preschool compensatory education programs designed to improve academic performance. (Mitchell, 1982)

The cultural deprivation theory had a wide acceptance by the majority culture. It did not, after all, lay the "blame" and responsibility for the "failure" on the American education system, and hence, the majority culture. Instead, the model put the blame on the victims—the students—and their respective cultures, languages, and experiences.

As a bilingual teacher in the early seventies, I began to question the deficiency model of education. I looked at my Latino students—both monolingual English and Spanish speaking. I spent many hours working with children in English and Spanish language, reading and writing, along with English as a second language. The contrast in the use of language among my students (e.g., English only, Spanish speaking, bilingual) could not be denied. Much of what I observed in some of my students was reminiscent of my own childhood (e.g., blank stares looking back at me as I introduced a new set of vocabulary words in the pocket chart). As a preservice teacher, I had been taught to teach through a linear, sequentially based approach to teaching (e.g., seven-step lesson plan, basal reading, skills-based instruction). I began to focus on finding other ways to assist my students. I wondered how I could structure learning for my Latino students (e.g., Mexican immigrant, Mexican American, Central American).

I increased my knowledge surrounding teaching and learning, especially for linguistically diverse children. While completing master's-level work in the seventies, I continued to focus on nonmainstream students who needed specialized help. Conceptually, I began to read and study various learning theories and to "rethink" how I taught children. In a sense, I began to undergo a paradigm shift, moving from linear-based instruction to more holistically based instructional modes. Conceptually, I underwent a change in the ways I viewed and valued my students. I began to take a closer look at my students, their respective backgrounds, and their specific needs, and to consciously define what my students brought into the learning situation.

Although most educators and policy makers may not consciously subscribe to a deficiency model in the 1990s, at the unconscious level, certain practices and policies continue to blame the victim for continued failure and "inadequate performance" in a still White-dominated educational mileu. At the unconscious level, teachers may interact with their students, organize learning situations, and implement standards and practices in a way that implicitly "blames the victim" for performances on a given task in a given situation. Another example of "blaming the victim" concerns the placement of children in remedial situations. In this instance, there is an underlying belief that with lots of skills-based instruction, repetition, and rote learning, the child can be "fixed." A gross extension of this practice shows kindergarten teachers who expect their students to come to school "ready to read"; when the student is unable to "read," he or she is labeled a "slow learner." One of the ironies of the deficiency-based perspective is that, in the 1990s, I still "see" and "hear" daily evidence of practices that place blame on the victims for their own academic failures.

As a doctoral student in the early eighties, I began to deepen my understanding of teaching and learning, mainly through the study of ethnography, communication, and sociolinguistics. I began to explore issues of active engagement and participation by students in the teaching/learning situation along with the role of sociocultural context. Thus, I was baffled when, as a parent of a first-grader, I was forced to "revisit" the practice of "blaming the victim" up close and personal.

In the mid-eighties, my family and I returned from the East Coast where I had completed doctoral coursework. We decided to settle in a suburban area of Los Angeles and enrolled our three children in the public schools. The youngest child, age 6, was placed in the first grade at the local elementary school. This child had been involved in multiethnic play-groups and attended preschool in Cambridge, Massachusetts. She had traveled throughout the United States and had been nurtured by myself, my husband, and our two older children. During her first semester at the neighborhood school, we were contacted by the first-grade teacher for a parent conference. In reviewing our child's progress report, we were informed that Gabriella was making good to normal progress in all of the designated areas. Thus, we were surprised when the teacher informed us that Gabriella had not met the "invisible standards" of this particular school. ("We at La Verne Heights expect all of our first-graders to come to us [from the kindergarten] reading. Since Gabriella did not have the benefit of the La Verne Heights kindergarten, I am recommending retention.") Although Gabriella was able to "read" the first-grade material and was in the first grade, we were told that it was not enough, because of the invisible standard—or boundary?

I set out to educate this teacher, and wrote a letter highlighting my concerns regarding the treatment of my child, and, by extension, the treatment of other children who do not necessarily fit into someone's notion of a "successful" student:

> *I understand that you feel Gabriella is very "passive" and "quiet" in her interactions at school. What does this mean? How do you define passive?*

Passive, active, and competitive behaviors do occur in classrooms. Yet, one is not "higher" or more "abstract" than the other—it is a matter of context and interpretation. Clearly, our interpretations do not coincide.

In the final example, recent immigrant Latino students are often taught by their parents and extended family members to show respect to adults by remaining silent and listening, rarely making eye contact. This type of behavior is often interpreted as disrespectful and/or "passive" in mainstream contexts. Maldonado-Guzman (1980) explored the process of differential treatment of students by the classroom teacher. He posed two significant questions: (1) How does the process of differential treatment occur? (2) Why do some teachers prefer some students over others? He suggested that some students are able to positively "get the floor" by playing "classroom politics" (p. 121). Some children know implicitly and/or explicitly what the behavior of an "ideal student" consists of in the eyes of the teacher. In an ethnographic study of student-student and teacher-student interaction in high, medium, and low Spanish reading groups, the notion of "classroom politics" and "getting the floor" were illustrated (Castaneda, 1989). Overall, students in the high reading group knew how to read teacher cues (e.g., knew when to sit and listen, when to provide an answer, how to get the teacher's attention, how to ask for clarification, and how to ask for information). Students in the high reading group were adept at getting their questions answered and completing the assignments. In whole-class, nonreading situations, these same students seemed to "gain and hold" the floor to a larger degree than their peers in the medium and low reading groups. Conversely, the classroom teacher provided more opportunities for students in the high group to answer questions and provide information.

Research shows that some students are able to read teacher cues in order to function as successful members of a given classroom situation. What about those students who are unable to decipher these critical cues? What about children who come to the learning situation with a different way of knowing and doing and showing what they know? Although these questions have been addressed by various researchers, what about a revisit to the notion of teachers' responsibility toward critical self-reflection, and thinking about their perceptions, beliefs, and biases toward children who do not "fit" into a mainstream context?

Approach to Research and Practice

As a researcher and coordinator of a teacher preparation program, I am challenged to revisit notions of cultural deprivation, cultural disadvantaged, and so on, deficit models of education. As a researcher, the approach I use is largely ethnographic, consisting of ongoing data collection in a given setting over an extended period of time. Through the use of fieldnotes, reflection, and constant updating and questioning of the data, I am able to learn about the "culture" of a given classroom or learning situation. Critical analyses of the data lead to the identification of patterns and categories present in a given situation. The approach leads to the formulation of propositions and implications for teaching, learning, curricula, and program development. The approach provides information on minority children that is not often portrayed or reflected in pure, quantitative designs. Although a vast majority of quantitative studies show that minority children do not perform at or near the levels of their majority culture counterparts, they fail to consider the cultural differences in learning styles, language differences and variation, communication and interaction, and, most importantly, the child, as an individual and "real" person. The approach departs from a linear framework and is holistic and multidimensional:

> *This concept involves the recognition that no phenomenon can be defined by one of a few objective dimensions. Both which should be given consideration by the researcher, and many of these dimensions are not even rooted in the specific time and place of a phenomenon's occurrence. In order to get to these dimensions the researcher needs the help of the members of the research site, and possibly the outsiders. The notion of multidimensionality also involves using the proper approaches and analyses—that the situation under study deserves. The researcher should be willing to find out or create the methods and theories that better suit that situation. (Maldonado-Guzman, 1980, p. v)*

The method of inquiry, coupled with my sociohistorical and sociocultural perspective, shapes my current approach to teaching, and learning. As a college professor, I engage my students in a variety of activities that require the application of the ethnographic method in their class readings and fieldwork component. Through readings, data gathering, and analysis activities, preservice teachers are able to learn about their students and to gather information that informs their future practice. Issues of sociocultural/ sociolinguistic competence, definitions of "successful" students, and ways that students show teachers what they know are explored at the preservice level. Courses are structured to move beyond the "obvious" (e.g., what is readily observable regarding students) to the "invisible" cultures that are at work in every classroom. Preservice teachers reflect on their own schooling experiences, within a sociocultural context.

As the coordinator of a teacher credential program that focuses on the preparation of preservice individuals to effectively and successfully address the needs of ethnically, linguistically, and culturally diverse students, nondeficit-based approaches to teaching and learning are introduced and critically analyzed. Issues of culture are explored, analyzed, and applied to students' fieldwork placements. A strength of the program is in the faculty that designed it cooperatively, to include a variety of readings, processes, activities, and discussions that merge theory and practice, within a sociohistoric, sociolinguistic, and sociocultural context. Faculty team-teach a core course for the (Bilingual) Crosscultural Language and Academic Development (B/CLAD) credential program that focuses on issues of culture—including generic notions of culture and macro/microanalyses, to more specific notions of culture and its role in communication, interaction, behaviors, beliefs, values, and implications for practice. The faculty who team-teach are also specialists in their respective content areas (e.g., bilingual education, language and literacy, learning, and instruction, educational leadership, math and science, and the social sciences). *Issues of culture transcend across the content areas.* Issues related to the education of culturally, racially, and linguistically diverse children are treated and presented simultaneously and are "on par" with the treatment of mainstream students in mainstream situations. This is an important distinction in that, traditionally, attention to "minority" needs are often thought of as an "add on" to an already developed program. The work currently underway at my university reflects a critical if not drastic departure from addressing minority issues as simple "additions"—to their inclusion in a comprehensive teacher-education program that delivers the same content and curricula to all its preservice students.

Growing up "Mexican American" in the United States and becoming "Chicano" has impacted my work as a teacher, researcher, and college professor. Growing up Mexican American allowed me to develop biculturally, with great adeptness at moving in and out of two worlds—that of the mainstream, dominant culture, and that of the Mexican-American community. As a young child, I was already bicultural. As an adolescent, I came to the realization that biculturalism is not a "guarantee" when it comes to moving in and out of mainstream situations with ease. Because of this rude awakening, I believe I am a stronger yet more sensitive individual, and this has informed my research and practice. Because of the many obstacles placed in front of me—beginning in the first grade, carrying into secondary education, and to some degree continuing in postsecondary education—I prepare individuals, regardless of their ethnicity, linguistic background, or race, to "think" about their ideas, notions, and stereotypes about children, in general, and children of color, specifically.

My personal narrative is not unique, but it must be noted that, although I grew up in the sixties, many of the same issues are still relevant today. A wide variety of recent immigrants from many countries and other children of color are entering the nation's schools for the first time. Concomitantly, the nation's children of color, the historically disenfranchised (e.g., African-American, Mexican-American, Puerto Rican), continue to drop out of school, continue to score low on standardized tests, are underprepared to enter postsecondary education, and are at great risk of becoming involved in "high-risk" behavior (e.g., gang activity, substance and/or alcohol abuse, teen pregnancy). Nonmainstream students are in critical need of focused and informed educational experiences to be implemented by a teaching force that is largely middle class and White. These teachers are in an unprecedented position to increase student achievement and success in a school context through critical self-reflection and sociohistoric and sociocultural analyses that move beyond the basic teacher preparation curricula.

References

Castaneda, Lillian Vega. (1989). An ethnographic study of the communication and interaction of first grade Hispanic children in a high Spanish reading group: A comparative view of children as they engage in classroom life. Unpublished doctoral dissertation, Harvard Graduate School of Education.

Cazden, Courtney, & Hymes, Dell. (1980). Narrative thinking and storytelling rights: A folklorist's clue to a critique of education. In Dell Hymes (Ed.), *Language and education: Ethnolinguistic essays*. Washington DC: Center for Applied Linguistics.

Hernandez, Marita. (1983). Generation in search of its legacy. In *Southern California's Latino Community, Los Angeles Times*.

Hymes, Dell. (1981). Ethnographic monitoring. In Henry T. Trueba, Grace P. Gutherie, & Kathryn H. Au (Eds.), *Culture and the bilingual classroom: Studies in classroom ethnography*. Rowley, MA: Newbury House Publishers, pp. 56–68.

Maldonado-Guzman, Abel. (1980). A multidimensional ethnographic framework for studying classroom organization and interaction. Unpublished Qualifying Paper, Harvard Graduate School of Education.

Mitchell, Jacquelyn. (1982). Reflections of a Black social scientist: Some struggles, some doubts, some hopes. *Harvard Educational Review, 52*(1).

Ogbu John. (1974). The next generation: An ethnography of education in an urban neighborhood. New York: Academic Press.

Ogbu, John. (1978). *Minority education and caste: The American system in crosscultural perspective.* New York: Academic Press.

Phillips, Susan Urston. (1983). *The invisible culture: Communication and community on the Warm Springs Indian Reservation.* New York: Longman.

Bibliography

Allen, W. B. (1993, November). Response to a "White discourse on White racism." *Educational Researcher, 22* (8).

Arvizu, Steven F., Snyder, Warren A., & Espinoza, Paul T. (1980, June). Demistifying the concept of culture: Theoretical and conceptual tools. *Bilingual Education Series, 3* (11). Los Angeles: Evaluation, Dissemination and Assessment Center.

Banks, James A. (1993, Winter). Multicultural education as an academic discipline: Goals for the 21st century." Multicultural Education.

Carrasco, Robert L. (1981). Expanded awareness of student performance: A case study in applied ethnographic monitoring in a bilingual classroom. In H. T. Trueba, G. P. Guthrie, & K. H. Au (Eds.), *Culture and the bilingual classroom: Studies in classroom ethnography.* Rowley, MA: Newbury House.

Castaneda, Lillian Vega. (1991). *Social organization of communication and interaction in exemplary SAIP classrooms and the nature of competent membership.* Paper presented at the annual meeting of the American Educational Research Association, Chicago.

Cazden, Courtney. (1988). *Classroom discourse: The language of teaching and learning.* Portsmouth, NH: Heinemann.

Garcia, Eugene. (1994). *Understanding and meeting the challenge of student cultural diversity.* Boston: Houghton Mifflin.

Garfinkel, Harold. (1972). Remarks on ethnomethodology. In John J. Gumperz & Dell Hymes (Eds.), *Directions in sociolinguistics.* New York: Holt, Rinehart and Winston.

Gegeo, Karen A. Watson, & Gegeo, David W. (1986). Calling out and repeating routines in Kwara'e children's language socialization. In Bambi B. Schieffelin & Elinor Och (Eds.), *Language socialization across cultures.* New York: Cambridge University Press, pp. 17–50.

Gegeo, Karen A. Watson, & Gegeo, David W. (1983, March). The social world of Kwara'e children. Acquisition of language and values. In Jenny Cook Gumperz, William Corsaro & Jurgen Streck (Eds.), *Children's worlds and children's language.* Berlin: Mouton de Gruyter, pp. 109–128.

Gilmore, Perry, & Glatthorn, Allan A. (1982). *Children in and out of school* Washington DC: Center for Applied Linguistics.

Glaser Barney G., & Strauss, Alslem L. (1967). *The discovery of grounded theory.* New York: Aldine.

Grant, Carl A. (Ed.). (1992). *Research and multicultural education: From the margins to the mainstream.* London: Falmer Press.

Gumperz, John J. (1971). *Language in social groups.* Stanford, CA: Stanford University Press.

Gumperz, John J., & Hymes, Dell (Eds.). (1972). *Directions in sociolinguistics.* New York: Holt, Rinehart and Winston.

Gumperz, John J. (1982). *Discourse strategies.* Cambridge: Cambridge University Press.

Gumperz, John J. (Ed.). (1982). *Language and social identity.* Cambridge, Cambridge University Press.

Heath, Shirley Brice. (1978). Teacher talk: Language in the classroom. In *Language in Education: Theory and Practice.* Washington, DC: Center for Applied Linguistics.

Heath, Shirley Brice. (1983). *Ways with words: Language, life and work in communities and classrooms.* Cambridge: Cambridge University Press.

Hymes, Dell. (1972). Models of the interaction of language and social life. In John J. Gumperz & Dell Hymes (Eds.), *Directions in sociolinguistics.* New York: Holt, Rinehart and Winston.

Hymes, Dell (Ed.). (1974). *Reinventing anthropology.* New York: Vintage Books.

McClaren, Peter. (1994). *Life in schools: An introduction to critical pedagogy in the foundations of education* (2nd ed.). New York: Longman.

Nava, Alfonso, Molina, Huberto, Cabello, Beverly, de la Torre, Bill, & Castaneda, Lillian Vega. (1994). *Educating Americans in a multicultural society.* New York: McGraw-Hill.

Peñalosa, Fernando. (1980). *Chicano sociolinguistics: A brief introduction.* Rowley, MA: Newbury House.

Scheurich, James Joseph. (1993, November). Toward a White discourse on White racism. *Educational Researcher, 22* (8).

Sleeter, Christine E. (1993, November). Advancing a White discourse: A response to Scheurich." *Educational Reseacher, 22* (8).

Spindler, George D. (1987). *Education and cultural process: anthropological approaches* (2nd ed.). Prospect Heights, IL: Waveland Press.

About the Author

Lillian Vega Castaneda is associate professor of education at California State University San Marcos. Castaneda coordinates the (Bilingual) Crosscultural Language and Academic Development (B/CLAD) teacher preparation program. She teaches in the areas of language and literacy, bilingual/multilingual education, and language and culture. Castaneda's primary research areas include the identification and description of exemplary educational practices for at-risk students, bilingual and cross-cultural education, and the nature of language and literacy in mainstream, multiple-language and bilingual contexts. She was the associate study director of A Descriptive Study of Significant Features of Exemplary Special Alternative Instructional Programs, a national study commissioned by the U.S. Department of Education. Currently, Castaneda is conducting applied research in the area of effective curriculum, instruction, and program implementation for at-risk students in a comprehensive service-based alternative learning environment. Castaneda has a wealth of experience as a bilingual teacher, site-based coordinator, district-level staff and curriculum developer, university instructor, and researcher. She has been invited to provide input by national governmental and academic educational agencies. Castaneda holds a doctorate in Teaching, Curriculum, and Learning Environments from Harvard University.

Footholds on an Icy Slope

One Chinese-American Story

AMY LING

To paraphrase the saying, "You are what you eat," I am what I have read. This is to say that I have been largely shaped by my education in U.S. public schools, from the first grade through a Ph.D., by both the reading assigned to me and those books that I chose for myself. As a member of a racial minority in the United States, however, I have also been shaped by the places, the times, and the social climates in which I grew up, and because these often seemed cold, books offered a warm escape. Though now a tenured professor in the English department of a large state university, I began my life in America many years ago as an F.O.B. (Fresh-off-the-Boat), a small child from China, knowing not a word of English.

Still haunted by the fear of red balloons signaling the arrival of Japanese bombers, the drone of planes penetrating the damp walls of air-raid shelters dug into the mountainside, the deep bomb craters in the smoking streets of Chungking (my earliest memories), I found myself, at age 6, thrust into a classroom of strangers all speaking a language I didn't understand and smelling of cow's milk, a liquid I had never tasted. It was my first day at an American school—Miss May's first-grade class in Stevens Elementary School, Allentown, Pennsylvania. I felt overwhelmingly lost, and I struggled to find a foothold on what seemed a steep, ice-covered slope while those around me found the terrain comfortably flat and not in the least slippery.

My sense of total bewilderment in school gradually melted away when, by keen attention and the mimicry natural to young children, I learned to communicate in English—a process that (according to my mother) took only a few months. With the language, however, came the value system of the culture, and I just as quickly learned to aspire to and admire everything American and to reject and feel embarrassed by everything Chinese. These were the years when assimilation and homogenization were the guiding educational principles; when America, using Israel Zangwill's words, believed itself to be the great "melting pot." I pledged allegiance to the flag with my classmates and sang "land where my fathers died" with heart-swelling, patriotic pride without any consciousness that these words were not appropriate to my own personal history.

Living amid Euro-Americans in Pennsylvania, and later Mexico, Missouri, and finally Brooklyn, New York, I often thought of myself as White. Like the child Janie Crawford in Zora Neale Hurston's *Their Eyes Were Watching God*, who didn't recognize herself in the group photograph, I would, more often than I'd now like to admit, walk past a mirror and do a double-take. "Who is that Chinese girl?" I'd wonder. Then, with a start and a sinking feeling, I would realize that "that Chinese girl" was me. I didn't feel foreign or strange inside, but in acquiring the visual perspective of Euro-American eyes, I'd become self-estranged. Just when I would begin to feel some measure of security about knowing the footholds of a place, I'd see myself in the mirror, or meet someone new, and be accosted by such ice-making questions as, "How come your face and nose are so flat?" "Why don't you open your eyes more?" "Your skin really *is* kind of yellow, isn't it?" or "Where'd you learn such good English?" And I'd be sliding on my back down the ice-covered slope again.

In all those years of American public schooling, the only Chinese I ever encountered in any of my reading was in Bret Harte's poem, "Plain Language from Truthful James," commonly known as "The Heathen Chinee," which my fourth-grade teacher assigned. The poem was one of her favorites, and she clearly savored it as she read it aloud. I, however, was red-hot with humiliation and embarrassment at being of the same race as Ah Sin, with his queue down his back and his cards up his sleeve, noted "for ways that are dark and for tricks that are vain." I didn't feel Chinese, which is to say heathen, exotic, and strange. I was reading fairy tales, and pictured myself a long-haired blonde princess being rescued by a handsome prince. (It had not escaped my notice that, with the exception of Snow White, black-haired women tended almost always to be witches.)

At about age 12, I discovered Jane Austen, Charles Dickens, William Thackeray, and George Eliot, and immersed myself in English classics. I identified so thoroughly with the characters in these books that I experienced a huge gulf between my interior and exterior selves, which seemed to have nothing in common. The exterior "I" was a small Chinese girl with straight black hair that would not hold a curl despite my mother's best efforts to make me Shirley Temple ringlets. The interior "I" agreed with Henry James: "There are few hours more agreeable than the hour dedicated to the ceremony known as afternoon tea" taken, or even imagined, on rolling green lawns of large English country estates.

How was one to bridge this yawning gulf? Being a Gemini helped. Born under the sign of the Twins, I was comforted by the thought that it was my fate to be split. It was natural that I ate with chopsticks each evening and lived and breathed Jane Austen novels the rest of the day. Life was full of things that didn't match up, that couldn't be neatly explained, that spilled out of the boxes seeking to contain them, that broke boundaries.

A naive, bookish 16, I entered one of the free public colleges of New York City. There again, books sheltered me from life while offering me many lives. My first college assignment, however (40 pages of Aristotle for a course called Contemporary Civilization), was daunting in its abstractness—another slippery slope with no foothold. I quickly learned, however, that outlining helped, and soon friends were borrowing *my* notes to study for exams. After a protracted struggle with my father, who wanted me to be a kindergarten teacher and warned me that no one would ever hire a Chinese English teacher, I became an English major. For me, it was an obvious choice, for it sanctioned and validated my love of reading.

I was introduced to and fell in love with Chaucer, whose love of life in all its variety came through brilliantly despite the hurdles of a language that seemed more difficult than French. Shakespeare and Donne, Hardy and Joyce, Hawthorne and Twain—I was keeping company with the world's greatest minds and souls, profound and exciting writers. This was heady stuff: ambrosia of the gods! My four years as an undergraduate were years of intellectual efflorescence, of exploration and expansion. I was reading *Don Quixote, Crime and Punishment*, and *Madame Bovary*—the world of literature and the literature of the world were mine to savor.

Then it all came to an abrupt end. Graduation. And what was I to do now? No one would pay me for loving to read and to paint, or for being Phi Beta Kappa. They only wanted to know how fast I could type. (I typed slowly and poorly.) The solution seemed to be to get the highest-paying job available, which turned out to be with the airlines or in insurance. I became a reservations agent for Trans-Canada Airlines. After one year of regimented, unstimulating work (rewarded by a brief trip to Europe at 75 percent discount fare, a free trip to Quebec City, and another to Vancouver), I decided that I'd rather be back in school. Choosing the graduate school that would take me farthest from home, I applied to the University of California at Berkeley. When the Davis campus offered me a teaching assistantship, I headed west.

Again, I majored in English and American literature, and took more of the courses I had enjoyed as an undergraduate: immersion in a century, a movement, or a great author (at this time all White males). When I finished a master's degree, my father became alarmed at how far I'd gone from my Chinese roots and decided to send me to Taiwan, hoping I'd return with a Chinese husband. There, my uncle found me a position teaching English literature in the Foreign Language Department at Chengkung University in Tainan.

My year in Taiwan was a catalyst in many unexpected ways. My sense of self was both deepened and more confused. Though I had been made conscious of being Chinese in America, in Taiwan I learned that I was, in fact, very American. For the second time in my life, I was thrown into a strange land where, being ignorant of the language (my so-called mother tongue), I was illiterate, deaf, and dumb. My Chinese face alone was hardly enough to make me feel comfortable. On the other hand, certain smells and tastes released locked childhood memories, and my extended family—paternal grandmother, uncle, aunt, and four cousins—all received me warmly as one of them. I was at home, yet *not* at home. Again, no footholds; again, I did not fit neatly anywhere, and I realized that perhaps I never would.

The following year, I took a French liner to Marseilles via Bombay, Colombo, Saigon, and Dijbouti, and spent a few months in Paris improving my "best foreign" language. I finally returned home to New York in late 1963. After teaching for several years in the turbulent and exciting SEEK Program at City College, I began my doctoral studies in Comparative Literature at New York University. My intention was to study world literature and do a dissertation on a topic that would compare Chinese and Western literatures. I wanted to begin bridging the gulf dividing me. However, though the chairman of the Comparative Literature department knew nine languages, they were all European, and there was no one in the department (or at NYU) who could work with me on a East/West comparative topic. Furthermore, my own Chinese language skills were so rudimentary that I could not have done the research on such a topic without many more years of intensive language study. By default, I selected a topic that interested me because of my own love of painting: "The Painter in the Lives and Works of Thackeray, James, and Zola."

External prodding carrried me through, for I'd been told, "If you want to continue teaching at the college level, you'll have to get a Ph.D." But the process seemed more an ordeal than one that engaged me, heart and soul. I was jumping hurdles set up by others— the Eurocentric department within a Eurocentric university of a Eurocentric society. It was a path I had started down that I had to follow to its end, a mountain I climbed because it was there, and I had figured out where the footholds were.

Dissertation completed and degree in hand, I first read Maxine Hong Kingston's *The Woman Warrior*. It awoke something in me that had lain dormant for years: my sense of self. Apart from my immediate family, I had known no other Chinese or Chinese Americans. My best friends in high school were a Jew and an African American. I had spent a year in Taiwan learning how un-Chinese I was. But, here was another like me—a Chinese-American woman articulating, reflecting, and validating the mixed feelings we shared, expressing my own confusion, and making art out of the paradoxes of our lives. Here was a new category, a name for my identity, the place where I belonged. I felt I was looking in a mirror and finding Maxine Hong Kingston looking back at me, saying, "Yes, that's us! We're Chinese-American women, and we're literary as well." In reading her, I had the extraordinary experience of coming together. The gulf between the external and the internal was at long last bridged.

When told that I would have to write a book in order to keep my university teaching position, I decided (like Toni Morrison) to write the one I very much wanted to read but no one had ever written: a history of the contributions to American literature by women of Chinese ancestry. The civil rights and women's liberation movements, and Maxine's book, had changed my consciousness. I began to question why nearly all the writers I had been taught were White and male; why writing by peoples of color was never taught in American literature courses I had taken; why women authors, such as Harriet Beecher Stowe, were classified as "merely popular" and not worthy of serious study, if they were acknowledged at all.

The answers to these questions were given by the African-American and women's movements. We lived in a White patriarchal society and therefore White males had the power to decide what culture was and which books should be taught and read and which forgotten. Not surprisingly, they decided that Culture and Literature was the work of men like themselves. It was not always conscious sexism or racism that denied all of us who are not White and male our culture and our literature. It was simply the unquestioned belief of these men that Truth was in their hands and that there was only one Truth— theirs. Furthermore, they also were the arbiters of Quality and Beauty, and, since time and space are limited according to their dictums, there was no room or time for anything Different or Other. It took all the rest of us (women and peoples of color) together to convince them that their views were not Objective Truth, but only a single perspective among many equally valid perspectives. Our message is gradually coming through. Ethnic studies requirements are being instituted at many colleges and universities, and a sensitivity to multicultural perspectives is becoming more and more visible in textbooks and classrooms. Even the Educational Testing Service, the creators of the SAT and other standardized tests, are monitoring closely and seeking to eliminate possible gender and racial biases in their test questions.

As the director of an Asian American Studies Program and a professor in the Department of English, I have found the kind of position perfectly suited to me: bridging two worlds, with a foot in each camp—upholding the traditional "canon" while simultaneously advocating new additions to it. The English Department affiliation has satisfied my early love of Jane Austen and William Shakespeare. And interest in Asian-American literature has spoken to the inner longings of a long-repressed identity, one I had tried to ignore and even disclaim, but which remained silently insistent, etched indelibly as it was on my face. At long last, by the example of courageous and talented others, such as Maxine Hong Kingston, Amy Tan, and David Henry Hwang, this Asian-American identity has been given a voice, a respectability, a way to *be*.

Before discussing how my personal history fits into the story of Chinese Americans, I'd like to discuss how Chinese Americans fit into the larger picture of Asian Americans. The term *Asian American* covers a large number of Asian national ancestries, all of which own their separate histories, cultures, and customs. However, in this country, Asian Americans are lumped together, for the physical features of those of the Mongolian race are rarely very distinct or even always accurately distinguishable. We are not, however, opposed to this coalition because, despite our separate chronologies and histories, our relationship with the dominant culture has been much the same. Regardless of economic class or educational attainments, we have all been made to feel self-alienated and depreciated. Even in 1991, when we moved from Washington, DC, to Madison, Wisconsin, my 10-year old son sighed, "Now I'll have to face all those new kids again talking about my 'Chinese' eyes." (He's a Korean-American adoptee.) A few months later, he was sent to the principal's office for being embroiled in a playground scuffle while objecting to the term *slit eyes*.

The rhetoric and the practice of America have all too often been divorced from each other. Emma Lazarus's famous words carved on the base of the Statue of Liberty extend the official invitation: "Give me your tired, your poor, your huddled masses yearning to breathe free." But once the huddled masses of China arrive here, they face the much less beautiful sentiments expressed by Ralph Waldo Emerson, in his 1824 journal: "Even miserable Africa can say I have hewn the wood and drawn the water to promote the civilization of other lands. But China, reverend dullness! hoary ideot! [sic], all she can say at the convocation of nations must be—'I made the tea'" (Miller, 1974, p. 16). An attitude of superiority has historically been the stance of White America in its relations with peoples of color. The civil rights movement did much to adjust this attitude but, as we saw from the 1992 presidential campaigns, the rhetoric of the organization of the National Association of American Scholars, the attacks on "political correctness," and the revival of the KKK, white supremacy notions are far from dead.

How, then, does my personal story fit into the larger picture of educating bi- and multicultural students? Above all, it points out the considerable damage that results from a lack of models. As educators, our obligation to our multicultural students is to provide them *their* histories, *their* writers, *their* appropriate models. To do this, we must educate ourselves. This is sure to be a challenging task but at the same time an enriching experience for all concerned. Lynne Cheney's term "victim studies" is an insidious attempt to dismiss and belittle the histories of the various minority groups in America. For minority groups to be ignorant of their histories is to be cut off from a past that provides them a foundation for the future. Euro-Americans who remain ignorant of their treatment of minorities risk repeating the mistakes of the past. Hidden wounds fester, but when wounds are exposed to the light, healing can begin.

Since entire (and excellent) books have been written on the subject, I will now give only the briefest sort of outline about Chinese Americans. I hope that educators will pursue the suggested additional readings to deepen their understanding of this particular group.

The Chinese have experienced the strange paradox of being both greatly admired and greatly despised in the West. For at least two centuries, the works of Chinese hands—silk, porcelain, carpets, jade and ivory carvings, and paintings—have been greatly prized, and their possession, obtained at great cost over great distance, has been perceived as a sign of wealth and good breeding. However, the Chinese people themselves have been as greatly scorned and despised. They are the only people in the United States with the dubious distinction of having been specifically named in a discriminatory law passed against them: the Chinese Exclusion Act of 1882, a law renewed for 10 years in 1892 and indefinitely in 1902. It was not repealed until 1943.

The Chinese were the first Asians to migrate to the United States. In the mid-nineteenth century, some adventurous Chinese men, mostly from the area around the city of Guandong (Canton) in southern China, were lured by the promise of instant wealth to join the California Gold Rush. However, the majority of such early Chinese were brought to this nation as laborers. Dense rain forests needed to be cleared to create sugar plantations in Hawaii in the mid-nineteenth century; Chinese laborers were initially brought in, to be succeeded by Japanese and Filipinos. Then, in the late 1860s, after the Civil War had eliminated African slave labor, thousands of Chinese workers were hired to construct the difficult, mountainous western portion of the transcontinental railroad. White labor feared the competition, so Chinese workers found themselves victims of harassment and race prejudice. From nearly the beginning of their appearance in the United States, laws were enacted, particularly in California, directed solely against the Chinese, ranging from a petty queue tax to the serious deprivation of civil rights. No Chinese could testify in court against a White man, nor could Chinese obtain citizenship, own land, or marry White women. Various ordinances forbade Chinese from working in cigar factories, in shoe factories, in fisheries, in agriculture—until the only work allowed them were the jobs no one else wanted: "women's work" of laundry and cooking. This severely limited choice of occupation explains the tradition of houseboys, laundries, and restaurants among Chinese men in the United States. The belief that Chinese were both undesirable and unassimilable was a blatant case of blaming the victim. Only in 1954 were Asian-born people allowed to become naturalized American citizens and permitted to vote. Only after that date did the numbers of Chinese men and women in the United States begin to reach parity.

In the nineteenth century, Chinese women in America were a rarity. In 1852, for example, of the 11,794 Chinese in California, only 7 were women. The first recorded Chinese woman in America, Afong Moy, was a living display in Barnum's Chinese Museum and "caused a sensation in New York" in 1834 simply by sitting "amidst the exotic Chinese trappings in vogue at that time" (see Yung, 1986). By Chinese custom, wives remained at home while the men went to "Gold Mountain" to make their fortunes, but U.S. legal restrictions also made it very difficult for Chinese women to immigrate. In the ninteenth century, a few Chinese women made their way to this country either as servants of returning White missionaries or as prostitutes. The biographical novel based on the life of one nineteenth-century pioneer Chinese woman, Lalu Nathoy, in *Thousand Pieces of Gold* by Ruthanne Lum McCunn, should be of particular interest to junior high and high school students. Abducted as a child, transported to the United States, and sold on the auction block in San Francisco, Lalu Nathoy later became a respected homesteader on the Salmon River, the "River of No Return" in Idaho; hers is a colorful piece of American history.

Little is known about the history of Chinese in America, but Hollywood has contributed greatly to stereotypes and negative images of both Chinese-American men and women, stereotypes that have molded popular concepts and perpetuated ignorance. The smiling, docile houseboy; the devious, evil Dr. Fu Manchu; the asexual, blundering Charlie Chan—these are the primary stereotypes of emasculated Chinese-American males even as the shy, submissive Lotus Blossom and the treacherous, deadly Dragon Lady images have characterized representations of Asian-American women. Images of the Asian woman as an exotic, erotic curiosity has persisted from Barnum's Chinese Museum and Puccini's *Madame Butterfly* to the present day, and may be found in such films as *The World of Suzy Wong, Teahouse of the August Moon*, and *The Volunteers* and in the musical stage production of *Miss Saigon*.

Asian Americans have set themselves the task of breaking the stereotypes by which they have been bound. No longer content to remain the silent minority, to flow like water into low ground, but now emboldened by the example of African Americans, they have begun to speak for themselves. In the last 20 years, there has been a cultural efflorescence: in literature, theater, dance, painting, film, and other performing arts. Frank Chin's plays in the early 1970s, *Chickencoop Chinaman* and *The Year of the Dragon*, were early protests against the emasculation and exoticization of Chinese Americans. Chin's work was performed in New York City's American Place Theatre, the first plays to present a Chinese-American perspective. Maxine Hong Kingston's *The Woman Warrior: Memoir of a Girlhood among Ghosts* won the National Book Critics Circle Award of 1976. In her multilayered account of generational and cultural tensions, Kingston did much to dispel the stereotype of the silent Asian girl. Interlacing traditional Chinese tales with her own family's stories (sometimes comical, sometimes frightening or tragic), Kingston revealed the sexist and racist conflicts that she as a young girl faced growing up in Stockton, California. David Henry Hwang's *M. Butterfly* inverts the "exotic oriental" female stereotype in his 1988 Tony Award winning Broadway drama. Deborah Gee's 1989 film,

Slaying the Dragon, exposes Hollywood's role in creating and perpetuating stereotypes of Asian women, and Arthur Dong's recent *Forbidden City* shows a little-known side of Asian Americans: popular singers and dancers who provided the entertainment at a San Francisco nightclub in the 1940s.

The Chinese-American literary tradition has a 100-year history, beginning in 1887 with Lee Yan Phou's *When I Was a Boy in China*. Lee was a student in the Chinese Educational Mission created by Yung Wing, Yale class of 1854, the first Chinese to graduate from a U.S. college. Yung Wing's dream was to give other Chinese youths the advantages of an American education, like his, in order to bring China technologically into the twentieth century. However, undone jointly by American sinophobia and Chinese xenophobia, the Chinese Educational Mission lasted only a decade, from 1872 to 1882. Yung Wing's own autobiography, *My Life in China and America*, was published in 1906.

Asian-American fiction writing began with the work of two Eurasian sisters: Edith Maud Eaton (1865–1914), who used the Chinese pseudonym Sui Sin Far, and her younger sister Winnifred Eaton (1875–1954), who published widely under the Japanese-sounding name Onoto Watanna. Though their mother was Chinese (their father was English), the younger sister claimed a fictitious ancestry in order to satisfy the contemporary preference for Japanese. Sui Sin Far published one collection of short stories, *Mrs. Spring Fragrance* (1909), while Onoto Watanna has nearly a dozen best-selling novels to her credit, beginning with *Miss Nume of Japan* in 1899. Her second novel, *A Japanese Nightingale* (1901) was transformed into a play and performed on Broadway to compete with a pre-Puccini version of *Madame Butterfly*. From 1926 and 1931, Onoto Watanna wrote scripts for Hollywood films, becoming chief scenarist at Universal and MGM.

The Chinese-American story continued to be told in two autobiographies, Pardee Lowe's *Father and Glorious Descendant* (1943) and Jade Snow Wong's *Fifth Chinese Daughter* (1945). Both are rather restrained, somewhat humorous, and quite unique accounts of the experience of growing up Chinese American in San Francisco in the 1930s.

Throughout the 1950s and 1960s, with China hidden behind the so-called Bamboo Curtain and the United States in a panic about the threat of communism, the Chinese in America maintained a low profile, emphasizing their connections to Taiwan. During these two decades, little was published by Chinese Americans, but when diplomatic relations resumed in 1972, creating a favorable climate, interest in Chinese things—including Chinese Americans—began to flourish. The 1970s saw the beginning of the literary efflorescence in the publication of the work of Frank Chin and Maxine Hong Kingston, to which the novels of Gish Jen, Gus Lee, and Fae Myenne Ng, the short stories of David Wong Louie, and the plays of David Henry Hwang and Elizabeth Wang, continue to contribute. The fortunate confluence of public interest and individual talent can be seen most recently in the reception given Amy Tan's, *The Joy Luck Club* (1989). Many months on the *New York Times* bestseller list, *The Joy Luck Club* speaks to both the feminist movement and interest in cultural pluralism, as it interweaves the fascinating stories of four Chinese mothers and their Chinese-American daughters. As a film, *The Joy Luck Club* reached even wider audiences.

For the history of women writers of Chinese ancestry, from the late nineteenth century to the present day, see Ling's (1990) *Between Worlds: Women Writers of Chinese*

Ancestry. For accounts of the Chinese in the larger context of Asian-American history, the most recent texts are Ronald Takaki's *Strangers from a Different Shore* (1989) and Sucheng Chan's *Asian Americans: An Interpretive History.* For studies focused solely on the Chinese, there are a number of good older texts: Stuart Creighton Miller's (1974) *The Unwelcome Immigrant: The American Image of the Chinese, 1785–1882*, Betty Lee Sung's (1967) *Mountain of Gold*, Peter Kwong's (1979) *Chinatown, NY: Labor and Politics, 1930–1950*, and Jack Chen's (1980) *The Chinese of America.* For an excellent poetic re-creation of the experience of the pioneer Chinese-American laborers in Hawaiian sugar plantations and on the railroad, see Maxine Hong Kingston's *China Men* (1980). For those interested in graphic images, there are several interesting pictorial histories, among which are Him Mark Lai and colleagues' *The Chinese of America, 1685–1980* (1980) and Ruthanne Lum McCunn's *An Illustrated History of the Chinese in America* (1979).

Chinese have contributed to U.S. life and culture in a wide variety of fields. Most recently, and perhaps the best known, are the Nobel Prize winners, among them Tsung-dao Lee and C. N. Yang, who shared the prize for physics in 1957; Samuel C. C. Ting in physics in 1976; and Yuan T. Lee in molecular beam chemistry in 1986. In architecture, I. M. Pei has long been internationally renowned, while Maya Lin, then an undergraduate student of architecture, quickly rose to prominence by winning the national competition for the Vietnam War Memorial in 1981 and sparking a controversy with her unusual design. In its simplicity and symbolic resonance, and in the inevitably emotional interactions of mourners with the names of loved ones on the polished black wall, the Vietnam War Memorial has turned out to be more eloquent and moving than most conventional monuments.

Earlier Chinese Americans are less well known, but some of their stories and photographs may be found in *Chinese American Portraits: Personal Histories, 1828–1988* by Ruthanne Lum McCunn (1988). One of these, horticulturist Lue Gim Gong (1858–1925), was instrumental in developing the Florida citrus industry by developing a new orange that was large and juicy, transported and kept well, and withstood sudden frosts. Lue experimented with other plants as well, creating a strain of rosebush on which 17 varieties of roses bloomed in seven different colors. However, defrauded of the profits of his work, he died a pauper.

The stories are myriad, but to dwell too long on the accomplishments of Chinese Americans would be to fuel the "model minority myth" that overgeneralizes on the basis of a few, masks the continuing effects of racism on this group, and is a tool by which the majority tends to divide and conquer the various minority groups. We must recognize, for example, that no matter how much education people have had, and/or how many generations their families have lived and worked in this country, if they have Asian facial features, they are still primarily perceived as foreigners and treated as such. For example, when Congressman Scott Klug was campaigning on the University of Wisconsin campus during the fall of 1992, he gave fliers to everyone *except* people with Asian faces. His reasoning presumably went thus: "Asian features = foreigner, so why waste fliers on people who can't vote?" So many Asian-American students were offended (there are nearly 1,300 on campus) that one wrote an editorial about it for the university paper. When Asian Americans are seen as foreigners, undifferentiated from Asians, not only are they denied their American citizenship but such a phenomenon makes possible the case of Vincent Chin.

In June 1982, in Detroit, a 27-year-old Chinese American, Vincent Chin, on the night before his wedding, was murdered by Richard Ebens, a laid-off auto worker, and his nephew, Michael Nitz. Believing Chin to be Japanese and wanting to vent their anger, Nitz held back Chin's arms while Ebens beat him on the head, chest, and knees with a baseball bat, then left him bleeding on the pavement. Four days later, Chin died from his wounds. The murderers were given three years' probation and fined $3,000—a sentence that outraged Asian Americans nationwide. An appeal was filed and a retrial held in a different city (Cincinnati) in 1986. Ebens was acquitted of all charges. The Chin case reveals what a slippery slope the United States can still be for Chinese Americans.

We as educators can make a difference. We can help to create a different society, one made up of informed citizens, starting with students who both realize and celebrate the fact that the United States is and will increasingly become a nation of many races. When each of us meets the responsibility of learning the unique histories and particular cultural traditions of all the various peoples of the United States, when no group's stories are silenced or ignored, then we shall not have a "disuniting of America," as Schlesinger fears, but a more tolerant, more harmonious, stronger and truly equal *union*.

References

Chan, Sucheng. (1991). *Asian Americans: An interpretive history*. Boston: Twayne.

Chen, Jack. (1980). *The Chinese of America*. New York: Harper & Row.

Cheung, King-Kok, & Yogi, Stan. (1988). *Asian American literature: An annotated bibliography*. New York: Modern Language Association of America.

Chin, Frank. (1981). *The chickencoop Chinaman and the year of the dragon*. Seattle: University of Washington Press.

Far, Sui Sin. [Edith Maud Eaton]. (1994). *Mrs. Spring Fragrance*. Chicago: A. C. McClung, 1912. Republished by the University of Illinois Press, 1994.

Kingston, Maxine Hong. (1980). *China men*. New York: Alfred Knopf.

Kingston, Maxine Hong. (1976). *The woman warrior: Memoir of a girlhood among ghosts*. New York: Alfred Knopf.

Kwong, Peter. (1979). *Chinatown, NY: Labor and politics, 1930–1950*. New York: Monthly Review Press.

Lai, Him Mark, et al. (1980). *The Chinese of America, 1685–1980*. San Francisco: Chinese Culture Foundation.

Lee, Yan Phou. (1887). *When I was a boy in China*. Boston: D. Lothrop.

Ling, Amy. (1990). *Between worlds: Women writers of Chinese ancestry*. New York: Pergamon Press.

Lowe, Pardee. (1943). *Father and glorious descendant*. Boston: Little.

McCunn, Ruthanne Lum. (1988). *Chinese American portraits: Personal histories, 1828–1988*. San Francisco: Chronicle Books.

McCunn, Ruthanne Lum. (1988). *Thousand pieces of gold*. San Francisco: Design Enterprises.

McCunn, Ruthanne Lum. (1979). *An illustrated history of the Chinese in America*. San Francisco: Design Enterprises.

Miller, Stuart Creighton. (1974). *The unwelcome immigrant: The American image of the Chinese, 1785–1882*. Berkeley and Los Angeles: University of California Press.

Sung, Betty Lee. (1967). *Mountain of gold*. New York: Macmillan.

Takaki, Ronald. (1989). *Strangers from a different shore*. New York: Penguin.

Tan, Amy. (1989). *The Joy Luck club*. New York: Putnam.

Watanna, Onoto. [Winnifred Eaton]. (1901). *A Japanese nightingale.* New York: Harper.

Watanna, Onoto. [Winnifred Eaton]. (1899). *Miss Nume of Japan.* Chicago: Rand, McNally.

Wong, Jade Snow. (1945). *Fifth Chinese daughter.* New York: Harper.

Yung, Judy. (1986). *The Chinese woman in America.* Seattle: University of Washington Press.

Yung, Wing. (1909). *My life in China and America.* New York: Holt.

About the Author

Amy Ling is an associate professor of English and director of the Asian American Studies Program at the University of Wisconsin-Madison. She is the author of *Between Worlds: Women Writers of Chinese Ancestry*, a cultural history of the "flowers in her mother's garden," and *Chinamerican Reflections*, a chapbook of her own poems and paintings. She has written numerous articles on Asian-American literature and has coedited several books, including *The Health Anthology of American Literature, Imagining America: Stories from the Promised Land, A Multicultural Reader, Asian Americans: Comparative and Global Perspectives* and the forthcoming *Visions of America: Personal Narratives from the Promised Land, The Oxford Companion to Women's Writing in the U.S.* and *Reading the Literatures of Asian America.*

Chapter *8*

The Cuban-American Experience in Exile

ANDREA B. BERMÚDEZ

I hear shots...and screams...it's pandemonium. Go for cover!... Oh, it's just another student unrest! Close call. Militia searches, curfews, censorship—not a very pleasant way to live! If one dares to disagree, it's imprisonment, or death. What are my choices?...Leave home...Seek refuge elsewhere...Grim choice! No looking back. No alternative but to move forward. And here begins the tale of an exile...

Cuban migration has been a common phenomenon in south Florida as early as the nineteenth century, since only 90 miles separate the United States and Cuba. However, an estimate of the number of Cubans living in the United States prior to the Castro revolution of 1959 is a modest 40,000. Today, this estimate surpasses one million (Jorge & Moncarz, 1991).

On January 1, 1959, General Fulgencio Batista y Zaldivar was overthrown as President of Cuba by the Castro forces. His regime was a military dictatorship that spanned two interrupted cycles, each beginning with a military *coup*. The end of Batista's dictatorship marked the beginning of a promised democracy never delivered.

The establishment of a totalitarian regime became more obvious as time passed and eventually the Soviet-inspired model, adopted by the Castroist leadership, became publicly acknowledged. Complete control over individual life-styles was immediately assumed as the new ideology took shape. Those not in accordance with the new directions sought political asylum, most notably in the United States. Soon after the arrival of the first group of dissidents, the 1960 U.S. census reported 125,000 Cubans living in the

United States. This figure rapidly escalated to almost five times that number during the next decade, especially after the Bay of Pigs fiasco.

The ill-fated Bay of Pigs invasion of April 1961 was organized under the auspices of the Kennedy administration with the full support of the Central Intelligence Agency (CIA). Cubans received training and weapons to fight the Castro forces. Political advisors to President Kennedy deemed the invasion unnecessary and influenced the president to cancel support while the invasion was already underway. The Castro military was prepared to meet the anti-revolutionaries who were forced to surrender. The 1,200 survivors of Brigade 2506 were condemned to 30 years of hard labor imprisonment until their freedom was negotiated by the United States government in 1962 at a cost of $62,500,000 in baby food and medicine.

Since the Bay of Pigs, the number of Cubans in the United States has continued to escalate. A great majority still remain in south Florida, particularly in the Miami-Dade area. An old Cuban joke used to say that Cuba was the only known country in the world to have its capital in Moscow, its government officials in Havana, and its inhabitants in Miami.

The Exile Experience

Adapting to an alien culture is no easy matter. Being forced by circumstances to not have a choice is even more traumatic. This is the fate of an exile. The language, habits, and value systems that once made sense are no longer viable means of getting along in one's new surroundings. Unfamiliar patterns of thought, feeling, logic, and action govern the new setting and individuals often develop a feeling of disfranchisement. Overcoming these barriers is a lonely and lengthy experience. Some of these barriers are more subtle than others, exacerbating the challenges faced by immigrants who have not yet developed an adequate proficiency in handling the cultural patterns and "rules of the game."

The Cuban-American experience has been no different than any other immigrant's in feeling alienated from the mainstream. However, the loss of homeland has seemed to assist in accelerating their acculturation to the mainstream of the host society. Cubans came to stay as long as their homeland's regime remains in power. After more than three decades, many of them have become an integral part of their adoptive society. Nonetheless, the pain of adjusting to a new world has still been profound. Gonzalez-Montserrat (1990) described how an exile feels: "I was like an illegitimate child. An alien in someone else's home. I wanted to adapt to this world but I felt a distance. There was a distance ....I learned to look at everything from afar. That is how we, immigrants, look at life. This is how they look at us" (p. 18). The observer versus participant levels of social interaction precisely distinguish the individual's level of success in attaining cultural adaptation.

There are two ways to approach this phenomenon. The individual may respond to the environment or the environment may incorporate the individual's *modus operandi* by modifying previous conditions and regulations that are exclusive. The latter is slow at taking place; therefore, the responsibility for change rests entirely on the individual.

Sociocultural Adjustment to the Mainstream

In general, there are three distinct levels of adjustment in the sociolcultural continuum: (1) a marginal level in which both groups coexist with little or no linguistic and cultural interaction, (2) an integrated level in which a group relates to another in a functional way without acquiring all the cultural traits of the other, or without giving up any of the essential features of their culture; and (3) the fusion level in which the group totally assimilates to the value systems and mores of the other group (refer to Figure 1). Membership in any of these three levels depends on the following factors: length of residence in the United States, degree of dispersion within the country, and quality and degree of exposure to the mainstream language, values, and mores.

How long an individual remains exposed to a linguistic and cultural environment presents an opportunity for successful adaptation only if frequent interaction between the individual and the host culture occurs. There are many instances of generations born in the host country that remain attached to the language and values of the inherited culture. These situations are usually found when those individuals cling to their own segregated cultural enclaves, generally found in the inner cities of large metropolitan areas. This level is not necessarily indicative of economic failure, as many have been able to enrich themselves by relying totally on conducting business within the Spanish-speaking community.

There are examples of all three levels of acculturation within the Cuban-American population of the United States. For a large portion of Cubans who have made their permanent homes in south Florida, particularly the greater Miami area, a transplant home was created to replace the lost one. A visit to Miami's Calle Ocho indicates a presence of a Spanish-American mosaic of language, foods, clothing, religious items, jewelry, and music. Eighth Street is the main artery running through "Little Havana." Its yearly carnival attracts more than one million visitors and pumps $10 million into the economy of this area (Bergsman, 1989). Additionally, a view of the opulent downtown skyline is a reminder of the successful entrepreneurship of Cuban Americans.

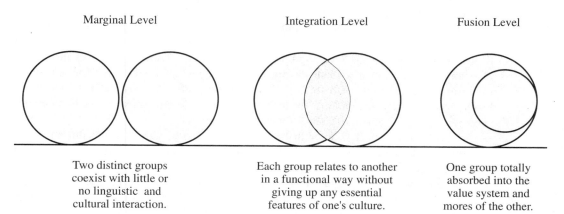

Marginal Level	Integration Level	Fusion Level
Two distinct groups coexist with little or no linguistic and cultural interaction.	Each group relates to another in a functional way without giving up any essential features of one's culture.	One group totally absorbed into the value system and mores of the other.

FIGURE 1   Levels of Adjustment in the Sociocultural Continuum

It is not uncommon to find groups of men playing an exciting round of dominoes and discussing in Spanish the fall of Castro while sipping an aromatic cup of *cafe cubano* (espresso). Others may have chosen to interact outside their enclave, to learn English, become highly educated, and/or go into business, sometimes for themselves. In short, they learned to function successfully in both worlds. Yet another group of Cuban Americans became totally assimilated to the language and life-styles germane to the mainstream. A large portion of this segment was born in the United States and became dispersed to other parts of the country in which the home culture was not so dominant.

One recent exodus, arriving in the Mariel boat lift, added a degree of controversy as many of the refugees were criminals forced out by the Castro regime. Castro's response to an embarrassing incident in which over 10,000 Cubans sought asylum in the Peruvian Embassy in Havana was to open the doors for Cubans to leave the island through the Port of Mariel. Approximately 125,000 arrived on U.S. shores, mostly blue-collar workers. It has been estimated that about 5 percent of that figure were convicted criminals.

These immigrants have been less welcome than the original groups as they have mostly faced deportation and internment. Considering the fact that this generation has been exposed to an entirely different cultural milieu, marked differences are found between these exiles and those preceding them. One visible difference is the lack of English language skills and background experiences that would prepare them to adjust to and succeed in a capitalistic and competitive environment.

Changing Perceptions Across Time

In general, the exile experience has forced Cuban Americans to redefine their sense of family, friendship, time orientation, and mobility. Dispersion has brought a geographical barrier to the extended family concept historically held by Cubans. The issue of distance has done away with traditional views and replaced them with a more nuclear family orientation. One example, the *compadrazgo* (a custom that welcomes godparents as an integral family member after assuming the lifelong spiritual responsibility for their godchild), has virtually disappeared (Queralt, 1984). Friendships have also become shaped by geographic distance, as "keeping up" becomes difficult with the daily responsibilities of a working world. Inherited longstanding family friendships are obsolete, and only those living in close proximity remain friends. Future orientation has replaced the tradition-laden views of older generations. A more capitalistic concept of time and efficiency has been adopted by the younger Cuban-American generation.

Mobility has been the factor that has accelerated or decelerated acculturation. As mentioned earlier, a large percentage of Cubans remained in south Florida. The minority who migrated have become splintered in many directions. It is common for a family reunion to show a third generation sporting accents from their various homes in Texas, New York, Virginia, and Boston! From this example, we can extrapolate that cultural differences will exist as well. Additionally, new class levels have emerged as economic success has allowed some to climb the mainstream social and political ladder.

Role of the Woman in the Cuban-American Family

There has been a widespread misperception of Cuban *machismo*. This term refers to the emphasis placed by a culture on the supremacy of the male role. It has been found that Cuban families presently in Miami still adhere to this ideology, continuing to view the female as passive and dependent.

In most Hispanic cultures, men have traditionally received a higher *locus standi,* while in reality homes have been governed by the women. It has been the Cuban woman who has taught values to the children, overseen their education, and offered the children the emotional support to deal with life's eventualities. The man's role has been to provide for the family and serve in the honorary role of disciplinarian.

Therefore, the role of the Cuban woman has been historically a very strong and significant one. Prior to the Castro revolution, women had already achieved a higher level

TABLE 1   Selected Economic Characteristics of Hispanic Persons of Cuban Origin by Sex

Occupation	Male (in percent)	Female (in percent)
Percent		
in civilian labor force	73.3	55.1
unemployed	5.2	8.0
Employed		
16 years and over (in thousands)	310	230
Managerial and professional specialty	21.6	20.0
Technical, sales, and administrative support	21.9	50.0
Service occupations	11.9	16.5
Farming, forestry, and fishing	1.0	-
Precision production, craft, and repair	22.6	2.6
Operators, fabricators, and laborers	20.6	11.7
Earnings of Persons in 1990	**Male (in percent)**	**Female (in percent)**
Number with earnings (in thousands)	340	251
Percent	100.0	100.0
Less than $10,000	25.5	36.1
$10,000 to $24,999	45.5	44.4
$25,000 to $49,999	22.2	17.4
$50,000 or more	6.8	2.0
Median earnings (dollars)	$17,455	$12,904

Source: U.S. Bureau of the Census (1991).

of parity with men than in most of Latin America, with the exception of Argentina and Uruguay (Queralt, 1984). The revolution supported this notion further, as women have actively served side by side with men in battle and in government.

Currently in the United States according to the most recent census report, 55.1 percent of the Cuban-American women, 16 years and over, are employed, in contrast with 73.3 percent of the men in the same age category. In addition, economic parity has not been achieved. Women's median income, for instance, was $12,904, as opposed to $17,455 for men, for similar or higher skill-level jobs (U.S. Bureau of the Census, 1991) (refer to Table 1).

Nature of the Hispanic Culture

The term *Hispanic* does not capture the wealth of cultural and linguistic differences among the different groups that it is meant to represent. Approximately 22 million individuals living in the United States are grouped under this umbrella. Mexican Americans, Puerto Ricans, Cubans, Spaniards, Central and South Americans—each represents a variety of cultural and linguistic experiences as well as ethnic backgrounds. This attests to the richness and diversity of their cultural and human contribution to the very fabric of this country. Music, literature, education, law, language, and architecture are among the various areas in which their significant mark has been left. A generic comparison between Mexican Americans and Cuban Americans serves to further illustrate this diversity. Several areas have been chosen for comparison: demographics, identity, reasons for migration, attitudes toward the United States, self- esteem, presence of the homeland, and choice of geographic locations to establish a family.

Demographics

Hispanics are the second largest, fastest growing, and youngest population in the United States. Cuban Americans are the third largest Hispanic group, whereas Mexican Americans are the most numerous. Before the Mariel boat lift, the 1980 U.S. census figures showed 803,226 Cubans living in the United States. This figure has grown to approximately 1,050,000, or 10 percent the population still living on the island (Leyva de Varona, 1991). Mexican Americans comprise approximately 5 percent of the total U.S. population, or 13,421,000 (U.S. Bureau of the Census, 1991). Other demographic differences include a higher median wage for Cubans, higher personal income and level of education, and a lower unemployment rate than all other Hispanic groups (U.S. Bureau of the Census, 1991). Table 2 documents these demographic indicators.

Identity

Cuban Americans of the pre-Castro era remain loyal to their Spanish-European roots. In contrast, Mexican Americans revere their Native-American ancestors, principally Aztec and Mayan, and resent the historical role of Spain in the devastation of their native heritage. The arrival of Spanish Europeans on U.S. soil has been the object of conflicting historical assessment. Most Mexicans perceive this role as exploitative and self-serving and exult the role of native cultures in their history.

TABLE 2   Selected Economic Characteristics by Type of Hispanic Origin

Household Characteristic	Mexican Origin	Cuban Origin
Mean number of persons	3.84	2.55
Median income (in dollars)	22,439	25,900
Percent less than $10,000	19.1	20.9
Percent $10,000 to $24,999	36.0	27.8
Percent $24,999 to $49,999	33.3	31.5
Percent $50,000 or more	11.6	19.8
Mean income in dollars	27,069	33,504

Educational Attainment (estimate in thousands)	Mexican Origin	Cuban Origin
Total 25 years and over	6,518	784
Percent completed less than 5 years of school	15.9	7.7
Percent completed 4 years of high school or more	43.6	61.0
Percent completed 4 years of college or more	6.2	18.5

Labor Force Status (estimate in thousands)	Mexican Origin	Cuban Origin
Total, 16 years and older in civilian labor force	5,839	577
Percent in civilian labor force	65.6	64.1
Percent unemployed	10.7	6.4

All Income Levels in 1990 (estimate in thousands)	Mexican Origin	Cuban Origin
Total persons for whom poverty status is determined	13,403	1,055
Less than 18 years old	4,999	181
18–64 years old	7,817	718
65 years old and over	588	155
Total persons below poverty level in 1990	3,764	178
Percent below poverty level	28.1	16.9

Source: U.S. Bureau of the Census (1991).

In addition, Cuban Americans received tremendous influence from the presence of Africans in the Caribbean region. Their music, language, literature, and attitude about life is a testimony of this symbiotic relationship; whereas Mexico embraced native cultures. Their language is influenced by the musical tonality and vocabulary loans from Nahuatl, the Aztec language.

Reasons for Migration

Cubans left their homeland for political rather than economic hardships. This factor has shaped the type of relations established with their new cultural environment. Having no homeland to return to has accelerated the process of adaptation to the mainstream U.S. culture. Reasons for Mexican Americans being in the United States vary from political to economic to historical. A portion of the Mexican territory, for example, was subsumed into to what had already become U.S. territory under the Guadalupe Hidalgo treaty, signed after losing the war to Texas. Considering the reasons for migration, together with the total sociohistorical context, allows one to better understand the feelings and attitudes that the group has developed toward the host culture.

Attitudes Toward the United States

The majority of Cubans harbor positive feelings toward the United States since, in a sense, U.S. hospitality was the Cubans' only hope for a home. In addition, Cubans arrived as the civil rights legislation was beginning to be enforced, thus avoiding some of the trauma caused by overt discrimination. Nonetheless, they have suffered their share of victimization by covert racism and stereotyping, especially the recent arrivals whose racial makeup, aspirations, and background are diametrically diferent from the earlier emigres. On the other hand, Mexican Americans were target to the separatist sentiments and oppressive actions preceding the sixties, which left them harboring bitter feelings regarding the mainstream.

Self-Esteem

Cuban emigres are proud of their courage to survive. This pride and self-confidence has often been misinterpreted as a sign of arrogance, however (Queralt, 1984). Since they came as political refugees from a communistic regime, they gained the status of "instant heroes." Children did not inherit the anger and frustrations of their older generations but a sense of superiority in having fought "the common enemy." Contrarily, Mexican-American children were exposed to blatant messages of inferiority. Their language was banned from schools and public places and their customs were reduced to disrespect and ridicule. The "Frito Bandito" stereotype hardly creates a climate to grow proud and self-assertive.

Presence of the Homeland

The Cuban American's loss of homeland precipitated the learning of survival skills, including language. The tragedy acted as a motivator to accommodate to and succeed in the new environment, which was fueled by their ability as entrepreneurs. The third generation has, for the most part, intermarried, and the young are being brought up in either bilingual or in non-Spanish monolingual contexts. This marks the beginning of a cultural transformation that will take future generations away from the Cuban cultural message. In contrast, Mexican Americans can either freely travel to Mexico or to the transplanted home that they have established in the United States. A majority lives in barrios, or homogeneous enclaves where the language and life-styles are kept alive in the community, providing the continuity necessary for the culture to survive.

Choice of Geographic Locations

Proximity and similarity of weather conditions and environment have made the Miami-Dade area a favorite site for Cubans. Some 59 percent of the emigres live in the state of Florida. Of these, 60 percent have settled in the Miami-Dade area (Strouse, 1992). They have impacted all aspects of its culture, including its economy, language, politics, education, religion, entertainment, sports, the arts, and the media (Boswell & Curtis, 1983), as well as exerted an influence on other Spanish-American groups who have recently migrated to the area. On the other hand, the existence of segregated Mexican-American enclaves, particularly in inner cities or in areas of greater concentration, strengthens their bond to the mother culture while it maintains a social and psychological distance from the mainstream.

Advocacy and Political Focus of Cuban Americans

Cuban-Americans' economic success and political acumen have provided their constituency with a strong political voice. In 1973, Dade County officials passed an ordinance that made the area officially bilingual. By the next decade, the backlash produced an anti-bilingualism ordinance forbidding public funds to be used in promoting bilingualism and from using a language other than English in the city's public affairs. The vote was cast along ethnic lines, with the Black vote opposing the English-only measure. This experience did nothing but strengthen what Leyva de Varona (1991) called the "flowering of Cuban political power" (p. 86). A result of an anti-immigrant campaign, the English-only movement has been mildly successful in promoting legislation to eliminate the use of languages other than English for public transaction. Its strength has been diminishing in the last few years in light of economic and leadership exigencies.

Generally, the decade of the 1980s marks the beginning of organized action. Examples include block voting to elect their own public officials, obtaining government sponsorship of radio transmissions to Cuba, and securing opposition to Castro-inspired revolutions in Angola, Grenada, Afghanistan, and Nicaragua.

In addition, several political groups, including the Cuban American Foundation, led by a small group of wealthy and well-organized exiles, have emerged to help Cuban Americans become active participants in the country's political system. Presidential candidates woo their votes as registered voters continue to increase, particularly in south Florida (Leyva de Varona, 1991). In addition, the number of Cuban Americans elected to public office continues to increase. Their economic contribution to the south Florida area—a buying power of $8.5 billion, high employment, and a hefty average annual income of $31,042 (Strategy Research Corporation, 1988)—serves as testimony of their enormous political prowess in that area. They have also shown an increasingly higher voter registration and participation in electoral politics (Leyva de Varona, 1991).

Their political interest focuses also on freeing the island from the present regime. One of the important contributions of the Foundation is Radio Martí, which transmits broadcasts into Cuba. The messages sent have eliminated the news censorship imposed by the Castro government. Furthermore, an informed people is a strong breeding ground for any anti-revolutionary effort. Plans for continuing the development of TV Martí are underway.

Spanish: The Language of Prestige

In spite of the anti-bilingualism ordinance in the Miami-Dade area, Spanish remains a common medium of daily communication. As a matter of fact, there are segments of the city (Calle Ocho, for example) where it is unusual to find English speakers. Some businesses even advertise an "English Spoken Here" sign, emphasizing the fact that 57 percent of the residents speak a language other than English (Balmaseda, 1992). The Cuban community is mainly responsible for the place of prestige that Spanish occupies within the community. The prevalent use of the Spanish among Cubans is an instinct for cultural preservation and a sign of undying pride. The English-only ordinance, according to Garcia and Otheguy (1985), reduced the majority's access to public-sponsored uses of Spanish, which has placed them at a disadvantage since now "all uses of Spanish are privately-sponsored and of difficult access to the majority" (p. 6).

Bilingual Education

During the early 1960s, Dade County experimented with one of the first bilingual programs in the nation. The Coral Way Elementary School started a new wave in education by reintroducing dual language instruction in the United States. It was not until 1968 that the U.S. Congress passed Title VII of the Elementary and Secondary Education Act, also known as the Bilingual Education Act. This law has been enacted in most states and is currently being argued for reauthorization. Its nature is transitional, as the focus is to teach English while students are developing content area concepts and literacy in their home language.

There are serious limitations as to how bilingual education has been implemented in the United States. Generally, when a minimal amount of English fluency is attained, the student exits the program and joins the mainstream classroom. Current educational research, however, strongly suggests that early-exit programs have been less successful in improving achievement of limited-English-proficient students than late-exit programs that keep students until the academic language and cognitive demands of more advanced content area material have been attained (Ramírez, Yuen, Ramey, & Pasta, 1991). Therefore, bilingual programs need to change direction from a "band-aid"-remedial focus to a more long-term and systematic treatment that will not only ensure mastery of language but also of academic concepts as well.

Additional Cuban-American Contributions to the United States

Most people living in the United States have developed a visual image of a Cuban as a quick-tempered, conga-playing, hen-pecked Ricky Ricardo-type, whose naive mixture of sweet and macho are his redeeming qualities. When we look at the Cuban experience, Ricky Ricardo takes on a very different light. The stereotype is replaced with a vivid image of a courageous and tough-minded survivalist who is determined to conquer adversity. Unlike the stereotype, Cuban-American contributions to U.S. society have been significant and generous. A partial discussion follows.

The Human Element

The most important contribution to the infrastructure of the total society has been the people themselves. Family oriented, hard-working, and gregarious, Cubans have shared with other Americans their humor, resilience, and courage for the last three decades. A visit to their transplant home in Dade County attests to the vitality and versatility of Cuban-American life-styles. Urban renewal, international networking, and religious and educational impact are areas that show the indelible presence of Cuban Americans. Early revitalization of Calle Ocho, the creation of well-kept suburban and urban enclaves with homes that they mostly own, and the revitalization of downtown Miami are but a few of the many testimonials of their presence.

In addition, the Miami-Dade area has become a center of international business whose bilingual character has facilitated close ties with Latin America. Bergsman (1989) stated, "Miami is second to New York in the number of foreign financial institutions located in a U.S. city" (p. 19). Geographic location, entrepreneurship, facilities, and efficient services make this area the hub of Latin business in the United States, as international insurance firms, banks, and other professional industries have made it their home base.

Local Business, Employment, and Income

There are more than 25,000 Hispanic-owned businesses in the south Florida area (Strategy Research Corporation, 1988). Banking, real estate, and small family-owned businesses exemplify the bulk of these initiatives. Labor force participation is high among Cuban Americans (refer to Table 2). The 1990 census reports an unemployment figure of 5.2 percent among males age 16 and over, and 8 percent among females—the lowest of all Hispanic groups. The median family income of $31,400 is well above other Hispanic family units. In addition, the report maintains that "proportionally more Cuban families had incomes of $50,000 or more than did the Mexican origin families"

(U.S. Bureau of the Census, 1991, p. 7). Other labor demographics appear on Table 1 and are the focus of an earlier discussion in this chapter.

Media

Besides Radio Martí and plans to develop TV Martí, there are several Spanish TV channels, including two with national audiences, Univision and Telemundo; 25 Spanish tabloids; 13 magazines with a monthly circulation of 300,000; and two daily newspapers, the *Diario de las Américas,* with 70,000 issues, and *El Nuevo Herald,* with 95,000 issues daily and 115,000 issues on Sundays (Cros Sandoval, 1991). Access to media is an important ingredient in maintaining close cultural ties and in enhancing the already solid political and economic power base at the continental and national levels.

Arts and Literature

The trauma of exile has made the Cuban people more introspective. Soul searching has opened the door to a flow of talent in the arts and literature. Painters, sculptors, musicians, and writers have left an indelible imprint with their bicultural message. Talented artists and writers, in the likes of Hilda Perera, Alma Flor Ada, Jorge Mañach, Humberto Calzada, Celia Cruz, and Guillermo Cabrera Infant, have excelled in sharing their very Cuban souls through their unique artistic medium. Among these, a new wave of dissenting artists have come to join this invaluable artistic heritage.

Postscript

The Castro dilemma remains unfinished business for Cuban Americans. What will happen when and if the island's regime changes and opens the doors to a safe return remains an unanswered question. Many Cuban Americans recognize the difficulty of transition between totalitarianism and democracy. Some 60 percent of the 10 million Cubans living on the island were born and bred during the Marxist-Leninist dictatorship. For those who will return to their homeland, collating these views and perceptions of life into the capitalistic, freedom-of-choice mentality of the exiles will be the challenge of living in the New Cuba.

Many Cuban Americans have uprooted and established a new identity that does not in any way deny the pride in their ancestry or in their homeland. To these, the opportunity to return to the island and replenish their spirit may provide the cultural continuity that every human being needs. To the U.S.-born-and-bred generation, the possibility of a visit can also result in a valuable self-energizing search for roots.

The life history of Cuban Americans is very compelling. Their strength of character and determination has allowed them to survive their tragedy with utmost dignity. Only time will tell how their destiny will be shaped.

References

Balmaseda, L. (1992, April). Old drugstore good for what's ailing Miami. *Miami Herald,* p. lb.

Bergsman, S. (1989, March). Carnival of cultures. *Hispanic Business,* 18–23.

Boswell, T. D., & Curtis, J. R. (1983). *The Cuban American experience.* Totowa, NJ: Rowman & Allaheld.

Clark, J. M. (1991). The social impact of Cuban immigration in Florida. In A. Jorge, J. Schlicki, & A. Leyva de Varona (Eds.), *Cuban exiles in Florida: Their presence and contribution* (pp. 39–61). Miami: University of Miami.

Cros Sandoval, M. (1991). Cultural contributions of the Cuban migrations in south Florida. In A. Jorge, J. Schlicki, & A. Leyva de Varona (Eds.), *Cuban exiles in Florida: Their presence and contribution* (pp. 13–37). Miami: University of Miami.

García, O., & Otheguy, R. (1985). The masters of survival send their children to school: Bilingual education in the ethnic schools of Miami. *Bilingual Review, 12* (1-2), 3–19.

González-Montserrat, I. (1990). *La Habana 1995.* Miami: Ediciones Universal.

Jorge, A., & Moncarz, R. (1991). The qualitatively different and massive nature of the Cuban outflow after Castro's revolution. In A. Jorge, J.

Schlicki, & A. Leyva de Varona (Eds.), *Cuban exiles in Florida: Their presence and contribution* (pp. 175–205). Miami: University of Miami.

Leyva de Varona, A. (1991) The political impact of Cuban-Americans in Florida. In A. Jorge, J. Schlicki, & A. Leyva de Varona (Eds.), *Cuban exiles in Florida: Their presence and contribution* (pp. 63–109). Miami: University of Miami.

Queralt, M. (1984). Understanding Cuban immigrants: A cultural perspective. *Social Work, 29* (2), 115–121.

Ramírez, J. D., Yuen, S. D., Ramey, D. R., & Pasta, D. J. (1991) *Final Report: Longitudinal study of structured immersion strategy, early-exit and late-exit transitional bilingual education programs for language-minority children* (Vol. I). San Mateo, CA: Aguirre International.

Strategy Research Corporation. (1988). *The 1989 south Florida Latin market.* Miami: Author.

Strouse, C. (1992, April). Non-Cuban Hispanic census count rising. *Miami Herald,* p. 1b.

U.S. Bureau of the Census. (1991). Current Population Reports, series P-20, No. 455. *The Hispanic population in the United States: March 1991.* Washington, DC: U.S. Government Printing Office.

About the Author

Andrea B. Bermúdez has been a professor of multicultural education and the director of the Research Center for Language and Culture at the University of Houston-Clear Lake. Bermúdez is a native of Cuba. She has earned a Bachelor of Arts from Randolph-Macon Woman's College, a Master of Arts from the University of Virginia, and an Ed.D. from the University of Houston. Bermúdez has conducted extensive research on educational issues of language minority students and currently serves as the editor of the *Bilingual Research Journal.*

The Hawaiian Islanders

DAVID PEDRO

For over a century, the Hawaiian Islanders have been the connecting link between East and West, demonstrating understanding, tolerance, and respect among their variety of peoples and cultures. Living together harmoniously appears to be an inherited trait. The early Polynesians had a strong inclination to welcome foreigners with warmness, tolerance, and understanding—a natural friendliness. A review of the names of the Hawaiian Islanders' elected officials shows strong evidence of their support of and respect for good leadership, regardless of the individual leader's racial background. The people believe that "a healthy democracy balances direct participation and representative government" (Morris, 1979, p. 47). On a Direct Democracy Index used by the International City Management Association (Morris, 1979) to evaluate each state's citizens' access to the public decision-making process, Hawaii ranked highest.

All of Hawaii's peoples came from someplace else. They include Native Hawaiians, Caucasians, Japanese, Chinese, Koreans, Portuguese, Filipinos, Samoans, Blacks, and others. Of the 50 states, Hawaii is the only one whose primary ethnic roots are Asian rather than European.

The first settlers of Hawaii were members of the Polynesian family group that included Marquesans, Easter Islanders, Maoris, Tahitians, and Samoans. From legends and genealogies, Hawaiian ethnic history began in 300 A.D. Before the Portuguese, Spanish, English, Dutch, and French explorers arrived, the Polynesians were making the long voyages to Hawaii (2,400 miles) and were discovering, exploring, and populating the widely scattered islands in the Pacific Ocean. They built island societies and lived on the Islands undisturbed for at least 4,000 years before the Europeans arrived.

The early Polynesians were outstanding navigators and they performed navigational feats that were unmatched by any other primitive society, including the Europeans. Without compasses, they guided their ocean crafts using the sun, clouds, birds, winds, currents, and waves during the day, and the stars at night, as navigational markers. Over the centuries, their explorations covered thousands of square miles within what today is called the "Polynesian Triangle" (Kuykendall & Day, 1961, p. 5). The points of the triangles are Easter Island to the east, New Zealand to the southwest, and Hawaii to the north.

The early Hawaiians did not have a written language for centuries, but rather preserved the memory of important events and persons by word of mouth. Their history, legends, and traditions were told and retold to each new generation. One of the ancient legends so preserved is about the discovery of Hawaii by a chief called Hawaii-loa, a well-known fisherman and navigator from Kahiku-ku (some foreign land). During his explorations to the northeast, he discovered the Islands, naming one of them Hawaii and another Maui. After making several trips back and forth, he settled on Hawaii with a large company of followers (Alexander, 1899, p. 20).

In ancient times, the Hawaiian society was divided into two major classes—the so-called commoners and the chiefs. The Kahuna, who were the priests, healers, and keepers of the spiritual power of each "family," were included with the chiefs. The local populations were organized into "family" units called *'ohanas*. Loyalty to the elders and the family was more highly valued than feelings of individuality; each person was a member of an 'ohana before anything else. The practices of sharing and of amity were so pervasive that words and expressions of gratitude were never needed in that old language. Today, the word *mahalo* is used as an expression of thanks, but formerly it was an expression of *praise.*

The name Kamehameha is used extensively in the Islands. There are Kamehameha schools, Kamehameha highways, and Kamehameha buildings. Kamehameha is a hero to the Hawaiian Islanders, and especially to those familiar with the Islands' history.

A member of the royal family, King Kamehameha I (1810–1819) was the first Hawaiian leader to unite the Islands under a strong governing system. That system survived well enough to protect the Islands' independence during the early critical years when American and European traders, whalers, and explorers exploited their resources. Uniting the Islands did cause 10 years of civil tension and fighting, and left them in a weakened condition—but Kamehameha showed his innovative leadership qualities as he quickly restored their economy. He encouraged the chiefs and their followers to grow food, and even led them by laboring among the chiefs and the commoners alike. They said of him, "He is a farmer, a fisherman, a maker of cloth, a provider for the needy, and a father to the fatherless" (Kuykendall & Day, 1961, p. 28).

By 1798, a little over a decade before Kamehameha assumed the throne, the Islands had reached the highest state of agricultural cultivation in memory. Native products were breadfruit, coconuts, plantain, sweet potatoes, taro, yams, and bananas. The products introduced to the Islands were watermelon, muskmelon, pumpkin, cabbage, and most of the current garden vegetables. Ethnic cultivation through immigration had not yet begun to peak. But by the end of Kamehameha's reign, just over 20 years later (when he died), the Islands were well on their way to becoming a racial melting pot, fairly brimming with people whose ethnic roots lay in England, the United States, China, Ireland, Africa, and Portugal. (An observant visitor estimated that there were more than 200 foreigners in Hawaii at that time.)

In 1816, four Hawaiian youths who had shown an aptitude for learning were sent to New England and enrolled in a school established by the American Board of Commissioners for Foreign Missions. The Commissioners' intention was to send these foreign students back to the Islands, to Christianize other natives, after their commencement. In late 1819, a group of 14 young newlywed American couples, soon to be missionaries, and the four now-certified Hawaiian youths organized in Boston under the title "Sandwich Islands Mission" (Kuykendall & Day, 1961, p. 43). Within less than a week's time, the group sailed from Boston, bound for Hawaii to fulfill their common religious goal.

The 18 were welcomed by the Islanders, but King Kamehameha II (1819–1824) was reluctant to grant them permission to remain in the Islands. It took 12 days of ardent missionary rhetoric before the governors granted them permission to stay for one year. The missionaries' ambitious plan for that year was to wholly uproot the sins of the heathen Hawaiians—and, according to their records, they were most successful. The fact is that, at the end of the first year, the question of the missionaries' leaving was not even raised. Indeed, within the missionaries' first 10 years there, more than 40,000 natives were receiving their religious instructions! The missionaries, it appeared, could rightly claim extraordinary success in Christianizing the "heathen" Hawaiians.

Under King Kamehameha III (1825–1854), the American missionaries added two other areas of interest to their spiritual affairs: government and commerce. By 1850, some of the best official positions and judgeships were held by ex-missionaries or their sons who had given up the cloth for political careers. On the advice of a missionary who became a judge, the King repealed the law that prohibited foreigners from owning land (Barber, 1941, p. 27). Following this repeal, a new law was enacted that allocated about a third of the King's land to the commoners. The foreigners, by extending credit to native landholders, soon had ownership of some of the choicest property. This was a sad period for the Hawaiians. While they were concentrating on learning the three Rs, much of their cultivatable land was coming under foreign control. They were even forfeiting their land through games of chance or exchanging it for goods such as a few yards of brightly dyed cloth.

As early as 1852, evangelists were purchasing thousands of acres of the best land in Hawaii for $0.56 an acre. Along with their sense of God, piety, and the heavenly hereafter, the missionaries obviously had a highly developed sense of property ownership. Their offspring pursued—and were very successful in—the highly profitable businesses of factoring (purchasing and collecting accounts), shipping, sugar production, and banking. In a short time, they, not the native Hawaiians, were in control of the Islands. As the later native Hawaiians tell it: "The missionaries instructed the Hawaiians to look up to the heavens and pray for God's forgiveness, and while they were doing it, the land under their feet was claimed by the missionaries' sons. They acquired our land and we were left holding the Bible." What actually happened is the topic of a bitter historical dispute. Witness, for example, this quote: "Volumes have been written accusing or absolving the missionaries and their descendants of land-grabbing proclivities" (Barber, 1941, p. 26).

During the early 1850s, the White residents owned companies that had several thousand acres of sugar cane under cultivation. One of the critical problems they faced was the shortage of cheap labor. Initially, the native Hawaiians were the laborers. They cleared the land; built the irrigation ditches; planted, cultivated, harvested, transported the cane to the mills; and did the heavy work in the mills. They did not, however, readily accept the idea of small compensation for such arduous labor, and eventually refused to work for less than $0.25 per day. On top of this, the planters faced a second problem with the Hawaiian labor supply: the drastic decline in the Hawaiian population caused by epidemics such as measles in 1848 and smallpox in 1853.

To get a cheaper labor supply, they searched elsewhere. By late 1852, some 300 Chinese laborers were imported from Canton, China—brought in as indentured servants with contracts running for five years and compensated at a rate of $0.02 an hour for a 10- to 12-hour day. They were given a daily rice ration, and most of the time their sleeping quarters were in the plantation stable with the horses and mules.

Not surprisingly, many of the Chinese committed suicide. A few remained with the sugar industry or returned to their homeland when their indentures expired, but many others stayed and started their own businesses in the food, laundry, and tailoring areas. Now and again, one or more invested in and operated a vegetable farm or hog-raising endeavor. Some of the earliest interracial marriages occurred during this period. Chinese men often married Hawaiian females, resulting in the births of a considerable number of Hawaiian-Chinese children.

As more and more Asians were imported by the Islanders for labor during the 1880s, U.S. Secretary of State James Blaine concluded that it was just a matter of time before the Hawaiians would be "absorbed," creating a Hawaii that would be controlled by Asians. He bluntly insisted that the Hawaiian Islands must *not* be absorbed under an Asian system. To ensure such a course of action, he instructed the U.S. representative in Hawaii to lobby the Hawaiian government to pass homestead laws that would favor and encourage American colonists to settle in the Islands. His goal was to influence the Hawaiian government to assimilate and identify with the *American* system (Barber, 1941, p. 30).

During the reign of King Kalakaua (1874–1891), a large number of foreigners—mostly Americans—were highly active in Hawaiian governmental activities. They were always ready to provide large loans in exchange for prized sugar land or other concessions. They were also quick to plead the case for their sugar interests before the U.S. government. The passage of the Reciprocity Treaty in 1876 granted the Hawaiian sugar planters the privilege of exporting their sugar to the United States duty free.

The Reciprocity Treaty greatly increased the production of sugar in the years that followed 1876 and gave rise to the missionary-merchant-planter aristocracy in Hawaii. The labor import business also increased as laboring groups were brought from such countries and regions as Japan, China, Puerto Rico, Portugal, the Philippine Islands, the United States, Germany, Scandinavia, and the South Sea Islands. Nevertheless, a sufficient labor force for working in the fields remained a problem through the late 1940s. Even in 1948, labor was still being imported from the Philippine Islands.

When Captain James Cook and his ships first arrived in the Hawaiian Islands in 1778, he estimated the Hawaiian population to be about 300,000. Some 75 years later, after exposure to diseases such as measles and smallpox, that Hawaiian population dropped to 71,000. In 1986, the pure Hawaiian population was estimated to be less than 9,000 (Frazier, 1987, p. 2).

The decline of the native Hawaiian population and the ever-increasing demand for labor in the expanding sugar industry forced a search for laborers *wherever* they were available. This brought diverse racial groups into the plantation housing structure. It became a mixing bowl wherein cultural values and traditions were shared. Many of the current Hawaiian Islanders are descendants of the 400,000 foreign-born people brought to the Islands for use on the sugar and pineapple plantations. As we have seen, the first group of laborers were recruited from China. They were in turn followed by workers, sometimes with families, from Japan, Portugal, Puerto Rico, Korea, Spain, and the Philippine Islands. All were settled into plantation camps more cosmopolitan, racially, than any other place in the world. Surprisingly, they lived and worked together amiably.

In the process, Hawaiian Islanders produced a community open to diversity—a very positive outcome of the blending of races and cultures at an effective level of intergroup interactions. To this day, for the Hawaiian Islander, acceptance and status depend on personal achievement or merit, not on racial or cultural background.

Unlike that in the southern states of the United States, laws that legalized racial discrimination did not exist in Hawaii. Nevertheless, until the Japanese attack on Pearl Harbor on December 7, 1941, Whites had acquired most of the power, money, national prestige, and international connections. All of these were changed deliberately after World War II. During the war, the Hawaiian-Japanese community clearly demonstrated their loyalty and patriotism. They courageously participated in military combat in Europe, and at home they led in the purchasing of war bonds and the donation of blood. (Although less publicized, loyalty and patriotism were just as strong throughout the war years among the descendants of other ethnic groups.)

Other contributing factors to the reduction of racial barriers after the war were the unionization of the sugar and pineapple plantation workers—a process that forced the workers to organize their efforts across racial lines. Public education provided schooling for all children and furthered both their emancipation and their racial assimilation. Intermarriages also reduced racial barriers by establishing linkages across racial lines.

"Hawaii's greatest strength is its people. They have an innate friendliness—perhaps stemming from the Polynesian laissez-faire with a New England ethic laminated onto it" (Peirce, 1972, p. 333). The assimilation of the cultures of the many different racial groups is the most noteworthy quality of the Hawaiian Islanders. Peter Morse, a local composer-author, claims that there are three levels of interaction between and among people of different races. The first level is typified by pure prejudice: One person dislikes another person almost solely on the basis that the other person is different. At the second level, there is a recognition of difference but a tolerance for the person who is different—and an attempt is made to treat that person as a fellow human being. At the third level, differences are recognized and one is fully aware of them but is receptive to and fascinated by them. At this latter level, differences have *value*, and *all* groups can retain their racial, cultural, and intellectual pride (Peirce, 1972, p. 334). Although there most assuredly have been strains of racial exploitation throughout Hawaii's recent history, *most* Hawaiian Islanders today are at the third level.

The Native Hawaiians welcome other races with a spirit of warmness, which is defined by the Hawaiian word *aloha*. Depending on the occasion, the word could mean greetings, hello, goodbye, love, affection, compassion, mercy, kindness—or anything else that is lovable and beautiful in thought and feeling. The "aloha spirit" is still valued and practiced even today, a basic ingredient of a way of life based on acceptance of the equality and dignity of all human beings (Chaplin & Paige, 1973, p. 147). This value pervades the full range of interpersonal relations of the Hawaiian Islanders. Not surprisingly, because of its location as well as of its friendliness to one and all, Hawaii is the world's gathering place for minorities whose ethnic roots are primarily Asian rather than European. However, the Hawaiian Islanders are in fact world-class leaders in matters dealing with multiracial relations and unity.

The Hawaiian Islanders consider themselves Hawaiians—a seemingly simplistic identity that allows for the complexities of a delicate balance of all minorities, an adaptive mechanism enabling any one group to deal effectively with any another. It permits the continuous mixing of cultural factors and at the same time lets each group retain its racial/ethnic uniqueness. It is the foundation for sharing the Hawaiian identity and for developing a community spirit remarkably free of racial/ethnic tension and strife. "Perhaps more than in any other state in the union, the citizens of Hawaii identify themselves together, bound by unique customs, music, geography, and dress. Thus, a common bond, although loose and at first glance superficial, allows the citizens of this state to consider themselves 'Hawaiian,' an identification with a larger and earlier culture, unique to us as a group within the United States" (Chaplin & Paige, 1973, p. 168).

Historical traditions and racial diversity have produced cultural values that have led the way in both racial assimilation and the acceptance of multicultural diversity, bringing together most of the major cultural traditions of the Pacific region and allowing the relationships among them to flourish. There is continuing interest in keeping the values that allow these relationships to flourish.

There is also a growing realization that the survival of the Hawaiian culture—especially of the *'ohana*, *aloha spirit*, *ho'oponopono*, and *kokua* values—is directly linked to the family, the function of which is a matter of major concern. "Participation" in the family unit may involve a parent and older children joining in an activity, such as paddling a canoe, while the younger children watch and learn. The working and playing together of all family members is a basic factor in building and maintaining especially the *'ohana* value. The whole family participates in such activities as swimming, singing, playing musical instruments, dancing, taking trips to historical sites, and reading sessions. The *'ohana* emphasis is on family togetherness, and each member has a responsibility—not a choice—to take care of other family members.

The *aloha spirit* value, defined earlier as a way of life, is best characterized as an open acceptance of others. This is the state of mind that has made Hawaii a place where strangers can gather and become friends in a very short period of time.

The *ho'oponopona* value means the "setting to right of wrongs" and is a problem-solving approach within the *'ohana*. This approach provides an opportunity for problems to be presented openly to all the people concerned. Participants are invited to speak out in personal terms, making everyone aware of how they feel. A solution to the problem is determined by the group, and is binding on all members.

The fourth value, *kokua*, means emphasizing cooperation as more important than either competing or winning. This value may at times conflict with White American and other economic systems that emphasize competing *and* winning, rather than cooperation. These four values obviously have had long-term societal benefits for the Hawaiian Islanders. Some of these benefits have been:

- A natural flow of caring for one's community develops from an environment wherein each family member is responsible for caring for other family members.

- In a climate of respect and acceptance, despite outward differences, all family members tend to develop concern for others. Having all family members, from the elderly to the young, participate in family activities tends to support the development of self-esteem and personhood, from the beginning to the end of life. All family members participate in and contribute to societal activities.
- A problem-solving system that provides opportunities for resolving problems openly allows group members to speak about whatever is on their minds. It is a way of communicating and keeping everyone informed.
- Emphasizing cooperation over competing *and* over winning allows all persons to experience satisfaction in just participating—not just in the winning.

The Hawaiian Islanders are a striking example of what is possible in large-scale intergroup relations. They have dealt successfully with assimilation and multicultural diversity issues, and achieved both economic and political integration. The educational climate of Hawaii has *always* been a multicultural one.

References

Alexander, W. D. (1899). *A brief history of the Hawaiian people*. New York: American Book Company.

Barber, J., Jr. (1941). *Hawaii: Restless rampart*. New York: Bobbs-Merrill.

Bell, R. (1984). *Last among equals*. Honolulu: University of Hawaii Press.

Blackman, W. F. (1906). *The making of Hawaii*. New York: Macmillan.

Chaplin, G., & Paige, G. D. (1973). *Hawaii 2000*. Honolulu: University Press of Hawaii.

Frazier, G. (1987). *Ka Wai Ola O Oha* (Vol. 4, No. 8.). Honolulu: Office of Hawaiian Affairs.

Kuykendall, R. S., & Day, A. G. (1961). *Hawaii: A history from Polynesian kingdom to American statehood* (rev. ed.). Englewood Cliffs, NJ: Prentice Hall.

Morris, D. (1979). *The municipal year book*. Washington DC: International City Management Association.

Peirce, N. R. (1972). *The Pacific states of America*. New York: W. W. Norton.

Tabrah, R. M. (1980). *Hawaii a history*. New York: W. W. Norton.

About the Author

David Pedro is a retired administrator for the state of Wisconsin. He is currently working on a book about a lesser known Hawaiian Island called Kahoolawe. His father lived and worked on the island for 22 years until the start of World War II, when the U.S. Navy claimed and used the island—and continues to do so to this day—for target and bombing practice. The state of Hawaii currently has a commission that is conducting an in-depth study of Kahoolawe and an attempt to reclaim it for Hawaii. Pedro spent three years as a high school teacher in the Milwaukee Public School system. After graduate study at the University of Missouri, he joined Martin-Marietta Corporation at Cape Canaveral, Florida, and later the Collins Radio Company in Dallas, Texas, as director of training. In the mid-1960s, he became director of training for Wisconsin's Division of Mental Hygiene and later administered employment and training programs for the state of Wisconsin.

C h a p t e r *10*

The Japanese-American Experience

KISHIO MATOBA

Formal relations between Japan and the United States began with the arrival of Commodore Matthew Perry's squadron of gunboats in Tokyo Bay on July 8, 1853. Perry had been sent by the U.S. government to force Japan to open its ports to American ships after they had been closed to Western nations over 200 years earlier.

At the time of Perry's arrival, Japan was a highly cultured and advanced society, with a long history of development as a nation, dating back to 300 A.D., when it was first unified under imperial rule. This development was strongly influenced by Chinese civilization, from which Japan borrowed on a massive scale for several hundred years from the fifth century on. In the twelfth century, the Japanese Imperial Government became impotent and was gradually supplanted by a military administration. The Emperor was reduced to a figurehead, and most of his power was assumed by the Shogun (generalissimo) who was designated commander-in-chief of all imperial troops.

This centralized rule, in turn, disintegrated during the fourteenth century when political dissension and civil warfare became endemic throughout the country. As local lords (called *daimyo*) gained nearly autonomous control over their domains, a system of government and land ownership evolved that closely resembled that of high feudalism in twelfth-century Europe.

Centralized shogunate rule was reestablished in 1603 when Ieyasu Tokugawa assumed the title of Shogun and began the 265-year reign of the powerful Tokugawa family. In order to ensure political stability and the maintenance of their dominant position, the Tokugawa froze the feudalistic system into a rigid four-class social hierarchy consisting—in descending order—of samurai (warriors), peasants, artisans, and merchants.

This system devised by the Tokugawa proved to be remarkably viable and maintained a state of relative peace and calm for over two centuries. By the end of this time, the dominant influence of Chinese culture had largely subsided, and most of the cultural developments of the Tokugawa period (1603–1868) were distinctively and uniquely Japanese. The visual arts, literature, theater, and fine crafts flowered in quality so high as to be recognized later in history among Japan's major esthetic contributions to the rest of the world. Advances were made also in educating the masses, so that by the end of this period, it has been estimated, 45 percent of men and 15 percent of women were literate.

The first signs of disruption in the tranquility of the Tokugawa era appeared early in the nineteenth century when, because of serious socioeconomic dislocations at all levels of the feudal structure, political unrest increased and peasant uprisings broke out with growing frequency. The major disruptive force that ultimately led to the downfall of the Tokugawa regime was the intrusions of Western powers, beginning with Commodore Perry's arrival and followed shortly thereafter by similar missions from European powers.

The powerlessness of the shogunate to prevent these intrusions soon became clear. This ineffectiveness led to a group of young samurai engineering a political coup, which finally toppled the Tokugawa shogunate in 1868. The emperor was reemplaced in a political move now referred to as the Meiji Restoration. In actuality, Emperor Meiji served mainly as a symbol of authority, and the powers of government were assumed by a small clique of court aristocrats and samurai who had led the overthrow of Tokugawa. Under the new and dynamic leadership, Japan actively proceeded to acquire knowledge of Western ideas, methods, and institutions. With amazing rapidity, it modernized its technological, industrial, military, political, and economic systems. By the turn of the twentieth century, Japan had developed a strong industrial base in such diverse areas as textiles, ship building, mining, and cement products. Railroad and telegraph systems were built. A stable currency and a strong banking institution evolved. The modern military forces showed their might by defeating the Russians on land and sea in the Russo-Japanese War of 1904.

In these early decades of the twentieth century, Japan emerged as a national power with which to be reckoned. However, despite the radical changes wrought by modernization, many of the cultural norms of the people remained relatively unchanged from those of the Tokugawa era. Indeed, the Meiji leaders instituted compulsory education to assure the inculcation of the traditional values and beliefs. A code of ethics—which emphasized such values as duty, obligation, obedience, respect for education, self-discipline, humility, and selfless service to the nation—remained strongly entrenched in the beliefs of the Japanese of the time. And, because most of the early Japanese immigrants to the United States were born and educated during the Meiji era (1868–1912), it can be safely assumed that they were strongly bound to those principles. From earliest Japanese history, the imperial personage has been revered as a divine being. By the first half of the nineteenth century, however, as daimyos and Shogun vied for power, the position of Emperor had waxed and waned in governmental significance. The Meiji Restoration held the Emperor as figurehead only, but in the Emperor's name, the Japanese people reestablished the traditional codes of obedience and respect. This ethical system was to be a powerful influence on how Japanese immigrants to this country, and their children, were able to cope with their American life and times.

The Immigration Pattern

From early 1600s to late 1800s, Japan had not allowed international travel to its people. After Japan opened itself to the Western countries, however, several early organized emigrations occurred. In 1868, a group of 148 Japanese were brought to Hawaii as contract laborers to work on the sugar plantations. Difficulties experienced by this first group led Japan to suspend further emigration for almost two decades, however. The first settlement of Japanese immigrants on the United States mainland is believed to have been the short-lived Wakamatsu Tea and Silk Colony near Placerville, California, in 1869. Due in part to unfavorable climatic conditions, the colony lasted only two years.

From these halting beginnings, emigration to the United States grew gradually until slowed by the "Gentlemen's Agreement" under which Japan agreed to halt the emigration of unskilled laborers, beginning in 1908. However, anti-Japanese groups and demagogues pressed for further and more severe restrictions and sanctions in order to suppress the Japanese, who were proving themselves to be skillful agricultural (and thus economic) rivals. The pressure from these anti-Japanese forces led to the enactment of California's 1913 Alien Land Law, which prohibited Asian aliens from buying and owning land because of their being "ineligible for citizenship." The Alien Land Law was made even more restrictive in 1920 and again in 1922, when the U.S. Supreme Court upheld a lower court decision that immigrant Japanese were legally and thus correctly ineligible for citizenship according to certain archaic laws.

Inspired by these victories, the exclusionists pressed their cause at the national level and lobbied to have an exclusion act passed by Congress. As it turned out, their efforts coincided with a growing national reaction to waves of immigrants from southern and eastern Europe. The National Origins Quota Act was enacted in 1924, and, by a critical amendment slipped in during the legislative process, Japanese immigration was effectively shut off. The Japanese population in the United States topped off at about 280,000 in 1930. It remained about the same up to World War II, with half living in Hawaii and half on the mainland, concentrated in the Pacific Coast states of Washington, Oregon, and California. Although there was a small movement of Japanese back to Japan, and of American-born Japanese who had been sent back to Japan for their education and were returning to the United States (the Kibei), the Japanese population in this country was pretty well stabilized and set to make its way in America. It was a matter of the Issei (first generation), having established themselves in farming or business, committing themselves to the well-being and future of their children, the Nisei. The Nisei were just into their college careers when World War II interrupted everything.

Prewar Social Problems

For 50 years before the World War II, there was almost continuous evidence of racial discrimination and bigotry. Many motion-picture theaters, restaurants, shops, and service establishments snubbed and discouraged—or openly rejected—Japanese clientele. There were vigilante actions against Japanese communities and work places, there was restricted housing, and there was considerable evidence of unequal justice before the law. In 1906, the San Francisco Board of Education ordered all 93 Japanese children in the city to attend a segregated Oriental school. This action became an international incident when officials in Japan protested the action to President Theodore Roosevelt. The president had enjoyed close contact with the Japanese in his sponsoring of the treaty that ended the Russo-Japanese War, and had realized the world stature of the Japanese nation. He interceded, and the Board rescinded the order.

The hidden effect of the San Francisco segregation move, however, was that three small communities in the Central Valley of California just east of San Francisco segregated their schools into White and Oriental. The educational effect was disastrous: Many Japanese children ended up being quite inadequate in both English and Japanese. Common racial-social interactions simply never reached a comfortable fluency for these people who had been isolated from the White community since childhood.

Among many other rankling conditions, there was a not-so-humorous saying that it would take an engineering degree to get a job tending a fruit stand. Certainly there were successful professionals among the Nisei, but there were also some types of jobs that did not welcome Japanese-American workers. The paucity of opportunities made many consider moving east—and some did. However, there were those, reared in closed and comfortable Japanese communities, who had real trepidations about leaving their protective homes. The symbolic question was posed: Can a Japanese American be happy without soy sauce? Until after the war, soy sauce was almost exclusively a West Coast condiment. In these circumstances, the Japanese response tended to be stoic—even passive—on the face of it. There was resentment, however, and that resentment was often transformed into scorn and ridicule. For example, the Japanese word for "white man" is the literal *haku jin* but the scornful term often used is *ke to* or "hairy people."

The ability to fend off social and political abuse seemed to rise from two cultural forces that fortified the Japanese. First, the Japanese are openly pluralistic about many social institutions and ideas. On religion, for example, a family can be Buddhist, keep a Shinto shrine, and send their children to a Baptist Sunday School with no qualms. They tend not to think dichotomously—that is, they do not often insist that something is either this or that. They can accept both, which viewpoint leads to their tolerance of what they see as strange American actions. They are confident that such acceptances do not override (or even seriously challenge) Japanese values and traditions. This belief system is what (in part, at least) allowed the Issei to be faithful to their Emperor even while being completely patriotic Americans during the war.

Second, the Japanese held deep pride in their national history and tradition, which had roots going back 2,000 years, whereas the Americans had (at that time) less than one-tenth that history. Thus, Americans were often seen as people without either a solid culture or a national ethic. It was not that they were all necessarily bad—indeed, many Americans earned great respect by their kindliness, honesty, and helpfulness—but the Japanese saw most Americans as naive, unsophisticated, and childlike in their thoughts and actions. Rightly or wrongly, the Japanese tended to believe that they were a more mature and wiser people than Americans, and thus able to tolerate, if not accept, the nastiness of the "young" Americans.

The Japanese, even under strong racially directed duress, believed they could make their way toward the American Dream because of their ability to distance themselves from the reality of American prejudice. They believed that simple-minded White people's actions could be circumvented through diligent efforts toward their own excellence in all endeavors.

The World War II Detention Program

Although the attack on Pearl Harbor cannot be fully comprehended without reviewing the history of Western imperialism in Asia, including the ramifications of Commodore Perry's foray into Tokyo Bay, its more immediate cause was the breakdown in negotiations between the United States and Japan over the latter's military aggression against China. Although the American public was aware of the growing animosity between the two countries, the attack on Pearl Harbor was a stunning surprise to most of the nation.

For the Japanese on the West Coast, the attack was a long-dreaded scenario come true. Almost immediately, West Coast newspapers once again began publishing racial tirades against the Japanese "Yellow Peril." They printed rumor-driven and wholly unverified stories of purported acts of espionage and sabotage committed by Japanese Americans. These stories gained considerable credibility when some high-government officials tacitly acknowledged them, although they did not possess any way of proving the accusations. As a result, there was growing fear among the White public, and the old racist groups and other people who had brought about earlier repressions now reemerged in full force and hatred. A concerted clamor for removing the Japanese was opposed by only a few Quaker groups and some American Civil Liberties Union chapters.

Finally, on February 19, 1942, President Franklin D. Roosevelt issued an executive order that authorized the military to remove the Japanese from the three West Coast states. The reason given for the issuance of the order was "military necessity," meaning that, whether citizens or not, the Japanese posed a threat to the internal security of this country. It is now generally agreed that the actions taken against the Japanese on the West Coast were primarily the result of racism, economic opportunism, and political expedience rather than military necessity.

The president's executive order affected more than 110,000 Japanese, more than two-thirds of whom were native-born citizens. Beginning in March 1942, often on only a few days' notice, the Japanese were rounded up and moved en masse into such facilities as racetrack stables and livestock pavilions. The people were allowed to take only meager personal goods that they could carry with them. Later, they were transferred to 10 concentration camps, euphemistically called "relocation centers." The camps, hastily erected in barren and desolate areas in various isolated regions of the country, consisted of tarpaper barracks surrounded by barbed-wire double fences guarded by machine gun-armed soldiers in watch towers. Although they cannot be compared with the death camps of Nazi Germany, they had all the trappings and formalities of concentration camps.

The Japanese, for the most part, cooperated with the government edict and tried to make the best of the situation. This is not to say that the camps were without conflicts. At least seven people are known to have died at the hands of military sentries; many more were seriously wounded, and hundreds were beaten and jailed. Generally, however, life in the camps tended to be desultory, meaningless, and demoralizing. Although everyone was expected to do useful work, the pay was $13 a month for nonprofessionals (which was most of the people) and $19 a month for doctors, lawyers, architects, and other highly trained and specially qualified people.

The biggest problem for the internees was the breakdown of the family structure. The traditional family, with the father as the breadwinner and decision-making head of the household, was effectively neutralized because the children had as much social and political power outside the family as did their parents, and also earned as much as the father. Looking up to or receiving advice from the patriarch became an empty process. Here was a case of reality overriding tradition; family conflicts and breakups occurred much more frequently than would be the case otherwise.

Additional evidence of the economic pragmatics rather than military need for removing the Japanese from the West Coast was the fact that the Japanese in Hawaii were not interned. They had a longer history of immigration from Japan and were strategically much closer in distance to their homeland, so they rightly should have been far more suspect than mainlanders. However, their exclusion—and the resultant loss of their labor and management skills—would have been a disaster to the Hawaiian farm and business economy. Whatever anybody feared about the Japanese-American threat to national security suddenly disappeared when money reared its powerful head.

There was very little White-Oriental animosity in Hawaii, as compared to the social situation on the mainland. This would seem to further indicate that racism was a strong force leading to removing the Japanese from the mainland; the general population in Hawaii were not the bigots and hate-mongers of the West Coast.

The Postwar Years

After their release from detention, the majority of the Japanese Americans hoped to rebuild their lives by returning to the West Coast. A significant number, however, moved to the East and the Midwest to try new surroundings. Most of the internees had lost everything during the war; their total losses were conservatively estimated by the Federal Reserve Bank to be $400 million. Other estimates reach that figure in California alone. Thus, for the most part, the returning Japanese Americans were starting from scratch.

The early period of return was not without incident. There were bombs and bullets and vicious tirades against the Japanese. This misdirected brutality was particularly virulent on the West Coast, where, in the eyes of the natives, the Japanese seemed to have come back to reclaim what they had lost to the locals. However, since this perception did not occur to residents east of the affected coastal states, the Japanese fared much better away from the West Coast.

In a few years, hostile feelings in the West began to wind down, and the general attitude of the public toward Japanese Americans gradually improved. In 1952, Congress passed laws granting citizenship rights to the alien Japanese, restored a token quota of immigration from Japan, and provided a meager, partial compensation for properties lost due to the exclusion. The alien land laws were gradually repealed or declared unconstitutional, although the last one remained on the books until 1967. Several cases involving individual Japanese Americans who had resisted the evacuation order and had lost their cases in the courts were reviewed, and these several people were freed of all charges.

The final chapter in correcting the injustice came in the Civil Liberties Act of 1988. In the name of the U.S. people and nation, Congress acknowledged that the Japanese had been summarily deprived of their civil rights during the war, and that a redress was in order. To each and every one of those who had been incarcerated and were still alive when the act was signed by President Ronald Reagan, both a personal letter of apology from the president and a check in the amount of $20,000 were to be tendered. Over several years, most of the individual cases were so resolved but there seems to be a few that are still pending.

Since 1970, Japanese Americans have made substantial gains, and their median levels of education and income are clearly above those of White Americans. Studies over the past three decades also have shown consistently that Japanese Americans have among the lowest rates of crime, delinquency, divorce, and mental illness of any ethnic group. (Given these facts, some writers have referred to them as the "model minority.") These data point out general characteristics—but of course they do not indicate the differences that can and do exist among individuals in a group. Thus, the "model minority" notion should be viewed as a useful sociological abstraction, but not as an expectation or a standard to be used in dealing with Japanese Americans.

Today, Japanese Americans of the third and fourth generations are active in our society. Spanning a wide range of achievements and accomplishments, they are found in every sector of activities. The Nisei tended toward technical fields because there the only measure of success was in cold, objective accomplishments; race, facial features, and stature were irrelevant. After the war, the younger Nisei and the Sansei seemed to gravitate toward teaching, nursing, and other human services—professions that are insulated from racial pressures from superiors and colleagues alike. It has finally come to a point in history where Japanese Americans have a clear and open field to opportunities in this country.

Values and Held Beliefs in Human Interactions

Any purposeful human interaction, such as teaching and learning, is effective only to the extent that the participants recognize the working values of the others in the group. The issues of right and wrong, of good and bad, rest in each of us, and we resolve those in our own particular ways. There is a broad range of how each of us deals with values—and how we deal with them derives, to a good extent, from how we obtained them.

Very few people are able to construct value conclusions through rigorous logic alone. Almost all values held are borrowed from or pressed upon us by our culture. Parents, teachers, clergy, peers, government officials and systems, and other such individuals and groups provide the value propositions. We then accept or reject them by using criteria that can be wholly subjective, or objectively weighed and calculated, judgments.

Value propositions can be held tentatively or they can be set strongly and uncompromisingly. The range and limits of tenacity vary with individuals, so that some people will seem to live with drifting values while others will stubbornly hold to their value beliefs. As in most such qualities, people at the extremes are rare. The people in the middle of the group will hold many values that are essentially flexible propositions, some which are more firmly established, and a few which are sacrosanct.

In a working relationship, people may have some aspects of their background that are outside the norm for the group with which they are involved. For example, a child from a rural setting, thrust into an urban school; a student from a depressed community, being given a scholarship to a prestigious prep school; or, of course, children with ethnic or national backgrounds, entering into U.S. schools.

Teachers in any of these situations who insist on dealing with children only in terms of their own personally encapsulated values will be sure to have conflicts, covert or overt. There can be classic cases, however, of a teacher with unyielding values and beliefs who will still be effective through sheer kindness and gentleness. However, a new teacher who counts on such a rare personal competence is more apt to be disappointed. Teachers, therefore, need both to recognize and understand values held by children from other ethnic, racial, or national backgrounds.

Japanese-American Values

Earlier in this chapter, it was pointed out that the first Japanese immigrants were reared in the Meiji era, where the schools inculcated formal ethical concepts for human behavior. These principles, which were established quite strongly, became the basis for the Japanese ability to thwart the personal and group attacks of the Americans. It was not a matter of the strength just happening to them: They understood their own traditional rationale for resistance.

Their children, the Nisei, were exposed to Japanese culture in many ways. From the one extreme of sending children to Japan for their education, to the other of casual concession to their heritage, the parents were variously involved. The principle of the value of education, plus the pluralism of attitudes, resulted in a good majority of Nisei going first to American schools, and then to Japanese schools—either daily after American school sessions or on Saturdays. Both schools were deemed to be valuable in their own way.

Having gone to Japanese schools, remembering the rituals of homeland holidays, and most usually on a diet of their national cuisine, the Nisei were very much Japanese in mode, if not able to be quite so in a working setting. In school they excelled. They were obedient and their self-disciplined respect for education garnered much academic success. This generation, then, made their way in their schooling with their attitude incline somewhat toward Japanese values—and quietly sorted out intruding values.

The children of the Nisei, the Sansei, tended to break considerably from their Japanese heritage. Their parents tolerated—even encouraged—more American ways of their children because, by then, Japanese Americans were totally committed to America; anything else just didn't occur to them. Although the Nisei intermarried rarely, the Sansei did freely. Today, the Sansei are all adults, so they no longer impact on education to any significant degree.

Because it is the fourth- and fifth-generation Japanese Americans who now are subject to our schools, an assessment of their bicultural value system is difficult to make. The guess would be that they are totally American on the surface and a little deeper than that. Only their grandparents, the fairly well Americanized Nisei, might be a contact point with Japan. To assume that there are no vestiges of Japanese values left in these children may not be at all prudent; a long-hidden private perception may suddenly emerge now and again from one or another.

A Personal Vignette

The Lone Tree Grammar School was a one-room schoolhouse where I began first grade (there was no kindergarten) three months short of being 6 years old. The fact that I spoke no English seemed to be of little concern, for at last I was happily joining the big kids who had left me at home when they went off to school the years before. I was told that I would have to work a little harder, and that turned out to be all too true. The need to start from the realization that there was a heretofore unknown alphabet (whose parts came together in strange ways to make curious words, which then needed to be understood in reading and in speaking) did take some effort. But by simply asking classmates about the language at recess or when walking to and from school, the basic skills came about.

The independent and personal childish curiosity and subsequent urgency to learn seemed to be the driving force in my earliest schooling, but I wonder what would have happened had I been taught in a bilingual system. The question is: Might bilingual schooling actually reduce the drive to learn English because the communication status quo is more comfortable than the hard work required to grasp knowledge and skills in a different language?

At the end of the second year at Lone Tree School, I brought home a report card that informed my parents that I would be entering the fourth grade the next fall. I would be skipping a grade! But the summer that followed brought on a major change in our family. We moved to a farm about 70 miles south, where my father built a modest little house on rented property. The big change for me, however, was that Elk Grove Union Grammar School was a large brick building that had a room for every grade. There also was a kindergarten room, a cafeteria, a wood shop and home economics room, a practice room for the orchestra, and, in the center of the school, a large auditorium.

After I had spent a few weeks in the fourth grade, the principal came to me and took me to another room. That one housed the third grade. But I held my peace because Japanese obey even though what is happening to them doesn't seem reasonable. And what seemed unreasonable was that I could write and read and comprehend as well as the other fourth-graders. I also knew my multiplication tables, and my arithmetic was every bit as competent. However, as I soon learned, I was faulted because I could not do long division. Later (too much later), I realized that someone could have taught me long division in 15 minutes, and that would have put me at par with the other fourth-graders. My father considered my demotion for a few days, but finally concluded that it was probably for the best: A 12-year-old may indeed be too young to be in high school. I will never really know. And I will neither know whether my situation rose from racial prejudice or institutional insensitivity. I personally knew the principal to be a race-baiter, and on returning to the community over 50 years later and talking with my old teachers, I discovered that he had been fired long ago for general incompetence.

However anyone in our society perceives the Japanese among us, there is no escaping the fact that they are readily seen and identified as Oriental. There was in my home a keen sense that our heritage can never be shed by any of us Japanese for all generations to come, when my daughter came home from an apparently racial encounter with a first-grade classmate. She solemnly announced that she didn't want to be Japanese any longer.

About the Author

Kishio Matoba is Professor Emeritus of art education at the State University College at Buffalo. He was born in Elk Grove, California, and spent from 1942 to 1944 interned in the Manzanar Relocation Camp. Matoba received his B.A. and M.A. degrees from the University of Wisconsin, and earned his Ed.D. from Syracuse University.

Chapter 11

The Jewish Americans

NATHAN GLAZER

American Jews may be alternatively thought of as a religious group and as an ethnic group. Normally we do not think of a religious group as consisting of only one people. However, the Jewish religion comes down from a period—long before the rise of Christianity and Islam—when the distinction between "religion" and "people" was not made and when (for example) Greeks, Persians, Romans, and other peoples worshiped distinctive Gods.

Origins

The Jewish people originally settled in Palestine. When it came under Roman rule (in the first century before Christ), however, Jews began to disperse throughout the Roman Empire. They fled in even greater numbers after the failure of their fiercely fought rebellions against Rome in the first and second centuries of the Common Era.

During the Middle Ages the major Jewish communities were those of the Muslim world—Spain, in particular—as well as of France, Germany, and the Rhineland. The Spanish Jews became known as "Sephardim"; the French, Rhineland, and German Jews as "Ashkenazim." Both adhered to the same religious law. Both prayed in Hebrew, and wrote their religious and secular works in Hebrew.

However, the popular language of the Sephardim (Ladino) was a variant of Spanish mixed with a great deal of Hebrew, and written in Hebrew characters. The popular language of the Ashkenazim (Yiddish) was a variant of German, again mixed with a great deal of Hebrew, and also written in Hebrew characters.

After the dispersion from Palestine, the Jews of the Mediterranean and European worlds, almost uniquely among the people of the Middle Ages, were not primarily farmers. In the feudal Christian countries of the medieval world there was no easy way for a Jew to become a landowner or farmer. They were considered "strangers." As a matter of fact, in many countries Jews were not permitted to own land at all.

Thus they became merchants, artisans, and urban people in what was still an agricultural world. Because as a group they emphasized the virtue of learning the sacred scriptures in Hebrew, many became literate, and devoted themselves to studies in religion, philosophy, and medicine. Accordingly, even in the Middle Ages many of the doctors were Jews.

Despite the fact that Christianity began as a version of Judaism, early Christians soon broke with any Jewish connection (though they continued to consider the Hebrew Bible— called by Christians the "Old Testament"—part of their own holy books) and became very hostile to Jews and Judaism. Jews were banned in the middle ages from many countries of Medieval Europe. Often too, they were massacred, as during the First Crusade, or were confined in ghettos and forced to live in almost constant danger of loss of property, or even of life.

Large numbers of Jews were subjected to forced conversion—as in Spain, where in 1492, after the final victory by Spanish Christians over the Muslims, Jews were required either to convert or be forced to emigrate to whatever country would have them. Portuguese Jews suffered the same fate. This hostility to Jews stemmed from the fact that religion was the basis of social organization, and Jews, whether in Christian or Muslim lands, were "outsiders." (Christians were equally hostile to Muslims.)

In the United States

The first Jewish settlers in the United States were descendants of Portuguese Jews (Sephardim) who, forced to leave their homeland, eventually had settled in one of the few religiously tolerant countries of Europe at that time, the Netherlands. From the Netherlands a few had gone to settle in Brazil during a brief period (1630-1654) when that South American country was under Dutch rule. When Brazil was reconquered by the Portuguese, the Jews were forced to flee again, and a few finally landed in what is now New York (but was then New Amsterdam, still under Dutch rule in 1654). Thus was founded the first Jewish community in what became the United States.

Gradually, other Jews settled in other towns in the English colonies (Newport, Philadelphia, Charleston), so that by the time of the American Revolution there were a half-dozen Jewish communities in the United States, generally consisting of merchants. During the Revolution, Jews were active in support of the war, and one in particular, Haym Solomon, became known for his important work in helping to finance the revolutionary struggle. Jews found the new United States almost the only country in which they could live in freedom—without societal restrictions and able to practice their religion without penalty. Even the new American Constitution was in their favor, declaring unequivocally that no religion could be given preference at the national level. There was some discrimination at the state level, but in time it became established as law that no religious test for citizenship, for election to office, or for government employment or appointment, could be imposed.

Patterns of Immigration

In the 1830's there began substantial emigration to the United States from the various German-speaking lands of central Europe (this was of course before the formation of a unified Germany), where Jews still lived under medieval restrictions. Thus, to the American "Sephardim" of the earlier period of the seventeenth and eighteenth centuries were added great numbers of "Ashkenazim." By 1880, there were about 250,000 Jews in the United States, established in many communities and mostly engaged in trade, both small and large.

After 1880, just as immigration in general to this country shifted from Western, Northern, and Central Europe to Eastern and Southern Europe, so too it did for Jews. Many hundreds of thousands of Jews came to this country as immigrants from the Austro-Hungarian Empire, the Russian Empire, and Rumania. Jews left the latter two countries because they were subject to particularly fierce official persecution— economic, political, and religious. By the mid-1920's, when mass immigration from Europe came to an end (owing to the passage of stringent immigration laws), there were 4 million Jews in this country, constituting about 4% percent of the population.

There were small waves of immigration of Jews after the 1920's: some escaped from Hitler's Germany in the 1930's; some survived the Nazi effort to kill the Jews of Europe and came here in the later 1940's. There has in recent decades been some immigration of Russian and Israeli Jews. But this immigration is very small. In recent decades, there has been hardly any growth in the Jewish population at all, since Jewish families ordinarily are extremely small. Thus Jews now form about 2% of the American population, and their average age is higher than that of other American ethnic groups.

Almost all Jewish immigration to this country has been of Jews escaping from persecution. For this reason Jews, more than other immigrants, came with the intentions of staying and of becoming American citizens as rapidly as possible. They became active in American political life quite early, and many became successful economically. For example, early German-Jewish immigrants went into trade primarily, but many as very small traders indeed—in fact, as peddlers. However, some became quite successful: Such names as Bloomingdale's, Gimbel's, Abraham and Strauss, and Bamberger's, among department stores, reflect their success in retail trade. ("Levis" are named after Levi Strauss, who first produced the popular denim trousers for miners in Gold Rush California.)

On the other hand, later-arriving East European Jews were primarily workers. While they had been artisans and small businessmen in Europe, in this country the only work available for them was generally in the clothing or building trades. However, substantial numbers did go into business, and succeeded in a variety of fields: clothing, real estate, construction, scrap metal, automobile parts, mass entertainment (such as the movies), theater, television.

Some Accomplishments

Perhaps the most marked success of Jews has been in education. As is true of some other groups (for example, Japanese Americans), Jews eagerly took up opportunities for education. Since half of the East European Jewish immigrants in this country settled in New

York City, they had the opportunity to attend that city's tuition-free schools of higher education (the College of the City of New York, Hunter College, Brooklyn College, and others founded later), and for decades the student bodies of these institutions were predominantly Jewish. (The "free tuition" policy was changed in 1976. Newer population groups in New York City recognized that the change was forced by the city's financial problems, but called attention to the fact that the change came only when large numbers of non-whites began at last to be enrolled.)

As a result of the high proportion of their numbers going on to higher education, Jews proved to be prominent, out of proportion to their numbers, in such professions as law, medicine, and college and university teaching. Many of the American Nobel Prize winners in the sciences and medicine have been Jews. Similarly, a good number of distinguished Jewish legal scholars and lawyers have become judges. Jews are perhaps proudest of those who became distinguished Supreme Court Justices, such as Louis D. Brandeis, Benjamin Cardozo, and Felix Frankfurter.

Jews also have achieved high office politically: Herbert Lehman, who was a Governor of New York State, the first director of UNRRA (the post-World War II United Nations Relief and Rehabilitation Agency), and a notable Senator from New York; Jacob Javits, who served for many years as another memorable Senator from New York; Abraham Ribicoff, who was a Governor of Connecticut, the Secretary of Health, Education, and Welfare, and also a Senator (in his case from Connecticut); and Arthur Goldberg, who served as Secretary of Labor, Supreme Court Justice, and Ambassador to the United Nations.

Indeed, American Jews have been active in seemingly all spheres of American culture: as writers (Saul Bellow, Bernard Malamud, Philip Roth, Lionel Trilling); painters and sculptors (Ben Shahn, Mark Rothko, Louise Nevelson); composers (Aaron Copland); and in particular as composers and lyricists of popular music (George Gershwin, Irving Berlin, Rodgers and Hart, Kurt Weill).

Varieties of Religious Groups

This success in American life has been paralleled by many changes among Jews. For example, few Jews in the U.S. now speak Yiddish; the great majority have been raised speaking English. Jewish religion has also undergone substantial change in this country. In the nineteenth century, German Jews changed Jewish prayers and services to make them more like those of American Protestantism, and substituted English for much of the Hebrew in Jewish religious services. Indeed, such substantial changes took place that an entirely new denomination, "Reform Judaism" (first established in Germany), spread among American Jewish communities. Jews engaged in more modest modifications establishing a second denomination—"Conservative Judaism." Many Jews, particularly those from Eastern Europe, remained faithful to Jewish religious practices unchanged since the Middle Ages, and are called "Orthodox." The most Orthodox Jews are the Hasidim, who comprise a number of sects which try to preserve traditional customs.

Although all of these people are Jews they disagree about many points, and their rabbis (Jewish religious leaders) are trained in different seminaries (Hebrew Union

College for the Reform, the Jewish Theological Seminary for the Conservative, and Yeshiva University and other institutions for the Orthodox). Individual congregations belong to different nationwide religious organizations. There is no hierarchy in the Jewish religion, no Pope or Chief Rabbi, no system by which some rabbis are formally raised over others. Each congregation is independent, though most are members of a congregational organization which reflects their point of view.

Other Community Organizations

Along with the institutions of Jewish religion in this country may be found many other Jewish organizations. Thus in each community one may find, in addition to Reform, Conservative, and Orthodox temples and synagogues (generally with associated religious schools), Jewish hospitals, old age homes, community centers, social service organizations, Jewish schools, and other cultural facilities. In addition, in each community there is generally a central fund-raising body which solicits funds for all these institutions.

Important as the focus of many of these fund-raising organizations may be, however, the spotlight remains on the needs of Jews in the state of Israel. American Jews have contributed heavily to help refugees from Europe and Arab countries in the Middle East to settle there, and continue to provide assistance toward the maintenance of social and welfare institutions in Israel.

Fighting Discrimination and Prejudice

Among Jewish organizations are also to be found some whose major aim is to fight anti-Semitism both in this country and abroad, and to protect the rights of Jews everywhere. The chief organizations that carry on these tasks are the American Jewish Committee, the Anti-Defamation League of B'nai B'rith, and the American Jewish Congress. Just as there is no central leadership in American Jewish religion, there is no central leadership in the defense of Jewish rights; each organization is independent and acts as it sees fit. These groups protect the civil rights of Jews, just as the NAACP protects the civil rights of Blacks, and operate by way of research, discussion, and legal action.

Organized anti-Semitism is not considered a major problem of Jews in this country today. In the past, however, despite the political freedom granted to Jews (as to people of all other religions), anti-Semitism has been a quite serious problem. In the late nineteenth century, for instance, as some Jews began to become wealthy and prominent, social clubs closed their doors to them. In the 1920's, as greater numbers of Jews began to attend Ivy League colleges, these began to discriminate by instituting quotas in order to hold down the number of Jewish students. At the same time, medical schools began to discriminate against Jews, many of whom wanted to become doctors.

In the 1920's, 1930's, and 1940's, discrimination against Jews was endemic in many occupations: among major corporations of almost every kind, in which Jews could not get jobs as executives; in colleges and universities, where Jews could not get jobs as teachers. This discrimination began to weaken only after the horrors of World War II, as our society became more liberal and tolerant. Fortunately, this movement to tolerance was aided by the passage of laws forbidding discrimination in employment, education, and housing.

Jews were among the most active leaders in the movement for such laws, and it was in states where Jews were numerous, like New York, where such laws were passed first and became most effective. In this work, Jews were closely associated with Black and other civil-rights leaders. Ultimately, this movement triumphed nationally in the Civil Rights Acts of 1964, 1965, and 1968, banning discrimination in public facilities, employment, government programs, voting, and housing. By the 1960's, discrimination against Jews had been quite reduced.

Whereas Jews were closely allied with Blacks in the fight for civil-rights legislation, developments since the late 1960's have created some tension and conflicts between Jews and Blacks. The emphasis by government on affirmative action in employment (the active effort, required by government, to hire larger numbers of certain minorities) and the rise of favored treatment for certain minorities in admission to medical schools and other competitive professional programs, have divided Jews. Having themselves been victims of quotas which limited them in the past, they are allergic to any policy which even looks like a quota. They question in particular the goals required by affirmative action for Blacks and some other minorities in employment, and the "goals" instituted by medical and other schools in order to enroll a certain number of minority students. Jews disagree on whether these policies are right or wrong, and Jewish organizations often are split on these difficult issues.

While to some minorities Jews may appear to be part of the "majority" (because they generally are white or light-skinned, and because many have achieved higher education, moved into rewarding occupations, and earn high incomes), Jews themselves are very much aware of their minority status and the dangers that may face them again one day. Hitler's effort to kill all Jews ended only with his loss of World War II in 1945, and he did succeed in killing most of the Jews of Europe—6 million. Almost every American Jew has relatives who died in the Holocaust; hundreds of thousands only barely escaped themselves. The permanent danger in which the small state of Israel lives also is something that reminds Jews of their minority status and the dangers they may yet face—even in America.

The Jewish Child in School

While Jews have a reputation for being good and eager students, this is of course not always the case. On the whole, though, there is little in American school practice that the Jewish student finds difficult to manage. Jewish students may be out of school for religious holidays (the number of holidays depends on how Orthodox they are in observance). They will probably not be happy if there is much emphasis on Christmas, and the more the specifically Christian and religious aspect of Christmas is emphasized, the less happy they will be.

Generally, their parents strongly urge them to do well in school, and to that end provide much support. The children generally are highly motivated academically—almost all Jewish children *expect* to go to college. Parents usually will be very willing to cooperate with teachers, requests for conferences included. In the past, Jewish children often were ashamed of their heritage, as was true of so many immigrant children. However, as Jewish children have become increasingly third generation, this has become much less true, and indeed many are quite proud of their heritage.

Relationships with Israel

The relationship of American Jews to Israel sometimes creates difficulties and misunderstandings with their fellow Americans. *Every* immigrant group has maintained close ties of friendship and concern with its homeland, and in this respect Jews are not different from other immigrant and ethnic groups. But it is also true that Israel is not an ordinary homeland. It was created by Jewish refugees from other countries, literally both before and after World War II.

Before Israel was founded in 1948, hundreds of thousands of Jews had settled in Palestine as refugees from Russia, Poland, and Germany, under the auspices of the Zionist movement (whose aim was to establish a national Jewish homeland). In 1948, the state of Israel was established. Great numbers of Jews who had survived Hitler's Holocaust, and others who faced persecution in Arab countries, fled to Israel. Nor has immigration to Israel ceased. In recent years, hundreds of thousands of Russian Jews have left that country to settle in Israel, and the entire Jewish population of Ethiopia—black Jews—has been evacuated from that country, where they faced terrible discrimination.

For a variety of reasons, most American Jews have an intense interest in Israel. Few American Jews come from Israel, but many of them have relatives and friends who may have settled there. Also, Israel has been for decades the most endangered country in the world. It is a small state surrounded by numerous and hostile neighbors who have never recognized its existence. Then, too, Israel plays a central role in the Jewish religion. It is thus understandable that Israel should play a central role in the consciousness of American Jews. And it does: They raise great sums of money for Israel's needs, and support the policies necessary for its defense on the American political scene.

The United States is closely tied to Israel: because Israel is a democracy, because we were instrumental in its birth, and because American Jews are passionately concerned that it should survive and prosper. But tensions may arise in the relations of any two states, no matter how closely allied, and they certainly do between Israel and the United States. And in these circumstances, American Jews often are placed in the difficult position of deciding whether they should support the views of the Israeli government or of their own. For example: Henry Kissinger, a Jewish refugee from Nazi Germany, was American Secretary of State for a number of years. As such, he represented the interests of the American Government in trying to move toward a stable peace in the Middle East. He negotiated with heads of all governments, even of those, such as Saudi Arabia, that are strongly anti-Jewish, as well as anti-Israel. His position admittedly was unique, but in different degrees other American Jews face somewhat similar dilemmas because of the extreme danger in which Israel lives, in which any misstep may lead to its destruction, and because of the importance of the United States in contributing to its defense.

A true peace in the Middle East would reduce anxiety among Jews in America as well as help to resolve economic and social problems in the Eastern Mediterranean. It has not been achieved during the first four decades of Israel's existence, but in recent years a number of Arab countries have agreed to recognize Isreal.

Problems of "Survival"

American Jews often talk about "survival." They mean many things by that term. They mean the simple brute physical survival of Israel as a Jewish state, and of its people, who are (so far) endlessly threatened. They also mean the survival of Jews *as* Jews in the United States, where the threats to survival take a very different form. For instance, Jews now have very small families. In fact, they already have achieved zero population growth. Whereas they were once almost 4% of the American people, they are now less than 3%; and, owing to their low rate of reproduction, they will become still fewer. Their political influence will of course then be smaller, as will be their power to advocate specific Jewish interests, such as the defense of Israel.

Jews also are concerned that their decline in numbers may become even more rapid because of intermarriage. Almost all American Jewish young people go to college, where they meet non-Jews, and many marry them. Will their children be raised as Jews, or not? Jewish schools already are often in difficulty because there are so few Jewish children. Will not intermarriage reduce their numbers further?

Jews are less worried about another ground for population loss—religious conversion to Christianity. This sort of departure from their faith was much more common in the earlier years of Jewish history in this country, when the Jewish minority was tiny and the attraction of the majority religion was greater. But conversion is still such an issue among Jews that in recent years certain prominent political personalities have become nagging reminders to them of the ongoing possibility of further losses to the Jewish faith through it. For example, Senator Barry Goldwater came from a Jewish family which had been converted to Christianity some generations back. And such other leading personalities of Jewish birth in America as James Schlesinger and Michael Blumenthal have converted to Christianity.

"Survival," to American Jews, refers not only to simple physical continuity, but also to *how* one survives—to the *quality* of life. There are many concerns in this respect. For example: When Jews were concentrated in the large cities (principally New York), they could support many institutions of all types, and therefore it was easy for them to participate in religious, cultural, political, and educational activities. That capability became more difficult as they (along with other middle-class Americans) were suburbanized and so no longer lived in dense concentrations. The Jewish population of the great cities has dropped considerably. In fact, many large cities are almost *without* Jews, as most have moved to the suburbs. While they can maintain their synagogues and temples in the suburbs, they cannot retain the variety of institutions they once had when their numbers were greater and more concentrated.

Immigrants knew and experienced the more intense Jewish lives in Eastern Europe. Their children, far removed from that life, know little Yiddish, and less Hebrew. Their children's children—and American Jews are by now predominantly third-generation—

know even less about traditional Jewish life. They still are Jews, attend synagogues (at least on the holiest days), and contribute to Jewish organizations and causes. But as their spiritual roots become more and more thinned by extension there is great concern among the more tradition-minded Jews as to how (indeed, whether) the spiritual quality of Jewish life can be maintained.

Jewish Traditions and Customs

Jewish life traditionally has been rich in observances, festivals, holidays, and customs. One observance involves the dietary laws that prescribe foods which may or may not be eaten, and the manner in which animals are to be slaughtered if they are to be considered "kosher"—that is, fit to be eaten by "observant" Jews. Although many Jews maintain these observances, a growing number have departed from these ways,

Although Jewish tradition prescribes a number of religious holidays, there is considerable variation among Jews in America as to the attention paid them, since now some are regarded as more important than others. Passover celebrates the Jewish exodus from ancient Egypt, where they had been enslaved. During this period matzos (the kind of unleavened bread that the Jews leaving Egypt prepared for their journey into the desert of Sinai) is eaten. Chanukah celebrates the deliverance of the ancient Temple in Jerusalem from the Greek-Syrian rulers of Palestine by the heroic Maccabees. Rosh Hashana and Yom Kippur are, respectively, Jewish New Year and (soon afterward) the Day of Atonement. Rosh Hashana and Yom Kippur are days for solemn prayer and personal penitence, and their observance is quite different from the joyous celebration of the secular New Year. Succoth (the feast of Tabernacles, a harvest festival) and Shevuoth (celebrating the giving of the Laws on Mount Sinai) are holidays on which the ancient Israelites would make pilgrimages—as also on Passover—to the Temple in Jerusalem. Whereas Jewish children generally will not attend school on Rosh Hashana, Yom Kippur, Succoth, Passover, and Shevuoth, there is considerable variation of opinion and pratice among Jewish families as to which holidays require absence from schools.

A marked tradition among Jews is "tsedakah," the giving of charity. This extends from small contributions of pennies in a charity box kept in the home, to the endowment of hospitals, universities, and cultural institutions. In most cities there is a federation of charitable and cultural institutions for which an annual fund drive is made through the United Jewish Appeal. In addition, the Jewish tradition of philanthropy is exemplified in generous support by individuals to universities, hospitals, museums, cultural centers, neighborhood houses, and social causes sponsored by secular and non-Jewish religious communities alike. The Jewish Hospital in many cities (whatever its formal name) gladly serves people who are not Jewish but are in need of help.

Of course, Jews retain the right not to agree among themselves on just what the specific spiritual content of American Jewish life should be. Some emphasize adherence to the old faith and its practices; some emphasize the pursuit of social justice—a theme first raised by the Jewish prophets; some believe that any form of liberal or progressive thought is Jewish, and that a good Jew must be either liberal or progressive. (Indeed, Jews overwhelmingly are left of center in their political views. Most Jews in public life are Democrats, and indeed liberal Democrats.)

Spiritual Revival

In recent years, we have seen among young Jews—as, naturally, among the young in other ethnic groups—new and serious efforts to revive Jewish spiritual life, even among those born in this country and with no direct knowledge of the intense Jewish life of the past. Young Jews have founded magazines, have established communities for Jewish living, and have begun to expand their interest in Jewish education. One sure sign of this is the increasing number of Jewish studies programs in our colleges.

In this attempt to strengthen Jewish life, Israel plays a unique role. Hebrew, the language of the Bible, is its daily speech; Jewish scholarship flourishes more actively there than anywhere else; it is by intention a Jewish state; and it offers a unique experience in kinds of Jewish living to young Jews. Israel becomes the curriculum of the Jewish education that most young Jews get.

As against many other ethnic groups, Jews, defined by religion as well as by peoplehood, and linked to Israel through ties of both spiritual and actual kinship, are not in much danger of losing their identity in American life. However, as they become more remote in time from the dense and whole Jewish life that their forefathers knew, they nevertheless wonder what the content of that identity may become.

Suggested Readings

Cohen, Steven M. *American Modernity and Jewish Identity*. New York: Tavistock Publications, 1983. A study, based on survey data, of changes in the Jewish community of Boston.

Cohen, Steven M. *American Assimilation or Jewish Revival?* Bloomington: Indiana University Press, 1988. A study, based on survey data, of the Jewish community of New York. Glazer, Nathan. *American Judaism*. Chicago: University of Chicago Press, 1957, 1972. A brief account of the development of the Jewish religion in America, presented in the context of Jewish social and economic development.

Howe, Irving. *The World of Our Fathers*. New York: Harcourt Brace Jovanovich, 1976. This is a detailed study of the life of the Jewish immigrants from Eastern Europe who settled on the lower east side of New York City. That community (and others like it) is the kind of place where the forefathers of most of today's American Jews first lived on arriving in this country. Rich and detailed, this study explains why American Jewish culture is the way it is.

Silberman, Charles E. *A Certain People: American Jews and Their Lives Today*. New York: Summit Books, 1985. A comprehensive survey of the American Jewish community in the early 1980s.

Sklare, Marshall. *America's Jews*. New York: Random House, 1971. An informed study of the contemporary American Jewish community.

Sklare, Marshall. *The Jew in American Society* and *The Jewish Community in America*. New York: Behrman House, 1974. These two books are collections of important studies of American Jews dealing with their history, politics, economic role, community, and religion.

About the Author
Nathan Glazer is professor emeritus of education and sociology at Harvard University. He is the author (with Daniel P. Moynihan) of *Beyond the Melting Pot, American Judaism*, and *Affirmative Discrimination*.

Chapter *12*

The Korean Americans

HAROLD CHU

Korean Americans have displayed the very same qualities of hard work, adaptability, self-confidence, and strong faith in opportunity that are represented by America. Every group migrating to the United States has experienced a certain degree of culture shock, adjustment stress, and sociocultural disruption, caused mainly by that group's distinctive culture and language, limited English proficiency, and unique physical characteristics. Among Koreans, these problems have been most severe for the younger generation, individuals caught in the middle of transition as they exist between the rather different worlds of school and home.

One of the most crucial areas challenging educators of newly immigrated Koreans is that of biculturality. Because children's thought patterns and values are formed and developed early in life through education and interaction between the school and the home, the role of educators becomes extremely important in the socialization and acculturation process of the young. Biculturality becomes a useful contrast for realizing that children can develop both new values and cultural orientation in America, even while understanding and developing cultural traits represented by the Korean family and community.

Although Korean Americans are less well known than other Asian-American groups, the presence of Korean-American communities in the five major cities (Los Angeles, New York, Chicago, San Francisco, and the Washington, DC, area) is so significant that they are now a major factor in the social and economic life in those cities. The 1970 census indicated that there were approximately 70,000 Koreans in the United States; but, what with their high immigration rate of roughly 30,000 a year, their numbers have grown significantly. At the time of the 1980 census, 354,529 Koreans were living in the United States, an increase of 413 percent between 1970 and 1980. The number of Koreans living in the United States as of the 1990 census report was 798,849, an increase of 125.3 percent over the 1980 figure.

The existence of a Korean community in the United States dates back to the early 1900s, when the initial wave of Korean migrants (mainly laborers and their families) began to reach the West Coast via Hawaii (Kim, 1978). The very first Korean migrants— 55 males, 21 females, and 25 children—sailed for Hawaii in 1903. The males were farmers who had agreed to contract with Hawaiian plantation owners. They also were lured by promises of payment in American gold. However, they were paid between $16 and $18 a month, averaging from 65 to 70 cents a day, working 10 hours per day in the hot sun, Monday through Saturday. The plantation owners worked out a policy of drawing workers from Asia because, for example, whereas recruiting and transporting one Caucasian laborer cost about $250, the cost for one Asian was only $70 (Choy, 1979). Some 7,226 Korean migrants arrived in Hawaii on 65 different ships between 1903 and 1905 (Choy, 1979). Koreans from Hawaii came to the West Coast because the railway companies needed manpower and offered slightly higher wages than Hawaii plantation owners. In addition, job opportunities for Orientals were better and more varied on the mainland; agricultural work in California, and railroad and mining jobs in Oregon, Washington, Montana, and Utah were wide open. General housework, cleaning, restaurant work, janitorial work, and other underpaid jobs involving hard physical labor were available in the urban areas (Choy, 1979). About 1,000 Koreans entered San Francisco from Hawaii between 1904 and 1907 and then scattered up and down the West Coast, although most remained in California.

After the Protectorate Treaty of 1905, when Japan occupied Korea, Korean migration to the United States was suspended because Japan assumed jurisdiction over Korea's relations with foreign nations. There is no way to determine the actual numbers of migrants between 1905 and 1945 because Koreans entered the United States with Japanese passports. Technically, no Korean migrants were admitted to the United States until the Immigration and Naturalization Act of 1952 allocated to Korea an annual quota of 100 (Lee, 1975). The Immigration Act of 1965 reopened the gates to immigrants from Asia, including Korea, allowing a quota of 20,000 immigrants a year for each country and also the entry of family members on a nonquota basis. Currently, half of all immigrants entering the United States are Asian (Takaki, 1989).

Unlike the earlier Korean migrants who came alone under labor contracts, the recent arrivals from Korea have come for permanent residence, already accompanied by young children as well as elderly persons. There are three major reasons for recent Korean immigrants: (1) educational opportunity, (2) economic improvement, and (3) family reunion. Koreans come with the intention of completing their education at a college or university rather than getting advanced job training in their fields. Their desire for higher education for their children also may be important in motivating some of the adults to immigrate. They do not immigrate with the idea of getting additional job training in the field; rather, they come looking for better-paying positions in their present ones so that they will be able to enjoy a better standard of living. When they arrive they usually have relatives already living here who may well be somewhat less recent arrivals.

Culture and Acculturation Process

Korean Patterns

Korean philosophical and other value systems have been formulated by means of a combination of several different roots. The three main ones are (1) Korean indigenous belief systems that have evolved since prehistoric periods and usually have been categorized as Shamanism, (2) Confucianism that originated in China, and (3) Mahayama Buddhism that sprang up in India but was imported to Korea through China (Yum, 1987). To understand Korean thought and communication patterns, it is necessary to have some understanding of these systems and to explore the extent of the impact of each.

The religious and philosophical systems that have had the greatest impact on the social, behavioral, and thought patterns of Korea, China, and Japan are Confucianism, Buddhism, and Taoism. Buddhism rules the mind, Taoism the body, and Confucianism the political society (Lew, 1970). Buddhism can be said to rule the mind because it strives either to control or to eliminate worldly desires so that suffering and pain will disappear from the world. Confucianism is the philosophy of human nature and proper human relationships, which together are the basis of society. By emphasizing practical human activities and relationships in society, it rules the social order. Taoism is mainly a philosophy of nature and an attempt to transcend the artificial human-made culture and society. It tries to bring one into closer harmony with nature, sometimes by withdrawing from the world and entering into the isolation of the mountains, where one practices a kind of training and asceticism that results in good health and long life. In this sense, Taoism rules the body. These generalizations are somewhat superficial, but they do demonstrate the tendency of each system.

Buddhism approaches the understanding of man through the understanding of the mind; Confucianism through human nature; and Taoism through the understanding of feeling (Kim, 1974). Buddhism advocates the cultivation of *sim* ("mind"), Taoism of *ki* ("energy"), and Confucianism of *no* ("reason"). As a way to transcend the falseness of the world and the suffering due to worldly concerns, Buddhism advocates the cultivation of the mind.

Taoism was based on the mystical concept of Tao, or Way of the Universe—the idea that man can achieve his salvation by obeying the Way or the underlying principle of the universe. This concept is based on a cosmological theory of *yin* and *yang*, representing the female principle and the male principle, respectively. Yin and yang are thought to produce all universal phenomena through their mutual interaction. Taoism, with its mystic and naturalistic inclination, was appealing to the early Koreans and it found the congenial soil and slowly took roots in the depth of Korean mind.

Confucianism, on the other hand, advocates that it is reason that rightly absorbs and unifies both *sim* and *ki*. The principle of Tao, or Way, constitutes the essence of all things in the universe. As man's mind partakes of this principle, its power of reason enables man not only to know what all things are but also to understand how they ought to be and to work harmoniously. Human relations and conduct, therefore, are determined by the principle or reason that underlies all phenomena.

In Korea, Taoism has not developed into a separate religious or philosophical system but rather has been absorbed into other belief systems, especially Buddhism. Among the three belief systems, Confucianism has had the most profound impact because it was the official philosophy of the Yi Dynasty (1392–1910). It was thoroughly institutionalized and systematically diffused to the people. Confucianism is a philosophy of humanity. In studying human nature and motivation, Confucianism suggests that there are four human natures from which the right conduct arises: *jen* (humanism), *i* (righteousness), *li* (property), and *chih* (wisdom). By contrast, the seven human natures by which people deviate from proper conduct were identified as joy, anger, sorrow, fear, love, hatred, and desire. Therefore, Confucian education strived to elevate and develop the four principles and suppress the seven human passions. However, it helps to know that the concept of *jen* and the concept of man are the same in meaning. Therefore, to ask the meaning of *jen* is to ask the meaning of man, since they are one and the same question, in the sense that the goal of human nature, the kind of man we are to become, the kind of man we should become, and the kind of man that would exist, all is summed up in jen (Yi, 1973). In Confucianism the ideal man who is really and fully man is called a man of jen.

As a philosophy of humanity, Confucianism is most elaborate in explicating proper human relationships and providing appropriate ways to handle the rituals that function to maintain social order (Chu, 1978). Confucianism devised five moral codes to regulate the five basic human relationships: (1) intimacy between father and son, (2) orders between elders and youngers, (3) loyalty between king and subject, (4) distinction in duties between husband and wife, and (5) faith between friends. The original meaning of the five moral principles is better described as (1) father love, son filiality; (2) elder brother brotherly love/younger brother reverence; (3) king justice/subject loyalty; (4) husband initiative/wife obedience; and (5) friends' mutual faith.

Affection Between Father and Son

Traditionally, affection is never demonstrated openly between father and son; however, one would give his life for the other. The father is the disciplinarian and is very strict. Relationships between young and old are orderly and formal. The father is the respected and unquestioned head of the family and he (theoretically at least) rules with almost absolute power, if he so desires. He has full responsibility to feed the family; to find work for the members; to approve all decisions and marriages, and to approve the future life of the younger members of the family, especially the son. During the lifetime of the father, the son must submit to his father's desires and advice. The son must regard his own plans and desires as secondary and subject to the father's approval.

This relationship is still maintained to a high degree in Korean-American homes, where father and son are friends, and as "pals" they will go fishing, make major purchases such as a house or car, and do things together whenever they find time (without the wife and other female members of the family). The father, of course, prefers to remain in his traditional role, but this desire sometimes can be thwarted by practical circumstances. For example, when children bring in homework and ask for fatherly help and he has only limited English proficiency, he is placed in a hopeless situation. Naturally, the father must maintain his dignity, and yet this unhappy situation can force his children to lose confidence in him. As a result, the son may well become disrespectful toward his father, and the father might lose his prized dignity and become upset. Eventually, the father and the son may reach a state of continual frustration. This is a condition directly contrary to family aims, and thus thwarted at every opportunity.

Respect for Elders

Relationships among members of the family are always vertical rather than horizontal. According to traditions (usually strongly enforced), elders are superior in the home, and so should be revered and honored, both in word and deed. Because of the Korean cultural patterns of both nuclear and extended families, the grandparents are the most respected. To be called "Grandfather" or "Grandmother" is a sign of great respect. For example, every home in Korea, no matter how poor, allots the best room in the house, and serves the finest delicacies, to the honored grandparents. The manner in which elderly people are sometimes shunted aside in the United States and the concept of an "old people's home" are considered extremely shocking to Koreans.

In the United States, a clash of values has taken place. No longer are the Korean-American grandparents given the best rooms or meals. Instead, perhaps for economic reasons, things are shared more equally. However, grandparents still are warmly respected, and their status in the family still is unquestioned. For example, in Korean-American households, children now exposed to the American way of living are questioning the one-way communication at home, except in the case of their grandparents, whom they almost invariably continue to respect.

Korean-American speech still is expected to be highly honorific toward elders and superiors, and much more often than not it is. Traditionally, the eldest son's obligation is to care for his parents, boys enjoy freedom, and girls are restricted, but all this has changed to a great degree. Now both boys and girls of appropriate age cooperate in the care of at least the elderly, and, in some cases, supplement the family income. Proper role behavior is, as usual, taught during childhood and adolescence, but has been modified greatly by the new Korean immigrants. Girls now are taught home management, housekeeping, sewing, and culinary arts and enjoy more personal freedom than ever before. They are, in fact, joining women of many other backgrounds in entering new fields of unaccustomed endeavor.

Loyalty Between King and Subject

For centuries, Koreans were subject to the caste system that divided their society into the *Yangban* nobility and the commoners. This experience colored latter Korean-American school of thought. The fall of the Yi Dynasty (1910), and consequently equality for all, came in the early 1900s, due mainly to Christian influence. Koreans have great respect for learning and scholastic achievement—education is taken very seriously by nearly every Korean. Therefore, teachers are held in the highest esteem. Respect for the teacher has been carried over to the United States, where teachers are considered "parents away from home" and should never be contradicted.

It is rude to call a person by name without due discretion. An honorary title has to follow the name of an older and more prominent person. The Korean language is devoid of an acceptable title equivalent to, for example, "Mr." There, the most widely used Korean term is *sunsaeng nim* (teacher) for one's superior. When a younger person becomes a professional and is then higher in social standings, the parents' acquaintances address the younger person in a formal manner. The younger person can demur and ask not to be honored.

Distinction in Duties Between Husband and Wife

Men still feel superior to women. Traditionally, women are faithful, cooperative, quiet, and unquestioningly dutiful. The wife's place is at home, and she is expected to fit into her husband's family or to perish. The historical life of Korean women always has been one of obedience and humiliation. If we look at the Confucian Way of the Three Female Obediences and Seven Reasons for Expelling a Wife, if she does not make her marriage life successful, we may well know the traditional women's situation. The three obediences are the following: when young, woman is obedient to her parents; when married, to her husband; and when old, to her son. The seven reasons for expulsion are the following: if she does not serve her parent-in-law well, if she has no children, if she is lecherous, if she is too jealous, if she has an incurable disease, if she talks too much, and if she steals.

Christianity has introduced a new appreciation of the value of the individual, and especially of the women. The impact of the combination of Christianity and modernization has greatly changed the status of Korean women. They now are more verbal and more involved in the care of the children, as well as in the area of household management. The working mother in a Korean-American home, having won her independence, has become more assertive within her family because she is now her husband's equal.

Faith Between and Among Friends

To be ready to help, guide, and counsel a friend is a very strong principle with the Koreans. For example, in Korea, an alumni association of high school or college is one of the most powerful organizations of friendships for life. *Sunbae* (seniors) and *hubae* (juniors) have a vertical relationship not only while they are in school but also after their graduation. The sunbae always takes care of the welfare of the hubae in terms of finding a job, financial assistance, family matters (especially arranging marriage and counseling, should there be a marriage problem), and other important personal matters. It is considered that the business of the alumni association for friendships takes precedence over all other personal business. Even in the United States, numerous Korean alumni associations are the extension of the practice in Korea.

Cross-Cultural Differences in Nonverbal Behavior Between Americans and Koreans

In the United States, Korean children in school, at home, and in whatever environment are going through an intense period of cultural transition and adjustment, and therefore must try to modify and reorder their ingrained values, attitudes, perceptions, and beliefs. Cultural differences in the nonverbal behavior of Korean Americans could well be one of the most important areas through which variations from any "norm" of nonlinguistic communication with Americans can be understood.

Whether Americans or Koreans, we are unique individuals. There are differences in behavior and therefore there are differences in judgments about the behavior of others. The most consistent of the differences between Americans and Koreans can be described as cultural. Many of us tend to think of a culture in terms of tangible things such as housing, food, clothing, festivals, holidays, and the like. Culture can also be defined as the material and nonmaterial aspects of a way of life that are shared and transmitted among members of a society. All of this is *learned* behavior. Much of the learning is informal and starts when we are first beginning to speak and to understand our environment. The early years of childhood are tremendously important in terms of both learning the nonmaterial aspects of one's culture and the development of one's personality.

Cross-cultural differences between Americans and Koreans in nonverbal behavior are mentioned here in terms of (1) expressions of thought, (2) manners and courtesies, and (3) privacy, gifts, and gestures.

Expressions of Thoughts

Expressive and Nonexpressive

The American way of both thinking and showing facial expression reflecting reactions to thoughts is direct, accurate, and candid. The Korean way can be said to be vague, indirect, nonexpressive, and passionless. The U.S. teacher who has Korean children in the classroom should expect that it will take a certain amount of time for them to adjust to the American way. Meanwhile, the Korean child is most likely to behave in a passive, nonparticipatory manner unless the teacher calls him or her by name or requests anyone at all (unnamed) to answer a question. The Korean child will hardly volunteer to answer, especially if the child has limited English proficiency and has not been acculturated. Acculturated Korean-American parents are quite likely to show enthusiastic facial expressions. This is usually an indication that the teacher can communicate with the parents at ease.

American couples smile at the time of their weddings, looking happy, but in Korea, neither the bride nor the groom is supposed to smile at that time. They should look serious at least before and during the ceremony. In Korean society, one is regarded as lighthearted or frivolous if he or she show enthusiasm in such a circumstance.

Whether one is overjoyed with another person's magnificent generosity or faces sad affairs, it is considered a virtue to hide one's own feelings. In such and similar cases, Koreans can detect whether others are really pleased or dissatisfied with them by what is called *nunchi*. This is the ability to guess or sense another's feelings, sentiments, and thinking by perceiving the environment and atmosphere that surround a situation.

Americans tend not to compromise or concede when it is contrary to common sense, regardless of the rank of the other person. In the case of Koreans, however, if they try to explain something to a superior on the basis of common sense, this is regarded as impertinent and reproachable. Therefore, there is no other way but to solve problems with *nunchi*, detecting the other person's facial expressions (kinesics and occultism) as well as inner feelings. For example, it is not unusual for parents to scold their child by saying, "Don't you have *nunchi*?" when he or she says or does something wrong or unexpected. *Nunchi* is an effort to cope with the individual and unique feelings, attitudes, desires, and tastes of especially one's superior. This effort too often leads to a loss of ego in the sense that one's behavior is motivated by the desire to please ostensibly significant others.

The Korean method of social intercourse, to pretend to like something though it is bad and to pretend to dislike even though it is good, has different implications than the American method that publicly dissects and analyzes everything. However, when Koreans get angry and lose their tempers, they do not hesitate to reveal their feelings in angry words or fistfights, regardless of onlookers. Paradoxically, they change from lambs to lions.

Another vital concept to understand in Korea is *kibun*, which is one of the most important factors influencing the conduct and the relationship with others. The word literally means inner feelings. If one's *kibun* is good, then one functions smoothly and with ease and feels like a million dollars. If one's *kibun* is upset or bad, then things may come to a complete halt and one feels depressed. The word has no true English equivalent, but "mood" is close. In interpersonal relationships, keeping the *kibun* in good order often takes precedence over all other considerations.

In business functions, businessmen try to operate in a manner that will enhance the *kibun* of both persons. To damage the *kibun* may effectively cut off relationships and create an enemy. One does not tend to do business with a person who has damaged one's *kibun*. Much of the disturbance of *kibun* in interpersonal relationships has to do with lower-class persons disturbing higher-class persons. Thus, for example, a teacher can scold a student in the class and no individual feels hurt or no one's *kibun* is especially disturbed.

Proper interpersonal relationships are all important among Koreans, and there is little concept of equality in relationships among Koreans. Three of the five major ethical principles based on Confucian teaching are: (1) orders between elders and youngers, (2) discretion between husband and wife, and (3) loyalty between king and subject. These three principles in terms of age, sex, and status establish the strict vertical relationship. The vertical relationships also are reflected in the Korean language. Thus, for example, there is no word for "brother," but there is for "younger brother" and "elder brother"; the same is true for "sister." This is in contrast to American horizontal relationships in terms of equality reflected in the English language. It is essential for one to know the level of society (status, age) and to know one's place in the scheme of things. In relationships, it is often necessary to appear to lower oneself in selfless humility and give honor to other people. A well-respected Korean often assumes an attitude of self-negation and self-effacement in social and business contacts. To put oneself forward is considered proud arrogance and worthy of scorn.

Protocol is extremely important to Koreans when meeting others; if you do not appreciate one's actual position and do not give the position due recognition, then you might as well withdraw on some pretext and try to avoid future contacts with that individual. A representative of another person or group at a meeting is treated with even more care than that person or group because the substitute might be sensitive to slights, either real or imagined, and report his interpretation back to his colleagues. This is very difficult for Westerners to understand, but a Korean who fails to observe the basic rules of social exchange is considered by other Koreans to not even be a person, but an "unperson." Foreigners, to a certain extent and in a certain sense, are considered by Koreans as unpersons. Koreans show very little concern for unpersons' feelings, comfort, or whether they live or die. In short, an unperson is not worthy of much consideration. When relationships are broken among Koreans, some people tend to resort to violence, but every effort must be made to remain within the framework of polite relationships.

Direct and Specific versus Indirect and General

The American way of thinking is direct, whereas the Korean's way is indirect. When Americans love, they confess, "I love you," but Koreans, even if they are acculturated in America, do not directly say the word *love*. Love and hate are emotions subtly shown by expressions on the face instead of being stated. In Korea, one does not praise another's generosity, kindness, hospitality, and honesty by verbalizing it directly. One just appreciates the other's goodness from one's inner heart.

Americans tend to move from the specific and small to the general and large. Most progress from personal and local issues to those of the state and finally of the nation. Koreans tend to move the other way around. It is more comfortable for Koreans to start with a general or larger part and then narrow down to specific facts. If a Korean businessman, for example, asks an American counterpart about an overall goal, a basic theory, or a principle, he is confused by a flood of statistics or a long description of methods before he hears of any overall purpose or plan. Americans, on the other hand, feel equally frustrated when they ask for a specific fact or detail only to be subjected to 20 minutes of theory or philosophy without a single concrete fact. This totally opposite approach to thinking affects negotiations, plans, and attitudes. This is perhaps the influence of contrastive structural and functional characteristics in the two languages. English is an SVO (Subject-Verb-Object) language; Korean is an SOV (Subject-Object-Verb) language. Since language is inextricably bound to culture, the teacher might need a certain degree of patience when the Korean child tries to tell something and it takes quite a while before he or she gets to the point. In response to a negative question in Korean, for example, one says "yes" when one wants to answer it in the negative, and one says "no" when one wants to answer it in the affirmative. The Korean "yes" does not necessarily mean a positive answer but simply means "what you've said is correct"; the Korean "no" means "what you've said is incorrect." So if someone asks a question in a negative way, the Korean answer turns out to be the opposite of English "yes" and "no," which affirms or denies the *fact* rather than *statement* of the fact. For example, in response to a negative question, "Are you not late?" the Korean answer is "yes," which means "No, I am not late," or "no," which means "Yes, I am late." The teacher might have experienced this kind of situation with the Korean child in communication.

Manners and Courtesies

Eye Contact

When a teacher talks to an American child he or she expects the child to look straight into the teacher's eyes and listen. However, a Korean child would not look straight into the teacher's eyes; instead, the child's eyes and head would be held down or to the side, a cultural trait of showing respect for one's teacher. Many U.S. teachers misunderstand this form of nonverbal behavior and tend to misjudge the child from then on, based on this first impression. It might take a while to readjust.

Drinking

In Korea, one does not fill one's own glass; someone always pours for someone else. When you finish your drink, you pass the empty glass to a friend, elder person, or superior, holding it with both hands. He takes the glass, you pour wine into his glass, using your right hand, with your left hand lightly supporting your right arm. Everything is passed this way, with the right hand holding the object and the other hand lightly supporting the right arm. Not to do so is an insult. The Korean child is most likely to do this in the same manner when he or she gives something to the teacher.

Eating

Many Americans seem to find silence uncomfortable. They babble on to fill any quietness if it extends for more than a moment. Koreans eat solemnly and it is perfectly all right for one to make noise while chewing or having soup. Koreans chew and suck audibly, an indication that one is enjoying the food. In the United States, it is considered impolite for one to make noise while eating or drinking, though it is necessary to talk. In Korea, even during the meal, belching, coughing, or hiccuping is all right, but blowing one's nose is impolite. In the United States, quite the opposite is true. One has to excuse oneself for belching, coughing, or hiccuping, but blowing one's nose is permissible. Picking one's teeth after a meal is perfectly all right, whereas in America, it is impolite and should be avoided until one has privacy.

Privacy, Gifts, and Gesture

Privacy is extremely important in the United States; in Korea, there is not even the word *privacy*. Thus, it is difficult to translate the word into Korean. Therefore, when a Korean greets someone, his or her first questions are usually "How old are you?" "What is your income?" or "Why don't you get married?" Koreans are curious to know others' personal affairs by saying in their greeting, "Where are you going?" or "How come you are here?"

Americans find it awkward to stand close to one another (proxemics) and they often back away a few inches. Koreans do not avoid bodily contact. While getting on a bus or train, in a crowded market place, or while watching sports, Koreans do not hesitate to push others, whereas in America touching, let alone pushing, is taboo. This is due to a larger "personal space" that Americans feel they must maintain to feel comfortable, unless they are with family or close friends.

Gifts of a certain nature in America are usually small and single—a gesture rather than a gift. In Korea, however, the gift is rather expensive. Gifts should not be opened in the presence of the giver, but in the United States, gifts are usually opened in the presence of the giver to show immediate appreciation. In Korea, even a gift of food offered to the house is not opened in the giver's presence or shared for fear this would be embarrassing. Thank-you letters are vague and do not mention the nature of the gift in the letter. Here again, the idea of directness and indirectness is involved.

In terms of gestures, Americans put a sympathetic or warm hand on a person's shoulder to demonstrate warmth of feeling or put an arm around a person in sympathy or affection. In Korea, younger persons are socially prohibited from putting their hands on elders' shoulders or from tapping the shoulders of elders, although these restrictions do not apply to seniors tapping the shoulders of people younger than they. Putting one's hands in one's pockets while talking with others, especially with seniors, is avoided among Koreans.

Forming a circle with your thumb and your second finger signifies "money" in Korea; in America, this means a strong "okay." Koreans use their palms as scratch paper to practice or memorize by writing Chinese characters, foreign words, or to do simple arithmetic, but Americans seldom write on their palms. Shrugging one's shoulders with a light movement of hands implies "I don't know" or "I don't understand" in America Koreans do not have the same movement, but just shake their head horizontally to show the same meaning. Shaking the head vertically means "I know or understand" or "yes."

In America, "thumbs up" indicates "okay" or consent, and "thumbs down" indicates disagreement or "no"; in Korea, "thumbs up" means "the best," "number one," or "boss." Waving of a hand, palm outward, with a vertical motion means "good-bye" in America, whereas the same movement signifies "come here" in Korea. Koreans count 1 to 10 by bending fingers from the thumb to the small finger in order with one hand, while Americans use two hands.

Religion

The people of Korea have been strongly influence by Shamanism, Buddhism, and Confucianism. Confucianism has been a strong force influencing social and governmental institutions. Confucian teaching of interpersonal relationships is still the core of Korean cultural patterns, with some modifications by Korean Americans. Christianity influenced Korea in terms of modern education, the Western work ethic, social mobility, and the democratic and humanistic ideals.

Shamanism

Korea had its own unique religion from prehistoric times, a form of animism or nature worship involving a national foundation myth that told of a son of the supreme deity who descended to earth, married a bear (which probably means a woman from a tribe whose totem animal was the bear), and founded the first Korean state. Animism persisted in coloring the Korean versions of other world religions as they reached the peninsula, and still survives today in the continuing reliance by simple rural people on the ceremonies conducted by Shamans (female), or *mudang*, to ward off bad luck, ensure success, and cure illness by invoking the power of nature spirits, or placating the vengeful wrath of ancestral spirits with some grievance against their descendants.

Buddhism

Perhaps the earliest foreign religion to attain wide acceptance was Buddhism, which was brought to the country via Chinese and Indian missionaries in 372 A.D. The new faith was accepted due to alleged miracles performed by saintly monks when the royal family adopted Buddhism, and the rest of the country rapidly followed suit. Soon the hillsides of Korea erupted in temples, shrines, hermitages, pagodas, and stone *miruk* images. Buddhist architecture, sculpture, painting, and theological scholarship flourished.

The fingerprint of a persisting animism within the Buddhist system is still found at nearly all Buddhist temples, where a small side-shrine is devoted to the Mountain Spirit and his national totem animal. This subsidiary shrine often is the object of more fervent devotion than the main Buddhist sanctuary with its stately gilt images. The old man with the tiger who embodies the Mountain Spirit derives in part from Chinese Taoism, an esoteric variety of refined nature mysticism that has never had a creed, scripture, or clergy, much less a formal organization, and which, therefore, can be said to survive only in its influence on other religions.

Buddhism was blamed for political revenges suffered by Korea during the Koryo Dynasty. When the Yi Dynasty took power in 1392 A.D., the Buddhist clergy was banished from the capital and it was no longer the state religion. This did not, however, prevent the first Yi king and his descendants from remaining devout Buddhists. In recent years, Buddhism has experienced a revival in Korea, modernizing its outlook, seeking ties with sister movements in other countries, and espousing ideals of social service and ecumenical cooperation like other world religions.

Confucianism

There is endless argument about whether the tenets of the Chinese sage, Confucius, and the social institutes based on these tenets, constitute a religion. It is true that there is no deity in the Confucian system (Heaven, when referred to, represents Fate or Things As They Are or the Moral Imperative by Kant, not a personified God) and no cosmogony. On the other hand, Confucianism does embrace a moral and ethical system, a philosophy of life and interpersonal relations, a code of conduct, and a method of government, all viable enough to have taken the place of more orthodox religious beliefs in China for thousands of years, and the same held true in Korea.

The philosophy of Confucius was introduced to Korea at nearly the same time as the religion of Buddha, and it had a strong influence on social and governmental institutions. It was not until the establishment of the Yi Dynasty (1392), and its ousting of Buddhism from political influence in the late fourteenth century, that Confucianism was elevated to the status of state cult, a position left vacant by the disestablishment of Buddhism.

Education in Chinese classics, and particularly the ethical and philosophical books of Confucius, became the sole basis of education; erudition represented the only path to social and political success. State examinations, which many failed and took over again while dependent on their families for support as students, determined the criteria for advancement of the scholar-administrator, the only career that a man of talent and breeding could honorably pursue.

Confucianism at best ensured stability and security within the system, but was woefully inadequate to meet challenges from outside, whether military, political, or social. For this reason, Korea became the "Hermit Kingdom" until the painful period late in the nineteenth century when the old system went into protracted death agonies due to overwhelming incursions from Japan and the Western powers.

To this day, many aspects of Confucianism remain central to the Korean character, for better or worse. This is illustrated under the section of Korean patterns. The Korean is intensely loyal to family and clan—a positive virtue. But the Korean government tends to be stultifyingly bureaucratic, which is hardly an advantage in the modernization process. Both circumstances are a heritage of Confucian thought.

Christianity

Christianity began in Korea with the indirect influence of Western ideas brought back from China by Korean tributary emissaries, who met Catholic missionaries in Peking (Beijing). The earliest such recorded contact was 1783. For some years, there was no priest to serve the Korean converts-by-hearsay; when foreign missionaries entered the country by stealth and ordained Korean clergy, so that the religion began to grow in influence, it suffered severe persecution from the dogmatically Confucian government that regarded the foreign creed as little better than devil worship. Nevertheless, by 1853, there were an estimated 20,000 Catholic converts. At this point, the most severe persecutions began, not coincidentally at a time when the government was locked in a last-ditch struggle to drive off all foreign influence. Thousands of converts died, several of whom have since been beatified by the Vatican as martyrs deemed worthy of eventual sainthood. Then came the treaties with Western governments signed under pressure in 1882, and suddenly Korea was wide open as a mission territory, with the lives and rights of missionaries and converts guaranteed by the government, however unwillingly. The nation rapidly became one of the most active Christian mission fields worldwide.

The reasons were not entirely involved with theology, although it is certainly true that the discrediting and demise of Confucianism as a formal philosophic system left a vacuum in Korean moral values that cried out to be filled. More important perhaps was the fact that the missionaries championed modern education, the Western work ethic, social mobility, the comforts of affluent Western society, and the humanistic and democratic ideals of the liberal parliamentarian nation, and thus became a rallying point for resistance to Japanese encroachment, both before and after Korea's annexation by Japan (1909). Christianity, therefore, recruited to its ranks many of the brightest and most progressive youths in Korean society, with the result that a disproportionate number of the nation's leaders and shapers have been Christians since the early years of the century.

Typical Classroom Behaviors: Korean Americans

Traditional Korean Values

Korean youth:
1. Should bow to show respect, but should not initiate a conversation with an elder.

2. Must choose differentiated vocabulary and verb forms in order to speak politely to a "superior."

3. Will never use the name of an adult when speaking face to face. Will call the instructor *sun-saeng-nim,* meaning "teacher," rather than by name.

4. Will not insult the teacher's efforts by saying "I don't understand." Will nod politely while not understanding and attribute the difficulty to their own lack of diligence.

5. Should remain silent rather than exhibit faulty understanding or command of a skill. To put forth a mistaken answer or an unperfected skill is a personal embarrassment and an insult to the teacher and the discipline.

6. Will hesitate to express their own opinion for fear that it may sound presumptuous or run contrary to the feelings of the teacher.

7. Must always defer to the judgment of superiors and must never openly disagree with anyone. To be contentious is a sign of conceit.

American Values

American youth:
1. Should smile and make friendly conversation when greeting an elder.

2. Do not differentiate word choices as radically when speaking to teacher or a parent's friend. Do not even perceive these adults to be "superior." Will "be oneself" in all situations.

3. Politely call adults "Mrs. Jones" or "Mr. Smith." It is rude to address an instructor merely as "teacher."

4. Should speak up whenever they do not understand. This is a favor to the teacher and other students as well. Perceive their own learning to depend on "good" or "bad" teaching.

5. Will give their best effort to answer a question or do a particular task, because trying is more important than being absolutely correct. Though just beginners, they will not hesitate to demonstrate a skill or speak about a particular subject.

6. Should be able to give their own view on a topic when called on by the teacher and to defend their statements with reasonable arguments.

7. Is encouraged to develop an independent viewpoint and to express it in contrast to the view of the teacher or other students. Debating is a high-level oral skill.

Key Relationships for Korean Americans

Parent-Child Relationship

- Have high respect for school administrators and teachers.
- Parents' role is to respect, listen, and follow the professional judgment of teachers and administrators.
- Their limited English proficiency makes them reluctant to participate in school functions and to confer with teachers.
- Parents' life-style in the United States is complicated by varying rates of acculturation and language learning.
- Biculturality-Korean parents hold ambivalent and often inconsistent expectations concerning the cultural choices of their children.
- Koreans' are dedicated to developing and maintaining a strong family unit, based in part on the Confucian tradition of Korean society.
- The inherent value of Confucian philosophy is placed on educational attainment.
- Children are reminded by their parents that education is to be valued, teachers are to be respected, and assignments are to be completed. Education comes first in the family.
- Parents believe that a positive parent-child relationship depends on their children's obedience to their wishes (another part of the Confucian ethic).
- Parent-child interactions are complicated by varying rates of acculturation and language learning and these differences create conflicting attitudes between parents and children over questions of cultural identity and adaptation.
- Confucian ethics have not prepared parents for open, frank communication between parents and their children.
- Parents are committed to helping their children be successful in school. However, some of the strategies they may use are counterproductive. Authoritarian parenting strategies have been shown to correlate highly with low grade-point averages of children.

Educator-Student Relationship

- Students represent many of the positive status characteristics used by teachers to form high expectations of the students' academic ability (neatly dressed, follows directions, educated parents, etc.).
- Students with poor academic achievement may be victims of interrupted schooling due to their immigration, cultural conflicts with their parents, deviant peer groups, or psychological problems.
- As members of a minority group, they are often exposed to racial hostility manifested by violence, harassment, rejection, and other forms of prejudice.
- A lack of understanding among educators of the sociopsychological background of Korean students may result in difficulty in assessing and responding to students' needs.
- They are reluctant to seek help from others because of the humiliation that their shortcomings will bring to their family.

- Being regarded as members of a "model minority" with exceptional academic ability creates special pressures on Korean-American children. (With little room for error, many believe that they have to make all *A*s, learn English, master American culture, and prepare for college—all at once).
- Through cooperative learning activities, Korean-American students can learn not only academic content but they may also learn how to lead a group, how to help others who are having trouble, and how to master the oral language skills that are important for success in a group.

Parent-Educator Relationship

Educators

- Korean-American students' academic, language, and psychological success is dependent in part on the quality of the relationship between their parents and those responsible for educating them.
- Educators are frequently unaware of the Korean community and institutions in it that could help the school improve the students' education (Korean churches, community-based organizations, weekend schools, etc.).
- Recognizing the dynamics of parents' cross-cultural adaptations will help educators better understand Korean students' needs and how the school can build on their out-of-school experiences.
- Participating in Korean-American community activities, educators will demonstrate to parents their respect for Koreans and their dedication to learn more about them.

Parents

- It is essential for Korean-American parents to understand the U.S. educational system (common discipline strategies in U.S. schools, the course requirements for high school graduation, the process of applying to college, etc.).
- Most importantly, Koreans' traditional views regarding the role of teachers differ significantly from those held by teachers in the United States. They entrust to the teacher full responsibility for not only the academic but also the social development of the child.
- Regarding parents as key partners in the educational process, teachers expect parents to work closely with school staff to support their child's education.
- Parents' failure to respond to written school communiques and absences at parent advisory committee meetings are a sign of deference to the teacher, not evidence of the parents' lack of interest in school.
- Discontinuities between the hierarchical and authoritarian family structure and the democratic and individualistic environment of the school complicate the schooling of Korean children. Teachers have difficulty in identifying and treating Korean students' psychological and emotional problems. On the other hand, Korean parents have their own problems accepting and coping with their children's emotional problems.
- The social stigma attached to having "problem" children may cause parents to deny the problem rather than seek help from educators or other professionals. (Koreans rely more on themselves than on groups or on agencies outside the family to solve personal problems.)

- Parents and teachers are disadvantaged by their lack of information and their misconceptions about each other. Teachers who take a more personal approach and demonstrate a knowledge of Korean culture will be most successful in eliciting parent support—for example, school personnel can establish good relationships with community organizations and Korean news media to announce school activities in Korean. Another example is a telephone "hot line" at the school with prerecorded information in Korean about current events of interest to parents.
- The most important step is for the educators to establish personal contacts with the parents. (Koreans place heavy emphasis on cultivating networks of relationships and personal contacts as resources for assistance in obtaining information and assistance needed to accomplish tasks and solve problems.)

Implications Regarding Role Relationships

- Students, parents, and educators are disadvantaged by their lack of information and their misconceptions about each other. As a result, the roles that they assume to further the education process are often contradictory, thereby weakening the emotional and academic support system that the children need during their school experience.
- It is important that students, parents, and educators increase their knowledge of themselves and the cross-cultural milieu in which they live and work.
- Educators, parents, and students are themselves cultural beings who are growing and changing as they adapt to one another and other sociocultural forces around them. As they learn more about each other's strengths, they can become advocates of one another, appreciating the resources that they represent to each other in succeeding in the educational process.
- Educators need to become more familiar with Korean immigrants, their communities, and their children.
- Parents need to understand the culture of the United States and the function of schooling in transmitting American values.
- Students need to improve their ability to function as intermediaries between the culture of the school and the culture of their family, facilitating not only the cross-cultural growth of their teachers and parents but also their own development as Korean Americans.

Summary

Recent waves of immigrants with values and customs newly encountered by Americans are changing the face of the United States. The impact of new immigrants on America is already considerable and promises to be even more significant in the future. Korean Americans have displayed qualities of hard work, adaptability, self-confidence, and strong faith in opportunities represented by the United States. Every group immigrating to the United States has experienced a certain degree of culture shock, adjustment stress, and sociocultural disruption, caused mainly by a distinctive culture and language, limited English proficiency, and unique physical characteristics. Among Koreans, these problems have been most severe for the younger generation—individuals caught in the middle of transition as they exist between the rather different worlds of school and home. Typical Korean-American parents are in their late 30s, usually have two or three children of elementary school age, and most often have a high school or college education. In most households, both parents are employed full time outside the home, in contrast to their life pattern in Korea. The parents' expectations for their children at school, in both academic and social areas, are very high.

One of the most crucial areas challenging educators of newly immigrated Koreans is that of biculturality. It has been indicated that Korean parents hold ambivalent, and often inconsistent, expectations concerning the cultural choices their children make in finding their place in U.S. life. Because children's thought patterns and values are formed and developed early in life through education and interaction between the school and the home, the role of educators becomes extremely important in the socialization and acculturation process of children. Biculturality becomes a useful construct for realizing that children can develop new values and cultural orientation in America while understanding and developing cultural traits represented by the Korean family and community.

Teachers play an important role in affecting Koreans' efforts to adjust to the culture of the United States. By having their cultural uniqueness reflected in school programs, Koreans can more easily overcome their feelings of inadequacy and lack of self-confidence brought about by language difficulties and bewildering cultural phenomena found in the United States.

Korean-American students and their parents need the support of educators in preserving their cultural traditions and adapting them to the American context. As they promote their cultural heritage and adjust to their new life, Koreans create a new culture—a Korean-American culture that enhances their own lives and those of all Americans.

One of the principles of multicultural education is that individuals need to function effectively between and among other ethnic groups. Teachers need to be concerned with developing and enhancing communication skills that will be taught ultimately to both language minority and mainstream public school students. It is not enough for these pupils to simply understand the concept of cultural pluralism: rather, they must be given the verbal and nonverbal communication skills necessary for transcultural functioning (Chu & Levy, 1988).

References

California State Department of Education. (1992). *Handbook for teaching Korean American students*. Sacramento, CA: CSDE.

Choy, Bong Youn. (1979) *Koreans in America*. Chicago: Nelson-Hall.

Chu, Harold. (1983). Linguistic interferences in acquisition of ESL for Korean LEP students. In R. V. Padilla (Ed.), *Theory, technology, and public policy on bilingual education* (pp. 231–252). Rosslyn, VA: National Clearinghouse for Bilingual Education.

Chu, Harold. (1981). *Testing instruments for reading skills: English and Korean (Grades 1–3)*. Fairfax, VA: George Mason University.

Chu, Harold. (1978). *A contrastive analysis between Korean and English for ESL teachers*. Arlington, VA: Arlington Public Schools.

Chu, Harold. (1978). The Korean learner in an American school. In Edward K. Lake (Ed.), *Teaching for cross-cultural understanding* (III-D, pp. 1–13). Arlington, VA: Arlington Public Schools (Ethnic Heritage Project).

Chu, Harold, & Levy, Jack. (1988). Multicultural skills for bilingual teachers: Training for competency development. In R. F. Macia (Ed.), *NABE Journal, 12* (2), 153–169. Washington, DC: National Association for Bilingual Education.

Chun, Shinayong (Ed.). (1982). *Buddhist culture in Korea*. Seoul: Si-sa-yong-o-sa Publishers.

Crane, Paul S. (1967). *Korean patterns*. Seoul: Hollym Corporation.

Fairbank, John K., Reischauer, Edwin O., & Craig, Albert M. (1978). *East Asia: Tradition and transformation*. Boston: Houghton Miffin.

Ha, Tae Hung. (1962). *Korea: Forty-three centuries*. Seoul: Yonse University Press.

Han, Woo-Keun. (1974). *The history of Korea*. Honolulu: The University Press of Hawaii.

Harris, Philip R., & Mohan, Robert T. (1987). *Managing cultural differences*. Houston, TX: Gulf.

Joe, Wanne J. (1977). *Traditional Korea: A cultural history*. Seoul: Chungang University Press.

Kim, Bok Lim C. (1978). *The Asian-American: Changing patterns, changing needs*. Montclair, NJ: Association of Korean Christian Scholars in North America, Inc.

Kim, Hyung-chan, & Patterson, W. (1974). *The Koreans in America: 1882–1974*. Dobbs Ferry, NY: Oceana Publications.

Kim, J. T. (1974). Li-Jo Yu-hak-ye it-su-su byukidan inyum gwa juntong (Byukidan ideology and tradition in Yi Dynasty). *Journal of Kukje University, 2*, 339–359.

Korean Overseas Information Services. (1978). *A handbook of Korea*. Seoul: Ministry of Culture and Information.

Lee, C. S. (1975). The United States immigration policy and the settlement of Koreans in America. *Korea Observer, 4*, 412–451.

Lew, S. K. (1970). Confucianism and Korean social structure. *Chulhak Yon-goo (Philosophical Studies), 5*, 13–38.

National Institute of Education. (1988). *Education in Korea*. Seoul: Ministry of Education.

Takaki, Ronald. (1989). *Strangers from a different shore: A history of Asian Americans*. Boston: Little, Brown.

Yi, H. D. (1973). Foundation of Confucian ethics in Korea. *Korea Journal, 13*, 10–16.

Yum, June-Ock. (1987). Korean philosophy and communication. In D. L. Kincaid (Ed.), *Communication theory: Eastern and Western perspectives* (pp. 71–86). New York: Academic Press 71–86.

About the Author

Harold Chu is an associate professor and director of the Center for Bilingual/Multicultural/ESL Teacher Preparation, Graduate School of Education, George Mason University. He received his Ph.D. from the University of Minnesota in 1973. His reasearch interests include bilingual/ multicultural education, Asian languages (Japanese and Korean) and cultures, and English as a Second Language.

The Mexican Americans

ESTEBAN HERMÁN GARCÍA

Encino, New Mexico, was my place of birth. It is a ranching and railroad town situated about 75 miles southeast of Santa Fe, a mostly homogeneous community of Mexican-American working-class people. Growing up in a rural area permeated and colored my view of the world from the time I was a very young child.

My great grandparents came to *El Nuevo México* from what is today a northern territory of Mexico. I am a sixth-generation Mexican American. I now refer to myself as a *Chicano*. For the purpose of clarifying for the reader the use of that term, I offer an enigmatic but operational definition. There are many terms and labels used today for identifying Spanish-origin groups: *Latinos, Latins, Hispanics, Spanish Americans, Spanish-speaking Americans*, and so on. Two terms, *Mexican American* and *Chicano*, will be applied interchangeably in this chapter. These two terms are my choices.

Before entering public school, I never struggled with my ethnolinguistic identity. My days were filled with Spanish-language activities involving my mother, grandparents, brothers and sisters, and neighborhood friends. I experienced few cultural conflicts because all of the affairs of the community that affected me were conducted in Spanish. I remember going to my *tío's* store with my *hermano mayor* to buy *chorizo*, to church for the *misa*, and watching my *mamá* and *abuela* make *tortillas*, all of these stressed terms of course delivered in Spanish, the first language of the Mexican Americans in Encino. Indeed, my idea of the world was formed in the context of my Spanish-speaking home community and I knew who I was as a person within, and had a strong sense of my identity because of its boundaries.

My Elementary School Years

My identity was harshly assailed when I entered elementary school. I, of course, was prohibited from speaking my first language, Spanish, and teachers punished me for using it even though I had no other means of clearly or extensively communicating. I spoke but a few words in English, but I was struck on the palm of my hand several times with a ruler each time I spoke Spanish! I was encouraged while in school to *forget* Spanish because, according to the teachers, it could only hurt my academic development. The messages I received in school soon began to make me feel uncomfortable, even with my familiar home-community surroundings.

There were several new teachers hired each year. Among them there were the local or regional teachers, a few of whom were Mexican American but most of whom were White. As I recall what they were like, it seems to me now that all of them had bought into the notion that only certain children can or should achieve.

If one considers the few minority teachers who enrolled and made it through teacher-education programs during that period in history (1940s and 1950s), it is not difficult to understand their relatively high levels of acculturation, but also to a large degree, their rejection of both themselves and their own ethnic culture. In some cases, minority teachers were even more oppressive than their White counterparts, because they were on the proving ground. It appeared that they wanted their White colleagues to know that they were different from (better than) the Mexican-American children who were struggling academically in the classrooms. It may be that the struggle of Mexican Americans in classrooms was and is more cultural than academic. The education they received had denuded them of any consciousness or human agency for dealing with their own ethnic and class identity and struggle. Thus, individuals such as myself were left to figure it out on our own. Given the low status of our cultural currency, we were not allowed to demonstrate our developmental abilities, but instead were subjected to a set of predefined behaviors and low expectations by most of the minority teachers.

Also, among the new teachers hired each year were the Whites, who came from many different parts of the United States. There were both males and females, but with similar dispositions regarding their minimum expectations of the Mexican-American students. Most came totally unprepared to provide a sound education because they did not understand us culturally, linguistically, or in any other way. They did, however, function from a set of preconceived assumptions that proved in more cases than not dreadfully harmful to most of us. This does not mean they were all batches of bad teachers. This had more to do with their inability to read the world for which they had no understanding or previous experience (Freire & Macedo, 1987). A few of them operated from a compassionate demeanor but were at a great loss to understand the spread between state and national high standard test scores and our low performance academically. Compassion certainly was not sufficient to take care of our schooling, cultural, and linguistic needs. Most assumed that we were simply an inferior group incapable of improving our lot in life.

Their shortcomings as educators in a predominantly language-minority community did little to sustain and promote our providence in life. As I mentioned a little earlier, minority teachers back then did not do better because they were trained in the same teacher-education programs as their White counterparts. Minority and White teachers simply "plugged" into the schooling machinery with its ideological steadfast notions of learning as a neutral, transparent experience totally removed from the axis of history, power, and its societal context.

My school experience involved learning about my ethnicity early. I remember being called a Mexican in the derogatory sense of the term. The legacy of hate that the Mexican

American War of 1846 created lingers in a variety of public, legal, and political domains. From this conquest of a nation was born the derogatory terminology associated with being Mexican—dumb Mexican, stupid Mexican, lazy Mexican, dirty Mexican and, on and on went the list that formed a vast number of negative stereotypes. These stereotypes carried over to the educational arena and became part of the broader experiences of Mexican Americans throughout the southwestern United States.

The term *Mexican American* is what I call a government label; it is used to identify Americans of Mexican descent. It is a term that attempts to represent Mexican Americans as full-fledged members of American society. However, by adding the ethnic/national marker *Mexican*, it relegates them to a subtle form of second-class citizenship. The term *Chicano*, for its part, has been in the Mexican-American community since the 1930s and 1940s. It became associated with the tumultuous but healthy civil rights ruptures of the 1960s and 1970s in the United States. It was with the Mexican-American community's struggle for civil rights that the term *Chicano* became a marker for a new self-identity (Hernández, 1970). That struggle is ongoing.

I didn't always refer to myself as a Chicano. The process of becoming aware of my ethnic identity took several years. In the 1960s. while I was still in high school, the United States was experiencing an exciting social transformation. As an ethnic-American community, we were being transformed in spite of our struggle against acculturation. However, those characteristics about my ethnicity and colonization were subtly (and at times not so subtly) pointed out during my school years through a variety of experiences. Even at that nexus in my life, however, I was not yet completely aware of my working-class, Mexican-American ethnicity. For example, I felt that school and most of the teachers were not totally accepting of my person. I was constantly told not to speak only English. In an uninformed way, I wondered why we spoke Spanish at home but doing so was unacceptable at school.

One difference between then and now is that teachers then had no access to multicultural and bilingual education awareness, whereas today there is a higher quantity of those knowledge bases. The issue today becomes one of quality and access. My changing identity outside my family community eventually destabilized my identity and sense of cultural confidence. There was no guidance or assistance as I connected with new cultures and languages. There was only the unspoken understanding that learning English at the expense of loosing Spanish was the right thing to do. I never totally lost the Spanish language, but I did for several years have an inferiority complex about my first language and culture.

As I went through school, I frequently sensed (mostly through my feelings) that there was something erroneous about how I was being treated and regarded. For example, I remember teachers overtly favoring the few White children, and those Mexican Americans from middle-class backgrounds who could speak English during class activities. Teachers, both monolingual and bilingual, would spend more one-on-one time with those children than with me or others like myself. When I would get home from school, I would always feel warm and wonderful about my family (we were 10 children, and to this day enjoy visiting our mother; our father is deceased). The butterflies and mixed emotions that had dominated my thoughts and feelings at school were submerged at home in the presence of my family. I believe those feelings were regularly negated by the neglectful behavior that teachers rendered in the classrooms with monolingual Spanish and limited-English-speaking and culturally diverse children such as myself. My elementary school years were trying ones due to the poor schooling experiences.

Who I have become as a person today is wedded to a variety of experiences, including my elementary and secondary schooling intervals and college background. Of course, many people have influenced my thinking which has shaped my personal and professional character.

My Junior High School Years

My entrance into junior high school was in itself a status promotion, especially since I was developing into an athlete, a change that gave me a new and improved identity. Finally, I was getting positive attention in school, from both peers and teachers, for my talents. Although it was a small school in which almost anyone could participate in sporting events, it was still exciting for me to be able to play a valuable role there.

Within the community, I still was just an average kid, even though I did respond well to the positive output of adults. My father owned and operated a small business and was an active politician. In fact, he was at one time or another a county commissioner, the mayor, a city council member, and a Justice of the Peace during the 1960s and 1970s, and a little into the early 1980s. His involvement in politics definitely had a positive effect on my life. He also was influential in attracting federal assistance programs such as the Community Action Programs (CAP) to Encino and surrounding communities—more an activist politician within, inspired by the Kennedy and Johnson eras. I was able to observe all those activities firsthand because my father used his gas station as a center for organizing politics. Many politicos would drop by daily to discuss things with him but it was always, local politics with which he was more or less concerned. He pushed for voter registration within the Mexican-American community during those years, although not as we know it today. Unfortunately, my understanding of those events, both great and small, really did not become part of my working knowledge and understanding until years later. In relation to my schooling experiences, those home, community, and broader political events affected me more as an adult pursuing a higher education than the immediate postyears the events occurred.

Although I am not into party politics, I learned later in life, from my father's activities as a politician, that one had to be politically involved at various levels in creating one's voice and struggling for representation of one's interests through sociopolitical commitments. In junior high, I was barely involved in student politics, my main goals being to play sports and to try to figure out the bizarre behavior of my hormones. Academically, I was not well grounded, but at least maintained a moderate enough grade-point average to be able to play sports. I still believe that my motivation for academic achievement had been brutally tormented by the teacher types in my elementary schooling years.

Reflecting on my lower-than-average academic achievement during those years, I can recall that I received little or no support or other encouragement from any of the teachers or staff to attend any form of postsecondary education, vocational or otherwise. It appears to me now, as I recollect those years, that there was no need to discuss the future; it seemed as if the future had already been forged and that it would be the best it could ever get. The most I could hope for, as I was told by one school counselor, was to work at menial and manual jobs unless I joined the military. It so happened that several years later I was "asked" (drafted) to join the military.

Although junior high presented formidable enough years for me as an athlete, it was also during those years that I felt I had to develop a strong resistance toward school authoritarianism. It is not that I understood it then as resistance, but as I now recall resistance was what I felt toward both school in general and the teachers and administrators that I didn't like in particular. It was the result of a feeling of constantly being put down, even though words were not always spoken. For example, there were times when I wanted to reply to a question a teacher had about a class assignment. If kids who were perceived to know more than I also raised their hands, they invariably would get called on first. It was frustrating. Teachers need to provide opportunities for *all* children to respond, even if that takes a little longer!

The teachers' attitudes toward me and many of the other Mexican-American students was patronizingly friendly, but I nevertheless felt then (and still do) that they were insincere in their attempts to provide us with an education that would be beneficial to the transformation of our educational and social posture. I know that this statement is itself quite naive, especially given what I know now about the role of education. However, assuming that an education is truly supposed to change one's lot in life, that rarely happened within my predominantly language-minority community where I grew up and went to school. It was hegemony at its best.

Every year, new White teachers would arrive. Many of them came with a missionary mentality. They had come to save the "Mexicans," as we were frequently referred to even though all of us were fourth-generation or higher Americans of Mexican descent. I personally do not mind being called a Mexican, but it is the *way* in which the term is used that makes it impudent. Even the teachers who came and ended up staying for several years never truly came to understand, but instead contributed to our subjugation and never served our plight.

The junior high experience consisted of formidable years in my life. John F. Kennedy was assassinated and America's involvement (aggression) in Vietnam had escalated. The social and civil eruptions were causing great concerns for the nation. As I see and understand events, conditions, and circumstances now, it was my *location* that contributed generously to my naiveté. Many historical events simply remained unknown to me for several years—for instance, Vietnam and its immorality, its initial popular support and then the gradual dissipation, and its long-term social and economic consequences, with which society was poorly equipped to deal. Also, although I was aware of the civil rights activities occurring in different parts of the country at the time, I did not clearly understand until years later its struggles and what they meant.

My High School Years

High school is memorable to me for a variety of reasons. First, I continued to develop both my athletic talents and to survive academically. I'm sure now that, had I been encouraged to develop my academic talents as much as my athletic ones, I would have surfaced from high school rather better prepared to face the world.

Second, I entered high school in 1964, when much of the world was undergoing a massive social, cultural, and political revolution. As I stated earlier, in rural New Mexico it was not uncommon either to be uninformed or to have important historical events totally bypass us. Small towns have a life of their own, and therefore often are not affected directly by the actions or events of the larger society, or even the world. With television being such an impinging medium on children and older youths today, they have much greater access to society's and the world's events than I did in the 1960s. Teachers need to take greater advantage of such technological advances in order to more fully inform students of global undertakings that affect them in their daily lives.

There were times in high school when I had my doubts about graduating, and even about wanting to graduate. However, my parents kept silent concerning whatever doubts I had in spite of my relatively poor academic performance; they were *not* going to let me leave school. Thus I graduated, courtesy of both state and social promotion policies.

When I finally left Encino, I had no real conception of the urban cultural shock I would experience, and the longing I would have for my familiar rural surroundings. I was unprepared to deal with large doses of city life. My high school experiences did little to prepare me (or anyone else in our school) for entry into the world of work. As I recall now, most of us were content to enter totally working-class, unskilled employment. The few that attempted college or any other form of postsecondary education also experienced varying degrees of culture shock. Of those who attempted college, not many finished. This revolving-door policy for minority students continues here and there even today, in colleges and universities.

As in junior high, most of my high school teachers were unprepared to deal with our cultural diversity. The attempt then, as it is now in most schools, was to assimilate us; the ideological stir was total cultural and linguistic genocide. There was little or no regard for the problems associated with language minority and their ethnic diverse status.

I recall one Mexican-American teacher who came to town and stayed for many years, always demonstrating his compassion and identifying with local Mexican-American youths and others. It may have been that his own background—which was similar to ours in terms of his working-class, semi-rural, and predominantly Mexican American language-minority credentials—was what motivated him to extend a helping hand and use encouraging language. He remained in the community until his tragic death in an auto accident. To many of us, he was a special teacher, coach, and friend who accepted us for who we were and never hesitated to support and inspire us to do our best. With more teachers like him, our schooling experiences would have enhanced our chances of developing our other potential and academic abilities.

During my senior year, there was a small group of us who talked about going on to postsecondary schooling, although for most of us it remained only talk, primarily because we didn't have the money to go to college. The few who did go were counseled and encouraged by the school to do so, and were presented with financial-aid applications. A probable explanation regarding the difference between myself and the students who went to college is that they were not resistant to teachers' repressive tactics, and thus their good behavior was interpreted as intelligent and more capable.

My Post-High School Years

The condition, threat, and concern that remained a constant during my high school years of the 1960s was the Vietnam War. The military state of mind of America had already summoned my two immediately older brothers to volunteer for military service. That episode began in 1965.

After graduation in 1968 at the age of 18, I began working at a variety of jobs from town to town across New Mexico. As any high school graduate who has gone job hunting can attest, it is a time when one still thinks that one knows it all, but few employers seem to believe it. There are in one's immediate past too few significant work experiences, if any, that can serve as useful. That is when teenagers rely heavily on their feelings of invincibility in order to encounter both the overt and the covert rejections from the job market. It is also the beginning of yet another phase on which one can embark with a negative attitude.

During this period, I was also in close observation of the draft. My two older brothers variously had served or were serving in Vietnam, and advised me not to volunteer—instead, they suggested, I should wait for the draft. I waited patiently (but not long) while I floated from unskilled job to unskilled job. A year and two months after graduation, I was drafted. Just a month earlier, I had applied to college for the fall semester and had been rejected because I applied too late into the year. I applied to college because I felt it would improve my chances to find a better job, although in fact I had very little confidence in myself about even going to college. The reply letter I received from the admissions office stated that my high school academic record was in poor shape, and I would be considered for admission only under probationary status for the following semester. I remember thinking I would probably *never* go to college.

I never made it to college before being drafted. Needless to say, I was not aware of the international politics of the Vietnam War. I was not politicized to the degree necessary to understand America's imperialistic role in Southeast Asia. At that time, I believed that the war was justifiable. The media and the politics had so legitimated it vis-à-vis the daily TV news reports that by the time I arrived in Vietnam at age 19, 1 thoroughly believed in it.

Vietnam

The sole purpose, I now believe, of my being drafted into the Army was to serve time in Vietnam. It seems to me that this became the only reason why so *many* of us (Mexican Americans were overrepresented proportionately in Vietnam) were drafted. I was the *third* one from my *immediate* family to serve in Vietnam. What the hell are people talking about when they say minorities are unpatriotic? We weren't buying one-way bus and plane tickets to Canada or Mexico! Yes, I later protested the war but it was my *right* to do that in this democracy. In doing that, I joined the, perhaps, not totally popular but, to my way of thinking, totally right struggle to end the genocidal madness "over there."

The whole military experience allowed me to see the world in a much different way than I had before I was drafted. It made me think that if I was good enough to serve in a war for the nation, then I was good enough to participate in the benefits it offered its citizen soldiers. I began to think then of what I would do later, after having served in both Vietnam and Germany. The experiences and friendships I gained in the military had provided me with a new confidence about my overall abilities—including my intellectual ones. From Germany, I applied to the university and was accepted on probationary status. In the fall of 1971, at the age of 21, I entered as a freshman.

The military also had an impact on my identity. I was now Herman S. García! The machinations of the military had not quite ended, however. It managed, in fact, to affect my identity. The Army bureaucracy had changed Esteban, which is on my birth certificate, to Steven—and Steven was further reduced to an initial (S.)! Later, I decided on adding accents on Hermán and García, and thus became Hermán S. García. Schoolchildren should not compromise their Spanish names. Teachers should not alter children's names unless both the children and the parents either initiate or agree to such changes.

My Postsecondary Education

Entrance into the university was a major challenge for me because, given my poor preparation in high school, I was not—as I quickly learned—ready to participate in an enriching academic or scholarly college student life. I had to discipline myself anew to study, which was not an easy task. The first two semesters in particular were quite difficult, in part because I also had to make various adjustments to civilian life. Before long, though, I felt more comfortable about a number of things, including making independent decisions. I no longer depended on my parents or the military to make decisions for me.

My undergraduate years were in a sense a renaissance period in my life. Inevitably, I got involved in student politics and movements. It was an exciting time in U.S. history, because people were attempting to openly exercise their democratic wings. Yet it also was a frustrating time, in that language-minority populations' civil rights still were in their infancy—not that we are now *without* the need for civil rights, but we *have* come a distance within the Chicano community toward understanding our civil rights, however diminished they may remain (of course, this allegation may be an illusion on my part). The 15 years that I look back on as I write this witnessed immense losses of civil rights for *all* people in this country—even those who would like to think they are totally exempt from needing to insist on their fulfillment. One special point here: Classrooms are sites where children *could* and *should* learn about democratic processes. Unfortunately, there are too many teachers there who themselves remain in denial of the need for improved human and civil rights.

My political development as an undergraduate set the tone for what I would pursue over the next 15 years. I selected teacher education as my major, and, as of my involvement in this book, have been in the field of education for 17 years, both as student and as teacher. I have helped to develop Chicano Studies Programs at various universities, and have been active in the political activities that go with such programs. As a result of getting involved in Chicano Studies/Ethnic Studies, bilingual education, and multicultural education, I was motivated to develop my writing and reading skills. By the time I entered graduate school, my academic and study skills had improved considerably.

I married when I entered graduate school and fortunately had my wife's full support from the start. In fact, we had our first two children while I was in graduate studies. Those were trying times for the whole family as we endured difficult years of low-income housing, shopping, clothing, and cars, and all the other frustrations that went with being on a tight budget while I tried to master my courses.

I experienced varying degrees of racism while in graduate school. Many of the White faculty members were anesthetized to the question of cultural and linguistic diversity. In addition, a fair share of minority faculty didn't care to get involved collectively in the struggles of minority faculty and students: They were simply the recipients of benefits and gains that were accorded via the struggles of other minority faculty and students.

I believe that what helped me persist throughout graduate school was a new understanding of the social, cultural, and economic inequalities prevalent in U.S. education. However, as contradictions will have it sometimes, it was also in graduate school that I made conceptual gains from some of the minority and nonminority faculty and students. It was there that I learned that the educational system can make individuals learn either to succumb to what it wants them to become or to resist its molding patterns.

Other Schools and Universities

I taught in public schools for five years. It was a fruitful yet frustrating experience for me because I rarely seemed to fit the system. I found public school teaching to be regimented, rule ordered, and lacking creativity. For example, there were no alternative methods allowed for helping children learn in diverse ways who could not, for whatever reason, sit quietly, be more serene, and work on the assignments I gave them. I asked counselors and administrators to consider different approaches, but my pleas and suggestions were to no avail. In those classrooms I saw the images of my own student life in public school and immediately became an advocate on behalf of marginal students. When I did implement teaching strategies that worked, I was asked, Why are you doing that?—as if to imply that, I was making other teachers look bad because my unorthodox ways in the classroom yielded positive results. I learned that I *did* like teaching, though it had to be in a setting where academic freedom was valued and respected. It also had to be in a setting where I could express myself without fear of reprisal by insecure administrators and teachers. The implication here seems to suggest that insecure administrators and teachers do not exist in colleges and universities, but that is not the point. Insecure people exist everywhere. Rather, the implication here is that colleges and universities, by their very nature, allow for more academic freedom and individual teaching style.

College and university teaching has always involved politics for me. The nature of university teaching, research, and service is surprisingly political. The pedagogies and knowledges acquired and implemented in universities are value laden, and so require faculty to take up positions that announce their views as being within the locally standardized academic boundaries. Frequently, those who wish to establish themselves outside of those boundaries are seen as dissidents. They are tolerated only to the degree that they pose no great threat to the monolithic yet legitimated canons of the institution and the culture it promotes.

I would like to consider myself a developing scholar, both critical and radical. "Radical," to me, is meant to apply to swift and therapeutic change. For several years, I worked within the boundaries of the "academy"—without, I feel, having my efforts recognized, no less reciprocated. It was a one-way experience: I gave, they took, period. It seems to me that in order to achieve some degree of balance between the large number of conservative academics and the small number of critical and radical ones in universities, a lot of new-breed scholars must weigh in before we can even *begin* to make sides more equal. The new breed must include academics from a pool in which gender, ethnicity, class, and race representation are not the stuff of academic hang-ups, but rather as sought-after aspects of the kind of diversity that the entire educational world needs.

It is my intent as a developing critical educator to continue to make contributions toward the transformation of our society, to one in which people's dreams for a better life are not suppressed by injustice, bigotry, lack of financial resources, hatred, and other social, cultural, and institutional afflictions (Aronowitz & Giroux, 1991). My relative successes to date can be attributed to many things. I needed but a little encouragement to believe in myself, to work at fulfilling my potential, and to understand that learning is both developmental and unending. Much of this I did myself, but there were significant others needed to help me to do the rest. Had I received their sort of input initially, I now would write in a more obliging and benevolent language about my early schooling experiences.

Teachers need both to know and to believe that they *can* make a difference in the lives of *all* the children they meet with almost daily. They must also know and believe that the only way to achieve this goal is to work empathetically with them rather than self-righteously.

References

Aronowitz, S., & Giroux, H. (1991). *Postmodern education: Politics, culture, and social Criticism.* Minneapolis: University of Minnesota Press.

Freire, P., & Macedo, D. (1987). LITERACY. *Reading the word and the world.* South Hadley, MA: Bergin and Garvey.

Hernandez, D. (1970). *Mexican American challenge to a sacred cow.* Chicano Studies Center Monograph, UCLA: Aztlan Publications.

About the Author

Hermán S. García was born in Encino, New Mexico, where he graduated from Encino High School. After military service, he attended New Mexico Highlands University, Washington State University, and New Mexico State University, respectively. He taught in public schools for five years. He has also taught at Eastern Washington University, Texas Tech University, Texas A&M University, and is currently teaching in the Department of Curriculum and Instruction at New Mexico State University in Las Cruces. García specializes in the broad area of language-minority educational issues, including bilingual education, critical pedagogy, international education, and curriculum and instruction.

Chapter *14*

The Middle Eastern Americans

BARAZANDEH "BARAZ"
SAMIIAN

G. PRITCHY
SMITH

> *We must now go on a long journey. Something, I am not sure what, will happen on the way. Those of you who have absorbed enough to enter this stage will be able to accompany me—Indries Shah in* Thinkers of the East

Middle Eastern Americans belong to a long list of excluded, invisible players in the development of contemporary America. Historically, multicultural education as an aspect of American teacher-education programs has centered the focus of its advocacy for inclusive school curricula on African-American, Hispanic-American, Native-American, Asian-American, and European immigrant cultures. In addition, more recent literature on multicultural teacher education reflects a broadening emphasis on the need for curricula to feature the diversity of nonethnically designated populations such as the differently abled, women, poor White rural and urban, and gays and lesbians. School curricula have relegated in the past, and too often continues to relegate, all of these and other unmentioned groups to invisibility as insignificant contributors to America's unique development as a nation. The purpose of this chapter is to focus the spotlight of discussion about excluded groups on the cultures of the Middle East and American descendants from these cultures who populate U.S. classrooms in greater numbers than most educators recognize.

The average citizen in the United States is embarrassingly ignorant about the Middle East and its diverse cultures. Additionally, American teachers typically do not know much about the Middle East. Too often, what teachers do know and transmit about the Middle East through school curricula does not transcend the denigrating stereotypes that are perpetuated by popular print and television media—the "camel jockey"; the fanatical religious zealot; the oil-rich, selfish Emir who is unconcerned with the poor; the tyrannical military leader; the impoverished, "crippled" street beggar; the secretive, untrustworthy plotter; the swarthy thief; the fierce warrior-horseman; the "belly-dancer"; and the veiled, subjugated woman who struggles vainly without benefit of equal rights in male-dominated societies. The list of examples of ignorance seems almost endless and definitely is appalling. In fact, just as people from other countries know Americans by the stereotypes of them that are projected abroad, Americans know Middle Easterners through incalculable distortions of information. Equally appalling are the unfortunate consequences of this cultural illiteracy about the Middle East that continues to be perpetuated throughout U.S. society and its schools. Two obvious, unfortunate results are that students of Middle Eastern heritage find little in American schools' curriculum to affirm their cultural worth, and that their classmates from non-Middle Eastern backgrounds find little to counteract historically perpetuated prejudices.

This present presentation of information about the Middle East, its cultures, and the relevance of their accurate portrayal in school curricula is deliberately limited to selected topics and requires preliminary discussion of several caveats in order to accomplish its purpose (rather than to contribute to an already existing body of harmful half-truths). The topics addressed include (1) a broad historical and cultural overview of the Middle Eastern peoples, (2) a discussion solely about the Iranian Americans and their homeland's historical and cultural roots, and (3) a consideration restricted to the Arab Americans, their homeland connections, and their cultural roots. Thus, this chapter does *not* discuss, for example, the diverse peoples of Cypress, Turkey, Israel, and other Middle Eastern countries. A discussion of their cultures and patterns of immigration to the United States must become the responsibility of other writers committed to multicultural education. Because information and data are largely restricted to Iranian Americans and Arab Americans, the authors readily concede that what is presented is at best better than the unacceptable, distorted information presented in most American school curricula but at worst considerably short of the comprehensive *accurate* information that should be presented about all Middle Eastern cultures in school programs of the future.

With regard to other caveats, it should be noted first that the brevity of information imposed by an essay-length chapter cannot do justice to the many separate Middle Eastern cultures that contribute to the rich texture of the larger Middle Eastern world. Second, the dynamics of long-standing amiable and hostile interactions alike among these many separate peoples cannot be treated comprehensively and sensitively. Third, only broad brushstrokes of 5,000 years of history and culture can be presented, thus preventing the meaningful capture of either the glories of past and present civilizations in the Middle East, or the cyclical flow of emerging and receding cultures. Not even the European and American interactions with the Middle East can be discussed with any serious depth. Moreover, only the most simplistic introduction to the rich diversity of religions can be presented. In fact, given the number of essential elements of culture (such as religions, customs, traditions, languages, and histories), and the material artifacts of art, music, literature, and other manifestations of the creative spirit, this treatise cannot help but fall short of the expectations of most readers. Omissions are due more to the limitation of the scope of this study than to any purposeful authors' bias—and are, therefore, not meant to offend.

The Middle East: An Overview

The term *Middle East* is rather vague to the average American. It loosely refers to a region that is a combination of Near East and Middle East in relation to Western Europe, and in contrast to the Far East (the Orient). The Middle East, in general, consists of the following countries: Afghanistan, Pakistan, Iran, Iraq, Turkey, Cyprus, Syria, Lebanon, Israel, Jordon, Kuwait, Saudi Arabia, Bahrain, Qatar, United Arab Emirates, Oman, Yemen Arab Republic, People's Democratic Republic of Yemen, and Egypt. As such, this region, in size, equals that of the continental United States.

From the earliest times, the Middle East has been considered by scholars as one of the world's wondrous cradles of cultural diversity. In fact, most archeologists agree that the Middle East *is* the cradle of civilization, what with Mesopotamian, Egyptian, and Persian civilizations dating back to between 4,000 and 3,000 B.C. and continuing through the Islamic civilization that began in the seventh century. From earliest times, too, the Middle East has been metaphorically considered the crossroad of trade routes between and among three continents: Asia, Africa, and Europe. Consequently, many cultures and civilizations have met, interacted, and flourished in the region. The Middle East not only is considered the cradle of civilization but it also is the birthplace of three major world religions—Judaism, Christianity, and Islam—with Jerusalem (old Palestine) considered the Holy Land equally revered by all three. As they did in the past, today's people of the Middle East speak many languages, including Arabic (the language of the majority of the Middle Eastern nations), Persian, Turkish, Aramaic, Kurdish, Armenian, Assyrian, Greek, and Hebrew.

Most Western historians trace European interest in the Middle East at least back to the Romans and Greeks of 400 to 300 B.C. They emphasize European interest in the Middle East as being manifested by the Christian Crusades and other invasions that have occurred since the eighteenth century—a broad expanse of time during which the Europeans (specifically the French, British, and Russians), through various pacts, divided the region into their own spheres of interest. As early as World War I, U.S. interest in the Middle East became evident; obviously, it has not only continued but has greatly expanded since then. Long-standing Russian interests in the region have been basically for economic and military reasons as well as for access to warmer waters and open seas through the Persian Gulf. Modern European and American interests, in general, also have been *economic* because of "the oil," *political* in order to exert influence and control in and over the region, and *military* with respect to the region's strategic location—not only during World War II but also throughout the Cold War with Russia.

Because of vast oil reserves in the Middle East, most present-day countries worldwide have had an abiding interest in the delicate balances of power among both the countries of the Middle East and the Western superpowers—who have maintained complicated overt and covert interactions with various Middle Eastern nations. In truth, most scholars of history and politics would agree that, more often than not, Middle Easterners perceive European, American, and Russian interaction with various countries of the Middle East as having been motivated by self-interest, and more akin to intrusive exertions of power than to relationships characterized by integrity and respect. In short, a long history from ancient to modern times—is replete with instances of invading armies, attempts to colonize, and nefarious treaties and agreements—is sufficient reason for most contemporary Middle Eastern citizens not to trust the idea that the rest of the world respects or believes in the Middle Eastern nations' right to self-determination.

The Middle East: A Brushstroke of History and Cultural Contributions

Archeological investigations in the Arabian Peninsula, although still in the infancy stage, indicate that ancient Semitic civilizations (such as the Dilmuns) thrived along the Persian Gulf coast—areas known today as Kuwait and Bahrain—as early as 4,000 B.C. A study spearheaded and edited by Nyrop (1984) of the American University asserts that "in about 3,500 B.C. two parallel migrations [from the central Arabian Peninsula] occurred—one by the western route northward to the Sinai Peninsula and into Egypt, where the immigrants mixed with the indigenous people to produce the historical Egyptians; the other by the eastern route to Sumer where they amalgamated and became known as Babylonians" (p. 7). Moreover, there is historical evidence that tribes of Arab nomads, from around 3,000 B.C., migrated northward to the Fertile Crescent (an arching crescent from Persian Gulf to modern Israel) and settled in northern and eastern Syria, becoming progenitors of the Aramaean and Akkadian kingdoms. The language spoken by this population was Aramaic—a Semitic language that (in much later years) was used by Jesus, the Apostles, and in the Old Testament.

Whereas there have been long-standing civilizations (such as the Assyrians, Babylonians, Egyptians, Persians, and Sumerians) in the region—some dating as far back as to over 4,000 B.C.—it was not until the seventh century that the peoples of Arabia became dominant players in the Middle Eastern region. In A.D. 622, with the dawn of Islam, the people of Arabia emerged as major contributor to the world civilization through an Islamic world that expanded from India, China, and Central Asia through Asia Minor and North Africa, and onto Southern Europe (Rosenfeld & Geller, 1979).

The vast Islamic world was administered by and large through a "caliphate" government centered in Baghdad (now the capital of Iraq). The Islamic rulers had the ability to recognize what was best in other cultures, adopt it, add to it, and then pass it on to other peoples. The Islamic caliphs (rulers of the Islamic Empire) welcomed to their courts artisans, writers, scholars, and scientists and encouraged them to innovate, to expand, and to develop new concepts that formed a distinguished culture for some 800 years. The Muslim scientists and writers were especially influenced by the philosophy and science of ancient Greece, Persia, India, and Egypt, and important works (of Greeks in particular) were translated into the Arabic language. During this period, life-saving discoveries in medicine, predicated on previous Greek and Egyptian findings, were made, and various diseases—such as measles and smallpox—were described and diagnosed. All available medical knowledge was collected and published in several huge volumes. In fact, the medical book *al-Qanun*, written in the eleventh century in the Arabic language by Ibn-e Sina (Avecinna), an Iranian born in Bukhara, became a basic medical book used in

European medical schools for several hundred years. The Islamic rulers also promoted the advancement of the study of astronomy, the development of effective astronomical instruments, and the construction of observatories.

Many significant mathematical, literary, and architectural contributions taken for granted in the West today came to Western civilization by way of Arabic influence during the pinnacle of Islamic civilization. For example, our present-day mathematical knowledge, including calculation principles, originally came from Hindus in India who had used zero and a numerical system for many, many years. Since the Arabs introduced this mathematical numbering to the Western world, today we commonly refer to its basic units as "arabic numerals" (Hourani, 1991). Algebra, too, is a contribution to the scientific world that came to the West by way of Arab peoples' expansion. The historical literature often identifies Diophantus, a Greek mathematician (ca. A.D. 200), as "the father of algebra," even though its principles were earlier known to (and used by) Chinese, Iranians, Egyptians, and peoples of India and Mesopotamia (Assyrians, Babylonians, and Sumerians) for thousands of years.

In fact, the word *algebra* comes to us from the title of a book by Al-Khwarazmi, an Iranian mathematician who taught at the mathematical school of Baghdad. Between A.D. 813 and 833, Al-Khwarazmi collected, studied, and improved on previous knowledge in the field of mathematics, and wrote his treatise in the Arabic language under the title *Ilm al-Gebr wa'l Muqabalah*—meaning, in Arabic, "the science of reduction and cancellation" (Smith, 1958). Of course, it was not until the 1500s that the European scholars began to understand and appreciate thoroughly the value of this symbolic language in mathematical calculations.

The exquisite art and architectural designs as represented by the decorative arts, paintings, geometric forms and shapes, and beautiful mosques and palaces were also gifts from the Islamic civilization to the Western world. The world-renowned Alhambra (meaning "red" in Arabic) Palace in Grenada, Spain, is the finest example of Islamic design and influence on the European continent. Many historians describe the Islamic civilization of this period as magnificent, splendid, and brilliant.

The Islamic world, however, started to decline sometime after A.D. 1200, and by A.D. 1600 the European civilization began to surpass that of the Islamic. In fact, around the middle of the tenth century it was evident that there was no longer any real unity in the Muslim world. The Caliphs, who had become lofty and extravagant, were not able to rule the vast Empire easily; and other non-Arab peoples who were under the domination of the Arab rule, such as the Iranians and the Turks, sought independence. Between 1097 and 1291, the Christian Crusaders (who conducted seven Crusades to the Middle East and one to North Africa), in support of the Byzantine Empire—to recapture the Holy Land— added to the decline of the Muslim rule (Rosenfeld & Geller, 1979). The greatest destruction, however, was wrought in the thirteenth century by the Mongols—nomadic horsemen who came from the steppes of Central Asia. Under the leadership of Genghis Khan, these hordes swept through the Middle East fiercefully. They conquered Iran, Asia Minor, and Syria. Baghdad, the capital of the Islamic world, fell in A.D. 1258. The Mongols slaughtered hundreds of thousands of people, and destroyed the cities, towns, and villages. As the invaders created misery and disorder by their invasions, industries declined, and the normally safe internal and cross-continental trade routes became both dangerous and broken down. In fact, for many decades, commerce and culture alike stagnated. Toward the end of the fifteenth century, the utilization of an all-water route between Europe, the Indian subcontinent, and the Orient contributed even further to the decline of the Middle East—whose once prosperous cities all too fully ceased to be centers of culture, commerce, and trade.

Religious Diversity in the Middle East, and the Islamic Traditions

The Middle East is the birthplace of Zoroastrianism, Judaism, Christianity, and Islamic faith—all of whose followers believe in the supremacy of the one and only God, Who created the universe. Consequently, peoples of the Middle East are not only Muslims and Jews but also Christians (Protestants, Catholics, Eastern/Greek/Armenian Orthodox, Coptic, etc.) and Zoroastrians. The majority of the Middle Easterners, however, are of the Muslim faith, which includes the followers of the Sunni, Shi'a, Ismaili, and Baha'i sects, and a number of smaller derivations thereof. The differences between the Islamic sects is more political in practice than theological, as all the sects believe in *Alläh* (meaning "God" in Arabic), Mohammed as Prophet and the Messenger of God, and the *Koran*—the Muslim Holy Book. The "Five Pillars of Islam" include (1) declaration of faith ("There is no God but Allah, and Mohammed is the Messenger of Allah"), (2) prayer (five times daily), (3) almsgiving (sharing a portion of one's possessions and wealth with those of lesser means), (4) fasting (from dawn to dusk during the month of Ramadan), and (5) pilgrimage (to Mecca, at least once in one's lifetime).

Aside from "the oil" and the politics of the Middle East, a prevailing contemporary question often is focused on the Islamic view of women. The Arab people prior to Islam, in fact, had very little regard for women and female children. However, the Islamic doctrine did much to strongly promote equality and respect for not only all peoples and all races but also for both genders. The following passages (Abdul-Rauf [Trans.], 1977) from the *Koran* illustrate pertinent Islamic sentiments:

On Religious Duties

And the believing men and the believing women owe loyalty to one another. They enjoin noble deeds and forbid dishonor, they perform the prayer, and pay the alms, and obey God and His Messenger. On them will God have mercy; God is All-mighty and All-wise. (Koran IX:71)

The Muslim men and women, the believing men and women, the devout men and women, the truthful men and men, the charitable men and women, and the men and women who engage much in God's praise—for them God has prepared forgiveness and a great reward. (Koran XXXIII:35)

On Human Equality

*O mankind, We created you all from a male and female, and made you into races and tribes, that you may know one another. Surely the noblest among you in the sight of God is the most God-fearing of you. (*Koran *XLIX:13)*

On Gender Equality in Wage Earning and in Receiving Inheritance

*To men there is a share of what parents and kinsmen leave; likewise to women there is a share of what parents and kinsmen leave; whether the property be small or large—a determinate share. (*Koran *IV:7)*
    *To men there is a right in what they have earned, likewise to women there is a right in what they have earned. (*Koran *IV:32)*

The Islamic religious doctrines indeed apply equally to both genders. Women, the same as men, are required to participate in *all* religious duties—including the learning and teaching of the doctrine (there is no ordained priesthood in Islam). The only major concession made for women is that they are to refrain from active prayers and fasting during menstruation or pregnancy. Islamic women have the *right* to retain their own name (that is, their birth/maiden name, even after marriage) and to control their own funds, properties, inheritances, finances, and earnings totally independent of their husbands, fathers, brothers, and all other potential male impediments. The possibility of divorce (resolution of a marriage) is sanctioned by Islam, as evidenced by the following passages (Abdul-Rauf [Trans.], 1977): "Live with them honorably, or part with them honorably" (*Koran* II:231); and "No matter how you may try or endeavor, you cannot do full justice to women. However, be not unfair to a wife [when] separating from her with no determined decision. But if you come to a friendly understanding and practice self-restraint, God is forgiving and merciful" (*Koran* IV:129).

A Muslim woman has the Islamic legal *right* not only to *choose* her own husband but also to *refuse* an arranged marriage. Furthermore, she has the *right* to stipulate in her marriage contract the right to divorce her husband at will, to be notified if her husband intends to become polygamous, and the right to divorce her husband should he practice polygamy without her explicit permission (Abdul-Rauf [Trans.], 1977). However, because there is a measure of discrepancy or contradiction in some of the surahs and passages in the *Koran*, certain "selective" interpretations have led to the outrageous discriminations now existing in many Islamic nations. For example, the passage "And [women] have rights equal to the rights incumbent on them according to what is equitable; and men have a degree over them [women]" (*Koran* II:228) contradicts the passage "And their Lord answered them: Verily I will never cause to be lost the labor of any of you, be you a male or a female—the one of you is as the other" (*Koran* III:195); or a passage from *Hadidth* (Pronouncements by the Prophet:) "All people are equal, as equal as the teeth of a comb. There is no claim of merit of an Arab over a non-Arab, or of a white over a black person, or of a male over a female. Only God-fearing people merit a preference with God" (Abdul-Rauf [Trans.], 1977).

Middle Easterners in the United States of America

Records indicate that immigration of Middle Easterners to the United States began in the early nineteenth century, and has increased steadily as political and economic upheavals forced individuals to leave their respective homelands. Immigrants to the United States, in general, fall within two categories: (1) those who enter the country with an immigrant visa obtained from the U.S. consular services abroad and (2) those whose visa status is adjusted to immigrant status (Permanent Resident) while they are in the United States. The term *American*, however, refers broadly to those members of our society who are U.S. citizens by birth or through naturalization. Naturalized citizens enjoy all the same rights as the U.S.-born citizens except for being eligible to stand for election to the office of president or vice president of the United States. Permanent residents, who in effect, are not considered Americans, can neither vote or stand for election, but can enjoy most other rights enjoyed by the U.S. citizens.

In addition to the children of both naturalized U.S. citizens and permanent residents, there are a large number of foreign students (individuals with student visas) from various Middle Eastern nations in our educational institutions. Larger yet is the student population of first-, second-, or third-generation Americans who, in fact, self-identify their nationality as American, but remain largely as Middle Easterners in culture and values. Together, these young people constitute a significant student population whose history, traditions, and ethnic contributions unfortunately are typically left out of school curricula. Also, they seldom find teachers who are empathetic, or even know how to be culturally responsive, to their needs, their cultural values, or their learning styles.

It is indisputable that we, as educators, need to enlarge the circle of our knowledge of, and respect for, the diversity of our students beyond that of race, gender, or mental ability if we are to succeed in reaching *all* our students. To this end, the next two chapters will discuss two distinctly different peoples of the Middle Eastern heritage: the Iranian Americans and the Arab Americans. It is important to note that the Iranians are not Arab and that the terms *Arabs* and *Arabic* do not equate with "Iranians," although the term *Middle Easterner* applies to both, as well as to a host of other peoples who share the same geographical roots.

References

Abdul-Rauf, M. (1977). *The Islamic view of women and the family*. New York: Robert Speller & Sons. *Al-Ghazaly Minaret Newletter*. (1991, October). 1(1).

Hourani, A. (1991). *A history of the Arab peoples*. Cambridge, MA: Belknap Press.

Nyrop, R. F. (Ed). (1984). *Saudi Arabia: A country study* (4th ed.) Washington, DC: United States Government.

Rosenfeld, E., & Geller, H. (1979). *Afro-Asian culture studies* (4th ed.). Woodbury: Barron's Educational Series.

Smith, D. E. (1958). *History of mathematics*. New York: Dover.

About the Authors

Barazandeh "Baraz" Samiian is adjunct professor of management, College of Business Administration, University of North Florida, and lecturer on the topics of organization theory and design, cultural diversity in the workplace, business and professional ethics, and multicultural communication. Baraz serves as instructional program coordinator, Telecourse program, at the Florida Community College at Jacksonville. She has authored numerous handbooks for human resources development programs.

G. Pritchy Smith is a professor of curriculum and instruction, University of North Florida. He is a founding member of the National Association for Multicultrual Education (NAME). He has authored articles on minority recruitment in teacher education and multicultural education. Smith has conducted research on the impact of teacher testing on the racial composition of the national teaching force.

15

The Iranian Americans

BARAZANDEH "BARAZ"
SAMIIAN

G. PRITCHY
SMITH

Make thy ownself pure, O righteous man! Anyone in the world here below can win purity for his own self, namely, when he cleans his ownself with good thoughts, words, and deeds.—Vendidad 10:19 (Adapted from Hopfe, 1991)

The poems of Omar Khayyam, the Persian lamb, the Persian melon, the Persian Gulf, crisis, the American hostages in Iran, the Persian cat, and the Persian carpet all provoke an emotional seesaw in the typical American. Iranians experience a similar sensation when they reflect on their history and culture. Indeed, the history of the Iranian peoples consists of cyclical peaks and valleys of civilizations—empires, invasions, victories, defeats, glories, cultural stagnation, and cultural achievements. As a nation, in fact, Iran is a multicultural confederation of a people called *Iranians* (Persians, from Persis by the Greeks), which includes an extremely diverse citizenry: Turks, Kurds, Lurs, Arabs, Jews, Armenians, Assyrians, Georgians, Turkamans, Balluchis, and a host of others, in addition to the original Aryans.

Historical documents (as well as some 4,000 year-old legends) unfold the story of Aryan tribes who migrated south from Central Asia, some on horseback, to settle in various parts of a plateau between the Caspian Sea and the Persian Gulf, which became known as Iran—meaning "the Land of Aryans." The tongue in which they spoke was related to what is come to be known as the Indo-Iranian language group, derived from the Indo-European linguistic family from which the Germanic, Latin-Romance, and Greek languages also take their root. This common-language parentage accounts for the similarities existing in many basic words and terms in Persian (Farsi), German, English, and Latin (for example: *brother* (English), *bárãdár* (Persian), *frater* (Latin), *bruder* (German); *father* (English), *pédár* (Persian), *pater* (Latin), *vater* (German); *mother* (English), *modár* (Persian), *mater* (Latin), *mutter* (German).

A Brushstroke of Iranian History and Culture

The height of the Iranian civilization was reached during the reign of the Hakhamanish Dynasty (Achaemenid in Greek). By 546 B.C., Cyrus the Great, the most renowned King of this Dynasty, had secured the control of the Aegean coastal territories of Asia Minor (today's Turkey) and Armenia, some of the Greek colonies, and Egypt in North Africa. Cyrus is noted with reverence in the Old Testament for having released the Jews—who were kept captive in Babylon—and allowing them to return to Palestine. The Achaemenid kings were called *Shahanshah*, meaning "King of Kings," largely because the Iranian Empire comprised many smaller kingdoms. The hallmark of the Iranian rulers of this period was a sound and far-sighted administrative system, brilliant military organization and maneuvering strategies, and—most important of all—a humanistic and egalitarian worldview. Pope (1965) wrote, "The remarkable Achaemenid achievements were due not merely to courage, strength, and enterprise, but also to superior intelligence: a capacity for large-scale planning and practical administrative ability. These capacities were reinforced, moreover, by humane sympathies, products of a noble faith that inspired racial, religious and cultural tolerance, in which a highly developed sense of justice played an important role" (p. 22).

The remarkable Achaemenid achievement indeed was based on a democratic and sound infrastructure that consisted of a strong central government—which oversaw the general and external affairs of the nation—and 20 independently governed *satrapies*, or states (a concept similar to the U.S. system). During the reign of Cyrus and his descendent, Darius I (Dariyush the Great), vast highways and roads were built throughout the Empire, linking the 20 satrapies together to facilitate expansion in commerce and interchange. In fact, Pope (1965) noted that the highways between Susa, Persepolis, and Ecbatana (in western Iran) were even paved. To accommodate the Phoenician merchant fleet's navigation from the Mediterranean Sea to the Persian Gulf, the Persian engineers constructed a canal between the Nile River and the Red Sea—a forerunner for the Suez Canal of some 2,000 years later. Moreover, an efficient "Pony Express" was established whose fame went beyond the Empire's borders; to the extent that the Greek historian Herodotus (ca. 484 B.C.), in praise of the Persian postal system, wrote "There is no mortal thing faster than these messengers. Neither snow nor rain nor heat nor gloom of night stays these couriers from the swift completion of their appointed rounds" (postal history, the *World Book Encyclopedia,* 1970, p. 626). Interestingly enough, the last part of this quotation is inscribed on the architrave of the main entrance to the General Post Office in New York City.

To ensure the fair treatment of the population, the Iranian kings had established a bureau of royal inspectors called "eyes and ears of the king." These inspectors regularly toured the Empire and reported back to the king the state of affairs therein. The Persian justice system, too, was designed so that the legal decisions reached at the satrapy-level courts could be appealed to the next higher court of the central government (a concept similar to today's U.S. Supreme Court) and even to the king. Although the common language used in most of the Empire was Aramaic (a Semitic language), the Persian language served as the "official" language of the Empire and was used for the inscriptions, official documents, and royal proclamations. In transmission to various parts of the

Empire, however, official documents always accompanied a translation in respective local language—as the Iranian kings believed in the rights of each people to preserve their own culture, language, and religion.

The elaborate and efficient infrastructure of the administration of this period facilitated a very healthy commercial activity, trade, and exchange of commodities among the populations in the far reaches of the Empire. Consequently, a variety of words as well as commodities were introduced to other Middle Eastern peoples and, over time, found their way into the Western world—and, eventually, into today's English language. For example, the word *bazaar*, and familiar commodities such as *shawl, sash, turquoise, tiara, orange, lemon, melon, peach, spinach, asparagus, tulip*, and *narcissus* (as well as other botanical favorites of the Western world) have their origins in this era.

The reign of the Achaemenid Dynasty came to an end in 331 B.C. when the Persian Empire was conquered by Alexander of Macedonia, who envisioned a new world based on infusions of Greek and Iranian cultures and ideals. To have this vision realized, Alexander, after conquering Iran, commanded his officers and some 10,000 of his other soldiers to marry Iranian women—at a mass wedding held at Susa in 324 B.C. (Metz, 1989). It is important to note that in the Iranian culture and literature Alexander is referred to as "Alexander of Macedonia" rather than "Alexander the Great" (as labeled by Western historians). The Iranian value system regards "greatness" in relation to wisdom, statesmanship, and nobility of mind. Alexander is regarded by the Iranians as a military genius, but one who lacked sagacity—as evidenced by his order, after a night of drinking and merry-making, to set ablaze the great palace and the seat of government in Persopolis. This event destroyed the library, and with it the bulk of the historical documents and literature of the ancient Persians.

Alexander's untimely death in 323 B.C. in Babylon (he died of a fever at age 33) left a vacuum that resulted in anarchy due to the lack of an organization sound enough to rule his vast conquest that reached from Egypt to India, and even to the Chinese borders. Eventually, four of his generals established individual small kingdoms throughout the conquered territories. Thus, most of Iran came under the control of the Seleucid Dynasty for some hundred years, during which time the use of Hellenistic motifs in both the arts and architecture became prevalent.

The Parthians, who prided themselves in being descendents from both the Greeks and the Persians, defeated the Seleucids, then ruled Iran for over three centuries. They spoke a language similar to the old Persian, used Pahlavi script for their writing, and established an administrative system based on the Achaemenid system of government. It was not, however, until A.D. 224 that the nation was again governed by native Iranian rulers. Ardeshir, who claimed to be a descendant of a legendary hero named Sassan, overthrew the last Parthian king and established the Sassanid Dynasty, which lasted for 400 years.

The Sassanid kings reestablished the title of Shahansha—king of kings—as they expanded their territory and empire over smaller kingdoms and rulers, resurrected the Iranian culture and traditions by eliminating the Greek cultural influences, and reestablished Zoroastrianism as the state religion. The most celebrated king of this dynasty was Anooshiravan "the Just" (Chosroes I, according to the Greeks)—a title bestowed on him because of his fairness and accessibility to his people. He established provincial administration and a taxation system, founded new towns, provided patronage for the arts, and commissioned the construction of great buildings, some of which are still in existence.

The Sassanid kings brought back from India scientific and academic manuscripts and had them translated into the Pahlavi language; many of these found their way into Islamic literature and Western civilization in later years. Harris (1977) reported that, according to later Arab sources, the grand hall of the Sassanid royal palace at Ctesiphon (the capital of the Empire) was carpeted with a magnificent floor covering woven of fine wool, silk, and silver and gold yarns, depicting a springtime garden with streams and reflecting ponds. Unfortunately, after the Arab invasion in A.D. 642, this legendary piece of art was cut up and carried away as souvenirs, and thus lost to the world.

Following the fall of the Sassanid Dynasty, and beginning with the Arab conquest, the Iranian people were invaded and governed by alien rulers for more than 800 years (from 642 to 1501). The Iranians' contention for the Arab incursion, however, precluded the conversion of the majority of the population into the Islamic faith until the ninth century. Meanwhile, a great number of Zoroastrian Persians, who did not convert, steadily moved on to India, where today the "Parsees" form a large community of educated, cultured, and respected citizens.

Between the eight and eleventh centuries, several native Iranian dynasties challenged the Arab rulers by establishing provincial governments within the Iranian plateau—but none could last long enough to mount sufficient resistance to counter Arab rule permanently. During the eleventh century, Iran was dominated by the Seljuk Turks, and then in 1219 was invaded and virtually destroyed by Genghis Khan. The Mongols, 700,000 strong, invaded Bukhara, Samarkand, Neyshabur, and other cities—burning, looting, and killing while conquering lands from east to west. The Mongol presence in Iran lasted into the fourteenth century. In 1381, Timur Leng (Tamulane), who has variously been described as of either Mongol or Turkic origin (Metz, 1989), invaded Iran and established yet *another* nonnative government. The descendants of Timur Long ruled Iran until the dawn of the Safavid Dynasty in 1501, the first native Iranian dynasty after almost nine centuries of foreign invasions and rulers.

The reign of the Safavid kings (until 1736) is noted as the Renaissance of Iranian culture and civilization. This revival manifested itself in all areas of the arts and architecture: spawning magnificent bridges, palaces, mosques, bazaars, caravanserais (an ancestor of today's motel concept); miniature paintings; textiles; enamelwork; ivory inlaid wooden objects and furniture; gold and silver vases and plates; pottery and porcelains of all types; and of course, the much admired and exquisite Persian rugs and carpets. The zenith of the Safavid Dynasty was reached during the reign of Shah Abbas the Great, who "transformed Isfahan into a capital of such splendor that the more remains of its brilliant filed facades and domes still makes it one of the wonders of the East" (Harris, 1977, p. 22). Under the Safavids, too, the Shi'a (or Shi'i, or Shiite) sect of Islam became the state religion—which has remained so to the present.

The subsequent native dynasties—Afshar and Zand, in particular—also made their mark in the Iranian history. For example, Nadir Shah Afshar's victories in India resulted in immense wealth of jewels, gold, and magnificent artifacts that were handed over to him in 1739 by the ruling Mongol Emperor in Delhi in exchange for peace. Although much of that enormous treasure has been lost through the years, what has remained today is still a resplendent and priceless treasure that is kept in a depository vault in Tehran, as backing for the Iranian currency (the same principle as U.S. gold bullion, kept in Fort Knox, KY). The most famous trophies in this collection were the Peacock Throne and the Kooh-i-Noor (meaning "Mountain of Light") diamond. After Nadir Shah's death (at the end of eighteenth century), the legendary Peacock Throne disappeared from the collection, although, in later years, a similar one was built, which became the royal chair of state for subsequent Iranian monarchs (*The Crown Jewels*, 1964). The magnificent Kooh-i-Noor diamond, too, was pilfered and subsequently (in 1849) was taken to England and presented to Queen Victoria (*The Crown Jewels*, 1964). Today, it adorns the British Royal Crown and can be viewed at the Tower of London.

From 1794 to 1925, Iran was ruled by the Qajar Dynasty. During this period, Iran was engulfed in internal and international intrigue that witnessed secret pacts between European powers competing to expand their spheres of interest and influence in the Middle East. Although the Qajar kings tried to secure the independence of the nation through their emissaries to the British and Russian royal courts, contradictions between overt and covert agreements cost Iran the loss of its northern territories to Russia, while the British occupied the regions along the Persian Gulf. The discovery of oil in 1901 in Iran established the British as a "partner" as they continued to manipulate the Iranian government. Also through deception, European archeologists (French and British in particular) carried away many of the historical treasures of the Iranian past.

In 1925, a far-sighted patriot—a commoner with military training—seized the reins of power, established the Pahlavi Dynasty and a parliamentary system of government, and embarked on modernizing a backward and sparsely educated nation. The historical records indicate that under the Pahlavi monarchy the nation made giant leaps into the twentieth century with the establishment of universities and compulsory education for youths (males and females alike); the unveiling and emancipation of women; the granting women the right to vote and stand for election; the improved health-care services and practices; the refinement and expansion of the banking system; the development and expansion of industries (including the oil industry and refineries); the building of roads, waterways, and railroads; the construction of dams for electricity and irrigation; the improvement of farming practices and food productions; the creation of hotels and recreational facilities; the preservation of historical sites and religious shrines; and the patronage of scientific research, the arts, literature, music, and Iranian culture and traditions as well as combating the production and export of narcotic drugs. However, much in the long list of major achievements and revolutionary social reforms contradicted the wishes and ideals of the Shi'a clergy who, in 1979, brought down the monarchy in Iran and established a parochial form of republican government.

Iranians in Islamic Civilization

Iranian influence on the development of the Islamic civilization is recorded in historical documents. The Arab *caliphs* (rulers) used the Iranian system of government and administration—including the office of *vizier* (minister) and bureaus and ministries for registration and control of revenues and expenditures. They also used the Sassanid coinage systems and Iranian court ceremonial practices and traditions. Iranians also became prominent in the caliphate administrations, as well as in such areas of Islamic civilization as literature, history, geography, jurisprudence, philology, philosophy, and the sciences (including mathematics, astronomy, physics, chemistry, and medicine). Among many outstanding Iranians who contributed to Islamic civilization were the ninth-century physician al-Razi, the Chief of Baghdad Hospital, who developed the use of seton (a procedure that facilitates the drainage of blood and fluids to eliminate or control infection) in surgery, defined the first clinical identification of smallpox, and effectively diagnosed and treated bladder and kidney stones; and the tenth-century physician lbn-e Sina (also a philosopher, astronomer, and poet), whose comprehensive medical books were used in Europe for over 600 years. Other examples include Al-Battani, who presented revolutionary ideas in trigonometry, and ratios that led to the field of spherical trigonometry and the most distinguished eleventh-century mathematician, Omar Khayyam (also a world-renowned poet), who made pivotal contributions to the science of astronomy. These notable people constitute only the start of a long, long list of Iranian scientists and academicians who have made, and continue to make, significant contributions to the world of science (Fisher & Ochsenwald, 1990).

Iranians under both the Seljuk and the Mongol Muslim rulers also distinguished themselves not only in science but also in literature and poetry as well. For instance, Firdawsi's (eleventh-century) *Shahnamah*—a great national epic—unfolds the history of legendary Iran in massive volumes of poetry (over 10,000 verses). Saadi's (thirteenth-century) poems and philosophical essays in *Gulistan* (meaning "Flower Garden") and *Boustan* (meaning "Orchard"), and Hafiz's (fourteenth-century) *Deevan* (meaning "Collection of Odes")—a masterpiece of Persian lyric poems—represent the richness of the Persian language and culture.

Although the use of Arabic as the official and academic language became widespread under Arab rule, the Iranians continued to use the Persian language. However, they adopted the Arabic script and incorporated a number of the Arabic "loanwords" into their language. The manuscripts produced by Iranians from the seventh through the fifteenth centuries often were written in the Persian language if in literature, and in Arabic if in science. It is important to note that in spite of similarity of script, the two languages are decidedly different—much the same as is, for example, the English language from French. It is also noteworthy to mention that the Persian (Farsi) alphabet contains 32 letters, including those that are purely of Indo-European roots, as opposed to the Arabic (a Semitic language) alphabet, which has 28.

Spiritual and Religious Beliefs: The Bases of Iranian Culture

In Beny's (1975) *Persia: Bridge of Turquoise*, Seyyed Hossein Nasr wrote that "Persian history separated by distinct periods yet unified within a whole is most directly reflected in religion, the backbone of Persian culture in every phase of its existence" (p. 25). The vast majority of Iranians today are Muslims, but prior to the Islamization of Iran they were of Zoroastrian faith for some 1,500 years. Hopfe (1991) stated that the religious beliefs of the earlier Iranians is veiled in mystery. What *is* known about these early beliefs, however, comes to us through the *Gathas*, hymns of early Zoroastrians (the *Gathas* are to Zoroastrianism as the *Torah* is to Judaism), which indicates that the early Iranians worshiped Daevas—gods associated with the Sun, the Moon, the Earth, fire, and water.

The Zoroastrian religion was founded by Zoroaster (the Latinized version of Zarthusht), who was born in the western region of Iran. The historical records are not very clear regarding Zoroaster's date of birth, although many ancient Greek writers, at various periods of time, placed his birth somewhere between 1,000 and 600 B.C. More recent investigations into the *Gathas* present the possibility of a much earlier date—between 1,400 and 1,000 B.C. (Hopfe, 1991).

In his early years, Zoroaster was trained for the priesthood as he continued questioning the worship of various gods, searching for answers, and seeking the *truth*. At about age 30, Zoroaster received revelations from Ahura Mazda (meaning "Lord All Wise"), disclosing to him that there was only one true god—the Creator—and designating Zoroaster as His Messenger. During the next several years, Zoroaster received other revelations from Ahura Mazda, and began to preach, gathering converts while facing great opposition to his advocacy of monotheistic belief. The Aryan people finally came to accept Zoroastrism, and the religion began to spread. Eventually, it became the state religion of the Iranian Empire during the Achaemenid dynasty in sixth century B.C.

Zorastrian religion is based on the concept of self-discipline through "Clean Thoughts, Clean Words, and Clean Deeds," and on the practice of respect for purity, nature, and the environment. One surmises that it is because of their concern for the lattermost two considerations that, in order to prevent polluting the earth or waters, the Zoroastrians did not bury their dead. Instead, they placed the body—after it was washed and purified—on a high platform in an open space (the tower of silence) where the flesh rotted away or was picked clean by vultures, and the sun's rays eventually dried and purified the bones. The remains then were gathered and stored in special chambers. Thus, there are no remnants of ancient graves or burial places for the ancient Iranian peoples, and only less than a handful of chambers—carved high in the mountain—for some Achaemenid kings.

To what extent the Zoroastrian religion has influenced other religious beliefs is a matter of ongoing discussion. For example, Hopfe (1991) explained that the Hebrew literature dating before 586 B.C. had no references to such themes as Satan, the resurrection of the body after death, heaven and hell, the end of the world, or the Day of Judgment—which were all a part of Zoroastrian teaching. However, much later narratives from Hebrew literature and documents not only addressed these themes but also developed them further, as a vital component of contemporary Judeo-Christian and Islamic religious beliefs.

Another Zoroastrian practice was the rite of passage—the induction (at a certain age) of Zoroastrian youth into the religion, through an investiture ceremony very similar to that practiced now in both Judaism and Christianity. The egalitarian worldview, which was the hallmark of the Iranian kings, also is of Zoroastrian teaching. It is a concept that corresponds to today's ideal of a true democratic society.

The ancient Greek philosophers and other scholars displayed great interest in Zoroaster's life, philosophy, and religion—as evidenced by, for example, Plato's attempts to travel to Persia to study with the Magis (the Zoroastrian priests). Although Plato was forbidden to do so because of the wars between Greece and Persia, interest in Zoroaster and Zoroastrian ethics and philosophy continued anyway—in fact, throughout the Western world. For instance, Friedrich Nietzsche, the renowned nineteenth-century German philosopher, chose the title *Also Sprach Zarathustra* (*Thus Spoke Zarathustra*) for one of his important works in which he proclaimed that religion (in his time) had lost its meaningfulness, and thus individuals must critically examine their moral values and foundations.

Patterns of Immigration to the United States

Iranians who have migrated to the United States of America generally have been individual families or persons. In fact, from the mid-1800s until after World War II, not more than 1,000 Iranians (those who listed Iran as their country of origin) so immigrated. From the mid-1940s, however, the number of immigrants rose steadily to upward of a thousand per year, totaling by 1976 around 34,000 (Lorentz & Wertime, 1980), although—as might be expected—a larger number came as students. In contrast, the Iranian revolution of 1979 evoked a major exodus which is reflected in the number of Iranians who migrated to the United States—as shown in the Table 1. It should be noted that the data in this table does *not* include the Iranian "foreign" students, nor does it reflect the number of those of first-, second-, or third-generation Iranian Americans (those born in the United States), who together form a yet larger Iranian/Iranian-American population in the United States. The largest Iranian community in the United States is in California, and particularly in southern California. Other large Iranian communities are located in the Washington, DC, metropolitan area (including northern Virginia and Maryland), New York and northern New Jersey, Texas, Florida, Illinois, Michigan, and Pennsylvania.

Iranian Americans are active in all aspects of professional arenas, especially such consumer trades as carpeting, food, clothing, and cosmetics production and sales; the entertainment industry (including film/cinema, theater, television, and music); the arts and literature; all areas of the sciences (notably mathematics, physics, engineering, computer and information systems, and medicine); jurisprudence; scientific and academic research, education, and publication; architectural design and construction; and political and governmental services on all levels (local, state, and national). They also are homemakers, educators, business executives, and students.

TABLE 1.   Iranian Immigrants and Naturalized Citizens

Years	Immigrants	Naturalized Citizens
1972–75	10,997	2,811
1976–80	31,708	5,544
1981–85	62,460	10,880
1986–90	92,397	24,274

Source: U.S. Immigration and Naturalization Service.

Culture and Characteristics

Characteristically, Iranians are a people of integrity, with notable dual capacities for assimilation and, at the same time, a great ability to influence profoundly the cultures and peoples with whom they interact. Hospitality, however, is the hallmark of the Iranian culture. A guest in one's home is considered "a gift from God" in the Iranian culture.

> *Come with me to an Iranian home and let yourself be treated as a prince or princess, for the Iranians will open their home and their heart to you and toy lavish on you, and share with you, all of what they have selflessly. Your Iranian host or hostess will respect your values, beliefs, and culture; and will accommodate your every needs, wishes, and desires. At the end, when you leave, however, you will be subliminally touched by their cultural generosity; and you will be influenced by their genuine friendship and hospitality. (Samiian, 1991)*

This attitude of hospitality, cordiality, and humility is also maintained throughout the Iranian people's business practices, whether those of the shopkeeper, the corporate executive, or the physician.

Although Zoroastrianism is the religion of only a minority of Iranian people today, its philosophy and traditions are woven into the fabric of everyday Iranian life. For example, Iranians still celebrate the first day of spring—March 21st (March 20th on leap years)—as their New Year (*Nuw Rooz*, in Persian) with a traditional table set with seven items from nature-depicting substance, strength, harmony, life, beauty, rebirth, and spiritual renewal. The Iranian "New Year" celebration continues for 13 days, during which time individuals visit each other to renew friendships and other relationships and to bridge misunderstandings and resolve past conflicts. This is a tradition that has lasted for over 3,000 years in the Iranian culture! The festivities end with ritualistic "thirteenth-day" picnics, at which families and friends gather together in gardens, prairies, or parks to rejoice in the endless rebirth of nature as manifested in the dawn of yet another spring. Perhaps at no other time do the Iranian expatriates feel as lonesome and estranged, in lands where no distinctive effort is made to welcome the wonders of all nature's "now life," as they do during the *Nuw Rooz* each March.

Traditionally, Iranians carry on an almost mystical romance with life and all that it offers. Nasr (1975) wrote "To understand fully the meaning of life for the traditional Persian one must penetrate into the deep sense of joy (*farah*) combined with a sorrow (*hozn*) which complements it on the human plane" (p. 29). This entwining of joy and sorrow is continuously reflected in the Persian poetry, literature, and music, as well as in the daily display of humanistic emotions among the Iranian people. The love of beauty (another characteristic of Iranian people) also serves as a foundation for arts and architecture witnessed by "delicacy, precision, clarity of forms, harmony of colors and of parts." Again, Nasr (1975) wrote, "The appreciation of beauty of every walk of life, far from leading to sensuality and worldliness, has served a positive spiritual function for the Persian who has never been opposed to asceticism and self-discipline" (p. 29). The expression of this love for beauty and harmony is manifested in Persian poetries and paintings. However, as noted by Lowry and Nemazee (1988), "Indeed, it is impossible to understand the idealized elements of Persian painting without appreciating the conventions and texture of Persian poetry. By examining the interaction between these means of expression.... the viewer becomes an active participant in the comprehension and interpretation of the works, engaging in an associative and symbolic dialogue with the artist" (p. 57) beyond the sheer brilliance or eloquence of either form.

Family unity and commitment, respect for elders and teachers, and responsibility toward the education of the young also rank very high in the Iranian people's value system. The meaning of "nuclear family" in the Iranian culture goes beyond the parents and children to include also grandparents, aunts, and uncles. "Family," then, means cousins, including second and third cousins. Hence "relatives" are those who have married into the "family." Thus, the circle of interpersonal commitment, and due respect, is for the Iranian people much larger than that of Western comprehension. Educating the young is not only considered a responsibility but a parental *duty* in the Iranian culture. The meaning of "education," too, goes beyond schooling, to include the teaching of the epistemic (holistically balanced) view of life and piety, due respect in relationships, and Iranian cultural values and traditions to a generation that is expected to function at all times with reverence, honor, and self-discipline. Thus, when Beny (1975) wrote, "How can I open the gate and guide my readers across the Bridge of Turquoise?" he was referring allegorically to a bridge spanning between Eastern and Western cultures and civilization, *and*, subliminally, to a perplexingly delicate balance that the Iranian Americans strive to achieve for themselves and their children raised within these two diverse cultures.

Resources for Educators

To enable Iranian-American students to find an appropriate balance between Eastern and Western cultures, and therefore to prosper academically in American educational institutions, educators need to know far more about Iranian history and culture than has been typical among them. For some teachers, *self*-education is necessary, since colleges of education usually offer only limited training in appreciation of cultural diversity. Fortunately, most educators already have the research skills necessary to locate appropriate resources on Iranian and other Middle Eastern cultures. Whatever your *own* skill of that nature, you might begin with the resources listed in the reference section of this chapter.

Educators committed to developing culturally responsive curricula in this present subject area would benefit from numerous publications on Middle Eastern cultures that are available in most public and educational institutions' libraries. Futhermore, the following should be considered as excellent starting points for this educational journey: Foundation for Iranian Studies (4343 Montgomery Ave., Suite 200, Bethesda, MD 20814); local Iranian Cultural Associations; the *Harvard [University] Encyclopedias of American Ethnic Groups* (1980); the Smithsonian Institution, Washington, DC; and the American Council on Education, Washington, DC (for the list of colleges and universities conferring degrees in the Iranian Languages and the Middle Eastern and/or Near Eastern Studies).

References

Beny, R. (1975). *Persia: Bridge of turquoise,* London: Thames and Hudson. *The crown jewels.* (1964). Tehran: The Central Bank of Iran.

Fisher, S. N., & Ochsenwald, W. (1990). *The Middle East: A history* (4th ed.). New York: McGraw-Hill.

Harris, N. (1977). *Rugs and carpets of the Orient.* London: Hamlyn Publishing.

Hooglund, E. J. (Ed.). (1987). *Crossing the waters.* Washington, DC: Smithsonian Institution.

Hopfe, L. M. (1991). *Religions of the world* (5th ed.). New York: Macmillan.

Lorentz, J. H., & Wertime, J. T. (1980). Iranians. In S. Thernstrom (Ed.), *Harvard Encyclopedia of American Ethnic Group* (pp. 521–524). Cambridge. MA: Belknap/Harvard University Press.

Lowry, G. D., & Nemazee, S. (1988). *A jeweler's eye: Islamic arts of the book from the Vever collection.* Washington, DC: Smithsonian Institution.

Metz, H. C. (Ed.). (1989). *Iran: A county study* (4th ed.). Washington, DC: United States Government.

Nasr, S. H. (1975). Essay. In R. Beny (Ed.), *Persian Bridge of turquoise* London: Thames and Hudson.

Pope, A. U. (1965). *Persian architecture.* London: Thames and Hudson.

About the Authors

Barazandeh "Baraz" Samiian is adjunct professor of management, College of Business Administration, University of North Florida, and lecturer on the topics of organization theory and design, cultural diversity in the workplace, business and professional ethics, and multicultural communication. Baraz serves as instructional program coordinator, Telecourse Program, at the Florida Community College at Jacksonville. She has authored numerous handbooks for human resources development programs.

G. Pritchy Smith is professor of curriculum and instruction, University of North Florida. He is a founding member of the National Association for Multicultural Education (NAME). He has authored articles on minority recruitment in teacher education and multicultural education. Smith has conducted research on the impact of teacher testing on the racial composition of the national teaching force.

Chapter *16*

The Arab Americans

PATTY ADEEB   *G. PRITCHY SMITH*

> *Acquire Knowledge. It enables its possessor to distinguish right from wrong; it lights the way to heaven; it is our friend in the desert, our society in solitude, our compassion when friendless; it guides us to happiness; it sustains us in misery; it is an ornament amongst friends, and an armor against enemies.—Prophet Muhammah,* Hadith *(Adapted from Al-Ghazaly Minaret Newsletter)*

With the exception of Arab Americans themselves, the typical citizen of the United States has been exposed to little information that provides humanistic and realistic insight into the identity of the Arab peoples. Shaped by a lack of multicultural education and a prejudicial, uninstructed film industry and print and television media, American perceptions about Arabs range from the overly romanticized to the harmfully negative. Quoting from W. Thesiger's *Arabian Sands*, Salah (1979) provides an example of a romantic image of Arabs, based on the desert bedouin: "I shall always remember how often I was humbled by those illiterate herdsmen, who possessed, in so much greater than I, generosity and courage, endurance, patience, and light-hearted gallantry. Among no other people have I felt the same sense of personal inferiority" (p. xiii). Although Thesiger's description captures a measure of the bedouins' nobility, it is also an image (like some of the romanticized images in such films as *Lawrence of Arabia*) that leaves uninformed Americans with incomplete and inaccurate perceptions about Arabs. Apart from their potential for being offensive and sometimes insulting, romantic images of Arabs, however, do seem somewhat harmful, and fewer in number, than the many negative images of Arabs that abound in the larger U.S. society.

Many Americans narrowly stereotype Arabs as greedy billionaires, corrupt sheiks, terrorists, desert nomads, camel-riding chieftains, slave traders, oil blackmailers, sex maniacs, harem girls, enslaved maidens, belly dancers, and veiled women. Arabs are often described as barbaric, uncultured, uneducated, committed to a religion dedicated to war, quick to torture and behead, and responsible for the conflict with Israel. Shaheen (1984) cited Shelly Slade's 1980 poll, for example, to illustrate that the American public perceives Arabs as "anti-American," anti-Christian," "cunning," and "war-like," while having little or no knowledge of the Arab peoples' rich heritage and accomplishments. Unfortunately, the 1990s have brought little change in the way Arabs are perceived or depicted. Inspired by romanticism or prejudice, the Arab caricature in the United States continues to be dehumanizing and continues to deprive the Arab Americans of deserved respect and ethnic pride.

Despite—indeed, perhaps because of—the continuation of negative Arab images, a countertrend to dispel misconceptions about Arabs arose during the 1980s and continues today. This trend to combat defamation of both Arabs and Arab Americans has been regularly influenced by a number of factors. Increasing numbers and visibility of Arab immigrants, and the rapidly expanding economic and political relations between the United States and the Arab World, for example, have sparked a much-delayed interest in Arab Americans and their counterparts abroad. Educated immigrants, as well as foreign students in colleges and universities, have played an important part in the political and cultural revival of the Arab-American communities and the revitalization of the doctrines and traditions of Islam. Furthermore, the Iran hostage situation, the war between Iraq and Iran, Suddam Hussein's invasion of Kuwait, the Israeli Palestinian conflict, the Russian occupation of Afghanistan, civil wars in Lebanon between Christians and Muslims, oil boycotts, and the control of the major natural resources of the area have magnified the need for the American educational system to present accurate information about Middle Eastern cultures.

Who Are the Arab Americans?

Arab Americans are citizens of the United States who are immigrants or descendants of immigrants who came to the United States primarily from the countries that constitute the present Arab World—Syria, Lebanon, Jordan, Saudi Arabia, Iraq, Kuwait, Egypt, Libya, Algeria, Tunisia, Morocco, Oman, Yemen, Bahrain, Qatar, United Arab Emirates, and the newly declared Palestinian state. Thus, Arab Americans are extremely diverse with regard to their country of origin, the beginning of their family ancestry in America, and their religion. A study by Zogby (1990) indicates, however, that most Arabic-speaking Americans are descendants of Lebanese immigrants, and that 90 percent are Arab Christians.

Many Arab Americans trace their family ancestry in America to the 1890–1940 wave of Arab immigrants who were primarily from Lebanon and Syria. Others trace the family beginnings in America to the early post–World War II wave of Arab immigrants who were predominantly Muslim and hailed from various independent Arab states. Other Arab Americans trace their ancestry to the wave of Palestinian immigration that followed the Palestinian Israeli wars. Still others trace their Arab-American ancestry to none of these well-known waves of immigration.

Because Islam is the predominant religion of the larger Middle East and the smaller geographical region known as the present Arab World, many uninformed, non-Arab Americans erroneously consider the term *Arab* to be synonymous with *Muslim*, but these are *not* interchangeable terms. In the present Arab World, an Arab is a person whose native tongue is Arabic and who lives by Arab cultural traditions and values. A Muslim is an adherent of the religion Islam and may or may not be Arab. Thus, whereas all Arab Americans do possess Arab ancestry and heritage, they nevertheless reflect considerable religious diversity among their numbers.

Religious diversity is characteristic of both the Arab World and the Arab-American population. Although it is true that Islam is the religion of the majority of Arabs in the Arab countries, as Shabbas and Al-Qazzaz (1989) noted, many Americans are often surprised to learn that of the 190 million Arabs living in Arab countries (including North Africa), nearly 14 million are Christians and 10,000 are Jews. Arab Christians comprise the Catholic, Orthodox (Greek and Roman), and Protestant sects and believe in the *dual* nature of Christ. Other Arab Christians are loyal to either the Assyrian Church of the East, the Coptic Orthodox, the Syrian Orthodox, or the Armenian Orthodox, and believe in the *singular* nature of Christ. The Greek Orthodox who do not recognize papal supremacy are also known as Unites or Eastern Rite Catholics. The vast majority of Arab Americans are Christians; whereas the preponderance of Arabs in the Arab World countries are Muslims. It is significant to note, however, that Arab Muslims are increasing in number among recent immigrant populations. It is also significant to note that Islam is (after Christianity) the second largest religious group in the United States. In fact it is estimated that the United States has 6 million Muslims who worship in approximately 800 mosques throughout the country. Some of these 6 million people are Arab Americans, but the majority are Muslims of non-Arab ancestry with their origins in such countries as Indonesia, Pakistan, India, Bangladesh, Russia, China, Malaysia, Iran, Turkey, Afghanistan, and numerous nations on the African continent.

Arab Americans live throughout the United States, but Zogby (1990) noted that the Northeast remains the geographical location where most Arab Americans reside. The Detroit-Dearborn area boasts the largest Arab-American community with approximately 250,000. Michigan (Arab population of 250,000), New York (Arab population of 250,000), and California (Arab population of 350,000) feature the largest and perhaps the most visible Arab-American communities. Massachusetts has one of the largest percentages of Lebanese, and Rhode Island has one of the highest percentages of Syrians.

To understand and appreciate the Arab American, one must remember that Western civilization owes a large measure of its heritage to the Arab World of the past. One must also remember that people of Arab descent have made modern contributions in almost every field of endeavor. In truth, the impact of the Arab-American's presence has never been greater, and the reality of what is observed does not fit the stereotypes harbored by many Americans. Most Americans should, for example, readily recognize the names of Arab Americans such as John Sununu, former White House Chief of Staff; George Mitchell, U.S. Senate Majority Leader; Doug Flutie, former professional football player; Rony Seikaly, professional basketball player; Abe Gibron, Chicago Bears coach; Casey Kasem, Paula Abdul, and Paul Anka, music entertainers; Marlo Thomas and Jamie Farr, television entertainers; the late Danny Thomas, entertainer and founder of St. Jude's Hospital (recognized for research and treatment for children afflicted with cancer and leukemia); Helen Thomas, senior White House correspondent and United Press International journalist, Najeeb Halaby, former head of the Federal Aviation Administration, holder of the aviation record for the first transcontinental solo jet flight across the United States, journalist, and father of Lisa Halaby, Queen Noor of Jordan; Vance Bourjaily, prominent novelist and author of *The Man Who Knew Kennedy*, Jim Haggar, founder and CEO of Haggar Slacks and Co.; Emile Khouri, creator of the Disneyland architectural conception; Dr. Michael DeBakey, pioneer heart surgeon and inventor of the heart lung bypass pump; Candy Lightner, founder of Mothers Against Drunk Drivers (MADD); Christine McAuliffe, first teacher in space and one of the seven crew members who died aboard the shuttle *Challenger*; and Ralph Nader, consumer advocate.

For years, Arabs were ignored by Americans. In the fall of 1973, however, when Arab states cut back oil production while at the same time the Organization of Petroleum Exporting Countries (OPEC) raised oil prices sharply, Americans for the first time had great reason to think about the Arab World and the millions of Arab Americans, both American born and foreign born. As the U.S. economy suffered and worldwide panic evolved, it was realized by many that a bridge between Americans, Arab Americans, and the Arab World was essential. Subsequent events of international significance, particularly the U.S. military action against Iraq in 1991, brought this realization into greater focus. The American people began a struggle to recognize and understand their newest, and one of their fastest-growing, ethnic groups. Establishment of Arab organizations to preserve Old World traditions and combat negative stereotyping and gross misconceptions grow in number. These groups established positive roles through which to help build an ethnic identity for Arab Americans, and laid a foundation for a bridge of acceptance, understanding, and respect between Americans, Arab Americans, and the peoples of the Arab World.

The following sections seek to further answer the question: Who are Arab Americans? Understanding Arab Americans requires an examination of their unique heritage of history and culture, both ancient *and* modern. The discussion in the first section centers on the Arab World, and includes a discussion of the modern Arab World with emphasis on education, social life, and the effects of modernization on selected Arab traditions. The second section discusses Arab immigration to the United States. This section also presents the effects of acculturation and assimilation on people of Arab descent in America. The final section features educational implications.

The Modern Arab World: An Era of Political, Economic, Educational, and Social Changes

The nineteenth and twentieth centuries brought new changes that impacted the Arab World's political and economic status, educational systems, and social life. Political and economic changes were influenced greatly by foreign interference and the internal dynamics of the evolving, present-day Middle East countries. In the mid-nineteenth century, European colonial powers began to gain economic power in the Middle East and undermine the control and the power of the Ottoman Empire. The impact of the West, in fact, influenced all of Syria, and most notably Mount Lebanon. The positive focus by the European powers on the Christian sects eventually led to an even more pronounced division between the Muslims and Christians.

By the end of World War I, Arab agitation for independence broke out in a revolt against the Turks. In 1918, France and Britain designated boundaries of political control over Arab lands, thus ending the rule of the Ottoman Empire and adding yet another piece to the mosaic of the Arab culture. During the ensuing period of European rule, the Arab World was faced with requests for the reform of Islamic law. Some of these reforms centered on equality for both Muslims and non-Muslims, both males and females. Many modernistic attempts to reformulate the interpretations of Islam were being addressed in ways that would make it responsive and acceptable to modern life. Later, numerous Arab sectors resisted the European domination and again began their struggles for independence.

In 1948, lasting and devastating effects of the Jewish holocaust influenced the British to play a key role in the creation of a Jewish state in Palestine, causing the exile of thousands of Arab Palestinians from their homeland. When people view the Arabs as the source of conflict between the Israelis and Palestinians, it is wise to reflect back on their history of religious tolerance and to remember that the Israelis exiled the Palestinians from a homeland where Jews and Arabs (many of whom were Christians rather than Muslims) were already living and sharing. The final conquest of Jerusalem by the Israelis in 1967 caused again the exile of thousands of Palestinians, and further confused feelings of allegiance by many for both the Israelis *and* the Palestinians. The Palestinians and the Israelis have *both* suffered great human losses; and to the outsiders, both often seem guilty of wrongdoing and killing one another. In their historical quest for the right to a homeland, each continues to express perceived legitimate grievances through methods deemed illegitimate by the other. Presently, no solution seems plausible for either the Israelis *or* the Palestinians, and the possibility of an international state to be recognized as a holy place for Judaism, Christianity, and Islam has not been eagerly received by most Israelis and Arabs.

Since World War II, the modern Arab World has experienced many other changes. The desire for Arab nationalism, social justice, acquisition of education, and closer unity has been prevalent throughout the Arab countries. Economic growth has been rapid due to oil resources. Resentment toward colonial policies, and a growing sense of national solidarity, have led to widespread appeals for Arab independence—the latter followed by revolts, riots, and wars. The death of Egyptian President al-Nasir weakened the illusions of independence but also gave birth to many Arab organizations that helped the Arab countries to grow closer; it generated a kind of solidarity, a feeling that there *was* such a thing as an Arab nation in the making.

With the end of British and French political dominance, the influence of the United States increased but carried with it both benefits and costs—particularly during the Suez conflict in 1956, the peace talks between Egypt and Israel in 1978, and various military conflicts in more recent times. The Arab World continues to find itself limited with respect to military power, and to experience disunity due to separate interests and economic dependence. Yet, despite the various elements of this disunity, it remains strong in cultural ties. The bottom line seems to be that the individual Arab countries practice differing, vacillating relationships with the United States and European countries, due at least in part to the fact that individuals within Arab countries perceive the United States and European countries differently.

Social Life: Family, Honor, and the Role of Women

The roots of modern Arab family life are found in the Old World traditions. Old World Arabs cherished strong family ties and group loyalty. The family constituted the basic social and economic unit of production and was the center of social organization through which persons and groups inherited their religion, social class, and cultural identities in all three Arab patterns of living (bedouin, rural, and urban), and in particular among tribesmen, peasants, and urban poor. Family bound its members in work and in leisure; everyone worked to preserve its status, honor, and welfare. It provided economic and emotional support to its members in exchange for allegiance. Family was the source of unity among the immediate and extended family members, to the extent that the family's survival was placed above individual needs. Family honor represented a sense of pride for the Arab people—the essence of their identity. The reputation of the family was preserved by behaving properly and maintaining family honor. As Naff (1985) has noted, a strong sense of family honor and loyalty was at the core of Arab life. Combined with the competitive spirit of individualistic behavior, family honor could lead to clannishness, jealousy, factionalism, and volatile emotionalism. Combined with generosity, compassion, and warmth, family honor and pride underlie Arab hospitality. Naff wrote, "When the Arab's pride and honor are engaged, tables often groan under the weight of ostentatious quantities of food and, in a duel of etiquette, servings are pressed on the guest" (p. 50).

During the twentieth century, the Arab World has undergone changes with regard to the roles of the women and the structure of the family. But even with the reformation of Islamic laws, social customs that have been deeply rooted in the core of the Arabic culture have been slow to change—especially the social customs that preserved the domination of the male, the early marriage of girls, and arranged marriages.

From the ancient beginnings of Islam, relationships between the genders have always been complex, and often misunderstood. As Najda (1976) asserted, the *Koran* and the teachings of Muhammad afforded great respect for women and assigned them equality with men rather than relegation to secondary roles. Islam afforded women the same rights as men with respect to the "Five Pillars of Faith," and their rights to possess property, keep their name after marriage, retain guardianship over their minor children, undertake professions, sue in court, and individually tailor a marriage. In the main, however, throughout the Arab World the social order remained male oriented with respect to rights, inheritance, and power. Thus, females were expected to yield their own interests and goals to the male members of the family. The male child was a symbol of the father's masculinity and the continuance of his lineage—the birth of a son was greatly celebrated, whereas the birth of a daughter was received in silence.

The Arab woman's sexuality was intertwined with the honor of the Arab family and was the responsibility of all the male kin to protect. Describing this male duty, Kayal and Kayal (1975) wrote, "A man of honor sees that his daughter and other females of his lineage do not act wantonly toward men, or that the sons do not misbehave toward daughters of other men" (p. 117). To protect family honor, Muslim women endured strict limitations on freedom and independence to ensure their chastity and respectability. Restrictions ranged from periods of isolation to the complete veiling of the body and hair to prohibit communication and stares of nonfamily males. Many young Arab women were wed to older men to protect their moral and economic position. Even differences in age were not viewed as undesirable, but couples who crossed the *religious* barriers invited harsh penalties. Marriages were arranged, and dowries were received from the bridegroom as a form of insurance if divorce should occur. Divorce was frowned on but was always an option for the male and (if written into the marriage contract) could be initiated by the female.

The *Koran* recognized polygamy but limited the number of wives to four with the provision of equality for all four. Unlimited concubines were allowed unless prohibited in the marriage contracts. Today, according to Shabbas and Al-Qazzaz (1989), polygamy is illegal in many Arab countries and represents only about 5 percent of all marriages. Where polygamy *is* permitted, approval of the first wife and proof of ability to provide equal financial support are required—or a document certifying the first wife is sterile. The harem (meaning "forbidden"), composed of a family's womenfolk and dominated by the mother or grandmother of the eldest male, is almost nonexistent today, and in fact never was the prevailing living arrangement.

The Prophet Muhammad wrote of the importance of good and educated mothers, but due to political, historical, and economic reasons, the education of Arab women lagged in the past. Progress in women's education accelerated with the Arab World's independence from colonial rule. Greatly encouraged by the *Koran* and considered a duty of all Muslims, education became the key to advancement for Arab women. Presently, the education of women is given high priority, the rapid rate of women's enrollment in all levels of education is evident. According to Shabbas and Al-Qazzaz (1989), in 1985 there were 20 million Arab women enrolled in education programs of all levels. Today, Arab women are more likely to enroll in all-girl schools and to study science and math. They score higher on national examinations than do Arab boys, and compete for top places in medical and engineering schools. Women also hold key positions in teaching and administration, especially in universities, and are greatly recognized as writers, journalists, painters, sculptors, poets, reporters, doctors, lawyers, and engineers. However, they are still isolated from government in many areas, except as elected officials and cabinet ministers.

Modernization has taken root, but for most Arabs, life is still organized around their religion, and their values are expressed in relation to the family. Some Arab countries still adhere to the very strict limitations for women that evolved during ancient times. Saudi Arabia still forbids women to drive, prohibits coed educational institutions, and demands complete modesty by women when they are outside the home. In both Iraq and Saudi Arabia, the women must be veiled and cover their arms and legs when in public or in the presence of most nonfamily males. All Arab families, even the poorest, guard their daughter's honor with the greatest circumspection. In 1974, the advanced family law finally gave both women and men the freedom to choose their own marital partners. Marriage is still based on contract, however, and both may have to pay alimony. Women can sue for divorce, but they stand to lose the dowry agreed upon in the marriage contract. The Arab woman living in seclusion is rare; today she is educated and works in the professions. The modern Arab woman helped greatly during the struggle for independence from colonial rule and continues to be active in the resistance movement especially in Palestine (Kayal & Kayal, 1975).

In the final analysis, despite common and dominant strands of culture throughout the Arab World, there are also vast differences. During the nineteenth and twentieth centuries, the separate Arab countries have often responded in their own chosen ways to the influences of the various Western powers. Even without the influence of foreign intrusion, notable dissimilarities in cultures, ideologies, languages, and religions already existed. As Naff (1985) has noted, it is difficult to define and describe an Arab culture that is characteristic and common to *all* Arabs. Indeed, the separate Arab countries reflect unique cultural differences, and individuals in each of these separate countries are as different from each other as are individuals of Western countries.

Arab Immigration: Trials, Triumphs, and Assimilation

Knowledge about the Arabic-speaking immigrants in the United States was virtually nonexistent until the 1970s when independent Arab-immigration research efforts were initiated. Further accurate data on incoming Arab immigrants was obtained in the 1980 census, the first ever to ask Americans to declare ancestry. Three distinct emigration waves have been identified: (1) the first wave, 1890 to 1940, was influenced by the Arab immigrants' strong desire for economic security; (2) the second wave, or post–World War II group, emigrated for political and economical security and educational opportunities; and (3) the third wave was a result of the Israeli occupation of Jerusalem in 1948 and 1967, which led to the exile of approximately 4.4 million Arab Palestinians (Shabbas & Al-Qazzaz, 1989). Originally, Arabic-speaking immigrants generally did not consider themselves to be Arabs, but rather Turks. The Arabic Christians never considered themselves Turks; instead they were identified on the basis of religious affiliation rather than nationality. The term *Syrians* came gradually to convey a geographic and ethnic meaning and was the term officially adopted by the United States to identify Arabic-speaking immigrants from the Ottoman Empire Syria. The term remained a mark of identification until the 1940s, when the term *Arab* became more acceptable (Hooglund, 1987).

From the Arab World, the region where most prominent Islamic civilizations once existed, young generations of Arabs, motivated by political reasons and the hope of living in a land where dreams come true, began the first wave of migration to America. Between 1890 and 1940, the era of tremendous industrial growth in the United States, more than 250,000 Arab immigrants from the provinces of the Turkish Ottoman Empire, now known as Lebanon and Syria came to America to seek better economic opportunities and to escape the impending military draft for Christians (Khalaf, 1987). Some 90 percent of the first wave were Arab Christians of the Middle Eastern Rite sects—mainly Maronite, Melkite, and Eastern Greek Orthodox—with the remaining 10 percent being Muslim and Druze Syrians (Zogby, 1990). They were barely perceptible in the great wave of all immigrants, approximately 27 million, who entered America during the high (1881 to 1914) and low (1915 to 1925) tides of immigration (Hooglund, 1987). The historical tendency of the Arab people in their original homelands to integrate with, rather than reject or destroy, other cultures augmented the development of a rich heritage of their own. This tendency appeared to carry over as they quickly entered the mainstream of American culture with relative ease, placing assimilation above ethnic identification.

First Wave

The majority of the first-wave Arab immigrants were fairly young unmarried males, not well educated. They came to America with little capital, limited skills, and speaking little or no English. Female immigration increased during the 1900s as the males realized that wives and relatives could facilitate the accumulation of wealth. Bureau of Immigration accounts indicate that illiteracy was high, particularly for the women (Naff, 1985). They struggled hard to achieve success as laborers, peddlers, shopkeepers, merchants, and workers in grocery stores and restaurants. Few entered the industrial labor force, although some did take factory jobs (Zogby, 1990). The majority who were peasants provided the human power that helped to transform the United States from a semiagricultural economy to one of the world's prominent industrial powers by 1914. The immigrants mainly worked diligently as pack peddlers, a trade they knew both before and after the rise of Islam in the Arab World. Individualism, loyalty, pride, determination, hard work, perseverance, resourcefulness, conservatism, close family relationships, and traditional values allowed the Arab immigrants to endure the hardships of America when they first arrived in the 1800s. To succeed in the United States was a matter of family honor, the main impetus for their hard work and hardships.

Peddling hastened the acculturation process—but it also contributed to its demise. With the accumulation of capital also came new values and aspirations to enter occupations of greater prestige and to become permanent citizens. It took time for the immigrants to reach a level of comfortable success; they often lived clustered together in ghettos and appeared to other Americans as clannish. However, throughout these difficult times the first-generation wave of Arab immigrants never lost sight of the value of family, both within America and at home in the Arab World. Age and wisdom were highly regarded, as was the tradition of giving help to the extended family. Much of the money they accumulated was sent back home to provide for the needs of their extended families or to provide passage for them to come to America—a culturally induced commitment to make a better life for *all* of their family members, both near and far.

The earliest Arab-American communities were predominantly in fast-growing urban and industrial area, such as Toledo and Detroit-Dearborn, and were built around a network of paddlers selling their wares and achieving a great degree of affluence quickly. Within the settlements, commonly known to many as the "Little Syrias," the Arab immigrants reveled in a sense of belonging and lapsed back into time through fellowship and the legacy of Arabic food, drink, song, and dance. The settlements offered a touch with the past. Contacts with other Arab immigrants provided not only a social network but also an economic one that helped newer immigrants to secure employment and housing and to maintain ties with their Arab language and culture.

The relatively high degree of Americanization among the first generation and the rather low degree of ethnic consciousness in the second generation of first-wave immigrants are two indications that the assimilation process penetrated sectors of Arab communities more deeply than expected (Zogby, 1990). Although many of the first generation enjoyed the prosperity that was now afforded them in America, their bliss was not without personal conflict as they watched many of their old customs dissipate. The first generation experienced many changes in their way of life as they struggled emotionally to maintain loyalty to the values and customs of the old country, while justifying the changes that seemed inevitable. In contrast to the Arab Christians, the assimilation was much more difficult for the Arab Muslims because of their strong adherence to Islamic faith and law.

The establishment of the first Islamic mosque in 1926 in Highland Park (Detroit) finally provided a place for the Arab Muslims to gather and to discuss the problems they were experiencing. The Mosque was a place to study the *Koran* and to reinforce their cultural ties to the mother country. Through the compulsory system, intimate contacts with classmates and teachers, the acquisition of a language other than Arabic, and an opportunity to compare two different cultures and ways of life, the second and third generations (American born and American reared) played a transitional role between the old and the new cultures and became agents of social change in Arab communities. These generations acquired more naturally and with less effort the language tools of the U.S. culture. Knowledge of the harsh socioeconomic conditions experienced by their parents in the old country made their assimilation into the now culture much easier.

The second generation often walked a fine line in trying to balance religious and social pressures exerted on them by the home-and-ethnic community and by the school-and-larger community. The Arabic values of family honor, and obedience to and respect for parental authority, became less restrictive for many Arab families, but still remained more of a source of control than did comparable values in most American families. The formal institution of education gradually replaced the role of the patriarchal head in providing knowledge and wisdom to succeed in the American society, and the devout adherence to the practice of Islam was influenced by cries for Islamic reform. As the assimilation process took place, the revered habits of fasting during Ramadan, prayers five times a day, and abstaining from the eating of pork were often difficult and impractical. The Islamic rituals of *qada* and *kafara* (meaning respectively "to satisfy a claim or duty" and "atonement") made it easier to make certain changes with respect to some traditional Muslim practices because prayers, acts of penance, and sacrifices *could* be performed as acts of forgiveness. Being different just made life too difficult in America, which gradually accelerated abandonment of a number of the cherished ancient Arab and Islamic customs.

Thus, the traditional Arab family was forced to change in the American setting. Personal attitudes toward such complex cultural matters as interethnic marriages were altered as a more liberal attitude was accepted. Many Arab Americans, males in particular, married Americans from other cultural and ethnic ancestries, which in turn affected the social structure of the Arab family. The restrictive customs pertaining to marriage (such as parallel cousin weddings, parental choice of the bride's husband, and the wife's role within the social hierarchy of the family) quickly underwent significant change as Arab women entered the work force in order to help provide economic security for the family. A breakup of the traditional patriarchal, extended family also reinforced both the rise of the Arab woman's status within the family and the beginning of the nuclear family unit. The notions of female obedience, sacrifice, and chastity, and the idea of male superiority, however, were precious slow to change.

Eventually, the vagaries of change were such that even divorce was no longer viewed by the Arab-American woman as equivalent to social and economic death. In time, diverse responsibilities even compelled working Arab women and homemakers alike to have fewer children and to cook many less time-consuming Arabic meals. Visiting, an important function in the Arab World practiced for the sake of reinforcing and creating relationships, became practically impossible to continue due to the newly imposed time constraints. The art of following a specific clocked schedule soon precluded hours formerly spent with a special friend or relative.

As Arab Americans experienced assimilation into the American culture, newly created paradigms continued to impact traditional and revered practices. For example, according to Naff (1985), "Even the time-honored preference for male children began to lose much of its force" (p. 287). Furthermore, the Arab-American children were no longer prepared to live a life of dependency, or expected to be a means of security for the aged parents or extended-family members, as in the old country. The American spirit of competition and independence had become yet another new way of life for the Arab American.

Naturally, the assimilation process of the Arab immigrants was not without pain or agony of choice regarding the preservation of their culture and traditions. Additionally, many suffered the prevailing ethnic and racial discrimination directed to minorities in America *in general*. Many of the dark-complexioned Arabs experienced extreme prejudice while perceived as being non-White *and* adherents of suspect religions (Hooglund, 1987). Ironically, the discrimination served in the main to *solidify* Arab unity and *reinforce* their identity. Through churches, clubs, and neighborhood functions, the immigrants reaffirmed their roots and preserved their customs as best they could under the enticing pressures to assimilate quickly within the U.S. culture.

The fairytale images of America and the American people that the immigrants hold before they arrived, coupled with the wonder and awe they experienced in accumulating economic security, only heightened their desire to remain in America come what might. Their food, customs, and norms had been Arab, and great energy was expended to preserve them in that mode. As their economic status and adjustment improved, they united to combat racial ostracism and to preserve their cultural heritage. The introduction of Arabic newspapers helped greatly to preserve the language and opened lines of communication for the Arab immigrants. While the immigrants simultaneously struggled to prevent what they thought might become the amalgamation (and perhaps the complete destruction) of their native traditions and values, there abound among them nevertheless an acceptance of American assimilationist views of patriotism, citizenry, and hard work.

Second Wave

A second wave of immigrants, nationals of various—and often competing—Arab nations known collectively as the Arab World, flourished following World War II, sparked to a large degree by political turmoil, civil war, foreign invasion, the creation of Israel, and poverty in the Middle East. This wave continues even now, and its members are recognized as being more educated, more ethnically conscious, more politically vocal, and more determined to retain their cultural heritage than were first-wave Arabs. According to Zogby's (1990) study, the second wave is predominantly concentrated in the Northeastern and Midwestern urban areas of America, and as a group are younger than the U.S. population as a whole and other ethnic groups. Zogby documented that the age level for the second influx of immigrants is (or at least was, as of the time of his study) between 20 and 44 years of age, with the median age being 25. He further described their communities as more likely to be foreign born and less likely to be assimilated with respect to both marriage outside their ethnic group and/or speaking a language other than Arabic in the home. This post–World War II group emigrating from independent Arab nation-states is made up of many individuals with college degrees, those who come to earn degrees, and people seeking professional positions—again, characteristics differing from those of the farmers and artisans who migrated during the first wave. The second wave is also more affluent and better educated that both the U.S. national average and many other ethnic groups. They continue to show a degree of independence with a much higher rate of self-employment and participation in retail trades.

Indeed, the postwar wave of immigrants do differ—greatly—from the first group who made that long journey to follow their dreams for a better life economically. The second group is dominated by Muslims, in contrast to the first wave of Arab Christians. They are less likely to assimilate at the cost of losing their ethnic identity, and reflect a more active political disposition. A growing concern for the crisis situation in the Middle East, a resurgence in the study of Arabic in community schools and universities, and a more devout adherence to the practice of Islam have greatly deepened the interest of second- and third-generation Arab Americans in both their Arab culture and their ties to the Arab World. Although the newer immigrants appear to hold stronger ties to Islam and Arabic customs, the second- and third-generation Arab Americans—descendants of the first-wave immigrants—still tend to be greatly removed in both tradition and religion as recognized and practiced in the present-day Arab World. At times, they even lack a meaningful grounding within the Arabic language and cultural practice.

Third Wave

A third wave can be identified among post–World War II immigrants who continue to arrive in America due to the escalating Palestinian-Israeli wars (Orfalea, 1988). Arab Palestinians have flocked to America's shores since 1967, when the Israelis took full control of the remaining sectors of Palestine, the West Bank, and Gaza. Between 1968 and 1985, close to 350,000 Arabs migrated to the United States. According to the U.S. Immigration and Naturalization Service's records, Palestinians account for a majority of the combined second and third waves of Arabs entering America. Mixed emotions over support given by the United States and Britain during the initial 1948 Zionist occupation has remained a continuous source of resentment among Arab Americans, and indeed the Arab World. In recent times, the United States has rejected Israel's actions of 1967 to place Jerusalem under Israeli jurisdiction, the rejection based on an interpretation of international law that posits that there can be no legal settlement by an occupying power in the territory it holds. It is somewhat of a paradox that so many Palestine refugees would come to the country that supported the forces they consider the cause of their exile.

According to the 1980 census, Arab Americans, both native born and foreign born, have a higher educational achievement level and a significantly higher number of high school and college graduates than the United States population as a whole *and* than most other ethnic groups. Many of the second-wave immigrants have come already educated, or specifically for the purpose of obtaining higher education. Presently, most of the third-wave Arab Americans are Muslims, as are the majority of Middle Eastern students that come to America to study. Religious mandates of ancient origin such as "God will raise up in the rank those of you who believe and have been given knowledge" (*Koran*, 58:11) and the Prophet Muhammad's "Seeking knowledge is the duty of every Muslim" (*Al-Ghazaly Minaret Newsletter*, 1991) are powerful motivational forces that drive educational achievement in the Arab culture. The data contradict the general American perception that Arab Americans are uneducated and are politically and globally naive. Educational achievement is abundantly evident among recent Arab immigrants, despite their having endured during most of their lifetime the tragedies of war.

Today, Arab Americans constitute a growing, sizable minority group in the United States. Zogby's (1990) study notes Arab immigration as a main source of new Americans and provides information on Arab immigration trends. For example, in the 1980s, the Arab nations accounted for 3.7 percent of the total of naturalized citizens, ranking tenth in the total number of immigrants coming into America, superseded in number only by that of the Western Hemisphere and other parts of Asia. Lebanon was the primary nation of origin of immigrants coming over from the Arab World during the 1980s. Immigrants from Egypt and Iraq recently surpassed Syrian immigrants. Many of the immigrants from Jordan and (to a lesser degree) other Arab nations are Palestinians. Additionally, a considerable number of nonimmigrants are university students who come to the United States to study and then return home, although some from the war-torn countries, particularly Lebanon and Iraq, choose to remain. The Lebanese and Syrians, however, still account for nearly 9 of every 10 Arab Americans. Regardless of the specific countries of origin, the collective Arab-American population is predicted to increase in number and so warrant increasing recognition—and inclusion—in U.S. society.

Implications for Education

The presence of 3 million Arab Americans, increasing numbers of visiting Arab students, and burgeoning population of new immigrants from Arab countries all have noteworthy implications for the U.S. educational system. In general, students of Arab heritage face problems similar to those of students from other nonmainstream cultures in America. That is, cultural and behavioral norms, and the curricula of U.S. schools, have been based primarily on Western traditions. In addition, according to Law and Lane (1986), classroom teachers are "no more accepting of various ethnic groups than the national samples spanning 6 decades" (p. 8). Furthermore, there exist extreme displays of overt and covert prejudice and discrimination toward people of color (Oakes, 1990). In this context, then, the first general implication is that education that is multicultural should become the rule rather than the exception in the U.S. school system. Secondly, teachers must learn to become culturally responsive to unique needs of students of Arab descent.

To accomplish outcomes implicit in these two general implications, and to better understand Arab-American students, teachers require first a broad and in-depth command of both the ancient and the modern histories that undergird today's Arab and Arab-America culture. Thus, the histories, cultures, religions, and contributions of Arab Americans, which are largely ignored in the pages of American textbooks, must be placed alongside those of other previously excluded groups in the school curricula. Respect for and acceptance of diversity and the inclusion of multicultural education within our educational institutions are the life support systems to enable *all* students to define their role in history and to legitimize their own cultural values, beliefs, customs, and ideas— improving the education and economic and social survival of *all* students. While understanding Arab cultures broadly, it is equally important that teachers at the same time recognize the great diversity within Arab culture and see the child of Arab descent as an *individual*. Indeed, what Naff (1985) wrote about the Arab World is also true for the persons of Arab descent in America: "No one religion, ideology, national identity, or sense of history and heritage defines all Arabs...[and] one cannot overlook the complexities imposed on any generalization by Arab history, geography, and society" (p. 15). To keep in mind individual differences and also be culturally responsive to students of Arab descent, teachers need to be cognizant of a number of factors that may characterize their students.

Teachers should know, for instance, that Arab-American and Arab-"foreign" students often face social and psychological displacement when confronted with a new language, methods, and curriculum that are foreign to the culture they know. Many students feel that it is their responsibility, their duty, to maintain their native culture; yet they need to feel comfortable with the culture of their new target language, English. In addition, behaviors reinforced within the Arab home are often not regarded in the same way outside the home, especially in school settings. The learning required by two different cultures (home and school) may lead to a lack of "fit," which may have detrimental effects on the development of adolescent self-esteem. For example, an important characteristic of Arab culture concerns the idea of "face." Teachers may very often find that the parents of Arab students are very sensitive to public criticism, thus, criticism should be shared in a way which will minimize loss of "face" and honor for both the student and the family.

Also, teachers of Arab-American students and visiting Arab students should realize the problems of acculturation. Many Arab children are bilingual or trilingual, and so may speak Arabic, French, and/or English. Matters of religion, diet, hygiene, gender roles, proxemics (social distance), and punctuality reflect cultural differences that are often misunderstood. Arab Americans vary from adherence to total assimilation to rejection of almost everything that is Western in nature. In some instances, it is important for teachers to remember that visiting Arab students have already been dealing with cultural conflict in their own countries, as the opposing Western modernism and Islamic conservatism clash within the Arab World.

In addition, teachers should be aware of other problems unique to Arab assimilation into U.S. society. In efforts to retain aspects of their culture and religion, the foreign-born Arab-American students, as well as the Arab visiting students, often feel insecure and experience feelings of loneliness, hostility, indecision, frustration, sadness, and homesickness. They are caught between cultures, not sure of which one they belong to, and may sense both a loss of membership in their original reference group and an increasing identification with the new group in an effort to become bicultural. Cultural stress or shock may pass rather quickly, but then of course it may also linger on.

Similarly, in reference to cultural problems, Arab-American students, and particularly the Arab visiting students, must confront harsh American perceptions of their way of life and the differences that tend to isolate them from the mainstream. For examples, Arab Americans are a people who enjoy close proximity to one another when talking, and members of the same gender are often known to walk arm in arm or hold hands—a behavior normal for them yet often unaccepted within mainstream America. Additionally, features of their language, such as loudness, and intonation patterns—perfectly acceptable in their own mother tongue—unfortunately can have connotations of rudeness, anger, and/or hostility as they attempt to speak in a new language.

Teaching within a pluralistic society further entreats educators to be aware that traditional Arab customs and values, especially among students from a Muslim heritage and sometimes other cultural religious heritages, pose unique circumstances in typical U.S. school settings. For instance, male students who have never been exposed to female authority figures may have difficulty in following orders from female teachers and administrators. Also, a lack of familiarity with deodorant has often led to the use of washing hands and face with cologne, usually reinforcing the U.S. perception of being unclean when in reality cleanliness is greatly valued, but culturally addressed from a different perspective. Punctuality, in contrast to the value placed on it by most middle-class Americans, may also present a problem. Some Arabs may place little significance on being a little late—tardiness is not considered a sign of disrespect. Forbidden to eat pork, Muslims often find it served as a main entree in school cafeterias.

Again, their differences are often brought to the forefront without any attempt to understand the rationale that gives value to them. Furthermore, many Muslim students fast during the month of Ramadan, and may appear tired or irritable during this period. Teachers should be understanding of the strength and endurance required by these young people to commit to the doctrines of their faith. Ramadan is a chance for them to reaffirm their cultural traditions and values that maintain important links to their home culture. Non-Muslim teachers need an extra measure of patience and should provide support during this period when some students may withdraw from or be isolated by classmates who perceive differences as being strange, wrong, or unacceptable.

Furthermore, it is instructive for teachers to recognize the differences and similarities between previous and new immigrant groups within the larger Arab community. As Zogby (1990) has noted, the first wave is now both older and more affluent in contrast to the newer immigrants some of whom are struggling near poverty. However, employment status of the second wave reflects the greater exposure to the professions, management, and student status. Whereas household income averages for Arab Americans tend to be higher than the national average, there is a greater percentage of Arab-American households below the poverty level than for the U.S. population as a whole. This paradox exists because a large number of Arab immigrants are earning less than poverty income and have a higher unemployment rate.

Early images of Arab immigrants as peddlers or merchants standing in front of a grocery store, adorned in a white apron, contrast greatly with the present Arab Americans' unparalleled need for independence. As noted, new immigrants are more likely to be self-employed entrepreneurs, or work as corporate, health-care, or educational professionals—*all* sharing a demonstrative success orientation. In contrast, adherents of Islam are found in increasing numbers among the new immigrants, when compared to the second-wave immigrants who were predominantly of the Christian faith (Shabbas & Al-Qazzaz, 1989).

Nevertheless, both the "newcomers" and the "established" Arab Americans are bound by a common ancient heritage, language, and culture. Indeed, in spite of the effects of enculturation and acculturation in U.S. life-styles, it is clear that family unity, honor, religious beliefs and practices, strong feelings of identity with their homelands, in addition to many other traditional values and customs, remain strong symbols of reverence in the Arab-American culture.

Conclusion

Recognizing the great importance of preparing young people for their roles as thoughtful and informed citizens of the twenty-first century challenges society to acknowledge that the U.S. involvement with the Middle Eastern nations and the world of Islam is certain to remain significant for many years. As Americans, we must realize that "we" and "they" are in a state of mutuality and interdependence. For example, the Arab countries provide the United States with 80 percent of its oil, serve as a market for American goods and services, and provide a place for employment for many Americans in the Persian Gulf area, Saudi Arabia, and other countries in the region. In turn, the United States opens its schools to provide quality education for the Middle Eastern youths, and continues to be a country which, for many reasons, still draws thousands of Middle Eastern immigrants to its shores annually. If the current trends of immigration, birth rates, and family sizes continue to rise, the Middle Eastern-Americans population and culture will become ever more visible.

Thus, an essential goal for educators ought to be to increase awareness and understanding of the Middle Eastern peoples through the study of their history, culture, religion, and contributions. An equally important educational goal should be to dispel the misconceptions and stereotypes about the Middle Easterners—Arabs and Arab Americans or Iranians and Iranian Americans, for example—that continue to be promoted through the media. In truth, the Arab caricature in America, for instance, continues to be dehumanizing, depriving the Arab Americans of much-deserved respect and ethnic pride. We as educators have a great opportunity, as well as a moral and ethical responsibility, to address aggressively these heinous forms of bigotry.

Finally, living within a pluralistic society should make it virtually impossible for ordinary people and highly sensitized educators alike to ignore the value of any of its citizens as contributing and distinctive members. Education *must* become the vehicle for eliminating stereotypes and replacing them with understandings. Educators are fortunate indeed to be in a position that allows them to reach out to *all* cultures in order to form bonds of friendship, savor shared memories, and create mutual respect for cultural traditions. In truth, the embracing of diversity is and will remain essential to America's social health and prosperity. Thus, teachers should not few diversity; rather, they should enjoy its gifts.

References

Al-Ghazaly Minaret Newsletter. (1991, October). *1*(1).

Hooglund, E. J. (Ed.). (1987). *Crossing the waters.* Washington, DC: Smithsonian Institution.

Kayal, P. M., & Kayal, J. M. (1975). *The Syrian-Lebanese in America.* Boston: Twayne.

Khalaf, S. (1987). The background and causes of Lebanese/Syrian immigration to the United States before World War II. In E. J. Hooglund (Ed.), *Crossing the waters.* Washington, DC: Smithsonian Institution.

Law S., & Lane D. (1986 April). *Multicultural acceptance by teacher education survey of attitudes toward thirty-two ethnic and national groups.* Paper presented at the annual meeting of the American Educational Association, San Francisco.

Naff, A. (1985). *Becoming Americans: The early Arab immigrant experience.* Carbondale: Southern Illinois University.

Najda. (1975 April). Women in ancient Egypt. *Najda Newsletter.*

Oakes, J. (1990). *Multiplying inequalities: The effects of race, social class, and tracking and opportunities to learn mathematics and science.* Santa Monica, CA: Rand Corporation.

Orfalea, G. (1988). *Before the flames: A quest for the history of Arab Americans.* Austin: University of Texas.

Salah, N. (1979). *Costumes and customs from the Arab world.* Altamonte Springs: International Promoters of Art.

Shabbas, A., & Al-Qazzaz A. (Eds.). (1989). *Arab world notebook.* Berkeley. Women Concerned About the Middle East.

Shaheen, J. G. (1984). *TV Arab.* Bowling Green: Bowling Green State University.

Zogby, J. G. (1990). *Arab American today: A demographic profile of Arab Americans.* Washington, DC: Arab American Institute.

About the Authors

Patty Adeeb is director of Excelling in Clinical Education Learning (EXCEL), College of Education and Human Services, University of North Florida, and adjunct professor and lecturer in the areas of multicultural education and cognitive learning styles. She has published articles on continued learning for terminally ill children and on intervention strategies for behavioral and academic classroom management.

G. Pritchy Smith is professor of curriculum and instruction, University of North Florida. He is a founding member of the National Association for Multicultural Education (NAME). He has authored articles on minority recruitment in teacher education and multicultural education. Smith has conducted research on the impact of teacher testing on the racial composition of the national teaching force.

Seasons in Retrospect

An Ojibwe Woman Looks at Fifty Years

ROSEMARY ACKLEY CHRISTENSEN

I am reluctant to provide biographical data—or, in simpler terms, to tell my story. I am not special. I have not skills or talents earned through my personal efforts. Skills and talents, if any, are gifts freely given by the Master of Life. We Indians are raised within the warm, comfortable, total (when intact) environment of the Tribe. This means to me that although I am a fiercely independent human being, I belong to the group. I have been raised to allow the group, and especially Elders within the group, to mitigate my behavior while yet demanding that each person not interfere with my personal independence. This difficult (yet simple) convolution is what powers Tribal individuals. The notion of a biography, or autobiographical detail on a single individual, is silly in the context in which I was raised. We do not raise ourselves above our group, our *dodaym*, our clan. All our lives we defer to our Elders—as is the proper thing to do.

When individuals are so gifted by the Creator that through their gifts they provide unusual events to or through their group, they strive very much to diminish gifts within the group. It is unusual for individual Indians to seek the attention of, or allow the sort of attention focused through, with, or by either the biographical or the autobiographical form. I am aware that this form (or structure) of writing is not of great age even in the White man's world, anyway. Isn't it precisely why the relative latecomers Boswell and Johnson became so famous?

When Tribal people *do* allow this form to be used in a personal context, they are very careful and cautious in using personal names and places—especially since many of our modest Elders, for example, will not allow attributable quotes. The reason for this is that when what is said or otherwise known is passed on verbally (orally), which is often, it does not then belong to the speaker. Anything that is used is strictly personal, and the person so talking takes any blame to be administered.

Always, when we speak (as I in effect do in this article), we say, as those who have gone on before us, "The mistakes *I* make, and there are many; I beg the pardon of my Elder-Teachers; it is *I* who make the mistakes. Please excuse my ignorance, my lack of modesty, and take pity on me. *Megwitch!*"

Our Beliefs

I live, work, teach, and learn in Big Lake Country, on the shores of Lake Superior. I was born on Gitchee Ojibwe Gaming after the Great Depression, during the Second World War. People like me have always lived here[1]—the *New World*, in Columbus's words. It is not new to us. We have been here forever. Yes, it looked new once upon a time, when we took care of it.[2] When hordes of people came to live here, our beliefs and values were derided, forgotten, and dammed for some time.

How long have we been here? Yes, we know what the history books say. They say we came here via the land bridge of long ago. We came from Asia, they say.[3] It is a theory, *we* say. It is *called* a theory in most books. Western scientists say a theory is not proven. Proof is something written. It is documented. It is old.

Our old ones say we have been here a long time. Yes, it took us a while to get to this inland sea, but we were headed this way all that time, our old ones say. We traveled here because we were told to by the Elders. Ojibwe with excellent manners just about always do what the old ones say. What is the point of absolute personal independence if there is not an exception built in? And what exception makes sense? That of an old one who has lived long years. They know lots of things. If they are asked properly, they will tell the young ones some things. As they get older, if they have the gift, they know how to ask those who know things hidden from us in this cycle, these puny seasons, in this world.

We were following a light, pursuing a Grail of sorts. Some of the old people called it the "pack of life." I found out when I went to school, that scholars say we came over the Bering Strait land bridge and were not born in the woodlands at all. Do I believe that?

Naah! Negative! No! *Gaween Gunigay.* Our old ones say we were created right here. This land, our world, was made for the red man[4] and he is part of Mother Earth forever. Our roots go deep in Mother Earth. People who dig in the earth for scholarship proofs, and hence a living, must go far down in the earth, *our mother*, to get beyond the bones of our ancestors.

We were given this land and our Ojibwe language by the Creator. It is the language of our forebears. It is the chosen language of Ojibwe prayer. It is the language the old ones speak; and if we cannot understand, we lose their message.

Differences in Customs

When I was born to my Indian mother for my father, both were of Ojibwe lineage, of the *dodaym*. In 1939, the birth certificate noted in a small box under "race" that I am "Red." I was born a citizen of the United States by virtue of the 1924 Indian Citizenship Act, although my parents, born earlier, were noncitizens born in Wisconsin, United States of America.

Red is a sacred color of the universe. It is the color of the East "whence spring the light and where the morning star lives to give men wisdom."[5] It is one of humankind's primary colors. I knew too much about that color in my universe to allow name-callers in high school to get too far beneath my 15-year-old skin. "Smoked Meat" they called me. Of course it was embarrassing, and of course I used the weapons I had to try and ridicule those who called me names. When they came to me for help in subjects I excelled in, I could just barely do my duty. When I did help them, it was in a derisive, sullen, sarcastic voice. A 15-year-old is no saint.

It was then that I missed my home village where we were the largest number. Everyone there looked like me. There was no one to ask the proper thing to do in the White world I found myself in at a young age. It was impossible for me to ask my Elders. The old ladies were long gone who used to tell me a story or a cautionary tale wherein I could figure out the proper behavior by myself while I helped in their gardens. Anyway, I lived in White society, where Indians were few. Those in high school were mostly my own age and struggling themselves to understand the society of the White man.

Later, when my young son had to listen to ridicule about his long hair and obvious Indian blood in his ninth-grade class in a suburban Minnesota city, I connected him with Indian men older than he was. Some acted as an older brother, others as mature men, one to another, and they talked to him of their experiences. He was a golfer and still is. Some he talked to while they were playing golf. Many Indians like the game of golf. I have spent many a pleasant moment in my leisure time assisting in Indian golf tournaments, on the recording side of the game. I see it as a civic duty, much like Junior League ladies on their civic rounds.

My son took a survey of these men, as he is wont to do when he has a problem. He told me later that he guessed he just had to go through this experience as others had before him. He was probably lucky that it happened when it did, he said—early enough to get it over with and late enough for him to handle it.

We learn to handle the slurs the White world dishes out to our loved ones. We try to help as our fathers and mothers tried for us. In Indian country, among my peers, we call that "fighting and dying," as in "You mean we fought and died to get those kids scholarships and they are not attending college classes?"

Tribal Citizens

We are citizens of the Algonkian Nation. We are the Three Fires. We are the Keepers of the Faith. Our skins resemble this earth. Our flesh resembles the red pipestone we reverently use when we smoke our pipes to the Creator. It is unique to Turtle Island. Our people have always known about the pipestone quarry. All human beings quarry there in peace. It has always been the Law of human beings. Dakota friends upheld the Intertribal law. We were told we should celebrate and honor our Creator by addressing him through our flesh-made spiritual: the redstone pipe. *Asaymah* carried to the Creator in fragrant coils of smoke is a petition he looks on with favor.

We have always known about Tobacco. Folks on Turtle Island gave it its name. Our ancestors gave it to Sir Walter Raleigh and today we still use it to petition our old people. They cannot refuse us, our relatives say, if we give tobacco and make our request.

Pipestone—they named it after the man who brought it to the government's attention; they called it *catlinite*.[6] It had to have the name of its "discoverer," I guess.

Ojibwe Language

We know we have been here a very long time. The names of the places are our names. The animals, the living things, understand the language of our old ones. Why not? They heard for thousands of years the magnificent, splendid, stirring discourse of Tribal tongues. Remember: We lived as relatives with all living things. We asked their pardon, offering *Asaymah* when we needed them to live. Remember: We know; the Old ones tell us so. We struggled to get to Gitchee Ojibwe Gaming. We worked hard to get to Moningwauna-kauning. We know through our history dances, meant to teach the young ones our history. We migrated here through a long period of time.

The Americans made fun of our dances. Weren't they all the same, they asked? They did not know that humankind in this part of the world may pray to their Creator using their whole bodies. We did not use just our hands as Western man does when he addresses his God. We did not bow our heads or kneel. We held our heads high so the Creator could see our faces, and we stood to show respect, as we still stand today.

Americans still poke fun when they gather at sporting events and call teams by names that may also mean our kind. They talk about killing or hurting through slogans in derisive chants hollered at the opposite side. This is said to all be good American fun.

Migration

When we traveled to our new homes, our old ones marked each stop on pages of birchbark. Those that stayed and those who moved on were mentioned in the old prayers. This is how it used to be with us, and how it continues with us. As long as we know and use the language of the people, Ojibwe culture will continue to exist—it exists only with the language. *Ikidowug dush chiayaahg, dabiashaysh kahmagud, eeshpin, gaygate wedo-kodahdiyung.*

Those wiser than us say tribal memories stir within us—within our DNA coil, circular, as life is a circle. The Circle represents, holds, brings back, and contains what has gone on before our present cycle.

Religious Conflicts

The black-robed men didn't like Ojibwe, Huron, Odawa, Algonkian, Three Fires stories of long ago. Theirs was a jealous God. No other Gods could exist in the minds of the people. Our people's minds were destroyed by men who believed that one path led to the Creator; it had to be their path, in their way, spoken in their language.

They did not listen to our old ones say "We must not fight over religion." "Each individual is free to worship the Creator as he was instructed in his dreams while he was alone with his thoughts, following the guidance of his advisor, and his belly was empty of food," the old ones admonished long ago.

The Ojibwe language spoke of other ways to address our Creator. Those who came to "save heathen souls" said the language was misshaped and misused. It was intentionally misunderstood as it was written down by visiting priests. Insulting names were coined for our long, old, revered ceremonies. Our old men were fools that *howled,* according to the Austrian Bishop that one day in Cincinnati.[7]

Our pages of birchbark were rolled into dust and stored on shelves far away from their true faith-keepers. Those who came after the faith-keepers quarreled over the children's lessons. The language was not taught, or taught imperfectly, or kept intentionally and institutionally from the people. This twentieth century, near the twenty-first, around Gitche Ojibwe Gaming, Great Sea of the Ojibwe, the sea beings hear infrequently the voices heard so long.

The Ojibwe Knew

The Little people who sail the waters and live in the caves around its perimeter look unfailingly for the Shinobs. Finally, after years have passed without hearing the drum resound around the waters, they ask, " Where are the *shinobs?* When will we hear again the beautiful language taught to us by friend Great Rabbit? Have they gone away forever? It must be—we only hear the tongue of Englishmen, the Long Knives. Is it true the children are afraid of us? How can that be? They used to make us such nice canoes our size. They always sent it packed with a load of tobacco."

Tribal memories remain within us, deep within DNA life circle. When I look at a river as I pass over it in my car, I cannot repress the idea that perhaps the canoes won't get through today. And I worry about it, perhaps the ways my mothers did before me. How odd, when I have not had to try to get through nearly frozen-over rivers in a canoe in my lifetime.

Our Beautiful Places

I visit the mouth of the Bad River as it joins the Great Lake. I look at the driftwood strewn there as if the world were new. I wonder what the grandfathers and grandmothers are saying. This important place is as stunning, glorious, and inviolate as Chartres Cathedral seemed to be to Henry James.

Once upon a time, when I was a young girl, not long a mother, a young man, to please me, pushed a long piece of driftwood for three miles in that cold lake water so we could take it home as a reminder of that superb place.

I picnic sometimes when I can take the time during hot August days, on the shores of this great lake, making fires on its friendly shores, as human beings have made fires for thousands of years before me. Sometimes, in June, I make a quick stop, driving in three miles to the lake from the highway, on my way to or from somewhere. I seek the juicy, red, sweet berry that tastes so good because, the old ladies said, it grew so close to the lake. I know if I look closely, I will find the wild strawberry patch I knew when I was young. If I drive toward home just right, I will see Odanah clay made famous when our fathers worked for the WPA during Roosevelt's time.

Clan Relatives

Going home to Duluth, I sight great Chequamegon swans that have always been here, where others have been before. Perhaps I will see Great Blue Crane as he walks in the marshy shoreline next to the marina. Once I remember talking to the Crow princess as we ate dinner, and my relative, Big Blue was stuck in the marshy bottom. Laughing and whispering quietly, so as to not tempt diners that evening to assess us as nuts, we sneaked outdoors and attempted to get close enough to assist that crabby old bird.

If I come in the fall and boat through Kakagon Sloughs, I will see unique green rice that grows where the fresh waters of the lake kiss the muddy waters of our river. "Green gold" I call it when I exchange it for my Tlingit friend's "red gold." He gives me salmon he catches in the cold waters near his home in Alaska. We have been trading for decades—from the time we met at a Princeton University conference. As colleagues at graduate school in Cambridge, Massachusetts, we continued to trade, just as our old, old ones did in the Tribal past on Turtle Island. Now we teach at different universities. He is at Stanford in California, and I teach in Duluth at the University of Minnesota.

I take manomin sticks and place them carefully on top of my bookcase in my home in Duluth. These were made by my brother for his nephews, my sons. He carved each carefully, and told Dane why it was important to do it just so. He also showed Barry what kind of wood to use. He taught them how to grow rice in the waters of our father's ancestral land. I realize, now that I am older, the care he took with my two sons during that fall season years ago.

That brother is in his fifties, as I am. We three, with our younger brother, must depend on our memories to remember our village of 50 years ago. Our younger brother remembers what it was like to dance, especially when I remind him how he looked the day he left, as our mother took him to dance at a field named Soldier, in an onion swampy place then and now called *Chicago*. The name sounds very much like *shigag*, does it not? It is our Ojibwe word for *skunk*

When we can take the time we follow the routes our elders took from the Eastern sea shore, we ponder why they left. What was the lesson they learned, never to forget? The sea voice from the great salt waters calls and we must hear its voice once again before facing our journey westward.

Raising Children

My sons were carefully taken there when they were little to know and follow the old trails of our relatives. I told them how we were related to people who were here before us. The people who lived in the beautiful Smokies were our relatives. The people who lived in this place, I said, as we came close to Illinois, were called the Sac and Fox by the French and Englishmen. They are now living in Iowa and Oklahoma. These Indians, as we got closer to the Wisconsin River, I said, are the rice eaters. They are Menomonie. They are our relatives. These people who went before us, who sailed the rivers, who still come back each fall to Rock Island from Oklahoma because they are lonesome for the woodland of their early youth, are our relatives.

Recently, I traveled to Rock Island with my attorney. She is Sac and Fox raised in Oklahoma. She and her brother, also an attorney, are Tribal Judges for their tribe. She wanted to see the lands the old ones lamented, so we went to Illinois. They, the relatives, were meeting there on that September day because they have always met there at that time—since time immemorial. They look like us.

"Remember, my sons," I told them recently, phoning from Minnesota to North Carolina, "When you wish to see your mother as you travel in your time to the spirit world, remember how to say, as our people have said it, 'Help me, for I am pitiful. Help me, for I am of the people. Help me, my name is your name. We are your relatives."

"Learn and speak it in your language. It is only then that you will know how to ask the Anishinabeg you see on your journey the questions they will answer. The road is marked with the footbeats of thousands of our folks who have gone before us. The softness, the lightness of their footwear marks the road we follow. The path of the wingtip and cowboy boot is not our path. Our old ones before us have joined the eternal Circle and wait for us to begin anew. It is as Black Elk said when he talked of Crazy Horse's grave, 'It does not matter where his body lies, for it is grass; but where his spirit is, it will be good to be."[8]

I watched my mother stack things around the edge of her diningroom in her urban apartment in Milwaukee, just the way our grannies did in teepees long ago—probably around this very lake, or one like it close by. Can I help choosing to believe that it is ever so much more civilized to learn to close one's ears in a small space, thereby allowing privacy, than to build many rooms and then close doors? It is a civilized learning from my folks who had to live in a small space of a teepee. They passed this civilized behavior from ear to ear until it reached mine in the forties of this century. I was careful to pass this civilized manner to my two sons.

I know as a Tribal woman that life follows the seasons. One season segues to another as my mother before me traveled through her seasons, and so on into time. I easily trace our family tree to names of our Elders and quickly, it seems, I arrive to Ojibwe names only on the register.

We must teach the children the Elder habits. We must continue, always, our work for the next generation. It was ordained in our families long before we were born. I remind my sons they must pay back soon, and they say, as I did when I was young, "Yes, ma, we know." Everyone in our lineage pays back into the Circle when he is mature. It is that way for me, and it shall be that way for my sons.

Season follows season. The lake changes slightly, if at all, during our little lives. We gaze at its great unchanging face continuing to fish, work, rice, and play on its shores. We thank the Creator daily for the sustenance provided through his gifts.

Cultural Education

Our first teacher, the splendid, magnificent, adroit, changing, funny, kind, sneaky, human, strong, handsome, ordinary, appealing Waynabosho, continues his sleep in the Bay of Thunder. Thunderbird travels still over his sleeping friend. Once, long ago, I was told by old ones that he sleeps there and will wake when the Anishinabeg need him. Frequently, I asked, "Will he wake up (while we live)?"

I remember I dragged my small sons around the great lake specifically to visit him. Young Barry wanted to know if Waynabosho would wake up that day, as we jockeyed for a good place to see him from the bushes up overlooking the bay and the fort town.

The great Circle is what we traveled around the big lake, Gitchee Ojibwe Gaming. I told the children how important this sea is to us, we Ojibwe. It reminds us of that faraway eastern seashore. Listening to the sea is in our blood. Once upon a time, we migrated away from the salt water and traveled west. I listened as my sons listened to me, telling how our old ones named these places. We wonder at the beauty of our universe, as we try to figure out the "real Ojibwe" names of the places. We ask someone who knows the old words.

Medicine Elders

The powerful man of Medicine told me that *Winnipeg* means dirty water. *Assinaboine*, the river there, is named for the people who lived there, "But it is in your language, and you should be able to figure it out," he said. "Okay," I said, "*Assin* means rock or stone, but what does *boine* mean?" "Remember," he said, " people did not speak our language correctly. Actually, it is the word, or *our* word for *Sioux*." "Oh," "I said," you mean it is *Bwaan*? Does it mean *stony Sioux*?" "Yes," he laughed, "it sort of means that."

Later, after our business was concluded, he gave me a quick but thorough smudging, to get me home safely. When he leaped about like Tolkien's Tom Bombadil to do this homey task, he seemed as quick, effervescent as our Earth.

I marveled at the beauty of the Manitoba Prairie. I could see why Ojibwe came so far. That old powerful man was a Supplier of pharmaceuticals. His was a prairie pharmacy. He collects, makes, and supplies the medicine needed by our Old Doctors. The cedar, sage, sweet grass, and other good medicine plants lose their power when they live in the cities too long. And sometimes only a few of the old men of wisdom still speak the language of the plants that once people knew as everyday knowledge. So the medicine people travel far and wide for the plants needed to cure and help the people. Once, that kind of travel and trade among intertribal people was normal. Now, we must stop at borders, lines drawn by the White man, and explain what we have or are fetching for our elders.

That man living on the western highway is a medical colleague of our Medicine Doctor. They converse when they feel like it on the phone. They converse in Ojibwe. In the old days, before phones, old men conversed in their heads, one to another over long distance.

The modern world of telephone, telegraph, and fax machine is used but these men are not limited to these taken-for-granted communication tools. They know of other skills passed by those who have moved on. But for those who listen, and have the patience to hear, the old men tell stories of travels. What skilled storytellers they are!

Elders Tell

I listened for several hours on the phone to that long-lived person, Roger Jourdain, former chairman of the Red Lake Band. For 31 years, 1959 to 1990, he was Chairman of the Red Lake Band of Chippewa Indians of Minnesota. Now he is out of office, losing, they say, by 135 ballots? He asked the Tribal court and the chief Judge, Margaret Treuer, to hear his case, but she ruled he was ineligible even to be *considered a candidate*, therefore he was not a plaintiff in the case. Jourdain's attorney in the case was not allowed in Treuer's court room.

Roger Jourdain stood up and was counted time and time again for Indian Sovereignty, for Indian control of Indian gaming, for good use of our environment. He had enormous difficulty receiving a pension from the people he served for over 30 years—unlike other men who held positions similar to his. Nixon sat in his power library at our expense. Ford has his pension. Carter, helping build homes for poor people, has a pension. Reagan has built his library in California. Governors of states have pensions. Our Ojibwe Elder, the former chairman who lived and worked to keep Red Lake for his Ojibwe people, sat at home in Bemidji without a pension for a long time. Strange behavior.

I like his stories. He told me how he had to yell at the then governor of Minnesota during his first years to keep the lakes of Red Lake clear and clean. The forests had to be protected from those who would sell them for short-term gain. The fishery had to be protected. He is funny. I laughed when he told me how he tried to get the full leather outfit back from H. Humphrey, III, that was given to Humphrey's father, the former senator and vice president. Humphrey, no novice when talking to Tribal Chairmen, told Jourdain to ask his mother, Muriel, for it.

Lots of people hate him, I have been told. I am interested in that old man, though, and I will do what I can to help his friend Mikinahkowajiwanongenini, Donald K. Allery of Montana, write the Jourdain biography. Young men and women need to know strong Ojibwe leaders existed in the twentieth century.

He told me how he and two other boys found their way home from boarding school. They traveled miles over this territory, sometimes by train, sometimes by thumbing it, but eventually they got home. "How old were you?" I asked him. "Oh, about 13 or 14, I guess," he said. I am astonished at the toughness of that old man and all our old men who learned about the White men first. They had to figure them out first.

Roger Jourdain knows and has so much in his head about the way it used to be and how it was for us. When he tells these stories now to the young ones, "they have no patience," he said. "They don't understand the language," he said. "And they don't know the territory," I add silently. He remembers how it was in the logging camps of his youth. He remembers giving food to Indians at commodity centers. He told me a favorite story of how he gave more food to an Indian woman because she asked for more in Ojibwe. He was so glad to hear someone speak the language that he gave her more—and got yelled at by the superintendent in charge because of it.

We Must Ask the Elders

The Elders say that we educated young ones know so much. Their old knowledge seems to be of no account. It is then I learned what has always been known. If the old people are not asked for their wisdom gleaned from a lifetime of living, they won't tell what they know. We will suffer a loss again, as we move from season to season, cycle to cycle.

Who is to know what has been lost because of the loose lips of the young? Who is to know what knowledge departed with the old ones who knew, who learned, who practiced, who listened when the world was new? They listened to the animals and never forgot how to talk in that language. Now, we hunt them during special seasons and we cage them for our amusement in zoos. How strange. How barbaric. How uncivilized. Who is to know what knowledge has departed with the Elders because some young green kid said, "That ain't what we learned in school; that ain't scientific; my teacher said something else."

Did Bird Tribes of long ago, sighting by marvels that made sense only when seen from the air and high in space, wonder how long we would remain cognizant of languages of all living things? Are they wondering, What will happen to the beautiful blue and green marble in space? How did our old ones know so much? How were they so wise when they said everything was round—that space curved, and the wind swirled in curves. Yes, they told us that, and much, much more in stories we heard as children.

"Yes," we said, "You are just an old man living in the woods. There is a big world out there over Birch Hill. What does it hold, old man? What does it mean when the clouds swirl and make noise? Is it really the thunderbirds, as you say? Or is it St. Peter bowling, as the nuns say?"

"Aaaa," said the old man, "You don't really know, do you child? Wait. The next time it thunders, look up and you will see the terrible eyes of that powerful being. His eyes will flash and his wings will be heard as he passes over. Be careful, child, that you do not anger him. Yes, he is friend, and he is busy teaching his young now, but be careful, as he may forget you are related to Nanabush. He remembers when they strolled the lake from shore to shore. He remembers when he roiled up the water for his friend. He visits him where he sleeps. I heard the White people there at that old fort now call him the "sleeping giant." They say he is just an old stone. But remember, my girl, how he got there."

Recently, as I traveled to Grand Forks to see a friend, and on to Winnipeg to see another friend, I noticed the sky was pitch black the way the Lakota say it is when the sky is filled with black powerful steeds on their way somewhere. But I looked again—me, a child of the forest and a listener of the Thunderbird stories. Once again, I saw with the eyes of the innocent child that, yes, the thunderbirds were coming in that immense sky, and their wings were enormous. Wave after wave of feathers were there to see. As I looked and wondered anew at the skills and mind pictures of storytellers of my youth, I noticed the drops. It was beautiful. It was awesome. It rained. *Gimiwunmigud.* And it rained. I could not see from my little car. I did what any child knowing about Thunderbird does. I looked for my pouch of Tobacco. I stopped at the next nearest exit. It happened to be where everyone was stopping. I got soaked running into the small luncheonette, even though I was sheltered under a very large golf umbrella.

Bad River: Yesterday and Today

The Bad River reservation and the Odanah village I knew in my youth are gone. They are alive only in my memory and that of my age-mates. I make the same lament others made. They, too, recollected how it used to be when they were young. So many "used to be's."

Once, they said, our territory stretched for miles and miles. It could not be walked in a day or two. Once, we could go for miles and see only Shinobs. In my time, it had to be east because 10 miles from our village was the village of Ashland on Chequamegon Bay.

This big town had many people. Many were not Indian. We would go there from our school and village to be in parades. We would wear our faked Indian costumes because that is what the tourists liked to see. They liked to see little Indian kids sitting on a float, stirring nonexistent food in a big fake black kettle strung up over make-believe fire. We would laugh at such nonsense as we rode through town. But it was fun to be in the parade.

Later on, when I was 17 years old, and a freshman in college, I went to visit my father at a fake Indian village set up for the tourists near Hayward, Wisconsin. Although most of what was shown was fakery, it was colorful and it gave the suited-up Indians employment. My father's wife, Fancy Feather, worked behind the bakery counter in her Fancy Feather costume selling big cookies, good-looking pies, and donuts. She was pretty in her pow-wow finery.

The young men were directed by my father, and he worked for the boss who owned the place. The tourists loved it, I guess; they sure came in droves. Later, my father would drive over to the center of town in his car, still in his leather costume, to deliver a speech to the tourists gathered in the town square. I would sink down in the car and listen to him giving a speech, and wonder, "God, why me? Why can't I have a normal father?"

Later on, I wandered into the cards section of the store. I saw my father and his wife in their costumes posing on postcards. I took my children when they were young to the very same place years later, and he was still there, on the postcards. I bought some and showed them their grandfather outfitted in an Indian costume on postcards. But when I was age 17 and trying to figure out what is what, I didn't have too much time to listen to my father, or anybody else for that matter. What is life about then? Isn't it about college, sophistication, young men, their attentive behaviors, dances before football games, and trying to look just like every other freshman?

In those days gone by, that is what seemed to be important. There was no time to ask my father what was really important about his buckskin outfit, or what he valued or fancied about Fancy Feather. What did he and the boss talk about to make the Indian village more colorful and more exciting to tourists that came in droves? What did he think when he looked out over the tourists listening to him talk up there behind the microphone? What did he think about the postcard?

What about Bad River? Why did he and his brother George leave their village to live in Odanah? Why did his brother George marry him to my mother on New Year's day? Why did his brother Ray go to Michigan? What did it mean that he was born in the state of Wisconsin, yet was not considered an American citizen until 1924?

Boarding Schools

How did his father, my grandfather, like the boarding school where he learned to be an elementary teacher? What were those boarding schools really like on the East Coast? Should I go to boarding school where my mother went in far-off Kansas or should I insist on staying home, in Odanah? I see the school there, near the railroad tracks, across from the river. It was near the church and run by the nuns. What were they? Who were they? Why did they dress so funny? Why did they think they could tell our uncles and fathers what to do? Who let them come to our village and build the big barn, the small cottage, and the pretty church? Why did the man say he was the father, an O.F.M. (we thought it stood for Old Fat Man)? He lived by himself, held himself aloof from our uncles and fathers, and smoked big cigars, yet did not use the tobacco or pipes of our old men. Why was it okay for those black-robed men to gather in that pretty church decked out in pictures painted by Peter Whitebird, wearing long dresses, with trousers sticking out underneath, yet make fun of Indians dress? Yet, I was willing to admit, they were an awesome lot when they got together on a feast day, put on their white lacy, shorty gowns, and marched single file into church down the aisle, singing in their deep voices, the Litany of the Saints, smelling slightly, but definitely of cigar? I don't know where they all came from on those days, but they were there. Why did only the boys get to learn the nice-sounding Latin? Sometimes they couldn't remember it, so we had to help them.

What fun we had at our marble tournaments in the spring, when Halfaday would win with his big steely, or the Maday girl would jump rope with the bigger girls, and we wished we could look like her, or perhaps even like that Poupart girl who was so pretty and could ice skate so well. How hard we worked when the Bad River flooded in the big flood that one spring. The bigger girls knew how to wear hats so smartly, and they could roller skate too. On Friday evenings, we could go to the movies in the gym, courtesy of Mr. Whitebird. He had the movie machine, and he would sometimes provide popcorn. We would all sit in the gym and watch the cowboy and Indian movies. We wondered out loud why the Indians always lost, even though it was apparent how good they were on their horses.

Village Dances

On Saturdays or the weekends there would sometimes be a dance. The boys would don their outfits, the old men would gather around the drum, and we girls would braid our hair, put on our buckskin dresses, and dance, trying to be as graceful as the three beautiful women who were called the Andrew Sisters of the Chippewa. They were called that, we were told, because there were three sisters everyone knew that could sing as well as these three Odanah ladies. *"Hohwah!"* we would say, which sort of means "Wow!"

Some days we would be allowed to help out at the rummage sale the nuns held in the small house next to the church. The old Indian ladies of the village would gather on the little porch, perhaps sitting and visiting on the one and only bench provided there. The ladies would discuss us as if we weren't there and as if they couldn't see us. We would sit and listen to them until we got bored, then we would run down to the river banks to see what was going on there.

The River

I remember a woman was found in the river once. Her corpse was bloated and big. I was fascinated at how she looked as we were shooed away. I didn't find out until I was grown up that she was a black lady. I did know she was the mother of one of my classmates. We didn't know that other kind of stuff in those days. Other times there was no one to shoo us away from the bridge and the river, so we would scale across, hoping not to fall to the rocks below. They looked mighty sharp and very big. I guess they were, because one day a girl fell.

The Woods

Sometimes we would be taken on a walk, perhaps to the Catholic cemetery over the river and through the woods. The Catholic cemetery looked so different from the Indian cemetery. The little Inidan cemetery is now part of an historical marker on Highway 2 and is no longer in use. The small, comfortable, cozy grounds are long gone—so too is the post office where the men and women of the village came to pick up their mail and chat one with another. Sometimes the postman, Mr. Maday, would let a kid have a cookie from the glass display case.

Village Life

We could see Mr. Maday everyday from our schoolroom window waiting by his car, down by the railroad tracks, for the train to come puffing through, over the Bad River bridge, and drop the mail. The train did not stop, where he stood to pick up the thrown mail bag and take it down to the post office to sort.

Sometimes, if we got there in time, we could stand by the railroad track and those men in the caboose would throw us a small nickle bag of candy. What fun that was. It didn't occur to us to tell anyone. We just thought that that is what trains did in those days. The other thing trains did was to take away our boys.

I remember how we went to the side of the tracks when the train did stop. It stopped for lots of our young men. A war was on, and the White people wanted our boys to help out. So they went off to war. We sent them off with a proper war dance. It was fun, it was exciting, but I forever mixed up Pearl Harbor with the poles that I was by when I heard them talk about that place. I thought Pearl Harbor had something to do with the tall light poles. We saved cans of vegetables for the war effort, and we planted war gardens. The windows at the school were pasted over with black shades, so the planes going over wouldn't see our lights flickering down on the ground. But some of those boys from our village families didn't make it back. My big sister from my father's first family cried because her big brother Richard died in Italy. He was finally shipped back to us years later. We wondered about that.

"Indiannish Behavior"

It was at the post office once that I heard Albert Whitebird picked up one of his friends. "Let's go for a ride," said Albert. His chum got in the car and forgot to ask where they were going. Not asking questions is typical Indian manners. He likely dozed off, as it was probably a nice day, and you know how drowsy one can get in a comfortable car like

Albert ran in those days. I saw his friend in Albuquerque after that ride. He was very mad at Albert, sitting in the lobby of the hotel, wondering how he got there without any change of clothes or luggage. "Sure, it was okay for Albert," he said. He had his stuff with him, and, as a matter of fact, was busy next door dancing up a storm at the pow-wow. I went and looked, and sure enough, cousin Albert was having a whee of a time, dancing his posturing dance in one of his best outfits. I told Mr. Maday that the next time someone asked him to go for a ride, he shouldn't be Indiannish, but should ask questions, or who would know where he would end up?

I don't interrupt our old ones when they tell stories because that is what I learned when I was young growing up in Bad River, Wisconsin, between the Bad River and the Big Lake. Now in the nineties, I teach and, once in a while, write. As I get older, I believe it is my right as an older person to say how it was with us, what was important.

Elderhood Season

I have learned about the White man, at one of his finest colleges, and now I listen to our old ones. I try to learn the language that was mine for the learning when I was young, but I was too smart and too concerned then about how I looked or appeared to the White people. I try to teach our young ones who will listen.

I try to write curriculum based on the values and world view I was taught by those old ladies and all the other people in my home village where I lived until the summer of my fourteenth year. I remember again how and what I learned as I played with all the Indian kids who lived and grew in Bad River in those years of the forties.

I know now that our lives go on much as our fathers did before us. We live, play, and work around these waters. We try to tell people not of our blood and lineage how it is with us. Maybe someday we will all like each other again, as it once was when the world was new, and all living things spoke one to another.

Endnotes

1. There are many documents to verify who lived here; see, for example, George Irving Quimby's *Indian life in the Upper Great Lakes*, (University of Chicago, 1960), or listen to the stories of our Elders who heard from their Elders, and so on into the dim reaches of time. The annual reprise tell us of our migration routes to these waterways from the great salt water of the East. Our people who have written are Lolita Taylor, (*Ojibwe the Wild Rice People* and *Native American Contributions to Progress*, Wisconsin Indianhead Vocational, Technical and Adult Education District Office, Shell Lake, Wisconsin, 1976), Anishinabe friend, Timothy G. Roufs, (*The Anishinabe of the Minnesota Chippewa Tribe*, Indian Tribal Series/ Phoenix and The Minnesota Chippewa Tribe, 1975— unfortunately out of print, but libraries may have copies), and see *History of the Ojibwe Nation*, written by our relative, William Warren, Ross and Haines, Inc., Minneapolis, Minnesota (reprint 1970 by the Minnesota Historical Society, St. Paul).

2. For an interesting and informative discussion of this point of view, Jack Weatherford, *Native Roots: How the Indians Enriched America*, Crown Publishers, New York, 1991.

3. See Russell Thorton, *American Indian Holocaust and Survival*, University of Oklahoma Press, Norman Oklahoma, (1987). See pages 5–9 for Thorton's discussion and conclusions.

4. These pronouns in English are used as a convenience. When speaking of men and women in terms like this, the Ojibwe people do not differentiate between men and women as English speakers do.

5. John G. Neihardt, *Black Elk Speaks*, Pocketbook, New York, 1972. Published originally by William Morrow and Company, Inc., 1932.

6. See George Catlin, *Letters and Notes on the Manners, Customs, and Conditions of North American Indians* (2 volumes), Dover Publications, New York, 1973. See page xi in Volume I.

7. Friedrick Baraga, "Chippewa Indians: Religion and Mythology," pp. 99–110, an article presenting the copy of the speech given by Baraga for getting money for "his Indians" in Cincinnati, Ohio. He said, "Men howling, running up and down, and with a great drum, those who can howl the loudest are the medicine men." The article is available from the Minnesota Historical Society Library, St. Paul, HS #BX940.A2. Volume 5.

8. John G. Neihardt, *Black Elk Speaks*, Pocketbook, New York, 1972. Published originally by William Morrow and Company, Inc., 1932.

About the Author

Rosemary Ackley Christensen is an enrolled member of the Lake Superior, Wisconsin, band of Chippewa Indians. She belongs to the Mole Lake band of her father. She grew up in the home village of her mother on the Bad River Indian reservation located 10 miles east of Ashland, Wisconsin, on the south shores of Lake Superior. She graduated from an all-Indian school located in Odanah, Wisconsin, attended an Ashland high school for one year, and graduated from high school in Drummond, Wisconsin. Her undergraduate college years were spent in Wisconsin, first at Stout, subsequently at Eau Claire. After transferring to the University of Minnesota, she left there with 15 language credits lacking for a bachelor's degree. Harvard University accepted her without a B.A. for a master's degree program. She graduated from Harvard in 1971 with an Ed.M., with major emphasis on curriculum. Further graduate work was completed at the University of Minnesota. She completed all the coursework toward a Ph.D., with educational administration as the major, and curriculum and Indian studies as the other concentrations.

In addition to devoting large amounts of time to her work with the Ojibwe language, researching teaching theory, and curriculum efficiency, with her laboratory colleagues, and Ojibwe language teacher, Amik Larry Smallwood, and Julie Corbine, she teaches at the University of Minnesota, Duluth, in the Indian Studies Department.

Chapter *18*

The American Indians

JOSEPH COBURN   PATRICIA A. LOCKE

ANITA B. PFEIFFER   JACK B. RIDLEY

SHARON M. SIMON   HENRI MANN

Editor's Note: In some ways, this ethnic vignette is like most of the others in this book. It was written by members of the ethnic group under discussion and it stresses the wide diversity within that group. There, however, the similarity ends. As you will notice, six authors are responsible for this chapter. Each represents one of the Indian tribes in the region of the United States being treated. Yet even having six authors is inadequate to indicate the great diversity of the more than 300 tribes presently in our country.

Moreover, the uniqueness of the American-Indian experience has no exact parallel among those of the other ethnic groups included in this text. In some aspects, the experiences of some Mexican Americans and some African Americans do suggest parallels. However, neither of these groups was colonized to the degree that has been true of the American Indians. In addition, neither suffered efforts at extermination to the same extent.

Only if you bear in mind what happened to the men, women, and children who were on this continent when the White Europeans first came to our shores can you fully understand the situation and needs of present-day American Indians. One stark set of statistics illuminates that situation in bold relief: In 1492, there were at least 8 million American Indians in America (some estimates range as high as 75 million); in 1910, there were only about 220,000 American Indians left in the United States. According to the 1990 census, 1,959,234 American Indians and Alaskan Natives live in the United States.

A earlier version of this chapter appeared in *In Praise of Diversity*. It is reprinted here with permission of the authors and publisher.

Actual warfare against the American Indians, it must be remembered, ex-
tended over our centuries: It was only a little more than a hundred years ago
that the United States Army finally forced the American-Indian tribes into
submission. Another instrument of American Indian destruction was the
forcible removal of tribes from their native lands to reservations, usually
west of the Mississippi. Hundreds of thousands died of starvation and disease
as they were forced to march thousands of miles to new areas. Particularly
destructive was the march of the Cherokees from Georgia to Oklahoma, in
1838 and 1839, that became known as the "Trail of Tears." Equally disas-
trous with this physical destruction was the cultural destruction that accom-
panied it—and continued in government schools and on reservations as often
well-intentioned but misguided White men and women, in accordance with
U.S. government policy, tried to "civilize the heathens."

Fortunately, this tide has begun to turn. Moving with the waves of civil-rights
reform and the War Against Poverty, American Indians are beginning to take
the lead in their cultural and economic revival. The authors of this chapter
all are playing an important part in this revival—particularly in the area of
education. They highlight what American Indians are doing, and what
teachers can do, to help restore American Indians to their rightful place in
their native land.

Introduction

Throughout the United States today, the descendants of our continent's original Indian
inhabitants are now experiencing a significant revival. Although the nature and extent of
the renascence may vary from tribe to tribe and reservation to reservation, most share at
least in a revival of hope. American Indians today comprise 510 federally recognized
tribes and 278 reservations (reservations, pueblos, rancherias, communities, etc.), and
speak 187 different languages. Because space does not permit detailed treatment of all of
these tribes, those that *are* included are grouped by geographic region.

In addition to linguistic differences, cultural characteristics vary greatly among the
many tribes. Even neighboring tribes may have totally different world views, complex
belief systems, social structures, governance and political systems, oral histories, ceremonies, arts, music, dance, and material cultures. Sex- and age-behavior expectations also
differ widely among the tribes. Thus, teachers can no more adopt a single teaching
strategy for children of the many culturally different Indian tribes than they can for
students of any other ancestral group. (It may help the teacher to recognize this diversity if
he or she thinks of Alaskan Eskimos and Florida Seminoles in America as comparable in
geographic separation to Laplanders and Sicilians in Europe.)

Since the mid-1960s, there has been an overt resurgence of pride among American
Indians. It is indeed remarkable that this tribal pride has endured, even to the degree that it
has, in spite of some 400 years of systematic attempts by the government and other
powerful forces to destroy the tribes and their cultures—especially their belief systems.
One might conclude that such tenacity is a result of the intrinsic beauty and validity of the
tribal cultures.

Many American Indians feel an obligation, as hosts of this continent, to offer as gifts
to our guests certain kinds of knowledge of the Beauty Way. Sensitive and perceptive

teachers of American-Indian children will find that a two-way exchange of knowledge and information can be most satisfying.

Tribal people often teach their children that they must learn two paths of knowledge. One is the path of the tribal-specific culture, including value systems that often are diametrically opposed to the value systems of the dominant society. The American-Indian child will be inclined to accept this tribal-specific path of knowledge as the good and right way of knowledge for him—or her—as a tribal member. The second path to be learned is that of is dominant society wherein the value systems (intrinsic to contemporary non-Indian America) of individualism, acquisitiveness, and mercantilism prevail. These latter values must be learned by American-Indian children as social and economic survival skills, not as values to be internalized. The American-Indian values of concern for the group, generosity, and disdain for material possessions are reinforced constantly in tribal ceremonies. Youngsters are expected to emulate persons who exemplify such values.

It is difficult, for American-Indian children to learn and to sort out simultaneously two different value systems, especially when school curricula, the media, and teacher behavior and attitudes usually give positive valences to the *dominant* culture's value systems. A sensitive teacher will realize the dichotomy inherent in formal schooling that an American-Indian child must face, and will present fairly both tribal *and* societal values. The teacher needs to be still more sensitive to differences when there are children from several different tribes within a single classroom. In such cases, it would seem appropriate to emphasize cross-cultural similarities.

It is important to realize that many American-Indian children are successfully learning *both* cultures, solely in their tribal languages, in at least some remote cultural enclaves. These fortunate children experience the delight of hearing teachers speak to them, for example, in Yupik Eskimo, Navajo, and Miccosukee—the languages of their parents, grandparents, and extended families. Their grade-level achievement surpasses those of less-fortunate children, who are forced to learn a foreign language (English) in the early grades. In many situations a *bilingual* approach is necessary. Exercising their rights as educational decision-makers, parents and tribal leaders have chosen this bilingual path as *the* desired approach for their children.

Teachers of American-Indian children also must realize that these people are dual citizens. They are first citizens of their tribes, which have an inherent sovereign status reaffirmed by treaties and the United States Constitution. In addition, since 1924, when American Indians became citizens of the United States, they have been entitled to all educational and related services. Indian Nations traded the majority of their vast land holdings in exchange for education, health, and other services that the United States agreed it has a moral obligation to provide "as long as the grass shall grow." Indian Nations, as an aspect of their sovereignty, have a legal right to be accorded a different status than are "communities" of other citizens. These differences are important for teachers to understand as they teach about Indian rights, and relationships with the U.S. government.

Teachers of these children have a challenging task if they wish to teach with understanding, compassion, and knowledge. The teachers must be willing to accept and appreciate values and perceptions of the world that differ from their own. As we have pointed out, the American Indian has different concepts of time, of space, and of an individual's relationship to the universe and to other creatures in the world—two-legged, four-legged, winged, finned, and crawling—and to the ones that are rooted in the earth.

The teacher of American-Indian children must suspend his or her ethnocentrism and seek to learn about students from the leaders and traditional members of a tribe. If a teacher in an urban setting finds that tribal elders are not available, he or she should read about students' tribe and talk to their parents and grandparents. There are several excellent resources available to assist teachers in understanding their American-Indian students better. They are listed in the Suggested Additional Readings section at the end of this chapter.

Unfortunately, most teachers of American-Indian children have not been equipped with appropriate preservice or other academic training to provide them with the competencies that are needed to teach culturally and linguistically diverse children. As a result, the responsible teacher must design his or her own in-service training program. The teacher should aim to achieve an understanding of tribal cultural and linguistic diversity, the resurgence and tenacity of tribal cultural pride, the validity of tribal-specific value and belief systems, the dichotomy of Indian and non-Indian cultural values, and the utilization of parents, tribal elders, and books to learn about specific tribal cultures.

As you read the following sections of this article that describe tribes from the major geographical areas of our country, it is hoped that your curiosity will be challenged and that you will read further and learn how, as the Navajo says, "to walk the path of the Beauty Way."

Some General Observations

There is a great gap between the realities of the American-Indian world and the myths and misconceptions that have traditionally been presented in accounts written by White historians. These accounts generally have focused on war-like struggles and have used them as a basis for presenting concepts of American-Indian character, philosophy, and way of life.

Before the advent of White "civilization," little is known through the literature about what kind of person the American Indian was. In his account to his sponsors of his first landing in America, Christopher Columbus said of the American Indians, "I swear to your majesties that there is not a better people in the world than these; more affectionate, mild and affable. They love their neighbors as themselves. Their language is the sweetest, the softest, and the most cheerful for they always speak smiling." Despite these words, Columbus's brutality toward American Indians was unparalleled.

When the American Indians did fight the White man, it was because the conflict was forced on them. The aggressors were the Whites, and the concept of Manifest Destiny[1] was developed to justify the aggression. Every method and means was utilized in the long struggle to dispossess the American Indian from his lands. On occasion, they won temporarily or were able to compromise or restrain White aggression long enough to bargain for restoration of part of their own land. Although American Indians suffered tremendously and their cultures did experience great changes, the White man's impact—with all of its technological superiority, aggressiveness, and zeal to conquer and refashion the American Indians in the White image—did not fully or finally end American-Indian life.

Prior to Anglo-European contact, this Turtle Island—as some tribes named America—was inhabited by culturally diverse tribal peoples, who today are referred to as "American Indians." The name has been accepted as a permanent misnomer after Christopher Columbus so named the natives he found here in the belief that he was in the Indies.

Spread over this wide country, now, as in 1492, there are more than 300 individual tribes, speaking a number of languages classified into 11 distinct linguistic groups. Because space limitations do not permit individual treatment, they are considered in this chapter according to the major regions in which they live.

Emergence Accounts

Handed down through an oral tradition, there is a different account of each tribe's emergence or origin—or, as one might say, the creation of the world. This view of creation colors much of the tribe's world view. These accounts do not jibe with some anthropological theories of Indian migration from Asia over the Bering Straits to Alaska, down the Pacific Coast through the Northwest and California, and eventually to the Southwest (and Mexico and Central and South America). Whatever the scientific explanation, the meanings that carry cultural significance for American-Indian tribes are the traditional beliefs, such as the illustrations that follow.

For example, the Cheyenne account starts with the Creator who ordered water, light, sky and air, and created the water peoples. He asked the assistance of the water peoples in creating land. After three unsuccessful attempts on their part, the lowly coot dived to the bottom of the salty water, bringing up a ball of mud that was placed on the back of grandmother turtle. Under the power of the Creator's hands, this ball expanded to become the earth, our grandmother or mother. Taking dirt or mud, the Creator made a human being, blew breath into this being's mouth, and gave it life.

Another example is the Hopi tradition:

> *The Grand Canyon in Arizona is a place of awe for the Hopi Indians because deep in the bottom of the gorge is the original* sipapu, *the mystic opening which links the world of the living and the world of the dead. The Hopis believe that they emerged from the Underworld at this sacred place. Mythically, the dying Hopis return to this chasm as wisps of vapor drifting downward into the canyon on their return to the Underworld. The Hopis who formerly ventured to the bottom of the canyon to bring back salt (a deposit which is found near the sipapu) returned with eerie tales. For example, if one passed just before rounding the last bend to the sipapu, the laughter and singing of happy people could be heard. However, as one approached it, the voices faded away and only the sound of the river remained. (Wright, 1975, p. 6)*

And the Navajos:

> *The Navajos believe they emerged through four worlds. At the beginning, there was a place called the Black World where only spirit people and Holy People lived....Man was not in his present shape and the creatures living in the First World were thought of as Mist Beings. Then Altse Hastiin (First Man) and Altse*

Asdzaa (First Woman) were formed. The Second World was the Blue World where many blue-feathered Beings lived. The journey continued to the Third World—The Yellow World; in this world small animals lived—the Spider People, the lizards, and snakes. The group then emerged into the Fourth World—the Glittering World—through a great female reed. The place of emergence is called Hajinnei. In the Fourth World, the First Man and First Woman formed the four main sacred mountains from the soil that First Man had gathered from the mountains in the Third World. (Yazzie, 1971, pp. 9–17)

Creation and/or emergence accounts are not alone in tying together the human and spiritual. Sweet Medicine, a Cheyenne prophet, is reported to have predicted the coming of the White man. He foretold the arrival of "good-looking, light-haired and white-skinned people" who would come "from where the sun rises." They would be a numerous, aggressive people who would be seeking gold, and they would bring "strange gifts such as flashing objects." Sweet Medicine said that they would decimate with a loud and deadly weapon the buffalo and other animals given by the Creator. He predicted war between the Cheyenne and the newcomers, with the loss of Cheyenne children to the ways of the new people. Finally, he noted with a heavy heart that his people would become crazy, and desecrate Mother Earth along with the White people, and forget his teachings.

Despite such prophecies, American Indians initially welcomed the White immigrants from across the water. However, early Anglo-European contact was marked by continuous dislocation of tribal peoples and other tragedies that Sweet Medicine foretold.

Maintenance of Identity

Despite White society's efforts to eradicate the American-Indian culture, American Indians have kept up the struggle to maintain their identity, their world views, their ways of life, and some portion of the land in which their identity is deeply rooted. As American-Indian country has survived the onslaught of civilization, so has the concept of "Indianness." Many cultural elements are still vigorously present and persist—such as traditional systems of governance, arts, oral traditions, language, belief systems and other aspects of national culture.

American Indians have struggled to gain a social and economic foothold in a national political economy that historically has rejected them. In doing so, they have been forced to encounter problems that are unique to them. For example, they are the only persons born in the United States who were denied citizenship until 1924—and this in their own homeland! American-Indian nations suffered conquest in their homeland under the theory of "manifest destiny." However, they have treaties and a special relationship with the U.S. federal government, which affirms their political status as nations and is recognized by international law.

Current Problems

The majority of the American-Indian people have not found it easy to adjust to the social or economic structures of the dominant White society. These people have been forced to live within a society that is both philosophically and historically alien to them.

The great Lakota chief, Sitting Bull, expressed his thoughts on this problem of adjustment as follows: "I am a red man. If the Great Spirit had desired me to be a white man he would have made me so in the first place. He put in your heart certain wishes and plans; in my heart he put other and different desires. Each man is good in his sight. It is not necessary for eagles to be crows. Now we are poor but we are free. No white man controls our footsteps...."

Until recently, American Indians have not been permitted to control their own destiny. On the contrary, the federal government has dictated a policy that has vacillated to include genocide, assimilation, and acculturation. From earliest colonial times, Indians have not been permitted any variation from a prescribed path. Only recently has self-determination become an explicit policy. Here is the way government policy was articulated by the Commissioner of Indian Affairs in 1889: "The reservation system belongs to the past, Indians must be absorbed into our national life, not as Indians but as American citizens, the Indian must be individualized...the Indian must conform to the white man's ways, peaceably if they will, forceably if they must...."

In spite of adversity as well as vast and seemingly unsurmountable obstacles, the American Indian continues to live and, in most instances, survive most vigorously and brilliantly. Today, more than ever before, leadership of a high quality exists among American-Indian people in the areas of education, health, social services, and economic development. To upgrade the quality of life of their people, American-Indian laymen, scholars, professionals, artists, historians, linguists, and religious leaders all are striving with great zeal and singleness of purpose.

Bureau of Indian Affairs

In 1824, Congress established the Bureau of Indian Affairs (BIA) within the War Department, giving it responsibility for American-Indian relations. The Bureau was transferred to the Department of Interior when that department was organized in 1849, and BIA remains there today as a federal agency. Headed by an Assistant Secretary of the Interior, the BIA is obligated to provide varying services to Indian tribes. These include many services that non-American Indians receive from state and local governments. The BIA has offices (agencies) on reservations that are responsible to the respective tribal governments and that are fiscally responsible to the Bureau of Indian Affairs Office in Washington, DC.

Health services are now provided to American Indians by the United States Public Health Service. This responsibility was transferred from the BIA to the U.S. Department of Health, Education and Welfare jurisdiction in 1955. As Alan L. Sorkin commented in 1971:

> It was thought that Public Health Service would have greater success in recruiting physicians to work on reservations, partly because of higher salaries and better fringe benefits. Furthermore, Congress was not as hostile to HEW appropriations as to those of the BIA. Indian health has improved substantially in the decade and half since that time, largely because of increased appropriations, which tripled on a per [capita] basis between 1955 and 1966.

Agricultural development also is sponsored by the BIA. These extension services were transferred to the U.S. Department of Agriculture (USDA) in the late 1950s, but funds for the program still are provided by the BIA on a contractual basis. Other services administered by the BIA are industrial development, roads, natural resources development, manpower development, property and income management, welfare services, and various housing improvement programs.

There is a housing crisis among American Indians—more than three-quarters of reservation housing is substandard; half of it is beyond repair. Educational achievement and levels of health are far below those of the general population. Agricultural productivity of the reservations is low; industrial development is proceeding too slowly to keep up with employment and consumer needs. Unemployment on reservations hovers at the level of 50 percent.

BIA employment assistance programs are minimally effective, having a minor impact on reservation economies. Forced termination of federal responsibility for American-Indian tribes is widely opposed by significant numbers of American Indians and has been found to be an unwise policy, but states with large populations are unwilling to assume financial responsibility for certain American-Indian welfare services. To improve the lot of the American Indians in all these respects will require new policies, changes in old policies, and increased government appropriations.

One of the most important BIA functions has been in the area of education. Initial efforts to extirpate American-Indian cultures have given way to a more enlightened pluralism. Today, there are various degrees to which various tribes are making their own educational decisions. In numerous instances, programs are initiated by members of these tribes.

Beginning in July 1976, American Indians were amazed to be asked to participate in planning BIA educational programs. Response throughout American-Indian country was widespread (i.e., American Indians attended several meetings to take part in reorganization of the BIA educational structure. Another cause for hope and new vitality at the BIA has been the implementation of the American-Indian preference policy in hiring. Significant numbers of American Indians had not been employed at high levels previously. However, beginning in the early 1970s, they were appointed at professional levels.

The BIA is still the only agency that assures Indians of guaranteed financial resources because of the federal trust relationship. About 87 percent of BIA employees are American Indian, largely due to preference in hiring and promotion. Under federal law, a non-American Indian cannot secure a position if a qualified American Indian has applied for the position.

Significant Legislation

American-Indian history has been marked by a series of Congressional legislative acts and policy statements. Early legislation by the U.S. Congress was assimilationist in purpose, attempting to coerce American Indians into the mainstream and to turn them away from tribal cultures. Recent enactments have been more pluralistic in tone. These include the Indian Citizenship Act of 1924; the Indian Reorganization Act and the Johnson O'Malley Acts of 1934; creation in 1946 of the Indian Claims Commission; President Nixon's 1970 Indian policy statement; the 1972 passage of the Indian Education Act (Title IV, PL 92-318); the Indian Self-Determination and Education Assistance Act of 1975 (PL 93-638); and Public Laws 95-561 and 101-297.

The Indian Education Act gave decision-making powers to American-Indian boards. The Indian Self-Determination Act is a landmark for tribal decision making. The four latter acts provided for tribal self-government, appropriated funds for meeting the unique needs of American-Indian children, created a mechanism to correct injustices through compensation, affirmed treaty relationships, and established a means for tribal self-determination. Today, most tribal governments contract BIA services to a large extent, thus providing local control, jobs, and equal if not better services.

Spiritual World Views (Religion)

Spurred on by the depth of their own convictions, Christian missions acted as agents in destroying American-Indian cultures. Although introduction of Christianity on this continent caused many of the native ceremonials and rituals to go underground, the missions did not completely succeed in their aim of assimilating the American Indians and eradicating their religion. This is evidenced today by the Plains Indians, who have been the vanguard for the renascence of the Sun Dance, which was prohibited by the U.S. government during the period from 1904 to 1935. Several tribes support their Native-American church, which has a membership of over 225,000. Other tribal religions are flourishing and are valid in their own right.

The Indian Ecumenical Conference, which has been held intermittently since 1968 on the Stoney Indian Reserve (a reservation in Morley, Alberta, Canada), offers additional evidence of the great rebirth of the belief systems of Indian peoples in the United States, Mexico, and Canada. Men and women, singers, healers, holy men, herbalists, and philosophers and others representing tribes from throughout this continent attend so that the core of tribal beliefs can be transmitted to the younger members by their elders. This gathering and similar gatherings ensure the vitality and the very essence of tribal cultures—religion—and attests to the strength of American-Indian belief systems. This conference makes it clear that American Indians are not acculturated, and that they nurture a deep and continuing sense of tribal identity.

Adaptation, Survival, and Renewal

Despite governmental policies of displacement and relocation to urban, metropolitan areas, American-Indian tribes continue to adapt and modify their tribal cultures to accommodate to the contemporary situation. It is a reality that American Indians no longer can live as before because of geographic relocation; however, in view of the importance of the family structure and because their cultures are dynamic, surrogate extended families have been created.

American-Indian tribal groups are creative and collaborative. Consider, for example, the large encampments of tribes such as that of the Lakota Cheyenne and the Arapaho at the Little Big Horn. Here, they performed ceremonials, shared spiritual gifts, and socialized, getting together for sheer pleasure. This continuing phenomenon is also illustrated by the camps of the Indian Exposition at Anadarko, Oklahoma, of the Crow Fair at Crow Agency, Montana, and the annual intertribal meetings of such organizations as the National Congress of American Indians, the National Indian Education Association, and the International Native Languages Issues Institute. These gatherings are an echo of the great encampments that were a routine aspect of American-Indian life. They demonstrate intertribal appreciation and the recognition of cultural differences.

Differences in language, customs, and traditions are found in many American-Indian families today. There is much tribal intermarriage, facilitated by friendships made in the government boarding school system, which includes Carlisle Institute, Haskell Indian Junior College, and the Institute of American Indian Arts.

Education, in general, is taking a multicultural-multilingual or bicultural-bilingual direction. In addition, there are some 22 tribally chartered colleges. Cultural knowledge and lifeways also are slowly being incorporated into the curriculum of the U.S. public school system. The final report of the Indian Nations at Risk Task Force, of the U.S. Department of Education, has formulated some goals for American-Indian education. Not all Indian Nations have approved these goals as written. The Task Force goals are:

- *Goal 1: Readiness for School.* By the year 2000 all Native children will have access to early childhood education programs that provide the language, social, physical, spiritual, and cultural foundations they need to succeed in school and to reach their full potential as adults.
- *Goal 2: Maintain Native Languages and Cultures.* By the year 2000 all schools will offer Native students the opportunity to maintain and develop their tribal languages and will create a multicultural environment that enhances the many cultures represented in the school.
- *Goal 3: Literacy.* By the year 2000 all Native children in school will be literate in the language skills appropriate for their individual levels of development. They will be competent in their English oral, reading, listening, and writing skills.
- *Goal 4: Student Academic Achievement.* By the year 2000 every Native student will demonstrate mastery of English, mathematics, science, history, geography, and other challenging academic skills necessary for an educated citizenry.
- *Goal 5: High School Graduation.* By the year 2000 all Native students capable of completing high school will graduate. They will demonstrate civic, social, creative, and critical thinking skills necessary for ethical, moral, and responsible citizenship and important in modern tribal, national, and world societies.
- *Goal 6: High-Quality Native and Non-Native School Personnel.* By the year 2000 the numbers of Native educators will double, and the colleges and universities that train the nation's teachers will develop a curriculum that prepares teachers to work effectively with the variety of cultures, including the Native cultures, that are served by schools.
- *Goal 7: Safe and Alcohol-Free and Drug-Free Schools.* By the year 2000 every school responsible for educating Native students will be free of alcohol and drugs and will provide safe facilities and an environment conducive to learning.
- *Goal 8: Adult Education and Lifelong Learning.* By the year 2000 every Native adult will have the opportunity to be literate and to obtain the necessary academic, vocational, and technical skills and knowledge needed to gain meaningful employment and to exercise the rights and responsibilities of tribal and national citizenship.
- *Goal 9: Restructuring Schools.* By the year 2000 schools serving Native children will be restructured to effectively meet the academic, cultural, spiritual, and social needs of students for developing strong, healthy, self-sufficient communities.

- *Goal 10: Parental, Community, and Tribal Partnerships.* By the year 2000 every school responsible for educating Native students will provide opportunities for Native parents and tribal leaders to help plan and evaluate the governance, operation, and performance of their educational programs.

A White House Conference on Indian Education, held in January 1992, recommended many of these and other goals that emphasize the native languages and cultures in the education process.

All of this activity reaffirms the fact that American-Indian cultures are dynamic and that they fully represent the vitality of a continually evolving people of diverse tribal backgrounds who reside in many parts of the United States.

Tribe of the Eastern and Southern States and the Great Lakes Area

In the area of the United States where the original inhabitants first met the White man, there has been the greatest dislocation. The few tribes living east of the Mississippi River are the least known and the least visible American Indians in the United States. Only a few have federally recognized status. Some groups live on state-recognized reservations but most have no reservation at all. Most of these groups are seeking federal recognition. American-Indian country, however, still manages to survive, even though it is a patchwork of tribal lands. In some cases, White-owned resorts and vacation cabins sit on leased American-Indian lands.

Early Tribal Groups

From the days of the first frontier, Indians were one of the principal determinants of historical events. The tribal peoples of New England and the eastern seaboard Algonquins were the largest linguistic family on the East Coast, stretching from what is now Maine to Virginia and straddling the Canadian border to the Rockies.

The Iroquois family, probably the most powerful in the area, occupied most of the St. Lawrence region, the basins of Lake Ontario and Erie, the southern coast of Lake Huron, all of New York, central Pennsylvania, the shores of the Chesapeake Bay and parts of Tennessee, Virginia, and the Carolinas.

Often included among the Indians of New England were those of the "Woodlands" or members of the Siouan family and the Muskogean group (Choctaws, Seminoles, Chickasaws, and the Ojibway). There were 20 or more tribes of Maine that made up the Abnaki Confederacy. The more significant tribes were the Micmacs, Passamaquoddy, and the Penobscots. Today, these tribes live on reservations exchanged for all of what is now the state of Maine.

The Penacook Confederacy of New Hampshire included 13 other tribes and the Penacooks themselves. A few Penacooks still live in New Hampshire near Manchester.

The state of Massachusetts is named for the Massachusetts Indians who occupied the Massachusetts Bay Territory in the early seventeenth century. This tribe also owned and occupied what is now Boston. A few Pequat Indians still occupy their own lands in part of Connecticut and there are some Mohegans near Norwich.

Where Are the Eastern and Great Lakes Indians Now?

In Rhode Island, two groups of Narragansetts live in Washington and Providence counties. The most visible concentration of American-Indian populations in New York may be found on several reservations.

Descendants of tribes that once occupied the Great Lakes region, or that were moved into this area from the eastern seaboard, live today on more than 25 reservations or small tracts of trust land in the states of Minnesota, Michigan, and Wisconsin. In Illinois, Indiana, and Ohio, there are other remnants of tribes who do not live on reservations and are not under any supervisory agency. Some descendants of the Miami tribe still live in Indiana.

In the Upper Great Lakes region, Michigan now has the largest American-Indian population—more than 55,000; Wisconsin has more than 39,000; and in Minnesota there are about 50,000. There also are three Sioux tribes living in southern Minnesota. In Wisconsin, there are 10 reservations and a population of Chippewas and Oneidas as well as Winnebagos, Potawatomis, and Stockbridge-Munsees.

The Menominees comprise most of the population of the county of Menominee in Michigan. The Menominees have achieved complete restoration of federal recognition. American Indians in Michigan include more than 1,000 Chippewas living on small tracts of land in the Bay Mills, Isabella, and Keenewa Bay communities. There also are a few Potawatomis as well as some Ottawas living in Michigan.

The majority of the American Indians in Florida reside on or near four reservations: Big Cypress, Brighton, Hollywood, and a Miccosukee community on the Tamiami Trail. Today, near Philadelphia, Mississippi, live most of the remaining Choctaws, once the most numerous tribe in the Mississippi-Alabama region. Some Creek Indians live in eastern Alabama.

The Cherokee people originally occupied vast sections of land in the states of North and South Carolina, Virginia, Tennessee, Georgia, and Alabama. However, as with so many other tribes, war, disease, and deliberate dislocation diminished the Cherokees as well. With the Treaty of New Echota, there followed the tragic period of the "Trail of Tears" during which 14,000 Cherokees began the forced march to a new Indian territory in what is now the state of Oklahoma. At the time of the removal decreed by President Jackson, a number of the tribe fled to the mountains to survive as the present-day Cherokees in North Carolina. This eastern band of Cherokees comprises the largest single group of American Indians in North Carolina and is the state's only federally recognized tribe. There are several other vestigial groups, but none of these is recognized federally by the Department of the Interior.

Two Eastern Tribal Cultures

The diversity among tribal cultures is illustrated by the differences between two tribes, both of which are in the same geographic region.

The Iroquois

From the early colonial period, the Iroquois Confederacy and the motivating spirit of its great prophet, Deganawida, set the tone of a quest for universal peace that the White man still searches for today. Deganawida had a vision of a great spruce tree with its top reaching through the sky to the land of the master of life. The tree stood for the sisterhood of all tribes, and its roots were the original Iroquois nations. Deganawida visualized the "Great Peace," a kind of world federation, as follows: "I, Deganawida, and the Confederated Chiefs, now uproot the tallest pine tree, and into the cavity thereby made, we cast all weapons of war. Into the depths of the earth, deep down into the underearth currents of water flowing to unknown regions, we cast all weapons of strife. We bury them from sight and we plant again the tree. Thus shall the Great Peace be established."

The teaching of the Iroquois league was idealistic and religious and its members were instructed to practice three pairs of principles: (1) health of body and mind, and peace among individuals and tribes; (2) right conduct, thought and justice, and respect for human rights; and (3) preparedness for defense, and keeping and increasing the spiritual power, known as *orenda*.

Deganawida's first follower was Hiawatha, whom tradition credits with the principal role in creating a working league. Faced with the original resistance of the Onondaga chief, Totadaho, Hiawatha united the Onondagas, the Senecas, the Cayugas, the Oneidas, and the Mohawks into a true union—the League of the Iroquois. In the eighteenth century, they were joined by the Tuscarora tribe, which moved north from Cherokee country. This strong League is still functioning today.

The Cherokees

While the Iroquois furnished the spirit for universal peace, the Cherokee nation furnished the foundation for U.S. policy and action in American-Indian affairs. They met every test in trying to negotiate and keep peace with the U.S. government. As with other tribes, however, the federal government consistently and repeatedly breached its treaties, both in the spirit and in the letter of the law. Despite this, the Cherokees made progress on their own, under the leadership of one of their great men, Sequoyah, who invented an alphabet that helped the Cherokee to become literate. Not only did the Cherokees write a constitution but they also established a legislature, a judiciary, and an executive branch of governance.

American-Indian life in the East has survived and now reflects a world in which many aspects of conquered peoples and nations have begun to change. In many ways, there is no longer an all-controlling force that dictates how, where, and under what conditions American Indians may fulfill their tribal and individual purposes in life.

Tribes of the Central States

In this section, there will be a general overview of the American-Indian tribes currently located in the central states region: Iowa, Kansas, Montana, Nebraska, North Dakota, Oklahoma, South Dakota, and Wyoming. Residing within this area are the following major tribes:

Kansas, Nebraska, and Iowa: Iowa, Kickapoo, Omaha, Ponca, Potawatomi, Sac and Fox, Sioux, and Winnebago

Montana: Assiniboine, Blackfeet, Chippewa, Cree, Crow, Gros Ventre (Atsina), Kootenai, Northern Cheyenne, Salish, and Sioux

North and South Dakota: Arikara, Chippewa, Dakota/Lakota (Sioux), Hidatsa, and Mandan

Oklahoma: Arapaho, Caddo, Cherokee, Cheyenne, Chickasaw, Choctaw, Comanche, Creek, Delaware, Iowa, Kaw (Kansas), Kickapoo, Kiowa, Kiowa-Apache, Osage, Otoe-Missouri, Pawnee, Ponga, Ouapaw, Sac and Fox, Seminole, Seneca-Cayuga, Shawnee, Tonkawa, and Wichita

Wyoming: Arapaho and Shoshone

Linguistic Groupings

Linguistically, the majority of these tribes fall predominantly into three of the linguistic groups into which American-Indian tribal languages are divided: Algonquian, Aztec-Tanoan, and Hokan-Siouan. Within each of these major groupings there are families or land areas, which provide for further subdivisions. Within any geographical area, one may find each of these groups represented.

Their Dwellings and Culture

Not only are the tribes of the central states linguistically diverse and geographically dispersed but they are also culturally unique. For example, and contrary to popular belief, many but not all of the tribes lived in skin-covered *tepees*, the Dakota name for this common type of mobile shelter. The Blackfeet, Comanche, Crow, and Shoshone used a four-pole structural base for the tepee; the Arapaho, Assiniboine, Cheyenne, Cree, Gros Ventre, and Kiowa utilized a three-pole structural foundation. The earth lodge, another type of shelter, was lived in by the Arikara, Hidatsa, Mandan, and Omaha. The Wichita resided in permanent grass lodges. The Osage house, an oval or oblong dome-like structure covered with mats, served as home for the Osage people.

Although the tribes differed from each other in many ways, the cultures of the majority of the tribes discussed in this section were shaped by the horse and the bison or buffalo. The horse became a common means of transportation, and the dog travois[2] was adapted to the horse. In addition, the horse became a standard of value in which the wealth of an individual was measured by the number of horses one owned or gave away. The buffalo provided the tribes of the great plains with a stable economy.

Commenting on the Dakotas, Clark Wissler (1966) wrote:

> *Their domestic economy was based upon buffalo; his flesh was used for food, his bones for tools, ornaments and arrow points, his horns for spoons and small containers, his dewclaws and hoofs for rattles, his hair was twisted into ropes for horses, tendons for thread, skins for robes, tepees, moccasins, etc. They even used skin for binding and joining where we would use nails. They made serviceable knives from buffalo ribs.*

One generalization that applies to all tribes involves their showing of respect for elder members. Each tribe's continuity is dependent on these teachers and transmitters of culture, history, wisdom, and knowledge. Other relationships, basically of respect but characterized more often as nonverbal, are those that exist between brothers and sisters, between a daughter-in-law and father-in-law, and between a son-in-law and mother-in-law as represented by Arapaho tribal culture. Evidencing concern for the well-being of others and placing tribal concerns above those for oneself were and are dominant values of the tribes in this region.

Reliance of the individual and/or tribe on the spiritual also is characteristic of these regional peoples. *There is no dichotomy between the spiritual and all the other aspects of the life process.* Most plains Indians (except the Pawnee, Wichita, and Omaha) observe the Sun Dance to reaffirm their dependence on the spiritual.

As typified by the Dakota, the tribes in this area have unique and numerous ceremonies, as well as a complex ceremonial life, which is necessary for maintaining harmony with the world about them. Attendance and proper conduct at tribal ceremonials is upheld by extended families.

Governance

Tribal governance was exemplified by the six-nation Iroqois Confederation to which the Seneca and Cayuga belonged; the Creek Confederation, composed of four similar tribes, in which there existed strong local village governments; and the Cherokee national government, which also rested on strong local control. An outstanding feature of these governments was their practice of democracy in following the will of the governed—the people.

Prior to the arrival of European immigrants, as diverse as tribal life-styles were, American-Indian life in all tribes was founded on the concepts of democracy, coexistence, humanitarian respect for the visions of others, and an attitude of respect and tolerance for other cultures—what we now refer to as *cultural pluralism.* This was highlighted in *American Indian Tribal Government Studies* (1976): "In spite of these vast differences, all of the many cultures appear to have had at least one thing in common—the knowledge that the earth was a good and beautiful place and that all living things were, in some way, dependent on all other living things, an idea that has only recently gained wide acceptance in the European cultures that now occupy the same lands." The U.S. government was heavily influenced by the League of Iroqois. Democracy and communist governments were influenced by the "Village Council" governing practices utilized by the majority of tribes in pre-Columbian America. Forms of this practice survive today.

Displacement of Tribes

In the 1800s, the lands of Oklahoma became home for many displaced Indian tribes. The first of hundreds of treaties was signed with the Delaware Tribe in 1778, which, like others, promised certain benefits and privileges in exchange for land. The Kickapoos joined in Tecumseh's alliance in 1800, and along with the Winnebago joined others in Black Hawk's War of 1832 in a desperate effort to resist White westward expansion. The Indian Removal Act of 1830 moved tribes west so that the White man's "destiny could be manifested." The Cherokee, Creek, Chickasaw, Choctaw, and Seminole were moved to Oklahoma between 1828 and 1846, in which period thousands of Cherokee died when they were illegally forced to leave Georgia. The Delaware tribe was removed 15 times.

Not only were the tribes removed and moved again but they also were brought into contact with diseases for which they had no immunity. Sometimes blankets given to the tribes were deliberately infected with smallpox. In 1831 and 1836, respectively, the Pawnee and Winnebago lost many tribal members through smallpox. The next year, the Arikara, Mandan, and Hidatsa tribes were greatly reduced by the same disease. The Pawnee and the Cheyenne were decimated by cholera epidemics in 1849, and smallpox reduced the Kansas (Kaw) tribe in the mid-1800s. Loss of family and relatives was as devastating as was severing ancient ties with their homelands.

In the 1840s the discovery of gold in California led to new treaties and non-American Indian abuse of American-Indian lands that had been reserved by treaty agreement. In 1856, the Omaha were placed on a reservation in Nebraska. In 1862, unfulfilled promises for annuities caused retaliatory action by some Dakota Santee in Minnesota; 300 Indians were later sentenced to hang, but President Abraham Lincoln commuted the sentences of all but 38.

In 1863 and 1864, the remnants of the Winnebago tribe were moved to Nebraska. In 1864, the troops of Colonel J. M. Chivington attacked a peaceful camp of Indians in Colorado Territory, slaughtering several hundred Cheyenne and Arapaho men, women, and children—an event known as the Sand Creek Massacre. Three years later, the Sac and Fox were removed to Oklahoma pursuant to their 1867 treaty.

The 1868 Fort Laramie Treaty assigned Ponca lands to the Dakota and the Ponca were removed to Oklahoma. It also guaranteed the Black Hills as Dakota land, but gold was discovered there by the expeditionary force of General George A. Custer. In 1868, he led an infamous attack on Black Kettle's Cheyenne camp on the Washita River in Indian Territory, killing nearly 100. In 1874, 174 Montana Blackfeet were massacred by Colonel E. M. Baker's troops.

On June 25, 1876, Custer attacked and fought the combined forces of Lakota, Cheyenne, and Arapaho in a battle on the Little Big Horn, which culminated in a decisive Indian victory over the United States Army. The following year, 900 Northern Cheyenne were sent south, but one-third walked back to their northern homelands. As a result, they were assigned a reservation in southeastern Montana. (In 1879, in the case of Standing Bear, a Ponca chief, it was determined that an American Indian was a person!)

The coveting by non-American Indians of lands reserved for American Indians caused Congress in 1887 to pass the General Allotment Act, which provided for the distribution of 40, 80, or 160 acres of land to certain American Indians, and legally sanctioned the taking of 90 million acres by the federal government.

In 1888, the majority of American-Indian tribes of the northern plains were confined to reservations. The last hope offered by the Ghost Dance of a return to the old ways culminated on December 29, 1890, at Wounded Knee Creek with the ruthless murder of several hundred Lakota followers of Big Foot.

Some Indian Contributions

After many centuries, the innate human capabilities of the American Indian are only now being accepted. Yet, U.S. society has benefited from an assortment of contributions from a wide range of tribes: Major General Clarence Tinker of Osage descent, who assumed command of the Air Force in Hawaii following the Japanese attack of 1941; Jim Thorpe of the Sac and Fox tribe, football star and Olympic champion; and Dr. Henry Roe Cloud, Winnebago, coauthor of the 1928 landmark Meriam Survey Report which served to modify American Indian policies. American-Indian talents have been significant in many fields. The wide range (from a variety of tribes) includes Pulitzer Prize-winning novelist N. Scott Momaday; artist R. C. Gorman; physicist Dr. Fred Young; and physicians George Blue Spruce and Kermit Smith.

Some outstanding American-Indian leaders in the past have been known to many Americans; however, members of their tribes revere them for vital contributions to their day-to-day survival. These leaders include Little Raven (Arapaho), Sequoyah (Cherokee), Black Kettle (Cheyenne), Stone Child (Chippewa, Quanah Parker (Comanche), Plenty Coups (Crow), Sitting Bull (Hunkpapa Sioux), Satanta (Kiowa), Crazy Horse (Oglala Sioux), Black Hawk (Sac and Fox), Tecumseh (Shawnee), and Washakie (Shoshone).

Highly talented and creative persons of American-Indian tribal descent are continuing to contribute to the beauty of American life. By no means a complete listing of tribes, the following are but a few of the individuals who continue to contribute much to our nation as well as to American-Indian betterment:

> *Atsina*: Gary Niles Kimble—attorney, legislator, and educator
> *Blackfeet*: Victoria Santana—attorney
> *Cheyenne-Arapaho*: A. Whiteman—artist
> *Cree*: Buffy Sainte-Marie—folksinger
> *Creek*: Allie Reynolds—professional baseball player
> *Comanche*: LaDonna Harris—administrator
> *Mandan*: Tillie Walker—child welfare advocate
> *Oglala Sioux*: Billy Mills—Olympic gold medalist
> *Osage*: Maria and Marjorie Tallchief—ballerinas
> *Quapaw-Cherokee*: Louis Ballard—composer
> *Salish-Kootenai*: D´Arcy McNickle —author and educator
> *Sioux*: Oscar Howe—artist
> *Winnebago*: Reuben Snake—administrator and author;
>   Ben Campbell—U.S. House of Representatives.

In addition, the Montana legislature had two senators and three representatives in the 1991 session. Individuals such as the aforementioned continue to perpetuate Indian tribal-specific cultures and contribute to a renascence of native cultural life patterns in a contemporary world.

Tribes of Alaska and the Western States

Alaskan Natives include the Tlingit, Haida, Tsimsian, and Athabascan Indians, and the Aleuts, Yupik, and Inupiat (Eskimos). The Athabascans inhabit the vast interior of Alaska. They live along the interior rivers and in wooded areas. A basic source of their subsistence is provided by the seasonal salmon runs in the rivers. They have traditionally supplemented their diet with game animals such as caribou and moose. Of course, contemporary diet has been influenced by the influx of whites.

The Tlingit, Tsimsian, and Haida live in the southeastern part of the state along the coast facing the Gulf of Alaska. Most of the territory from Controller Bay southward is the home of the Tlingits. The Haidas live principally on Prince of Wales Island and surrounding areas of Canada.

Although the Tlingit and the Haida speak different languages and have unique cultural features, they have many similarities. Both of their economies are based principally upon fishing. Salmon, halibut, and cod are the main sources of food but they also eat shellfish and sea mammals. As with all Alaskan Natives, Tlingits and Haidas occupy permanent villages during the winter months, and frequently move to fish camps during the summer months.

The Aleuts live in coastal villages on the islands that make up the Aleutian chain. They are considered to be more closely related to the Eskimo than they are to the Indian. Aleuts traditionally have been hunters of seals, sea lions, and whales. They still supplement their diet with roots, berries, and birds—and also their eggs—which are found in great abundance on the Aleutian islands. They, too, have adopted non-Native diets to some degree.

The Inupiat and Yupik Eskimos live in the northern and western coastal portions of Alaska. They have permanent villages that are located along the coast in such places as the mouths of rivers or the favorable bays and coves. The major source of food for the Eskimo comes from the seas and the rivers running into the sea.

The northern or Inupiat Eskimo have traditionally been hunters of whale, walrus, and seal in the Arctic Ocean. The western, southern, or Yupik Eskimo live along the Bering Sea coast and are still hunters of the bearded seal and salmon. Both groups of Eskimos supplement their sea-based diet with large game (including caribou) and with fish found in rivers. The subsistence economy of the Alaskan Natives often is at odds with the rapid influx of technological changes. Natives ask, "Must one way of life end, so that another may prevail? Or is it possible for the Native and non-Native to exist side by side?"

The Alaskan Native Claims Settlement Act

To deal with the problems of land claims in Alaska, the United States Congress passed the Alaskan Native Claims Settlement Act on December 18, 1971 (P.L. 92-203). Under this law, the Alaskan Natives retained title to 40 million acres of land and relinquished all rights and claims to the rest of Alaska for a monetary consideration of 962.5 million dollars. Twelve regional corporations were established with each Native having rights as a shareholder. It is worth noting that the Alaskan Natives Claims Settlement Act is but one of many legal actions in recent years designed to adjudicate American Indian rights and land claims.

Northwest Coast Indians

The Northwest Coast Indians live in an area stretching from northern California to southern Alaska. The earlier Natives in this area made their living from the sea and the coastal rivers. They supplemented their sea food with land animals and plant foods. Salmon taken in the annual spawning runs can still be considered to be one of the major sources of food for the people of the Northwest Coast.

Contemporary American Indians in this area still rely in large measure on ocean and river fishing and aquaculture. The Makah, Quiliute, Quinault, Swinomish, Lummi, Chehalis, and Tulalip are some of the major tribes in this area. Over 20 smaller tribes are encompassed within STOWW (Small Tribes of Western Washington). Today, the northwest coastal tribal reservations are largely made up of numerous small tracts, particularly in the Puget Sound area of Washington. Many of the Indians still fish for subsistence and are also involved with commercial fishing. The Northwest Affiliated Tribes is a politically strong organization that is deeply concerned with education and that is vocal about educational issues. Plateau tribes are included in this organization.

Northwest Plateau Indians

The Northwest Plateau Area consists of parts of the states of Washington and Oregon, northern Idaho, and the northwestern portion of Montana, situated between the Cascade Mountain range on the west and the Rocky Mountain range on the east. The plateau tribes share some of the culture and customs of their neighbors on the coast and have some similarities with those of the American Indians of the plains. The tribes that lived near the Columbia River and its inland tributaries were able to obtain the abundant fish found in these rivers—particularly the salmon, steelhead, sturgeon, and eels—as they made their spawning rounds. The Columbia River also served as an avenue of communication and trade among the plateau tribes and the northwest coastal tribes.

As another example, the Coeur d'Alenes, Nez Perce, and Salish-speaking tribes (Flatheads and Kootenai) hunted buffalo and used tepees during the summer months. However, they had permanent villages that they occupied during the winter months. Along with fish, buffalo, and other big game, the Plateau tribes ate the abundant berries and plant roots found in the area.

Some of the major tribes found in this area are the Salish (Flathead and Kootenai), Coeur d'Alene, Nez Perce, Colville, Spokane, Yakima, Umatilla, Warm Springs, and Klamuth. As with the Northwest Coast tribes, some of the present tribes of the plateau region are composite tribes, made up of several smaller tribes. For example, there are 14 tribal subgroups that make up the Yakima today. The Colville and Warm Springs tribes also have several different and distinct subgroups.

The Plateau tribes are now located on reservations that have timber, crop, or range lands. American Indians living on the reservation engage either in farming or ranching, or work in the various industries located on or near their reservations. Nearly all of the reservations in this area were opened at one time for homesteading, and today they are a mixture of American-Indian and non-American-Indian owned lands.

The tribes in this area are engaged in legal efforts to retain their rights to hunt and fish within their aboriginal territory. They are striving to continue their traditional forms of government, social structures, ceremonies, dances, arts, and languages.

The Basin Area Indians

The Basin Area consists of tribes living within the states of Nevada, Utah, southern Idaho, and parts of southeastern Oregon and southwestern Wyoming. This area is bordered on the west by the Sierra Nevada Mountains, on the east by the Wasach Mountains in Utah, and on the North by the Blue Mountains of Oregon. Much of the Basin Area is classified as semi-desert owing to its scarcity of rainfall. This scarcity, in turn, limits the amount of vegetation that can exist, which thus prevents any large concentration of game animals. There are few lakes and streams in the Basin Area.

The tribes of this area are the Paiute, Shoshone, Ute, Bannock, and Washoe. Although there are many subgroups of the Paiute, Ute, and Shoshone, by and large they consider themselves today as either Paiute, Shoshone, or Ute.

The tribes of the Basin Area can be subdivided into two distinct groups: (1) those of the eastern edge (such as the Ute, eastern Shoshone, and Bannock) who used the horse and hunted the buffalo as part of their way of life and (2) the other tribes in this area (which are generally classified as "seed gatherers"): the Washoe, the northern and southern Paiute, and the western and southern Shoshone. Their main sources of food have traditionally included pinon nuts, antelope, and other small game.

Owing to the sparcity of plant and subsequent animal life for food, the Native population in the Basin Area was of low density. Tribes lived along the small streams and lakes in the area. Annually, they collected the nuts from the pinon trees during the fall and used this basic substance in a variety of ways together with the small-game animals and birds found along the streams and small lakes.

Today, the American Indians of the Basin live on large reservations or in small colonies located near the cities and towns in this area. Those who live on the reservation often make their living from livestock, whereas those who live in the colonies may be employed in the surrounding communities. Many of the American Indians in this area have retained their language and other cultural customs. Their attendance at public schools and churches is considerable. As with other American Indians, they have strongly retained their tribal affiliations and thus have insisted on certain rights to hunt and fish within their aboriginal territory. Approximately 1 to 1.5 percent of the population in this area is American Indian.

California Indians

Some of the major tribes in early California were the Hupa (Hoopa), Karok, and Yarok of the northern coastal areas. The Modoc were in the northwestern part of the state. The interior valley was the home of the Pomo, Wintun, Maidu, Miwoks, and Yokuts. Numerous tribes also were found in southern California: The Chumash and Yuman tribes lived on the coastal plains, with the Tehachapi, Cahuilla, Serrano, and related groups living in southeastern California.

The major food staples of the California Indians varied in accordance with their locality. However, from the numerous oak trees many tribes harvested the acorn, which was in earlier days a basic food source for most of the tribes. Fishing in the coastal bays and marshes also provided an important part of their diets, as did the pinon nuts for the natives in the southeastern portion of California. Today, diet is similar to non-American-Indian diet.

The diversity of the languages of the early California natives suggests that the area may have been first populated by several different tribes that traveled into the area over a period of several centuries. Once in this favorable and abundant environment, some settled and have continued to maintain their separate and distinct cultures and languages.

Present-day California American Indians, for the most part, have changed and evolved in many ways. Many of the early American Indians were annihilated by the Spanish and Anglo-American settlers. Today, the surviving California American Indians live on small and somewhat isolated rancherias and reservations scattered throughout the interior valley and foothills. The larger rancherias are scattered in the foothills of the southwestern tip of the state. There are nearly 70 distinct reservations and rancherias with government structures located in what is now called California.

The major reservations in California are located in the northern part of the state. The Hupa and Yurok reservation is located in the northwestern coastal area. The Pomo are located on the round Valley reservation, north of Ukiah. The original California American Indians made a series of treaties and agreements with representatives of the U.S. government but these never were ratified by Congress.

The policy of the federal government in the 1950s of relocating American Indians away from their reservations resulted in many American Indians from other states being translocated into the major cities of California. Today, most of the American Indians in California are from out of state and come from a variety of tribal backgrounds. There are centers in the major cities of the state that provide social and other services for all American Indians in California. Indigenous tribal American Indians of the region continue to observe and practice cultural and religious ceremonies away from the major population centers. Through their educational systems tribes are beginning to revive to an even greater degree their cultural practices and languages.

Some Tribes in the Southwest

In discussing the southwestern tribes, one must remember that cultural change is a continuous process and therefore the development of various tribes and individuals within those tribes is at different stages in the continuum of cultural change. Tribal members come from families that practice one of the following belief systems: (1) Traditional Native, (2) Protestant, (3) Catholic, (4) Native American Church, (5) Mormon, (6) none of the foregoing, or (7) a syncretic combination of two or more of the foregoing, which influence the daily decisions of their family. One also may find that within one family (consisting of the nuclear family, plus grandparents, perhaps uncles and aunts) there may be representation of several belief groups.

Christian churches have had a drastic influence on the southwestern tribes. The Spanish explorers first encountered the Tohono O'Odham (Papagos) and Pueblos in 1540, with the Coronado Expedition. Colonization did not occur until 1598 under the leadership of the first Spanish governor, Don Juan de Onate. The Spanish colonial frontier did not permanently reach Tohono O'Odham (Papagos) territory until 1687. The Reverend Eusebio F. Kino, a Tyrolian Jesuit trained in Germany, established the first mission among Northern Pimans in 1687. The first historical glimpse of Navajo culture was recorded by Fray Alonso de Benavides in 1630.

The Christianizing and proselytizing efforts among the various tribes were demeaning and not advantageous to the development of the tribes. For example, the following account is reported by Spicer (1961):

> *The encomienda (tithing) system in New Mexico aggravated conditions by exact-ing tribute from the Indians, while the missionary program vied with the encomienda system in forcing the Indians to abandon their native practices and was equally coercive and brutal.*
>
> *To supplement native ceremonial patterns and beliefs, missionaries bap-tized Indians, forced attendance at Mass and made instruction in Catholic doctrine compulsory in missionary establishments. A Spanish decree in 1620 permitted the creation of native officers among the Pueblos. These officers were expected to cooperate with Spanish civil and church officials in compelling their members to comply with the civilizing and Christianizing efforts of the Spaniards.*
>
> *The Pueblo Indians appeared to compromise by outwardly seeming to have accepted the Spanish-imposed cultural system. They adopted the externals of the new faith and conformed to its demands of labor and tribute, but they continued to practice their own indigenous religion and other customs behind closed doors, heavily guarded against church and civil authorities.*

Today, each of the Pueblo villages has a mission in its midst. Although most Pueblo people nominally have been Catholic for more than 300 years, the native religion is the basis of their system of belief. The two systems are maintained by a process which Pueblo scholar Alfonso Ortiz once described as "compartmentalization."

Five church denominations now exist among the Jicarilla Apaches (northern part of New Mexico); the Navajos have at least a dozen different denominations on their reserva-tion; and the Tohono O'Odham (Papagos) have at least three denominations.

Basic Data

To summarize the significant events in the history of the southwestern tribes is not possible within the space limits of this section. However, some key facts and a few highlights can be indicated here.

It is important to know that the American Indians of the southwest are not vanishing, but rather are increasing in numbers. For example, the Navajos (the largest tribe, whose reservation is comparable in area to France) have a population of some 143,405.

The tribe is comparatively young: The average age is 17 years, and 50 percent of all Navajos are under the age of 30.

The Jicarilla Apaches number approximately 2,300. The Mescalero Apaches have a population of approximately 2,500. The Tohono O'Odham (Papagos) number approxi-mately 4,000 to 5,000. The population of both the northern and southern Pueblos—excluding the Hopis and Zunis—number approximately 25,500. (The 1990 census reported that the population of the Zunis was 7,073 and the population of the Hopis was 7,061.)

Diversity

There is an erroneous tendency among non-American Indians to believe that American Indians all are of one group and little different from other educationally disadvantaged groups. In the southwest, as elsewhere, there is a great diversity of culture, language, economic conditions, and legal relations with the federal government.

The American-Indian languages spoken in the Southwest vary as follows: Athabascan-related languages are spoken by the Navajos, Apaches, Utes, and Paiutes; Pima, Yuma, and Tanoan—three dialects of Tewan—are spoken by six northern Pueblos tribes; Tiwa is spoken by two northern Pueblos and two southern Pueblos; Towa is spoken by one Pueblo; Zunian is spoken by one Pueblo; and Keresan is spoken by seven Pueblos.

Pueblo languages are highly diverse; they contain three completely unrelated languages: Tanoan, Zunain, and Keresan. The three language subgroups of the Tanoan—Tiwa, Tewa, and Towa—although obviously related, are mutually unintelligible; hence, they are separate languages. In addition, there are dialectical differences from pueblo to pueblo within each language group. Hopi and Tanoan have linguistic relatives outside the Pueblos; Hopi and Uto-Aztecan and Tanoan with Kowan. Both also are Hopi and Tanoan, which are linked by some linguists to Uto-Aztecan Tanoan. Zuni also may be distantly related to California Penutian.

The principal members of the Athabascan linguistic family are divided into the Northern group, the Pacific group, and the Southern group. The southwest Athabascan-related languages fall into the Southern group. The southwestern Indians today reside on trust lands situated in New Mexico, Colorado, Utah, and Arizona. These reservations are federally recognized and have been created by treaties, Congressional Acts, Executive Orders, and Agreements.

Life on the Reservation

The reservations of the Jicarilla Apaches consist of about 742,315 acres and are located in the Rio Arriba and Sandoval Counties of northern New Mexico. (The word *Jicarilla* means "little basket" in Spanish.) The northern area of the reservation is mountainous (with an average elevation of 8,700 feet). It is dotted by seven lakes and includes the Navajo River.

Originally, the Apaches were forcibly moved to this northern reservation as a "temporary" home. However, the reservation became permanent in 1887 through an executive order by President Grover Cleveland. The southern portion of the reservation (containing approximately 341,000 acres at an average elevation of 6,450 feet) is composed of rolling hills and sagebrush country. The major use of the southern reservation is for grazing of livestock: sheep, cattle, and horses. The southern portion of the reservation was acquired under the Executive Order of another President, Theodore Roosevelt, in 1908.

As was mentioned earlier, the Jicarilla Apaches speak Apache, which is a part of the Athabascan family language group. There are two clans in the tribe: The Ollero (mountain people) and the Lanero (plains people). Like other southwestern tribes, the Jicarilla Apaches are maintaining their indigenous religion as well as participating in non-American-Indian secular activities.

Special Jicarilla religious ceremonies are held seasonally, for special occasions or for healing purposes, as is the case with other southwestern tribes. The Go-Gee-Ya Feast (including a harvest and relay race between the two clans) usually is held in the autumn of each year. The Puberty ceremony (held for girls who are entering womanhood) continues for four days and is conducted by a medicine man who also conducts the Bear Dance, a healing ceremony for the ill. Extending for four days, the Bear Dance is held whenever it is deemed necessary.

Just as Navajo religious activities concern and involve all the members of the family and permeate the daily lives of individuals, so too is it among the Jicarilla. There is constant interaction between the adults and children. Furthermore, there are no special buildings erected to worship in; rather, the *hogan* (home) is the shrine, and major religious activities occur within it.

His home is where the Navajo youngster develops and refines his knowledge of the Navajo code of life (*Dine ba niilyaii* and *Dine yee hinanii*) and the Navajo way of life (*Dine yik' ehgo yigaalii*). The home is the place of births and of family celebrations such as that for a baby's first laugh, of *kinaalda* (puberty rites of a young woman), and of weddings. It also is the center for the judicial process and the place where maintaining good, health, happiness, and harmony with relatives, friends, and natural surroundings are all learned and reinforced through *Hozhooji* (the Blessingway ceremony).

The Navajo hogan also is the place where theology, law, and medicine are learned and reinforced. Bergman (1973) reported, "In a Navajo ceremony, there is no way to tell what is healing and what is worship. Everything is both. Moral guidance is also an inextricable element of ceremonial practice."

Southwestern tribes exhibit varying degrees of maintenance of their traditional history, stories, ceremonies, songs, prayers, and explanations of proper behavioral patterns. A mixture of these ingredients, which makes for proper living, is included within the teaching of each ceremony. For example, the Navajos sing some 70 to 75 ceremonial songs during their four-day puberty ceremony. The medicine man explains why certain songs are sung, how they relate to prayers and stories, and why certain behavioral patterns and expectations are required. The young woman being honored must observe strictly those behavioral patterns detailed to her during the four days since this will teach her to move about smoothly in the adult world she is entering. She also is taught about the responsibilities that she will shoulder during the course of her life among her people. In addition, encouragements are voiced concerning her acquisition of various skills, such as weaving, for example.

Currently, the question of water rights for the southwestern tribes is extremely critical. The Navajo River is the only usable river on the Jicarilla Apache Indian Reservation. This river is being turned around and, through a three-quarter billion dollar project, being taken into the Rio Grande. It has been pointed out by the American Indians affected that this diversion ordered by the Secretary of Interior will cause "the destruction of the Jicarilla, the Southern Ute, the Ute Mountain and the mighty Navajos." Furthermore, they have noted:

> The eternal verities of low rainfall, lack of surface water, and a limited number of mountain springs have been somewhat altered by deep tube wells in the alluvial valleys. Water remains the limiting factor in Papagueria (Spanish name for the land of the Tohono O'Odham).... What has changed most drastically in the environment of the Tohono O'Odham is migration of Mexican Americans, Anglo-Americans and Blacks into the same riverine valleys where the Tohono O'Odham historically and prehistorically supplemented desert resources.

Alfonso Ortiz summed up the situation as follows: "Today the Pimas are farming about one-half the acreage of their peak years a century ago, despite a doubling of their population since that time."

Some Educational Problems of the Navajos

The Navajo reservation extends into three states: Arizona (where the major portion of the land is located), New Mexico, and Utah—an area of approximately 25,000 square miles. Thus, the reservation is the size of the state of West Virginia, or larger than the combined states of Connecticut, Delaware, Massachusetts, and New Hampshire. Because of the size of its land area and the large population of the tribe (over 140,000), Navajo problems are complex. The situation in education will serve as an example.

About 39,000 of the tribe's children attend public schools extending over 18 varied districts. (In addition, the boundaries of these school districts do not coincide with those of Bureau of Indian Affairs agency divisions.) About 3,000 children attend 22 church schools, which are administered by at least 12 different religious denominations whose home office locations usually are on the East Coast. About 16,000 children attend 53 BIA schools, whose overall administrative office is in Washington, DC.

Since 1966, five Navajo schools have been established, each administered by its local community. Three of these schools have educational programs that include preschool through high school age children. About 1,500 children attend the five schools. There also are 102 Head Start sites and several day-care centers administered by the Navajo tribe, which serve over 3,000 children.

In addition to this complex web of educational administration, there are three U.S. Office of Education (USOE) regional offices that subdivide responsibilities for federal programs in the reservation schools. For example, the New Mexico schools that have federal programs are serviced by the Dallas USOE office; the Arizona schools by the San Francisco office, and the Utah schools by the Denver office. These programs include the public, contract, and Head Start school operations. The network of layer upon layer of administration—tribal, state, federal, and often church—causes slow development of programs and extreme levels of frustration for those in tribal positions who are attempting to make some changes for the benefit of the Navajo children.

The public school experiences of southwestern tribes generally have been detrimental to the growth of a positive self-image among American-Indian youngsters. The curriculum has been foreign, as have been the teachers, the language used, the administration, and the food served. Traditionally, public schools have not involved the Navajo community—its teachings, training, or diet.

In its effort to improve the education of its children, the Navajo tribe, through its own Division of Education, has set as its number-one priority the training of its first cadre of professional Navajos to be classroom teachers.

At present, the tribes 62,000 school children are taught by 4,800 teachers and 423 administrators. In 1984, it was reported that only 739 of the teachers were Navajos (not all of them bilingual) and that approximately 110 of the administrators were Navajos. Although only a small amount of teachers were Navajos, 1,160 of the 1,638 teacher aides were Navajos. According to the March 1976 issue of the *Navajo Nation Education Review*, 200 students were enrolled in the Navajo-sponsored teacher-education development program, with 100 expected to graduate in June of that year, bringing the total of Navajo teachers up to about 500.

This new corps of Navajo teachers is expected to make a difference in the lives of Navajo children, especially those teachers who are bilingual and who are knowledgeable about the life-styles, religions, cultures, and social influences that may not result in either the strengthening or weakening of the Navajo people. Navajo teachers and administrators are planning to combine their efforts and to establish a new coalition of educators from tribal communities who can assist in the teaching of the young. The Navajo tribe is hopeful that eventually it will have full decision-making responsibility for the education of all of its children and youth.

Over the last 10 years, some changes have been introduced in the education of American Indians, beginning with the community-based Rough Rock Demonstration School in Rough Rock, Arizona.

Early in 1977, the Navajo Division of Education and the Board of Trustees established the Navajo Academy in Window Rock, Arizona. A private high school "founded on the principle of cultural pluralism," it is open without charge to young Navajos "who wish to prepare themselves for future roles of leadership and service to the Navajo Nation and the United States."

An Editor's Concluding Note

Hopefully, reading this chapter has given you insights that will be helpful in the education of American-Indian boys and girls. From this reading, however, it should be clear that if your own particular questions have not been answered in the chapter, you must seek the answers in your own American-Indian community because the answers will be different for different tribal peoples.

If teachers make the effort to meet the family, they will find that individual members of the family will be inclined to meet them half-way. Establishing a one-to-one relationship with family members will make cultural differences easier to understand. Experience of the teacher as a mother or father may form a common bond with the parents of the American-Indian children and provide understanding rooted in human values.

Only by getting to know the local, American-Indian community—its problems and its values—can the teacher really meet the needs of the children in his or her classroom. For example, only if the teacher finds out that local American-Indian families have to walk miles for pails of scarce water will he or she understand why the children's school clothing cannot be sparkling clean at all times. Only if the teacher finds out that there is no electricity in his or her pupils' homes will he or she understand why they cannot do homework assignments at night.

To discover the value and belief systems of students' families or tribes, however, may require more subtle and painstaking explorations. It may surprise some teachers, for instance, to discover how deeply religious values pervade all aspects of American-Indian students' lives—how religion is something that they *live* seven days a week in all of their activities rather than observe only in church on Sunday mornings.

It also may surprise some teachers to discover the serious tribal responsibilities that American-Indian families place on the shoulders of their children—responsibilities as broad and far-reaching as helping to ensure the economic and spiritual survival of their tribes. Such a discovery will help explain why qualified American-Indian boys and girls are now being encouraged by tribal leaders to go into key fields such as medicine, law, economics, and business administration. Similar insights into tribal naming ceremonies will indicate their crucial roles in helping children to focus on the goals of their Indian Nations. For instance, in the first years of her life, a little American-Indian girl may be given the loving and playful name that means (in English) "She flies like a butterfly." At the age of five, however, at a tribal naming ceremony, she will be renamed to make clear her life's mission: "She flies to defend her nation."

Discoveries and insights such as these can help teachers realize what important roles they themselves may play in helping American-Indian students to achieve their individual potential and their tribal goals. Not only can a teacher reap intense personal satisfaction for his or her efforts but he or she also can help to make partial repayment of the debt all of us owe to America's Indians as they continue to share with us the riches of this "Turtle Island."

Endnotes

1. *Manifest Destiny* is a phrase that was coined before the Mexican American War to express expansionist sentiment in the United States to extend U.S. sovereignty from the Atlantic to the Pacific and even to the islands of the Caribbean.

2. A *travois* is a vehicle consisting of two trailing poles (travois poles) that serve as shafts for a dog or horse and that bear a platform or net for the load.

References

Bergman, Robert L., "Navajo Medicine and Psychoanalysis," *Human Behavior* (July 1973).

National Congress of American Indians, *American Indian Tribal Government Studies* (Washington, DC: Author, 1976).

Sorkin, Alan L., *American Indians and Federal Aid* (Washington, DC: The Brookings Institute, 1971).

Spicer, Edward H. (Ed.), *Perspectives in American Indian Cultural Change* (Chicago: University of Chicago Press, 1961).

Wissler, Clark, *Indians of the United States* (New York: Anchor, 1966).

Wright, Barton, *The Unchanging Hopi* (Flagstaff, AZ: Northland, 1975).

Yazzie, Ethelou (Ed.), *Navajo History* (Tsaille, AZ: Navajo Community College, 1971).

Suggested Additional Readings

Annotations have been adapted from the Social Science Education Consortium's *Materials and Human Resources for Teaching Ethnic Studies: An Annotated Bibliogaphy* (Boulder, CO: Author, 1975).

Bureau of Indian Affairs. *American Indians Today: Answers to Your Questions—1991.* Washington, DC: Bureau of Indian Affairs, 1991 (third edition).

Butterfield, Robin A. *Effective Practices in Indian Education: A Monograph for Using and Developing Culturally Appropriate Curriculum for American Indian Students.* Portland, OR: Northwest Regional Educational Laboratory, 1985.

Coburn, Joseph, and Steven Nelson. *Teachers Do Make a Difference: What Indian Graduates Say about Their School Experience.* Portland, OR: Northwest Regional Educational Laboratory, 1989.

Fuchs, Estelle, and Robert Havighurst. *To Live on This Earth: American Indian Education.* New York: Anchor Press, 1973.

An exhaustive study of the nature of the education that American Indians receive and have received in the United States. Deals with a number of important issues and problems, such as the identity and location of contemporary tribes and the difficulties and subsequent achievement levels resulting from cultural assimilation into American schools.

Hodgkinson, Harold L., Outtz, Janice Hamilton, and Obarakpor, Anita M. *The Demographics of American Indians: One Percent of the People; Fifty Percent of the Diversity.* Washington, DC: Institute for Educational Leadership, Inc., Center for Demographic Policy, 1990.

Josephy, Alvin M., Jr. *The Indian Heritage of America.* New York: Bantam Books, 1968.

An excellent book for both students and teachers. Each chapter covers a different tribe and the corresponding geographical location of each. Explored are attitudes toward American Indians, stereotypes, the White man's conquest, and American Indians today and their fight for survival.

Levine, Stuart, and Nancy O. Lurie. *The American Indian Today.* Baltimore, MD: Penguin Books, 1972.

Indian and White anthropologists explore the American-Indian identity today in the light of firmly rooted, traditional values. Their findings are supported by a series of case studies that examine current problems confronting American Indians. Nationalistic trends, current tendencies, acculturation, governmental relations, and education are major topics of this study. Included are highly detailed maps, topical bibliographies, illustrations, and a complete index.

Mander, Jerry, "What You Don't Know about Indians: Native American Issues Are Not History." *Utne Reader* (November/December 1991).

Moquin, Wayne, and Charles Van Doren. *Great Documents in American Indian History.* New York: Praeger Publishers, 1973.

A series of readings about some of the tribes in the United States. Authors note the similarities and differences among tribes and with American culture. They explore the texture of tribal life, the confrontation with the White man, and the problems facing American Indians today.

National Geographic Society. *The World of the North American Indian.* Washington, DC: National Geographic Society, 1974.

The narrative and illustrations, covering the history of American Indians, provide a vivid account of their beliefs, customs, crafts, and accomplishments. Historical events and discussions of customs are integrated into an excellent resource for both readers and nonreaders.

Pepper, Floy C. *Effective Practices in Indian Education: A Teacher's Monograph.* Portland, OR: Northwest Regional Educational Laboratory, 1985.

Pepper, Floy C., and Nelson, Steven R. *A Monograph on Effective Administration Practices in Indian Education.* Portland, OR: Northwest Regional Educational Laboratory, 1985.

U.S. Department of Education. *Indian Nations At Risk: An Educational Strategy for Action.* Washington, DC: Indian Nations At Risk Task Force, U.S. Department of Education, 1991.

Vogel, Virgil J. *This Country Was Ours; A Documentary History of the American Indian.* New York: Harper and Row, Inc., 1974.

A thorough, chronological history of American Indians from prehistory to the present. Through the use of a variety of materials (laws, treaties, letters, official reports, court decisions, and party platforms), Vogel reveals the injustices the White man has committed against Indians.

Weatherford, Jack. *Indian Givers: How the Indians of the Americas Transformed the World.* New York: Ballantine Books, 1988.

About the Authors

Joseph Coburn is a member of the Klamath tribe and was raised on the Klamath Reservation. Coburn graduated from Chemawa Indian School, University of Oregon, and Western Oregon State College. He has been an educator for 33 years, serving as a teacher, a coach, a counselor, and an administrator. For 20 years, he has served as the director of the Research and Development Program for Indian Education at the Northwest Regional Educational Laboratory. This Program has produced *The Indian Reading Series,* monographs on *Effective Practices in Indian Education,* and several reports on Indian education. For 10 years, Coburn has also served on the Klamath Tribal Executive Committee, which includes two years as Tribal chairman. He was chairman of the Restoration Committee, which obtained restoration of the Klamath tribe to federal recognition.

Patricia A. Locke, a Hunkpapa Lakota and Anishnabe-Mississippi Band, has helped 17 Indian Nations establish colleges on their reservations and is working with 12 Indian Nations to develop their education codes and departments of education. She also served as the coordinator and special editor of the topic American Indians.

Anita B. Pfeiffer is a Navajo educator from Kayenta, Arizona. She is presently director of education, Navajo Nation. She prepared this chapter's materials on the Southwest and contributed to the section General Observations.

The late **Jack B. Ridley** was director of the Center for Native American Development and associate professor of the University of Idaho in Moscow. A member of the Western Shoshone Tribe, he published widely on crop physiology and reservational land development and management. Ridley served as a consultant to the National Science Foundation for Minority Science Education. He prepared this chapter's material on Alaska and the Western states, and contributed to the section General Observations.

Sharon M. Simon, a member of the Mohawk tribe, Six Nation Bands, has served as an education program specialist for the United States office of Education in the administration of the Indian Education Act of 1972. She also has served as a curriculum and reading consultant for Indian schools and as an education specialist for the Bureau of Indian Affairs. She prepared the materials in this chapter on the Eastern Seaboard and the Great Lakes, and contributed to the section General Observations.

Henri(etta) Mann is currently director and professor of Native American Studies as the University of Montana, Missoula. A member of the Cheyenne-Arapaho tribes of Oklahoma, she was lecturer/coordinator of Native American Studies at the University of California, Berkeley, and has served as interim director of the American Indian Program and Visiting Lecturer, Graduate School of Education, Harvard University. In this chapter, she prepared the material on the Central States and contributed to the section General Observations.

Chapter 19

The So Called

PAZCUAL VILLARONGA

I am mixture
similar to h2O
I am american pie
the black-eyed peas
with plenty of salsa

I am the rhythm and blues
the classical lines
the pru-cu-ta-ca-ca-mambo

I am a potpourri of values and attitudes
the fact that men don't cry
but in reality they do
and don't die

I am a mixture
of beautiful paints
that picture
psychedelic tones
african blood
spanish blood
and Indian blood

transported
by economical
social
or political fact

from an island of joy
under a damn
cynical
implemented
ploy

to a jungle of cement
metal
and glass

to become a confused entity
a confused being
of meatloaf
and oxtails
and arroz con pollo

of beethoven
Isaac Hayes
and eddie palmieri

to struggle with my culture
their culture
and the loss of mine

goodbye three kings
hello christmas
and its mad capitalistic
season

the dropping of my accent
the implementation of
another language

mine is second
excuse me while I change
to another mother tongue

I am Puerto Rico
the u.s. of a.
and new york

spinning
trying to lose myself
in the sun
on the penthouse
in my place
in my slums
trying to become
what will constantly be denied

I am black
white
brown
uptown
downtown
all around
the damn town

I am here
I am there
I am everywhere
spread thin
so that my existence
my consistency
my reality

can be denied
mesmerized
until I boil down to nothing
at the bottom of the pot
"El Pegao"

which they don't know is the best
part of the meal
especially because I survive
to eat it

I am the music you can't exploit
because you don't
understand
comes from our corazones
speaks of our culture
our history
our minds

in a language you find
easier to destroy
because yours is better

I am caught in a flight
over a sea
of controversy

I am a piece of a puzzle
that doesn't fit
here or there

because both my vehicles of expression
are dulled and

downed
by my own
and my own

I am what has always been there
only with a different name
to fit the purpose
to play the game,
for someone's fame
other than mine

I am the P.R.
the rican
the spic
the new click
the so called New-Yor-Rican

The writing of the poem *The So Called* came about as a result of a committee presentation that I was a part of while at Hunter College. It was also a going against norms, sort of, in the class of a professor who was very conservative and expected a committee presentation, not a poetry reading. We were to *link the Puerto Rican born and living in Puerto Rico with the Puerto Rican born and living in New York City*. It was a topic that was interesting as well as challenging.

By group consensus, I wound up with the task of summarizing their thoughts and ideas, as well as coming up with a part about being a "Neoyorican"—a task that, to be very honest, I thought would be very easy. I should have been able to take what they had written and put it together into a great summary. And as far as being a New York-born Puerto Rican, *that* should have been easy. It turned out to be an agonizing experience.

I remember sharing with my wife, Carmen, how I had read everyone's part of the presentation and how they made me feel. How it had dredged open my own feelings, opened up my soul. How it felt when I had to exchange my mother tongue for another. How the simple fact of an expanding menu at home made me feel insecure, music changed, people's ways changed.

I remember that we had three weeks for the presentation, and everyone had given me their work and kept asking me about the ending. I read about how my friends had come here, or been born here and slowly but surely acclimated to New York, struggling with Puerto Rico within: the music, food, language, culture, habits all flowing within our bodies, yet we were Americanized—American pie, George Washington, and good old Abe Lincoln. I remembered going to school and hearing the biting remark, "That language isn't spoken here" (meaning my Spanish). In fact, American pie, George Washington, and good old Abe is all we ever celebrated. I remember singing "Oh, me name is MacNamara, I'm the leader of the band...," but I don't ever recall them celebrating *me* and *my* ways. Never!

I remember being part of the first Puerto Rican family to move onto the block on 105th Street between First and Second Avenues. I remember my mixing with those of Italian descent and hearing my father being called "Patsy" (short for Pascual, in Italian).

We were Patsy's kids and accepted. My father was very friendly. People named Margaret, Christina, and Mrs. Russo were our neighbors. Slowly, other families moved in—the Milans, the Maestres—and things changed. My soul blended with those of African descent; it was my Black experience. I remember learning that as a Puerto Rican I was part Taino Indian, African, and Spanish, and it fit inside of me so well because I seemed to have garnered something from every one of them as I grew up. I felt so special—yet *we* were still not celebrated in school.

Our presentation was due on the third Tuesday after it had been assigned. Everyone had handed in the parts. All that was left for me was to tie it together into a nice little package. One of the members of the committee had called me at home and asked me about it, and I remember reading it to her. She said it was good. But I knew better: It did not say what I *wanted* to say. I was not satisfied with it. My wife kept telling me that I should just say it the way I felt it. I tried to explain to her that this was college, that the work I had to summarize was high-caliber writing and technical in nature, and that although our topic was an emotional one, I was told that Dr. Rivera would not approve if anything other than the norm were presented. We were told that she was very conservative when it came to these presentations and that we had been, so to speak, "warned!"

I went to sleep in turmoil: I had abdicated to intellectualism minus the emotion. Still, I couldn't get the idea out of my mind that this was *more* emotional than intellectual.

At exactly 3:46 A.M. it happened. Suddenly I was up and, because I don't see well without my glasses, grabbed some odd-looking paper (graph paper, in fact), fumbled for my pen, and began. The turmoil, the emotion, the confusion of who I was exploded. And it began thus: "I am a mixture similar to H^2O/I am American pie/the black-eyed peas/with plenty of salsa/I am the rhythm and blues/the classical lines/the pru-cu-ta-ca-ca mambo…." It spoke of the blood that flows within, of food and music, of changing to "another mother tongue," of the root (raices) and how things are ripped from us (that isn't spoken here).

I read it to my wife—and, despite being awakened up at 4:30 A.M., she loved it and was very supportive. However, I still needed to get it past Dr. Rivera.

The next day, I read my summary and the poem to my committee members. They loved it—and one of the members (whose name also was Carmen) said, "Read the poem. We have to tell it the way it feels or else we continue to lie, to deny ourselves!" She was right—it was one thing to have someone else deny you, but wrong for you to continue to deny yourself. I especially knew that, now that my soul had been opened up. Except for one dissenting vote, we decided we would sink or swim with the poem as the summary. The support made me even more determined.

There is something that happens every once in a while to naturally add drama to life, and this time it did. We would be the last group of four to present. Carmen started the presentation, having been born in Puerto Rico the earliest, and it continued until we got to New York and being born and raised Puerto Rican there. I stood before the members of the class, looked over at Dr. Rivera, and read the poem. To say that it was very well received would be to understate the reaction to it: It got a "standing O." (The poem has in fact received many standing ovations, but *that* one has always been my favorite). Dr. Rivera herself was quite pleased in spite of the unorthodox ending.

The So Called has always been a poem to tell people that what one is will *always* be important, that what one is *cannot* be taken away if one is not willing to give it up. This is what I tell my students now, and will as long as I deal with the young. I will remind them too that there are so many things to learn that some will in time be forgotten—but that the knowledge of who one is *must* be maintained—and also celebrated. And I will say that we become a mixture of cultures as we grow, learning and living each as we go through life, and that even though each culture will surely have its effects on us, we most assuredly should keep ours *as well as* enjoy the new additions. (We must always remember who *we* are; we just can't lose sight of that.) Finally, I will tell them that this poem's energy is not so much out of anger, but rather more out of a burning desire to celebrate the many cultures within. And especially the ones that make me who *I* am!

About the Author

Pazcual Villaronga is presently teaching as a bilingual teacher in the Lola Rodriguez de Tio Bilingual School in Manhattan's District 4, in New York City's "El Barrio." His works include the well-received *Stereotypes and Cycles*, *Passages*, and *The Box*. His work appeared in the anthologies *All Around the Mulberry Bush*, *Windfall* (a women's poetry anthology), *FAHARI* (a Shaw University Publication) and *ALTERNATIVA* (a City College Publication). He has received the Golden and Silver Poet Awards in California and placed third in "La Cancion Bilinque—The Bilingual Song" competition in Washington, DC. Villaronga has recited his poetry at Columbia University, Teachers College, Hunter College, Hostos Community College, and Connecticut's Housatonic Community College. Along with his writing of poetry and short stories, he has established "IBEDGY," an Afro-Cuban Caribbean Percussion Ensemble consisting of children and young adults ranging from grades 4 to 12. (He credits master drummer/folklorist Louis Bauzo for this inspiration.) He is currently preparing several collections of poetry as well as two children's books for publication. His latest project is a collection of childhood stories, "Silver Streaks, Superglasses and a Watermelon balloon." Villaronga believes that one's culture can be kept alive by writing. "It doen't matter what the medium—poetry, prose, a play—what one is, needs to be preserved as well as expressed."

Part *III*

Diversity among the Diverse

Waiting to Excel

Biraciality in the Classroom

EVELYN REID

This chapter is the result of a research review aimed at understanding the issues and problems faced in our society and schools by biracial individuals with the hope of providing information that will help to shape our classrooms with those individuals' needs in mind. This chapter will attempt to briefly set the historical context that gave rise to dualistic thinking about race and culture in American society, then will present a review of the psychological research on biracial individuals, and finally, will close with recommendations for classroom teachers support of biracial students.

Introduction

In 1967, the Supreme Court (*Loving* v. *Virginia*) struck down antimiscegenation laws that previously had prohibited interracial marriages. As a result, such families gained legal recognition. Although these legal mandates provided equality and due process for interracial couples, the biracial offspring of these marriages are still currently embroiled within an intense struggle for recognition, acceptance, and respect for their civil rights in public schools. The contours of this biracial civil rights struggle in schools is framed within federal categories of racial groups and personal judgments about race. Primarily, these judgments about race are based on visible physical features such as skin color and those "above-the-neck-characteristics" such as hair, eyes, ears, and so forth. Biracial students are those individuals whose parental lineages represent two racial backgrounds.

Recent opposition to Ohio state law and local school board policy can be seen in the case of eight-year-old James McCray, who challenged the Cincinnati Public School

System for failing to provide a specific designation for biracial students. This opposition to law and policy serves as a reminder to educators about how both the government and school systems—as well as other societal institutions—exclude, and therefore ignore the specific needs of, biracial students (*Cincinnati Enquirer*, 1991, 1992). The unwillingness of biracial students to be forced into choosing one race over another highlights the particular dilemma these students are forced into by the "system." However, even more unsettling are the criteria for classification—ambiguous at best—that assumes clear-cut distinctions about racial heritage, therefore unwittingly perpetuating the societal notion that racial purity is the standard and that racial intermixing is somehow deviant, or at least not common enough to be acknowledged. These criteria for classifying the biracial segment of the population place individuals from racially mixed backgrounds in an especially compromising position—a position that is then exacerbated when their particular needs and experiences are also left unacknowledged in the classroom.

Historical data will demonstrate that the biracial segment of this country's population is not new. Woodward (1969) documented that in the state of Virginia in 1613, Pocahontas and John Rolfe married and had a biracial son. Woodward has maintained that the marriage between Pocahontas (an American Indian) and John Rolfe (an English widower) brought about peace between many English settlers and American Indians and their biracial offsprings. But Wardle (1988) observed that many interracial marriages and their biracial offspring faced human indignities in American society. For instance, Wardle noted that many non-Whites and language minorities were brought to this country for cheap labor. This cheap labor force intermixed and intermarried. Thus, their offsprings began a biracial mix (e.g., mixes of various American-Indian groups, Scottish/Black American, Amerasian, Mexican/White American).

It appears, then, that this group has been present in society since the 1600s and they have been both supported and abused. Thus, American society's lack of recognition of the group may be linked to political, social, and economic concerns within the system.

Demographic data on biraciality reveal that the majority of these families reside in urban areas of the North, Midwest, and West Coast, where they experience less overt racial prejudice and greater tolerance for diversity in family structures and life-styles (Gibbs, 1989; U.S. Bureau of the Census, 1987). Moreover, these data highlight that interracial families and their biracial offspring gravitate to metropolitan areas where a significant number of interracial families live—for instance, New York, Boston, Chicago, Minneapolis, St. Paul, Denver, Seattle, San Francisco, and Los Angeles (Collins, 1984; Gibbs, 1989). Although these researchers approximate the biracial population at 500,000 to 650,000, there is no accurate accounting of the group for various reasons. For instance, federal classifications ignore biraciality, federal data on interracial marriages primarily reflect Black/White unions with limited statistics on their offspring, and many interracial families fail to respond to federal data forms that ignore biraciality.

Biraciality—The Historical Context

The particular dilemma of biracial students stems from long-standing Western belief systems that implicitly accepted White race and culture as the "norm," while establishing other races and cultures as somehow deviant. This type of dualistic thinking is represented, for example, in biblical thought, where races originated from Noah's blessing on Shem and Japhet, fathers of the Semites and Indo-Europeans, and his curse on Ham, father of the African race—and the natural implications of good and evil that such interpretations imply.

Certain assumptions about race were also perpetuated by theories stemming from Darwin's *Origin of the Species*, whose ideas about "survival of the fittest" and "natural selection" were later used by Social Darwinians to explain away various political, social, and economic barriers to descendents of Africans and other Brown races as simply being a matter of their inability to adapt to their social environment. These explanations implicitly set up the "dominant" or accepted White race as superior and the "subordinate" or minority Brown races as marginal or inferior, placing them on the fringes of society.

In U.S. society, many of the elements embedded in these systems of thought have been perpetuated in the laws and government classification schemes for racial and ethnic groups. Events from American history show that during the period of slavery, society's view of race was radically dualistic, with Whites being the "pure" race advantaged by the system, and any other race or mix of race being the "Negro" race neglected by the system. According to Gordon (1964), legal mandates from this time period designated the following races as Negro: "American Indians, Ethiopians, Chinese, Japanese, Mongolians, Malays, Hindus, Mestizos, Half-breeds, and 'the Brown Race.'" These two types of classification (White/Negro), according to Gordon, superimposed group attributes that in society transformed into power and privileges for Whites, while denying the individual rights of, other races, thus implicitly supporting racially biased creationist and evolutionist views.

Although the Constitution had given certain Americans equal rights, and the Bill of Rights established democracy and equal representation under the law, slave statutes were instituted that rescinded or restricted the rights of anyone falling into the category of "Negro." White males were assumed to have natural rights and privileges; however, most persons with non-White ancestry were

> *considered Negro, and as such, was forced into slavery, with resistors being brutally beaten or killed. White male masters were granted the right to use unwilling African females to bear children for the slave labor force (Benson, 1981), with those children, in turn, becoming slaves. Intermarriage was allowed between Black slaves and White female servants, however the law stated that...if a free-born White woman married a Negro slave, she would be required to serve her husband's master through her slave husband's life, and further, that the children born of such marriages would be regarded as slaves. (Logan, Freeman, & McRoy, 1990, p. 222)*

In sum, then, the White/Negro dichotomy—implicitly carrying with it the connotations of "norm/deviant," "good/evil," or "superior/inferior"—has served in American history to grant privileges and power to the White majority, while denying basic rights to anyone with non-White blood. Caught especially in this false dilemma of race, and the implicit privileges granted or denied, were those biracial offspring of interracial heritage. Their fate in society would be governed by whether they could pass as White, or whether they would be identified as Negro, and thus be governed by societal constraints that limited their basic human rights.

In the 1950s and 1960s, non-Whites began to fight openly for their rights in society and schools. These civil rights groups mobilized societal support and placed pressure on federal representatives to fashion legislation in support of minority group rights (e.g., *Brown* v. *Board of Education of Topeka* [1954], the Civil Rights Act of 1964, ESEA [1965], Bilingual Education Act of 1968, and Education for All Handicapped Children Act [1975]. Yet even while new laws were being formed to protect the rights of minorities, the social stigma of being non-White—especially of being of mixed race—was being expressed in movies and popular writings of the period. For instance, Millard Kaufman's 1958 movie, *Raintree County* commented on the fear of having mixed blood: "The worst of fates to befall Whites is 'havin' a little Negra blood in ya'—just one little teeny drop and a person's all Negra" (Omi & Winant, 1986, p. 60) Also, Neila Larsen's book, *Passing*, in the 1960s chronicled the internal dilemmas that a young biracial (Black/White) female grappled with in attempting to resolve whether to pass for Black or White.

It appears then that, during this time, White fear of racial mixing expressed itself more in terms of social and cultural sanctions on those whose blood lines were not pure. Those social and cultural sanctions were damaging enough to persuade those of mixed race or heritage to deny one heritage for another in order to "qualify" for the advantages and privileges granted to Whites.

This pattern, for biracials, of having to "choose" one racial heritage over another no longer carries the legal ramifications it did during the period of slavery. However, the ghost-like assumption of racial purity, with its implicit biases against non-White individuals, is still reflected in the categories of race established by the federal government and used by school administrators to report student racial data. The categories automatically assume racial purity and, as such, are not relevant for those of mixed heritage. Moreover, the omission of a category that represents these individuals is indicative of a deeper neglect on the part of society in recognizing this segment of its people. This mindset, which ignores the existence of biracial Americans, coupled with the implicit biases inherent in a White/non-White system of categorization, has contributed to a situation wherein the potential for psychological harm to biracial Americans is quite high. As a result, educational institutions and individual educators must make themselves aware of the specific needs of biracial students with the hope that validating and supporting these individuals' experiences will eventually lead to a time when racial categorizations will no longer be necessary in helping to achieve individual civil rights.

Psychological Literature on Biraciality

Because biraciality is still a relatively new area of study, very little information has been gathered about the curriculum needs of biracial students in schools. In fact, studies of interracial families and their biracial offspring in community settings are also still relatively rare. As a result, this review of research relies mostly on clinical studies, with the assumption that information gathered from these sources can be used as a starting point for developing effective educational strategies for biracial students in classroom settings.

Much of the clinical literature points to identity formation as the major issue for biracial individuals. In a 1990 study, Poston argued that identity with a racial group and clarification of group characteristics are basic to the development of a healthy and independent personality. However, the study implies a distinction between racial identity and racial definition. Poston has maintained that racial identity is formed internally and focuses on shared characteristics. Racial definition is externally imposed and focuses on differences. This distinction is crucial in understanding the dilemma of biracial individuals because racial identity, unlike racial definition, need not necessarily consist of an either/or choice; instead, it offers the possibility of accepting biraciality or biculturality *as a racial identity*, thus eliminating the individual's necessity to choose.

Although most studies cite the biracial child's critical need for family, community, and school support in developing a healthy racial and ethnic identity (Benson, 1981; Chang, 1974; Chen, 1981; Erikson, 1950, 1959, 1963, 1968; Gibbs, 1974; Gibbs et al., 1989; Gordon, 1964; Gunthorpe, 1978; Ladner, 1977; Logan, 1981; McRoy et al., 1984; Payne, 1977; Piskacek & Golub, 1973; Poston, 1990; Teicher, 1968), several studies underline the need for recognizing the unique situation of interracial families and biracial children. For instance, several researchers found that in the family setting, biracial children's attitudes and perceptions about race develop differently from children of single-race families (Gunthorpe, 1978; Logan, 1981; Payne, 1977). One study noted that darker-skinned children of Black/White parentage tended to reject identification with the Black heritage and culture, perhaps suggesting that the darker-skinned biracial youth had a more negative self-image than those of lighter complexion. Another study (Piskacek & Golub, 1973) found that there is often conflict between the biracial youth's choice of racial identification and that of their parents. The underlying commonality of both studies, however, is a constant pressure on biracial children to *choose*—a situation that does not apply to children of single-race parentage and is often unfamiliar to intermarried parents, since they each have a single-race background. As Gordon (1964) emphasized, "[Often] well intentioned intermarried parents find it difficult to provide their children with the security that comes from 'knowing who I am and what I am'" (p. 317).

Teicher's (1968) clinical study of Black/White intermarriages and biracial children supports Gordon's statement. Teicher's study found that although more sophisticated parents (those who were open to, receptive to, and offered immediate and positive feedback to their biracial children's concerns about exclusion) were successful at helping their children feel confident with both parents' racial differences (the children felt good about their sexuality and felt comfortable interacting in White society). On the other hand, less sophisticated parents dealt with their biracial children's concerns by suggesting that "we are all human," which served to dismiss—and therefore deny—their children's frustration and confusion over issues of exclusion, racial bias, and the like. Such an approach, in distinct cases, led to intense problems with "identification with the minority parent, sexual-identity conflicts, and extreme problems of adjustment to a predominantly White environment" (pp. 249–256).

Although most of the research on biracial children is clinical in nature, some studies have specific implications for educators. In the area of socialization, several studies (Benson, 1981; Chang, 1974; Gibbs et al., 1989, Teicher, 1968) have found that biracial students may view their social place within the school as marginal. Even children who have satisfying social relationships in elementary school may confront this sense of marginality when entering junior high school and college, and young adults may also undergo a crisis of identity as they begin to consider a career choice. In addition, many biracial students may adopt their version of a Black identity when they fear rejection by their Black peers who may perceive them as "too studious or bookish." Such students may overidentify with their version of Black ghetto culture by adopting a negative attitude toward school and their studies, become truant, deliberately fail courses, and express antiachievement values.

Another growing body of literature (Cole, Glick, Gay, & Sharp, 1971; Hale, 1978, 1982; Kagan, 1977; Ramirez & Casteneda, 1974; Shade, 1989) finds that learning styles often vary among different groups. This research implies that the strategies learned at home for acquiring, organizing, and remembering information may reflect a child's racial identity—or, in the case of a biracial child, a combination of identities. Implications of this research suggest that teachers must consciously plan for the unique learning styles of biracial children.

Discussion and Recommendations

The complexity of the issues raised by the historical data and psychological research on biracial children and their interracial families presents a challenge to educators and teachers to work toward increasing their knowledge, awareness, and understanding about biracial children and their needs. There is a critical need for investigations of biracial children in community settings, especially schools and classrooms. Because no education research was located that reported the specific curriculum needs of biracial students, this void in the area represents a critically important field of study.

However, the psychological research does point to a set of specific areas in which educators can help address the needs of biracial children. The failure of society in general and educators in particular (and sometimes from the home, as well) to support biracial youth results in a critical need for support in classroom settings as these students refine their knowledge of themselves and the world. To achieve this support, educators and classroom teachers must work to create a climate that fosters the development of a healthy identity for all students through acceptance of religious, social, cultural, and other differences, as well as sensitivity to a variety of learning styles and socialization issues. It is not enough to incorporate biracial issues into a mainstream education program in a fragmented or cursory manner that is itself exclusionary; the most powerful element of change in the classroom is to infuse biracial issues throughout the total curriculum.

Certain psychological research suggests that teachers must consciously plan not only for the subject matter that they teach but also for their students' psychological, social, emotional, and cultural needs (e.g., Benson, 1981, Chang, 1974). This research also suggests that from an early age (i.e., two and three years), children recognize physical and racial differences (Erickson, 1959, 1963; Logan, 1981; Logan et al., 1990; McRoy et al., 1984; Wardle, 1988). Thus, the implication of the research suggests that one way teachers can become effective at working in classrooms with diverse student populations where biracial students are present is to select content carefully. Then, present it in such a way that young children are engaged not only in the physical differences of racial groups but also in discussions of racial oppression (history/migration of groups and economic, social, and political realities of groups) and its consequences. For example, Cullen's (1903–1946) "Incident" is illustrative of poetry for teachers to launch into a discussion of racial oppression and the need for students to reflect on their actions and observations of others in regard to racial slurs and its impact on others. This poetry allows for specific content (e.g., English literature) that may help teachers move away from overemphasizng the physical characteristics of racial groups and onto a discussion of the psychological, social, and emotional harm of oppression.

A psychologically based curriculum that shows sensitivity to process as much as content might also break down the competitive and unequal structures that exclude interracial parents and their biracial children from schools and classrooms. For example, teachers may use parents as resource persons in the classroom to explain how they have dealt with various forms of oppression (race, gender) in particular situations. Another consideration might be to use poetry similar in content to the Cullen's "Incident" to engage students in open classroom discussions and written expressions of their personal experiences with oppression. Also, this careful attention to content and process may aid teachers in supporting parents' rights to be part of a mixed marriage and support their understanding of their responsibility to raise healthy children. In addition, curriculum content and process sensitive to group issues will place teachers in a positive position to offer advice, support, counseling, and referrals based on individual needs of the family or child.

There is a need for teachers to develop an awareness of their views of interracial families and their biracial children. Wardle (1988) contended that a critically important starting point for teachers is to understand that people of different racial backgrounds have a right to marry and have children, and these parents can raise their children with a rich interracial identity void of choosing one parents racial background over another. However, the historical data and psychological literature highlighted the omission of federal classifications for biracial children, negative and conflicting messages from society, and the fact that often well-intentioned interracial couples have not yet decided their children's identity (Gordon, 1964; Teicher, 1968). Thus, this research implies that teachers must oftentimes be prepared to help not only biracial children figure out their racial identity but they must also be prepared to assist parents in this area as well. This is especially true in schools where forms omit a biracial category and require specific racial designations.

The research suggests that teachers must aid in the refinement of biracial children's identity so that they understand that regardless of the process of combining heritages, they are a single unit as other racial groups. (Perhaps in the future, racial categories will no longer exist or, as in the case of Brazil, a biracial category will exist for them nationally.) The research on biracial identity (Benson, 1981; Chang, 1974; Chen, 1981; Erikson, 1959, 1963; Gibbs, 1974; Gibbs et al., 1989; Gordon, 1964; Gunthorpe, 1978; Ladner, 1977) cautions community representatives, parents, and teachers not to automatically assume that biracial children must identify with the parent of color. Wardle (1988) suggested that teachers provide parents with suggestions for exposing their children to their heritage through festivals, books, art, music and drama, and community and religious organizations where other interracial families with biracial children are present, and to encourage parents and children to openly discuss all aspects of a mixed racial heritage, including skin, eyes, eye color, hair, ears, and so forth. Teachers must include in these suggestions to parents ways in which they might connect these discussions to conflicts stemming from societal prejudices. For example, teachers must provide parents and children with tools (words and phrases) to protect themselves from others who do not affirm human diversity and biraciality.

It is important that teachers recognize their critically important role in the classroom as the central value transmitter in the school lives of youth. As such, they must plan for the individual differences that all students bring to the classroom by responding to children's naturally curious questions. For instance, students may ask, "Why is your mother White and your father Black?" "Why do you look different from your parents?" "Can I touch your hair?" "Are you adopted?" Teachers must show sensitivity to these questions by openly and genuinely linking into children's interest and entering a discussion about valuing those physical characteristics inherited from parents. There are a number of specific classroom activities that teachers may use to teach about inherited physical features from parents. For instance, teachers might use family members (both sides) and go as far back as possible so that all children in the classroom develop family trees that expose inherited physical characteristics. Another suggestion is to provide activities for mixing colors: paints, food colors, colored plastic, tissue paper, and so forth. Still another idea for teachers is to avoid curriculum materials that divide the country and the world into neat distinctive racial and ethnic groups (or use supplemental materials). Yet another suggestion to teachers might be to conduct classroom activities that address the commonality of all people, such as creating a collage of hands or a poster of heads, having all children trace (or use prints) their feet onto butcher paper, or using a chart of emotions all children experience (noting that all children have parents, a language, clothes, and so on).

The research on learning styles (Benson, 1981; Chang, 1974; Gibbs et al., 1989; Shade, 1989) implies that teachers who work with biracial students must become sensitive to variations in children's learning styles. Perhaps classroom teachers might develop a cooperative classroom atmosphere where students learn to share their unique experiences and learning styles in a student-centered cooperative environment. In this regard, students are able to see their own identity reflected in the curriculum and are better able to accept and understand the content of that curriculum. The interactive nature of a cooperative process-oriented curriculum and classroom empowers the biracial student in ways that can provide a positive force in his or her understanding of self and community.

The process-based curriculum, with its emphasis on the lives and experiences of the students, also addresses the issue of relevant content. It allows the development of a curriculum that reflects multicultural issues and challenges societal assumptions about race and ethnicity—assumptions that are often especially harmful to biracial children. For example, engaging in a critique of U.S. history from a sociohistorical and social reconstructionist perspective can help the biracial student not only in understanding how he or she fits into society but also in viewing himself or herself as an agent of social change (e.g., see Sleeter & Grant, 1988). The process-based content-based curriculum will also support biracial students who face problems of identity in regard to marginality. For instance, Benson, Chang, and Gibbs pointed out that many biracial children may feel secure during the elementary years. However, upon entering junior high, high school, and even college, they may adopt negative attitudes toward their studies and school and/or their version of Black ghetto culture. Specific information on biracial Americans who have made major contributions to society can help to reinforce the students' sense of empowerment.

Conclusion

Though issues of race and ethnicity are receiving more and more attention in the classroom, the tendency to focus on single-group issues—though helping to raise consciousness about those specific groups—actually serves to exclude, and therefore discriminate against, those students with mixed racial or ethnic backgrounds. However, as interracial marriages and biracial children become more commonplace, increasing numbers of students will share the unique experiences derived from living in an integrated family environment. As educators charged with meeting both students' and society's needs, we must answer the challenge of making sure that our society recognizes and accepts these individuals. The simple omission of a category on an application form should serve to remind us that our societal institutions are a reflection of what we believe; when they no longer accurately represent those beliefs, we must move to change both the forms *and* the institutions.

References

Aragon, J. (1973). "An Impediment to Cultural Pluralism: Culturally Deficient Educators Attempting to Teach Culturally Different Children." In Stent, Madolon, et al. (Eds.), *Cultural Pluralism in Education: A Mandate for Change* (pp. 77–84). New York: Appleton-Century-Crofts.

Banks, J. A. (1981). *Multiethnic Education.* Boston: Allyn and Bacon.

Baptiste, P., and S. Cambell. (1985). "The Contemporary Interracial Child." *Communique,* April.

Benson, S. (1981). *Ambiguous Ethnicity.* Cambridge: Cambridge University Press.

Bilingual Education Act. (1968). PL 95-561 (92 STAT 2268).

Brown v. *Board of Education of Topeka, Kansas.* (1954). 74, Supreme Court 686.

Burkey, R. M. (1971). *Racial Discrimination and Public Policy in the Unite*d States. Lexington MA: Heath Lexington.

Chang, T. S. (1974). "The Self-Concept of Children of Ethnically Different Marriages." *California Journal of Educational Research, XXV* (5), 245–252.

Chen, J. (1981). *The Chinese of America: From the Beginnings to the the Present.* New York: Harper and Row.

Cincinnati Enquirer (September 9, 1991). Article by K. Ramsey, "A Box for the 'Other' Kids," p. A1.

Cincinnati Enquirer (January 2, 1992). Article by K. Ramsey, "Biracial Student Offered a New Designation," p. A1.

Civil Rights Act. (1964). PL88-352 (92 STAT 2268).

Collins, G. (1984). "Children of Interracial Marriage." *New York Times*, March 20, p. 17.

Cole, M., Gay, J., Glick J., and Sharp, D. W. (1971). *The Cultural Context of Learning and Thinking.* New York: Basic Books.

Condon, J. C. (1986). "The Ethnocentric Classroom." In J. Civikly (Ed.), *Community in College Classrooms* (pp. 11–20). San Francisco: Jossey-Bass.

Council on Interracial Books for Children. (1984). "Conference Addresses Needs of Interracial Children." *CIBC Bulletin, 15* (5), 13–14.

Cullen, Countee. (1991). *My Soul's High Song: The Collected Writings of Countee Cullen, Voice of the Harlem Renaissance.* New York: Doubleday, 1991.

Degler, C. N. (1971). *Neither Black nor White.* New York: Macmillan.

Denzin, N. K. (Ed.). (1984). *Studies in Symbolic Interaction, 5.* Greenwich, CT: JAI Press.

Education for All Handicapped Children Act. (1975). PL94-142 (89- STAT 773).

Elementary and Secondary Education Act. (1965). PL 89-10 (79 STAT 27).

Erickson, E. H. (1950). *Childhood and Society.* New York: Norton.

Erickson, E. H. (1959). "Identity and the Life Cycle." *Psychological Issues, 1* (1).

Erickson, E. H. (1963). *Childhood and Society* (2nd ed.). New York: Norton.

Erickson, E. H. (1968). "Race and the Wider Identity." *Identity, Youth and Crisis.* New York: Norton.

Gay, K. (1987). *The Rainbow Effect.* New York: Franklin Watts.

Germain, C. B. (Ed.). (1982). *Advances in Clinical Social Work Practice.* Silver Springs MD: NASW.

Gibbs, J. T. (1974). "Patterns of Adaptation Among Black Students at a Predominantly White University." *American Journal of Orthopsychiatry, 44,* 728–740.

Gibbs J. T., et al. (1989). *Children of Color.* San Francisco: Jossey-Bass.

Gordon, A. I. (1964). *Intermarriage.* Boston: Beacon Press.

Guerra, M. H. (1973). "Bilingual and Bicultural Education." In Stent, Madolon, et al. (Eds.), *Cultural Pluralism in Education: A Mandate for Change* (pp. 27–33). New York: Appleton-Century-Crofts.

Gunthorpe, W. (1978). "Skin Color Recognition, Preference, and Identification in Interracial Children: A Comparative Study." *Dissertation Abstracts International, 38* (10-B), 3468.

Hale, J. (1978). "Cultural Influences on Learning Styles of Afro- American Children." In L. Morris, (Ed.), *Extracting Learning Styles for Social/Cultural Diversity: A Study of Five American Minorities.* Washington, DC: Office of Education.

Hale, J. (1982). *Black Children—Their Roots, Culture and Learning Styles.* Provo, UT: Brigham Young University Press.

Harding, V. (1973). "Black Reflections on the Cultural Ramifications of Identity." In Stent, Madolon, et al.(Eds.), *Cultural Pluralism in Education: A Mandate for Change* (pp. 103–113). New York: Appleton-Century-Crofts.

Hauser, S. (1972). "Black and White Identity Development: Aspects and Perspectives." *Journal of Youth and Adolescence, 1* (2), 113–130.

Hauser, S., and Kasendorf, E. (1983). *Black and White Identity Formation.* Malabar: Robert E. Krieger.

The Holy Bible: New International Version. (1984). Grand Rapids: Zondervan.

Kagan, S. (1977). "Social Motives and Behaviors of Mexican-American and Anglo American Children." In J. Martinez, (Ed.), *Chicano Psychology.* New York: Academic Press.

Kaufman, Millard. (1958). "Raintree County." Culver City, CA: Metro Goldwyn Mayer.

Lack, D. (1957). *Evolutionary Theory and Christian Belief.* London: Methuen & Co.

Ladner, J. A. (1977). *Mixed Families.* New York: Anchor Press.

Lasker, G. W. (1961). *The Evolution of Man.* New York: Holt, Rinehart and Winston.

Logan, S. L. (1981). "Race, Identity, and Black Children: A Developmental Perspective." *Social Casework, 62* (1), 47–56.

Logan, S. L., Freeman, E. M., and McRoy, R. G. (1990). *Social Work Practice with Black Families.* New York: Longman.

Loving, Richard Perry et UX., appellants, v. *Virginia,* United States Reports 388, US 1.

Lyles, M., et al. (1985). "Racial Identity and Self-Esteem: Problems Peculiar to Biracial Children." *Journal of the American Academy of Child Psychiatry, 24* (2), 150–153.

The Madison Plan. (1988). University of Wisconsin-Madison: Office of Chancellor.

McRoy, R., et al. (1984). "The Identity of Transracial Adoptees." *Social Casework: The Journal of Contemporary Social Work, 65* (1), 34–39.

Norman, J. S. (1980). "Short-Term Treatment with the Adolescent Client." *Social Casework: The Journal of Contemporary Social Work, 61* (1), 74–82.

Ogbu, J. U. (1978). *Minority Education and Caste.* New York: Academic Press.

Ogbu, J. U. (1974). *The Next Generation.* New York: Academic Press.

Oldham, D. G., et al. (1980). "Clinical Assessment of Symptoms in Adolescents." *American Journal of Orthopsychiatry, 50* (4), 697–703.

Omi, M., & Winant, H. (1986). *Racial Formation in the United States.* New York: Routledge & Keegan Paul.

Payne, R. (1977). "Racial Attitude Formation in Children of Mixed Black and White Heritage: Skin Color and Racial Identity." *Dissertation Abstracts International, 38* (6-B), 2876.

Piskacek, V., and Golub, M. (1973). "Children of Interracial Marriage." In I. R. Stuart and L. E. Abt (Eds.), *Interracial Marriage: Expectations and Reality.* New York: Grossman.

Porter, C. P. (1991). "Social Reasons for Skin Tone Preferences of Black School-Age Children." *American Journal of Orthopsychiatry, 61* (1).

Poston, W. S. C. (1990). "The Biracial Identity Development Model: A Needed Addition." *Journal of Counseling & Development, 69*, 152–155.

Ramirez, M., and Castaneda, A. (1974). *Cultural Democracy, Bicognitive Development and Education.* New York, Academic Press.

Shade, B. (Ed.). (1989). *Culture Style and the Educative Process.* Springfield, IL: Charles C. Thomas.

Sleeter, C., and Grant, C. (1988). *Making Choices for Multicultural Education: Five Approaches to Race, Class, and Gender.* Columbus, OH: Merrill.

Sommers, V. S. (1964). "The Impact of Dual-Cultural Membership on Identity." *Psychiatry, 27* (4), 332–344.

Stuart, I. R., and Abt, L. (Eds.). (1973). *Interracial Marriage: Expectations and Realities.* New York: Grossman.

Taylor, R. L. (1976). "Psychosocial Development Among Black Children and Youth: A Reexamination." *American Journal of Orthopsychiatry, 46* (1).

Teicher, J. D. (1968). "Some Observations on Identity Problems in Children of Negro-White Marriages." *The Journal of Nervous and Mental Disease, 146* (3), 249–256.

UNESCO. (1952). *The Race Concept.* Paris: UNESCO.

United States Bureau of the Census. (1987). U.S. Department of Commerce. Washington, DC: U.S. Government Printing Office.

Wardle, Francis. (1988, November). "Responding to Individual Differences in the Classroom Setting." Paper presented for Child Care Services, Inc. and the Black/White Task Force, Shreveport, LA.

White, B. W. (Ed.). (1982). *Color in a White Society.* Silver Springs MD: NASW.

Wilkerson, I. (1991). "Black-White Marriages Rise, But Social Acceptance Lags." *New York Times,* p. A1.

Woodward, Grace Steele. (1969). *Pocahontas.* Norman: University of Oklahoma Press.

About the Author

Evelyn Reid is a member of the educational theory, research, and social foundation faculty at the University of Toledo. She earned the Ph.D. degree from the University of Wisconsin-Madison, where she studied teacher education with an emphasis in multiculturalism. Research publications and interests include the following:"Good Teachers Make a Lasting Impact," a chapter in Dr. Carl Grant's *Preparing for Reflective Teaching* (Allyn and Bacon, 1982), "Recruitment and Retention of Minority Teachers: An Analysis of One University," *Conference Proceedings on Recruitment and Retention of Minority Students in Teacher Education: Programs that Work,*" "Seeds of Change: One Group of Senior Preservice Teachers Responses to Issues of Diversity in one University Course," "Rites of Passage: The Transformation of African American Females in the Academy," "Moving to the Beat of Different Rhythm: The Making of Four Black Female Academicans," and "Meaning and Interpretation of Humor: Implications for Classroom Teachers."

Chapter 21

Challenges for Educators
Lesbian, Gay, and Bisexual Families

JAMES T. SEARS

Kim and Carolyn, a Boston area lesbian couple, took in Earl, a Black deaf boy, who at the time was five years old. Kim is also deaf, although she can speak and lip-read...Eventually Kim and Carolyn were formally approved as Earl's foster parents by Massachusetts social workers. Several years later the two women adopted Earl....[At age 11] Earl is a child who is different. He is deaf in a hearing world; Black in a predominantly white community; and the son of [white Asian] lesbians in a largely heterosexual culture. (Sands, 1988, pp. 46–47, 50)

Since I made the decision seven years ago to become a parent through anonymous donor insemination, the question that others have asked most frequently is, "But how are you going to explain this to your child?"...During breakfast today, in the middle of a discussion about Velcro closings on shoes, Jonathon [her five-year-old son] asked why he has only a mom and some people have a mom and a dad. I explained that there are all kinds of families in the world and gave lots of examples of those he knows: some with, some without kids; some big, some small. We talked about the fact that from the time I was 15, I just had a dad and no mom. I explained that there are no set rules for who family members can be; rather, families are people who love...one another. (Blumenthal, 1990/1991, p. 45)

A slightly different version of this chapter originally appeared in *The High School Journal*, 77 (1 & 2): 138–156. © 1994 The University of North Carolina Press. Used by permission.

The seven-year-old daughter [Alicia] asked her father some questions about "Gene" (the lover), and the father answered them honestly, explaining that he loved Gene and he loved Mommy. The daughter did not seem concerned, but shortly afterward she asked her mother, "Do you still love Daddy?" Mother assured her that she did. "Do you love Gene?" the daughter asked. "He's my friend," her mother answered, "but I love your father." (Matteson, 1987, p. 151)

Jennifer sits down at the kitchen table to eat her cereal and juice. "What will you be doing at school, today?" asks Patsy, her mother. "Mrs. Thomkins says we will make Christmas trees today." Patsy's husband, Bill, pours another cup of coffee and says: "Well, I guess that means that we won't have to go and chop down a tree this year!" "Oh, no!" Jennifer exclaims. "We're going to make them out of paper. When are we going to get our tree?" "Well," Patsy's mother says, "When Pam's ship returns for Christmas next week. Until then, you and Bill can talk about where we should go this year for our tree." Jennifer finishes her meal, kisses her mother and Patsy's husband goodbye. "Oh, I almost forgot. Where's Bob?" Bob, Bill's lover of five years, sits in the living room reading the morning paper. "I'm out here, Jennifer. Give me a kiss before you go to school."—An Alabama family (circa 1991)

The traditional American family—to the degree that it ever existed—represents a minority of all households in the United States today (Kamerman & Hayes, 1982). There are three major types of U.S. families: families of first marriage, single-parent families, and families of remarriage. Less than 1 in 4 students come to school from a home occupied by both biological parents. Single-parent households account for about one-quarter of all families in the United States; about 1 of every 2 African-American children (1 of every 4 White children) live with a lone parent (Glick, 1988). If current trends continue, 6 out of 10 children will be part of a single family sometime before they become 18 years of age (Bozett & Hanson, 1991). These single households are generally the product of divorce or separation. Remarried families account for one in six households with nearly six million stepchildren (Glick, 1987).

In recent years, alternative family arrangements have emerged in which either one or both partners are a self-identified lesbian, gay man, or bisexual person (Alpert, 1988; Pollack & Vaughn, 1989; Schulenberg, 1985).[1] Children, like Jennifer, from these alternative marriages may be the product of a prior marriage in which the partner has custody or visiting privileges, or a gay or lesbian couple's decision, like Kim's and Carolyn's, to adopt (Jullion, 1985; Ricketts & Achtenberg, 1987).[2] Other children, like Alicia, may live in a biologically traditional family but have one or both parents who are openly bisexual (Matteson, 1985, 1987). Children, like Jonathon, may also come to school from households of a lesbian or bisexual woman who has elected to bear and raise the child following artificial insemination or the departure of the father (Pies, 1985, 1987). And, of course, the parents of many other children never choose to disclose their bisexuality or homosexuality to their family (Green & Clunis, 1989).

The publications on alternative families, such as *Jenny Lives with Eric and Martin* (Bosche, 1983), *How Would You Feel If Your Dad Was Gay?* (Heron & Maran, 1990), and

Daddy's Roommate (Wilhoite, 1990), as well as the controversy surrounding the New York City Public Schools' adoption of the Rainbow Curriculum and the subsequent dismissal of its superintendent, Frank Fernandez, may mean that few of our students will understand the true diversity among the families whose children attend their schools. Deleting lesbian, gay, and bisexual families from the school curriculum, however, does not remove them from the day-to-day realities of school life. If we are to truly serve all of our students, then educators must become more aware of the challenges facing lesbian, gay, and bisexual parents and their children.

Challenges Facing Lesbian, Gay, and Bisexual Parents

> *How, the average person wants to know, can a lesbian possibly be a mother? If heterosexual intercourse is the usual prerequisite for maternity, how is it possible for women who by definition do not engage in heterosexual behavior to be mothers? If motherhood is a state which requires the expression of nurturance, altruism, and the sacrifice of sexual fulfillment, how can a lesbian, a being thought to be oversexed, narcissistic, and pleasure-oriented, perform the maternal role? How can women who are "masculine," aggressive, and assumed to be confused about their gender be able to behave appropriately within its boundaries, or to assume the quintessentially womanly task of motherhood? If lesbians are women whose lives are organized in terms of the relentless pursuit of clandestine pleasures, if lesbians are women who behave as quasi-men and who have been poorly socialized into their gender roles, then how can they expect to provide adequate models of feminine behavior to their children, to prepare them for their own sexual and parental careers? (Lewin & Lyons, 1982, p. 250)*

Such questions pose challenges to women (and men) who are homosexual but choose parenting. While the assumptions underlying many of these questions are flawed (Sears, 1991a), the coupling of parenthood with homosexuality to form categories of lesbian mothers and gay fathers may appear contradictory. This contradiction, however, is of social not biological origin.

The difficulties confronted by acknowledged lesbian mothers or gay fathers is, in many ways, similar to those faced by single parents and divorced households with the significant exception of the additional burden of wrestling with the social stigma associated with homosexuality. Two of the greatest challenges are securing or maintaining custody of their children and disclosing their homosexuality to their children.

Legal Barriers

In child custody decisions, the judge has a wide leeway within common law to provide for the "best interest of the child" and not to interfere with existing custody arrangements unless there have been "material changes in circumstances" (Achtenburg, 1985; Basile, 1974; Payne, 1977/1978). Although heterosexual mothers have generally not lost custody of their children for unfitness, the sexual orientation of a parent has played a prominent role in both circumstances (Pagelow, 1980; Rivera, 1987).

In general, gay fathers seeking custody face the double burden of being male where the female is presumed more nurturant and of being homosexual where heterosexual is considered normal. Moreover, in those cases involving a son, the court appears more concerned with issues of sexual development than those involving daughters (Miller, 1979b), and in custody disputes involving lesbian mothers, the woman loses 85 percent of those cases that go to trial (Chesler, 1986). A disproportionate number of cases are between the mother and another relative (Hitchens, 1979/1980), and in cases where lesbian mothers are provided custody, the courts have often demanded the absence of same-sex lovers in the household. One lesbian who won provisional custody of her five-year-old son lamented:

> *That is unjust! They don't put those kinds of restrictions on a heterosexual mother... for 13 years I'm forbidden to set up a living relationship with a sexual partner of my choice. Sure, I don't have to be celibate—I can sneak out somewhere or I can send my son away—but I want to be free to set up my home with someone I love. It's much better for a child to have more than one parent figure—I can't possibly be available to answer all of my child's needs alone. (Pagelow, 1980, p. 194)*

In deciding whether to award custody, or even visiting privileges, to a homosexual parent or to allow a lesbian or gay couple to adopt a child, judges often base their decisions on other unsubstantiated judicial fears such as "turning" the child into a homosexual, molesting the child, stigmatization of the child, and AIDS (Hitchens, 1979/1980; Payne, 1977/1978; Polikoff, 1987; Rivera, 1987). The willingness of the courts to entertain homosexuality as a factor for denying custody or restricting visiting rights has not escaped the attention of many lesbian mothers who, though themselves not a party to legal action, fear such a possibility (Kirkpatrick, Smith, & Roy, 1981).

Nonbiological parents and lesbians or gay men wishing to adopt also face significant legal hurdles. Six jurisdictions in the United States have ruled in favor of adoptions by same-sex parents (Alaska, Washington, Oregon, California, Minnesota, and the District of Columbia), and although only two states (Massachusetts and Florida) specifically prohibit gay men or lesbians from being foster or adoptive parents, most courts and agencies have allowed sodomy statutes (applicable in 25 states), prejudicial attitudes, or myths and stereotypes to affect their decision. In Minnesota, for example, one lesbian was denied visitation rights to a child she had raised with her former partner, and in Wisconsin, the court refused to enforce a coparenting contract signed by two former lovers. Even in states that have ruled in favor of adoptions, there remains bureaucratic and political resistance and, if approved, joint adoptions by gay men or lesbians are unusual (Achtenberg, 1985; Ricketts & Achtenberg, 1987).

Only recently have educational associations, state departments of education, and school districts developed policies and programs regarding the discrimination and harassment of homosexual students or the inclusion of sexual orientation issues in the school curriculum; little attention has been given to children with a lesbian or gay parent. As I will discuss in the final section of this chapter, these policies and programs will not only have a positive affect on the lesbian, gay, or bisexual student but also on the heterosexual student who comes from such an alternative family structure.

Disclosure to Children

Some, if not most, of our children from such families have not been told of their parents' sexual identity (Bozett, 1980; Miller, 1979a). In heterosexually coupled families with a gay, lesbian, or bisexual spouse, underlying tensions may create home problems (e.g., marital discord, emotional detachment from the child) that manifest themselves in a child's school behavior or academic achievement (Harris & Turner, 1985/1986; Lewis, 1980; Matteson, 1987). In those families, for example, where gay fathers have not disclosed their sexual identity to their children, Miller (1979b) found "their fathering is of lower quality than the fathering of more overt respondents.... The guilt many of these men experienced over being homosexual manifested itself in over-indulgent behavior.... Data also indicate that respondents living with their wives tended to spend less time with their children" (p. 550). Educators who are aware of this social phenomenon can integrate this knowledge with their classroom assessment while respecting the confidentiality of the family.

Parents often fear the impact of such disclosure on their children. In deciding whether to disclose the parent's sexual identity, the most common parental fears are rejection from the child, inability of the child to understand, and child rejection from peers (Shernoff, 1984, Wyers, 1984, 1987). The difficulties faced by the gay or bisexual partner in "coming out" to a child are well articulated by Matteson (1987) following his analysis of a nonclinical sample of 44 spouses in a mixed-orientation marriage: "Since the beginning, I've been saying, 'next year I'm leaving as soon as the children are bigger.' Now that they are in college, I can't leave because they are my judges. They'd never forgive me for doing this all these years to their mother" (p. 145; quoted from Miller, 1978, p. 217).

The most common time for such disclosure is during a separation or a divorce or when the gay parent elects to enter into a domestic partnership (Bozett, 1981b, Miller, 1978). In the case of still-married bisexual spouses, somewhere between one-third to one-half of their school-age children have been informed (Coleman, 1985; Wolf, 1985). The mean age of gay parental self-disclosure or child discovery ranges from 8 to 11 years of age (Turner, Scadden, & Harris, 1985; Wyers, 1984). According to Bozett (1987b): "The means by which the father discloses takes several forms. For example, with small children the father may disclose indirectly by taking children to a gay social event or by hugging another man in their presence. Both indirect and direct means may be used with older children in which the father also discusses his homosexuality with them" (p. 13).

Studies of gay parents and their children report different findings regarding the child's reaction (Bozett, 1980; Harris & Turner, 1985/1986; Lewis, 1980; Miller, 1979b; Paul, 1986; Pennington, 1987; Turner, Scadden, & Harris, 1985; Wyers, 1987). In her clinical study of 32 children from 28 lesbian-mother families, Pennington (1987) found the differing "children's reactions to mother 'coming out' generally range from 'Please, can't you change, you're ruining my life!' to 'I'm proud of my mom, and if other kids don't like it, then I don't want that kind of person to be my friend'" (p. 66). In his study of 40 gay fathers, Miller (1979b), on the other hand, found all of their children to have reacted more positively than their fathers had anticipated. Further, "children who showed the greatest acceptance were those who, prior to full disclosure, were gradually introduced by their parents to homosexuality through meeting gay family friends, reading about it, and discussing the topic informally with parents" (p. 549). In general, these and other studies (e.g., Gantz, 1983; Lamothe, 1989; Schulenburg, 1985) found the parent-child relationship was ultimately enhanced by such disclosure.

Challenges Faced by Children with Lesbian, Gay, or Bisexual Parents

> *Susan expected her family to be thrilled that she was finally "settling down" after a decade of working as a lawyer. Her mother's first reaction [to Susan's interest in having a baby], however, was "But you're not married!" After Susan explained that she was still lesbian and planned to raise the child with her lover, Susan's mother wondered, "But is it fair to the child? Everyone else will have a father; she'll feel different, she'll be treated badly." (Rohrbaugh, 1989, pp. 51–52)*

In the past, concerns about children growing up in a homosexual household focused on the household as the potential problem. Children were believed to be at a higher risk of developing a gender-inappropriate identity or sex-typed behaviors, acquiring a homosexual orientation, or exhibiting behavioral or psychological problems. While these fears are unjustified, the difficulties of growing up in a lesbian, gay, or bisexual household are linked to the homophobia and heterosexism pervasive in our society and tolerated, if not magnified, in our public schools.

Impact of Parental Sexual Orientation on Children

As the discussion of gay parenting becomes more public, fears about a child living with a lesbian or gay parent have been expressed. One concern is that the child may become homosexual or experience sexual harassment from either the parent or parental friends. Though persons generally do not identify themselves as gay or lesbian until their late teens or early twenties (Sears, 1991a; Rust, 1993), there is no greater likelihood that a son or daughter of a homosexual parent may declare a homosexual identity than those children from heterosexual households (Bozett, 1981a; 1981b; Gottman, 1990; Green, 1978; Miller, 1979b; Paul, 1986). Further, there is no empirical evidence that such children living with lesbian or gay parents face any greater danger of sexual harassment or molestation than those living with heterosexual parents (Hotvedt & Mandel, 1982; Miller, 1979b).

Another concern is that children living in homosexual families may suffer in gender development or model "inappropriate" sex-role behaviors. Here, research studies present a mixed picture. Some studies have found that homosexual parents, like their heterosexual counterparts, encourage their child's use of sex-typed toys (Golombok, Spencer, & Rutter, 1983; Gottman, 1990; Harris & Turner, 1985/1986; McGuire & Alexander, 1985; Kirkpatrick, Smith, & Roy, 1981; Turner, Scadden, & Harris, 1985); others have reported the opposite finding, including a greater emphasis on paternal nurturance or less preference for traditional sex-typed play (Hotvedt & Mandel, 1982; Scallen, 1981).

In general, studies comparing lesbian or gay men as parents with heterosexual single parents (Bigner & Jacobsen, 1989; Kirkpatrick, Smith, & Roy, 1981; Lewin & Lyons, 1982; Scallen, 1981) portray families that are either similar to the heterosexual norm or that excel in socially desirable ways (e.g., androgynous parenting behaviors, more child-centered fathers). Though the studies cited in this article varied in their methodology and samples, none found homosexuality to be incompatible with fatherhood or motherhood. Further, these studies do not reveal parenting patterns that would be any less positive than those provided by a heterosexual parent (e.g., Bozett, 1985; Golombok, Spencer, & Rutter, 1983; Hoeffer, 1981; Robinson & Skeen, 1982).

In fact, those men who are most open about their homosexuality, compared with other homosexual fathers, display fatherhood traits that many professionals consider to be desirable. These fathers, for example, used corporal punishment less often, expressed a strong commitment to provide a nonsexist and egalitarian home environment, and were less authoritarian (Miller, 1979b). Similar findings were available for lesbian mothers. For example, in comparing Black lesbian with Black heterosexual mothers (Hill, 1981), the lesbians were found to be more tolerant and treated their male and female children in a more sex equitable manner.

Those fathers and mothers who were the most publicly "out" were most likely to provide a supportive home environment. Ironically, given custody or visiting concerns as well as the general level of homophobia in society, those parents who are the most candid may be most vulnerable to denial of their parenting rights and visible targets for anti-gay harassment of themselves and their children.

Impact of Homophobia and Heterosexism on Children

The most commonly experienced problem or fear confronting children, most notably adolescents, from lesbian or gay households is rejection or harassment from peers or the fear that others would assume that they, too, were homosexual (Bigner & Bozett, 1990; Bozett, 1987a; Lewis, 1980; Paul, 1986; Wyers, 1987). An anecdote told to Pennington (1987) by a daughter of a lesbian mother illustrates the genuine acceptance of children *prior* to encountering stereotypes and harassment in school: "When I was around five, my mom and Lois told me they were lesbians. I said good, and thought I want to be just like my mom. Well, when I reached about the fifth grade ... I heard kids calling someone a faggot as a swear word, and I thought, " 'My God, they're talking about my mom.'" (p. 61).

Based on his study of 16 children with a gay or bisexual father, Paul (1986), as well as others (e.g., Riddle & Arguelles, 1981), found that it was during adolescence that these children had the most difficult time coping with their father's sexuality. An excerpt from a case study, written by a family psychotherapist (Corley, 1990) who worked with the two lesbians, Jane and Marge, and their eight children—a family for more than 10 years—is illustrative. During the next 3 years of therapy, the family began their first open discussions about the special relationship between the two women and the feelings of their children. The therapist continues:

> *Marge's two boys had difficult adjusting to do....By now everyone at their school knew Joe and Tom had two mothers. Both of them had come to their school as the primary parent. The children started to tease them about having "lesbos" for parents. Both of the boys [in their early teens] were rather stout in nature so many fights erupted over the teasing they received. Since Joe and Tom*

were embarrassed over what the children at school were saying, they usually told the teachers and principal that there was no reason for the fights. When Jane and Marge would question them about the fights, they would equally clam up.... Because of the lack of intervention, the boys continued to get in trouble at school and started to act out in other ways. Although the boys were only average students, they always passed. Now they were bringing home failing marks. Since these were the first failing grades for either of them, Jane and Marge felt the situation would improve. Unfortunately, the grade situation only deteriorated. Several parent conferences were called at school. Although both women showed up at the conferences together, nothing was ever mentioned about the family unit or their relationship. It was not until the family came into therapy that the boys revealed they were having problems. (p. 80)

A prominent researcher in the study of children of gay fathers, Frederick Bozett (1980) relayed a similar anecdote from a 14-year-old boy whose gay father had made several school visits: "All his jewelry was on. The teachers knew he was gay, and all the kids saw him and figured it out. It was obvious. They started calling me names like 'homoson.' It was awful. I couldn't stand it. I hate him for it. I really do" (p. 178).

According to Bozett (1987a), children generally use one of three "social control strategies" to deal with their parent's homosexuality. The first, *boundary control*, is evidenced in the child's control of the parent's behavior, the child's control of their own behavior vis-á-vis their gay parent, and the child's control of others' contact with the parent. Some of these controls are evidenced in an interview with two adolescent girls, both of whom have lesbian parents:

Margo: I try and hide stuff when people walk in, but probably most of my friends know.

Interviewer: Do they ever ask you directly?

Tania: My friends don't. My mother's girlfriend doesn't live with us. My mom keeps stuff out but I make a point of putting it away when someone is going to come over ....

Margo: I used to always walk between my mother and Cheryl. I used to make Cheryl walk at the curb and my mother inside and I'd walk right in the middle ....So it wouldn't be really obvious. But it probably was....People say, "Why do they live together?" And you make up all these stories and they don't even fit together....My mother tries to make up stories sometimes, but it doesn't work because they make no sense. "Oh my girlfriend, my brother's ex-wife's sister...." I used to be real embarrassed. One of my girlfriends asked me once and I was really embarrassed. I was like "No! What are you talking about? Where did you get that idea from?" But it turned out that her mother was gay too. (Alpert, 1988, pp. 100–102)

The second controlling strategy, *nondisclosure*, is evidenced in the child's refusal to share (and in some cases deny) their parent's homosexuality. One lesbian woman, discussing the difficulties she faced in her daughter's denials, commented:

When I asked Noelle [now age 13] what she would say if anybody asked her about me she said she would deny it. I was very very hurt. I talked it over with Cathy (a lesbian and a close friend). She said her son...had got into a fight at school about her and had come home really upset.... She told him that she didn't expect him to fight her battles for her.... That was fine by her and that really helped me because I realized I should not expect Noelle to fight my battles either.... I actually did tell my children that if they want to deny it that's fine and I think that helped them because they were caught a bit between loyalties.. (Lesbian Mothers Group, 1989, p. 126)

Some children, however, also employ nondisclosure to protect the parent who might be vulnerable to a child custody challenge or to job discrimination (Paul, 1986).

The third controlling strategy, *disclosure*, is evidenced by a child's selective sharing of this personal information. In Miller's (1979b) study of gay fathers, one 17-year-old son stated, "I don't tell people if they're uptight types or unless I know them well. I've told my close friends and it's cool with them" (p. 548). In Gantz's (1983) study, a 13-year-old child of a household with two lesbians noted, "I've told one person.... We'd go do stuff like shoot pool and all that down in his basement. I just told him, you know, that they were gay.... I didn't know how he'd react. He said he'd keep it a secret, so that made me feel a little better" (p. 68). Another male respondent commented, "You have to be sure they won't tell somebody else. I was worried [about] people knowing [because] I was afraid of what they'd think of me; maybe it would be embarrassing" (Bozett, 1987a, p. 43).

Further, according to Bozett (1987a), there are several factors that influence the degree to which children employ one or more of these strategies. Those children who identify with the father because of their behavior, life-style, values, or beliefs are less likely to use any social control strategy. Those children who view their father's homosexuality as "obtrusive," who are older, or who live with their father are more likely to employ these strategies.

Studies on children from gay families or homosexual mothers and fathers have been conducted within a Euro-American context. Only one study has examined minority homosexual parents (Hill, 1981), and there has been no research directed at minority children of a gay parent. Anecdotal writings by persons of color who are homosexual parents, however, convey some dissimilarities with their Anglo counterparts. For example, Lorde (1987) wrote:

Black children of lesbian couples have an advantage because they learn, very early, that oppression comes in many different forms, none of which have anything to do with their own worth.... I remember that for years, in the name-calling at school, boys shouted at Jonathan not—"Your mother's a lesbian"— but rather "Your mother's a nigger." (p. 222)

Research into the unique difficulties confronting lesbian or gay young adults who must cope with their emerging homosexual identity within the context of a nondominant culture underscores the difficulties of being a minority within a minority and suggests differences that minority children with gay or lesbian parents might confront (Sears, 1991a; Johnson, 1981). Morales (1990) explained:

What does it mean to be an ethnic minority gay man or lesbian? For ethnic minority gays and lesbians, life is often living in three different communities: the gay/lesbian community, the ethnic minority community, and the predominantly heterosexual white mainstream society. Since these three social groups have norms, expectations, and styles, the minority lesbian or gay man must balance a set of often conflicting challenges and pressures. The multi-minority status makes it difficult for a person to become integrated and assimilated. (p. 220)

This was evident in my study of young lesbian and gay African-American southerners (Sears, 1991a). Irwin, a working-class Black man, for example, stated: "When you're black in a black society and you're gay it's even harder. Blacks don't want it to be known because they don't want to mimic or imitate white people. They see it as a crutch and they don't want to have to deal with it" (p. 135). Malcolm commented, "If they are going to see you with a man at all, they would rather see you with another black man.... If they think you're gay and you're with a white man, they think that he's your sugar daddy or you're a snow queen" (p. 138). This is also evident in the anecdotal and autobiographical writings by people of color (e.g., Beam, 1986; Moraga & Anzaldua, 1981; Smith, 1983). A Chinese-American (Lim-Hing, 1990/1991), for example, wrote about her family's reactions to her lesbianism:

The implicit message my family gave me was not so much a condemnation as an embarrassed tolerance inextricably tied to a plea for secrecy.... At the end of my stay [with my father], he asked me if "they" would pick me up at Logan, although he knows Jacquelyn's name. My father's inability to accept my being a lesbian is related to his more traditional values: family first, make money and buy land, don't stand out. (p. 20)

A Puerto Rican (Vazquez, 1992) expressed his anger at racism encountered within the Anglo gay community: "I won't lay in my own bed with some Euro-American and do Racism 101. Nor do I want to sit down with the cute white boy I'm dating and deconstruct the statement, 'I love sleeping with Puerto Ricans'" (p. 90).

Children from some minority families may have a particularly difficult time coping with the homosexuality of a parent or may choose to cope with the information in a culturally different manner than researchers such as Bozett have found. Whether it is a child "coming out" to his family, a parent disclosing her homosexual orientation to the children, or both revealing this information to their extended family, they do so within different cultural contexts, perhaps facing greater risks than their Euro-American counterparts. Morales (1990) wrote:

"Coming out" to the family tends to involve both the nuclear and extended family systems. Such a family collective is the major support system for the ethnic persons and is the source of great strength and pride....For minority lesbians and gays coming out to the family not only jeopardizes the intra-family relationships, but also threatens their strong association with their ethnic community. As a result minority gays and lesbians may run the risk of feeling uprooted as an ethnic person. (p. 233)

Other difficulties faced by both Anglo and minority children of lesbian, gay, and bisexual parents may be the same as children from other families experiencing marital discord or integrating a new adult into the household (Hotvedt & Mandel, 1982; Miller, 1979b; Weeks, Derdeyn, & Langman, 1975). Like children of heterosexual divorces, adolescents generally experience the most difficult period of adjustment during the first year of separation. In one of the first studies of gay fathers and their children, Miller (1979b) found "problems of sexual acting out" in the biographies of 48 daughters and 42 sons. Only

> *two daughters reported premarital pregnancies and abortions; one admitted to engaging in some prostitution. Two interviewed offspring had problems in school, and one had had professional counseling for emotional difficulties. As studies of children of divorced heterosexual parents have revealed similar problems...these concerns may not result so much from the father's homosexuality as from family tensions surrounding marital instability, divorce, and residential relocation. Anger and bitterness toward parents are common to children with disrupted families, and respondents in this study were not immune to such feelings. (p. 547)*

In another study matching separated or divorced lesbian mothers with heterosexual mothers and using a variety of questionnaires, attitudes scales, as well as interviews for both parents and preadolescent children (ages 3 to 11), Hotvedt and Mandel (1982) concluded that there was "no evidence of gender identity conflict, poor peer relationships, or neglect" (p. 285). These findings were extended by Huggins (1989), who examined children's self-esteem through interviews and surveys of 36 adolescents whose head of household was lesbian. Compared with a match-set of heterosexual single female parents, Huggins concluded that "the mother's sexual object choice does not appear to influence negatively the self-esteem of her adolescent children.... The assumption that children of lesbian mothers are socially stigmatized by their mothers' sexual choice is not borne out by this study" (p. 132).

While this study does not imply that these children experienced no difficulties because of the stigma of homosexuality, it does mean that "the development of self-esteem is primarily influenced by the interaction between children and their parents or primary caregivers" (Huggins, 1989, p. 132). For example, one study found that one out of two children of lesbian mothers experienced relationship problems with other people due to the stigma of their mother's sexual identity (Wyers, 1987), and another (Lewis, 1980) concluded: "Although the findings are similar to those...of children of divorce, the particular issue of acceptance of the "crisis" is dissimilar.... Children's initial reaction to divorce was denial of pain; follow-up one year later revealed more open acceptance of the hurt. One reason for this difference may be that children of divorce have community support for their pain; children of lesbians do not" (p. 199).

Of course, parenting by lesbians, gay men, and bisexuals presents society with alternate approaches to family life that can challenge oppressive sexist and heterosexist myths and stereotypes. Sandra Pollack (1989), though acknowledging the legal necessity for demonstrating the sameness between homosexual and heterosexual families, challenges the "underlying assumption that the lesbian mother should be judged on how well she compares to the heterosexual norm." For example, do we really believe that, as a society, we want to foster the continued sex-role education of children?

Pollack has argued that rather than accepting the values associated with the heterosexual family, lesbian and gay parenting affords opportunities to challenge these norms in society and in the upbringing of their children. The "possible benefits of being a child of a lesbian mother" include "the children of lesbians may become aware (perhaps more so than other children) of their responsibility for themselves and their choices" (p. 322). For example, one study (Harris & Turner, 1985/1986) reported that lesbian mothers tended to use their homosexuality in a positive manner through assisting their children to accept their own sexuality, adopt empathetic and tolerant attitudes, and consider other points of view.

Central to the problems faced by children of lesbian and gay parents is the heterosexism and homophobia rampant in today's society. Homophobia—an irrational fear and hatred of homosexuals (Weinberg, 1972)—manifests itself in students' negative attitudes and feelings about homosexuality and the institutionalization of sodomy statutes which deny rights of sexual expression among persons of the same gender, thus restricting the legal definition of marriage and family. Heterosexism—the presumption of superiority and exclusiveness of heterosexual relationships—is evidenced in the assumption that parents of all children are heterosexual or that a heterosexual adult will *prima facie* be a better parent than one who is homosexual.

As two leading researchers on gay parenting stated, "Much ignorance regarding homosexuality is due to the propagation of myths. It is important for educators in many disciplines and at all educational levels to dispel myths, impart facts, and promote values clarification" (Bigner & Bozett, 1990, p. 168). It is at this juncture that educators' concern for the student with a newly identified lesbian or gay parent is married to their concern for the gay or lesbian student and for the heterosexual student harboring intensely homophobic feelings and attitudes. Each of these students can benefit from honest discussion about homosexuality in the school (Sears, 1987, 1991b), the adoption and implementation of anti-harassment guidelines (Sears, 1992d), the portrayal of the contributions and rich history of lesbians, gay men, and bisexuals (Sears, 1983), and the provision of gay-affirmative counseling services (Sears, 1989b).

Based on her interviews with children with lesbian mothers, Lewis (1980) concurred:

> *The children of lesbians seem not to have peer support available to them, since most of these children have either pulled away from their friends altogether or maintained friends but with a sense of their own differentness. Children of lesbians have been taught the same stereotypical myths and prejudices against homosexuals as the rest of society. Better understanding is needed about available family support systems and other systems that should be provided. These might include peer supports as well as educational supports, for example, dissemination of information about homosexuality. (p. 202)*

Homosexuality and the Schools

Though some teachers, administrators, and guidance counselors are reluctant to discuss homosexuality in schools (Sears, 1992a, 1992b), every major professional educational association has adopted resolutions calling upon schools to address this topic. The National Council for the Accreditation of Teacher Education (NCATE) has proposed the inclusion of sexual orientation in its anti-discrimination standard and in its definition of cultural diversity. Some school districts have adopted specific programs and policies, and a variety of recommendations have been made to integrate issues relating to homosexuality in the school curriculum. Educators who assume proactive roles not only benefit lesbian, gay, and bisexual students but are making inroads into the institutionalized homophobia and heterosexism that makes school life more difficult for children from homosexual families.

Gay and Lesbian Students and Professional Standards

Professional educational associations have adopted policies affirming the worth and dignity of lesbians, gay men, and bisexuals, and/or calling for an end to statutes, policies, and practices that effectively condone discrimination and harassment on the basis of sexual identity. Educators, school board members, and parents who have spearheaded these efforts acknowledge the simple social fact that being sexually different in a society of sexual sameness exacts a heavy psychological toll. Struggling to cope with their sexual identity, these students are more likely than other youth to attempt suicide, to abuse drugs or alcohol, and to experience academic problems (Gibson, 1989; Hetrick & Martin, 1987; Martin & Hetrick, 1988; Sears, 1989a; Teague, 1992; Zera, 1992). Other youth coping with their same-sex feelings may not display these symptoms but may excel in schoolwork, extracurricular activities, or sports as a means of hiding their sexual feelings from themselves or others (Sears, 1991a). By hiding, however, their emotional and sexual development languishes (Martin, 1982).

Five states (Massachusetts, New Jersey, Wisconsin, Hawaii, and Minnesota) have adopted some type of antidiscrimination statutes. Massachusetts became the first state to outlaw discrimination against lesbian and gay students in public schools. Wisconsin's statute Section 118.13 reads, in part, "No person may be denied admission to any public school or be denied participation in, be denied the benefits of or be discriminated against in any curricular, extracurricular, pupil services, recreational, or other program or activity because of the person's sex, race...marital or parental status, sexual orientation."

As part of the process of implementing its statute, the Wisconsin Department of Public Instruction issued a 59-page booklet that noted "the board shall adopt instructional and library media materials selection policies stating that instructional materials, texts, and library services reflect the cultural diversity and pluralist nature of American study" and cited lesbian/gay students as one underrepresented group.

Many major educational organizations, such as the National Educational Association, the American Federation of Teachers, and the Association for Supervision and Curriculum Development, have adopted statements affirming the rights of homosexual/bisexual students in K–12 schools and have called on their members to undertake proactive measures to combat the heterosexism and homophobia that are rampant in our nation's schools. For example, the American School Health Association issued a policy statement on gay and lesbian youth in schools that stated, in part: "School personnel should discourage any sexually oriented, deprecating, harassing, and prejudicial statements injurious to students' self-esteem. Every school district should provide access to professional counseling by specially trained personnel for students who may be concerned about sexual orientation."

Finally, the NCATE in its draft of the standards revision has revised one standard as follows: "policies and practices of the unit clearly demonstrate inclusiveness and do not discriminate on the basis of race, ethnicity, language, gender, sexual orientation, religion, age, or disability" (IV.A.54). Further, it has recommended altering its operational definition of "cultural diversity" to include sexual orientation.

School Polices and Programs

Since the late 1980s, the invisibility of homosexuality in education has lessened. Evidence of its being less invisible includes extensive sex education courses in this nation's schools (Haffner, 1990; Sears, 1992c) with some systems including units on homosexuality (Sears, 1991b); the first public funding of a school serving homosexual students, The Harvey Milk School, by the New York City public school system (Friends of Project 10, 1991; Rofes, 1989); the institution of the first gay-affirmative counseling service in a public high school, Project 10 within the Los Angles Unified School District (Rofes, 1989); the election of the nation's first openly gay school board member in San Francisco; and the formation of the Lesbian and Gay Studies special interest group of the American Educational Research Association (Grayson, 1987).

Several school districts have adopted antiharassment guidelines. In 1987, the Cambridge (Massachusetts) public schools included in their policies the following statement:

> *Harassment on the basis of an individual's sexual preference or orientation is prohibited. Words, action or other verbal, written, or physical conduct which ridicules, scorns, mocks, intimidates, or otherwise threatens an individual because of his/her sexual orientation/preference constitutes homophobic harassment when it has the purpose or effect of unreasonably interfering with the work performance or creating an intimidating, hostile, or offensive environment. (Peterkin, 1987)*

More recently, in 1991, the St. Paul school board passed a human rights policy forbidding discrimination on the basis of "sexual or affectional orientation." Several large urban school districts (e.g., New York, Washington, DC, Cincinnati, Los Angeles, Des Moines, San Francisco) have implemented anti-gay and lesbian discrimination policies. Perhaps the most publicized effort to meet the needs of homosexual students has been the funding of a public alternative school for gay and lesbian youth in New York City and the development of counseling services expressly for this target population in Los Angeles. The Harvey Milk School, established in 1985 under the sponsorship of the Hetrick-Martin Institute, serves about 40 students who are unable to function in the conventional school setting (Rofes, 1989). In Los Angeles, Project 10 at Fairfax High School has received international attention for the gay-affirmative services provided by its counseling staff. And, in 1993, the school district, under the auspices of Project 10, hosted the first conference for their high school gay youth at nearby Occidental College.

These policies and programs not only have a positive impact on the gay, lesbian, and bisexual student but on heterosexual students, faculty, and staff who often harbor homophobic feelings or heterosexist attitudes. Thus, these policies and programs can help to create a supportive school climate for heterosexual students who come from lesbian, gay, or bisexual households.

Curriculum and Staffing Recommendations

Elsewhere (Sears, 1987, 1991b, 1992b), I have discussed the importance of integrating issues of homosexuality into the school curriculum. When the issue of homosexuality appears in the school curriculum, the most likely subjects to be targeted are science in the form of human physiology or health in the form of HIV/AIDS prevention (Sears, 1992c). In contrast, I believe, sexuality can serve as a transformative tool for thinking about the construction of one's sexual identities vis-á-vis the interrelationships among language, history, and society (Carlson, 1992; Macanghaill, 1991). As such, sexuality no longer becomes the province of sex educators teaching separate units within physical education or biology but becomes a major strand woven throughout the curriculum (Sears, 1991b).

Educators have long argued that schools ought to be an embryonic environment for engaging young people in the art of democratic living and, in the process, moving society further along its democratic path (Dewey, 1916; Giroux, 1988; Rugg, 1939). In fact, however, the hidden curriculum of school fosters conformity and passivity while seldom encouraging critical thinking, ethical behavior, and civic courage (Giroux, 1988; McLaren, 1991, 1993). Within this environment, controversial ideas and individual differences are seldom welcomed. The discussion of homosexuality, the treatment of lesbian, gay, and bisexual students, and the restrictive definition of family are some of the most glaring examples.

Specific strategies and materials that foster an awareness of homosexuality and homosexual persons already have been proposed or developed (e.g., Friends of Project 10, 1991; Goodman, 1983; Hubbard, 1989; Krysiak, 1987; Lipkin, 1992; Sears, 1983; Wilson, 1984). Educators have been admonished by scholars and activists alike to sit down and talk with bisexual, lesbian, and gay adults to learn first hand about the special problems they faced in school; the importance of lesbian and gay educators as role models for homosexual students has been stressed, as has the need for public school systems to follow the lead of communities such as Berkeley and Cambridge in adopting anti-slur policies and nonharassment guidelines (Griffin, 1992; Hetrick & Martin, 1987; Kissen, 1991; Martin & Hetrick, 1988; Peterkin, 1987; Rofes, 1989; Sears, 1987, 1993; Slater, 1988; Stover, 1992). In some schools, anti-homophobia workshops with heterosexual students and educators have been conducted (Schneider & Tremble, 1986; Stewart, 1984). Professional educators as well as lesbian and gay activists ask, at the very least, for the construction of a nonjudgmental atmosphere in which homosexual-identified students can come to terms with their sexuality, the acquisition by school libraries of biographical books where students can discover the homosexuality of some famous people, and the integration of references to homosexual men and women as well as the topic of homosexuality into the high school curriculum (Jenkins, 1990; Sears, 1983, 1988).

It should be noted that there is no legal justification for systematically barring discussion of homosexuality and the inclusion of the contributions of lesbian, gay, and bisexual artists, politicians, scientists, and athletes from the school curriculum. A United States Court of Appeals ruling that a state statute prohibiting educators and school staff from "advocating, soliciting, or promoting homosexual activity" was unconstitutional was let stand due to a deadlock Supreme Court vote (*National Gay Task Force* v. *Board of Education of the City of Oklahoma*, 1984). Nevertheless, the integration of lesbian, gay, and bisexual topics or persons in the school curriculum appears too radical for many educators. Too few administrators refuse to acquiesce to a scissors and paste mentality of curriculum development in which only the most mundane, least controversial material survives the scrutiny of self-appointed moral vigilantes or the self-censorship of timid school officials (Sears, 1992d; Summerford, 1987; Tabbert, 1988).

In such an Orwellian school world, the curriculum is carefully crafted to omit (without the appearance of omission) the homoerotic imagery in the poetry of Walt Whitman, Sappho, and Langston Hughes or the visual arts of Donatello, Marsden Hartley, and Robert Mapplethorpe, the conflict between racial and sexual identities present in the literature of James Baldwin, Yukio Mishima, and Toni Morrison, or the conflict between the professional and personal lives of computer inventor Alan Turing, sports heroes David Kopay and Martina Navratilova, and political activists Eleanor Roosevelt and Susan B. Anthony. Just as sexuality is extracted from life and compartmentalized into units of sexuality education, so too is bisexuality and homosexuality exorcised from the body politic and tucked away in the curriculum closet.

In each of these areas, educators can play an important role in reducing homophobia and heterosexism. In the process, they can directly counter those litigants who petition courts to deny custody or visitation rights to lesbian or gay parents due to the fear of a "definite possibility of peer ridicule in the future" (Hitchens, 1979/1980, p. 90).

Summary and Recommendations

Summary of Research

Studies on bisexual and homosexual parenting as well as children of lesbians and gay men are far from complete. There are, however, some suggestive findings:

- Children are less accepting when a same-sex parent "comes out" than when a parent of the other gender discloses sexual identity.
- Children of a lesbian or gay parent are no more likely to define themselves as homosexual than children of heterosexual parents, nor are they any more likely to display atypical sex-role preferences.
- Lesbian, gay, and bisexual parents often seek to provide children with a variety of gender role models.
- The earlier the disclosure to the child the fewer problems in the parent/child relationship.
- Children of a lesbian or gay parent follow typical developmental patterns of acquiring sex-role concepts and sex-typed behaviors.

- Children of homosexual parents who have experienced marital turmoil face similar difficulties common to children of divorce.
- Gay fathers may have a more difficult time disclosing their sexuality to their children than lesbian mothers, children of gay fathers are less likely to know of their parents sexual identity, and the coming out process is more difficult for gay fathers with children at home.
- Sons are less accepting when learning their parent is gay than are daughters.
- As children enter adolescence, there is a greater likelihood that they will experience peer harassment about their parents' sexual identity and engage in a variety of self-protective mechanisms.
- Gay fathers are more likely to report their children experiencing difficulty with peer harassment because of the parent's homosexuality.

Recommendations for Educators

In several studies, researchers have noted the important role that educators can play in reducing homophobia and heterosexism that create difficult environments for children of lesbian or gay families to learn and for their parents to visit. Based on these and other writings (e.g., Clay, 1990; Casper & Wickens, 1992), educators should:

- Redesign school paperwork in order to be inclusive. Replace words such as *mother* and *father* with *parent* or *parent 1, parent 2.*
- When establishing associations, such as parent-teacher organizations, develop assistance for single-parent families (e.g., child care) and create or identify a safe space for homosexual parents (e.g., support groups). Encouraging gay parents to share their family status with school officials is important. Based on his extensive research with children of gay fathers, Bozett (1987a) stated:

> It is best for school officials to know about the father's homosexuality, especially if the father has child custody. Knowing about the family can alert school personal to problems which may have the home situation as their genesis. Likewise, if the father is known about by school officials, both the father and his lover may participate in school affairs, attend school functions, or the lover may pick the child up at school all without the parents or the child having to make elaborate explanations. (p. 53)

- Represent family/cultural diversity in classroom materials and books, on bulletin boards, and in everyday teaching practices.
- Ensure that books depicting alternative family patterns are included in school libraries (see following resource section for a few recommendations).
- Sensitize teachers and prepare guidance counselors to work with children as well as their gay parent as they confront issues ranging from the child's need for self-protection to the parent's need of respect for their sexual choices.
- Provide role models of gay or lesbian parents for students. Examples should reflect a multicultural emphasis rather than reinforcing the stereotype of homosexuality existing

only within the White community. Since some children in every school will identify themselves as lesbian or gay, it is important for them to have positive parenting role models, should they elect to bear or foster children as adults.

- Inform parents of any sexual harassment or intimidation directed at their child.
- Modify the school's anti-slur and anti-harassment policy to include sexual orientation and equally enforce violations against this policy.
- Interview potential teachers and counselors to ascertain their professional experiences and personal attitudes in working with sexual minorities.
- Revise hiring policies and procedures to enhance the likelihood of recruiting sexual minority faculty.
- Develop and publicize a counseling service for students who wish to discuss issues related to sexual identity.
- Hold a series of informal faculty meetings with gay and lesbian parents and faculty to identify needs and possible solutions.
- Meet with support services personnel (e.g., media specialists, counselors) to determine the adequacy of resource materials available for students and faculty about homosexuality and bisexuality.
- Review and revise accordingly student and faculty school-sanctioned activities that discriminate on the basis of sexual orientation (e.g., Junior ROTC, school dances, job recruitment fairs).
- Review school textbooks for biased or misleading information about lesbians, gays, and bisexuals.
- Review the school curriculum to identify areas within *every* subject matter where relevant information (people, places, events) about lesbians, gay men, and bisexuals can be included.
- Engage teachers and administrators in formal activities that address the cognitive, affective, and behavioral dimension of homophobia.
- Develop prejudice awareness among student leaders through after-school workshops.
- Invite former students and members of the community to address the student body on issues relating to homosexuality.

Resources for Educators

There is a wide selection of books, organizations, and journals appropriate for adults interested in lesbian and gay parents or their children. These include:

Alpert, H. (1988). *We are everywhere: Writings by and about lesbian parents.* Freedom, CA: Crossing Press.

Boys of Lesbian Mothers. 935 W. Broadway, Eugene, OR 97402.

Burke, P. (1993). *Family values: Two moms and their son.* New York: Random House.

Chain of Life. A newsletter for lesbian and gay adoptees. Box 8081, Berkeley, CA 94707.

Children of Gay/Lesbians. 8306 Wilshire Blvd., Suite 222, Beverly Hills, CA 90211.

Empathy: An interdisciplinary journal for persons working to end oppression based on sexual identities. Published twice a year (individuals $15, institutions $20), this 100+ page journal regularly includes essays on alternative family structures and issues relating to lesbian, gay, and bisexual youth. PO Box 5085, Columbia, SC 29250.

Gay and Lesbian Parents Coalition International. An advocacy/support group ⸜ parents with a quarterly newsletter. PO Box 50360, Washington, DC 20091 .

Gay Fathers (1981). Some of their stories, experiences, and advice. Toronto: Author.

Gay Fathers Coalition. Box 50360, Washington, DC 20004.

Gay Parents Support Packet. National Gay Task Force, 80 Fifth Ave., Room 506, New York, 10011.

Jenkins, C. (1990, September 1). *"Being gay: Gay/lesbian characters and concerns in young adult books."* Booklist, 39-41.

Jullion, J. (1985). *Long way home: The odyssey of a lesbian mother and her children.* Pittsburgh, PA: Cleis.

Lewin, E (1993). *Lesbian mothers: Accounts of gender in American culture.*

MacPike, L. (1989). *There's something I've been meaning to tell you.* Tallahassee, FL: Naiad Press.

Parents and Friends of Lesbians and Gays. PO Box 27605, Washington, DC 20038-7605.

Pollack, S., & Vaughn, S. (1987). *Politics of the heart: A lesbian parenting anthology.* Ithaca, NY: Firebrand.

Rafkin, L. (1990). *Different mothers: Sons and daughters of lesbians talk about their lives.* Pittsburgh, PA: Cleis.

Schulenburg, J. (1985). *Gay parenting: A complete guide for gay men and lesbians with children.* Garden City, NY: Anchor.

Wolf, V. (1989). "The gay family in literature for young people." *Children's Literature in Education, 20*(1), 51-58.

There is also a growing selection of books appropriate for children and adolescents about gay and lesbian families. These include:

Children's Books with Lesbian Moms

Newman, L. (1989). *Heather has two mommies.* Boston: Alyson.

Elwin, R., & Paulsee, M. (1990). *Asha's mums.* Toronto: Women's Press.

Willholte, M. (1993). *Belinda's bouquet.* Boston: Alyson.

Children's Books with Gay Dads

Heron, A., & Maran, M. (1991). *How would you feel if your dad was gay?* Boston: Alyson.

Bosche, S. (1981). *Jenny lives with Eric and Martin.* London: Gay Men's Press.

Willholte, M. (1990). *Daddy's roommate.* Boston: Alyson.

Children's Books with Lesbian & Gay Families

Willholte, M. (1991). Families: *A coloring book.* Boston: Alyson.

Willholte, M. (1993). *Uncle what-it-is is coming to visit!!* Boston: Alyson.

Valentine, J. (1991). *The duke who outlawed jelly beans and other stories.* Boston: Alyson.

Adolescent Books with Lesbian & Gay Family Themes

Homes, A. (1990). *Jack.* New York: Vintage

Salat, C. (1993). *Living in secret.* New York: Bantam.

Miller, D. (1992). *Coping when a parent is gay.* New York: Rosen

Endnotes

1. These real-world vignettes reflect the variety of lesbian, gay, or bisexual families. Although the number of children of lesbian, gay, and bisexual parents is speculative, researchers cite a range of 6 to 14 million children (Bozett, 1987a; Rivera, 1987; Schulenberg, 1985). Empirical data, itself subject to sampling problems, suggests that approximately 1 in 5 lesbians and 1 in 10 gay men have children (Bell & Weinberg, 1978; Jay & Young, 1979) with estimates of upwards of 1.5 million lesbians living with their children (Hoeffer, 1981). Until recently, these children were the result of defunct heterosexual relationships or marriages in which a spouses' homosexuality remains undisclosed (Brown, 1976; Green, 1987; Miller, 1979a).

Studies on lesbian and gay parents and their families have been limited in terms of sample size and methodology. For example, some studies (e.g., Weeks, Derdeyn, & Langman, 1975) have been clinical case studies and others have relied on anecdotal evidence (e.g., Alpert, 1988; Brown, 1976; Mager, 1975); others have studied small (1,040) groups of homosexual parents identified through gayrelated organizations (e.g., Scallen, 1981). Only a few studies have used larger samples with more sophisticated research designs (e.g., Bigner & Jacobsen, 1989; Hotvedt & Mandel, 1982). There have been no ethnographic, longitudinal, or nationwide studies conducted. Further, researchers generally have compared homosexual single parents with single heterosexual parents and, occasionally, homosexual parents living with a domestic partner with remarried heterosexual couples. Due to their incompatibility, no comparisons between homosexual parented households with the "traditional" two-parent heterosexual families have been made. Further, few of these studies present statistical analyses, control for the presence of a male role model in the home, take into account the desire to appear socially acceptable, include a majority of adolescent subjects, or focus on bisexual parents (Gottman, 1990). Finally, only a handful of studies have directly interviewed, surveyed, or observed children raised by a father or mother who is homosexual (Bozett, 1980, 1987b; Green, 1978; Huggins, 1989; Paul, 1986). For a review of much of this literature, see Bozett (1989).

2. One tragedy of failures to challenge successfully state sodomy statutes in the courts and the legislature is the difficulty that lesbians, gay men, or bisexuals have in obtaining child custody or visiting privileges in divorce hearings or approval from adoption agencies even for children whose prospects for adoption are slim, such as an older child or an HIV-infected baby (Hitchens, 1979/1980; Payne, 1978; Ricketts & Achtenberg, 1987; Rivera, 1987).

References

Achtenburg, R. (1985). *Sexual/ orientation and the law*. New York: Clark-Boardman.

Alpert, H. (1988). *We are everywhere: Writings by and about lesbian parents*. Freedom, CA: Crossing Press.

Basile, R. (1974). "Lesbian mothers and custody and homosexual parents." *Women's Rights Law Reporter, 2,*

Beam, J. (Ed.). (1986). *In the life: A black gay anthology*. Boston: Alyson.

Bell, A., & Weinberg, M. (1978). *Homosexualities*. New York: Simon & Schuster.

Bigner, J., & Bozett, F. (1990). "Parenting by gay fathers." In F. Bozett & M. Sussman (Eds.), *Homosexuality and family relations* (pp. 155–175). New York: Haworth Press.

Bigner, J., & Jacobsen, R. (1989). "Parenting behaviors of homosexual and heterosexual fathers." In F. Bozett (Ed.), *Homosexuality and the family* (pp. 173–186). New York: Haworth Press.

Blumenthal, A. (1990/1991). "Scrambled eggs and seed daddies: Conversations with my son." *Empathy, 2*(2) 45–48.

Bosche, S. (1983). *Jenny lives with Eric and Martin*. London: Gay Men's Press.

Bozett, F. (1980). "Gay fathers: How and why gay fathers disclose their homosexuality to their children." *Family Relations, 29,* 173–179.

Bozett, F. (1981a). "Gay fathers: Evolution of the gay father identity." *American Journal of Orthopsychiatry,* 51, 552–559.

Bozett, F. (1981b) "Gay fathers: Identity conflict resolution through integrative sanctions." *Alternative Lifestyles,* 4, 90–107.

Bozett, F. (1985). "Gay men as fathers." In S. Hanson & F. Bozett (Eds.), *Dimensions of fatherhood* (pp. 327–352). Beverly Hllls, CA: Sage.

Bozett, F. (1987a). "Children of gay fathers." In F. Bozett (Ed.), *Gay and lesbian parents* (pp. 39–57). Westport CT: Praeger.

Bozett, F. (1987b). "Gay fathers." In F. Bozett (Ed.), *Gay and lesbian parents* (pp. 3–22). Westport, CT: Praeger.

Bozett, F. (1989). "Gay fathers: A review of the literature." In F. Bozett (Ed.), *Homosexuality and the family* (pp. 137–162). New York: Haworth Press.

Bozett, F., & Hanson, S. (1991). "Cultural change and the future of fatherhood and families." In F. Bozett & S. Hanson (Eds.), *Fatherhood and families in cultural context* (pp. 263–274). New York: Springer.

Brown, H. (1976). "Married homosexuals." In H. Brown (Ed.), *Familiar faces, hidden lives* (pp. 108–130). New York: Harcourt Brace Jovanovich.

Carlson, D. (1992). "Ideological conflict and change in the sexuality curriculum." In J. Sears (Ed.), *Sexuality and the curriculum* (pp. 34–57). New York: Teachers College Press.

Casper, V., & Wickens, E. (1992). "Gay and lesbian parents: Their children in school." *Teachers College Record,* 94

Chesler, P. (1986). *Mothers on trial: The battle for children and custody.* New York: McGraw-Hill.

Clay, J. (1990). "Working with lesbian and gay parents and their children." *Young Children,* 45(3), 31–35.

Coleman, E. (1985). "Bisexual women in marriages." *Journal of Homosexuality,* 11, 87–100.

Corley, R. (1990). *The final closet.* N. Miami, FL: Editech Press .

Dewey, J. (1916). *Democracy and education: An introduction to the philosophy of education.* New York: Macmillan .

Friends of Project 10 (1991). *Project 10 Handbook: Addressing lesbian and gay issues in our schools* (third edition). Los Angeles, CA: Author. (ERIC Reproduction No. ED 337567).

Gantz, J. (1983). "The Weston/Roberts Family." In J. Gantz (Ed.), *Whose child cries: Children of gay parents talk about their lives* (pp. 49–96). Rolling Hills Estate, CA: Jalmar Press.

Gibson, P. (1989). "Gay male and lesbian youth suicide." *Report of the Secretary's Task Force on Youth Suicide. Volume 3: Prevention and interventions in youth suicide.* Washington, DC: U.S. Department of Health and Human Services.

Giroux, H. (1988). *Teachers as intellectuals: Toward a critical pedagogy of learning.* Boston: Bergin & Garvey.

Glick, P. (1987). *Remarried families, stepfamilies and stepchildren.* Paper presented at the Wingspread Conference on the Remarried Family. Racine, WI.

Glick, P. (1988). "Fifty years of family demography: A record of social change." *Journal of Marriage and the Family,* 50(4), 861–873.

Golombok, S., Spencer, A., & Rutter, M. (1983). "Children in lesbian and single-parent households: Psychosexual and psychiatric appraisal." *Journal of Child Psychology and Psychiatry,* 24, 551–572.

Goodman, J. (1983). "Out of the closet by paying the price." *Interracial Books for Children,* 9(3/4), 13–15.

Gottman, J. (1990). "Children of gay and lesbian parents." In F. Bozett & M. Sussman (Eds.), *Homosexuality and family relations* (pp. 177–196). New York: Haworth Press.

Grayson, D. (1987). "Emerging equity issues related to homosexuality in education." *Peabody Journal of Education,* 64(4), 132–145.

Green, G. (1987, August 28). *Lesbian mothers.* Paper presented at the Annual Convention of the American Psychological Association. (ERIC Reproduction No. ED 297205).

Green, G., & Clunis, D. (1989). "Married lesbians." In E. Rothblum & E. Cole (Eds.), *Lesbianism: Affirming non-traditional roles* (pp. 41–50). New York: Haworth Press.

Green, R. (1978). "Sexual identity of 37 children raised by homosexual or transsexual parents." *American Journal of Psychiatry,* 135(6), 692–697.

Griffin, P. (1992). "From hiding out to coming out: Empowering lesbian and gay educators." In K. Harbeck (Ed.), *Homosexuality and education*. New York: Haworth Press.

Haffner, D. (1990). *Sex education 2000: A call to action*. New York: SIECUS.

Harris, M., & Turner, P. (1985/1986). "Gay and lesbian parents." *Journal of Homosexuality,* 12(2), 101–113.

Heron, A., & Maran, M. (1990). *How would you feel if your dad was gay?* Boston: Alyson.

Hetrick, E., & Martin, A. D. (1987). "Developmental issues and their resolution for gay and lesbian adolescents." *Journal of Homosexuality,* 14(1/2), 25–43 .

Hill, M. (1981). "Effects of conscious and unconscious factors on child reacting attitudes of lesbian mothers." Doctoral dissertation, Adelphia University. *Dissertation Abstracts International,* 42 1608B.

Hitchens, D. (1979/1980). "Social attitudes, legal standards, and personal trauma in child custody cases." *Journal of Homosexuality,* 5(1/2), 89–95.

Hoeffer, B. (1981). "Children's acquisition of sex role behavior in lesbian-mother families." *American Journal of Orthopsychiatry,* 51(31), 536–544.

Hotvedt, M., & Mandel, J. (1982). "Children of lesbian mothers." In W. Paul, J. Weinrich, J. Gonsiorek, & M. Hotvedt (Eds.), *Homosexuality: Social, psychological and biological issues* (pp. 275–285). Beverly Hills. CA: Sage.

Hubbard, B. (1989). *Entering adulthood: Living in relationships. A curriculum for grades 9–12.* Santa Cruz CA: Network Publications.

Huggins, S. (1989). "A comparative study of self-esteem of adolescent children of divorced lesbian mothers and divorced heterosexual mothers." In F. Bozett (Ed.), *Homosexuality and the family* (pp. 123–135). New York: Haworth Press.

Jay, K., & Young, A. (1979). *The gay report.* New York: Summit.

Jenkins, C. (1990, September 1). "Being gay: Gay/lesbian characters and concerns in young adult books." *Booklist,* 39–41.

Johnson, J. (1981). *Influence of assimilation on the psychosocial adjustment of black homosexual men.* Unpublished doctoral dissertation, California School of Professional Psychology, Berkeley, CA. *Dissertation Abstracts International* 42, 11, 4620B.

Jullion, J. (1985). *Long way home: The odyssey of a lesbian mother and her children.* Pittsburgh PA: Cleis.

Kamerman, S., & Hayes, C.(1982). "Families that work." In S. Kamerman & C. Hayes (Eds.), *Children in a changing world.* Washington, DC: National Academy Press.

Kirkpatrick, M., Smith, C., & Roy, R. (1981). "Lesbian mothers and their children: A comparative study." *American Journal of Orthopsychiatry,* 51(3), 545–551.

Kissen, R. (1991). *Listening to gay and lesbian teenagers.* Paper presented at the Annual Meeting of the National Council of Teachers of English, Seattle, WA. (ERIC Reproduction No. ED 344220).

Krysiak, G. (1987). "Very silent and gay minority." *School Counselor,* 34(4), 304–307.

Lamothe, D. (1989). *Previously heterosexual lesbian mothers who have come out to an adolescent daughter: An exploratory study of the coming out process.* Unpublished doctoral dissertation, Antioch University, Yellow Spring, OH. *Dissertation Abstracts International* 50, 5, 2157B.

Lesbian Mothers Group. (1989). "'A word might slip and that would be it.' Lesbian mothers and their children." In L. Holly (Ed.), *Girls and sexuality* (pp. 122–129). Milton Keynes: Open University .

Lewin, E., & Lyons, T. (1982). "Everything in its place: The coexistence of lesbianism and motherhood." In W. Paul, J. Weinrich, J. Gonsiorek, & M. Hotvedt (Eds.), *Homosexuality: Social, psychological, and biological issues* (pp. 249–273). Beverly Hills, CA: Sage.

Lewis, K. (1980). "Children of lesbians: Their points of view." *Social Work,* 25(3), 198–203.

Lim-Hing, S. (1990/1991). "Dragon ladies, snow queens, and Asian-American dykes: Reflections on race and sexuality." *Empathy, 2* (2), 20–22.

Lipkin, A. (1992). "Project 10: Gay and lesbian students find acceptance in their school community." *Teaching Tolerance, 1* (2), 24–27.

Lorde, A. (1987). "Man child: A black lesbian feminist's response." In S. Pollack & J. Vaughn (Eds.), *Politics of the Heart: A lesbian parenting anthology* (pp. 220–226). Ithaca, NY: Firebrand.

Macanghaill, M. (1991). "Schooling, sexuality and male power: Towards an emancipatory curriculum." *Gender and Education, 3*(3), 291–309.

Mager, D. (1975). "Faggot father." In. K. Jay & A. Young (Eds.), *After you're out* (pp. 128–134). New York: Gage.

Martin, A. (1982). "Learning to hide: The socialization of the gay adolescent." In S. Feinstein & J. Looney (Eds.), *Adolescent psychiatry: Developmental and clinical studies* (pp. 52–65). Chicago: University of Chicago Press.

Martin, A., & Hetrick, E. (1988). "The stigmatization of gay and lesbian adolescents." *Journal of Homosexuality, 15*(1–2), 163–185.

Matteson, D. (1985). "Bisexual men in marriages: Is a positive homosexual identity and stable marriage possible?" *Journal of Homosexuality,* 11, 149–173.

Matteson, D. (1987). "The heterosexually married gay and lesbian parent." In F. Bozett (Ed.), *Gay and lesbian parents* (pp. 138–161). Westport, CT: Praeger.

McGuire, M., & Alexander, N. (1985). "Artificial insemination of single women." *Fertility and Sterility,* 43, 182–184.

McLaren, P. (1991). "Critical pedagogy: Constructing an arch of social dreaming and a doorway to hope." *Journal of Education, 173*(1), 9–34.

McLaren, P. (1993). *Schooling as a ritual performance* (second edition). London: Routledge.

Miller, B. (1978). "Adult sexual resocialization: Adjustments toward a stigmatized identity." *Alternative Lifestyles,* 1, 207–234.

Miller, B. (1979a). "Unpromised paternity: The lifestyles of gay fathers." In M. Levin (Ed.), *Gay men: The sociology of male homosexuality* (pp. 239–252). New York: Harper & Row.

Miller, B. (1979b). "Gay fathers and their children." *Family Coordinator, 28*(4), 544–552.

Moraga, C., & Anzaldua, G. (Eds.). (1981). *This bridge called me back: Writings by radical women of color.* Watertown, MA: Persephone Press.

Morales, E. (1990). "Ethnic minority families and minority gays and lesbians." In F. Bozett & M. Sussman (Eds.), *Homosexuality and family relations* (pp. 217–239). New York: Haworth.

National Gay Task Force v. *Board of Education of the City of Oklahoma,* State of Oklahoma, 729 Fed.2d 1270 (1984), 33 FEP 1009 (1982).

Pagelow, M. (1980). "Heterosexual and lesbian single mothers: A comparison of problems, coping, and solutions." *Journal of Homosexuality, 5*(3), 189–204.

Paul, J. (1986). "Growing up with a gay, lesbian or bisexual parent: An exploratory study of experiences and perceptions." Unpublished doctoral dissertation, University of California, Berkeley. *Dissertation Abstracts International,* 47, 7, 2756A.

Payne, A. (1977/1978). "Law and the problem patient: Custody and parental rights of homosexual, mentally retarded, mentally ill, and incarcerated patients." *Journal of Family Law, 16*(4), 797–818.

Pennington, S. (1987). "Children of lesbian mothers." F. Bozett (Ed.), *Gay and lesbian parents* (pp. 58–74). New York: Praeger.

Peterkin, R. (1987, June 11). Letter to Administrative Staff: *Anti-harassment guidelines.* Cambridge, MA.

Pies, C. (1985). Considering parenthood. San Francisco, CA: Spinster's Ink.

Pies, C. (1987). *"Considering parenthood:* Psychosocial issues for gay men and lesbians choosing alternative fertilization." In F. Bozett (Ed.), *Gay and lesbian parents* (pp. 165–174). Westport, CT: Praeger.

Polikoff, N. (1987). "Lesbian mothers, lesbian families: Legal obstacles, legal challenges." In S. Pollack & J. Vaughn (Eds.), *Politics of the heart: A lesbian parenting anthology* (pp. 325–332). Ithaca, NY: Firebrand.

Pollack, S. (1989). "Lesbian mothers: A lesbian-feminist perspective on research." In S. Pollack & J. Vaughn (Eds.), *Politics of the heart: A lesbian parenting anthology* (pp. 316–324). Ithaca, NY: Firebrand.

Pollack, S., & Vaughn, J. (Eds.). (1989). *Politics of the heart: A lesbian parenting anthology.* Ithaca, NY: Firebrand.

Ricketts, W., & Achtenberg, R. (1987). "The adoptive and foster gay and lesbian parent." In F. Bozett (Ed.), *Gay and lesbian parents* (pp. 89–111). Westport, CT: Praeger.

Riddle, D., & Arguelles, M. (1981). "Children of gay parents: Homophobia's victims." In I. Stuart & L. Abt (Eds.), *Children of separation and divorce.* New York: Von Nostrand Reinhold.

Rivera, R. (1987). "Legal issues in gay and lesbian parenting." In F. Bozett (Ed.), *Gay and lesbian parents* (pp. 199–227). Westport, CT: Praeger.

Robinson, B., & Skeen, P. (1982). "Sex-role orientation of gay fathers versus gay nonfathers." *Perceptual and Motor Skills*, 55, 1055–1059.

Rofes, E. (1989). "Opening up the classroom closet: Responding to the educational needs of gay and lesbian youth." *Harvard Educational Review*, 59(4), 444–453.

Rohrbaugh, J. (1989). "Choosing children: Psychological issues in lesbian parenting." In E. Rothblum & E. Cole (Eds.), *Lesbianism: Affirming non traditional roles* (pp. 51–64). New York: Haworth.

Rugg, H. (1939). *Democracy and the curriculum: The life and progress of the American school.* New York: Appleton-Century.

Rust, P. (1993). "'Coming Out' in the age of social constructionism: Sexual identity formation among lesbian and bisexual women." *Gender and Society*, 7(1), 50–77.

Sands, A. (1988). "We are family." In H. Alpert (Ed.), *We are everywhere* (pp. 45–51). Freedom, CA: Crossing Press.

Scallen, R. (1981). *An investigation of paternal attitudes and behaviors in homosexual and heterosexual fathers.* Unpublished doctoral dissertation, California School of Professional Psychology, Los Angeles, CA. *Dissertation Abstracts International*, 42, 9, 3809B.

Schneider, M., & Tremble, B. (1986). "Training service providers to work with gay or lesbian adolescents: A workshop." *Journal of Counseling and Development*, 65(2), 98–99.

Schulenberg, J. (1985). *Gay parenting.* New York: Doubleday.

Sears, J. (1983). "Sexuality: Taking off the masks." *Changing Schools*, 11,12–13.

Sears, J. (1987). "Peering into the well of loneliness: The responsibility of educators to gay and lesbian youth." In Alex Molnar (Ed.), *Social issues and education: Challenge and responsibility* (pp. 79–100). Alexandria, VA: Association for Supervision & Curriculum Development.

Sears, J. (1988). "Growing up gay: Is anyone there to listen?" *American School Counselors Association Newsletter*, 26, 8–9.

Sears, J. (1989a). "The impact of gender and race on growing up lesbian and gay in the South." *NWSA Journal*, 1(3), 422–457.

Sears, J. (1989b). "Counseling sexual minorities: An interview with Virginia Uribe." *Empathy*, 1(2),1, 8.

Sears, J. (1991a). *Growing up gay in the South: Race, gender, and journeys of the spirit.* New York: Haworth.

Sears, J. (1991b). "Teaching for diversity: Student sexual identities." *Educational Leadership*, 49, 54–57.

Sears, J. (1992a). "Educators, homosexuality, and homosexual students: Are personal feelings related to professional beliefs?" *Journal of Homosexuality*, 29–79.

Sears, J. (1992b). "The impact of culture and ideology on the construction of gender and sexual identities: Developing a critically-based sexuality curriculum." In J. Sears (Ed.), *Sexuality and the curriculum: The politics and practices of sexuality education* (pp. 169–189). New York: Teachers College Press.

Sears, J. (1992c). "Dilemmas and possibilities of sexuality education: Reproducing the body politic." In J. Sears (Ed.), *Sexuality and the curriculum: The politics and practices of sexuality education* (pp. 19–50). New York: Teachers College Press.

Sears, J. (1992d). "Responding to the sexual diversity of faculty and students: An agenda for critically reflective administrators." In C. Capper (Ed.), *The social context of education: Administration in a pluralist society* (pp. 110–172). New York: SUNY Press.

Sears, J. (1993). "Alston and Everetta: Too Risky for School?" In R. Donmoyer & R. Kos (Eds.), *At-risk students* (pp. 153–172). New York: State University of New York Press.

Shernoff, M. (1984). "Family therapy for lesbian and gay clients." *Social Work*, 29(4), 393–396.

Slater, B. (1988). "Essential issues in working with lesbian and gay male youths." *Professional Psychology: Research and Practice*, 19(2), 226–235.

Smith, B. (Ed.). (1983). *Home girls: A black feminist anthology.* New York: Kitchen Table/ Women of Color Press.

Stewart, J. (1984). "What non-gay therapists need to know to work with gay and lesbian clients." *Practice Digest, 7*(1), 28–32.

Stover, D. (1992). "The at-risk kids schools ignore." *Executive Educator, 14*(3), 28–31.

Summerford, S. (1987). "The public library: Offensive by design." *Public Libraries, 26*(2), 60–62.

Tabbert, B. (1988). "Battling over books: Freedom and responsibility are tested." *Emergency Librarian, 16*(1), 9–13.

Teague, J. (1992). "Issues relating to the treatment of adolescent lesbians and homosexuals." *Journal of Mental Health Counseling, 14*(4), 422–439.

Turner, P., Scadden, L., & Harris, M. (1985, March). *Parenting in gay and lesbian families.* Paper presented at the First Annual Future of Parenting Symposium, Chicago, IL.

Vazquez, R. (1992). "(No longer) sleeping with the enemy." *Empathy, 3*(1), 90–91.

Weeks, R., Derdeyn, A., & Langman, M. (1975). "Two cases of children of homosexuals." *Child Psychiatry and Human Development, 6*(1), 26–32.

Weinberg, G. (1972). *Society and the healthy homosexual.* New York: St. Martin's Press.

Wilhoite, M. (1990). *Daddy's roommate.* Boston: Alyson.

Wilson, D. (1984). "The open library." *English Journal, 43*(7), 60–63.

Wolf, T. (1985). "Marriages of bisexual men." *Journal of Homosexuality, 4*, 135–148.

Wyers, N. (1984). *Lesbian and gay spouses and parents: Homosexuality in the family.* Portland, OR: School of Social Work, Portland State University.

Wyers, N. (1987). "Homosexuality in the family: Lesbian and gay spouses." *Social Work, 32*(2), 143–148.

Zera, D. (1992). "Coming of age in a heterosexist world: The development of gay and lesbian adolescents." *Adolescence, 27*(108), 849–854.

About the Author

James T. Sears is an associate professor in the Department of Educational Leadership and Policies at the University of South Carolina. He is also a senior research associate for the South Carolina Educational Policy Center. Completing graduate degrees at the University of Wisconsin-Madison and at Indiana University, Sears's academic interests are curriculum and sexuality. His books include *Teaching and Thinking About Curriculum: Critical Inquiries* (with J. Dan Marshall) and the critically acclaimed *Growing Up Gay in the South: Race, Gender, and Journeys of the Spirit.* He is currently completing an ethnography that details how persons belonging to various cultural communities within the United States understand sexuality and the implications for sexuality education. Sears's writings have appeared in a variety of scholarly journals and popular magazines and he serves as coeditor of *Teaching Education* and editor of *Empathy.* He holds leadership positions in national organizations, including the Association of Supervision and Curriculum Development and the American Educational Research Association. Additionally, he serves on the editorial boards of the *Journal of Curriculum Theorizing* and the *Journal of Homosexuality.*

Culturally and Linguistically Diverse Students with Mild Disabilities

CHERYL A. UTLEY

One of the most serious challenges facing regular and special education teachers is the provision of individualized, appropriate instructional programs for culturally and linguistically diverse students with mild disabilities in regular and special education classrooms. In the majority of universities, teacher education programs have not established guidelines for the infusion of multicultural coursework in the departmental curricula. Consequently, regular and special education teachers are ill prepared, frustrated, and without the necessary knowledge and skills in their repetoire for implementing instructional programs that facilitate the mainstreaming of culturally and linguistically diverse students with mild disabilities.

The plight of culturally and linguistically diverse students with and without mild disabilities has served to focus efforts on the (1) misidentification of students into special education classes, (2) erroneous use of intelligence tests, (3) inequitable allocation of resources, and (4) quality of instructional programs in regular and special education. While these concerns have given rise to subsequent legislation and litigation, regular and special education teachers have been unsuccessful in teaching culturally and linguistically diverse students with mild disabilities, regardless of their placements in regular and special education classroom settings (MacMillan, Hendrick, & Watkins, 1988).

This chapter focuses on the (1) commonalities between multicultural and special education and the extent to which these two disciplines complement each other; (2) issues affecting the classification and subsequent placement of culturally and linguistically diverse students in special education; and (3) recommendations for special and regular educators for culturally and linguistically diverse students with mild disabilities. There are a number of important concerns related to culturally and linguistically diverse students who have either severe disabilities, sensory impairments, or physical limitations, or who are gifted and talented. However, the majority of the controversies surrounding culturally and linguistically diverse students primarily deal with students with mild disabilities (i.e., students who do not have obvious physical or biological anomalies that differentiate them from normal-achieving students in the general population).

Multicultural and Special Education Perspectives

The first prerequisite for a creative and productive interface between multicultural education and special education—one that assures maximally effective and appropriate educational experiences for every child—is informed educational personnel. (Chinn & McCormick, 1986, p. 96)

There is now widespread interest in defining the nature of the relationship between multicultural and special education and the extent to which these two disciplines are compatible with each other. The disciplines of multicultural and special education share several goals, two of which are promoting cultural diversity and understanding individual differences among students who have been underserved, neglected, or mistreated in the

TABLE 1   Teaching the Exceptional and the Culturally Different

Societal goals:	Help fit people into the existing social structure and culture
School goals:	Teach dominant traditional educational aims more effectively by building bridges between the student and the demands of the student
Target students:	Lower-class, minority, special education, limited English proficiency, or female students who are behind in achievement in main school subjects
Practices:	
Curriculum	Make relevant to students' experiential background; fill in gaps in basic skills and knowledge
Instruction	Build on students' learning styles; adapt to students' skill levels; teach as effectively and efficiently as possible to enable students to catch up
Other aspects of classroom	Use decorations showing group members integrated into mainstream of society
Support services	Use transitional bilingual education, ESL, remedial classes, special education as temporary and intensive aids to fill gaps in knowledge
Other schoolwide concerns	Involve lower-class and minority parents in supporting work concerns of the school

Source: Based on C. E. Sleeter & C. A. Grant (1988). *Making choices for multicultural education: Five approaches to race, class, and gender.* Columbus, OH: Merrill.

public school system. The multicultural approach, according to Banks (1988) and Sleeter and Grant (1988) consists of goals along several dimensions, which may serve as a foundation for regular and special education teachers to understand culturally and linguistically diverse students with and without mild disabilities (see Table 1).

A second commonality between multicultural and special education is that culturally and linguistically diverse students, with and without mild disabilities, have similar experiences and are often discriminated against because of cultural characteristics—poverty, language, and/or their disabling condition (Brantlinger & Guskin, 1988; Gollnick & Chinn, 1990; Harry, 1992; Poplin & Wright, 1983; Tinney, 1983). Amos and Landers (1984) have noted that the stereotypical attitudes, expectations, and practices related to culturally and linguistically diverse students are also similar to those experienced by persons with mild disabilities (see Table 2). These students face quadruple jeopardy due to a combination of factors, such as poverty, language, culture, and/or disabling condition and this has had devastating effects on their educational opportunities and makes them vulnerable to placement in special education. In the public school system, the most obvious forms of discrimination against culturally and linguistically diverse students, with and without mild disabilities, have been the tracking of these students into classes

TABLE 2   Stereotypical Attitudes toward Culturally Different and Persons with Disabilities

Culturally Different	Disabled
1. Categorized—"all alike" within the group.	1. Categorized—"all alike" within the group. Examples: "The mentally retarded have poor memory." "The learning disabled are hyperactive." "The cerebral praised score in the mentally retarded range."
2. Labeled—disadvantaged, culturally seen as mentally deprived.	2. Labeled—sometimes seen as mentally retarded or mentally ill.
3. Segregated—Even after the laws prohibited segregation in housing and schools, segregation is still widespread.	3. Segregated—in special, classes, special schools, and institutions.
4. Confronted with attitudinal barriers. Seen as misfits, aggressive, etc.	4. Confronted with attitudinal and architectural barriers. Seen as slow, incapable of growth and progress, ill, handicapped.
5. Considered communication or language deficient. Seen as unable to speak English, low IQ.	5. Seen as untestable, noneducable, deficient in academics, low IQ.
6. Adjudged as genetically inferior.	6. Adjudged as genetically inferior.
7. Seen as lifelong children, happy, unmotivated, carefree. Incapable of responsibility.	7. Seen as lifelong children, with need to be patronized, protected, sheltered.
8. Seen as financial drains on schools and agencies.	8. Seen as financial drains with money being diverted from regular students.
9. Seen as discipline problems—hard to manage and teach.	9. Seen as too hard to manage or teach.

Source: Based on O. E. Amos & M. F. Landers (1984). Special education and multicultural education: A compatible marriage. *Theory Into Practice, 23,* 145.

according to their ability level, their exclusion from the mainstream, and their placement into separate special education classes.

A third commonality is that both regular and special educators must be aware of the issues, knowledge base, and technological advances in multicultural and special education. Chinn and McCormick (1986) have noted that it is important for regular and special education teachers who work with culturally and linguistically diverse students with mild disabilities to be not only competent in the teaching of subject matter but also to possess the skills essential for establishing a classroom atmosphere that is accepting of cultural differences. One possible solution to establishing a positive classroom climate is the sensitization of regular and special education teachers to the concept of cultural pluralism.

Implicit within the notion of cultural pluralism is the fact that cultural groups are heterogenous. It is very difficult to attribute specific behaviors to all culturally and linguistically diverse students with and without mild disabilities (Watkins, 1989). Chinn and McCormick (1986) have also suggested that teachers who work with culturally and linguistically diverse students with and without mild disabilities must develop competencies such as (1) understanding of how their own cultural perspective affects the teaching/learning relationship, (2) the ability to scrutinize assessment practices, (3) the ability to incorporate the cultural experiences of students and parents into the curriculum, and (4) the ability to expand the students' knowledge of themselves and to develop an appreciation of differences in other individuals.

A fourth commonality is the relationsip between educational reform movements, as illustrated by the civil rights movement and special education litigation (Heward & Orlansky, 1992). The concepts of "equal protection" and "due process" have formed the basis for arguments upholding the rights of people who have disabilities. Under the equal protection clause of the 14th Amendment, persons with disabilities may not be denied access to educational programs because of their disability. Due process for parents of students with disabilities within the public educational system provides legal safeguards that acknowledge their rights and responsibilities to be notified of changes in their child's educational program.

Legal arguments against the segregation of African-American children in public schools supported lawsuits on behalf of persons with disabilities. This legal argument, for example, was used in the *Brown* v. *Board of Education of Topeka 1954* against the "separate but equal" philosophy and was the foundation for the right to education movement for the disabled. The "right to education" cases dealt with placement bias due to the overrepresentation of culturally and linguistically diverse students in special education programs. In the *Larry P.* v. *Riles* (1979, 1984) cases, African-American students were overrepresented in segregated special classes for educable mentally retarded (EMR) students. In the *Diana* v. *State Board of Education* (1970, 1973) and the *Guadalupe Organization* v. *Tempe Elementary School District* (1972) cases, the plantiffs argued that the overrepresentation of Hispanic students in special classes was due to inappropriate assessment practices. The rulings of several court cases, which are based on the equal protection clause of the 14th Amendment have been incorporated into subsequent legislation (e.g., PL 94-142).

Issues in the Education of Culturally and Linguistically Diverse Students with Mild Disabilities

There are a number of important concerns related to the variables of minority status, ethnicity, and education that are of relevance to students with mild disabilities. These concerns are focused on the issues of prevalence, labeling, psychological assessment, effective instruction, and parent-teacher communication involving culturally and linguistically diverse students with mild disabilities in special and regular education classrooms.

Prevalence Issues

One of the major issues in special education has been the variability in prevalence rates for culturally and linguistically diverse students who reside in low socioeconomic status (SES) environments. For example, estimates of the number of culturally and linguistically diverse students from low SES environments who experienced academic difficulties and social behavior problems were higher when compared to the estimates of the number of students from middle or higher SES backgrounds (Chinn & Gollnick, 1986; Dunn, 1968; Finn, 1982; Wright & Santa Cruz, 1983). More recently, conclusive evidence of this phenomenon is provided by student enrollment data collected by the U.S. Office of Civil Rights (OCR) Surveys of Elementary and Secondary Schools. Chinn and Hughes (1987) reported that African-American children continue to be overrepresented in classes for students with educable mental retardation (EMR) and moderate mental retardation (MR), for students with learning disabilities (LD), and for students with emotional disturbance (ED). Hispanic students, although not statistically represented in classes for students with EMR, are disproportionately represented in classes for students with LD. Native-American children are overrepresented in classes for students with LD and EMR.

Harry (1992) conducted a more recent analysis of survey reports on the placement rates of enrollment by race in special education programs. Using data from the OCR (1978), she identified trends in placement rates for seven states that represented the various population sizes of culturally and linguistically diverse students: Alabama, Alaska, Arizona, California, Hawaii, New Jersey, and New York. For example, in Alabama, where African-American students represent 37 percent of the school population, their placement rate in classes for students with MR was one and one-half times greater than the general school body. In Alaska, their rates of enrollment in classes for students with LD and ED were one and three-quarter times that of the total school population. In California and New Jersey, placement rates were twice the rate of the overall student population.

In school districts where Hispanic students represent 2 percent of all the students, there is no disproportionate representation. However, in school districts where Hispanic students represent 27 percent of all students, they account for 35 percent of students in the EMR category. In school districts where Hispanic students represent 26 percent of all students, they account for 30 percent of the LD category.

With regard to Native-American students in school districts where they represent 25 percent of all students, their highest placement rate is in the EMR category with these students one and three-quarter times greater than the general student body. In school districts in California, where they represent only 1 percent of the student population, there is no disproportionate representation. However, in Arizona, where the student enrollment is 6 percent of the student population, disproportionate representation is evident.

Asian-American students, on the other hand, present a very different pattern of enrollment in special education programs. Asian-American students are not disproportionately represented in the categories of EMR, LD, and ED, but proportionately represented in the trainable mentally retarded (TMR) category. In Hawaiian school districts where the Asian population is approximately 72 percent, the placement rate is 80 percent in the EMR category.

Labeling Effects

One controversial issue in the education of culturally and linguistically diverse students with mild disabilities is the assignment of labels for placement into special education (Ysseldyke, 1987). The relationship between labels and teachers' attitudes and behaviors is not a simple one because it is difficult to determine if the poor performance of culturally and linguistically diverse students with mild disabilities is due to their slower intellectual ability, culturally specific behaviors, or merely the low expectations of the teacher. More succinctly stated, there is a question as to whether or not the perceptions of teachers are affected by the term *EMR* which connotes low ability, or whether the EMR concept heightens teacher awareness of factors that may cause academic or behavior problems.

Evidence suggests that regular education teachers' expectations of culturally and linguistically diverse children result in a higher incidence of these children being defined as having mild disabilities than are majority group children (Chinn & McCormick, 1986), because they perceive culturally and linguistically diverse students as less compentent than their majority counterparts (Cheung, 1989; Harry, 1992; Parker, 1988), and erroneously identify culturally and linguistically diverse children for special education services (Gollnick & Chinn, 1987; Mercer, 1973). In addition, Gleason (1991) asserted that negative and false perceptions held by both teachers and children are manifested in their thoughts and actions, and that most school evaluation systems are set up so that only the academically oriented students are successful.

Given these facts, it is essential that regular and special education teachers recognize the characteristics of culturally and linguistically diverse students with and without mild disabilities and the extent to which they can affect their learning styles, academic achievement levels, and social interactions with other students (Shade, 1990; Valero-Figueira, 1988). As depicted in Tables 3, 4, 5, and 6, there are culture-specific characteristics and behaviors for African-American, Hispanic, Asian-American, and Native-American groups in relation to the categorical labels of MR, LD, and ED. For example, African-American students classified with the condition of MR are characterized as slow learners with a limited educational attainment level. African-American students have low performance on standardized intelligence and achievement tests. With regard to relevant cultural characteristics that affect learning, African-American students demonstrate higher performance levels on adaptive behavior tests and nonverbal tasks than on vocabulary tests. Because African-American students with MR are misdiagnosed, disproportionately repre-

TABLE 3 Characteristics of African-American Students with Mild Disabilities

Condition	Characteristics of Condition	Characteristics of Culture	Effects
Mental Retardation	Limited level of educational achievement	Historically, received little or no schooling	Family may give up on schooling
	Slow thinking	Tolerance for broad range of abilities	May not be perceived as disabled except related to academics
	Poor performance on tests of intelligence and achievement	Poor performance of tests normed on non-Black populations	Misdiagnosis: parental hostility, defensiveness
Learning Disabled	Achievement below ability	Ability often misjudged because of test bias	Students with learning disabilities misdiagnosed as mentally retarded
	Faulty perception of sounds, words, etc.	Words not spoken with familiar intonation	Child believed to have auditory perceptual problems when there is a failure to recognize meaning without the cues of dialect
	Hyperactive	Interactive style	Child engaged in interactive process may be viewed as hyperactive
Emotionally Disturbed/ Behavior Disordered	Delinquency	Youths may rebel against system when they believe they have little hope for success	Antisocial behavior may be used to achieve status when it cannot be achieved within the system
	Drugs and alcohol	Youths may become drug or alcohol dependent in environment where narcotics are commonly used as an escape	
	Aggressive, acting out, challenging, militant	Desire to assert racial identify	Needs to be directed into positive channels

sented in special education classes, and are not identified as disabled until they enter elementary school, parents are suspicious of the school system and are defensive toward school staff members. As long as culture-specific behaviors of culturally and linguistically diverse children are ignored in the teaching-learning process, the greater will be the probability of referrals for special education services increasing substantially.

TABLE 4   Characteristics of Hispanic Students with Mild Disabilities

Condition	Characteristics of Condition	Characteristics of Culture	Effects
Mental Retardation	Limited level of educational achievement	Historically, received little or no schooling	Dropout rate high, even among nondisabled
	Slow thinking	Adapts roles and expectations to abilities	Person assured of place in community in spite of limitations
	Poor performance on tests	Most tests are not appropriate	Frequent misdiagnosis
	Noncompetive	Noncompetitive	Best to use team or cooperative learning
Learning Disabled	Achievement below ability	Weak skills in both English and Spanish	Problem determining nature of learning problem
	Faulty perception of sounds, words, and so on	Many English words sound alike to Spanish speaker	Problem determining cause of misperceptions
Emotionally Disturbed/ Behavior Disordered	Depressed, anxious withdrawn	Youths may turn to drugs or alcohol in situations where family roles have broken down	Requires special extended family and community effort to combat abuse

Psychological Assessment Practices

One of the most controversial explanations of the overinclusion of culturally and linguistically diverse children in special education classes is the allegation of systematic bias, defined as "the unfairness or inaccuracy of results that are due to cultural background, the facts of the test rather than actual mental abilities or skills" (Reynolds, 1987). Critics have noted that (1) test developers systematically exclude culturally and linguistically diverse children in the stratified samples of the normative framework (Haywood, 1977); (2) standardized test norms, items, and indices of reliability and validity are inadequately constructed for use with culturally and linguistically diverse students with mild disabilities (Fuchs, Fuchs, Benowitz, & Barringer, 1987); (3) normative or standardized tests do not assess the "functional academic skills" essential for classroom performance (Gallas & Siegel, 1979; Shinn & Tindal, 1988); (4) traditional normative testing procedures are biased agained low SES examinees (Fuchs, Fuchs, Dailey, & Power, 1985; Fuchs & Fuchs, 1986); and (5) tests are primarily used for classification and diagnostic purposes,

TABLE 5   Characteristics of Asian-American Students with Mild Disabilities

Condition	Characteristics of Condition	Characteristics of Culture	Effects
Mental Retardation	Limited level of educational achievement	Social class and self-esteem determined by level of identify	May have poor self-esteem; family may feel shame
Learning Disabled	Achievement below ability	Value placed on high academic achievement, industriousness	Child may try to compensate for disability by working extra hard, memorizing material, etc., so as not to bring shame on family
	Faulty perception of sounds, words, and so on	Failure to perceive unfamiliar sounds; failure to remember words out of context for non-English speaking children	May lead to confusion in diagnosing problem
	Hyperactive	Self-controlled	Behavior may be a source of shame to parents and self; requires special understanding by educators of traditional cultural expectations
Emotionally Disturbed/ Behavior Disordered	Anxiety, psychosomatic complaints, hysteric blind and deaf reactions; school phobia from not being able to satisfy achievement demands of home and school	Traditionally, child is inhibited, conventional, subservient to authority	Requires special understanding by educators of traditional cultural expectations
	Suicide	Suicide	Japanese culture once reinforced this alternative as a way of ending a shameful situation
	Delinquency	Youths refuse to give unquestioning obedience to parental views	Less traditional youths may use crime as a statement of rebellion
	Anxiety, depressive reactions	Youths may become angry at racial barriers then feel guilty for denying their own ethnicity	Requires special effort to reduce racial barriers so youth will not desire to deny ethnicity
	Aggressive, acting out, challenging, militant	Desire to assert ethnic identify	May be particularly shame producing for more traditional parents

TABLE 6   Characteristics of Native-American Students with Mild Disabilities

Condition	Characteristics of Condition	Characteristics of Culture	Effects
Mental Retardation	Limited level of educational achievement	Social class and self-esteem determined by level of identify	May have poor self-esteem; family may feel shame
Learning Disabled	Achievement below ability	Value placed on high academic achievement, industriousness	Child may try to compensate for disability by working extra hard, memorizing material, etc., so as not to bring shame on family
	Faulty perception of sounds, words, and so on	Failure to perceive unfamiliar sounds; failure to remember words out context for non-English speaking children	May lead to confusion in diagnosing problem
	Hyperactive	Self-controlled	Behavior may be a source of shame to parents and self
	Depressed, anxious, withdrawn, suicidal	Feelings of unworthiness, due to conflict of values	Common syndrome; may not receive attention
Emotionally Disturbed	Delinquency	Inability to succeed may lead to rebellion	Ridicule may be more effective deterrent than other punishments
	Alcohol	Alcohol abuse	Requires special extended family and community effort
	Militant	Desire to assert cultural identity	Need to be directed to productive channels

Source: Based on J. N. Nazarro (1981). *Special problems of exceptional minority children. In culturally diverse exceptional children in school.* Washington, DC: National Institute of Education, ERIC Document Reproduction Services No. 199 993.

hence they are not prescriptive (Heller, Holtzman, & Messick, 1982; Utley, Haywood, & Masters, 1991).

The majority of allegations against standardized psychoeducational assessment procedures for culturally and linguistically diverse students, in general, are linked to the psychometric aspects of test validation: content validity, predictive or criterion validity, and construct validity. The empirical evidence, however, specifically related to culturally and linguistically diverse students does not refute claims of test bias. More specifically, the conclusions derived from empirical studies suggest that differences in test scores between culturally and linguistically diverse students and majority students are not due to the relative difficulty of the item content, an underestimation of the abilities of culturally and linguistically diverse students, and the measurement of different attributes for different culturally and linguistically diverse groups. The psychometic perspective has been extensively criticized because of the exclusion of ethical issues of fairness and unfairness and the consequences resulting from the sole use of test scores for evaluation.

One method of realizing fairness in the psychoeducational assessment of culturally and linguistically diverse students with and without mild disabilities is the theory of dynamic assessment, one that is anchored in the cognitive developmental theories of Feuerstein's system of structural cognitive modifiability and Vygotsky's notions of the social context of learning (Feuerstein, 1982; Haywood, Brown, & Wingenfeld, 1990; Vygotsky, 1978). Feuerstein (1982) asserted that cultures and subcultures possess the essential elements for adequate cognitive development and school achievement and that it is through "intergenerational cultural transfer" that the patterns of systematic thought, rules, rule-making techniques, attitudes toward learning, strategies of problem solving, and achievement motivation are passed on from one generation to the next.

The vehicles for transmitting optimal social and cognitive development are through direct exposure and mediated learning experience (MLE). Direct exposure learning occurs without external mediation and through successive encounters of environmental events that facilitate the acquisition of the basic cognitive functions in order to think logically, perceive the world in structured and orderly ways, and apply intelligence to problem-solving situations. Mediated learning experiences, on the other hand, involve child-rearing agents and/or caregivers (e.g., parents, grandparents, and teachers) who have the responsibility of helping children to "understand that events, objects, and persons have meaning beyond themselves, that the universe has predictable structure, that understanding that structure helps one to know what to do in a wide variety of future situations, that it is possible to make explanatory rules that help one to organize observations, and that it is essential to test the applicability of such rules in a wide variety of circumstances" (Haywood, 1987, p. 1). Without the adequate mediation of culture-characteristic ways of perceiving and organizing the world, children from these environments, particularly those individuals who experience academic difficulties, have been denied the benefits of their own culture and the essential components of good child rearing environments. Thus, the "unavailability of the processes of intergenerational cultural transfer" (i.e., MLE) results in inadequate cognitive development, the inefficient learning of both academic and social content, and a discrepancy between academic performance and potential.

The dynamic assessment approach differs from traditional methods of psychological assessment in several important ways. Differences between these two methods of psychological assessment may be observed along the following dimensions: goals, the method of administration, what is assessed, assumptions, and comparison groups (Haywood & Bransford, 1984). For example, the primary goal of traditional assessment procedures is that of classification and prediction, while the focus of dynamic assessment procedures is the identification of cognitive processes that can be changed so that the distance between the actual levels of performance and the true learning potential of students is minimized. In this method of assessment, the examiner utilizes a test-teach-test procedure to show

how much a person's performance can be modified when generalized cognitive principles of thought and understanding are taught during the testing sessions (Feuerestein, Rand, Hoffman, & Miller, 1980; Haywood, 1988; Haywood & Switzky, 1986). The traditional method of administration in standardized testing situations does not permit assistance from the examiner. On the other hand, dynamic assessment procedures involve a shift in the examiner-examinee relationship with the examiner being characterized as a passive recorder to an active participant. In this role, the examiner recognizes that learning and problem solving depends upon some prior knowledge, and that failure on a task may result from the lack of essential information or development of cognitive strategies and not from the lack of opportunity to learn from the environment. In addition, the criterion for learning in standardized assessment procedures is achievement test scores, whereas in dynamic assessment testing situations the focus is on learning new tasks.

Assessment Linked to Instruction

A frequently discussed and important issue that is continually debated is the use of "valid and functional" assessment procedures that are linked to effective instructional practices. Reschly (1982, p. 215) observed, "Assessment which does not result in effective interventions should be regarded as useless, and biased or unfair as well, if ethnic or racial minorities are *differentially* exposed to ineffective programs as a result of assessment activities." Heller and colleagues (1982) stated that one of the key components of the educational process is the evaluation of the effectiveness of interventions. They further stated that an evaluation must include categories of academically relevant skills, cognitive strategies, and adaptive/motivational skills by using systematic observations of teacher and student behaviors as a means of documenting academic outcomes in both regular and special education programs. Therefore, valid assessment procedures must focus on "functional" characteristics of students that are relevant to classroom performance and instructional practices that maximize the competencies of culturally and linguistically diverse students.

Dynamic Assessment

The argument in support of a "process orientation" to learning is the fact that specific "prescriptive" information can be obtained on the child's learning potential, strengths, weaknesses, nature and locus of cognitive impairments, and degree of modifiability (Arbitman-Smith & Haywood, 1980; Dale & Cole, 1988; Harth, 1988). The cognitive education approach is concerned not only with the modifiability of cognitive processes teaches but primarily with how one teaches those processes. Because MLE is a critical condition for adequate cognitive development, it is important for teachers to develop a teaching style that fosters positive adult-child interactions and effective, systematic patterns of perceiving, thinking, learning, and problem solving. The criteria for a mediational teaching style consist of intentionality, transcendence, communication of meaning and purpose, mediation of a feeling of competence, regulation of behavior, and shared participation. The specialized strategies for implementing qualitative mediated learning interactions involve process questioning, bridging, challenging, teaching about rules, and emphasizing order, predictability, system, sequence, and strategies.

Feuerstein and colleagues (1979) developed a cognitive education curriculum for culturally and linguistically diverse children, adolescents, and adults. This program, called *Instrumental Enrichment*, is widely used in Israel and has been translated to other languages, including English, Hebrew, French, and Spanish. The program consists of 15 curriculum units or "instruments" that are taught for one class period per day over two to three years. These instruments focus on deficient cognitive functions (e.g., impulsive responding) and are titled Orientation in Space, Analytic Perception, Numerical Progressions, Comparisons, Organization of Dots, Temporal Relations, Categorization, and Syllogisms. These instruments are content free and do not require the inclusion of specific curricular content for implementation.

A second curriculum program entitled *Cognitive Curriculum for Young Children* is designed for young children with and without developmental disabilities, ages 3 to 6. The focus of this program is the accession to concrete operations, as based on Piaget's principles of learning. It consists of 7 small-group units, outlines for content-oriented lessons, a cognitive-mediational behavior management system, theoretical systems, and parent participation components. These lessons are focused on the teaching of precognitive processes and generalizable cognitive principles and strategies. In addition, these lessons emphasize content (e.g., colors, number operations, etc.) with a specified cognitive function integrated into the unit in order to provide a means of understanding, organizing, and applying the newly acquired content knowledge.

Curriculum-Based Assessment (CBA)

This assessment-instructional model reflects a student's current level of performance on a specific component of the curriculum (e.g., reading fluency, math comprehension, etc.). Because CBA assesses exactly what is taught within a short instructional sequence, regular and special education teachers know when culturally and linguistically diverse students with and without mild disabilities have achieved the skills necessary to advance to the next unit of instruction. CBA also allows teachers to monitor the attainment of a series of short-term objectives (Fuchs & Deno, 1991).

Effective Instructional Practices

Regular and special education teachers are becoming increasingly concerned about the quality of academic instruction for culturally and linguistically diverse students with mild disabilities (Berliner, 1988; Larrivee, 1989). Bickel and Bickel (1986) have categorized effective teaching practices under the broad headings of (1) teacher-directed classrooms and (2) peer-directed lessons. Examples of teacher-directed strategies are the Exemplary Center for Reading Instruction (Reid, 1986) and precision teaching (White, 1986). Teacher-directed procedures are highly structured and consist of a comprehensive system of instruction, including classroom management, teacher-student interaction, and the design of curriculum materials.

Peer-mediated approaches, by contrast, are designed to provide direct instruction to target peers. Examples of peer-mediated practices were classwide peer tutoring (Delquadri, Greenwood, Whorton, Carta, & Hall, 1986), cooperative learning strategies (Johnson &

TABLE 7   Critical Elements of Effective Instructional Practices

Teacher-Mediated Strategies	Peer-Mediated Strategies
Clearly specified and sequenced learning objectives	Selection of peer partners or partner pairing procedures.
An explicit scripted step-by-step instructional strategy	Tutoring roles that involve tutor and tutee interactions (e.g., task presentation, error correction strategies, presentation of new material, point systems, positive reinforcement)
Development of mastery on each skill	Regularly scheduled tutoring sessions
Design of instructional materials that reduce the likelihood of student errors and misunderstanding	Adapted materials for use within a peer tutoring arrangement
Gradual fading from teacher-mediated activities toward independent work	Frequent testing to evaluate learning
Use of systematic practice across a range of example	Teacher monitoring of tutoring activities
Cumulative review and integration of newly learned concepts with previously mastered materials	

Source: Based on C. R. Greenwood, J. J. Carta, & D. Kamps (1990). Teacher-mediated versus peer-mediated instruction. A review of educational advantages and disadvantages. In H. C. Foot, M. J. Morgan, & R.H. Shute (Eds.), *Children Helping Children* (pp. 177–205). New York: John Wiley & Sons, Ltd.

Johnson, 1986), and social skills training (Strain & Odom, 1986). Greenwood, Carta, and Kamps (1990) define a peer-mediated approach as presenting prompts or task trials, monitoring tutee responses, using error correction procedures, and providing help. This approach is highly structured and based on teacher goals and the classroom curriculum. Aspects of this approach include a continuous program of moderate duration and specific tutor training (i.e., encouraging and praising correct responses).

As illustrated in Table 7, there are two categories of critical elements of instructional programs in teacher and peer-mediated approaches. Each of these approaches has advantages and disadvantages. For example, the one of the advantages of teacher-mediated approaches (i.e., direct instruction) is the heavy emphasis on the processes of academic learning time and structure. Small group instruction with unison responding is used so that students are given response opportunities. Instructional procedures include fast-paced sessions designed to maintain student attention and to cover large amounts of academic material. Disadvantages include the emphasis on rote learning rather than higher-order conceptual skills and the use of scripted lesson presentations. The positive effects of peer-mediated strategies include an increase in the time students spend engaged in relevant academic behaviors (e.g., academic talk, reading aloud, writing, etc.) that are related to learning specific academic tasks. Students are able to receive extra instruction, to practice, and to clarify concepts that enable them to feel successful in the regular classroom. Disadvantages include a deemphasis on the teaching of higher-order conceptual skills and the development of inappropriately sequenced reading materials.

Despite the recognition that cultural and linguistic variables influence the achievement of students with disabilities, the implementation of alterative psychoeducational assessment procedures and effective instructional practices into special education is a relatively new phenomenon (Rueda, 1989). Although one of the goals of special education is to understand individual differences that maximize the achievements for culturally and linguistically diverse students with mild disabilities, the educational inequities continue to affect the quality of programs available for these students. For example, *The Handicapped*

TABLE 8   Summary of Findings from the Minority Research Institutes

Assesment	Instruction
1. Special education placement leads to decreased test scores (IQ and achievement).	1. Special education produces little academic development.
2. Language proficiency is not seriously taken into account in special education assessment.	2. Few children receive primary language support before special education; even fewer, during special education.
3. Testing is done in English, often increasing the likelihood of establishing an achievement or intelligence discrepancy.	3. The behaviors that trigger teacher referral suggest that English-language-aquisition stages and their interaction with English-only programs are being confused for handicapping conditions.
4. Learning disability and communication handicapped placements have replaced the misplacement of students as EMR of the 1960s and 1970s.	4. The second and third grades are critical for bilingual children in terms of potentially being referred.
5. Home data are not used in assessment.	5. Individual education plans had few, if any, accommodations for bilingual children.
6. English-language problems that are typically characteristic of second-language learners (poor comprehension, limited vocabulary, grammar and syntax errors, and problems with English articulation) are misinterpreted as handicaps.	6. Prereferral modifications of the regular programs are rare and show little indication of primary language support.
7. Psychometric test scores from Spanish or English tests are capricious in their outcomes, though, paradoxically, internally sound.	7. The few special education classes that work for biliguals are more like good regular bilingual education classes (whole-Language emphasis, comprehensible input, cooperative learning, and student empowerment) than traditional behavioristic, task-analysis driven work sheet oriented special education classes.
8. The same few tests are used with most children	
9. Having parents who were born outside the United States increases the likelihood of being found eligible for special education.	
10. Reevaluation usually led to more special education.	

Source: From "Bilingual special education and this special issue" by R. A. Figueroa, S. H. Fradd, & V. I. Correa, *Exceptional Children, 56*(2), 1986, pages 174–178. Copyright 1986 by The Council for Exceptional Children. Reprinted with permission.

Minority Research Institutes (Garcia, 1985; Ortiz & Maldonado-Colon, 1986; Swedo, 1987) provided a series of reports that focused on the empirical state of special education for culturally and linguistically diverse students with mild disabilities. Illustrated in Table 8 is a listing of the findings on the topics of assessment and instructional services (Figueroa, Fradd, & Correa, 1989, p. 176).

✓*Parent Involvement*

The special educator's interest in working effectively with culturally and linguistically diverse parents who have children with mild disabilities is related to three factors: (1) federal and state laws provide statutory guidelines for parent professional interactions in regard to referral, testing, placement, and program planning; (2) many parents want to be involved; and (3) research and practice have convinced educators that their effectiveness can be significantly greater with the assistance and involvement of parents. Although Individuals with Disabilities Education Act (IDEA) (1990) describes specific rights of culturally and linguistically parents of students with mild disabilities, it also implies certain responsibilities. Parents must acquire specific knowledge about criterion-referenced tests and learn specific skills (e.g., participating in individual educational plan (IEP) conferences).

In spite of the emphasis on parental participation mandated by PL 94-142, empirical findings demonstrate that many families, particularly culturally and linguistically diverse families, do not actively participate in the IEP process. Professionals working with urban culturally and linguistically diverse parents who have children with mild disabilities must be aware of cultural differences. For example, professionals may perceive the attitudes of African-American parents differently than Caucasian parents with children who have similar disabling conditions. African-American and Hispanic parents were not as aware of the related services identified on the IEP when compared to the knowledge base of services by Caucasian parents. African-American parents may be less inclined to blame themselves or feel guilty for their child's learning problems. Professionals must recognize the potential for differences in values among parents that may create a different set of expectations and goals from those held by the school. It is also important to consider how some life-styles may serve as strengths in the family's attempt to cope with implications of an exceptionality.

Major barriers must be recognized as factors that influence the nature of the participation of urban culturally and linguistically diverse parents in the IEP conference. Empirical evidence has demonstrated that urban culturally and linguistically diverse parents of students with mild disabilities may not (1) understand the nature of the child's handicap (Heron & Harris, 1987); (2) be aware of the appropriate educational services available for their child (Lynch & Stein, 1987); (3) have different value and belief systems from mainstream society; and (4) have coping skills necessary for adapting to the school system. As depicted in Table 9, the barriers that prevent effective communication between urban culturally and linguistically diverse parents and regular and special education teachers may be categorized into the different areas: language and culture, logistics, and school-related factors. Each of these barriers influence one another and are not mutually exclusive.

TABLE 9 Major Barriers Affecting Effective Parent-Teacher Communication

Language/Cultural Barriers	Logstical Barriers
Lack of cultural sensitivity	Communication problems
Indifference to religious beliefs	Lack of understanding of public school system
Adherence to stereotypical assumptions of families	Uncertainty about child's disability
Differences in values and belief systems	Concerns about the role of parent and teacher
Language/dialectal differences	Transportation
	Time

School Barriers

Lack of information about special services
Uninformed about legal rights
Limited information about terms in special education
Feelings of inferiority to school personnel
Feelings of intimidation

Source: Adapted from E. W. Lynch, & R. Stein (1982). Parent participation by ethnicity: A comparison of Hispanic, Black, and Anglo families. *Exceptional Children, 54*(2) 105–111.

Despite the recognition of the aforementioned barriers, several authors have discussed the benefits of systematically incorporating parent participation as a part of the school's program. Their discussions include the following points. First, parents might facilitate the integration by helping their children learn the skills required in the regular classroom and by actively participating in the decisions made by the multidisciplinary team (Simich-Dudgeon, 1987). Second, the parents' active involvement will enable them to become advocates for their child so they can receive appropriate services (Met, 1987; Morgan, 1982). Third, the professionals' commitment to developing and maintaining a collaborative relationship with culturally and linguistically diverse parents provides the opportunities for them to develop support networks with other parents (Marion, 1980). Effective strategies for overcoming barriers that prevent culturally and linguistically diverse parental involvement have been discussed by Correa (1989) and Turnbull and Turnbull (1990). These include, but are not limited to, the following: (1) conducting a thorough assessment of the family's needs by a trained professional, (2) developing a knowledge base for understanding and becoming sensitive to different cultures, and (3) developing school behaviors that can assist families in establishing a positive rapport with teachers.

Recommendations

This chapter presents a review of issues and programmatic concerns of professionals in the fields of multicultural and special education. The multicultural component is a necessary element for the effective implementation of special education programs. The *ral* instructional program, according to Baca and Cervantes (1989, p. 81), "is ___ the diverse cultural backgrounds of students, including monolingual English ___ the classroom. Students' cultural experiences are considered and instruction is ___vided within the students' cultural framework. The students' self-concepts are enhanced as their cultural backgrounds are valued. Students are taught to value cultural diversity."

It is recommended that teacher training programs infuse or interface multicultural perspectives and goals into special education programs. Ramsey (1987, pp. 3–5) has outlined eight teaching goals from a multicultural perspective that may be incorporated into a special education program. These are:

1. To help children develop positive gender, racial, cultural, class, and individual identities and to recognize and accept their membership in many groups.
2. To enable children to see themselves as part of the larger society; to identify, emphasize, and relate with individuals from other groups.
3. To foster respect and appreciation for the diverse ways in which other people live.
4. To encourage in young children's earliest social relationships an openness and interest in others, a willingness to include others, and a desire to cooperate.
5. To promote the development of a realistic awareness of contemporary society, a sense of social responsibility, and an active concern that extends beyond one's immediate family or group.
6. To empower children to become autonomous and critical analysts and activists in their social environment.
7. To support the development of educational and social skills that are needed for children to become full participants in the larger society in ways that are most appropriate to individual styles, cultural orientations, and linguistic backgrounds.
8. To promote effective and reciprocal relationships between schools and families.

It is recommended that research focused specifically on culturally and linguistically diverse students with mild disabilities in both regular and special education classes continue to be directed on the issues of disproportionate representation and the identification of language, cognitive processes, and academic and social skills through the use of appropriate psychoeducational assessment procedures, and the implementation of effective instructional practices.

It is recommended that regular and special education teachers be provided with the opportunity to increase their knowledge base, to work collaboratively with each other, and to implement effective instructional programs. These programs can have a direct impact on the school-based outcome measures and the quality of services provided culturally and linguistically diverse students with mild disabilities.

It is recommended that regular and special education teachers be provided with alternative methods for differentiating cultural and linguistic factors from true learning problems. Arreaga-Mayer and Greenwood (1986) and Rueda (1989) suggest a comprehensive approach focused on prereferral interventions and the measurement of instructional environments as prerequisites for consideration, prior to special education placement. Such an approach would lead to a focus on alterable, school-related variables that have been found to affect student learning directly (e.g., functional assessment practices) and that lead to the improvement of instruction (The Executive Committee of the Council for Exceptional Children and Behavioral Disorders, 1989).

It is recommended that regular and special education teachers be provided with training focused on strengthening parent-teacher communication, identifying cultural factors that impede or hinder parents from being involved in the implementation of instructional programs, and developing parent skills that will improve the academic success of their children in school.

References

Amos, O. E., & Landers, M. F. (1984). Special education and multicultural education: A compatible marriage. *Theory Into Practice, 23*(2), 144–150.

Anderson-Inman, L. (1986). Bridging the gap: Student-centered strategies for promoting the transfer of learning [Special Issue]. *Exceptional Children, 52*(6), 562–572.

Arbitman-Smith, R., & Haywood, H. C. (1980). Cognitive education for learning disabled adolescents. *Journal of Abnormal Child Psychology, 8*(1), 51–64.

Arbitman-Smith, R., Haywood, H. C., & Bransford, J. D. (1984). Assessing cognitive change. In P. Brooks, R. Sperber, & C. M. McCauley (Eds.), *Learning and cognition in the mentally retarded* (pp. 433–471). Hillsdale, NJ: Erlbaum.

Arreaga-Mayer, C. & Greenwood, C. R. (1986, Winter). Environmental variables affecting the school achievement of culturally and linguistically different learners: An instructional perspective. *National Association of Bilingual Education*, pp. 113–135.

Baca, L. M., & Cervantes, H. T. (1989). *The bilingual special education interface*. Columbus, OH: Merrill.

Banks, J. A. (1988). *Multiethnic education: Theory and practice* (2nd ed.). Boston: Allyn and Bacon.

Baumeister, A. A., Kuptas, F., & Klindworth, L. M. (1990). New morbidity: Implications for prevention of children's disabilities. *Exceptionality, 1*, 1–16.

Berliner, D. C. (1988). The half-full glass: A review of research on teaching. In E. L. Meyen, G. A. Vergason, & R. J. Whelan (Eds.), *Effective instructional strategies for exceptional children* (pp. 7–31). Denver, CO: Love.

Brantlinger, E. A. & Guskin, S. L. (1988). Implications of social and cultural differences for special education. In E. L. Meyen, G. A. Vergason, & R. J. Whelan (Eds.), *Effective instructional strategies for exceptional children* (pp. 118–138). Denver, CO: Love.

Bratlinger, E. A., & Guskin, S. L. (1989). Ethnocultural and social-psychological effects on learning characteristics of handicapped children. In M. C. Wang, M. C. Reynolds, & H. J. Walberg (Eds.), *Handbook of special education: Research and practice (Vol. 1). Learner characteristics and adaptive education* (pp. 7–34). New York: Pergamon Press.

Brown v. *Board of Education of Topeka.* 347 U.S. (1954).

Carnine, D., & Silbert, J. (1979). *Direct instruction reading*. Columbus, OH: Merrill.

Chan, K. S., & Rueda, R. (1979). Poverty and culture in education: Separate but equal. *Exceptional Children, 45*, 421–428.

Cheung, F. K. (1989, May). *Culture and mental health care for Asian Americans in the United States*. Paper presented at the 1989 American Psychiatric Association Annual Meeting, San Francisco, CA.

Chinn, P. C. & Hughes, S. (1987). Representation of minority students in special education classes. *Remedial and Special Education, 8*(4), 41–16.

Chinn, P. C., & McCormick, L. (1986). Cultural diversity and exceptionality. In N. G. Haring & L. McCormick (Eds.), *Exceptional children and youth* (4th ed.) (pp. 95–117). Columbus, OH: Merrill.

Christenson, S. L., Ysseldyke, J. E., & Thurlow, M. L. (1989). *Remedial and Special Education, 10*(5), 21–31.

Correa, V. I. (1989). Involving culturally diverse families in the educational process. In S. H. Fradd & M. J. Weismantal (Eds.), *Meeting the needs of culturally and linguistically diverse students: A handbook for educators* (pp. 130–144). Boston, MA: College Hill.

Dale, P. S., & Cole, K. N. (1988). Comparison of academic and cognitive programs for young handicapped children. *Exceptional Children, 54*(5), 439–447.

Delquadri, J. C., Greenwood, C. R., Whorton, D., Carta, J. J., & Hall, R. V. (1986). Classwide peer tutoring [Special Issue]. *Exceptional Children, 52*, 535–542.

Deshler, D. D., & Schumaker, J. B. (1986). Learning strategies: An instructional alternative for low-achieving adolescents [Special Issue]. *Exceptional Children, 52*(6), 583–591.

Diana v. *State Board of Education* (1970, 1973). C-70, 37 RFP. (N.D. Cal., 1970, 1973).

Dunn, L. M. (1968). Special education for the mildly retarded—Is much of it justifiable? *Exceptional Children, 35*(1), 5–22.

Feuerstein, R., Rand, Y., & Hoffman, M. B. (1979). *The dynamic assessment of retarded performers: The Learning Potential Assessment Device, theory, instruments, and techniques.* Baltimore, MD: University Park Press.

Feuerstein, R., Rand, Y., Hoffman, M. B., & Miller (1980). *Instrumental enrichment.* Baltimore, MD: University Park Press.

Figueroa, R. A., Fradd, S. H., & Correa, V. I. (1989). Bilingual special education [Special issue]. *Exceptional Children, 56*(2), 174–178.

Final report on the national assessment of Chapter One. (1987). Washington, DC: Office of Research, Office of Educational Research and Improvement, U.S. Department of Education.

Finn, J. D. (1982). Patterns in special education placement as revealed by the OCR surveys. In K. A. Heller, W. H. Holtzman, & S. Messick (Eds.), *Placing children in special education: A strategy for equity.* Washington, DC: National Academy Press.

Fowler, S. A. (1986). Peer-monitoring and self-monitoring: Alternatives to traditional teacher management [Special Issue]. *Exceptional Children, 52*(6), 573–582.

Fuchs, D., Fuchs, L. S., Benowitz, S., & Barringer, K. (1987). Norm-references tests: Are they vaid for use with handicapped students. *Exceptional Children, 54*(3), 263–291.

Fuchs, D., Fuchs, L. S., Dailey, A. M., & Power, M. H. (1985). The effect of examiners' personal familiarity and professional experience on handicapped children's test performance. *Journal of Educational Research, 78*, 141–146.

Gallas, H. B. & Siegel, I. E. (1979). Cognitive-developmenal assessment in children: Application of a cybernetic model. In M. N. Ozer (Ed.), *A cybernetic approach to the assessment of children: Toward a more humane use of human beings.* Boulder, CO: Westview Press.

Garcia, S. (1985, Fall). Characteristics of limited English proficient Hispanic students served in programs for the learning disabled: Implications for policy, practice, and research (Part 1). *Bilingual Special Education Newsletter*, pp. 1–5.

Gersten, R., Carnine, D., & Woodward, J. (1987). Direct instruction research: The third decade. *Remedial and Special Education, 8*(6), 48–56.

Gleason, J. J. (1991, Fall). Multicultural and exceptional student education: Separate but equal? *Preventing School Failure, 36*(1), 47–49.

Gollnick, D. M., & Chinn, P. C. (1990). *Multicultural education in a pluralistic society.* Columbus, OH: Merrill.

Gottlieb, J. (1981). Mainstreaming: Fulfilling the promise? *American Journal of Mental Deficiency, 86*, 115–126.

Gottlieb, J., Agard, J. A., Kaufman, M. J., & Semmel, M. I. (1976). Retarded children mainstreamed: A study of practices as they affect minority group children. In R. L. Jones (Ed.), *Mainstreaming and the minority child.* Minneapolis: University of Minnesota Leadership Training Institute/Special Education, pp. 195–214.

Greenwood, C. R. (1991). Classwide peer tutoring: Longitudinal effects on the reading, language, and mathematics achievement of at-risk students. *Reading, Writing, and Learning Disabilities, 7*, 105–123.

Greenwood, C. R. (1991). Longitudinal analysis of time, engagement, and achievement in at-risk versus non-risk students. *Exceptional Children, 57*(6), 521–535.

Greenwood, C. R., Carta, J. J., & Kamps, D. (1990). Teacher-mediated versus peer-mediated instruction: A review of advantages and disadvantages. In H. C. Foot, M. J. Morgan, & R. H. Shute (Eds.), *Children helping children* (pp. 177–206). New York: John Wiley.

Greenwood, C. R., Carta, J. J., & Hall, R. V. (1988). The use of peer tutoring strategies in classroom management and educational instruction. *School Psychology Review, 17*, 258–275.

Greenwood, C. R., Delquadri, J., & Hall, R. V. (1991). The longitudinal effects of classwide peer tutoring. *Journal of Educational Psychology, 81*, 371–383.

Greenwood, C. R., Delquadri, J. C., Stanley, S., Sasso, G., Whorton, D., & Schulte, D. (1981, Summer). Allocating opportunity to learn as a basis for academic remediation: A developing model for teaching. *Monograph in Behavioral Disorders*, pp. 22–32.

Greenwwod, C. R., Dinwiddie, G., Terry, B., Wade, L., Stanley, S. O., Thibadeau, S., & Delquadri, J. (1984). Teacher versus peer-mediated instruction: An ecobehavioral analysis of achievement outcomes. *Journal of Applied Behavior Analysis, 17*, 521–538.

Grossman, H. J. (1983). *Classification in mental retardation*. Washington, DC: American Association on Mental Retardation.

Guadalupe Organization v. *Tempe Elementary School District No. 3*, No. 71–435 (D. Ariz., January 24, 1972) (consent decree).

Harry, B. (1992). *Cultural diversity, families, and the special education system: Communication and empowerment*. New York: Teachers College, Columbia University.

Harth, R. (1988). The Feuerstein perspective on the modification of cognitive performance. In E. L. Meyen, G. A. Vergason, & R. J. Whelan (Eds.), *Effective instructional strategies for exceptional children* (pp. 118–138). Denver, CO: Love.

Haywood, H. C., Brown, A. L., & Wingenfeld, S. (1990). Dynamic approaches to psychoeducational assessment. *School Psychology Review, 19*(4), 411–422.

Haywood, H. C. (1988). Dynamic assessment: The Learning Potential Assessment Device: In R. Jones (Ed.), *Psychoeducational assessment of minority group children: A casebook* (pp. 39–63). Berkeley, CA: Cobb & Henry.

Haywood, H. C. (1982). Compensatory education. *Peabody Journal of Education*, 272–300.

Haywood, H. C. (1987). A mediational teaching style. *The Thinking Teacher: Cognitive Education for Young Children, 4*(1), 3–5.

Haywood, H. C., & Bransford, J. D. (1984, March). Dynamic assessment: Issues, research, and applications. Introductory paper for a *Symposium on Dynamic Assessment given at the XVII Gatlinburg Conference on Research in Mental Retardation*, Gatlinburg, TN.

Haywood, H. C. & Switzky, H. N. (in press). Ability and modifiability: What, how, and how much? In J. S. Carlson (Ed.), *Cognition and Educational Practice: An International Perspective*. Greenwich, CT: JAI Press.

Haywood, H. C. & Switzky, H. N. (1986). The malleability of intelligence: Cognitive processes as a function of polygenic-experiential interaction. *School Psychology Review, 15*, 245–255.

Haywood, H. C. (1977). Alternatives to normative assessment. In P. Mittler (Ed.), *Research to practice in mental retardation: Education and training* (Vol. 2) (pp. 11–18). IASSMD.

Heflinger, C. A., Cook, V., & Thackrey, M. (1987). Identification of mental retardation by the System of Multicultural Pluralistic Assessment: Nondiscriminatory or non-existent. *Journal of School Psychology, 25*, 121–1–121–7.

Heller, K., Holtzman, W., & Messick, S. (1982). *Placing children in special education: A strategy for equity. Report of the National Research Council Panel on the Election and Placement of Students in Programs for the Mentally Retarded*. Washington, DC: National Academy Press.

Heron, T. E., & Harris, K. C. (1987). *The educational consultant: Helping professionals, parents, and mainstreamed students*. Austin, TX: Pro-Ed.

Heward, W. L. & Orlansky, M. D. (1992). *Exceptional Children* (4th ed.). Columbus, OH: Merrill.

Johnson, D. W., & Johnson, R. T. (1986). Mainstreaming and cooperative learning strategies [Special Issue]. *Exceptional Children, 52*(6), 553–561.

Jones, R. L. (1988). *Psychoeducational assessment of minority group children*. Berkeley, CA: Cobb & Henry.

Larrivee, B. (1989). Effective strategies for academically handicapped students in the regular classroom. In R. E. Slavin, N. L. Karweit, & N. A. Madden (Eds.), *Effective programs for students at risk*. Boston, MA: Allyn and Bacon.

Larry P. v. Wilson Riles (1979). 495 F. Supp. 926 (N.D. Cal. 1979) No. 80.4027. (9th Cir., Jan., 1980).

Larry P. v. Wilson Riles (1984). United States Court of Appeals, Ninth Circuit, No. 80–427. January 23, 1984. Trial Court Decision Affirmed.

Lynch, E. W., & Stein, R. (1982). Parent participation by ethnicity: A comparison of Hispanic, Black, and Anglo families. *Exceptional Children, 54*(2), 105–111.

MacMillan, D. L. (1988). New EMR's. In G. A. Polloway & L. R. Sargent (Eds.), *Best practices in mental disabilities* (pp. 3–24). Des Moines: Iowa Dept. of Education.

MacMillan, D. L., Hendrick, I. G., & Watkins, A. V. (1988). Impact of Diana, Larry P., and P.L. 94–142 on Minority Students. *Exceptional Children, 54*(5), 426–432.

MacMillan, D. L., & Borthwick, S. (1980). The new educable mentally retarded population. Can they be mainstreamed? *Mental Retardation, 18*, 155–158.

Maheady, L., & Harper, G. F. (1987). A classwide peer tutoring system to improve the spelling performance of low-income third- and fourth-grade students. *Education and Treatment of Children, 10*, 120–133.

Marion, R. L. (1980). Communicating with parents of culturally diverse exceptional children. *Exceptional Children, 46*(8), 616–623.

Marshall et al. v. Georgia (1984). U.S. District Court for the Southern District of Georgia, CV 482–233, June 28, 1984.

Met, M. (1987). Parent involvement in foreign language learning. *ERIC/CLL News Bulletin, 11*, 2–3, 7–8.

Mercer, J. R. (1983). *Labeling the mentally retarded*. Berkeley: University of California Press.

Mercer, J. R. (1982). I.Q.: The lethal label. *Psychology Today, 95*, 44–47.

Meyen, E. L., & Lehr, D. H. (1980). Evolving practices in assessment and intervention for mildly handicapped adolescents. The case for intensive instruction. *Exceptional Education Quarterly, 1*(2), 19–26.

Morgan, D. P. (1982). Parent participation in the IEP Process: Does it enhance appropriate education? *Exceptional Education Quarterly, 3*, 33–40.

Nazarro, J. N. (1981). Special problems of exceptional minority children. In J. N. Nazzaro (Ed.), *Culturally diverse exceptional children in school*. Virginia: ERIC, 1–12.

Nazarro, J. N. (1981). Special problems of exceptional minority children. In J. N. Nazzaro (Ed.), *Culturally diverse exceptional children in school*. Virginia: ERIC, 13–52.

Office of Civil Rights. (1978). *Elementary and secondary civil rights survey. Sample selection*. Washington, DC: U.S. Department of Health, Education, and Welfare.

Ortiz, A., & Maldonado-Colon, E. (1986). Recognizing learning disabilities in bilingual children: How to lessen inappropriate referral of language minority students to special education. *Journal of Reading, Writing, and Learning Disabilities International, 43*(1), 47–56.

Parker, W. (1988, October). Keynote speech at the 35th Annual Conference of the Southeastern Regional Association of Teacher Educators, Lexington, KY.

PASE (Parents in Action on Special Education) v. Joseph P. Hannon (1980). U.S. District Court, Northern District of Illinois, Eastern Division, No. 74 (3586), July, 1980.

Patrick, J. L., & Reschly, D. J. (1982). Relationship of state educational criteria and demographic variables to school-system prevalence of mental retardation. *American Journal of Mental Deficiency, 86*(4), 351–360.

Polloway, E. A., Epstein, M. H., Patton, J. R., Culliham, D., & Luebke, J. (1986). Demographic, social, and behavioral characteristics of students with educable mental retardation. *Education and Training of the Mentally Retarded, 2*, 27–34.

Polloway, E. A., Epstein, M. H., Polloway, C. H., Patton, J. R., & Ball, D. W. (1986). Corrective reading program: An analysis of effectiveness with learning disabled and mentally retarded students. *Remedial and Special Education, 7*(4), 41–47.

Polloway, E. A., Patton, J. R., Smith, J. D., & Roderique, S. (1991). Issues in design for elementary students with mild mental retardation: Emphasis on curriculum development. *Education and Training in Mental Retardation, 58,* 142–149.

Polloway, E. A., & Smith, J. D. (1983). Changes in mild mental retardation: Population programs and perspectives. *Exceptional Children, 50,* 149–159.

Poplin, M. S. & Wright, P. (1983, Fall). The concept of cultural pluralism: Issues in special education. *Learning Disability Quarterly, 6*(4), 367–371.

Ramsey, P. G. (1987). *Teaching and learning in a diverse world: Multicultural education of young children*: New York: Teachers College Press.

Reid, E. R. (1986). Practicing effective instruction: The Exemplary Center for Reading Instruction Approach [Special Issue]. *Exceptional Children, 52*(6), 510–519.

Reschly, D. J. (1988). Minority mild mental retardation overrepresentation: Legal issues, research findings, and reform trends. In M. C. Wang, M. C. Reynolds, & H. J. Walberg (Eds.), *Handbook of Special Education: Research and practice: (Vol. 2) Mildly handicapped conditions* (pp. 23–43). New York: Pergamon Press.

Reschly, D. J. (1982). Assessing mild mental retardation: The influence of adaptive behavior, sociocultural status, and prospects for non-biased assessment. In C. R. Reynolds & T. B. Gutkin (Eds.), *The handbook for school psychology* (pp. 209–242). New York: John Wiley.

Reynolds, C. R. (1987). Race bias in testing. In R. J. Corsini (Ed.), *Concise encyclopedia of psychology* (pp. 953–954). New York: John Wiley.

Sainato, D. M., Strain, P. S., & Lyon, S. R. (1987). Increasing academic responding of handicapped preschool children during group instruction. *Journal of the Division of Early Childhood, 12*(1), 23–30.

Shinn, M. R., & Tindal, G. A. (1922). Using student performance data in academics: A pragmatic and defensible approach to nondiscriminatory assessment. In R. L. Jones (Ed.), *Psychoeducational assessment of minority group children: A casebook* (pp. 383–407). Berkeley, CA: Cobb & Henry.

Simich-Dudgeon, C. (1987). Involving limited-English proficient parents as tutors in their children's education. *ERIC/CLL News Bulletin, 10,* 3–4, 7.

Slavin, R. E. (1987). Ability grouping and student achievement in elementary schools. A best-evidence synthesis. *Review of Educational Research, 51*(3), 293–336.

Sleeter, C., & Grant, C. A. (1988). *Making choices for multicultural education: Five approaches to race, class, and gender.* Columbus, OH: Merrill.

Stanley, S. O., Greenwood, C. R. (1983). Assessing opportunity to respond in classroom environments through direct observation: How much opportunity to respond does the minority, disadvantaged student receive in school? *Exceptional Children, 49,* 370–373.

Strain, P., & Odom, S. (1986). Peer social imitations: Effective interventions for social skills development of exceptional children [Special Issue]. *Exceptional Children, 52*(6), 543–552.

Swedo, J. (1987, Fall). Effective teaching strategies for handicapped limited English proficient students. *Bilingual Special Education Newsletter,* pp. 1–5.

The Executive Committee of The Council for Children with Behavioral Disorders. (1989). Best assessment practices for students with behavioral disorders: Accommodation to cultural diversity and individual differences. *Behavioral Disorders, 14*(4), 263–278.

Tinney, J. S. (1983). Interconnections. *Interracial Books for Children, 14*(3 & 4), 4–6+.

Turnbull, A. P., & Turnbull, H. R. (1990). *Families, professionals, and exceptionality: A special partnership* (2nd ed.). Columbus, OH: Merrill.

Twelfth Annual Report to Congress on the Implementation of the Education of the Handicapped Act. (1990). Washington, DC: U.S. Department of Education.

Utley, C. A., Haywood, H. C., & Masters, J. C. (1991). Policy implications of psychological assessment. In H. C. Haywood & D. Tzuriel (Eds.), *Interactive assessment.* New York: Springer-Verlag.

Utley, C. A., Lowitzer, A. C., & Baumeister, A. A. (1987). A comparison of the AAMD's definition, eligibility criteria, and classification schemes with state departments of education guidelines. *Education and Treatment in Mental Retardation, 22,* 35–43.

Utley, C. A., Haywood, H. C., & Masters, J. C. (1991). Policy implications of psychological assessment. In H. C. Haywood & D. Tzuriel (Eds.), *Interactive Assessment*. New York: Springer-Verlag.

Valero-Figueira, E. (1988). Hispanic children. *Teaching Exceptional Children, 20*(4), 47–49.

Vygotsky, L. S. (1978). *Mind in society: The development of higher psychological processes*. Cambridge, MA: Harvard University Press.

Watkins, A. V. (1989). The culturally diverse student population. In J. Wood (Ed.), *Mainstreaming: A practical approach for teachers*. Columbus, OH: Merrill.

White, O. R. (1986). Precision teaching—Precision learning [Special Issue]. *Exceptional Children, 52*(6), 522–534.

Wright, P., & Santa Cruz, R. (1983). Ethnic composition of special education programs in California. *Learning Disability Quarterly, 6*(4), 387–394.

Ysseldyke, J. E. (1987). Classification of handicapped children. In M. C. Wang, M. C. Reynolds, & H. J. Walberg (Eds.), *Handbook of special education research and practice: Learner characteristics and adaptive education* (Vol. 1.)(pp. 253–271). New York: Pergamon Press.

Acknowledgments

The research reported in this chapter was supported by the Post-Doctoral Program in Research Concerning Effective Instructional Practices for Minority Group Students with Handicaps at the Juniper Gardens Children's Project, Office of Special Education and Rehabilitative Services, Grant #H029D00085. However, the opinions expressed do not necessarily reflect the policy of the U.S. Department of Education. I gratefully acknowledge the assistance of Charles R. Greenwood and Barbara J. Terry for their review of the manuscript. I would also like to acknowledge Bernadine Roberts for her graphic talents in the preparation of the manuscript.

About the Author

Cheryln A. Utley is an assistant scientist at the Juniper Gardens Children's Project (JGCP), Schiefelbusch Institute for Life Span Studies at the University of Kansas, Lawrence, Kansas. She received her doctorate in behavioral disabilities with a minor in curriculum and instruction from the University of Wisconsin-Madison. Prior to joining the faculty at the JGCP, she worked as a research assistant professor, Department of Special Education and Research Associate, John F. Kennedy Center on Mental Retardation, George Peabody College of Vanderbilt University, Nashville, Tennessee. Her research interests include classification issues in mental retardation, attentional modifiability of students with mild mental retardation, and the use of dynamic assessment procedures as an alternative to standardized psychological assessment instruments. She also taught undergraduate and graduate courses on exceptional children and psychological measurement. Currently, Utley is project director of a research program that examines students with and without mild mental retardation. She also directs a special project that is focused on the in-service training of regular and special education teachers who educate multicultural students with mild disabilities in integrated classroom settings.

Part IV

Diversity in Schools:
Applying What We Know

Challenging Customs, Canons, and Content

Developing Relevant Curriculum for Diversity

GLORIA LADSON-BILLINGS

Introduction

In my former university teaching job, I taught a course to preservice teachers entitled Curriculum Foundations and Methods. One of the culminating activities in that class involved asking the students to imagine that they were invited to a very upscale cocktail party in which the other guests were doctors, lawyers, accountants, computer specialists, and other high-powered and highly paid professionals. I then ask them to imagine that they have arrived late to the party and when asked why they were late they replied, "Oh, I had to finish my project for my curriculum class." The questioner stands dumbfounded for a second or two and then asks, "What *is* curriculum?" My students are asked to frame an answer to this question that is coherent for this audience.

With a full quarter of instruction behind them, I found that many of them still struggled with being able to articulate just what is meant by curriculum. They were capable of reciting educational jargon and explanations but were at a loss when the task required them to explain curriculum to laymen. Given the ambiguity and confusion surrounding much of educational thought, it is not surprising that the students did not have a simple and plain vocabulary with which to explain this term. In this chapter, I will attempt to discuss a variety of curriculum conceptions, offer a useful definition of *curriculum* for this discussion, outline the national curriculum debate, and suggest some relevant curricula for diversity.

ake a look at ways in which the curriculum can be conceptualized. Elliot
eth Vallance (1974) suggested that there are at least five conceptions of
m which teachers, administrators, and educational policymakers have to
e conceptions include an academic rationalist position, a cognitive
, a self-actualization position, a social adaptation/social reconstructionist
riculum as technology position.

cademic rationalist position suggests that the point of schooling is to
prepare students to be conversant with the thinking of the "great" minds of history as
presented in the "great" books. This position presumes that there is a codified body of
worthwhile knowledge and knowledgeable authorities select from this body of knowledge
to construct the curriculum. Thus, this position has no room for subjects such as driver's
education or vocational training. For example, reading of Shakespeare or Dickens along
with maintaining courses in Latin or Greek are unquestionably part of the curriculum
using the academic rationalist approach. This position is best actualized in the work of E.
D. Hirsch and others with their notion of a core curriculum.

The *cognitive processes* position suggests that the curriculum should provide students
with appropriate skills that they may apply to a variety of content areas and real-life
circumstances. Thus, teaching students reasoning or critical thinking skills is what constitutes the curriculum. Here, the content is not nearly as important as the process. For
example, one might teach a student how to measure, conduct an interview, or solve a
problem, with an emphasis on reinforcing these skills for later life application.

The *self-actualization* position reflects the curriculum orientation of the Progressives
of the 1920s such as John Dewey. This position believes that the curriculum should help
all students develop to their fullest potential. Thus, the focus is both on the individual and
the here and now, not just a notion of schooling as preparation for some future time.
Schools and classrooms that allow students to exercise a range of choice regarding what to
study and work on may represent this position. Certainly, the notion of the "open
classroom" of the late 1960s reflects this position.

The *social adaptation/social reconstruction* position represents opposite sides of the
same coin. Both positions reflect the curriculum's concern with the larger society, but the
approaches are oppositional. In the social adaptation position, the curriculum is designed
to help students adapt to society and, consequently, represents maintaining of the status
quo. The social adaptation approach may emphasize "good citizenship" via role models,
obedience and allegiance to the existing social order, and vocational training that permits
students to fit into existing employment slots. The social reconstruction position suggests
that the curriculum should equip students to change society. Often it is implemented
through a problems approach or alternative school.

Finally, the *curriculum as technology* position suggests that the curriculum should be
prespecified, well ordered, and packaged. The students are assessed, placed at a particular
level, and move through the content at their own pace and can have control over the rate
and reinforcement of the learning. This curriculum can be both commercially or teacher
produced as long as it is undertaken in a step-by-step manner with little student-to-student
interaction. Examples of this approach are found in vocational training modules and
commercial programs of programmed instruction like the popular Science Research
Associates (SRA) reading labs.

Each of these curriculum approaches can be found to varying degrees in many of this nation's schools. Some disciplines, by virtue of their structure, seem more comfortable employing one of these approaches rather than others. At the same time, elementary teachers, because of their need to teach a variety of subject areas, may use each of these approaches to some extent depending on what they are teaching and who they are teaching.

I would like to propose here a broader vision of the curriculum—one that extends beyond the classroom, throughout the school, and into the larger community. For the purposes of this discussion, I will suggest that the curriculum encompasses *everything* that students experience under the aegis of the school. This means that despite the fact that two schools may have identical advertised curricula and course guides, the school climate, extracurricular activities, staffing patterns, tracking, parent support and involvement, student population, and so on may render the curriculum in School A different from that of School B. Perhaps the following scenario will illustrate this more clearly:

City High School and Lawnview High are in the same state. They are subject to the same state curriculum guidelines. City High School serves a multiethnic, linguistically diverse student population in the heart of a large urban area. Lawnview's students are predominantly White and reside in the suburbs. City's principal is an African-American female and her staff is a mixture of White, African-American, Latino, and Asian teachers. Lawnview has a White male principal, one African-American male teacher, a physical education teacher who coaches basketball, and one Asian teacher who teaches mathematics. The only other people of color on the Lawnview staff are custodians and cafeteria workers.

Lawnview students can select the courses that appeal to them. Every classroom has a chart on one of the bulletin boards that lists the requirements for getting into the various state universities and colleges. Lawnview sends a large proportion of its graduates to the state's most prestigious university. City High students are more often routed to specific courses of study. Thus, the most academically challenging courses are populated by Asian students and the few Whites who attend the school.

Lawnview students can choose from a wide range of extracurricular activities, including major team interscholastic sports, interscholastic individual sports like golf and tennis, intramural sports, band, spirit team, and clubs. At City High, students are restricted to the major interscholastic team sports, band, and a few clubs. The senior class trip at Lawnview is to Hawaii. City High does not offer its seniors a class trip.

Discipline policies at the two schools are different also. At City High, when students are late to class they are required to report to the office and secure an "admit" slip so they can inform the teacher that they are late. Three tardy's means detention. Failure to report to detention can mean suspension. Every student receives a copy of the discipline code each school year. At Lawnview, students are urged to be "good school citizens" and are reminded of a few school rules at a welcome back to school assembly. There is no tardy policy at Lawnview. Tardy students assume responsibility for speaking to the teacher about the reasons for their lateness. Lawnview has no schoolwide detention policy.

A large number of students from Lawnview attend the state's most prestigious colleges and universities as well as high-status colleges throughout the nation. Those City High students that attend college typically take advantage of the state's junior colleges and smaller, less expensive state colleges. A few attend historically Black colleges and universities in the South.

I developed this scenario based on years of teaching in a large urban school district and supervising student teachers in both urban and suburban schools. Despite overt similarities regarding curriculum guides, courses, or standards, students at different high schools can and do experience the "curriculum" differently. When we envision the curriculum in its broadest sense, we must ask deeper more fundamental questions about the opportunities for equitable school experiences for all of our children. While it may be true that few City High students may be interested in learning golf or tennis, some of this comes from the lack of opportunity to even experience these sports, even on a club or intramural level. At the same time, Lawnview, with all of its "advantages," provides a "curriculum" that distorts and "disadvantages" its students' perspectives regarding the full spectrum of experiences and life in the United States. How will the predominantly White staffing impact these students' views of possibilities for others? Will they be prepared to work and grow in college classrooms and on the job with professors and supervisors of color? Will they be immune and disinterested to issues of racism, sexism, class difference, and disability? Will the "curriculum" they experienced at Lawnview prepare them for a demographically shifting society in which important issues surrounding equity and fairness will need to be decided?

Having taught a large number of "Lawnview graduates," I am concerned about the "miseducation" of these students as well as the "undereducation" of the "City High graduates." Because of the rapidly changing demographics of this nation, the miseducation and undereducation have consequences for all students. Some of the female Lawnview graduates will reflect the majority of the nation's public school teachers for the foreseeable future (Haberman, 1989; Grant, 1989). In college preparation courses, these students are more likely to be ignorant of and resistant to substantive information about difference and what they can do to initiate change (Ahlquist, 1990; King, 1990; King & Ladson-Billings, 1990; Ladson-Billings, 1990). At the same time, City High graduates who fail to enter college will find themselves ill equipped to cope with a rapidly changing economic structure that has no place for them in the work force. Not only will the typical stereotypes and structures stay in place but they will be reinforced with dire consequences for a nation that has a vision of itself as both equitable and excellent. A vision of the curriculum that narrowly defines itself as academic course content is both dangerous and foolhardy. In the next section, we will examine what this view has precipitated in the form of national debate and policy.

Canon Wars and Skirmishes

During the 1989 and 1990 academic years, debate took place at Stanford University over a proposal to change a traditional freshman course offering entitled Western Civilization. This course represented what I have described previously as the academic rationalist position. It was a course taught by history, English, and humanities professors designed to examine the "great ideas" promulgated by the "great thinkers" who laid the foundation of Western civilization. As the campus moved toward recruiting and retaining the "best and brightest" from diverse racial, ethnic, and cultural backgrounds, there came a demand for a reexamination of the Western Civilization course. Some students and faculty members believed to more accurately reflect the foundations of Western civilization, books and ideas other than those of European males would need to be considered. Lively and spirited debate resulted on campus from this demand for reexamination—the kind of debate one might hope is supported and encouraged in the academy. But, once a decision was made to make some "minor"[1] changes in the reading lists and the course title, both the media and several national leaders entered the debate.

One of the national leaders that figured prominently in the debate was the former Secretary of Education turned Drug Czar, William Bennett. Most interesting about Bennett's appearance at Stanford in defense of the "sacred canon" was the obvious contradiction in his stance. Previously, Bennett had underscored the need for the federal government to take a hands-off approach to the curricular decisions of local schools but he departed from this stance at a private university filled with eminent scholars declaring that he knew what was the best curriculum for Stanford.

Bennett's defense of the canon was bolstered by the earlier publications of conservative scholars Bloom (1987), Hirsch (1987), and Ravitch and Finn (1987). Each of these scholars and others have argued that every American must be indoctrinated into a high culture that is based on a view of Western civilization that locates all knowledge in classical Greece and Rome with some input from the Hebrews.

When scholars who take a different position—one that looks at a longer continuum of Western tradition and asserts that both Africa and Asia have contributed to the European scholarship and thus are joint heirs to the western tradition (Asante, 1987; Bernal, 1987)—they are castigated and accused of sloppy scholarship. And while most conservative scholars will acknowledge the influence of Egypt on the West, there is a subtle pattern of distortion that lifts Egypt out of Africa and reconstructs the racial composition of Egyptian society. Another component of this elevation of the West is the denigration of courses that examine, explore, and celebrate other traditions—African American, Latino, Asian. In addition to representing this conservative agenda, some of these scholars have become self-proclaimed advocates of a new version of multiculturalism (see Ravitch, 1990; Glazer, 1991) that has no connection with the ongoing scholarships of multiculturalism (see Banks, 1981; Sleeter & Grant, 1987; Gay, 1983).

The debate over college and university course offerings has spread to the precollegiate level. In states such as California, Texas, and Florida, there have been vigorous debates over the inclusion (and infusion) of multicultural perspectives in the curriculum and textbooks (Waugh, 1991). These debates center as much on the quality of inclusion as they do on the quantity. One feature of the debates is the pitting of people of color (and others representing multicultural interests) against an alleged "national agenda" that fails to recognize the importance of cultural diversity (Cuban, 1990).

The national goals set forth by President Bush and the Department of Education[2] are both lofty and admirable; however, they fail to address the need for multiple curricular perspectives in a multicultural nation. The assumption that children can be homogenized

into a monolithic whole and spoonfed a "national curriculum" is both naive and dangerous. The need for a curriculum reflecting multiple and multicultural perspectives is
necessary because of our changing demographics and our growing global interdependence. Students from diverse ethnic, cultural, and linguistic groups must have an opportunity to see themselves and their heritages represented in the curriculum if they are to
ultimately see themselves as Americans. At the same time, White students will find
themselves in work and living environments that are increasingly diverse. They will need
perspectives and skills that prepare them to successfully encounter diversity.

The Search for Relevant Multicultural Curriculum

One attempt at developing more multicultural curriculum has been a search for
"centeredness." Centeredness represents an attempt to place children, regardless of their
culture and/or ethnicity, in the center of the curriculum. This means that the curriculum
must make students from diverse ethnic groups the subject rather than the object of study
(see Asante, 1990). One specific attempt at a centered curriculum has been an approach
known as "Afrocentrism" (Asante, 1987), which has become the object of much of the
conservative venom.

In charges and countercharges (Asante, 1991; Ravitch, 1991; Adler et al., 1991),
proponents and opponents of Afrocentrism have made multiculturalism the site of struggle.
For proponents of Afrocentrism, their philosophy is a necessary prerequisite to
multiculturalism; for opponents, it is racist and divisive. For some multicultural educators, this argument places them in the middle of an unpleasant philosophical and political
battle. The inclusive nature of multiculturalism does allow for consideration of Afrocentrism
as a philosophical and curriculum strategy in much the same way Black, Latino, Asian,
Native American, Feminist Studies, and bilingual education have come under the umbrella
of multicultural education.

In the early years of both ethnic and multicultural studies, many of the attempts at
curriculum change at the precollegiate level resulted in superficial add-ons and trivialization
(McCarthy, 1988) and produced an assimilationist curriculum that provided students with
no opportunity to participate in social action and consider real change. Growing frustrations with this "food, fun, and festivals" approach caused many teachers to drop multicultural
education as a curriculum reform sometimes in favor of self-esteem programs or back to
business as usual.

The current conservative agenda has produced a cultural literacy curriculum designed
to foster an academic rationalist approach in the early elementary grades (Meyer, 1991).
This curriculum claims to identify what every youngster should know at each grade level.
Examples of what first-graders should know include the following:

1. *What kind of matter—solid, liquid or gas—are these things: tree, sidewalk,
   grass, rain?*
2. *Which were built for the pharaohs in Egypt: castles, mosques, pyramids?*
3. *What does it mean when people say we should live by the Golden Rule?*
4. *What happened to the tea at the Boston Tea Party and why did it happen?*

5. *What war began with the "shot heard round the world"? (Meyer, 1991, p. 36)*

It is possible to argue that Hirsch's "core curriculum" includes multicultural content. It is not possible to assert that this curriculum addresses multicultural education's highest aims—connecting children's lives and experiences to the curriculum in meaningful ways, empowering and encouraging social action, and working for social change.

One of the things that makes developing a multicultural curriculum so difficult is the fact that multicultural education is as much an ideal as it is a reality (Banks & Banks, 1989). Like democracy, it is never finished. However, this more esoteric nature of multicultural education does not absolve educators from the responsibility of working toward developing relevant and multicultural curriculum. In a subsequent section, I will provide examples that illustrate how the curriculum can be conceived as more relevant and multicultural.

Both of these issues—relevance and multiculturalism—are important in curriculum development for educating students in a democratic and diverse society. The multicultural aspect is evident because of the national commitment to equality, justice, and freedom. However far off these ideals may appear, the concept of equity—fairness and impartiality—must operate in the here and now. The multicultural aspect is necessary also because of the need to have accurate information upon which to make critical decisions. Thus, if you understand the dynamics of the Chinese Exclusion Act of 1882 and the fact that many Chinese men had immigrated to the United States without their wives, you have some basis for understanding the high rate of elderly bachelors that resided in the San Francisco Bay area and the rise of Chinese associations that provided food, friendship, and family for these men. Monocultural information is inaccurate and incomplete. It perpetuates myths and stereotypes that are detrimental to a democracy.

The issue of relevance is important also. This concept seems to have fallen out of favor in the educational literature after the curriculum (and cultural) revolution of the late 1960s. Many educators assumed that *relevance* was a buzzword for lack of substance, intellectual shallowness, and gripe sessions for people of color. However, in this context, the term *relevance* refers to the ability of the curriculum to make deep and meaningful connections with the lives of the students. The need for these connections are related to the likelihood that deep and meaningful connections will mean that students really *learn* something in school rather than memorize endless bits and pieces of information for testing purposes but later forget them and can in no way apply them to their real lives. Critical theorists assert that "critical pedagogy always strives to incorporate student experiences as 'official' curriculum" (Giroux & Simon, 1989, p. 250). This means that relevance is addressed in all curriculum decisions. The success of many White middle-class youngsters is imbedded in the fact that the status quo curriculum in some ways makes sense and is relevant to them. However, more recently, even these students have recognized that their schooling experience has lacked vital information about those they have come to know as "others" (Ramirez, 1990). The following vignettes are based on research articles and papers that illustrate ways in which the curriculum can become more multicultural and relevant.

Social Action in the Barrio

A group of Latino high school students attend an alternative school in their community. Most of the students have been unsuccessful in the traditional school. The science teacher has alerted the students to the fact that there might be a toxic waste dump in their community. The students engage in reconnaissance to discover whether or not the teacher's report is true. After several visits where the students take photographs and notes, the dump site operators erect a fence to keep the students out and block their line of vision. The students present their "evidence" to the borough leadership and level a charge of "environmental racism" at the dump site operators. The students call themselves the "Toxic Avengers." Their teacher is not certified but he is a geologist and has the scientific knowledge that aids the students in their research efforts. Over the course of the project the students engage in writing, scientific research, and social action. They are engaged in their own schooling in a new way. (Torres-Guzman, 1989)

This first example of making the curriculum more relevant and multicultural tackles an area of the curriculum—science—that some would argue is beyond the scope of multicultural education. However, the teacher (who happens to be a scientist) has helped the students to understand that interest in the environment cannot be left to professionals and politicians; it must be critically examined in their own contexts. The students' use of a central multicultural concept—racism—in a new way, linked with the environment, is useful in helping to explore the broad dimensions of racism. Rather than concluding that racism is practiced merely in individual acts of prejudice and discrimination, the students are developing a broader picture of how the presence of racism in a society does more than victimize people of color—it also privileges others. This broader meaning may help students understand why racism is so difficult to eliminate. Although the historical information about racism is important, this tangible, close-to-the-community example provides a fertile site of critical analysis and investigation. Surely, the dump site operator can counter with charges of economic viability, zoning regulations, and his freedom to operate a business, but these too can serve to provide students with a better understanding of how economics, politics, and special interests are tied to the interests of particular groups and society in general.

Second, in addition to applying multicultural concepts to a curriculum area, this example illustrates the use of curriculum relevance. The dump site is located in the students' community. Any contamination or health risks present may have consequences for them and their families. The gathering of data, documenting the problem, analyzing their findings and drawing conclusions is not merely an exercise in the use of the "Scientific Method." The students are acquiring these skills in a meaningful context. They are learning the value of the skills and developing a conceptual framework for using them again in other contexts.

Island Dreams

The classroom seems similar to most U.S. elementary classrooms. A group of four students are seated at a table with their teacher preparing to read a story from a basal reading text.... As we look closely at the group there are some obvious differences from an elementary classroom in "middle America." The teacher is Hawaiian. The students are also Hawaiian and native speakers of the local dialect. In general, the students are poor.... They are in Hawaii, the land of island dreams, but they are living the urban nightmare. What seems to spare them the pain of academic failure is the teacher's use of their linguistic style to make connections between the knowledge they bring with them and school knowledge. As the teacher begins the lesson she encourages the children to share their own experiences. To someone unfamiliar with Hawaiian talk story the lesson may seem somewhat chaotic. Students are speaking out of turn, they are completing each other's sentences, and talking at the same time as other speakers. The teacher appears very comfortable with the thrust of the conversation and does not reprimand students for this conversational style. There are instances when the teacher has the floor and requires the attention of the entire group but during the discussion phase of the lesson, the students are free to engage in a talk story like format. To the surprise of doubters, the seemingly chaotic reading environment produces literate students with improved standardized test scores. (Au, 1980)

This example demonstrates that even in a more conventional setting, such as a reading lesson, there are possibilities for developing a multicultural and relevant approach to teaching. Although the teacher in this example is using a basal, she has capitalized on the diverse linguistic competence of the students to make the lesson more multicultural. She shows that she *values* what they bring with them by incorporating it into the reading lesson, not as an occasional activity but as a primary interactional strategy.

The teacher also makes reading relevant to the students by helping them understand that the way in which they communicate and use language is pivotal to their acquisition of greater literacy skills. Rather than impose a different linguistic style on the students, they are learning how their linguistic style "translates" to that of the basal. However, they are free to discuss the content of the basal in their own linguistic style. They are learning to make the basal more meaningful through their use of language.

Boyz N the Hood

Ann Lewis's[3] sixth grade class in a low income district in Northern California looks much like other low income urban California classrooms. The student population is diverse. The predominant group is African American. The largest single group in Ann's classroom is both African American and male. A few of Ann's African American male students have been retained in previous grades and are now larger and older than the typical 6th grader. Ann is white and has been teaching in this district her entire 16 year teaching career. Ann *lives* in this community and has lived here most of her life. Because of her linguistic style, people who do not know her look with puzzlement when she is engaged in casual conversation. Ann's linguistic style uses an African-American dialect. In her classroom, there is a friendly, flexible atmosphere. Ann's class is studying international conflict and nuclear proliferation. There are no reading groups. The entire class is reading a novel about an African American 6th grader whose quest to better understand her dad, a Viet Nam war veteran, leads her to participate in a group project on Viet Nam. Ann's students keep "metacognitive journals" as they read the novel. They are viewing films dealing with nuclear war, reading about the Sadako Monument in Japan, and making origami cranes as symbols of their desire for world peace. The students are interviewing family members who have been involved in war. Three of Ann's students have first hand experience with war. One student is from Viet Nam and the two others are from Nicaragua. The classroom often has lively debates about whether or not violence is ever justified. The classroom discussions often are lead by the African American males. Despite their trendy haircuts, athletic apparel, and devotion to rap music, which might suggest to some a lack of interest in school-type endeavors. Ann's students are actively involved in the class. Many of them have cumulative records that document school problems, suspensions, and failure to conform. However, in Ann's class all are engaged. Ann has organized them into teams and whenever students are off task, Ann reminds them not to let their team down. Ann offers lots of praise for student achievement but she is not afraid to chastise them when they deserve it. Discussion in this class is high level, intellectually stimulating, boisterous, and inclusive. Students discuss how the brain functions, community history and development, Ancient Egypt, personal problems and solutions. The classroom is a festival of student to student and student to teacher interaction. It is intellectually stimulating and emotionally gratifying and the African American males are the intellectual *leaders* of the class. (Ladson-Billings, field notes)

This example provides us with an illustration of how a teacher can move beyond the preconceived notions of what "certain" students can do. In this class, the teacher has made the world of the students the site of curriculum inquiry and who better to investigate that world than the students themselves. Ann has capitalized on the knowledge that students bring with them to the classroom (an often overlooked resource in diverse classrooms) and found ways to use that knowledge to improve student performance in all areas. She made the curriculum multicultural by searching for examples of war protests throughout the world and she made it relevant by constantly tying it to the lives her students were living in a community severely impacted by drugs and crime.

Rather than be afraid of or intimidated by the African-American male students, Ann has found ways to channel their knowledge, understandings, and skills about the community and larger world into meaningful investigations for a sixth grade classroom. Ann has helped to uncover the competence that some of the students were beginning to think they never had.

Using a School to Save a Culture

Schooling for Maori youngsters in New Zealand has many of the features of minority schooling in the U.S. The Maori youngsters do less well on all standard measures than their Euro-New Zealand counterparts. The unemployment rate for Maori men is extremely high and the longer the students stay in state sponsored schools, the more divorced from their home culture they are. As an option to this situation, community based schools, called Kura Kaupapa Maori emerged. They were designed not only to rescue students but to rescue Maori culture. The continued urbanization of Maori people is responsible for a steady loss of Maori language skill. Thus, building upon a successful community based pre-school language immersion program, the community developed the Kura Kaupapa Maori (KKM). KKM is designed to reinforce the legitimacy and validity of Maori language and culture and to develop a fully bilingual, bicultural Maori citizen. These efforts represent a critique of New Zealand schools and have forced some much needed change. (Rata, 1991)

In this instance, we have an illustration of how dissatisfaction with the schooling process prompted parents and community members to develop their own, culturally specific schooling to not only ensure that their students were "educated" but to ensure that their culture did not vanish. Nothing that the school provided could guarantee employment for the students or preservation of their native culture. The parents and community members' decision to find their own way represents a strategy for developing relevant and diverse curriculum.

The curriculum was multicultural because it included both Maori knowledge and language and Pakeha (non-Maori) knowledge and language. The curriculum was relevant because it built upon what the students had learned at community preschools and how they and their parents lived their lives.

Prospects for the Future

I began this chapter with a discussion of curriculum conceptions and the way in which arguing over the curriculum has led to deep political and philosophical schisms. I later attempted to give illustrations of what I have termed a culturally relevant curriculum. The vignettes were intended to be illustrative, not prescriptive.

Two points need to be made about the nature of the illustrative vignettes. First, there is no *one* right way to teach diverse groups of students. However, each of the teachers in the examples attempted to find meaningful ways to link up the knowledge that students bring *with* them with additional knowledge that may or may not be within their experiential and/or cultural background. This is not unlike what teachers of White middle-class students do. But the experiences of White middle-class students so often parallel the experiences that schools provide, that the teachers are unaware that they are making these linkages (Gee, 1989). I am arguing that they need to be conscious of these efforts and do the same for diverse groups of students.

Second, although this chapter ostensibly is about making relevant curricula for diverse learners, the instructional connections are inescapable. Although we sometimes discuss curriculum as if it exists in a vacuum, we know that no matter how exciting and compelling the curriculum, without complementary instruction, it loses its power. The illustrative vignettes attempted to make the teachers' instructional strength apparent. They had to *do* something with the curriculum to make it come alive and engage the students. Also, they had to make decisions about how, what, and why that something had to be done at particular moments in the classroom. I believe this reflects what Shulman (1987) calls "pedagogical content knowledge." According to Shulman, this is the "blending of content and pedagogy into an understanding of how particular topics, problems, or issues are organized, represented and adapted to the diverse interests and abilities of learners, and presented for instruction" (p. 8). These teachers also demonstrated what Shulman calls the "wisdom of practice"; that is, they used their own experiences and successes to guide their instructional decisions and practice. They were not "flying by the seat of their pants." They knew what they were doing and were deliberate and decisive in the classroom.

This chapter has attempted to answer some questions about the need for relevant curriculum for our increasingly diverse student populations. What are the possibilities for the creation of widely disseminated and implemented relevant and multicultural curricula? If we attempt to answer that question based on the current sociopolitical climate, we have to say the possibilities exist but the probabilities are few. The current move to develop "standard" ways of knowing in each discipline are discouraging experimentation and creativity in the content areas. Various political forces are making those who advocate a multicultural curriculum approach seem out of step ideologically and philosophically with "American" aims of education (Schlesinger, 1991). No where in the president's "National Goals for Education" (Cuban, 1990) is there a call for a curriculum that meets the needs of our increasingly diverse student population and society.

However, there are some glimmers of hope. Classroom teachers are becoming increasingly frustrated and anxious about the kinds of curricula with which they are faced and the student response to it. There are small but significant rumblings in many urban areas, suggesting that the curriculum can be a site of struggle over issues of diversity and relevance. Urban communities are tired of schools that render their children unable to cope with the demands of a sophisticated technological society and unable to communicate and live effectively with diverse peoples. Efforts toward a more multicultural and relevant curriculum are appearing in both independent and public schools. Some are small-scale experimental programs (Hollins & Spencer, 1990; Chrichlow, Goodwin, Shakes, & Swartz, 1990); others are more systemic in approach (Comer, 1980). The verdict is still out on both. However, we know that what we have been doing with students has not helped to prepare them for the complex, diverse world they must face. In the final analysis, they, along with their parents and teachers, must not be afraid to challenge the customs, canons, and content they have inherited from a simpler, less enlightened era. They must not be afraid to participate in knowledge construction and pedagogical strategies that help answer essential questions for their lives and positions. In a time when we see the peoples all around the world rising up to take back those freedoms they never ceded to the state, we must ensure that our children, parents, and teachers feel free to take back, create and re-create that curriculum that is rightfully their own.

Endnotes

1. I refer to these as minor changes because the structure of the course remained in tact. What was changed was the expansion of the reading list to include writings from women and from men and women of color. The crux of the debate was about who (of the European males) was to be excluded in order to make room for these new "others." The name of the course was also changed from Western Civilization to Culture, Ideas, and Values (CIV).

2. The National Goals include the following: By the year 2000, (1) all children in America will start school ready to learn; (2) the high school gradua-

tion rate will increase to at least 90 percent; (3) American students will leave grades 4, 8, and 12 having demonstrated competency in challenging subject matter, including English, mathematics, science, history, and geography; and every school in America will ensure that all students learn to use their minds well, so that they may be prepared for responsible citizenship, further learning, and pro-

ductive employment in our modern economy; (4) U.S students will be first in the world in mathematics and science achievement; and (5) every adult American will be literate and will possess the skills necessary to compete in a global economy and to exercise the rights and responsibilities of citizenship.

3. The name, Ann Lewis, is a pseudonym.

References

Adler, J., Manly, H., Smith, V., Chideya, F. & Wilson, L. (1991). African dreams. *Time.* September 23, pp. 42–45.

Ahlquist, R. (1990). Position and imposition: Power relations in a multicultural foundations class. *Journal of Negro Education, 60*(2):158–169.

Asante, M. K. (1991). Multiculturalism an exchange. *The American Scholar, 60*(2):267–272.

_____. (1990). The Afrocentric idea in education. *Journal of Negro Education, 60*(2):170–180.

_____. (1987). *The Afrocentric idea.* Philadelphia, PA: Temple University Press.

Au, K. H. (1980). Participation structures in a reading lesson with Hawaiian children: Analysis of a culturally appropriate instructional event. *Anthropology and Education Quarterly, 11*(2): 91–115.

Banks, J. (1981). *Multiethnic education: Theory and practice.* 2nd ed. Boston: Allyn and Bacon.

Banks, J., & Banks, C. (Eds.). (1989). *Multicultural education: Issues and perspectives.* Boston: Allyn and Bacon.

Bernal, M. (1987). *Black Athena: The Afro-Asiatic roots of classical Greece and Rome* (vol. I). New Brunswick, NJ: Rutgers University Press.

Bloom, (1987). *The closing of the American mind.* New York: Simon & Schuster.

Chrichlow, W., Goodwin, S., Shakes, G., & Swartz, E. (1990). Multicultural ways of knowing: Implications for practice. *Journal of Education, 172* (2):101–117.

Comer, J. (1980). School power: Implications of an intervention project. New York: Free Press.

Cuban, L. (1990). Four stories about national goals for American education. *Phi Delta Kappan, 72*(4): 264–271.

Eisner, E., & Vallance, E. (Eds.). (1974). *Conflicting conceptions of the curriculum.* Berkeley, CA: McCutcheon.

Gay, G. (1983). Retrospects and prospects of multicultural education. *Momentum, 14*:4–8.

Gee, J. (1989). "Literariness," formalism, and sense making: The line and stanza structure of human thought. *Journal of Education, 171*(1):61–74.

Giroux, H., & Simon, R. (1989). Popular culture and critical pedagogy: Everyday life as a basis for curriculum knowledge. In Giroux, H. & McLaren, P. (Eds.), *Critical pedagogy, the state and cultural struggle.* Albany: State University of New York Press, pp. 236–252.

Glazer, N. (1991). In defense of multiculturalism. *The New Republic.* September, 18–22.

Grant, C. (1989). Urban teachers: Their new colleagues and curriculum. *Phi Delta Kappan, 70*(10): 764–770.

Haberman, M. (1989). More minority teachers. *Phi Delta Kappan, 70*(10): 771–776.

Hirsch, E. D. (Ed.). (1991). *What your first grader needs to know: Fundamentals of a good first-grade education (1st ed).* New York: Doubleday.

Hirsch, E. D. (1987). *Cultural literacy: What every American needs to know.* Boston: Houghton Mifflin.

Hollins, E., & Spencer, K. (1990). Restructuring schools for cultural inclusion: Changing the schooling process for African American youngsters. *Journal of Education, 172*(2):89–100.

King, J. (1990). Dysconscious racism: Ideology, identity, and miseducation. *Journal of Negro Education, 60*(2): 133–146.

King, J., & Ladson-Billings, G. (1990). The teacher education challenge in elite university settings:

Developing critical perspectives for teaching in a democratic and multicultural society. *European Journal of Intercultural Studies, 1*(2):15–30.

Ladson-Billings, G. (1990). Beyond multicultural illiteracy. *Journal of Negro Education, 60*(2): 147–157.

McCarthy, C. (1988). Rethinking liberal and radical perspectives on racial inequality in schooling: Making the case for nonsynchrony. *Harvard Educational Review, 58*(3): 265–279.

Meyer, P. (1991). Getting to the core. *Life.* September, pp. 36–39.

Ramirez, P. (1990, May 7). Students feel unprepared for life in a multicultural society. *San Francisco Examiner,* p. A1+.

Rata, E. (1991). Kura Kaupapa Maori. *PPTA Journal.* Aukland, New Zealand, pp. 30–32.

Ravitch, D. (1991). Multiculturalism: An exchange. *The American Scholar, 60*(2):272–276.

_____. (1990). Multiculturalism. *American Scholar, 59*(3):337–354.

Ravitch, D., & Finn, C. (1987). *What do our 17-year-olds know? A report on the first national assessment of history and literature.* New York: Harper and Row.

Schlesinger, A. (1991). *The disuniting of America: Reflections on a multicultural society.* Knoxville, TN: Whittle Direct Books.

Shulman, L. (1987). Knowledge and teaching: Foundations of the new reform. *Harvard Educational Review, 57*(1):1–22.

Sleeter, C., & Grant, C. (1987). An analysis of multicultural education in the United States. *Harvard Educational Review, 57*(4):421–444.

Torres-Guzman, M. (1989, May). *Stories of hope in the midst of despair: Culturally responsive education for Latino students in an alternative high school in New York City.* Paper presented at the Tenth Anniversary colloquium of the College Board's Council on Academic Affairs, New York.

Waugh, D. (1991). California's history textbooks: Do they offend? *California Journal, 22*(3):121–127.

About the Author

Gloria Ladson-Billings received her Ph.D. from Stanford University and is currently an assistant professor in the Department of Curriculum & Instruction at the University of Wisconsin-Madison, where she teaches courses in social studies methods, multicultural education, and culturally relevant pedagogy. She has published several articles on multicultural education and culturally relevant teaching. She is a 1988–1989 recipient of the National Academy of Education's Spencer postdoctoral fellowship, and is a member of numerous national committees and advisory boards, including the Equity and Cultural Diversity Panel of the National Board for Professional Teaching Standards, the State University of New York-Buffalo History Center, and the National Council for the Social Standards Task Force.

The Power of Culture

Building Culturally Affirming Instruction

VALERIE OOKA PANG *ROBERTTA H. BARBA*

Once upon a time, I was a 'socially disadvantaged' child. An enchantedly happy child. Mine was a childhood of intense family closeness. And extreme public alienation. (Rodriguez, 1981, p. 3)

Traditionally, the educational community has tended to view culturally diverse students as coming from a deficit model—that is, from the perspective that somehow these students lack "the right stuff," the correct prior educational experiences necessary for their success in school. Rarely have schools and educational institutions viewed culturally diverse students as being "culture rich" and not an "at risk." Schools should be places that excite rather than inhibit the learning of culturally diverse students. When children are not allowed to incorporate their prior knowledge with new experiences provided in the classroom, learning is slowed and the child constructs a disjointed view of the world.

The purpose of this chapter is to help teachers identify research-based instructional and curricular strategies that focus on the belief that we have "culturally rich" children in our classrooms not "culturally deprived" children. Although this chapter focuses primarily on ethnic cultural context and content, culture is a broad concept and also includes categories such as social class, religious preference, sexual orientation, age, interracial issues, and special educational needs of children.

The key to effective instruction is to build bridges between children's prior knowledge and new information that the child is to learn in the school environment. The heart of learning, according to Tobin (1991) is negotiating meaning—that is, comparing what is known to new experiences and resolving discrepancies between what is known and what seems to be implied by new experiences. Culturally diverse children do not come to school as "disadvantaged" or "different"; instead, they shine with hope and are eager to learn. Culturally diverse learners come to schools with a wealth of prior knowledge, ready to negotiate meaning from the educational environment (Trueba, 1989; Moll & Greenberg, 1990; Philips, 1993; Shade, 1994).

The Importance of Culture in Instruction

It is not uncommon today for a class of children to bring 20 to 30 languages and cultures into a single classroom (California Department of Education, 1990). It is impossible for us as educators to be experts in each cultural group's history, values, traditions, rituals, behaviors, and language. However, we can begin to look at life from the world view of the students in our classrooms and try to create congruency and continuity between home and school (Gay, 1988). We need to allow children to work in classrooms that enable and encourage them to use their language, personal beliefs, metaphors, and preferred learning styles as tools for learning new information.

As teachers, we need to know the local communities that we serve in order to create connections between the home and the school. Children have been nurtured by their parents within a cultural context. Just as we are comfortable in the way(s) that we were raised, our students are also comfortable with the ways of their parents and communities. In creating an affirming learning environment for culturally diverse children, our methods of instruction need to parallel those of the community from which the children in our classrooms have been reared.

Schools need to be places that help children make sense of the world in which they live rather than being alien environments. Too often, the culture of the school experienced by children is very different from the culture of the family and community in which the child lives.

As teachers, we frequently operate on overgeneralized feelings and attitudes about students who come from cultural backgrounds different from our own. For example, we may believe that since the few parents we are "having trouble with" do not seem to care about their children, all parents in that neighborhood or community hold similar attitudes. Goldenberg and Gallimore (1991) found that teachers doubted that parents of their students in a Hispanic community could read or were willing to help their children with their school work. Direct observations and interviews in the homes of these children, conducted as part of the study, revealed that although the skills of parents varied, all homes contained evidence of literacy in the form of letters written to relatives in Central America or Mexico and sale flyers written in Spanish. The parents of students in this study did believe in education and felt that schooling was important to the future success of their children. Additionally, they did not know much about the school system and indicated they did not know what to do to support the work of teachers.

This study could help us to examine our own perceptions about Hispanic/Latino children. As educators, we may have a gap between our perceptions of children's home and family life and the reality of that life-style. Because parents are not literate in English, teachers sometimes assume that the parents are illiterate. The teachers in the previously cited study had not considered the possibility that the parents were literate in Spanish. Understanding the community's cultural values and milieu can only strengthen our work as teachers in developing effective instruction.

Culturally Affirming Instruction

We learn in many different ways that are frequently culturally dependent. When we learned how to cook pancakes in our home, our mother or father may have stood next to us flipping the pancakes, saying, "Turn pancakes over when most of the bubbles have popped." Some other parents may have not said anything, but expected us to watch how they cooked and to have learned from their example. One of these *familia* teaching models is a demonstration method and the other entails step-by-step verbal instruction.

Children have ways of learning that are natural and culturally derived. Parents are our first teachers, and as such they may employ instructional strategies that are very different from the instructional models used in schools. Children who come from a family that expects careful observation to be the primary instructional strategy may become bored with lengthy expository teaching techniques in school.

The writings of Vgotsky (Trueba, 1989; Moll & Greenberg, 1990) indicate that new learning needs to be built on prior knowledge—on that which children already know. This prior knowledge also includes the sociocultural context within which learning occurs. Children have been nourished and grown within a cultural environment. Teachers can use culturally familiar strategies and content to make conceptual bridges between the child's world and new knowledge to be learned within the classroom. Instruction can be created that is culturally congruent where aspects of children's culture are incorporated into classroom activities (Au & Kawakami, 1994). When teachers examine what children already know and what children are comfortable with, they can help children solve new problems, sometimes using child-generated approaches (Saxe, 1985). Otherwise, children may need to build new schema to accommodate new learning when previous learning is not connected to the current learning. Gilbert and Gay (1985) explained why teachers need to adjust their instruction to the world view of students:

> *The means appropriate for teaching poor, urban black students differ from those appropriate for teaching other students because teaching and learning are sociocultural processes that take place within given social systems. When different social systems interact, the normative rules of procedure often conflict. This is the case when the school culture comes up against the urban black culture. Many of the instructional procedures used by schools stem from a set of cultural values, orientations, and perceptions that differ radically from those of poor black students. (p. 134)*

Instruction may or may not be culturally familiar to students. If students speak English as a second language or if they grew up with a different cultural belief system from mainstream Americans, students may not understand the expectations, value orientations, ways of teaching, concepts, and ideas that are presented in school. To help facilitate learning, teachers can utilize culturally familiar content and contexts in the classroom. Culturally familiar instructional strategies and content may include interactional patterns, group processes, analogies, concepts, materials, motivational values, and the physical environment.

When teachers build on these culturally familiar components, they are creating a culturally affirming learning environment that reinforces the importance of what children bring to the classroom as it increases students' conceptual development and comprehension. When instructional strategies are culturally familiar, they include and stress a whole-language approach to reading, the learning cycle approach to science, a hands-on problem-solving approach to mathematics, and an issues-centered approach to social studies. See Figure 1 for a model of a culturally familiar learning process that has been broken into curriculum and instruction components.

Parents entrust their children to teachers in the public schools and it is our job to understand their dreams, hopes, and aspirations for their children. Historically, teachers lived in the communities in which they taught; they were part of the world of their students and they understood their students' values, life-styles, and cultural heritage. Today, it is not uncommon for teachers to live in suburban areas while working in urban environments many miles from their homes (California Department of Education, 1990). As a result of this, teachers lack a connectedness with the community that they serve. As Wiggington (1992) has written:

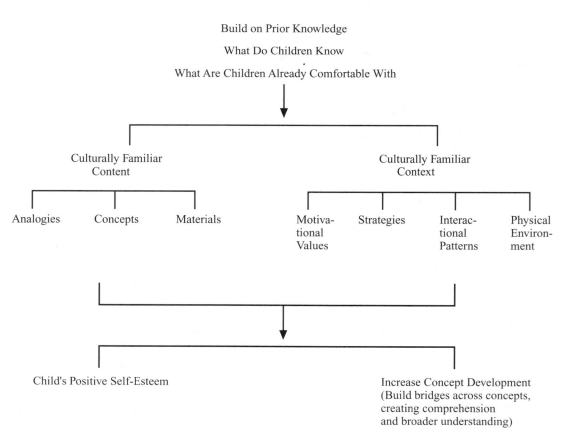

FIGURE 1   Building a Culturally Affirming Curriculum

Urban teachers routinely commute an hour each way, teaching in a city but living in a suburb. Teachers on Indian reservations live in all-white isolation from their students, sometimes in compounds surrounded by fences. At a recent workshop, a teacher admitted to me that part of the difficulty she was having with her students probably stemmed from the fact that she was from the urban East, was teaching in the rural South, and just didn't know anything about her students or how to get through to them. (p. 217)

Wigginton (1992) enjoyed living in the small rural town of Rabun County, Georgia, and felt he was getting to know the community, yet he still felt he had placed a barrier between himself and the community.

But it was not until I had made a real attempt to understand it [the community] that I realized the terrible traps into which I could fall by trying to impose my middle-class values on my students and their families, by trying to impose certain types of literature and poetry that I had considered appropriate on students to whom it was alien and false and inappropriate. Such behavior is as wrong headed as insisting that poor Southern blacks or migrant Chicano children learn to read best from Dick and Jane readers. It is like a white teacher of Indian children insisting that they all start a magazine like Foxfire, only to discover that the culture forbids the writing down and sharing of many cultural customs with the outside world. It is at such times we meekly say, "Oh. I didn't know," and we realize how far we have to go. (p. 219)

Instruction is interwoven with curriculum. The next section will describe how culturally familiar instruction can be built into our nation's classrooms. Much of this discussion centers on what children bring to the classroom in terms of the contextual nature of learning. The culturally relevant context of learning stems from the culture woven into the whole being of each of our students. The following three areas will be reviewed: (1) the use of culturally familiar interactional patterns, (2) the value of culturally familiar learning strategies, and (3) the use of a culturally familiar environment. The examples provided in this chapter may reflect ethnic, occupational, and/or regional cultural characteristics that may be generalized to other similar populations.

Culturally Familiar Interactional Patterns

Research on interactional patterns shows that children come to school with social systems of values and behaviors (Philips, 1972, 1993; Au & Kawakami, 1985; Moll & Greenberg, 1990). Teachers often request that students talk aloud in class and in front of other students and the teacher. The process of schooling frequently requires children to give answers to teacher-directed questions. Philips (1972, 1993) found that on the Warms Springs Indian Reservation in Central Oregon, Native-American children were not comfortable with verbal interaction and talked less as they progressed in school. Philips discovered that the social context of the situation directed how much children talked.

The role of adults in some cultures is quite different from the role of teachers in schools. The children of the Warm Springs community (Philips, 1972, 1993) have close relationships with various extended family members and other adults. Traditionally, these children may observe the work of an adult for a long period of time and work coopera- tively with an adult by helping with small portions of a larger task. This observation of the adult by the child does not include much formal discussion or verbal interaction with the adult. Children may ask some questions of the mentoring adult, but the adult does not give a lengthy verbal response nor lecture, as is often found in mainstream classrooms.

Philips also found that the Native-American children on the Warm Springs Reserva- tion responded best to hands-on activities. Teachers had students choose experiments with motors and batteries. It was more effective for children to conduct projects of their choice than to read about electricity and answer worksheet questions. These Native-American students were accustomed to being self-directed in a learning environment and tended to view the teacher as a facilitator of learning, rather than as an authoritative source of information.

In addition, the children at the Warm Springs school were more interested in the activities of their peers than the activities of the teacher during teacher-directed lessons. Often the Native-American children in this study were found to wander around the room while the teacher was lecturing. The children in this situation were performing in school in a culturally familiar way—that is, they were interacting with cousins, siblings, and other children in the classroom in the same fashion that they did at home. Teachers, not aware of the cultural context of the children's behavior, might be tempted to term the children as "disruptive" or "off task."

Warm Springs students also were not accustomed to being the focal point of interac- tion between the teacher in front of the entire class. They were more accustomed to a community participation model. During community gatherings, one person does not usually verbally direct activities or transitions to new phases. Rather, there is a procedure or ritual that is followed and everyone is invited to participate, youth and elders alike. The learning model used at home may lead to the reluctance of some Native-American students to answer teacher questions when the verbal and individual performance of students is required.

Additionally, a teacher is not always considered a leader simply because of his or her position. In the Warms Springs community, a person is a leader because others choose to follow that person due to the individual's knowledge or special abilities. Therefore, from the children's perspective, teachers must earn the children's respect before students will obey a teacher's instructions. Students follow a teacher's instructions because they have chosen to do so, not because they are compelled to do so.

The research of Au and Kawakami (1985) also demonstrates the importance of interactional patterns in creating the learning environment of Hawaiian-American students. These researchers looked at reading achievement among Hawaiian-American students and found that by structuring the reading setting around a culturally affirming and compatible learning style, students attended to the reading lessons almost twice as much as they did with "mainstream" teaching strategies.

Their research addressed the question of how teachers can structure learning so that children have equal access and control of information. In this study, the teacher of the experimental group allowed her sixth-grade children to engage in self-directed discussions of stories. Many of the children talked simultaneously, as in the culturally familiar interactional pattern called *talk story* (which is a culturally derived strategy where children tell a story together). One student does not do all of the talking, but rather various speakers enthusiastically "jump in" and provide their descriptive and contextual enhancement to the story. Group performance, rather than individual performance, is the focus of this cultural pattern of communication. The *talk story* approach encourages the group to generate a leader who encourages the participation of other children.

Au and Kawakami (1985) reinforced the importance of the idea that though children have discussion rights, it is the role of the teacher to keep students focused on the reading lesson. In the *talk story* approach, teachers allow children to voluntarily chime in while they themselves refrain from calling on individual students to participate in the discussion. The use of this approach encourages teachers to create a family of caring and sharing readers who value the input of each class member, rather than to utilize an expository teaching method.

Though many teachers believe that many Asian-American children are shy and do not talk much, the work by Cabezas (1981) found Asian-American mothers talked a great deal to their children, asking them questions, rather than modeling, prompting, or giving direct commands. These children, two to seven years old, readily talked and sought a great deal of verbal approval from their mothers. The reluctance of young Asian-American children to readily volunteer in class discussions may have more to do with lack of teacher encouragement than a lack of the desire to participate (Pang, 1990). When this is coupled with a belief that a person should not be too aggressive or demanding of the teacher's attention, students may be caught in a bicultural web. In a study of teacher-student interactions between 713 elementary-aged schoolchildren and their teachers in multicultural classrooms, the authors found that White-American males interacted with their teachers once every 14 minutes on average, whereas Asian-American females interacted only once every 60 minutes.

For Asian-American students, teachers may take on the role of parents in that they represent respected members of the community. Teachers need to understand their role in encouraging Asian-American children to participate in large group oral dialogue. In addition, since Asian-American children often grow up in close-knit families where group success is valued rather than individual initiative, some children prefer group activities rather than highly competitive individualized instruction. Teachers can use peer tutoring or cooperative grouping strategies to provide an inviting educational environment for students.

Gilbert and Gay (1985) have found that some African-American students grow up within a social context that integrates both intellectual, physical, and emotional development. When African-American students are asked to respond to teacher questions, they may show emotion, using hand gestures and changes in voice tonality. When African-American students are asked to participate in oral discussions, students may answer simultaneously or chorally because the students value expressiveness and community participation. If teachers are unaware that a choral response is an acceptable cultural tradition, they may interpret such behavior as disruptive or inappropriate in the classroom.

The research presented here directs us to consider the following instructional patterns:

1. Some culturally diverse children may be more comfortable with observing demonstration lessons and may prefer a limited amount of teacher lecturing.
2. Many culturally diverse learners are more attentive when they engage in hands-on exploration of a topic, rather than reading or writing about an idea.
3. Some culturally diverse children may prefer interacting with other children in a group setting rather than asking the teacher questions. If their peers come from the same cultural context, then they may better understand what is considered "acceptable behavior."
4. Some children may prefer self-directed discussions where group performance rather than individual performance is the focus.
5. Many culturally diverse children may be accustomed to the use of directed questioning strategies.
6. Some children of color prefer peer tutoring and cooperative grouping to individualized instruction.
7. Some children may prefer oral presentation of information and enjoy communal dialogue.

As we better understand the sociocultural context of children's lives, we also will better be able to choose the culturally familiar strategies that we can use in the classroom.

Culturally Familiar Strategies

We all adopt ways of finding new information or learning new skills. For example, we know teachers who are searching for new methods to use with children they are not reaching. These teachers use their peers as a data source to devise new teaching methods. We also know teachers who would not want to bother anyone; instead, they are voracious readers and try new instructional approaches that they find in professional journals and books. Children from various cultural groups also develop their own ways of learning. These methods may not be the same as those currently used in schools, but they are effective in the daily survival of the child.

The works of Saxe (1988a, 1988b, 1985), Ginsburg, Posner, and Russell (1981), and Gannon and Ginsburg (1985) are helpful in explaining how children develop mathematical strategies to solve real-world problems. For example, when 10- to 12-year-old street vendors in Brazil were asked to solve problems involving mental computation of bills or of ratio comparisons, their results were more accurate than those of children who were formally educated (Saxe, 1988a). These children had to be able to add large numbers quickly in selling candy bars and rolls of Lifesavers. Sellers (children who worked in the streets rather than attending school) would often regroup large bills and sum 500 + 500 and 200 + 200 + 100 in sets. The children did not need to use pencil and paper to do these problems accurately. During the time period of the study, Brazil's inflation rate was 250 percent, so these children had to be able to manipulate large numbers in selling and adjust for continual changes in the inflation rate. Saxe found that these children developed increasingly complex mathematical problem-solving strategies based on the currency system. In addition, sellers who had some school knowledge transferred that knowledge to practical problems.

Ginsburg, Posner, and Russell (1981) discovered that unschooled children 10 years old and older from the Ivory Coast also developed regrouping skills to solve mental addition problems. The regrouping was based on factors of 10 and may stem from the use of the base-ten Dioula numeration system in the culture. These researchers believed that the children rearranged numbers from $7 + (3 + 5) = (7 + 3) + 5$ because of their familiarity with the numeration system used in the marketplace. These unschooled sellers often put out merchandise in groups of 5 or 10, thus easing their mental computational efforts when dealing with buyers. Teachers could teach these culturally derived strategies as a formal instructional model in regular mathematics classes.

Peer and cooperative learning is another culturally familiar strategy teachers can utilize with culturally diverse students (Bradley, 1984; Gilbert & Gay, 1985). In many culturally diverse communities, groups arise naturally as a self-selection process, from the interaction between individuals. In many schools, cooperative grouping strategies involves teacher-selected leadership and the assignment of tasks to various members of the group. This continues the mainstream model of teacher-directed instruction, since the teacher controls the composition and leadership of the learning unit. When children are free to select their own groups and to elect their own leadership, the school environment resembles that of the community in which the children were nurtured.

Cooperative Learning

Though there is much literature on cooperative learning as an effective approach to instruction, we are concerned that teachers do not understand that the underlying assumptions and beliefs of cooperative learning may differ from group to group. Cooperative learning is not simply a matter of grouping students into heterogeneous teams. Effective use of cooperative learning means that teachers apply in the classroom the children's preferred style for group formation and interaction. Some children—for example, some African-American children—prefer to develop their own leadership structures. Other children—for example, Hispanic/Latino children and some Native-American children— prefer to work in mixed-age groups made up of friends and family members. Allowing students occasionally to work in groups of their own making allows children to more fully participate in their schooling.

Often children with limited English skills or those who come from family backgrounds where children are encouraged to work quietly may be less likely to be verbally active in whole group lessons and/or large group discussions. Working in small cooperative groups allows for more personal interaction where students can practice their skills and clarify or construct new information in a supportive environment.

Some children come to school from highly group-oriented communities (Philips, 1972; Au & Kawakami, 1985; Little Soldier, 1989; Shade, 1994). These communities may hold traditional values and teach these values through child-rearing practices. Little Soldier (1989) found cooperation and sharing to be core values in many Native-American communities. These groups are not centered on personal ownership and are characterized by large extended families. Children in these communities may tend to share what they have with each other, including homework and test answers, much to the dismay of their mainstream teachers. Little Soldier discovered that Native-American children had well-developed social skills like taking turns, working in groups, and sharing because of an underlying belief in the value of harmony of the community. Teachers sometimes misunderstand the actions of Native-American students. Though these students usually are not competitive individually, they may be extremely competitive team players.

Several advantages of cooperative learning are as followed:

1. Learning can take place in a smaller group, which allows students the opportunity to better articulate their ideas by interacting with their peers. In addition, students may have more chances to use their English language skills if English is their second language (Trueba, 1989).

2. Cooperative learning can foster cultural integration when children are mixed heterogeneously across ethnic groups because children can develop a sense of humanness as they work toward a common goal (Slavin, 1987).

3. The use of cooperative learning groups has found to be a more effective teaching strategy for Mexican Americans, Native Americans, and African Americans than for teaching White students in terms of student achievement. It is theorized that culturally diverse children perform at a higher level of learning in cooperative groups than with individualistic learning activities because these children prefer group learning (Slavin & Oickle, 1981; Slavin, 1987).

4. Cooperative learning shifts the responsibility of the learning from the teacher to all children, who work toward a mutually agreed upon goal (Little Soldier, 1989) or toward a socially negotiated meaning for information. It may be that peer tutoring is occurring in cooperative groups and that this facilitates language acquisition and/or concept formation among culturally diverse learners. From this perspective, peer tutoring is seen as a helpful strategy and not as "cheating" (Au & Kawakami, 1994).

In some cultural situations, tasks are directed to groups and not to individuals (Au & Kawakami, 1994). Children who have developed a support network among their peers learn within a culturally familiar context. Cooperative learning allows students more chances to negotiate conceptual knowledge within a group and to clarify their personal beliefs, concepts, and values.

When placing students into cooperative groups, teachers need to remember that children come to school with many preconceived attitudes about each other, just as adults do. If you are going to place children of different racial backgrounds and neighborhoods together, those students first need time to get acquainted with each other. Students who come from neighborhoods where individual physical power is an important means of survival may be easily threatened by a physical nudge or negative comment from other students. Sometimes students may not understand how their own nonverbal actions (such as the roll of the eyes or physical bumping of other students) may cause conflict within a group. As Gilbert and Gay (1985) have indicated, students come to school with a well-developed social system.

In assigning children to cooperative groups, teachers should be aware of the social class of children. For example, if a teacher has a student whose father is the chauffeur for another student's father, these children are aware of the social disparity between their parents' social status. Class differences between children may be addressed by social interactions brought about in cooperative working groups. When students interact with each other on a daily basis to solve shared tasks, class differences between students are minimized.

In understanding the workings of cooperative groups, teachers need to consider that each group may have a different pace of learning (Gilbert & Gay, 1985). Additionally, groups that function best—those that achieve the greatest gains in cognitive learning—are characterized by having a leader who is self-generated (Au & Kawakami, 1985) or selected by the students themselves. In many cooperative learning approaches, the teacher appoints children to a variety of jobs in order to give each student the opportunity to develop many skills. Many culturally diverse children may not, at first, be comfortable with this model. Teachers ought to encourage children to allow all members of the group to try each job in the group, but the actual selection of roles is best left to the students themselves in most instances. Children have a strong sense of fair play and will assume responsibility for the equitable divisions of labor with only minor teacher intervention.

Alternative Methods of Assessment

Culturally familiar ways of communication may also be integrated into the curriculum and used in assessing students' understanding. Many Native-American students shy away from oral reports in class. They may choose to construct a mural, painting, or written report about an event or activity rather than to report orally to the class. In contrast, African-American students may feel more comfortable with verbally demonstrating their learning by speaking in front of the class. Many African-American students are excellent verbal performers because the social system in which they were reared reinforces the importance of oral communication and of oral tradition (Gilbert & Gay, 1985; Shade, 1994). These students often are concerned with style of presentation as illustrated in the rhythm of their words, their use of dramatic elements, and their use of nonverbal gestures. Teachers may sometimes allow students to write scripts and put on plays, to tell a story, or to perform a poem. Children need to have some control over their learning environment. Utilizing skills they have developed in their homes and communities helps students understand that skills learned in school are relevant to real life.

Culturally Familiar Environment

We all come from an environment that we know well. We know what the houses look like on our block, where the dogs who bite walkers live, and the name of the closest grocery store to our home. When we see a sign with an icon of a telephone, we know we can make a call if needed. As we walk the streets of our neighborhood, our friends call out our name, people smile at us, and we are surrounded by familiar people, sights, music, and smells. Our neighborhoods are familiar and comfortable places for us. As educators, we can make our instructional environments more comfortable and safe for students if we understand the use of behaviors that reinforce trust and respect for students.

For many children, the classroom is a culturally unfamiliar environment—a place where the familiar people, sights, sounds, and smells are missing, often to be replaced by a harsh, alien world. Frequently, our classrooms are physically structured so that all chairs and desks are lined up with military precision and all children face the teacher who stands in the front of the classroom. Around each child's desk, there exists an invisible bubble, separating the child from others in the classroom. Sometimes, children are educated in classrooms where teachers display open hostility by pacing the perimeter of the classroom during the class period, carrying a meter stick in their hands as a symbol of their power and authority. When teachers require students to raise their hands and seek the teacher's recognition before asking a question, going to the bathroom, or moving from their desks, they may unknowingly convey unfamiliar or even hostile messages to their students.

In observing a poor, urban school, the authors observed the interaction between an African-American female teacher and her students. They noted that the classroom was filled with pictures and posters commonly found in the children's neighborhood. They also noted that the invisible bubbles that frequently exist in classrooms had been replaced by a warmer, nonverbal teacher-student interactional model that included (1) decreased contact distance between the child and teacher during verbal interactions, (2) increased eye contact between child and teacher, (3) light "touch control" used by the teacher to reassure the children of her presence, (4) positively reinforcing verbal feedback provided to children in liberal doses, (5) a "no contact hug" being used (where the teacher extended her arms around the child while the child sat at the desk), and (6) the disappearance of the invisible bubble that surrounds the child. Learning is maximized when the classroom resembles the environment in which children are used to interacting. Instruction does not occur in a vacuum.

Culturally Familiar Content

In creating a culturally affirming classroom, we are going to discuss the importance of using culturally familiar analogies, themes, materials, and environment as part of instruction. The use of these elaborative strategies builds bridges that connect the student's prior knowledge to the new knowledge presented in the educational environment.

Culturally Familiar Analogies

Culturally familiar analogies are examples or stories that students in the class are aware of and that are used to illustrate concepts taught in the classroom. For example, the authors had a student teacher in a fifth-grade class who was teaching a lesson about the natural instinct of female animals to protect their young. The students in the class had a general idea of what the student teacher meant until the student teacher said, "The mother cat may pull the young kitten into the protection of her belly." A fifth-grader thought the student teacher meant the mother cat was moved to scratch anyone who might try to take her kitten away. The fifth-grade boy did not quite grasp the meaning of protect in this situation.

The student teacher was also the volunteer coach of the fifth-grade football team. He remembered how well this particular young student had "protected" the ball during a scrimmage game. So the student teacher said, "What do you do to protect the ball when you are running down the field?" The young man answered, "I hold the ball close to my body so that no one can grab it from me." "That's a great answer," said the student teacher, "the mother cat holds her kitten in the same way." The student was an African-American male and the teacher used the culture of football to help the young man understand a new definition of *protection*. The teacher could also have used this analogy if the student had been a White female who knew football.

Another culturally familiar analogy was used by a teacher who was explaining the history of Thanksgiving to her second-grade class. Her second-graders focused on the clothes of the Pilgrims, but could not understand the circumstances that caused the Pilgrims to migrate to a new land. Then, the teacher said, "The Pilgrims did not have enough food when they landed and did not have the skills they needed to build cabins and to survive in a new country. They were lost in a scary new world." Rosa, a Guatemalan-American child in the class piped, up saying, "We're like the Pilgrims. My family doesn't have any money and we don't know anyone to help us." Rosa had made an important connection with history. Through her personal story of being an immigrant, she was able to help her classmates better understand how immigrants felt when they move to a new country. The other students had learned about the Pilgrims previously in preschool and kindergarten and first grade, but Rosa enriched their perception of the Pilgrims.

Rosa's friends then began to ask, "How do you like San Diego? What do you like about San Diego? What don't you like about San Diego? How is San Diego different from your home in Guatemala?" Though the initial information dealt with a community that arrived on the East Coast of the United States hundreds of years ago, the student's schemata or framework about the Pilgrims and refugees had been structured more concisely because of Rosa's modern-day contributions.

Culturally Familiar Themes and Concepts

Wiggington has been teaching English in Georgia for over 25 years and he has utilized the Appalachian culture as the vehicle to teach language arts skills to high school students. His students have published a quarterly magazine called *Foxfire* and numerous books about family life in that part of the United States. Wiggington uses a whole-language approach to teaching writing, reading, grammar, vocabulary development, and comprehension. The reason that his classes are so powerful is that he allows students to create a product about people, places, and traditions familiar to the students he is teaching. Though Wiggington deals primarily with White students in a rural community, his strategies and curriculum have been used with Southeast-Asian students in Portland and with African-American students in Mississippi.

Using the Wigginton model, students in Mississippi wrote *Minds Stayed on Freedom*, an oral history of the civil rights movement (Wiggington, 1992). These eighth- and ninth-graders came together because they wanted to record the grassroots civil rights movement in Holmes County Mississippi (Youth of the Rural Organizing and Cultural Center, 1991). In the introduction to *Minds Stayed on Freedom*, this is what the young Black writers said about the process of writing the book:

> *Our title comes from a freedom song that was used to make black people in struggle unite and become stronger. That's also what happened to us as we*

struggled over fourteen months to make this book—we united and got stronger. We also became prouder and prouder: proud of the way our people fought for their natural rights and proud of ourselves for capturing that history for all to read and learn from. (p. x)

Minds Stayed on Freedom, like *Foxfire*, is an example of how the cultural content of the curriculum can stem from the beliefs and interests of students. In both instances, the students believed in the project and became owners of the learning process. The culturally familiar concepts that they investigated and learned about were the vehicles for skills development and for stretching their capabilities as scholars.

A cultural content can also be woven into the curriculum by choosing from the everyday lives of the students. For example, if one of the students in a class works in a hardware store, the concept of supply and demand can be covered as it relates to the success of this retail business. In addition, Wigginton (1985) wrote that one of the overarching characteristics of excellent teachers is to make linkages between the local community, their students, the world, and the subject matter they are teaching. Wiggington wrote about specific types of lessons that teachers can incorporate into the curriculum which may stem from their daily existence:

Shopping lists and card games become math problems. Carpet dyes and gymnasium floor waxes and cans of beer become subjects of chemical analysis. The first spring flowers become targets of botanical scrutiny. And never in isolation, for each step inevitably leads to the next: Why do those spring flowers have color and fragrance? How do they acquire it? Of what is it made? What is the connection between flowers and bees? How do bees work? How do they communicate? How do they build? Why are the cells in their combs hexagonal? (pp. 200–201)

As teachers, we can spark student interest in learning by using that what they know to deepen student curiosity about new ideas, concepts, and values.

Culturally Familiar Materials

Culturally familiar materials help students make linkages between real-world experience and abstract concepts. In her ethnographic study of two communities, one Black and one White, Heath (1983) found that effective teachers often utilized culturally familiar materials. For example, Mrs. Gardner, a first-grade teacher who taught in Trackton (a Black-American working-class community) asked parents in her room to provide discarded tires and planks of wood for her classroom (materials available in all communities). The parents then helped her cut the tires into letters of the alphabet and placed them on the playground. These letters became part of the children's play and served to reinforced what students were learning in the classroom. Mrs. Gardner also pointed to letters found in the surrounding neighborhood; for example, there was an *I* in a telephone pole and an *O* in a cup.

Heath found other teachers using culturally familiar materials in the teaching of reading by gathering familiar advertisements, road signs, cereal boxes, and labels from mayonnaise jars and salad dressing. She noted that teachers could successfully teach reading and writing by showing children that everyone used these skills all the time. The children could see the link between school skills and their world when they were presented with price tags, labels on toys, and instructions on how to use those toys.

Bradley (1984) reported that teachers have often used culturally familiar materials like geometric patterns in Navajo blankets in their geometry classes. Loom-woven beadwork has been used to teach Euclidean geometry, coordinate geometry, number theory, and measurement. Students in this project were taught to write computer programs in Logo to design beadwork. The computer skills were integrated with culturally familiar materials and mathematical concepts. These culturally based patterns help students understand abstract concepts in geometry from the perspective of physical objects that are part of their everyday milieu.

Sometimes, students choose culturally familiar materials in their own work. Though not all Japanese-American students know origami, a Japanese-American student in junior high decided to use a large square of green paper as she told a story to her English class. This young student had taught herself simple origami at the age of five, so she was quite accomplished at paper folding. She chose to tell the story of the frog prince. While telling the story, she folded the green paper into various shapes to describe the prince's table, pants, and boat. Finally, at the end of the story, the young student made several small folds and as the story ended, the class laughed when the conceited prince demands that the princess kiss him. Though the princess wasn't excited about doing this, she smiled and as she kissed his cheek, the conceited prince turned into a frog and the young storyteller ended with the origami frog hopping off the stage.

Teachers have also developed math curriculum that uses foods, events, and dice sticks to create a culturally affirming curriculum for Native-American students. For example, a unit on probability can be introduced using Papago dice sticks or Loway bone dice and wooden bowl (Cheek, 1984). These materials are used in games of chance by many students who engage in street or group games. Street math—whether blackjack, craps, trading baseball cards, or pitching pennies—can help students to bridge the gap between their world and the formal language of mathematics.

Culturally familiar materials may also include intangible items from the environment. Goodman (1985) wrote that children begin to develop literacy at a young age when they make sense out of symbolic forms around them. Young children can read signs like "Stop," "Keep off the grass," "McDonald's hamburgers," and "No parking." Teachers can ask children to bring in materials from their homes to school. If they are learning about different communities in school, children can bring in their local community newspaper—such as *La Presa, International Examiner*, or *Black Voice*, in addition to the *Los Angeles Times*—into the classroom. School curriculum should involve children from the beginning by encouraging them to become empowered and make choices about their learning (Goodman, 1985).

When we teach with culturally based materials—whether these materials are worksheets, pinto beans, textbooks, bagels, milk cartons, tires, or origami paper—we bring the familiar environment of home into the classroom. When teachers bring in real materials from children's lives, children may not only be more comfortable but they may also be more interested in instruction (Bradley, 1984). Culturally familiar materials can be paired with materials from the school curriculum. This serves as a conceptual bridge which affirms the student's community while engaging the child in mainstream education.

Culturally Affirming Instructional Approaches

The teaching approaches described in this chapter are process-oriented rather than product-oriented strategies and they serve to encourage children to make interconnections between their lives and school learning. With the teaching approaches reported thus far, children select their data sources and gather information. These approaches encourage children to use their prior experiences and append new learning to existing schema as they negotiate conceptual meaning in the classroom. These strategies encourage children to judge the information they gather, to make inferences, to draw conclusions, and to make their own generalizations.

We do not believe that all learning must be culturally familiar; rather, we believe that some culturally familiar context and content should be embedded in our instructional programs. The purpose of this chapter was to help teachers better understand that it is important to structure learning experiences "where students are" (Suzuki, 1985) in order to help children develop linkages with mainstream school culture. It is important that all children have the opportunity to learn within the comfort of what they know best and to be affirmed in who they are. Culturally diverse students are especially at risk of not knowing the "culture of power" (Delpit, 1988). Teachers can reach all children in using their own culturally familiar strategies and content in order to help them be successful in mainstream schools. Culturally diverse students are "culture rich" and not "culturally disadvantaged." We must affirm our children's families and cultures by building bridges between what they know and mainstream knowledge. Our children hunger for an "equal chance" and we can provide an educational experience that excites rather than alienates all our children.

References

Au, K., & Kawakami, A. (1985). Research currents: Talk story and learning to read. *Language Arts, 62*(4), 406–411.

Au, K., & Kawakami, A. (1994). Cultural congruence in instruction. In E. Hollins, J. King, & W. Hayman (Eds.), *Teaching Diverse Populations* (pp. 5–23). Albany: State University of New York Press.

Bradley, C. (1984). Issues in mathematics education for Native Americans and directions for research. *Journal for Research in Mathematics Education, 15*(2), 96–106.

Cabezas, A. (1981). *Early Childhood Development in Asian and Pacific American Families: Families in Transition.* San Francisco, CA: Asian, Inc.

California Department of Education. (1990). *Fingertip Facts on Education in California,1990.* Sacramento, CA: Department of Education.

Cheek, H. N. (1984) Increasing the participation of Native Americans in mathematics. *Journal for Research in Mathematics Education, 15*(2), 107–113.

Delpit, L. (1988). The silenced dialogue: Power and pedagogy in educating other peoples' children. *Harvard Educational Review, 58*(3), 280–298.

Gannon, K., & Ginsburg, H. (1985) Children's learning difficulties in mathematics, *Education and Urban Society, 17*(4), 405–416.

Gay, G. (1988). Designing relevant curricula for diverse learners. *Education and Urban Society, 20*(4), 327–340.

Gilbert, S., & Gay, G. (1985). Improving the success in school of poor black children. *Phi Delta Kappan,* 66, 133–137.

Ginsburg, H., Posner, J., & Russell, R. (1981). The development of mental addition as a function of schooling and culture. *Journal of Cross-Cultural Psychology, 12*(2),163–178.

Goldenberg, C., & Gallimore, R. (1991). Local knowledge, research knowledge, and educational change: A case study of early Spanish reading improvement. *Educational Researcher, 28*(8), 2–14.

Goodman, K. S. (1985). Growing into literacy. *Prospects: Quarterly Review of Education, 15*(1), 57–65.

Heath, S. B. (1983). Ways with Words. Cambridge: Cambridge University Press.

Little Soldier, L. (1989). Cooperative learning and the Native American student. *Phi Delta Kappan, 71*(2), 161–163.

Longstreet, W. (1978). *Aspects of ethnicity.* New York: Teachers College Press.

Moll, L., & Greenberg, J. B. (1990). Creating zones of possibilities Combining social contexts for instruction. In L. Moll (Ed.), *Vgotsky and Education* (pp. 319–348). Cambridge: Cambridge University Press.

Pang, V. O. (1990). Asian-American children: A diverse population. *Educational Forum, 55*(1), 49–66.

Philips, S. (1972). Participant structures and communicative competence: Warm Springs children in community and classroom. In C. Cazden, V. John, & D. Hymes (Eds.), *Functions of Language in the Classroom.* New York: Teachers College Press.

Philips, S. (1993). *The Invisible Culture.* Prospect Heights, IL: Waveland Press.

Rodriguez, R. (1981). *Hungry of Memory.* Boston: D. R. Godine.

Saxe, G. B. (1988a). Candy selling and math learning. *Educational Researcher, 17*(6), 14–21.

Saxe, G. B. (1988b). The mathematics of street vendors. Child Development, 59, 1415–1425.

Saxe, G. B. (1985). Effects of schooling on arithmetical understandings: Studies with Oksapmin children in Papua New Guinea. *Journal of Educational Psychology, 77*(5), 503–513.

Science Curriculum Improvement Study. (1974). *Teacher's Handbook* Berkeley, CA: Lawrence Hall of Science.

Shade, B. (1994). Understanding the African American learner. In E. Hollins, J. King, & W. Hayman (Eds.), *Teaching Diverse Populations* (pp. 175–189). Albany: State University of New York Press.

Slavin, R. (1987). *Cooperative Learning.* 2d ed. Washington, DC: National Education Association.

Slavin, R., & Oickle, E. (1981). *Effects of cooperative learning teams on student achievement and race relations: Treatment by race.* State of California Department of Education, Educational Demographics Unit Program Evaluation and Research Division, April.

Suzuki, R. (1985). Cultural transformation for multicultural education. *Education and Urban Society, 16*(3), 294–322.

Tobin, K. G. (1991). *Constructivist perspective on teacher learning.* Paper presented at the 11th Biennial Conference on Chemical Education, Atlanta, GA.

Trueba, H. (1989). *Raising Silent Voices: Educating Linguistic Minorities for the 21st Century.* Boston: Heinle & Heinle.

Wiggington, E. (1992) Culture begins at home. *Educational Leadership, 49*(4), 60–64.

Youth of the Rural Organizing and Cultural Center. (1991). *Minds Stayed on Freedom: The Civil Rights Struggle in Rural South.* Boulder, CO: Westview Press.

Zaslvasky, C. (1979). Symmetry along with other mathematical concepts and applications in African life. *Applications in School Mathematics.* Reston, VA: National Council of Teachers of Mathematics.

About the Authors

Valerie Ooka Pang is an associate professor in teacher education at San Diego State University. Her specialization is multicultural education. Her research interests include curriculum development, multicultural children's literature, and Asian-American youth. She is a former elementary-grade teacher. Her publications have appeared in *Harvard Educational Review*, *Educational Forum*, *Social Education*, *The Social Studies*, *The Reading Teacher*, and *Journal of Cross-cultural Psychology*.

Robertta H. Barba is an associate professor in the School of Teacher Education at San Diego State University, where she teaches preservice and graduate-level courses in science education. Barba is associated with the Center for Research in Mathematics and Science Education, where she conducts research into culturally diverse students' problem-solving strategies in the earth and space science classroom. She is a frequent presenter at NARST, NSTA, NCTM, and NECC conventions, and is author of more than 60 articles and chapters in publications dealing with science education issues.

Chapter 25

School Policy and Student Diversity

ROBERT CRUMPTON

"It takes a whole village to educate a child"—African Proverb

Introduction

The racial composition of our nation's schools is changing dramatically. By the year 2000, our nation's public schools (K–12) will be more than 50 percent minority (Hodgkinson, 1988). Today, every one of the 25 largest city school systems in the United States has a majority of Black and Hispanic students, most of whom are economically disadvantaged (i.e., from homes with incomes below federal poverty guidelines). These students of color offer a new set of challenges to the classroom. Their social, cultural, and linguistic backgrounds are often very different from those found in classrooms at the onset of the now-terminated Cold War.

The nation's public school system is not meeting the academic needs of all its students. Significant numbers of students of color are experiencing academic failure. The nation's education strategies are not keeping pace with the nation's changing demographics.

Among the most serious challenges presented to the schools by students of color is the issue of academic failure. One needs only to review or study the academic profiles of students of color in any large urban city to find that the nation's public education system is inadequate when it comes to educating students of color. Consider, for example, Wright (1991) reported that: (1) during the 1986–87 school year, Milwaukee's African-American high school students had an average grade-point average of "D" (1.46); (2) between 1978 and 1985, 94 percent of all students expelled from the Milwaukee Public Schools were African-American; and (3) Milwaukee Public Schools ranked third among cities in the nation in suspending more Black than White students from school.

Similar indices of academic failure can be found in other large large cities. For example, the average dropout rate for students of color in the Minneapolis Public Schools over the period from 1985 to 1990 was 54 percent. In other words, students of color represented more than one-half of all students who dropped out of the Minneapolis Public Schools during this period. It should noted that this is significantly higher than the average enrollment for students of color for the same period, which was 45 percent. More disturbing is the Minneapolis Board of Education report that indicates that the graduation rate of minority students in the Minneapolis Public Schools consistently declined from 1985 to 1990, from 72 percent in 1985 to 63 percent in 1990. And over the same five-year period, Asian-American students had the highest graduation rate of all students, with an average graduation rate of 87 percent as compared with 85 percent for White students, while the graduation rate of American-Indian students was the lowest, with an average graduation rate of 60 percent.

Although these examples are primarily from two midwestern cities, similar patterns can be found in large urban areas across the nation. For example, Wright (1991) reported that across the nation some 18 percent of African-American males drop out of high school.

The purpose of this chapter is to describe how the United States has responded to the new challenges presented by the increase in the number of students of color attending public schools. This chapter discusses and analyzes some of the current trends in the nation's school reform movement and the development of public policy to address the educational needs of students of color. In this chapter, three criteria are employed to examine six education policies and to give the reader a general idea of the nature of the nation's response to the academic challenges presented by the new students. *Policy*, as used in this chapter, means any report, legislation, or large-scale project designed to address the needs of students of color, or provide data for informed decision making to address those needs.

Since the early 1960s, educators have increasingly employed policy analysis as a key tool for improving government policies and programs and for solving (or at least reducing) social problems that have beset our public schools (Boyer, 1987; Coleman, 1984). Because schools generally have been viewed as one of the nation's primary means of solving social problems, policy analysis has been heavily applied in the public education arena. Policy analysis techniques will be employed in this chapter to examine the nature of several reports and pieces of legislation related to current school reform. Specifically, the following criteria were applied to six reports and/or pieces of legislation to depict the nature of the current school reform movement:

1. Use of multicultural curriculum tenets/ learning styles
2. Efforts to increase the number of minorities in the professional teaching force
3. Involvement of minorities in the educational decision making process, at all levels

The discussion will focus on the following state and national efforts:

1. State-mandated teacher education curriculum
2. Outcome-based education
3. Choice programs
4. Inclusive education
5. America 2000, Minnesota 2000
6. Reports and recommendations of national organizations

Discussion

During the past 10 years, state and national policy has had a dominant effect on educational issues, especially in the area of school reform. State educational reform initiatives in the early part of the 1980s focused primarily on raising student performance standards and providing the resources to achieve higher levels of performance. There was, however, very little attention in these reform efforts toward policy that would seriously deal with multicultural education. These reform efforts have been characterized by a variety of different strategies, such as outcome-based education, inclusive education, choice programs, and national standards.

States vary considerably in the types of education policies and corresponding approaches to the challenges presented by the new students of color to the public schools they have implemented. Although the following examples of reform efforts are primarily from Minnesota, they represent, in general terms, the wide variety of education policies being implemented across the United States.

Teacher Education Curriculum

Minnesota Statute 125.8700.2810 is an alternative teacher education program. It is designed primarily to assist Minnesota institutions that are approved to prepare persons for teacher licensure and their teacher education units with redesigning teacher education programs consistent with the goal of developing effective teachers. It is also designed to attract minorities and other specialized individuals from nonteacher training programs into teacher education. This legislation is divided into three components: (1) program development and implementation, (2) program outcomes, and (3) program evaluation.

The program development and implementation component describes the elements required to fulfill the legislation, including a statement of philosophy, and requirements that: (1) teacher education programs be based on the study of a variety of educational theories, including knowledge and understanding of the foundations of history, philosophy, sociology, and politics of education, and the application of this knowledge and understanding in clinical settings; (2) teacher education programs be results oriented, based on essential knowledge, current research, and sound professional practices; and (3) teacher education programs include regular and systematic experiential activities that relate to the acquisition of dispositions, skills, and knowledge.

The program outcomes require that each institution establish a set of experiences involving personal, programmatic, and clinical components that foster dispositions for beginning teachers toward self and others, learners, learning, teaching, knowledge, the education profession, and institutions. In all instances, teacher education programs are required to foster knowledge and understanding to assure that beginning teachers are aware of and sensitive to disabilities and issues of multicultural education and gender fairness.

The evaluation component provides 12 criteria to be used in evaluating the effectiveness of the program, including required program outcomes based on research, theory, and accepted practice; a liberal arts curriculum that is an integral component of the teacher education program and is coordinated with current knowledge in the liberal arts; the incorporation of a broad range of clinical and field experiences; evidence that the faculty and cooperating school personnel demonstrate effective teaching; and the use of evaluation results to improve courses, programs, and learning experiences.

Legislation of this kind clearly addresses the need for preparing teachers in a nontraditional manner to work with diverse student populations. Although its primary aim is to increase the number of minorities in the professional teaching force, it also addresses multicultural education issues, as well as the involvement of minorities in the decision-making process.

Outcome-Based Education (OBE)

Outcome-based education (OBE) purports to change schools from input-based (time, courses) to outcome or results-based systems. OBE is programs designed and implemented in a manner that assures alignment of three basic elements: learner outcomes, assessment and feedback process, and instructional process. OBE includes an emphasis on personalized learning for students and the attainment of specific outcomes. This implies that schools or learning sites should be formed according to how outcomes can best be achieved, rather than size or cost alone. OBE is not simply a change in language, but, done properly, would require wholesale transformation of schools. There are numerous OBE efforts currently underway in Minnesota.

There is no single philosophy or educational theory that describes these efforts. The OBE movement seems to be developing as a belief system and as a shift of educational focus from the teacher to the learner. The activities within Minnesota are very diverse, including curricular revision, individualized educational planning for all students, new scheduling (including a 12-month year), integrated curriculum, nongraded activities, state-mandated OBE high school graduation requirements by 1996, and nontraditional assessment. Many of these activities are closely related to other educational reform efforts.

The Minnesota Department of Education (MDE) has sponsored several week-long workshops and summer "clinics," and encourages educators and schools to use learner outcomes as the focus of educational planning. *A Minnesota Vision for Outcome-Based Education* (1990) is a recent state publication that suggests some direction for curricular outcomes and/or objectives. The model recommended by the MDE incorporates the following eight activities under which all district activities fit:

1. Planning, evaluating, and reporting to the local community
2. Defining expectations (goals and outcomes) for students
3. Assessing student progress toward those expectations
4. Designing instruction that leads to achievement of the expectations
5. Dealing with individual parent/student abilities and aspirations
7. Partnership activities
8. Management of the educational enterprise

While there are specific suggestions for curriculum development and graduation requirements, the primary problems with the OBE movement in Minnesota are (1) it does not specifically address or mention the unique needs of students of color, (2) it does not include a strategy for increasing the number of minorities in the professional teaching force in Minnesota, and (3) it does not speak to the involvement of minorities in the education decision making process.

Choice Programs

After the dramatic 1983 report *A Nation At Risk* warned educators that the public schools were sinking in "a rising tide of mediocrity," national attention turned to ways to improve public schools in order for the United States to regain a competitive economic advantage internationally. State policy makers in Minnesota did not rush, as did many other states, to mandate a host of changes such as longer school days, statewide competency testing, or tougher graduation requirements. Instead, the questions being raised in Minnesota were whether learners would be better served by incentives for innovation rather than mandates to bureaucratic school systems.

Minnesota had already begun taking steps to encourage educational innovation. As early as 1982, legislation was passed that allowed high schools to enter into agreements with postsecondary institutions to enable high school students to enroll, with district approval, in courses that were not available at the high school. This was an attempt to assure academically talented students access to more advanced classes.

In 1985, Minnesota declared that choice belonged to all learners, regardless of where they lived or their ability to pay. A series of new laws placed the power to decide where a student attends school in the hands of families and learners themselves. This dramatically changed the picture for parents, learners, and schools.

Recognizing that no one school or program is best for all learners, the Minnesota choice programs provide a way for educators to assist learners in accessing the best educational experience for their needs and interests. All of the programs are designed to lead to a high school diploma. The choices include:

- *Postsecondary Enrollment Options* allows eleventh and twelfth-graders to attend, full or part time, a technical college; a community college; a private, liberal arts college or university; or any of the state universities for high school credit.

- *School District Enrollment Options or Open Enrollment* permits kindergarten through twelfth-grade students to apply to attend any school outside the district in which they live.
- *High School Graduation Incentives* encourage learners who are having difficulty in school or who have dropped out of school to complete their high school credits in alternative settings. Qualifying students may attend another traditional high school inside or outside their district, an Area Learning Center, an Alternative Program, or a private, nonsectarian school.
- *Diploma Opportunities for Adult 21 and Over* encourages adult learners to return to an educational setting. All of the enrollment options are available to eligible adults, with the exception of private alternative programs.
- *Area Learning Centers* provide year-round, nontraditional education for students 12 years of age through adult on a full- or part-time basis. Students develop, with an instructor, learning plans that best fit their course needs and learning styles.
- *Public/Private Alternative Programs* are designed to provide learners with alternative settings at a variety of sites and/or institutions where the education program is designed to meet the individual needs of the learner.
- *Programs for Pregnant Minors and Minor Parents* is designed to ensure that young women and men who have not finished high school and are either pregnant or a parent have the opportunity to choose an educational program that will lead them to a high school diploma.

The opportunity to choose any of these programs offers people a much larger role in their own or their children's education. Choice places greater responsibility on learners and their families to be active in determining the goals they have for education, to acknowledge the needs and interests of the learner, and to assess the school's ability to provide an excellent educational experience.

However, the Minnesota choice programs leave several issues that need to be addressed if they wish to meet the needs of the new students of color. None of them specifically address issues of multicultural or inclusive education. Rather, they allude to providing opportunities for all Minnesota students. Nor do these choice programs speak to increasing the number of minorities in the professional teaching force, or to involving minorities in the educational decision-making process. Furthermore, none of the choice programs have a specific strategy for inviting students of color to participate in their respective program.

Choice has fostered an atmosphere in which everyone is taking a closer look at schools. Educators and education policy makers across the country are taking a fresh approach to what makes a good school. Nathan (1989) suggested that as we have opened up more opportunities for choice among public schools, we have seen other results: (1) greater parental involvement, (2) more exciting opportunities for teachers, (3) greater support for levy referendums, (4) better schools, and (5) higher-quality education for our young people.

Inclusive Education

The Minnesota Rule for Multicultural and Gender-Fair Curriculum (3500.0550) was adopted by the State Board of Education in December 1988. The Rule requires districts to adopt a written plan for an inclusive educational program, requires districts to address all aspects of the curriculum development process, and suggests specific procedures in planning, evaluating, and reporting. Each plan must be developed in consultation with people of color, women and men, and people with disabilities. However, the Rule is specifically aimed at individuals who are currently students and teachers, rather than at increasing the number of minority individuals in the teaching force. It should be noted that the Rule specifically requires involvement of persons affected or impacted by the Rule, especially representatives from the four primary minority groups in Minnesota: African Americans, American Indians, Asian Americans, and Hispanic Americans.

Minnesota 2000

Minnesota 2000 is a clone of America 2000. Both are long-term strategies that build on the themes of earlier reform reports from the past 10 years. Both attempt to establish clear performance goals for all students—goals that will make us internationally competitive. However, a major limitation of this new strategy is lack of a specific discussion about how our nation's children will become knowledgeable about the diverse cultural heritage of this nation and about the world community. Indeed, this is characteristic of most of the earlier reform reports that give little or no attention to the unique educational needs of students of color. Although the strategy does address curriculum issues, it does not specifically speak to multicultural or inclusive education issues—nor does it suggest any strategy for increasing the number of minorities in the professional teaching force.

Reports and Recommendations of National Organizations

Science for All Americans (American Association for the Advancement of Science, 1989) is an example of a major report of a national organization. The report sets forth goals that suggest changes in our educational systems that are as profound and as radical as those occurring in the broader society. In the report, the American Association for Advancement of Science argues that schools need to pay more attention to the education of students of color, especially in the areas of science and technology area. The report further argues that (1) curriculum must be changed to eliminate rigid subject matter; to pay more attention to the connections among science, mathematics, and technology; and to present the scientific endeavor as a social enterprise; (2) the effective teaching of science, mathematics, and technology must be based on learning principles that derive from systematic research; (3) education reform must be comprehensive, focusing on the learning needs of all children, covering all grades and subjects, and dealing with all components and aspects of the educational system; and (4) reform must be collaborative. Additionally, the report points out the need to involve administrators, university faculty members, and community, business, labor, and political leaders as well as teachers, parents, and students themselves in the curriculum development process.

Although this report can be applauded for the attention it focuses on the education of students of color, like many other national reports, it fails to specifically address teaching and learning from a multicultural perspective. Additionally, it does not address any issues involved in increasing the number of minorities in the professional teaching force of our public schools.

Summary and Recomendations

The preceding reform efforts were presented to give the reader a general idea of the nation's varied response to the challenges presented by the increasing number of students of color in our public schools. States are indeed experimenting with a wide variety of strategies. However, few of these initiatives suggest specific strategies for increasing the number of minorities in the professional teaching force, or for involving minorities in the education decision-making process.

In order to address the critical issues concerning the academic failure being experienced by students of color in our nation's public school system, the federal government will need to assume larger responsibilities for setting goals and defining outcome standards; stimulating local inventiveness; and establishing assessment and evaluation systems linked specifically to inclusive education goals.

If state departments of education are to help students and staff gain an understanding and appreciation for cultural diversity, they will have to institute long-range planning in the area of inclusive education. It is especially important that these plans reflect the cultural diversity of the the United States and the historical and contemporary contributions of women, men, and disabled persons in our society.

State departments of education will need to develop policies that stimulate local creativity and inventiveness. The development and implementation of effective inclusive education programs will require new school structures that are flexible and allow for more instructional arrangements, more collegial interaction among students, teachers and parents, and more teacher involvement in curriculum development. The question of how schools could be restructured to best meet the objectives of inclusive education has not yet been well defined or developed. New inclusive education concepts must, therefore, come through carefully supported local efforts, where new ideas can emerge from, and be empirically tested against, the realities of schools and classrooms.

Although there is no single philosophy or educational theory that describes or summarizes the state and national reform efforts discussed in this paper, some commonalities can be seen among them:

1. There was very little attention in these reform efforts toward policy that would seriously deal with multicultural education. That is, issues of multicultural education were typically ancillary to the main idea, rather than integrated into the concept.
2. Specific minority involvement in the education decision making process was the exception rather than the rule.

3. Although these reform efforts generally speak to a focus on the learning needs of all children, generally they fail to specifically address teaching and learning from a multicultural perspective. (Indeed, a major limitation of the reform efforts discussed in this chapter is lack of specific discussion regarding the need for education about the diverse cultural heritage of this nation.)

In conclusion, the need for training in inclusive education in order to accommodate the full range of students of color is strongly suggested by the nation's dropout and graduation rates. State departments of education, as well as the federal government, should give the highest priority to providing leadership in at least the following five areas to establish a significant inclusive education research base:

1. Specifically, articulate a vision of inclusive education (i.e., there should be greater efforts to define and identify some standard tenets of inclusive education).
2. Encouraging local experimentation with different approaches to inclusive education should encourage local school districts and other education agencies to test different approaches to inclusive education to determine its effectiveness in increasing school achievement.
3. Provide an on-going implementation support and technical assistance, as well as financial assistance, to schools and districts trying new approaches to inclusive education. The federal government staff, as well as the staff of state departments of education, should increase their own level of expertise so that they can more effectively provide technical assistance to schools and local districts bringing out new approaches to inclusive education.
4. Research and disseminate results of effective inclusive education programs to schools and districts. The federal government should encourage collaborative efforts with state departments of education, colleges, and universities designing relevant policy studies, and teacher education programs. These collaborative efforts should make a special effort to ensure that people of color are involved in the education decision-making process.
5. Provide an appropriate set of sanctions and incentives attached to accountability mechanisms so that together they can stimulate increased participation in the development of effective inclusive education programs. This also calls for increased collaboration between colleges, universities, and state departments of education, especially in the area of licensing.

These five areas do not exhaust the critical policy issues regarding inclusive education that need to be addressed. Indeed, the suggestions herein are presented in an effort to start a national debate on school policy and diversity. Much remains to be learned about the most effective methods of designing and implementing an effective inclusive education curriculum. Research efforts should be increasingly oriented in this direction. Additionally, state and federal support should be provided to evaluate experimental programs designed to incorporate inclusive education approaches in the school's curriculum.

References

American Association for the Advancement of Science. (1989). *Science for all Americans: Project 2061*. Washington, DC: Author.

Boyer, E. L. (1987). *A Blueprint for Action II*. Paper presented at the National Conference on Educating Black Children, sponsored by the Washington Urban League, Washington, DC.

Coleman, J. S. (1984). "How might policy research in education be better carried out?" *Improving Education: Perspectives on Educational Research*. Pittsburgh: National Academy of Education, University of Pittsburgh.

Crumpton, R., et al. (1992). *Communities of Color Education Profiles*. A communities of color education assessment project sponsored by the St. Paul Companies, Inc., St. Paul, MN.

Grant, C. A., & Sleeter, C. E. (1985). "Equality, equity, and excellence: A critique." In P. G. Albach, G. P. Kelly, & L. Weis, (Eds.), *Excellence in Education: Perspectives in Policy and Practice*. Buffalo, NY: Prometheus Books.

Hodgkinson, H. L. (1988). *One Third a Nation*. Washington, DC.: The Institute for Educational Leadership, Inc.

Minneapolis Public Schools. (1990). "The nation's report card goes home: Good news and bad about trends in achievement." *Phi Delta Kappan*, 72C2, 127–133.

Minnesota Department of Education. (1990). *Multicultural and Gender Fair Curriculum, Planning for Inclusive Education in Minnesota*. St. Paul, MN.

Minnesota Department of Education. (1990). *A Minnesota Vision for Outcome-Based Education*. St. Paul, MN.

Mitchell, B. (1988). *A National Survey of Multicultural Education*. Cheney, WA.: Western states Consulting and Evaluation Services.

Nathan, J. (1989). *Public Schools by Choice: Expanding Opportunities for Parents, Students and Teachers*. St. Paul, MN: The Institute for Learning and Teaching.

New York State Department of Education. (1990). *A Curriculum of Inclusion: A Summary of the Task Force Report on Minorities: Equity and Excellence*.

Randall, R., & Geiger, K. (1991). *School Choice: Issues and Answers*. Bloomington, IN: National Educational Service.

U.S. Department of Education. (1983, April). *A Nation at Risk: Imperatives for Education Reform, Report of the National Commission on Excellence in Education*. Washington, DC: U.S. Government Printing Office.

U.S. Department of Education. (1991, April). *America 2000: An Education Strategy, Report of the National Goals in Education*. Washington, DC: U.S. Government Printing Office.

About the Author

Robert Crumpton is presently the supervisor of the Eisenhower Math/Science Program for the Minnesota Department of Education. Over the past 13 years, Crumpton has served in a variety of capacities for the Department, including manager of the Elementary/Secondary Education Section, basic skills supervisor, assistant manager of the Chapter I Program, and acting manager of the Equal Educational Opportunity Office.

Crumpton has just returned from a two-year leave of absence at St. Cloud State University, where he was an associate professor of education in the Teacher Development Department and director of the Minneapolis Public Schools/St. Cloud State University Partnership Program, a program designed to increase the number of minorities in Minneapolis's teaching force; enhance the teacher training programs at SCSU, and develop a professional development school for

Minneapolis teachers. During his tenure at SCSU, Crumpton wrote and published several articles on school policy and student diversity, including "Policy Analysis of State Multicultural Education Programs," "Profiles of American Students in the Minneapolis and St. Paul Public Schools," and "Preparing Teachers for Diversity: An Alternative Preparation Licensing Program."

Ethnic Labeling and Mislabeling

HARRY N. RIVLIN   *DOROTHY M. FRASER*

Everyone knows that there are laws and regulations against mislabeling canned goods. The weight of the contents of a can of food and the ingredients the can contains must be stated on its label.

Don't we also need ethnic "laws" against mislabeling people? Especially the children in our schools?

For many years, effective teachers have studied their pupils to identify the particular characteristics of each one—that is, their "individual differences." They have done this in order to plan for varied activities and materials to include some that would be suitable for each child in the class. Teachers examine basic data about such factors as the pupil's health, stage of maturation, intelligence quotient, reading level, scores on achievement tests, major interests, and family background.

There is, however, a basic inadequacy in using studies of individual psychology as the sole basis for developing teaching strategies. Psychological and sociological research are demonstrating that learning is an aspect of social psychology rather than of only the individual's psychology. In a sense, every classroom in the country is crowded because each child brings not only himself but also his friends, his family, his community, and the culture into which he has been born and is being raised.

Teachers already have taken a giant step forward when they realize that a child's coming from a cultural background different from that of the teacher, or from that of most of the other children in the class, is not automatically a handicap. Fortunately, the expression *culturally disadvantaged* that was used so commonly only a decade or two ago is hardly ever heard today.

This chapter originally appeared in *Praise of Diversity.* Its message is still relevant today. It is being reprinted in this text with a few minor changes and updates.

Pupils from other cultures bring customs and values that can enrich our own. We should appreciate the humanistic orientation of a Chicano who judges a man by the way he treats other people rather than by his wealth. We have to understand the absence from school of a minority ethnic child whose working parents had him stay home from school to take care of a younger sibling. Is this pupil just another truant or are there differences in values to be discussed? These days, when we wonder whether the structure of the American family seems so often to be deteriorating, we have much to learn from other ethnic cultures in which parents and grandparents are held in great respect.

The culture values and customs of another ethnic group may be different from our own without necessarily being either superior or inferior to ours. It is not the responsibilty of teachers to evaluate other cultures, but to understand them so that they may better understand and teach the children coming from those ethnic groups.

Yet even here we must express a caution. Although the last few paragraphs may make sense, they also illustrate the common fallacy of thinking of various cultures as though all of the members of that group are alike in their values and in their adherence to the customs and values of that group.

In recent decades, sociological and psychological research have revealed how important socioeconomic and cultural backgrounds are as influences on a child's learning. Studies of the traditions and life-styles of various ethnic groups in our heterogeneous society have provided significant clues for understanding a child's motivations, interests, and behavior patterns in the light of his cultural background. A wealth of information of this kind is now available.

Such information can help teachers take off the cultural blinders that all of us inevitably wear if we are ill-informed about ethnic groups other than our own. It can free our minds of widely circulated stereotypes which have denigrated particular ethnic groups as shiftless, or stupid, or lawless, or without merit in other respects. Erroneous labels or stereotypes such as these have done irreparable damage to generations of children and adults in our society. If we can get rid of such stereotypes, we will have taken a giant step forward.

However, as scholars draw together authentic information about the various cultural groups in our nation, it is essential to remember that the resulting pictures are perforce highly generalized. Data about thousands or even millions of specific situations must be pulled together. Outstanding values, customs, traditions, and other characteristics of an ethnic group are, therefore, often described in summary fashion. We may begin to think in terms of a *typical* Asian American, or Puerto Rican, or Black, when there really are no single individuals who can be considered typical of a whole culture.

There is danger that new labels will be used—labels that are possibly more valid and more appropriate than those based on the prejudices of the past—but that nevertheless are correct only in a generalized sense. Uncritical use of such labels as a basis for working with pupils of a particular ethnic group will mislead the best-intentioned teacher. Some teachers may feel sophisticated when they speak of knowing how to teach Black or Slavic children, when in truth they are simply thinking in terms of stereotypes.

When we speak of Blacks, for example, are we thinking of southern Blacks who have moved to the North? of Blacks in our northern ghettos who are trying to move into the mainstream of American life? of Blacks recently arrived from Africa? or of Blacks from the Caribbean islands? Not all southern Blacks are displaced share croppers. Some are former school superintendents, principals, and teachers who knew their professional status would have to be sacrificed if integration were to come into their schools, and yet fought for integrated schools. Even speaking of Caribbeans as a group is too vague, for few people know that the Caribbean Federation failed because the Trinidados, for example, thought they were so different from the inhabitants of other Caribbean islands.

The Problem of Ethnic Classification

Taking an ethnic census contributes to the use of labels that may mislead. Consider for a moment some of the other broad groupings that have been used in the collection of data about the student population of some large school systems.

Spanish surnamed, for example, is a recognized category. It includes such disparate groups as Puerto Rican, Mexican-American, and Cuban children, as well as those from Venezuela, Colombia, and other Latin American countries. Even Sephardic Jewish children, whose names reflect the sojourn of their ancestors in Spain many centuries ago, may be counted in the *Spanish surnamed* group despite the marked differences in religion, language, and many aspects of culture from others also classified as *Spanish surnamed.*

Again, *American Indian* is a classification which includes more than 300 separate tribal groups. From one to another, these groups differ enormously in language, tradition, political organization, and social structure. Even within one tribe, such as the Hopi, there are traditional communities that reject many accommodations to twentieth-century America that have been accepted by other, less conservative communities located only a few miles away. And there are the Native American Indians of many tribes who have left their reservation to work and live in urban areas. Yet the label for all reads *American Indian.*

For a final example, think of *Asian Americans.* This category includes children whose ancestors came from China, Japan, Korea, India, the Philippines, or one of the countries of Southeast Asia. No matter that there are huge contrasts in the history, religion, governmental organization, social traditions and life-style of the peoples of these nations—and of groups within each nation. Yet, in classifying the children in our schools, all are given the label of *Asian American.*

Looking Under the Ethnic Label

Of course, a system of classification must be simplified into broad categories to be manageable in collecting and organizing enormous amounts of data. To be sure, no qualified scholar whose lifework is the study of a particular ethnic or cultural group is misled by these broad categories. But the problem of mislabeling because of overgeneralization must be dealt with by teachers who seek to understand their pupils in the light of their ethnic backgrounds. A first step is to become aware of labels that hide as much or more than they reveal. Then, one must consider a range of factors that contribute to a particular child's sense of ethnicity and so to his individuality.

Within every ethnic group there are wide-ranging differences that have arisen from many interrelated factors. Some are socioeconomic in nature. Others have to do with variations in the traditions of subgroups within the larger ethnic cluster, or may be related to how many generations the family has been in the United States, and the circumstances of its arrival and first settlement.

Let us return to the example of the *Spanish surnamed* category which is used in classifying children by their ethnic origins. We have noted above the many and varied groups that are included in this category. Clearly, to look under the broad label of *Spanish surnamed,* we must find out whether the child's family background is Puerto Rican, or Chicano, or Cuban, or is derived from still another branch of Hispanic culture.

Those who have come to the United States, moreover, may not be typical of the population of the land from which they have come. The Cubans who came to the United States as soon as they could get away from Castro's Cuba were more likely to be middle-class business and professional people who stood to lose much from revolutionary changes rather than to be impoverished Cubans to whom Castro seemed to offer new hope and new opportunity. By contrast, those who moved from Puerto Rico to the mainland—they were not immigrants because Puerto Ricans are American citizens—were more often, but not always, the poorer ones who saw the mainland as a source of better jobs and a higher standard of living.

The Cuban exiles, moreover, knew that they could not return to Cuba while Castro was in power. On the other hand, Puerto Ricans who moved to the mainland know how easy it is to return to their old home for a visit or to remain there whenever they think they will be better off in Puerto Rico—and many do go back.

How much do teachers gain in understanding a child when they lump all Puerto Rican and Cuban children into the single category of *Spanish surnamed* and then also include Mexican Americans and Latin Americans in the same category?

Having determined that Maria, one of our pupils, is of Puerto Rican ancestry, we have a more definite idea about where to begin in understanding her ethnic background. But—is there a single model of "Puerto Rican-ness?" Researchers point, for example, to the greater difference that skin color makes to Puerto Ricans on the mainland than it does in Puerto Rico. Do *all* Puerto Rican families conform to a definite pattern with regard to the roles of family members and religious practices? Will all children of Puerto Rican ancestry react in the same way in a given situation? The answer is obviously "No." We must learn much more about Maria's specific experiences and those of her family in order to gauge the impact of her ethnicity on her reactions in school.

We must never forget, either, that Maria is not only of Puerto Rican background, but she is also an 11-year-old fifth grader. She is, thus, both a child and a Puerto Rican. We can expect, therefore, that she will sometimes act as a child, as all children do, and sometimes will reveal her Puerto Rican culture as she responds in ways typical of many Puerto Ricans.

The picture will become even more complex a few years later when Maria is a 16-year-old adolescent high school student.. Then, she will be torn between following the example of her adolescent classmates, for instance so far as dating is concerned, and living up to the wishes of a family that still looks askance at having 16-year-old girls going off on dates unescorted by a responsible adult. As an adolescent, moreover, Maria is not in a transition stage between childhood and maturity but is both child and adult at the same time, sometimes wanting both the freedom of an adult to do as one pleases and also the protection of her family that a child expects.

While knowing something about the culture of Puerto Ricans, and the hopes, fears, and problems of Puerto Rican families living in the United States helps the teacher understand why Maria acts as she does, any teacher who labels Maria as a Puerto Rican and lets it go at that, is far from knowing how to deal with Maria as a student or as a person in her own right.

Rich, Poor, and In-Between

To avoid ethnic mislabeling, we must recognize the social-class differences exist within every ethnic group. There are upper-class, middle-class, and lower-class Japanese Americans, Blacks, Jews, Chicanos, Italian Americans, and so on through the roster of ethnic groups.

Regardless of ethnic origin, every individual reflects in his or her life-style the socioeconomic class of which the person is a part. This is not to say that all lower-class. upper-class, or middle-class persons are carbon copies of one another—but it is to recognize the influence of social class on the individual.

If, for example, we consider Coretta King, Jesse Jackson, Clarence Thomas, Andrew Young, Bayard Rustin, and Barbara Jordan, we must be aware that each has his or her own distinctive life-style but that each follows a pattern of America's Black ghettos.

The children of a Chinese-American, or Puerto Rican, or Polish-American college professor undoubtedly have a different life experience from those of the same ethnic group whose family is below the national average in income, educational level, and other factors that go into social-class identification. Indeed, daily life in a middle-class Black family may bear more resemblance to that of a middle-class family of Italian American, or Chicano, or WASP ancestry than to the life-style of a poor Black family. How many teachers realize, for example, that more than 10,000 Black children in Washington D.C. attend private schools and do not enroll in the public schools?

One part of looking beneath a child's ethnic label, therefore, is to learn about his socioeconomic background. A middle-class setting is likely—but not guaranteed—to mean that the pupil has had broader and more varied experiences, such as travel, exposure to magazines and books, attendance at concerts, and visits to museums, than if he came from a lower-class background. He is likely to be more accepting of school tasks and more highly motivated to do well at them. His social attitudes and vocational aspirations probably will be influenced to a considerable degree by the socioeconomic milieu in which he lives.

Much is being said these days about the subculture of poverty. Being continually hungry is debilitating, regardless of ethnic background. Being unemployed is psychologically as well as economically threatening, especially in a culture like ours that answers the question of what a person is worth in terms of dollars.

Unfortunately, most of the minority ethnic groups discussed in this book know at firsthand what it means to be poor and to be discriminated against in the search for jobs and desirable housing. All to often, the differences in learning or behavior between the white middle class and the various other ethnic groups, regardless of whether the ethnic group is numerically a minority or a majority, can be explained more accurately as resulting from differences in socioeconomic level than from differences in cultural values.

Regardless of ethnic background, it is difficult for a student to concentrate on Greshman's or Keynes's theories of money when there was no money at home that morning to pay the rent. Why should an adolescent worry about staying in high school when he sees how many high school graduates in the neighborhood are either unemployed or are holding jobs that are unrewarding economically, socially, and personally?

Even so, we should not use *poor* as another stereotype. There is a world of difference between the kind of poverty referred to by the humorist Sam Levenson—who said of his family, "We weren't poor; we just didn't have any money"—and that of another family which sees itself as not only poor but also as helpless and hopeless.

Variations within Cultural Groups

Each ethnic group has important traditions that mark its cultural identity. Many elements are involved, including language, religious beliefs and practices, family structures and roles of family members, forms of artistic expression, and dietary customs.

Within each ethnic complex, however, there are variations of these cultural elements from one subgroup to another. Some of these variations may be traced to contrasting conditions and customs in different regions of the homeland of the family's forebears. In the enormous land area of China, for example, there are contrasts between the people living north of the Yangtze River and those of the southeastern regions in physical appearance and in aspects of daily life, such as dietary habits. Chinese Americans whose progenitors lived in northern China and those whose forefathers came from southeastern China may reflect those differences. There also are marked differences in values and behavior between the Chinese immigrants of past years and the more recent Chinese immigrants from Hong Kong.

Some variations may be the result of differences between rural and urban life in the land of origin—the peasant from southern Italy brought different cultural values and customs to his new homeland than did the immigrant from an urban commercial-industrial setting in northern Italy. The members of a particular ethnic group do not all follow the same religion nor worship in the same manner, even in cases where one church dominated in the original homeland. Orthodox Jews in the United States, for example, follow a lifestyle that is different in many ways from that of members of Reform or Conservative Jewish congregations.

Yet another element we must think of in order to understand the meaning of children's cultural backgrounds is the depth of their identification with their particular ethnic group. A child whose family is the only Slavic or Black or Italian family in the neighborhood, or is one of the few families of that background, experiences a different world from one who lives in an ethnic enclave where contacts are almost exclusively with members of the same cultural group.

How long the family has been in the United States may have considerable bearing on the degree and nature of a child's ethnic awareness. The Japanese Americans even use different names to designate the various generations. The first generation of immigrants in this country is referred to as Issei; the second generation, as *Nisei;* and the third generation as *Sansei.*

Among the ethnic groups which made up the late nineteenth and early twentieth century wave of immigration from southern and eastern Europe, members of the second generation often rejected their ethnic identity, sometimes as a response to the discrimination they encountered here and sometimes out of enthusiasm for their newly chosen land. Change of name, refusal to speak the language of their parents, and breaking away from traditional customs were among the forms this rejection took. As their children and grandchildren have moved into the mainstream of American life, however, there often has been a renewal of ethnic identification among members of the third and fourth generations. Many take pride in their traditional heritage and search for roots in the culture of their ancestors.

We must not assume, moreover, that the process of shedding old customs to become "like all the other Americans" is a continuous process. It often happens that first-generation immigrants are encouraged by their children to dispose of all the old-fashioned things they had brought with them from their old home. The third generation, interested in their ethnic heritage, may buy back from antique dealers at much higher prices what their parents and grandparents had disposed of as junk. Similarly, many members of the second, third, fourth generations often show greater interest in the old customs and traditions than did the original arrivals here or their children.

Among non-Whites, whose physical appearance establishes their ethnic group for all to see, there are varying reactions to their own ethnicity. "Black (or Brown, or Red, or Yellow) is beautiful" is felt deeply by some, and not at all by others. One cannot generalize about the degree to which a non-White child accepts his or her ethnicity any more than one can assume that all White children feel the same degree of identification with their particular ancestral group.

We must also recognize that many individuals in contemporary America have little or no sense of their ethnicity. They simply are not aware of it. Such lack of conscious ethnic identification probably is most common among people whose ancestors came early to the American scene, but it is not limited to them

For example, not all third- and fourth-generation Americans are seeking out their cultural beginnings. While they may no longer harbor the overtly negative reactions of their second-generation parents or grandparents, they simply are not aware of nor concerned about their own ethnicity.

We can smile tolerantly at the 10-year-old boy who says, "Girls are all alike," and decides not to have anything more to do with any of them from now on. We know that he will change his mind and act differently as he matures. We cannot afford, however, to be equally unmoved by teachers who say, "All Blacks are alike" or "All Chicanos are alike."

Stereotypes are harmful regardless of whether the stereotype is favorable to the group or insulting. We recogize as bigoted such generalizations as "Blacks are lazy," "American Indians are all drunks," and "Orientals are sly," although some of them are, as are some members of all other ethnic groups. A supposedly complimentary stereotype also may be

ading, such as is expressed when we say that Blacks have a natural sense of rhythm
t American Indians are good with their hands and are natural-born artists.

: is unrealistic to update Rousseau's picture of "the noble savage" and expect every
member of a minority ethnic group to be a paragon of virtue as it is to assume that none of
them can ever succeed in our often too-competitive world. People are people, and people
from all ethnic groups vary considerably among themselves.

Why should we be shocked when some members of a minority group who are elected
to the legislature prove to be demagogues and some prove to be statesmen? Does one have
to be a middle-class White in order to be demagogue? Similarly, why should we be
surprised to see some poor minority adolescents fight against many social and economic
obstacles, work their way through high school and college, and attain success as adolescents and as adults? Are only White middle-class adolescents ambitious and conscientious?

Labeling Also Can Be Useful

Labeling can be beneficial if it is used to start a series of interrogative rather than
declarative sentences. The teacher who starts by saying, "This girl is Oriental and that boy
is Chicano," is probably wrong if the next sentence is a declarative one such as, "Therefore she is…" or "Therefore he will do…" There is more likely to be a positive result if,
instead, the teacher then asks, "How can I get to know her better?" or "How can I use his
background to enrich the other children in the class?"

Labeling can be useful if the teacher labels the child as "child" and realizes that all
children have much the same emotional needs, even when they vary in the ways those
needs are satisfied. Thus, all children want to know that they are accepted as people and
are not ridiculed, either publicly or privately. They all want to feel the thrill of success,
even though they may vary in the degree to which they want this success to be acknowledged publicly. They all want to know that the teacher respects them and their family and
they are all pleased by the teacher's attempts to know more about them, provided, of
course, that the teacher does so out of obvious interest rather than as a surprised reaction
to a cultural oddity.

Preparing to Teach Children of Other Ethnic Groups

Teachers can never be adequately prepared in advance to teach the children of all the
ethnic groups they may meet in the course of a rich professional career. Teachers are
mobile and pupils are mobile. In one school, for example, where the experienced teachers
had learned to understand the cultural background of the Black students who filled the
school, the faculty found that their classes now included many Haitian children, who
spoke a different language and had different customs.

The interested teacher can learn much about the cultural characteristics of whatever
ethnic groups are represented in his class. This book deals with many of the large ethnic

groups in America, and there are other sources to which teachers may turn for information about almost every ethnic group to be found in American schools.

Though the information which a teacher learns about one ethnic group is ordinarily not readily transferable to other groups, the attitudes with which a teacher approaches one group can be generalized to apply to other groups. In general, the approach to another culture is either a positive one of willingness to accept what is different or a negative one of conscious or unconscious fear and rejection.

Virtually every ethnic group that has migrated to America has had to contend with prejudice and discrimination as its members struggled for survival. The compassionate teacher understands the problems of children with a cultural background different from the teacher's and possibly different, too, from that of the other members of the class.

No child should have to feel that he must reject his parents' culture in order to be accepted. Indeed, his chances of adjusting successfully to his school, to his community, and to the larger society are enhanced if he is not encumbered by feelings of shame and of inferiority because he was not born into a different family and a different culture. To speak of any child as "culturally disadvantaged" merely because of ethnic origin is damaging not only to the child but also to society, for it deprives the nation of the contribution that can be made by each of the many groups in our country.

While it surely helps teachers to understand and to work with children of diverse ethnic groups when teachers understand these groups, teachers should not forget that they teach *individuals* and not ethnic groups. Nor can teachers afford to ignore Kant's dictum: "So live as to treat every individual as an end in himself, not as to means to an end."

About the Authors

The late **Harry N. Rivlin** served as dean of the Graduate School of Education of Fordham University and university dean of Teacher Education of the City University of New York prior to his death in 1992. As director of the Leadership Training Institute for the United States Office of Education program, Training the Teacher Trainers, he helped the various TTT programs to focus attention on multicultural education, culminating in the book *Cultural Pluralism in Education: A Mandate for Change*. He coauthored this chapter as director of the Multicultural Component of the New York State Teacher Corps Network.

Dorothy M. Fraser was the professional assistant to the director of the Leadership Training Institute for Training the Teacher Trainers. She has been a social studies specialist in the U.S. Office of Education and is a past president of the National Council for the Social Studies. She is a professor emeritus at Hunter College, where she served as coordinator of social sciences in the teacher education program.

Chapter 27

Cultural and Gender Identity in Early Childhood

Anti-Bias, Culturally Inclusive Pedagogy with Young Learners

BETH BLUE
SWADENER

BETSY CAHILL

MARY SMITH
ARNOLD

MONICA MILLER
MARSH

Introduction

Patrick (age 5, painting his body tracing):   My mother has more melanin than I do. She has freckles and I don't.

Robert (age 6, mixing paint):   Look, I think that's the right color. Maybe should I add a little more yellow?

Kevin: Make it exactly like your skin (holding his arm up to Robert's). It is like my color! Let me help you!

For many years, strategies for multicultural education and strengthening human relations have been applied to progressively younger children. Often, these applications have taken an additive and superficial approach, focusing on holidays, foods, festivals, and customs of "other people, other places," or promoted a "tourist curriculum" (Derman-Sparks, 1988), rather than being implemented in a developmental framework for encouraging positive identity formative, perspective taking, or increasing social sensitivity and responsibility. Although many early childhood educators and child and family advocates have embraced multicultural education (Ramsey & Derman-Sparks, 1992) and have struggled with creating more culturally compatible and inclusive programs for children from diverse backgrounds, it has only been within the past decade that a concerted effort to promote *anti-bias* education in early education (e.g., preschool through primary) has been initiated.

The National Association for the Education of Young Children (the largest professional association of early childhood educators in the United States) has supported the anti-bias approach to early education through participation in an Anti-Bias Task Force, the publication of the *Anti-Bias Curriculum: Tools for Empowering Young Children*, and the inclusion of several multicultural criteria in their accreditation guidelines. A national network of early childhood educators committed to implementing anti-bias curriculum with young children has also been established, and qualitative action research, including that described in this chapter, has begun (e.g., Paley, 1984; Jones & Derman-Sparks, 1992; Marsh, 1992; Ramsey, 1987; Romero, 1991; Swadener, 1988, 1989).

The purpose of this chapter is to raise a number of issues and questions regarding anti-bias education with young children, and discuss observations and recommendations based on the literature and on our collective experiences working with young children, early childhood educators, and parents. Following a brief review of the literature and a framing of the "landscape" of multiculturalism in early childhood, we will share both individual stories and dialogue, drawing from our related teaching, research, and anti-oppression experiences. We have chosen to focus primarily on gender, race, and ethnic awareness and identity in young children. In the early childhood literature, as well as in our own experience of attempting to implement anti-bias curriculum, these are interrelated and emerging phenomena that have many linkages. Also, as women, these have been life issues to us; we ascribe to feminist principles and value the process of "unpacking" our own internalized oppression and assumptions about difference. The following paragraphs provide some background information on each of us.

Betsy is completing a doctorate in early childhood education, with 15 years' teaching experience in preschool through primary. She is a co-founder and owner of a child-care center in Columbus, Ohio, from which several of her examples are drawn, and she has completed masters research on reconstructing gender identity using life history interviews with adults. Betsy has been active in the anti-bias movement and social policy issues in early childhood, and continues to do research on gender identity and oppression using interviews with adults, adolescents, and observations of children.

Monica is currently a doctoral student in early childhood education. At the time this was written, she was a kindergarten teacher in a full-day enriched kindergarten in an urban public school. For three years, she implemented an anti-bias curriculum in her classroom, and has conducted action research on this process, including the children's responses and interactions, and her own growth as a teacher. This work was done in collaboration with Beth, a university researcher. Prior to teaching kindergarten, Monica taught in a fifth-grade gifted program and taught preschool and kindergarten children in a university child development center.

Beth, an assistant professor in early childhood education, has been conducting qualitative research on anti-bias and culturally sensitive education with young children for the past nine years, and has also done research on pre-primary education in Senegal and The

Gambia. Beth has taught preschool and kindergarten and has coordinated a full-inclusion campus child-care center. Her work has been increasingly collaborative in nature, including a two-year collaborative ethnography of conflict mediation in a Friends Elementary School and the more recent collaborative anti-bias research with Monica.

Mary is an assistant professor in counselor education with an emphasis in community counseling. She teaches marriage and family therapy courses and counsels families on a regular basis. Currently, she is conducting a research project that involves talking with African-American mothers about experiences as parents and how and what they do to fortify their children to thrive in spite of oppression. She is particularly interested in what families do to support the academic and social achievement of children. Mary has been involved in anti-oppression movements for many years, and during the past seven years has facilitated unlearning racism workshops for educators and social service personnel. Beth and Mary work together on an Institute for Education That Is Multicultural, focusing on school change in five urban schools, and often do unlearning oppression workshops together.

We draw heavily, in the format as well as the spirit of this chapter, from the work of such teacher-researchers and collaborative writers as Janet Miller (1990), Marilyn Cochran-Smith (1992), Vivian Gussin Paley (1979, 1984), Bill Ayers (1989, 1992, 1993), Gloria Ladson-Billings (1990), and Mary Louise Holly (1989, 1990). This work, which has moved teachers and teacher-researchers' voices to the foreground, has drawn from interpretive theory, life history, and autobiographical work, and provides examples of many ways in which early childhood educators are collaborating for empowerment and struggling for curricular transformation. We have each used qualitative research methods rooted in "every day lived experience" of children and adults in educational settings (van Manen, 1990), and have been influenced by interpretive theory (Page & Valli, 1990). As Bill Ayers (1992) stated, "Recovering the voice of the teacher—usually a woman, increasingly a person of color, often a member of the working poor—is an essential part of reconceptualizing the field of early childhood education." We share the view that authentic collaboration with teachers and listening to what early childhood teachers have to tell us (Kessler & Swadener, 1992) are essential in the enactment of an anti-bias, culturally inclusive early education.

Several approaches to multicultural education have been described by Sleeter and Grant (1987). These include: (1) teaching the culturally different, (2) single group studies, (3) human relations, (4) multicultural education, and (5) education that is multicultural and social reconstructionist. Of these five approaches, human relations is the model most frequently applied to early childhood settings. The goals of this approach include helping children communicate with, accept, and get along with people who are different from themselves, reducing or eliminating stereotypes, and helping children develop a healthy self-esteem and identity, often including an individual differences approach (Swadener, 1989). A major focus in the human relations approach, as well as in other approaches to multicultural education, is on the importance of teachers and caregivers using nonstereotypic materials with children. An identified weakness, however, of the human relations approach is that it seems to suggest that people should get along, communicate, and appreciate each other within the existing stratified social system. Issues such as poverty, institutional racism, sexism, ableism, heterosexism, and other forms of oppression in dominant society are not fully addressed in the human relations literature nor in their early childhood applications.

The single group, or ethnic studies, approach is far less frequent in early childhood settings, although it can be seen in the growing area of Afrocentric education (Asante, 1987, 1988; Delpit, 1988; Hale, 1986, 1992; Hilliard, Payton-Stewart, & Williams, 1990; Kunjufa, 1987) and some bilingual child-care and early education programs (Soto, 1991; Williams & DeGaetano, 1985). A growing movement within curriculum studies and education reform is the recognition that many of the unexamined assumptions about what should be learned and how it should be taught are grounded deeply in a Eurocentric world view, including assumptions about how children learn. This is particularly problematic in early childhood education, in which many of the prevailing assumptions of child development theory and "best practice" have been either colorblind or based on Eurocentric, often middle-class, notions of optimal early childhood experiences, communication with children, and what should be emphasized in programs for young children (Kessler & Swadener, 1992). Thus, voices for Afrocentric approaches to curriculum, including early childhood curriculum, have been growing rapidly in the past decade.

Teaching the culturally different was one of the first educational approaches to multiculturalism in the United States, and is based largely on assimilationist principles. Although the approach is often diminished in contemporary early childhood programs, a number of major early childhood projects and programs that emphasize early intervention (e.g., Head Start) or prepare dominant culture teachers to work with poor children and children of color embody this model. It is also applied to counseling, with courses such as Counseling the Culturally Different frequently offered. One of the ways in which this approach is problematic is in its framing of the "other," and the implication that there are dominant culture members and there are those who are culturally "different." We share the view that all classrooms are diverse and that we must interrogate ourselves, while learning about others.

Our work falls largely within the theoretical framework of education that is multicultural and social reconstructionist (Sleeter & Grant, 1988, 1987). Education that is multicultural goes beyond more typical forms or interpretations of multicultural education to include race, class, gender, age, and exceptionality. Particularly when applied to older children, this construct also emphasizes preparing students to analyze and challenge oppression based on race, social class, gender, and ability, in their school, community, and society (Sleeter & Grant, 1987). The importance of addressing these issues in developmentally appropriate (i.e., ways understood by young children), as well as culturally authentic, ways with young children is addressed by Clemens (1988), Derman-Sparks (1988), Phillips (1988), Ramsey (1987), Soto (1991) and Swadener (1988, 1989) and will be emphasized throughout this chapter. Phillips emphasized the importance of developing multicultural education into a process of action through which adults gain clarity about the conditions of our society and how to change them, and then design appropriate curricular strategies for schools and early childhood programs.

The *Anti-Bias Curriculum: Tools for Empowering Young Children* (Derman-Sparks, 1988) presents one of the first curricula to apply education that is multicultural to toddler through kindergarten settings. In applying an anti-bias or social reconstructionist perspective to early childhood programs, a number of challenging issues are apparent. The first concerns young children's lack of "developmental readiness" or cognitive capacity to deal with cultural content, beyond their own lived cultures, such as the significance of traditions to cultures, a sense of the history and issues of a group of people, or even recognizing a stereotype. Arguments against addressing complex cultural information with preschool and kindergarten children tend to emphasize the child's egocentrism and relative lack of understanding of time, distance, history, and symbolism, making it difficult for children to avoid superficial or stereotypic conceptions. The risk of providing children with only a caricature of diverse cultures is a very real concern. The importance of first enhancing young children's sense of self, power to make authentic choices, and opportunities to interact with diverse peers cannot be underestimated in any multicultural recommendations for caregivers, teachers, and parents working with young children. Children in bilingual or multilingual, mainstreamed, and other diverse settings have many natural opportunities to learn firsthand about individual differences and experience the richness of cultural and human diversity.

It has also been argued that young children can better understand information about ethnic diversity—for example, after they have had a number of concrete experiences dealing with shared human needs, self-awareness, and acceptance of individual and family differences. To assume that early childhood curricula, teachers, and environments need not reflect or incorporate the diversity of cultural, gender, linguistic, class, and racial perspectives is, however, to shirk from the responsibility of finding—and creating—developmentally appropriate ways to do so.

What does the growing body of research on children's early concepts of race, gender, and physical difference tell us? The development of racial and gender identity and attitudes is also of great importance to early childhood programs attempting to promote education that is multicultural or antibias education. By ages three to four, most children are aware of color and racial differences (Abound, 1988; Katz, 1976), as well as gender differences; and by age four, race or color becomes affectively laden, though the child may lack a highly developed understanding of race. Racial identification appears to develop similarly to gender identification, with girls tending to use gender for identification more than race. Racial awareness tends to develop earlier in children of color, and prejudice tends to develop earlier in White children.

Recently, it has been argued that gender identity is largely socially constructed, within the boundaries of the dominant U.S. culture in which hierarchies are established to maintain the distribution of power (Cahill, 1991; Davies, 1991; Morawski, 1990). In fact, one of us will argue that gender identity theory is in need of interrogation and reconstruction, drawing from an interpretive feminist perspective and informed by such approaches as life history interviews.

Another theme that has grown out of the blurring of boundaries between special education and early childhood education, as well as out of the mainstreaming movement, is the promotion of full *inclusion.* Creating an inclusive school or early childhood program in which all children feel acknowledged, valued, and respected, according to Sapon-Shevin (1992, p. 1), "involves attending to what gets taught in addition to how the curriculum is delivered. Not only must teaching strategies be designed to respond to a broad range of student differences, but the curriculum itself must address the many ways in which students differ." Although not a major focus of this chapter, children's understanding of developmental differences, and early childhood mainstreaming and full inclusion represent an integral part of anti-bias education. One of us has done research on mainstreaming in the context of early childhood multicultural education (Swadener, 1988, 1989) and another has taught in the field of gifted education for four years.

Finally, we would like to state some of our basic assumptions concerning bias and oppression. We share the assumption that racism and other forms of oppression are learned at an early age, and are not our fault; that oppression hurts everyone; that we, as adults, as well as the children we work with, stand in the shoes of both victim and perpetrator of oppression; and that oppression and bias can be unlearned, including through the process of participating in anti-bias education, parenting, and other early experiences.

Moving Anti-Bias Curriculum from the Margins to the Center of Early Childhood Education: A Conversation

In this section, we begin a dialogue describing our classroom experiences and research in areas of anti-bias education, particularly focusing on ethnic and gender identity formation. This section forms the bulk of our chapter and is divided into a discussion of two basic questions: (1) What are some of our personal and professional experiences in anti-bias early education, and what barriers, resistance, or dilemmas have we encountered? and (2) What do young children bring to anti-bias education, and how have children responded to anti-bias activities and discussions? In discussing these questions, we draw from our research, which has utilized life history interviews, interpretive theory, and action research approaches. Monica has kept a journal during the first two years of implementing an anti-bias curriculum in her kindergarten classroom, and we will be discussing a number of her journal entries. The dialogue that follows is drawn from several sources, including our meetings to discuss shared themes, dilemmas, and issues in our anti-bias work with children and teachers, previous research that we have published or presented, and personal-professional journals and field notes.

Monica: I wrote a comment in my journal: "I expect sexism in my classroom, and therefore accept it, in my classroom, more than I do racism." It's so subtle, and I'm used to hearing "You can't do that because you're a girl" or "Being a teacher is the perfect job for you because then you can raise a family." But I'm not used to racism—so I will accept sexism before I will accept racism. And I'm just now beginning to really look at sex oppression in a deeper way.

Mary: It sounds like you're coming to a new awareness of sex oppression, and you have an old awareness of racism, and that there's discomfort in trying to resolve these issues in your classroom. You're learning to unpack both sexism and racism, and you haven't grown up experiencing racism. It's important to consider how we are going to work with that tension. We need to find ways of thinking that allow us to support children in trying to debunk myths and dismantle oppression in our work.

Of course, as an African-American, I see racism everywhere—and sexism, and heterosexism, and anti-semitism, and all the other forms of oppression all the times everyday. One of the things which is transferable about different forms of oppression is that it is *pervasive*, and that it's the unspoken that really represents oppression. And so your parents said, "Be a teacher so you can raise a family," and didn't say, "Be an attorney, so you can raise a family." So the unspoken message to you as a female is that you cannot become an attorney. So, if we would begin to notice the unspoken, we'd have a real clear picture of how oppression operates.

Beth: This is similar to my frequent question "Who's not at the table?" or "What issues are not on the table?" and I think some of that comes out of my work on the implicit curriculum. What are the messages that even though we're doing some intentional, observable things to multiculturalize education, when we look at the overall structures, we're still operating in systems that perpetuate oppression and differential power relations? And that's where social reconstructionism comes in, and makes the whole project a more political one.

I also feel that it's important to interrogate my own White privilege, and have been using an essay "Unpacking the Invisible Suitcase: White Privilege" (McIntosh, 1992) with my predominantly White students and colleagues, in order to encourage examination of ourselves, our assumptions, and ways in which we are unknowingly reinforcing the status quo, which is based in large measure on power relations that privilege White, male, Christian, able-bodied, and middle-class perspectives (Meyers et al., 1991). I've also been looking at ways in which heterosexism gets played out in early childhood contexts, and so little has been written about that (Clay, 1990).

Monica: It's just that the more you're involved in anti-bias education, the more you learn about yourself. And sometimes it's comfortable and sometimes it's not.

Mary: That's the work. That's how oppression gets dismantled. By people doing the kinds of self interrogation that you're doing.

Beth: And I think you just keep upping the gradient on yourself, and how much you're willing to allow anti-oppression work to be pervasive in your life. Experiences of putting yourself in situations where you are a minority, and having more cross-cultural experiences so deepens the authenticity of our work, when it's carried out in more aspects of our lives than just in the classroom.

Betsy: The transferring of parallel types of oppression is part of what we're struggling with. I think that oppression—across gender, race, and class—is transferable, and that this is an assumption we should state up front. I've been very self-conscious of making the claim that racial identity is similar to gender. My research suggested that it is, but I can only hypothesize. African-American adults I interviewed remember identifying around race and then, later, around gender in similar ways, though much of this was unspoken in their childhood.

Mary: I don't think it's that clearly transferable or quite that neat. I think there are lots of parallels and lots of intersections between various forms of oppression, but you can't pick up one process and apply it to another one without a real critical review. Your comment, however, that gender identity may come later than racial identity with African Americans fits with so much of what I've always believed. One of the biggest dialogues in the women's movement, as you know, is that African-American women see themselves as African Americans before they see themselves as female, which I don't believe, either. But that would somehow confirm and try to expand our awareness about that issue if you have noticed that in your work.

Beth: I remember that from an African-American male you interviewed—that the gender messages were entirely unspoken, although many implicit gender identification messages were given and received.

Betsy: Yes. He referred to unspoken "positive indicators" for him as a male, so he didn't really have to think about gender. But as a Black man, he knew race right up front the whole time, and many of these were "negative indicators."

Mary: I had an older brother, so I think I was pretty much in touch with gender, but this example resonated because of the many discussions we've had over the years about how we see each other, and it is something that needs to be worked on.

Personal and Professional Experience with Anti-Bias Education

Beth: Maybe we can talk more about how we've interpreted or enacted an anti-bias perspective with young children. Let's start fleshing out just what it means to be an anti-bias educator. What kinds of work have we had to do on ourselves, with the parents of the children we teach, on curriculum design, and on making curriculum materials where few have been available? Henry Giroux (1992) has recently described teachers as "cultural workers"—what does it look like and feel like when we do this work?

Mary: Bell Hooks does a beautiful job explaining how her early childhood teachers served as cultural workers. She was taught a pedagogy of liberation—one that called into question the injustices of racism and challenged her to step beyond the limitations of racial stereotypes. This is what Giroux is saying—as cultural workers we can either support the systems of exclusion and oppression in society or we can teach children to question these systems. We can teach children that knowledge is more than what's contained in books; we can give children a critical world view.

Monica: For me, as a teacher, the first thing I would do is look at the makeup of children in my classroom. And if I want to have an anti-bias or inclusive curriculum, I would try to include each one of those children, so that what I am presenting to them becomes more meaningful and relevant to each one of them. For example, this year I have three Asian students, and last year I had only one, so this year I'm going to do even more on Asian heritage, traditions, and perspectives. So I make available a kindergarten curriculum, and infuse the activities which are anti-bias and which I try to make directly related to their experiences, with many opportunities to question, think about, and understand issues of equity.

Betsy: I think also being aware that we do live in a racist society, and recognizing that I have been a part of that socialization, and that I've bought into the unconscious messages about what it means to be a woman. And I've attempted to unlearn the messages that I've received which separate—or marginalize—people, and make that part of my curriculum. And so, it's not just working on sort of a psychological area such as self-identity and esteem and making children feel good about themselves, but it's also that I'm aware that there's racism and other forms of oppression out there. My goal, I think, is to promote social change—similar to what has been called "social reconstructionist" education.

Monica: The longer I teach an anti-bias curriculum and the more I add to it, the more I go though stages. Maybe you've already been through some of these. For me, now, I have deeper feelings about it. I'm not as nervous to present the information, and I'm more confident, but I'm also more amazed at myself and the different kinds of ideas and biases that I still want to hang on to. Unlearning a lifetime of dominant culture values, many of which you had never questioned before, can be a painful process. I'm beginning to really look at the fact that so many of my unexamined assumptions are based on very Eurocentric values and information. And this reexamination of old assumptions is an essential process if anti-bias education will ever become a reality.

Betsy: Probably the biggest step I took before there was even an "anti-bias curriculum" to follow, was to *answer questions honestly.* Kids would always ask us the questions, and we weren't always prepared to answer them.

Beth: Yes. The questions which children ask us often contradict some of the arguments from critics of anti-bias early education which emphasize a colorblind point of view—that children don't see difference, or don't read the nonverbal cues that someone is nervous around someone else and moves away, or that children don't respond to the stereotypes to which they are exposed daily. To be around children, I found that it was very hard to hang on to the idea sometimes found in the early childhood literature that children don't really see difference until they are five or six, and then may not see it until you point it out to them.

I think that children are naturally curious and accepting, and human differences don't yet have a negative connotation. It seems that so much of what we're dealing with in society is the assumption that difference equals deficit or that we, or the dominant culture, have to give something up in order to allow for diversity. I've been using a James Quay (1990) quote which states that in the U.S. we don't have to choose between a common legacy and diversity when we recognize that diversity *is* our legacy! It's a false dichotomy that we create between allowing for diversity and maintaining a national identity, and if we view our national identity as embodying diversity, it would be a lot easier to move forward with our efforts to education *all* children in a culturally relevant way.

Betsy: And it's interesting that when we're taught about how children learn, and Piaget's concept of schema, and if we accept this as a way in which children categorize and understand the world, it would just make sense that noticing differences and the subtleties, as well as the more obvious differences, is just part of who children are.

Beth: Yes. I've often used that as an example. If preschool children can do complex classification tasks, like class inclusion and different kinds of perceptual sorting tasks, and if that's part of children's predictable cognitive development, in the "typical" course of development, I question why we would argue that children do not see difference in skin color, features, hair texture, physical mobility, and other aspects of human diversity?

Monica: That always makes me think of one of the kindergarten boys last year who walked in early one morning and said, "Two little kids, two big kids, two black kids, and two white kids." And it was perfectly normal to notice that.

Beth: We've already begun discussing how young children notice and learn about human diversity and their own identities. This leads well into the second question we wanted to discuss, which is the issue of how children have asked for, questioned, or responded to our attempts to use anti-bias curriculum and culturally inclusive teaching.

What Children Bring to Anti-bias Education

In this section we continue to discuss the "specifics" of anti-bias education, including a number of recent classroom examples from Monica's kindergarten children and the children and families in Betsy's child-care center. We continued our discussion and critique of the assertion that children are "colorblind," and Monica provided several examples that demonstrated young children's awareness of racial and religious diversity and the ability to make connections across related issues of oppression.

Monica: Early in the school year, Douglas said to our Assistant Teacher, who is African-American, "Mrs. Martin, I have black hair and so do you, but yours has some white in it." Mrs. Martin said, "That white is gray, Douglas, because I am older than you." Douglas responded, "Oh! Well, I have black hair and I'm Chinese. You have black hair, what are you?" After talking about Martin Luther King, Jr., Derrick said to me, "Mrs. Marsh, skin color and different colors of skin are called race."

Children also became interested in religious diversity and its relationship to racial and cultural diversity. The following is a November entry in my journal:

> There was an argument after lunch today. Larry said that he was Jewish. Kevin said that he could not be Jewish because he was black. Larry: "Yes, I am Jewish and I am celebrating Passover." Kevin (pointing to children around the room): "Billy, Nirij, Patrick, and Stephanie cannot be Jewish because they are not white. I only see white people at temple!" Larry was very upset and protested this idea. The incident led to a discussion about skin color, nationality, and religion. I explained that most Jewish people were fair skinned but I did know there were African Americans who practiced Judaism. I gave the example of Sammy Davis, Jr. I later questioned Larry's mother about their religious back-ground. Although they are not Jewish, their closest friends are and the two families celebrate many of the Jewish holidays together.

Another recent example of the children's informal discussions of religion involved Allen, who was talking with a small number of children about the second coming of Jesus, and Joe L. said, "I'm glad I'm Jewish, which is much better than being a Christian!" I intervened, saying, "But Joe L., I'm a Christian. Does that mean that you're better than me—is that what that means?" And he said, "Yes, it does. We're luckier—we have more holidays! Look how long Hanukkah is! Eight days to celebrate and Christians only have one." You know, you really have to listen.

Betsy: I have an example of interrupting heterosexism with children. One of the boys at our child-care center has an aunt who is in a Lesbian-committed relationship, and they spend time together, and Brian is at the point of trying to understand what that means. One day at the lunch table, I heard Brian yelling at another child at the lunch table, "No, no, two men can't get married and have babies. No, it's not allowed!" almost looking like he was searching for some sort of answer because he was confused. For some children, this is out of their experience, but for Brian, here's this aunt that he spent every summer with, and so we just talked about what society thinks about a variety of life choices. It started with a conversation about two boys who were best friends wanting to get married and have a baby together. I just said, "You could adopt together. But, no, Brian's right, in most places two men could not legally get married." I really felt that Brian just wanted me to say it was fine. I also noticed that I was wondering how this conversation might be discussed with some of the parents that night, which brought up some of my internalized heterosexism. The reason I bring this up is that one of the things we all struggle with is how much information we should give children, because they do ask hard questions.

Monica: And how much do you hold back your own values?

Beth: Have you encountered any racist events at school or fostered ways of interrupting racism with your children?

Monica: Here is a January entry in my journal related to exclusion based on race.

> *While we were outside at recess today, Monyea came over to me crying as I was walking with Chad and Dan.*
>
> Monyea: *Those girls won't let me play with them.*
> Mrs. M.: *I'll bet if you go ask them again they will let you play.*
> Monyea: *No, they won't!*
> Mrs. M.: *Why not?*
> Monyea: *Jean said that I couldn't play with them because I was black!*
> Mrs. M.: *You're kidding. (Later I thought about how this may have been an inappropriate response, but it was my first reaction—one of disbelief. I mean, these are the only two girls of color in my classroom, and Jean is Asian!)*
> Chad: *Where are they? I'm going to go and take care of that!*
> Dan: *Yeah! Me, too. I thought that ended with Rosa Parks!*
> Mrs. M. (to Monyea): *Let's go and find Jean. I think we need to talk to her about this right now. Jean, would you please come here?*
> Jean: *Yes, Mrs. Marsh.*
> Mrs. M.: *I understand that you won't let Monyea play with you. Could you please tell me why.*
> Jean: *I just didn't want her to play with us.*

Mrs. M.:   *Monyea said that you told her that she couldn't play with you because she was black. Is that right Monyea?*
Monyea: *Yes.*
Mrs. M.:   *Jean, did you say that?*
Jean: *Yes.*
Mrs. M.:   *Why would you say something like that? Especially since we've been talking about Rosa Parks and Dr. Martin Luther King, Jr. and that it's not fair to judge a person by their skin color or eye color or type of hair?*
Jean: *I'm sorry, Mrs. Marsh.*
Mrs. M.:   *Please don't tell me that you are sorry. You didn't say it to me, you said it to Monyea. My feelings are hurt because I know that Monyea's feelings are hurt. It you are going to apologize to someone, I think it should be Monyea.*
Jean (turning to Monyea):   *I'm sorry. (I later noted that this may have been inappropriate, but I was taken aback and it was my first response.)*

Shortly after this incident, I received a note from Monyea's mother. Evidently this was not the first time a racist remark was made to Monyea in our classroom. It had happened twice before. I telephone Monyea's mother that evening.

Mrs. P. (Monyea's mother):   *Mrs. Marsh, I just wanted to know if you dealt with racism in the curriculum.*
Mrs. M.:   *Yes, especially at this point of the year when we are discussing Martin Luther King, Jr. and the civil rights movement.*
Mrs. P.:   *I just wondered. Monyea is too young to deal with racism in kindergarten. I know she will have to deal with it all her life but not now, she's not strong enough yet. She's too young. She came home and asked my why she had brown skin. Why did I give her brown skin. I said, Monyea, look at Mommy! Look at Mommy's brown skin, and then I explained the melanin and I used the idea of apples. They have different colored skin but they're all apples.*
Mrs. M.:   *I like that analogy. May I use that with our class?*
Mrs. P.:   *Yes, of course.*
Mrs. M.:   *Do you have any other suggestions of ways that I could help the children better understand the concept of race?*
Mrs. P.:   *Yes, sometimes I use cars. They make cars in all colors. Black, white, yellow, but no matter what the color, it's still a car.*
Mrs. M.:   *I like that analogy too. I am sorry that this happened to Monyea and I will address the issue of racism again. I will also help the children come up with some strategies that they could use to interrupt racism when they see it. If they are ready to make racist comments, then they are old enough to identity this kind of behavior and take action to stop it.*

Mary: We're always teaching and learning at the same time, and this would be a good time to use the "it's not our fault" assumption. I think when we work with kids, we have to find ways to let them be blame free. I'm wondering if finding a way to find out "what does the color black mean to you?" or to give her a list of questions would help Jean further explore why she didn't want to play with Monyea. As we work with children, we want to use some of the same strategies we've been using with ourselves, in terms of interrogating our own assumptions. It feels to me here that it gets cut off.

Monica: Jean is Chinese and there are only two girls of color in the class, and my perception is that Jean is often left out of things because she has a difficult time socializing with other children, and that was a way for her to be the leader at that moment.

Mary: Since this is an Asian child, are we seeing divide and conquer or internalized oppression?

Monica: I could feel myself being caught off guard, because I'm doing all these anti-bias activities, so how could the kindergartners say those kinds of things (laughter)? Sometimes you want to explore more but aren't sure how far to go.

Betsy: I think children learn very young that there's great power in some words and actions, including the power of exclusionary language—even when they don't say things with truly intentional or malicious intent. They see the reaction that some words and actions get from others and are experimenting with this effect.

Monica: And sometimes children just want to know more than we're telling them. The following is a dialogue from my journal in January, during a discussion of *A Picture Book of Dr. Martin Luther King, Jr.* They were asking for more information as they tried to make connections between three historical happenings.

Allen: *You know that man that killed Martin Luther King Jr. was a white man.*
Chad: *Well, what I want to know is how fast did he die? Where did he get shot? He got shot just like that other president for helping the black people.*
Allen: *Do you mean Abraham Lincoln?*
Andrew: *Yes, he, Abraham Lincoln, got shot for trying to free the slaves.*
Chad: *No, I mean Kennedy—I think his name is J. F. Kennedy. Is that right, Mrs. Marsh?*

Beth: Do either of you have examples of children's sense of justice or advocacy efforts which may have been influenced by anti-bias curriculum and related discussions?

Monica: Kevin was very involved in the discussion revolving around Dr. Martin Luther King, Jr., and nonviolent ways of protesting unequal treatment. The day after the war in the Gulf was announced, Kevin stated, "Dr. King wouldn't agree with this at all!" Kevin made a series of posters depicting Dr. King, including one of him giving the "I have a dream" speech. One morning I noted the following incident in my journal:

Kevin: *I have to talk to Mr. G. (the school counselor).*
Mrs. M.:   *Kevin, what is the matter?*
Kevin: *You wouldn't understand! You can't do anything about it. Can I go?*
Mrs. M.:   *Mr. G. is not here this morning, but this seems urgent. Is it something we could write him a note about and leave in his mailbox up in the office? When he comes in, he can contact you.*
Kevin: *Well, I think so. Kevin dictated the following note:*

Dear Mr. G.,

Why are there no black boy crossing guards? If this school is peaceful and you're making conflict managers and we want freedom, we should have black boy crossing guards. They need to feel like a part of our school. Please send me a note back after you know.

Signed,
Kevin

Kevin is very aware of the crossing guard situation because he and his sister walk to school every morning. Kevin's sister is in fifth grade and she is a crossing guard and a conflict manager. Together we took the note down to the office and deposited it in Mr. G's mailbox. That afternoon Kevin got a reply.

Dear Kevin,

I asked some of my black male students if they would like to be at the doors of the school or if they would like to be outside at the corner. They preferred to be guards at the doors inside. They feel like a part of our school. Thank you for your concern.

Mr. G.

Kevin seemed to be comfortable with this answer.

Mary: This is a powerful example of a child noticing who's not there!

Beth: Yes. Kevin is beginning to actually notice what could be described as part of the hidden or implicit curriculum in his school environment. I also see Kevin as a budding ally for others in his school.

Mary: I'm a bit concerned about the school counselor's response, however. Mr. G. chose to speak for the African-American boys and this served to stop further action on Kevin's part. He also may have missed an opportunity to bring Kevin together with some of these older boys for a conversation, which would have encouraged Kevin to further explore issues of race in his school. This is probably a very good example of how children, who are acting on their sense of justice, get stopped or begin to feel a sense of powerlessness.

Monica: The children actively responded to the anti-bias activities associated with peace. When the kindergarten class was excluded from a peace march which included representatives from every class except the three kindergartens, Carli organized a class peace march on the playground. I described it this way in my journal:

Carli: *Come on, let's march for peace! We want peace! We want peace!*
Anna: *Peace on earth! We want peace!*
The line got longer and longer. Jack, Kevin and Patrick ran to get on top of the climber.
Jack: *Look, Mrs. Marsh! We made floats for the parade! Peace on earth!*
There was one student who started shouting, "We want war, we want more!"
Carli: *Scott, be quiet! Get in line!*

> *Scott didn't join in the march but he did stop shouting. The march lasted for the rest of the time that we were on the playground.*

Mary: That's another beautiful example of how children have a profound sense of justice.

Monica: Some of the most commonly accepted indicators of intellectual giftedness in young children include advanced understanding, exceptional use of knowledge, and a high level of concern regarding injustice. Having worked with children identified as gifted most of my teaching career, I began to wonder if this profound sense of justice was specific to this group of children. As I share stories with other educators, I realized that young children in general do indeed have strong opinions about fairness and equity.

Betsy: Yes, I can think of many examples of children demonstrating a strong sense of justice. I remember one day when I was teaching kindergarten, we had been talking about Martin Luther King and what life would be like if he hadn't been around. And Jake, who is White, was sitting with his arm around his best friend Celia, who is Black, said, "We couldn't have been friends."

Beth: I have observed many discussions among preschool and primary children that take a strong advocacy stance—whether it's about saving endangered species, dictating letters and drawing pictures about the importance of having a more wheelchair accessible community, or ending apartheid in South Africa—and have been so creative in expressing their feelings and taking concrete action. Children haven't yet learned to question whether they can make a difference; they seem to be "naturally empowered" until we teach them otherwise. One of the benefits of full inclusion, or even mainstreaming, is that children can find so many ways to be allies for each other. It is great when children both help and learn from a peer who is differently abled. Peer interactions can form the heart of anti-bias education.

Mary: Interesting. Children have a critical world view. They see things as they are, and they usually name them as they see them. Little children ask "Why?" all the time because they want explanations for things they often perceive and experience as unjust. Of course, they are little kids so they cannot fully articulate this capacity. Adults, because of their discomfort with questions or the subject matter, often shut children up (or down) with a half truth, a lie, a punishment, or some simple fantasy.

Monica: Discussing a subject that sparks the interest of kindergarten children usually leads to the generation of new topics and much peer teaching. After our discussion of Rosa Parks, and a role-play of the bus boycott, the children were very interested in struggles for freedom and justice. One story in particular that the children seemed impressed with was the story of Jackie Robinson. Here's another recent journal entry.

> Andrew: *Since we discussed Rosa Parks, would it be all right if I talked to the class about Jackie Robinson?*
> Mrs. M.:   *Sure.*
> Andrew: *This is my book about Jackie Robinson. He was the first baseball player to cross the color line.*

Mrs. M.:   *Do you have any idea what that would mean? (No response) Do you think he jumped over a line with all different colors on it? (some laughter) Let's see some hands. What do you think?*

Andrew: *Maybe because he was black?*

Mrs. M.:   *Yes, that's right. He was the very first African American who was given permission to play professional baseball.*

Andrew: *Not all of the players on his team wanted him to play because he was black, but the coach said that he was going to play. He had to promise that he would not get mad at anyone who said something about his color or he wouldn't be able to play anymore. He promised to be peaceful.*

The kindergartners discussed how it would be very difficult to be peaceful if the other players were making remarks to you about your appearance.

Mrs. M.:   *Do you think skin color would have anything to do with being a good athlete?*

Children: *No! No way!*

Chad: *Is he still alive?*

Mrs. M.:   *No, I don't believe that he is.*

Chad: *Did he get shot?*

Mrs. M.:   *No, I don't think he got shot. I'm not sure how he died. Let's look that up later. Thank you, Andrew, for sharing your book with us.*

Andrew: *I'll leave it on the table so everyone can look at it.*

Beth: How do you think parents feel about all your discussions and anti-bias related activities? You described the mother who asked you to do even more. What other reactions have you gotten?

Monica: One mother told me that when her daughter came home and was talking about Rosa Parks and boycotts and Martin Luther King, Jr., she told a friend, "This is why we send Elizabeth to the public schools as opposed to parochial or private. You can never get a richness like this other than in the public schools." She told me she thought what I'm doing with the kids was great. Parents continue to be so willing to volunteer, share their ideas and cultural resources, and support this effort.

Beth: Let's branch out from our discussion of issues of race in the early childhood classroom and discuss gender and gender identity issues as they relate to anti-bias curriculum.

Monica: Yet another example from our recent bus boycott activities and discussions comes to mind. We were reviewing the bus boycott with Andrew since he had been absent for the role-play. I asked the children, as an aside, where they thought the word *boycott* came from. Here were their responses.

Andrew: *Maybe because more boys refuse to do things than girls.*

Claire: *Maybe because more men are bus drivers than women.*

Heather: *No, they are not! I have a woman bus driver!*

Claire: *Back then there weren't!*
Katie: *I think it's because more boys will refuse to do things than girls.*

I shared the "correct" answer with them, but they seemed to like their ideas much better.

Beth: This reminds me of some of my observations in a case study of two child-care centers that were trying hard to teach in nongender stereotypic ways. I remember children inventing language that was more inclusive. For example, when the dramatic play area was set up as a restaurant and one girl was repeatedly told by some of the boys that she couldn't be a chef, because "Chefs are men and waitresses are girls," she responded, "Then I'll be a Cheffa!" and entered the kitchen.

Not all my observations were so encouraging, however. I remember during an extended community helpers unit, another girl was often pretending to be the fire chief in dramatic play. The next time I visited her classroom, I noticed that she was the reception-ist and didn't seem too happy about it. When I asked her about her "job," she responded, "We went to the fire station, but no women were there. I can't be a fire chief." Another incident, during a week focusing on health and medical "helpers," two visitors had come in to talk with the children—a female doctor and a male nurse. Later, I overheard two children arguing strongly with a girl that she couldn't be a doctor (again, in dramatic play). When I reminded them of their recent visitors, one boy said, "They lied!" One striking finding in my observations, which did consistently model nonsexist language and talk about ways to get away from gender-typed activities, was the creative ways in which children used language. I also remember them playing with words—for example, when some children were playing airport, one said, "I'm the control tower boy," and a girl responded, "Then I'm the control tower girl," and another girl said, "No, you're both control tower people!"

One child-care center I studied had both a racially and gender integrated staff, including three male caregivers. It was interesting to observe one caregiver reading a story to his group of three-year-olds about "What Makes a Boy and What Makes a Girl," during which some of the children asserted that boys could not have long hair or pierced ears. What made this particularly interesting was that this teacher had long hair, worn that day in a pony tail, and had a pierced ear. Even when he pointed this out, some of the youngest children said, "You're not a boy; you're a teacher!" I was delighted on a couple of occasions to meet Marge, the plumber, who came to the center, and to hear children go to female caregivers to get help in fixing things. The most resistant community helper term, however, was *milk man.* Why? They never saw a woman deliver the milk. Similar to the girl who didn't see any women at the fire station, they do need concrete "proof" of sex equity sometimes.

Betsy: My research has taken a more theoretical, as well as adult-informed or life history-based, perspective on gender identity development. I've had problems with much of the dominant developmental psychology literature on gender identity, particularly in the ways in which researchers have decontextualized the process of identity making, thereby ignoring the powerful influences of cultural bias and discrimination. Frequently, children gain knowledge about gender identity through widely accepted principles regard-ing socialization, traditional role acquisitions, stereotypes, femininity, and masculinity

(Morawski, 1990). Children unavoidably gain an understanding of "gender-appropriate" behavioral roles because our society strongly dictates culturally acceptable norms.

My reading of the literature, as well as my research, leads me to think of the gender identity process as a cognitive construct created by children and adults as they attempt to belong in their world. Furthermore, I do not view the process of acquiring gender identity as separate from other identity formations. Instead, the process can be thought of as a continuum on which people travel at individual paces as critical incidents, experiences, and people assume central importance in their lives. This process is sometimes easy and other times painful, depending on an individual's awareness of membership in or exclusion from the mainstream culture. I view this process as fluid and continuous throughout a lifetime.

Beth: Is this one of the reasons you approached early childhood gender identity through "adult eyes" using life history interviews?

Betsy: Yes. To illustrate the various dimensions of this process, a visual image may be helpful. I've been thinking about various forms of identity as similar to the many wires inside a phone cord. Self-identity is like telephone wire—a flexible, encapsulated tube full of multicolored wire. Each wire represents an identity strand such as race, ethnicity, gender, sexual orientation, class, religion, or age. Surrounding the telephone wire is an individual's cultural experiences. Imagine pushing into the wire; this represents one or more of many life issues, and the push impacts the entire identity tube. In other words, as children and adults live, certain identity issues become of greater importance due to critical life issues and experiences. Each of these identities are formed within the boundaries of the dominant culture in which hierarchies are established that allow greater privilege and social value for some people.

To get at the gender identity process, I interviewed adults about their early memories of learning about gender, and about their first memories of an awareness of sex differences. I'd like to share a couple of quotes from these interviews. The first one is from an African-American woman, Veronica.

> *I remember this one kid—I guess I had been fascinated with the boys and wanted to find out what they had that was different from what I had. So he came over to the house and we were on the back steps, these wooden steps that led down from the back of the house. I was eating some Ritz crackers. And this kid, I don't remember how this came up, but this kid offered to pee in his hand if I would give him some Ritz crackers. I guess he was going to pee in his hand so I could see his penis. So, he was sitting there and he peed in his hand. So I got to see a penis for the first time. And I was like, "Well, so that's what it looks like." He was a little light-skinned fellow with his two little testicles and his little penis and he just peed in his hand and I gave him his Ritz crackers! I was real young, probably six years old.*

The process of noticing differences includes the powerful influence of social awareness and all the messages received concerning role acquisition and socialization. I think of socialization as the process by which a person is training to fit and function in the dominant culture. The process of socialization is often so pervasive that it is difficult to articulate specific incidences regarding early awareness of its existence. Here's another quote, from Bob, an African-American male.

> *Remembering when I grew up, it never was a matter of boys having to do certain things, it just was. Boys did these types of things and wore these clothes and acted in certain ways and girls wore other types of clothes and did certain things and acted in certain ways. This is the way it was.*
>
> *If I'm growing up and I don't conceive that there is a choice for me to play with dolls or I don't conceive that there is a choice for me to cook, my socialization does not affect me at all because I don't perceive it as an option.*

Beth: In other words, Bob felt comfortable with his early assigned sex roles and didn't resist these messages.

Betsy: Yes. But for others, there is a feeling that there are parts of the human experience in which they feel denied participation due to their gender, or feelings of exclusion. The message both men remember is that men do not cry; the feeling of being excluded from the female world where expression of hurt is an accepted part of being human. Chester, who is European-American, for example, described feeling uncomfortable because of his size.

> *I'm not very big. It makes me less attractive than if I was 6' 3". The closer I can get to the traditional image—a big, muscular guy—the easier a lot of things go.*

It was interesting to hear Chester describe his own four-year-old son's gender socialization.

> *I'm aware of the male culture I grew up in as I watch my own little boy. I took him to a playground and one of the other little boys started throwing rocks at him, and I know what he will have to do if he were to go back to that playground a lot...[He will] face up to this other little boy and demonstrate a willingness to fight back and if he doesn't do that, then, in the other little boy's eyes, he will lose stature. That's part of being a little boy, to demonstrate independence and assertiveness, and if needed, aggressiveness.*

The women I interviewed recall their childhood feelings of hurt and disappointment from being excluded from activities, decisions, and life choices because of their gender. Susan, for example, recalls many examples of differential treatment from her brother, or his preferential treatment in a number of ways.

> *We have a painting in our family that had hung in a museum in Europe—I look like this young woman in the paining. So all my life, at Christmas time, I would have to stand next to the painting and people would admire my face and her face. But is became real clear that the painting was going to go to the male in the family, not me. Even though it was my face.*

For Veronica, the recollection of exclusionary practices was apparent in the division of household chores and of messages about career possibilities.

> *My bother is three years older than me and he went to a special high school because he had decided he was going to be a doctor. So he was always busy working on that. I don't remember anybody saying, "Well, he's a boy and so he's this and that," but maybe that's what was happening—unconsciously.*
>
> *I don't know if it's because my brother was the only boy. There was three of us girls, but I look back now and it seems as though we did all the house chores and I don't remember my brother doing a lot of those things. I remember my brother was never there. I feel like I did a lot of the work that my brother or my father should have been doing.*

Role modeling of older siblings and same-sex parents were also part of my interviewee's gender socialization, although Susan recalls seeing her mother naked when she was very young and not identifying with her as a same-sex parent.

> *She was changing clothes. I was really little and I didn't identify with that at all. As far as I was concerned, her body was completely different from mine. Mine was so plain. She was as different as a male to me. She was seemingly so very big and rounded, with hair and breasts that looked so funny.*

Among Veronica's early childhood memories were her experiences as a "tomboy."

> *While we were growing up, we had a big field on the side of our house and I would be out there playing and Marie just wanted to play jump rope and tacks and I wanted to play baseball and basketball and run and play tag. So I noticed a difference there. I thought, "I'm just a tomboy." That's what everybody would call me and I just got used to it. Though I wasn't real comfortable with it. I remember that I was afraid that I was too much of a tomboy and that people would think that I was a homosexual. It was just fun stuff to do. Why were these people coming across this way? This was obviously a bad thing to be.*

Beth: How would you summarize your research on gender, and other forms of identity formation, as informed by your life history interviews?

Betsy: I found that adults can reconstruct childhood experiences as they relate to gender identity formation, and that the strong influence of adult role models, parental and nonparental, was apparent. I also found that making connections was an important step in gender identity making. Within this category, three themes emerged from interviewees' perceptions of belonging in the world: either feeling included, excluded, or exceptional. The multiple identities of class, race, gender, and sexuality were interwoven. A final category to emerge from the interview process I refer to as "facilitating change." The change making articulated by the participants included self-acceptance, transformation, and norm-challenging behaviors. This reinforced my belief that gender and other forms of identification are continuous life course issues, with strong themes from early childhood, but not limited to the "formative years."

Parting Reflections on Anti-Bias Work in Early Childhood

We have tried in this chapter to raise a number of issues related to the personal and professional struggle to implement anti-bias education with young children, while bringing ourselves fully to the work of unlearning oppression. We have attempted to share a series of conversations in which we interrogated our own and each other's interpretations and enactment of anti-bias. Approaches have included examples of things that get in the way of empowering students and working for larger social change. This work includes looking at the things we carry in our "invisible baggage" (McIntosh, 1992) and the old meanings we bring to new words and work.

One of our reasons for struggling to weave a tapestry of four voices—working across a variety of different background experiences, world views, and assumptions—is that we want to emphasize multiculturalism in action. We have much to learn from each other when we can trust ourselves and our colleagues enough to be honest and can care enough about each other to listen to other perspectives. We also share the concern that too much educational discourse is framed in subject-object relations, including many of the studies of young children's acquisitions of attitudes concerning human diversity. In other words, much of the literature on children's race and gender awareness and identity focuses on the children only, or on children's responses in a decontextualized research setting. We feel that implementing anti-bias education or education that is multicultural with children requires a thorough examination of teacher beliefs, assumptions, and understanding of the dynamics of oppression. As Mary puts it, "If we're not part of the unpacking, we continue to reinforce the status quo, and do not interrupt the process of learning oppression at an early age."

References

Aboud, F. (1988). *Children and prejudice.* Oxford: Basil Blackwell Ltd..

Asante, M. (1987). *The Afrocentric idea.* Philadelphia: Temple University Press.

Asante, M. (1988). *Afrocentricity.* Trenton, NJ: Africa World Press.

Ayers, W. (1989). *The good preschool teacher: Six teachers reflect on their lives.* New York: Teachers College Press.

Ayers, W. (1992). Disturbances from the field: Recovering the voice of the early childhood teacher. In S. Kessler & B. Swadener (Eds.), *Reconceptualizing the early childhood curriculum: Be-* *ginning the dialogue.* New York: Teachers College Press, pp. 256–266.

Ayers, W. (1993). *To teach: The journey of a teacher.* New York: Teachers College Press.

Cahill, E. (1991). *Reconstructing gender identity theory.* Masters thesis, Kent State University.

Cahill, E. (1992, February). *The social construction of gender.* Paper presented at the Ethnography in Education Research Forum, Philadelphia.

Clay, J. (1990). Working with lesbian and gay parents and their children. *Young Children, 45*(3), 31–35.

Clemens, (1988). Martin Luther King Jr. curriculum: Playing the dream. *Young Children, 43*(2), 59–63.

Cochran-Smith, M., & Lytle, S. L. (Eds.). (1992). *Inside/outside: Teacher research and knowledge.* New York: Teachers College Press.

Davies, B. (1991). The accomplishment of genderedness in pre-school children. In L. Weis, P. Altbach, G. Kelly, & H. Petrie (Eds.), *Critical perspectives on early childhood education.* Albany: State University of New York Press.

Delpit, L. (1988). Power and pedagogy in educating other people's children. *Harvard Educational Review, 58*(1), 54–84.

Derman-Sparks, L. (1988). *Anti-bias curriculum: Tools for empowering young children.* Washington, DC: National Association for the Education of Young Children.

Giroux, H. (1992). *Border crossings: Cultural workers and the politics of education.* New York: Routledge.

Green, G. M. (1991, February). *African-American four-year-olds' self-esteem: A field study of a southern rural Head Start program.* Paper presented at the annual Ethnography in Educational Research Forum, Philadelphia.

Greenman, N. (1991, November). *"Dealing with" diversity: Perception of difference and the shaping of meaning for multicultural education.* Paper presented at the annual meeting of the American Anthropological Association, Chicago.

Hale, J. E. (1986). *Black children: Their roots, culture, and learning styles,* Revised Edition. Baltimore, MD: The Johns Hopkins University Press.

Hale, J. E. (1992). Visions for Children: African-American early childhood education program. In S. A. Kessler & B. B. Swadener (Eds.), *Reconceptualizing the early childhood curriculum.* New York: Teachers College Press.

Hilliard, A. G., Payton-Stewart, L., & Williams, L. O. (Eds.). (1990). *Infusion of African and African-American content in the school curriculum.* Proceedings from the First National Conference, Atlanta, GA, October, 1989. Morristown, NJ: Aron Press.

Holly, M. L. (1989). *Writing to grow: Keeping a personal-professional journal.* Portsmouth, NH: Heinemann Press.

Holly, M. L., & McClure, M. (1990). Special issue on life history and autobiography. *Cambridge Journal of Education.*

Hooks, B. (1989). *Talking back.* Boston: South End Press.

Jones, E., & Derman-Sparks, L. (1992). Meeting the challenge of diversity. *Young Children, 47*(2), 12–18.

Katz, J. (1979). *White awareness: Handbook for anti-racism training.* Norman, OK: University of Oklahoma Press.

Katz, P. A. (1976). The acquisition of racial attitudes in children. In P. A. Katz (Ed.), *Towards the elimination of racism.* New York: Pergamon.

Kessler, S. A., & Swadener, B. B. (Eds.). (1992). Epilogue. *Reconceptualizing the early childhood curriculum.* New York: Teachers College Press.

Kunjufa, J. (1987). *Developing positive self-image and discipline in black children.* Chicago, IL: African–American Images.

Ladson-Billings, G. (1990, April). *Making a little magic: Teachers' talk about successful teaching strategies for black children.* Paper presented at the annual meeting of the American Educational Research Association, Boston.

Marsh, M. M. (1992). Implementing anti-bias curriculum in the kindergarten classroom. In S. Kessler & B. Swadener (Eds.), *Reconceptualizing the early childhood curriculum: Beginning the dialogue.* New York: Teachers College Press, pp. 267–288.

McIntosh, P. (1992). Unpacking the invisible suitcase: White privilege. *Creation spirituality* (January-February), 33–35, 53.

Meyers, L. J., Speight, S. L., Highlen, P. S., Cox, C. I., Reynolds, A. L., Adams, E. M., & Hanley, C. P. (1991). Individual development and world view: Toward an optimal conceptualization. *Journal of Counseling and Development, 70,* 54–63.

Miller, J. L. (1990). *Creating spaces and finding voices: Teachers collaborating for empowerment.* Albany, NY: State University of New York Press.

Morawski, J. G. (1990). Toward the unimagined: Feminism and epistemology in psychology. In Hare-Mustin & Marecek (Eds.), *Making a difference.* New Haven, CN: Yale University Press, pp. 150–183.

Page, R., & Valli, L. (1990). *The differentiated curriculum.* Albany, NY: State University of New York Press.

Paley, V. G. (1979). *White teacher.* Cambridge, MA: Harvard University Press.

Paley, V. G. (1984). *Boys and girls: Superheroes in the doll corner.* Chicago, IL: University of Chicago Press.

Phillips, C. B. (1988). Nurturing diversity for today's children and tomorrow's leaders. *Young Children, 43*(2), 42–47.

Quay, J. (1990). Indroduction. In E. C. DuBois, & V. L. Ruiz, (Eds.), *Unequal sisters: A multicultural history of women in the United States.* New York: Routledge, p. xiii.

Ramsey, P. (1987). *Teaching and learning in a diverse world.* New York: Teachers College Press.

Ramsey, P., & Derman-Sparks, L. (1992). Multicultural education reaffirmed. *Young Children, 47*(2), 10–11.

Romero, M. (1991). Work and play in the nursery school. In L. Weis et al. (Eds.), *Critical perspectives on early childhood education.* Albany, NY: State University of New York Press.

Sapon-Shevin, M. (1992). Celebrating diversity, creating community: Curriculum that honors and builds on difference. In S. Stainbach & B. Stainbach (Eds.), *Adapting the regular classroom curriculum: Enhancing student success in inclusive classrooms.* Baltimore, MD: Paul H. Brooklee.

Sleeter, C. E., & Grant, C. A. (1987). An analysis of multicultural education in the United States. *Harvard Educational Review, 57*(4), 421–444.

Sleeter, C. E., & Grant, C. A. (1988). *Making choices for multicultural education: Five approaches to race, class, and gender.* Columbus, OH: Charles E. Merrill.

Soto, L. D. (1991). Understanding bilingual/bicultural young children. *Young Children, 46*(2), 30–36.

Swadener, E. B. (1988). Implementing education that is multicultural in early childhood settings: A case study of two day care programs. *Urban Review, 2*(1), 8–27.

Swadener, E. B. (1989). Race, gender, and exceptionality: Peer interactions in two child care centers. *Educational Policy, 3*(4), 371–387.

Taylor, D. (1991). *Learning denied.* Portsmouth, NH: Heinemann Press.

van Manen, M. (1990). *Researching lived experience: Human science for an action sensitive pedagogy.* Albany, NY: State University of New York Press.

Williams, L. R., & DeGaetano, Y. (1985). *ALERTA: A multicultural, bilingual approach to teaching young children.* Menlo Park, CA: Addison-Wesley.

About the Authors

Beth Blue Swadner is an associate professor of early childhood education at Kent State University. She has been conducting qualitative research on mainstreaming, and culturally inclusive antibias education with young children for the past 10 years, and has also done research on preprimary education in Senegal, the Gambia, and Kenya. Her articles and book chapters focus on cultural diversity, home-school relations, and collaborative research. She edited, with Shirley Kessler, *Reconceptualizing the Early Childhood Curriculum, and Children and Families "At Promise": The Social Construction of Risk* with Sally Lubeck.

Betsy Cahill, M.A., is a Ph.D. candidate in early childhood education at Kent State University and has 15 years of teaching experience in preschool through primary. She is a cofounder and owner of child-care center in Columbus, Ohio which has implemented a multicultural, antibias curriculum, and has done research on reconstructing gender identity theory, using life history interviews. Cahill has been active in social policy and equity issues in early childhood education and care. She has presented her work on gender identity at two national conferences and will be publishing a book chapter on this work.

Mary Smith Arnold is an assistant professor in counselor education, with an emphasis in community and family counseling. She teaches marriage and family therapy courses and counsels families. Currently, she is completing a research project that involves talking with Black mothers about experiences as parents and what they do to fortify their children to thrive academically and socially, in spite of oppression. Arnold is a member of the Iowa City Women Against Racism group and is coauthoring a book based on this work. Mary Smith Arnold and Beth Blue Swadener work together at the Institute for Education That Is Multicultural and cofacilitate workshops that focus on unlearning oppression.

Monica Miller Marsh, M.A., is a Ph.D student in curriculum and instruction at University of Wisconsin-Madison. She was a kindergarten teacher in a full-day kindergarten in an urban public school, where she implemented an antibias curriculum in her classroom and conducted action research on this process. Prior to teaching kindergarten, Marsh taught in a fifth-grade gifted program and taught preschool and kindergarten children in a university child-development center. She has presented her work at national conferences and at a collaborative training seminar in Nairobi, Kenya, and has published a book chapter on her implementation of antibias curriculum.

Chapter *28*

An Interpretation of Multicultural Education and its Implications for School-Community Relationships

KATHLEEN DENSMORE

A fundamental paradox of our time is that after 30 years of reforms intended to meet the needs of low-income students and students of color, we are farther away from our goals in key areas than we were when we started (Kozol, 1991; Hawkins, 1992). Politically marginalized groups argue today, as they did decades ago, that our public schools are not serving their children's needs nor those of their communities. We are faced with increasing racial tensions in many areas throughout the country, as well as growing disparities in the relative educational and socioeconomic fortunes of other races and ethnic groups vis-á-vis Whites. Data on average grades, suspensions, and dropout rates from high schools on both coasts and in the midwest document sustained inequities in educational outcomes between White students and students of color. Once again, we are asking the question: What could really be of use, particularly in the lives of people of color, women, and working people? It is in response to this concern that different multicultural curricula have been developed.

In this chapter, I will first outline various rationales that have been offered for why we need multicultural education. Second, I will examine various policies that have been implemented accordingly, noting some of their successes and failures. Third, I will suggest that a key reason behind the limited and mixed successes of multicultural education has been the insufficient attention given to the school-community relationship. Last, I will conclude by offering some guidelines for future directions. The outline of rationales and goals of multicultural education will be presented in the framework of a brief historical overview.

My central concern in this chapter is to suggest that curricular changes have to be embedded in a context where we simultaneously (1) rethink our notions of and commitment to democratic education; (2) make challenges to existing institutional relations, particularly those concerning school-community ties; and (3) involve neighborhood communities to a much greater extent in the educational process. Thus, as part of a general concern with the relationship of education to sociocultural factors, I propose that the promise of multiculturalism will be realized only as we come to define its democratic content and character, especially the implications for community involvement in the educational process. My argument is part of the larger contention that the educational system, including efforts toward a multicultural education, will serve progressive goals to the extent that the surrounding public is simultaneously involved and committed. This is a lesson that needs relearning.

An understanding of the context of multicultural education must include an examination of the historical relations between our educational institutions and students of color. These relations embody another historic tension that continues to define key educational debates today: that between democratic and elitist visions of schooling. As with many working people, schools have long been a source of both hope and frustration for racial and ethnic minorities. For most of our history, educational policies have been informed by assimilationist assumptions that schools could and should serve as vehicles through which non-Anglo groups would come to conform to White, middle-class practices and values and thereby be effectively incorporated into the American mainstream (Kaestle, 1983; Kliebard, 1986). But as White ethnics benefitted from assimilationist policies, racial minorities continued to be subjected to profound racism and discrimination (Steinberg, 1981; Banks, 1981). Thus, it is not surprising that as the policies of assimilation lost ground, our nation experienced the civil rights movement and the actions of more militant racial and ethnic groups such as the Black Panther Party. These activist organizations can be considered the early advocates of multicultural education (Gay, 1983).

During the social movements of the sixties, questions of whether and how public education should become involved in trying to improve interracial and interethnic relations came to the fore. Activists during this period called for a restructuring of existing differential power relations in both society at large and within specific social institutions, including schools (Banks, 1988). Arguing that traditional educational structures and processes were not serving the needs of their communities, they demanded more control over schools and other social institutions. Demands for redistributing power in schools and school districts were accompanied by calls for greater minority representation in curricula and in teaching and administrative positions. Demands for community schools and scholarship and courses on racial and ethnic histories and cultures were advanced (McCarthy & Apple, 1988). Calls for "democratic" education implied that quality education meant equality in education. Multicultural education, in particular, was (and is) perceived as having the potential to preserve diversity, reduce social stratification, promote equal opportunity, and remediate ethnocentrism, thereby ameliorating racial tensions and furthering minority academic, political, and economic participation and success.

More recently, the argument has been made, often implicitly, that multicultural education is a misnomer: it really just means quality education. In this sense, multicultural education is a crystallization of our implicit values and notions of what education should be in a diverse society. At issue is one's orientation toward the entire educational process, rather than, for example, a particular kind of education (Grant, 1978).

Thus, three key rationales for multicultural education have been to promote (1) assimilation, (2) the maintenance of diversity, and (3) a particular perspective toward the educational process (Sleeter & Grant, 1988). I will now discuss select educational policies that have been implemented, at least since the sixties. Sometimes these reforms have been adopted in the guise of one of these rationales and sometimes they combine different rationales.

Perhaps the most important victory to arise from the popular awakenings of the sixties was the enlargement of access to public education for those previously disenfranchised. We have also witnessed a multitude of forms of multicultural education intended to redress racial inequalities in schooling. Prescriptions for reform have included modifications in curricula and textbooks (Banks, 1981; Banks & Lynch, 1986); teacher behavior—for example, raising teacher expectations and displaying cultural sensitivities in varying teaching styles (Ramirez & Castaneda, 1974; Garcia, 1982) and cooperative learning strategies; testing, counseling, and similar schooling practices (Atkinson, Morten, & Sue, 1979); and bilingual education programs (California State Department of Education, 1981). Despite some differences in theoretical perspectives, scholars from varying disciplines generally agree that students of color have attained unacceptable levels of educational achievement and that major school-related changes are necessary. Cultural factors are seen as largely responsible for these relatively low achievement levels. For example, the cultural and social structure of the school is often contrasted with that of (language) minority homes, resulting in student alienation from school. Culture, including language, is thus perceived as the level at which changes should be made in order to facilitate both educational and social success for students of oppressed nationalities.

Various approaches to multicultural education emphasize such curricular strategies as an appreciation of and sensitivity to different cultures, the preservation of ethnic identities and languages, and increasing the school and therefore future economic success of individual students of color. These approaches are improvements on earlier assimilationist models in that they place greater value on "difference" and cultural distinctiveness. These models are also beneficial to the extent that individual teachers are implicated in unequal schooling. For example, significant progress has been made in raising teachers' consciousness about sex-role stereotyping and excluding the accomplishments and histories of diverse peoples. Students' rights to literacy in both their first and second languages are also being advanced. Last, some of the approaches connect curricular changes to larger social and economic changes, such as job opportunities for targeted high school graduates (Grant & Sleeter, 1989).

Yet, the extent to which these approaches actually explain or confront the problem of racial inequality is problematic. In fact, the kinds of reforms we tend to find make it easy to forget that systemic racial and social inequity is the problem facing us today. Multicultural reform has, for the most part, been concentrated in the areas of curriculum and instruction. An individual's attitudes and values typically receive more attention than structural issues of power and control in society at large (McCarthy, 1991). Even when this is not the case and students learn, for example, about histories of exploitation and cultural oppression, students are not necessarily empowered as a result. In part, this is because students' relations to what they are learning are only abstract. The relationship between the knowledge and skills students acquire and the problems they face daily is uncertain.

Generally speaking, the persistent belief among educators that either (1) educators cannot really make any fundamental social or economic changes anyway or (2) the changing of individuals' attitudes can influence the kinds of multicultural reforms we find in schools today that contribute to the worsening education crisis. One problem with the second belief is that attitudinal change is often attempted at the ideational level only and not the experiential level. Further, insufficient attention has been given to the precise values and attitudes we are striving toward, their manifestations and implications. Most important, attitudinal change is often viewed as the most we, as educators, can accomplish. Perhaps because of this we tend to overrate its significance. The emphasis that we place on attitudinal change reflects, I believe, a cynical retreat from what might accrue if, for example, we were to define our role as including active community work directed at the social and economic factors underlying the problems before us. In this way, rather than simply changing students' opinions and ideas, their activities are changed as well.

In the discussion that follows I will address these two beliefs by contrasting the two notions of multicultural education as (1) primarily specific content to be taught and (2) a particular notion of "quality education" for a diverse society. I will conclude by arguing for the latter and explain how it requires that greater attention be given to school-community relations.

Multicultural education tends to be defined in terms of particularistic content believed to be appropriate for specific racial and ethnic groups in order to address the historical under- and misrepresentation of these groups and their subordinate status in the dominant culture. Using these same criteria, women and low-income peoples are often included in multicultural agendas. Thus, typical assumptions held by teachers who want to give attention to diversity are that (1) African Americans need to learn African-American history, (2) females need to learn about famous historical women, and (3) students from low-income backgrounds need to learn a trade or labor history. In some cases, changing teaching styles in order to take into account possible differences in learning styles among these groups is also proposed.

These assumptions and approaches are understandable given, for example, issues around identity development and maintenance (Bullivant, 1981). For the past two decades, minority and female scientists, writers, mathematicians, and so on have been "rediscovered" and serve as a source of pride and as people with whom many alienated youth can identify. Further, these approaches reflect our striving, as educators, to deal more accurately with the contributions of diverse peoples and to question the implications of the dominance of White, middle-class males in society. Indeed, increasing numbers of people have been forced to reexamine "dominant" history and literature and to raise important intellectual, cultural, and social questions. This questioning is critical, especially given recent immigration trends (both legal and illegal). These trends suggest that our society will increase in its racial and ethnic diversity. In the state of California, for example, we have matrices of Japantowns, Chinatowns, Koreatowns, barrios, and so forth. These changes, together with the intellectual questioning we are engaged in, are changing and enriching our notions of what it means to be an "American" (Schlesinger, 1991).

Multicultural education is intended, in large part, to affirm the worth and dignity of those students who have been historically marginalized. Even though conservative critics have recently been trying to create the impression that ethnic-centered curricula have been imposed in schools nationwide, in fact, changes in the ethnic diversification of curriculum content are not yet widespread. This constitutes an area in which we will have to continue to struggle for a long time.

At the same time, I believe we have confused the need to target and advocate the educational needs of those who systematically and institutionally wield marginal control in society with giving students of color special curriculum content. A separate though related dilemma is that, in practice, multiculturalists often ignore categories of social class, sexual orientation, and disabilities.

This neglect contributes to multicultural reform being interpreted as supplemental curriculum content designed for specific racial and ethnic groups. Teaching African-American adolescents about Martin Luther King or Malcolm X appears radical, but often it means little more than substituting one content for another. Especially when taught via conventional pedagogy, this new content *may not* be what best serves students' needs. Memorizing who Emilio Zapata was does not necessarily advance the interests of Chicano students. This *may* be "relevant" for some students but not necessarily. This may be true, for example, if by "relevant" we mean responding to an interest that a given student brings with him or her to the classroom on any given day. But even this is problematic. Historical figures, or that which is selected about them for textbook inclusion, even when having membership in conventionally excluded groups, typically do not have either the class identity or ideological commitments that fundamentally challenge existing power relationships.

For example, Martin Luther King was not only a leader of African Americans but he was also a world leader for peace as well as a leader of the Vietnam anti-war coalition in the United States. He was a leader of the struggle for the interests of all poor peoples. He grew increasingly critical of the many forms of exploitation in our society. This kind of information about Dr. King receives scant attention, if any. Further, the significance of these contributions transcends race and ethnicity and properly forms part of our national and international heritage. Finally, if our struggle against racism is to take root, then we must also aim this content at White students.

There are three issues here—one is the very real importance of content selection, another is which students receive which content, and the third refers to limiting change to curriculum content. With respect to the latter, content substitution alone avoids rethinking possibilities for and requisites of democratic education, active citizenship, and questions about the larger purposes of education. Failing this, new curricula cannot address the underlying needs of students and their communities that multicultural education was meant to respond to.

Let me be clear. I am not arguing against the need for Black history, women studies, and so on. In large part because of this work we now understand that to study any subject at all, including "American" traditions *is* to study diversity; influences, patterns, traditions, and events are best understood in relation to others. This contrasts with the Eurocentric assimilationist model.

Logically, then, might not multicultural education really be what we have in mind when we speak of quality education—for all? The issue presupposes questions of aims and commitments. Depending on one's definition of the purpose of education, different kinds of reforms will be suggested. While most people likely agree that schooling should lead to the development of both individual potential and social betterment, the questions of individual potential for what, and what kind of social betterment we have in mind is answered in different ways by different peoples. If, for example, one views the purpose of public education as ultimately to contribute to economic growth believing that a strong, internationally competitive economy is the most fundamental answer to both social and educational questions and problems, you might think of developing individual potential in order to increase one's capacity for economic achievement From this perspective, quality education might be defined as that which most efficiently and effectively prepares students for the world of work

If, on the other hand, you view the purpose of education as primarily to reduce or eradicate social injustices, believing that social betterment depends on socioeconomic, political equality as much as economic strength, you might think of developing individual potential for the purpose of enabling all students to critically engage with society. From this perspective, quality education might be defined as that which starts with and builds on students' experiences, teaching them to analyze such things as the interests that underlie various things that we take for granted; who they have become in relation to their cultural historical, economic context and in relation to who they want to be (Simon, 1987) and the canon in our disciplines, in relation to popular works.

My own perspective combines elements of both of the preceding viewpoints. The purpose of education in general, and of multicultural education in particular, as I see it, is to simultaneously prepare students to function effectively in existing institutional structures—the world of work being no exception—and to enable students to transform existing social and economic inequities while working toward a more just society. Quality education in this sense is that which provides a critical understanding of how society works and of how social values and priorities are defined. Quality education has as a goal educating students to distinguish between that from our diverse pasts that needs to be discarded and that which we can build upon. Students should be taught to draw on their own cultural resources as a basis for engaging in the development of new skills and to critically appropriate forms of knowledge that exist outside of their personal experiences. Various works, including the canon, should be read as both cultural and historical products.

Thus, in addition to curriculum content that is inclusive of diverse contributions and critical of structures of oppression, multicultural education also involves a particular perspective from which one approaches subject matter, whether it be math or English literature. Further, minority cultural experiences, or "diversity" would not simply be "confirmed" or celebrated but compared and contrasted in diverse contexts and examined like everything else, identifying strengths as well as weaknesses. Last, but not least, the lessons we prepare for students would be closely connected to the realities of the larger society. In this way, citizenship can begin to take on real meaning.

The kinds of skills quality teaching implies include basic general skills of analysis and abstraction where students, for example, move from the general to the particular and from the concrete to the abstract. Students would distinguish between information, ideas, and knowledge. Intellectual work should be experienced as having tangible efficacy for everyone, enhancing the expression of diversity in our society. To the extent that students have had experience with exercising capabilities of reasoning, questioning, creating, and imagining, they will be better able to facilitate social cohesion and reduce the polarization of peoples that is currently jeopardizing the quality of life in our society. Both intellectual and cultural growth depend on serious questioning, criticism, and change.

The failure of public schools to enhance students' capacities to think critically, acquire social understandings, and develop and encourage active citizenship is not separate from the failure of schools to achieve equality of outcomes. While everyone has a right to receive quality education, where students learn, for example, to analyze problems and create and design their own projects, these kinds of learning activities tend to be found most often in economically privileged schools. This (historic) tension between democratic and elitist visions of schooling may help explain why in so many instances we find supplemental curricula—content for students to absorb—sufficing for multicultural education. Such reforms can be condescending; they are sometimes used in attempts to placate targeted populations, where teachers complacently reason the new content renders their classrooms relevant. It is not surprising that the response among many oppressed nationalities is less than enthusiasm. Treating multicultural education as either supplemental curricula or as curricula especially suited for students of color is similar to meritocratic school practices that explain school failure by attributing it to individual (or cultural) deficiencies, rather than to educational practices that do not serve students in general well. Thus, a contradiction exists for those who understand that educational "underachievements" are not due primarily to individuals, families, or cultural traits and yet advance culturally specific content for minorities as "solutions." Isn't it reasonable instead to make all curricula multicultural?

Most education reforms designed to address the needs of our diverse society have focused on intraschool change—namely, curriculum and instruction. The search for reforms that will fit into existing institutional constraints is understandable given, for example, teachers' needs for hands-on materials as they face the ever-present question, "What will I do tomorrow in class?" At the same time, these reforms have failed to redress the worsening plight of low-income women and people of color. The rebellions occurring in our urban areas testify to this, as do the various forms of racial oppression and overt acts of racial hostility in our schools and workplaces. Low-income students and racial and ethnic minorities continue to "underachieve" in school, obtain lower-paying jobs, receive fewer promotions, and on and on. In the broader scheme of things, such interrelated factors as prolonged economic stagnation, the shifting of national priorities away from social spending, the demise of social movements, unresponsive bureaucracies, and the isolation of teacher professionalism from school communities (Densmore, 1987) have combined to largely resist, coopt, or fragment the early multicultural demands for far-reaching educational and social changes. Still, as educators, we must continue to search for ways to improve our practice.

To conclude this chapter, I will now discuss the need for teachers and students to work more closely with parents and other community members in identifying and working toward common goals. "Relevance," with this approach, takes on new meaning as students come to understand themselves in multiple and overlapping dimensions and as all of us find new terms of unity.

Educators generally agree that public schooling can and should play a role in preparing students to participate in and enhance our democratic, diverse culture, yet it is astonishing how the specification of what this role is or might become continues to receive scant attention. Despite scholarly calls for debate and clear articulation of our goals and priorities, whether we're talking about "anti-racist" teaching, "critical" pedagogy, or a "revitalized public sphere" (e.g., Liston & Zeichner, 1987; Aronowitz & Giroux, 1985), most often the "solutions" offered are those that individual teachers can obtain within their classrooms. For example, teachers are exhorted to engage students in democratic "discourse" where they critically examine structures of oppression and possibilities for social transformation. Drawing on John Dewey, the argument is that democracy demands particular habits of mind and citizenship skills and that these qualities must be learned and practiced. Sometimes the reasonable though vague argument is made that teachers engaged in "critical" pedagogy must also link up with progressive organizations or movements and simultaneously struggle for democracy outside of more narrow school issues. Rarely, but occasionally, there are more specific calls for political action such as campaigns against budget cuts or the arms race (Shor, 1986).

Progressive educators are familiar with these proposals; they are not new. Yet a glaring silence exists regarding how to carry them out. Indeed, that these proposals need organizational mechanisms and that educators have a responsibility to work with noneducators toward this end is disputed, or, more often, ignored. The political space opened by these arguments remains neglected.

The organizational mechanisms and political space I have in mind refer to the need to systematically secure community (e.g., civic organizations, unions) involvement in and support for our goals as progressive educators. Earlier in this chapter I argued that the primary rationale for multicultural education should not be simply curriculum content but, in addition, skills of analysis and active citizenship. But how are these skills best learned? In practice, many educators advocating "multiculturalism" place greater emphasis on holding "relevant" discussions with their students than teaching or reinforcing the use of analytical abilities. This is, I believe, a serious mistake. First, even if a student displays "progressive" values or bits of knowledge, that does not empower him or her to resist indoctrination (from the left or right) or assess new and problematic situations. Second, isn't the acquisition of these skills (including reading, writing, and computation) one major expectation that parents have of schools? Third, given that this expectation is a prerequisite for a democratic society, educators must give it serious attention. Last, this kind of classroom practice reinforces the notion that multicultural education is less than intellectually rigorous. This notion is held not only by many members of the general public but by many educators as well and must be addressed.

At the same time, the exercise of informed citizenship cannot be learned in the abstract. Reading civics books or even holding mock elections in the classroom falls short of imparting a broad understanding of education and social responsibility in the lives of students. Democratic, multicultural education must be more than a mode of discourse. To date, most "critical" pedagogy has been confined to classroom practice, and even still, often with no clear intellectual objectives. This unnecessarily limits students' understandings of society and, in particular, those sections that are most closely linked to schooling. As educators, our social and intellectual objectives necessarily require going outside of the classroom with our students. Both the reasons for and implications of this are manifold. In the absence of vibrant working relationships between schools and communities, it is difficult for students to experience and recognize the applicability of what they learn in school for their life outside of the classroom. This is especially true for low-income and minority students whose life experiences are typically not reflected in school practices.

Ethnically diversified curricula should articulate strategies for how teachers and students can work with and learn from diverse community members in working toward their common concerns. For example, as students are studying how historically different peoples under different circumstances have improved their lives as well as the quality of life for others, they can also be learning about struggles taking place in their own communities against racism, poverty, and the like. Meeting with adults who are working to arrest crime in their neighborhood, fight substance abuse, or reverse state budget cuts provides an experiential basis from which students can give meaning to the curriculum in their schools. This principle applies to all students regardless of community affiliation. In this way, we also stand firm on the responsibility that schools, as public institutions, have to serve not only their students as individuals but their communities as well. In this way, we can simultaneously begin to better understand and solve the underlying problems that are largely responsible for the problems facing us today.

There is a tendency for educators to define academic curricula, even multicultural curricula, as properly distinct from engagement in solving social problems. Yet the impact of these problems (e.g., poverty) on the students in our classrooms means that we must confront them if we are serious about educating the students we have. Malnutrition and low self-esteem, for example, seriously impair a child's ability to learn. This means that in our efforts to realize the goals of a curriculum for diversity, we will confront and must address underlying social and economic factors. This can be best accomplished by teachers and community members working together. The specific problems to focus on will vary, especially at the initial stages of working together, depending on the community. Generally, however, schools and communities must create new institutional structures and political processes by which needs can be reprioritized and the means of satisfying them decided upon.

In my own neighborhood, for example, neighbors have recently come together to discuss possibilities for stopping drug transactions that take place at a corner grocery store. Equally important to the problem of drugs is that daily, as young, African-American schoolchildren go back and forth between their homes in the "projects" and school, they pass African-American males, young and old, congregated at this corner with little to look forward to in their lives. What sense do the students make of these daily realities in relation to what they are learning in school? In short, teachers have an immediate interest in joining community efforts to combat such issues, all of which critically impact students.

Vast economic disparities among families and communities mean that there are immense differences in the capacities of parents and local communities to address these problems and improve the quality of education in local schools. For example, it is simply unrealistic to assume that goals of equal opportunity can be met without certain commitments on the national level. We need new tax policies, job training programs, and a stronger safety net for the poor. This implies that community-school initiatives must, at some point, be connected to parallel efforts in other areas of the country to be effective.

Thus, as a public institution that many people still believe can and should contribute to social betterment, schools should not be disengaged from the growing social problems of their communities. Also, creative and critical thinking and cooperative learning are not only imperatives for a democratic society but are more intellectually engaging and more successful strategies for learning than conventional forms of pedagogy. Finally, the history of education reform as well as of multicultural education demonstrates that instituting reforms that ignore larger issues of power and influence prevents the interests of people of color and low-income students, as well as other disenfranchised groups, from being advanced.

Historically, school-community relations in urban areas have by and large been characterized by strategies devised by school administrators to secure parent involvement in assisting with and improving their children's academic performance. Parent involvement has also consisted of solicited support for various school activities. The assumption, or perhaps recognition, has been that schooling is not an integral part of community life and therefore formal planning is necessary in order to secure parent participation. While some school districts continue to offer little more than token opportunities or public relations programs, the increasing complexity of urban life and deepening fiscal crisis offer strong reasons for improving school-community ties.

Over the past two decades, a variety of mechanisms and policies have been pursued with reportedly positive results (McLaughlin & Shields, 1986). Rather than relying on informal community communication processes, as has traditionally been the case in rural areas, most urban schools today try some combination of newsletters (in few cases, bi- or multilingually produced), open houses, pupil handbooks, parent-teacher conferences, grade reports to the home, and home phone calls. School-based strategies—for example, PTA meetings—have proven most beneficial to middle- and upper-income parents; their value for low-income parents has been more limited. Some research suggests that parents of color and low-income parents become more engaged when interactions with school personnel take place in their home or some location other than the school (Henderson, 1981). Conventional wisdom holds that low-income parents are neither willing nor able to take an active role in their children's education. It is important, however, to understand why low-income parents and parents of color have often participated to a lesser extent than others.

Low-income parents, especially those of oppressed nationalities, face great economic pressures. These pressures may mean both parents or the single parent have to take jobs wherever they can be found. This often leaves little time, energy, or resources for child care or travel to their child's school. Further, school personnel often live outside the community where they work. This cultural distance, especially when coupled with the attitude common among teachers and school administrators that parents are best kept at a distance, results in parent intimidation, reluctance, and uncertainty about their role. These feelings are further reinforced by the fact that parents have been kept out of educational decision making; participation has generally meant providing support, sometimes input, into plans already developed. Thus, what is typically perceived as parent apathy may be better explained by parent realization that their participation is not valued.

Public schools today must work toward more responsive relations with their communities. The rapid and dramatic demographic economic and cultural changes that our country has undergone in the last 30 years have rendered ineffective traditional means of home-school communication. Today, the "family" or "parents" often mean parents sharing custody, parents who work at night, undocumented parents, homeless parents, parents with limited English proficiency, foster parents, or none of the above. "Building bridges" (Sleeter & Grant, 1986) must consist of more than suggestions for teachers to address school correspondence more sensitively, though such practical steps are not to be discounted.

More responsive school-community relations imply school initiatives to structure time with parents not only on the basis of specific knowledge about who the parents are but also in ways that hold schools more accountable. The issue of accountability lies at the heart of school-community relations. The various ways in which as a society we are currently addressing this issue deserve mention. Today, we find the following four tendencies: (1) local control of schools, (2) site-based management schemes, (3) parental "choice," and (4) greater national control of education policy. Though differences exist over formulations for implementation and to some extent underlying rationales, the first two "remedies" essentially assume a correlation between the quality of education within a particular school and its system of governance. Advocates of both options argue that student, parent, and community needs are more likely to be met if teams of parents, community members, and school personnel have control over such issues as teacher hiring, curriculum content, and teaching methods. Parental choice advocates recognize that parents have little influence over their children's schooling. Some "choice" advocates argue that market mechanisms are needed to create excellence in education (Chubb & Moe, 1990). Others, however, call for "diversity" within public school systems (Meier, 1991). The fact that our public school system has failed low-income students of color makes these options understandably attractive, especially in these communities.

Yet, at best, all three of these options are problematic. Problems arise given existing segregation in our urban areas and structurally underfunded school systems. Given these demographics, the extent to which issues of equity and genuine democratic involvement are dealt with varies considerably. The fourth remedy, tighter federal control of education policy (as federal funding for education decreases), is unlikely to further goals of diversity with greater curricular uniformity and schemes for nationally standardized testing.

These are complicated issues. The choices before us are not straightforward. There is no one answer to school reforms to give greater attention to diversity. In a very broad sense, I can only suggest that the democratization of education policy and control appears to be our strongest response to the proposals cited above and to the need for our praise of diversity to impact the critical situation we find ourselves in today (Jones, 1983). Reciprocal relationships where representative parents and other representative community members serve on school councils and committees as representative teachers participate in neighborhood activities and councils can get *all* of us more actively involved in the issues that must be addressed if we are going to improve the life chances of our young people.

Schools will benefit from the experiences of a wide range of persons as the public acquires greater awareness of school realities. For teachers, involvement in community issues can deepen their understandings of what active citizenship and multicultural sensitivities really mean for their students' immediate context.

These kinds of responsibilities presuppose a restructuring of teachers' work so that instead of adding to their already heavy workload they actually have time for community involvement, including home visits to students' parents. Teachers would also be encouraged to live in the same community where they work. More important, the councils and committees that teachers serve on would need to have responsibility for areas that are determinant in shaping the life circumstances of young people such as employment and health care. Similarly, community members' participation in the schools needs to address educational policies, such as curriculum content and goals. This would be instead of parents' traditional role of providing support, or, more generally, "token" participation on committees. The main point I wish to make, however, is that of the process of mutual participation. Paradoxically, from the standpoint that diversity *is* our common culture, we need to develop both a common education and a common culture. In no sense does this idea imply uniformity. Rather, the idea is for all peoples to have the opportunity to participate in society and in solving its problems. It is this joint participation, that can be our common culture (Williams, 1989).

Widespread community activism in working and minority communities declined with the decline of social activism in the early seventies. This decline is due, in part, to a changed economic context where, for example, adults must pay greater attention to matters of employment and family maintenance. These broad social and economic parameters today make it especially difficult for working and minority parents to play an influential role in educational institutions. Yet, it is important to understand how the historical precedents outlined at the beginning of this chapter contain a notion of multicultural education as part of both a specific (in the case of schooling) and general (i.e., something to be carried out throughout society at large) struggle to advance democratic and more equitable practices. In contrast, it is striking how educators today have to articulate ways we might possibly *link* multiculturalism *to* the imperatives of democracy. This shift is due, in large part, to our tendency as educators to ignore uncomfortable political questions and subsequently turn demands for structural realignment into smaller educational reforms that can be accommodated without making fundamental changes in existing institutional arrangements. This propensity results in a weak challenge to institutionalized unequal social relations and arguably has had much to do with the form and content of existing multicultural programs.

Nevertheless, there appear to be sparks of a renewed movement around a variety of educational issues given the deepening fiscal crisis attacks from the right against the institution of public education, and the sustained failure of our nation's schools to provide quality education for low-income students and students of color (Bastian et.al., 1986). This situation suggests that it is necessary to launch a defense of the public school as a multiracial, secular, and free institution that, by necessity, offers a democratic, multicultural education and whose mission is to serve the common good.

There are real limits to what an education for diversity can accomplish. Generally speaking, we can say that our notion of the common good must be allowed to change as it grows—for example, embracing the goal of educational equity, not just access. Increased educational funding must also be a key agenda item for multiculturalists, with new formulas for state and federal financial responsibilities in order to break the cycle where, for example, poor children go to bad schools. More specifically, in addition to the imperatives for mass participation discussed above, effective schools research demonstrates that reducing the distance between schools and their communities helps student performance (Purkey & Marshall, 1985). There are many varieties and possible levels for involvement. We must become familiar with and continue research in this area.

In our praise of diversity, multicultural reform should not be conceived of as curriculum content designed for students of color. Second, multiculturalism cannot be an isolated reform if it is to have efficacy. Pedagogical practices—for example, those that require critical and social student participation—are essential, as are fundamental social understandings or academic curricula. Finally, the institutional structures and political processes within which such reforms operate must also be refigured.

References

Anner, J. (1991–92, Winter). Reforming the Schools: Community Control or Corporate Con Game? *The Minority Trendsetter, 5*(1), pp. 15–31.

Aronowitz, Stanley, & Giroux, Henry A. (1985*). Education Under Siege: The Conservative, Liberal and Radical Debate Over Schooling.* Boston: Bergin & Garvey.

Atkinson, Donald R., Morten, George, & Sue, Derald Wing (Eds.). (1979). *Counseling American Minorities: A Cross-Cultural Perspective.* Dubuque, IA: William C. Brown.

Banks, J. (1981). *Multiethnic Education: Theory and Practice.* Boston: Allyn and Bacon.

Banks, J. (1988). *Multiethnic Education: Theory and Practice,* 2nd edition. Boston: Allyn and Bacon.

Banks, James A. (Ed.). (1981). *Education in the 80s: Multiethnic Education.* Washington, DC: National Education Association.

Banks, James A., & Lynch, James (Eds.). (1986). *Multicultural Education in Western Societies.* London: Holt, Rinehart and Winston.

Bastian, A., Fruchter, N., Gittell, M., Greer, C., & Haskins, K. (1986). *Choosing Equality.* Philadelphia: Temple University Press.

Bullivant, B. (1981). *The Pluralist Dilemma in Education: Six Case Studies.* Boston: Allen & Unwin.

California State Department of Education. (1981). *Schooling and Language Minority Students: A Theoretical Framework.* Los Angeles Evaluation Dissemination and Assessment Center, California State University, Los Angeles.

California State Department of Education, Bilingual Office. (1986). *Beyond Language: Social and Cultural Factors in Schooling Language Minority Students.* Los Angeles Evaluation Dissemination and Assessment Center, California State University, Los Angeles.

Chubb, John E., & Moe, Terry E. (1990). *Politics Markets and America 's Schools.* Washington, DC: The Brookings Institution.

Cummins, J. (1986). Empowering minority students: A framework for intervention. *Harvard Educational Review,* 56, pp. 18–35.

Densmore, K. (1987). Professionalism, proletarianization and teacher work in T. S. Popkewitz (Ed.), *Critical Studies in Teacher Education: Its Folklore Theory and Practice.* New York: Falmer Press.

Ellsworth, Elizabeth. (1989, August). Why doesn't this feel empowering? Working through the repressive myths of critical pedagogy. *Harvard Educational Review* 59 (3), pp. 297–324.

Garcia, Ricardo L. (1982). *Teaching in a Pluralistic Society: Concepts, Models, Strategies.* New York: Harper & Row.

Gay, G. (1983). Multiethnic education: Historical developments and future prospects. *Phi Delta Kappan,* 64, pp. 560–563.

Giroux, Henry A., & McLaren, Peter. (1986). Teacher education and the politics of engagement: The case for democratic schooling. *Harvard Educational Review* 56, pp. 213–238.

Grant, C. A. (1978). Education that is multicultural—Isn't that what we mean? *Journal of Teacher Education, 29.*

Grant, C., & Sleeter, C. (1989). *Turning on Learning: Five Approaches for Multicultural Teaching Plans for Race, Class Gender, and Disability.* Columbus: Merrill.

Hawkins Billy C. (1992, Spring). Declining black representation. *Thought & Action, The NEA Higher Education Journal* 3 (1), pp. 73–84.

Henderson, Anne. (Ed.). (1981). *Parent Participation-Student Achievement: The Evidence Grows.* Columbia, MD: National Committee for Citizens in Education.

Jones, Ken. (1983). *Beyond Progressive Education.* Great Britain: The Pitman Press.

Kaestle, C. (1983). *Pillars of the Republic: Common Schools and American Society, 1780–1860.* New York: Hill and Wang.

Kliebard, H. (1986). *The Struggle for the American Curriculum 1983–1958.* Boston: Routledge and Kegan Paul.

Kozol, Jonathan. (1991). *Savage Inequalities.* New York: Crown Publishers.

Liston, Daniel P., & Zeichner, Kenneth M. (1987). Critical pedagogy and teacher education. *Journal of Education* 169, pp. 117–137.

McCarthy, Cameron. (1991). Multicultural approaches to racial inequality in the United States. *Oxford Review.* 17 (1).

McCarthy, C., & Apple, M. (1988). Race, class, and gender in American educational research: Toward a non-synchronous position. In L. Weis (Ed.), *Class, Race, and Gender in American education.* Albany: State University of New York Press.

McLaughlin, Milbrey W., & Shields, Patrick M. (1986). *Involving Parents in the Schools' Les-*

sons for Policy. Draft paper prepared for the Conference of Effects for Alternative Designs in Compensatory Education. Washington, DC, June 17–18.

Meier, Deborah. (1991). Choice can save public education. *The Nation,* 4 March.

Olsen, Laurie. (1991, Fall). Whose culture is this? Whose curriculum will it be? *California Perspectives.*

Purkey, Stewart C., & Smith, Marshall S. (1985, January). School reform: The district policy implications of the effective schools literature. *Elementary School Journal.*

Ramirez, Manuel III, & Castaneda, Alfredo. (1974). *Cultural Democracy, Bicognitive Development, and Education.* New York: Academic Press.

Schlesinger, Arthur M. Jr. (1991). *The Disuniting of America.* New York: W. W. Norton & Company.

Shor, Ira. (1986, November). Equality is Excellence. *Harvard Educational Review, 56*(4), pp. 406–426.

Simon, R. (1987). Empowerment as a pedagogy of possibility. *Language Arts,* 64, pp. 370–382.

Sleeter, C., & Grant, C. (1986). *The Literature of Multicultural Education in the United States of America.* Paper presented at the meeting of the American Educational Research Association, San Francisco.

Sleeter, C. E., & Grant, Carl A. (1988). *Making Choices for Multicultural Education: Five Approaches to Race, Class, and Gender.* Columbus, OH: Merrill.

Steinberg, S. (1981). *The Ethnic Myth.* New York: Atheneum.

The Good Common School Making the Vision Work for All Children. Boston: Massachusetts National Coalition of Advocates for Students, 1991.

Williams, Raymond. (1989). The idea of a common culture. In *Resources of Hope.* London: Verso, pp. 32–38.

About the Author

Kathleen Densmore is an assistant professor of teacher education at San Jose State University, San Jose, California. She is currently engaged in research on the relevance of socioecomic and educational changes in Latin America for students of color in the United States. Recent publications offer a critical perspective on teacher professionalism in the United States.

Index